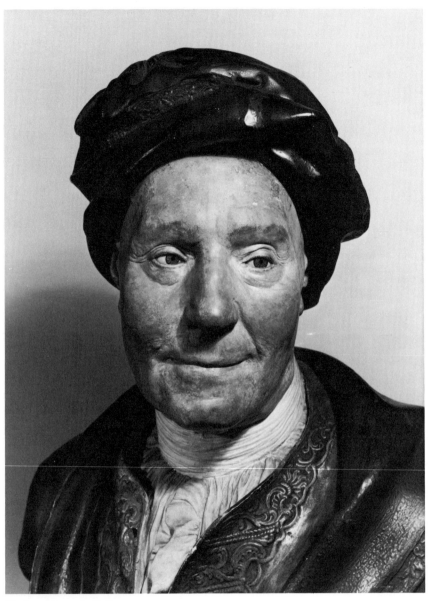

National Portrait Gallery

COLLEY CIBBER
bust, attributed to Roubiliac

A
BIOGRAPHICAL
DICTIONARY

OF

ACTORS, ACTRESSES, MUSICIANS, DANCERS,

MANAGERS & OTHER STAGE PERSONNEL

IN LONDON, 1660–1800

Volume 3: Cabanel *to* Cory

by

PHILIP H. HIGHFILL, JR., KALMAN A BURNIM

and

EDWARD A. LANGHANS

SOUTHERN ILLINOIS UNIVERSITY PRESS

CARBONDALE AND EDWARDSVILLE

Library of Congress Cataloging in Publication Data (Revised)

Highfill, Philip H., Jr
   A biographical dictionary of actors, actresses, musicians, dancers, managers & other stage personnel in London, 1660–1800.

   Includes bibliographical references.
   CONTENTS: v. 1. Abaco to Belfille—v. 2. Belfort to Byzand.—v. 3. Cabanel to Cory.
   1. Performing arts—London—Biography. I. Burnim, Kalman A., joint author. II. Langhans, Edward A., joint author. III. Title.
PN2597.H5   790.2′092′2 [B]   71-157068
ISBN 0-8093-0692-1 (v. 3)

List of Illustrations

FRINGE THEATRICALS: PLEASURE GARDENS, CIRCUSES, FAIRS, MASQUERADES, AND MINOR THEATRES

Volume 3

Cabanel to Cory

= C =

Cabanel, Mons [*fl.* 1789–1804?],
dancer? actor? pyrotechnist.

In the bill of Astley's Amphitheatre for
4 September 1789 appeared the name of
one "Mons. Cabanell, Sen." as Commander
of *H. M. S. Goliah* in a spectacle called *The
Royal Naval Review of Plymouth*. In the
same bill appeared a younger Cabanel who
must have been Rudolphe, later well
known as a machinist and a theatrical
architect.

The elder Cabanel, who was most probably Rudolphe's father, may have toiled
obscurely at Astley's and elsewhere both
before and after that date, as an actor and
possibly as a machinist. He surfaced in the
records only once more, when in 1804 the
"Messrs. Cabanell and Son" produced for
Astley a fireworks display on the Thames in
honor of the King's birthday.

Very likely Cabanel, Senior, was the husband of the dancer Madame Victoire
Cabanel and the father not only of Rudolphe but of Miss Eliza and Miss Harriot
Cabanel (later Mrs Helme), also dancers;
and if so he was also father of the Fredericka mentioned by Rudolphe in his will.

Cabanel, Eliza [*fl.* 1792–1800],
dancer. See **CABANEL, HARRIOT.**

Cabanel, Harriot, later Mrs Helme
[*fl.* 1791–1806], *dancer.*

Harriot Cabanel was, according to
Charles Dibdin the younger, the sister of
the machinist Rudolphe Cabanel and the
dancer Eliza Cabanel. She was thus probably the daughter of that Cabanel, actor and
pyrotechnist, who was active from perhaps
before 1789 until perhaps 1804. She became the wife of the actor and dancer
Helme about 1800.

So far as the bills show, Harriot danced
first in a ballet called *The Animated Statue*
at Astley's Royal Circus on 17 and 19 September 1791. She played some part in the
pantomime *Maternal Affection* at Astley's
on both 8 April and 24 October 1793, and
it is reasonable to suppose that she was in
the company between those dates.

Harriot's sister Eliza danced first at Astley's in the pantomime *The Good and the
Bad; or, Jupiter's Vengeance* on 11 June
1792. Another dancer in that pantomime
was a "Miss Victoire Cabanel"; but she was
billed on 3 April 1793 as "*Mad.* Victoire
Cabanel," and it seems likely that she was
the mother of the family. She was not noticed again. Harriot and Eliza were dancing
together at the King's Theatre on 2 June
1796 in "a new Indian Divertissement" by
Didelot, in which the girls were billed as
"Two Audalisques." This offering was popular during the season. One of the sisters
was listed as dancing in *L'Heureux naufrage*
on 7 July 1796, also at the Opera.

Nothing more was recorded of their activities in opera house or patent theatre for
three years, but "the Miss Cabanels" were
featured, along with the premier dancer
D'Egville, at the Royal Circus on 12 November 1798 in a piece called *Duncan and
Peggy; or, The Scotch Cottagers*; and, "in
the course of the pantomime" *Alexandria;
or, Harlequin in Egypt*, they presented "a
new Turkish dance."

At Covent Garden Theatre on 25 May
1799 "Miss E. and Miss H. Cabanel" were
featured dancers. During the evening Eliza
and Harriot danced with Bologna *Un pas*

de trois, Harriot danced *Un pas seul sérieux*, and Eliza and the male dancer Platt did *Un pas seul de demie caractère*. But they did not confine their efforts to Covent Garden, for the *Monthly Mirror* of April 1799 commended "the light fantastic toe of Miss H. Cabanels" as "the columbine" at Cross's New Royal Circus, and a bill of the Circus dated 29 May 1800 first called Harriot Mrs Helme. She was that night Columbine in the pantomime *Harlequin Highlander*. "Miss Cabanel" (Eliza) was billed as "principal dancer" in the pantomime, and Mr Helme played the lead part, Sawney Beane.

Perhaps Mrs Helme continued in the *corps de ballet* at Cross's establishment continuously, though she was seldom shown in the extant bills after 1801. She was, indeed, in the leading role of Maria Theresa when the spectacular *Louisa of Lombardy* came out at the Circus on 25 April 1803. She was probably the "Miss Cabanal" who danced at Lancaster on 22 May 1805. Charles Dibdin remembered engaging her as a Columbine at "either 4 or 5 G[uinea]s" per week to play at the Amphitheatre in Peter Street, Dublin, from 9 November 1805 through 14 February 1806. After the latter date all record of the activities of the sisters Cabanel ceases.

Cabanel, Rudolphe *1763–1839, architect, machinist, inventor, pyrotechnist.*
Rudolphe (or Rodolpho) Cabanel (Cabanal, Carbanel) was born, according to some sources, in Aix-la-Chapelle and, according to others, in Liège in 1763. The circumstances of his youth are obscure, but he belonged to a theatrical family, for Charles Dibdin in 1802 called him the brother of the "principal Dancer" Miss [Harriot] Cabanel who was by then Mrs Helme, and Miss Eliza Cabanel, Harriot's sister often performed with her during this period. Furthermore, the presence of a "Mons Cabanell, Sen[ior]" as a performer in a bill of Astley's Circus of 4 September 1789, in which "Cabanell" (presumably

Rudolphe) was first publicly credited in his function as a machinist, gives some grounds to suppose that his father may have been active in the theatre at that date. Rudolphe was still denominated "Cabanel, jun" on the Royal Circus bill of 25 March 1799.

The initial notice mentioned above was for devising, along with a machinist named Macquoid, workable small boats for a huge patriotic water spectacle called *The Royal Naval Review at Plymouth; or, Devonshire and Cornwall Royalty*. Doubtless Cabanel rose in his employment at Astley's, for by 1792 he had sufficient reputation to be commissioned by R. B. Sheridan, the patentee, and Henry Holland, the architect, to devise the stage machinery for the new Drury Lane Theatre. (He was evidently a man of uncertain temperament. In a letter from Sheridan to Holland of 27 October 1793, Sheridan says: "I have met Mr Cabanel here—and after giving me the trouble to draw up a contract according to what I thought he at least proposed he broke off. I offered him 9 *guineas* a week for *a year certain*. . . . I further told Cabanel that he should have a compliment if he exerted himself on the Stage.") The theatre's surviving accounts show an interesting series of payments in the first half of 1794 which demonstrate the scale of his responsibilities: for 12 March 1794 "Cabanel Build^g stage for new theatre on Acct. 130/0/0"; 15 March "Cabanel in full 8th March inclusive 102/7/6"; 28 March "Cabanel 2 weeks 22nd incl. 193.10.4"; 5 April "Cabanel . . . 140.5.0"; 14 April "Cabanel 50.0.0"; 3 May "for stage bldg. to this day 123.15.—"; 8 July "Riordan and Sealton 2 of Cabanels Men for Work 7.7.6."

Cabanel remained at Drury Lane as machinist, and often embraced as well the function on the one hand of chief carpenter (disbursing to and directing the subordinate carpenters) and on the other hand that of architect, through the season of 1796–97, in which season his salary was £5 per week.

He was also associated with the theatre in the season of 1804–5, when he laid out sums totaling £700 2s. 4d. from 5 January through 20 June. He ("Carbonel" in the bill) devised the machinery for the first dramatic performance in the new Drury Lane Theatre on 21 April 1794, presumably among other effects causing the witches to hover through the fog and filthy air when on this occasion John Philip Kemble played Macbeth in his own alteration of the play. Certainly next day's *Morning Chronicle* reported that "Hecate's companion spirit descends on the cloud and rises again with him [*sic*]." The writer added, however, "It would be better if they were not made to fly backwards."

On 9 June 1794 Cabanel prepared new devices and machines when Kemble's elaborate new afterpiece *Lodoiska* took the stage. Cabanel and Jacobs "designed and executed" the machinery for J. H. D'Egville's *Alexander the Great* on 12 February 1795, as they did also for James Hook, Jr's new mainpiece *Jack of Newberry* on 6 May, William Linley's *Harlequin Captive* on 18 January 1796, and the revival of the afterpiece *Robinson Crusoe* on 26 December 1796. In 1796 Cabanel earned an additional £150 for the season serving as machinist for the opera at the King's Theatre.

In 1794 Cabanel was called into consultation "respecting the machinery of the stage" of the Birmingham Theatre by its architect, George Saunders, and he made further alterations there in 1814. In the winter of 1801–2 he reconstructed the auditorium of Sadler's Wells, altering its shape from square to semicircular. He designed the stage and interior of the Royal Circus, Blackfriars Road, in 1799, and it was rebuilt "under the direction of Mr Cabanel, jun." The architect James Donaldson the younger employed him in further alterations to the Circus in 1805–6. Cabanel designed the auditorium of the Cobourg Theatre, Lambeth (later the "Old Vic"), in 1817–18. He invented a form of roof which was known by his name and is said to have invented several mechanical appliances, the exact character of which is not now known.

It is almost certain, also, that the following announcement of one of Philip Astley's spectacles in 1804 involves either Rudolphe and a son or, more likely, Rudolphe and his father:

the Fireworks are made under the Direction of Mr Astley, by Messrs Cobonell and Son, who will let them off on the Thames this evening at different signals from Mr Astley, Sen., who will be mounted on the Gibraltar Charger, placed in a Barge, in the Front of the line of Fireworks.

"Cabanal, jun" was credited with the machinery for *The Cloud King* at J. C. Cross's New Royal Circus on 30 June 1806 and for *The False Friend* at the Circus on 7 September of that year.

Cabanel died at his house at No 2, Mount Gardens, Lambeth, on 5 February 1839. By the terms of a will (signed "Rudolphe Cabanel" on 8 November 1838) he left in trust to his friend and executor John Stephen Spindler Hopwood of No 47, Chancery Lane, his leasehold factory and several messuages adjoining in Webber Street "on the East side of the Victoria [*quondam* Cobourg] Theatre, Lambeth" and all his patents and patent rights, to lay out in stocks and bonds for the interest of his widow Elizabeth, and, after her death, to his sisters Fredericka Cabanel and Harriot Helme. The residuary legatees, after the deaths of the sisters, were to be "Henry Davis and his wife Elizabeth of the Victoria Tavern Waterloo Road, tavernkeeper[s]." The will was proved by Hopwood on 5 June 1839.

Cabanel, Victoire [*fl.* 1792–1793], *dancer. See* **CABANEL, HARRIOT.**

Cabanes, Mr [*fl.* 1784], *violinist.* Mr Cabanes was listed by Dr Burney as a first violinist in the Handel Memorial Concerts at Westminster Abbey and the Pantheon in May and June 1784.

Cabell, Mr [fl. 1760], dresser.

In accounts of Covent Garden Theatre dated 22 September 1760, one Cabell is listed at a salary of 1s. per night under "Men Dressers Charg'd in the Wardrobe Bills."

Cable, Mrs d. 1767, house servant?

The treasurer of Covent Garden Theatre entered a payment of £3 8s. "for the funeral of Mrs Cable" on 13 January 1767. It is not known in what capacity Mrs Cable served the theatre.

Cademan, Philip b. c. 1643, actor.

Philip Cademan was one of four sons born to Thomas Cross, a wealthy apothecary, and his wife Anne, the daughter of an apothecary. Most evidence would suggest his birth to have occurred about 1643. Cross died early in the wars, and his widow married his friend Sir Thomas Cademan, then a widower. Though young Philip's brothers, Thomas, Paul, and John, kept the Cross name, Philip adopted Cademan as his surname—unless, as some sources say (but without clear evidence), he was actually Cademan's son. Documents dating about 1696 refer to him as Philip Cademan, alias Cross. Sir Thomas died in 1651 and in October 1652 Dame Anne remarried, again to a friend of her former spouse: Sir William Davenant.

Davenant, like Cademan before him, was a Cavalier in distress, and Dame Anne helped him to the tune of £1400, in recompense whereof Davenant married her and entered into a strange bond concerning her children in February 1654. He agreed to pay each of the boys £100 within a year and to maintain them or forfeit the £800 bond; this penalty was to be void if Sir William continued supporting the children until they received their £100 payments. He

contrived to avoid all the conditions of the bond, however, and have the boys cared for in other ways. Philip Cademan and Thomas Cross were put to work in Davenant's newly formed Duke's Company at the Restoration, and not until late in the century did they try to claim the money promised them.

Thomas Cross became the company's treasurer, and Philip Cademan pursued the career of an actor. His first recorded role was Sylvio in *The Duchess of Malfi* on 30 September 1662 at Lincoln's Inn Fields. For the next ten years he acted mostly small roles, such as Donalbain in *Macbeth* and Guildenstern in *Hamlet*. One may guess that even his stepfather could not make much of an actor out of him. His undistinguished career was cut short in 1673 by a dreadful accident. On 9 August 1673 he was playing, apparently, Don Lewis in *The Man's the Master*. John Downes the prompter described in 1708 what happened on stage:

Mr Cademan in the Play, not long after our Company began in Dorset-Garden; his Part being to Fight with Mr Harris, was Unfortunately, with a sharp Foil pierc'd near the Eye, which so Maim'd both the Hand and his Speech, that he can make little use of either; for which Mischance, he has receiv'd a Pension ever since 1673, being 35 Years a goe.

After the accident Cademan received a weekly pension of 30s., the equivalent of his regular salary in the 1660s. This was a fair sum for the time, but when the Duke's and King's companies united in the 1680s and Christopher Rich worked his way to a position of control, the treatment of Cademan changed. About 1696, in an effort to obtain the £100 promised him by Davenant many years before, Cademan went to court. Cademan testified that

in ye year 1673 as he was Acting his Part upon ye Stage, he received a Wound from

The Case of Philip Cademan. Gent.

Sr W.^m D'Avenant after K. Charles's Restoration had a
patent granted him for the Dukes Company of Players.
At wch time Sr W.^m stood indebted to Mr Cademan in a
Bond of 100.^{li} and in Consideration that Mr Cademan would
acquit Sr W.^m of y.^s s.^d debt and act as a player S.^r
W.^m promised to settle upon him 30 ♃ Week to be paid
out of ye profits arising from ye playhouse. W.^{ch} M.^r
Cademan did accordingly and received 30 ♃ Week
during Sr W.^{ms} Life and Several years after his
Death. And in ye year 1673 as he was Acting his part
upon ye Stage, he received a Wound from the late M.^r
Harris ye player w.th a foyle under his right Eye, w.^{ch}
touch'd his Brain. by means Whereof he lost his memory
his speech and the use of his right side, wch made him
incapable of acting any more. Notwithstanding wch his
Salary was continued until Mr Rich had ye management
of ye playhouse. (as indeed all persons had it for their
Lives that were disabled from acting by Sickness or
other Misfortunes, for wch there are several presidents)
And then Mr Rich thought it reasonable that M.^r
Cademan shou'd do Something for his Salary, and
order'd him to sit and deliver out Tickets wch he did
until he was disabled by Sickness in ye year 1695
But after he was restor'd to his health he offers

Public Record Office

The Case of PHILIP CADEMAN
Reproductions of Crown Copyright Records appear by permission of the Controller of H.M. Stationery Office

the late Mr Harris ye player wth a foyle under his right Eye, wch touch'd his Brain by means whereof he lost his memory his speech and the use of his right side, wch made him incapable of acting any more Notwithstanding wch his Salary was continu'd until Mr Rich had ye management of ye playhouse . . . and then Mr Rich thought it reasonable that Mr Cademan should do something for his Salary, and ordered him to sit and deliver out Tickets wch he did until he was disabled by Sickness in ye year 1695 But after he was restored to his health he offerd to serve in ye same Capacity he did before But Mr Rich refused to suffer him and has ever since denyd to pay him his Salary . . . by reason Whereof Mr Cademan is reduced

to ye greatest Extreamity of poverty, and is altogether Incapable of almost any Imployment by reason of ye s^d Hurt he rec^d upon ye stage.

The results of this pathetic plea are not known. Downes, writing in 1708, spoke of Cademan as though he were still alive, but he apparently was unaware of the old actor's distress or did not think it prudent to make public Rich's inhumanity.

The only other record of note concerning Cademan is a bequest in the will of the actor William Smith. On 19 November 1688 Smith directed that 10s. each for mourning rings be given to Thomas Betterton, Alexander and Thomas Davenant—all important members of the United Company —and Philip Cademan. The will was proved on 2 January 1696, about the time Cademan's fortunes were at their lowest, but this compassionate memento from Smith could hardly have helped much.

Cadet, Mr (*fl.* 1707–1711), *bassoonist, bass player.*

A musician named Cadet (or Cadot) was employed at the Queen's Theatre in the Haymarket, first as a bassoonist from 1 December 1707 to about 1710, and then as a bass player in 1711. Vice Chamberlain Coke's papers at Harvard University reveal that though Cadet asked for £1 nightly for his services, he was paid only half that. The Michael Cadette of St Paul, Covent Garden, who buried a son Isaac on 17 June 1704 and a son Michael on 22 March 1706 may have been the musician.

Cadet, Mr (*fl.* 1708), *house servant.*

On a list of Queen's company personnel dated January 1708 in Vice Chamberlain Coke's papers at Harvard University, one Cadett, possibly related to the musician in the troupe, was grouped with a pit keeper and a tailor and listed at a daily salary of 7*s.* 6*d.* His function is not known.

Cadman, Robert *d. 1740, ropewalker.*

Robert Cadman was for a brief period the most celebrated male performer on the rope in Britain and was exceeded as an attraction in this line only by Madame Violante. He is almost certainly the figure depicted sliding down the rope in Hogarth's celebrated picture of Southwark Fair, and like all the other figures there, stands as the emblem of excellence in his profession. The contemporary poem of "Southwark Fair" mentions him with his chief competitor:

Nor be our joys to earth confin'd,
But, light as air, swift as the wind,

Let Cadman cut the liquid sky,
And on the rope Violante fly.

Cadman, like the rest of his fraternity, was a nomad, playing seasonally probably all over the British Isles, in fair booths and circuses, almost always out of doors. The mode of his existence made him both famous and mysterious, and no details of his life and few of his movements are known. We are fortunate to have a contemporary account of one of his three-day stands, this at Derby in October 1732, where he offered his specialty, his rope slide. Here he affixed one end of a rope to the top of the steeple of All Saints Church and the other to the bottom of St Michael's tower, a horizontal distance of 80 yards, but an extremely steep incline. Cadman donned a breastplate of wood which was grooved to receive the rope. His walk up the rope consumed an hour, during which his small, muscular figure performed various acrobatic stunts on the slack rope. His descent was swift, requiring only six or seven seconds. It was also spectacular and noisy, for he fired pistols and blew a trumpet on the way down, and the friction of rope on breastplate left a plume of smoke billowing after him. During his three days at Derby he descended twice each day. In January 1740, descending from the steeple of St Mary Friars, Shrewsbury, he lost his balance, fell, and was killed. His fall was mourned in bad verse in the *Gentleman's Magazine.*

Owen, in *Account of the Ancient and Present State of Shrewsbury* (1808), citing the *Weekly Miscellany* of 17 April 1736, identifies the performer as Thomas Kidman.

Cadoret. *See* TERODAT.

Cadwell, Mr (*fl.* 1776–1777), *dresser.*

A person by the name of Cadwell was a dresser at Drury Lane in 1776–77 at 9*s.* per week.

Cady, Mr [fl. 1773], hairdresser.

According to the author of *The Secret History of the Green Room* (1795), a Mr Cady, who was a hairdresser to the Royal Circus, impressed by the talent of the child singer Maria Theresa Romanzini (later Mrs Bland) upon her arrival in London in 1773, helped her secure an engagement at Hughes's Riding School near Blackfriars Bridge.

Caff. *See* CLOUGH.

Caffarelli, Signor, stage name of Gaetano Maiorano *1710–1783, singer.*

Gaetano Maiorano, called Caffarelli, one of the most famous of the *castrati* singers of his time, and the greatest rival of Farinelli, was born at Bitonto, near Bari, on 12 April 1710. Recent research has exploded a long-held legend: that the young Maiorano was a child of humble parentage taken up by the musician Pasquale Cafaro (actually Caffarelli's junior by five years), who took him to Norcia to be castrated and then placed him under the instruction of Porpora at Naples, and that in gratitude for these services the boy adopted the name of his first teacher. Actually Maiorano's parents were respectable middle-class folk of the little town of Bitonto. His benefactor has been identified as one Domenico Caffarelli, "Razionale della Nunziatura," who also paid the expense of a Francesco Maiorano, "alias Cafarelli," when that youngster entered the Neapolitan Conservatorio dei Poveri on 8 May 1732. Yet a third boy, Pasquale Maiorano, also "alias Cafarelli," of Bitonto, was entered at the same conservatory on 5 November 1738 but was sponsored by Cardinal Spinelli. These latter youngsters no doubt were Gaetano's younger brothers, and their sponsors were, as Grove suggests, giving them a chance to repeat the success of their sibling.

Certainly, under Porpora's tuition, Caffarelli endured a most thorough and com-

Civiche Raccolte d'Arte ed Incisione, Milan

CAFFARELLI
engraving by Stuppi

prehensive discipline in the musical arts, so intense that it gave rise to the legend that after the master had long kept him to the study of a single page of exercise he dismissed the youth with the blessing, "Go, my son: I have nothing more to teach you. You are the greatest singer in Europe." (However, the same remark, after the same course of study, is attributed to Porpora as he bade goodbye to his even more famous pupil Farinelli.) At the age of sixteen, Caffarelli made his debut at the Teatro delle Dame, at Rome, in 1726, in the female role of Alvida in Sarro's *Il Veldemaro*. His reputation and the competition for his services grew over the next eight years during which he sang in the principal Italian theatres. At the Teatro Capranica at Rome in 1730 he caused a sensation as Pirro in Hasse's *Cajo Fabricio* and as Arminio in Porpora's *Germanico*. At Milan he appeared with

Amorevoli, Tesi, and Peruzzi in Lampugnani's *Ezio* and sang at Bologna in Hasse's *Siroe*. In 1734, at Venice, he sang with Farinelli in Giacomelli's *Merope*. The libretti of these operas describe him as "virtuoso di camera," suggesting that he was in the retinue of the last of the Medici, Gian Gastone.

Returning to Naples in 1734, where he sang in *Il castello d'Atlante* in July at the Teatro San Bartolomeo, he succeeded Matteuccio at the Royal Chapel there and established his home in that city for the rest of his life, though he traveled all over Europe for professional appearances.

In 1737–38, before his real maturity as a singer, Caffarelli joined Handel's company at the King's Theatre in London. On 21 May 1737, the directors of the opera had announced his engagement for the ensuing winter, as "the famous Caffariello, reputed to be the best singer in Italy." He made his first appearance on 29 October 1737 in the title role of *Arsace*, and subsequently sang the title role in *Faramondo* (3 January), Giascone in *La conquista del vello d'oro* (28 January), Claudio in *Alessandro severo* (25 February), Olinto in *Partenio* (14 March), and the title role in *Serse* (15 April). For an audience which had but recently been enchanted, almost crazed, by the powers of Farinelli, who had quitted England when the "Opera of the Nobility" had collapsed in the previous spring, Caffarelli proved to be a disappointment. Though he received praise, by Burney's report he was never well or in good voice all the time he was in England, and, in the exaggeration of Gray's letter to Walpole of 12 November 1737, he was left by the public "to screech by himself."

Caffarelli gave his last performance at London on 6 June 1738, as Olinto in *Partenio*, and returned to the kinder climate of Naples. During the next 30 years he made a considerable reputation throughout Europe as a most exquisite singer, appearing regularly at the San Carlo Theatre,

Naples, and at Madrid, Florence, Rome, Turin, Venice, Lucca, Modena, Paris, and Lisbon. He also earned a reputation for bad manners and eccentric behavior, in consequence of his feline brawls with other singers and his disrespect for audiences. Once, at a performance of *Olimpia nell'isola d'Ebuda* at Naples in 1741, he was so rude, behaving on stage in a "manner bordering on lasciviousness" with one of the female singers, that he was imprisoned for three days. Earlier, in 1739, because of an argument in which he came to blows with another singer in the church of Donna Romita at Naples, the quarrelsome *castrato* was brought before an ecclesiastical court but was acquitted in order that he might keep an engagement to sing at a royal wedding in Spain.

In 1750 Caffarelli sang at concerts in Paris by invitation of the Dauphine, and in October 1752 he performed before the King at Fontainebleau. In 1753 he was summoned from Naples again to Paris by Marshal Richelieu to sing before the Dauphin's wife, and he also sang at the Concert Spirituel once before returning to Italy. Garrick heard the tempestuous singer at the consecration of a nun at Naples and wrote to Burney on 5 February 1764 that "to crown the whole the principal part was sung by the famous *Caffarelli*, who, though old [now 54], has pleased me more than all the singers I have heard. He *touched* me; and it was the first time I have been touched since I came into Italy." Burney himself heard Caffarelli six years later in a concert room at Naples and reported that "though his voice was thin, it was easy to imagine, from what he was still able to do, that his voice and talents had been of the very first class." The singer lived out his last years in ease and affluence, having purchased a dukedom and two palatial homes, which upon his death at Naples on 31 January 1783 he left to his nephew. A portrait of him engraved by G. Stuppi was published at Milan in 1837.

Details of Caffarelli's career and exploits on the Continent may be found in the *Enciclopedia dello spettacolo* and in Heriot's *The Castrati in Opera*.

Caffariello. *See* CAFFARELLI.

Cafferielli. *See* CAFFARELLI.

Cagle. *See* KAYGILL.

Cahusac, William Maurice ₍*fl.* 1794–1829₎, *musician, music publisher, instrument maker, singer?*

William Maurice Cahusac was listed by Doane's *Musical Directory* in 1794 as a "canto," living at No 24, James Street, Westminster, a member of the Academy of Ancient Music, and a participant in the Academy's concerts, as well as a member of the Chapel Royal Choir. With his father Thomas Cahusac (d. 1798) and his brother Thomas he carried on a business in music-selling and instrument-making at No 126, the Strand, "at the sign of the Two Flutes and Violin," opposite St Clement's Church, from about 1794 until the father's death in 1798, after which he remained in part-nership with his brother. The partnership dissolved in 1800, with his brother estab-lishing his own business at No 41, Hay-market, and William remaining at the premises in the Strand until about 1811, when he moved the business to No 79, High Holborn. After his retirement about 1816, William Cahusac lived at Maida Hill, and then at Bexley, Kent, by 1829. A John Arthur Cahusac of the parish of St Mary, Islington, was married to Amelia Anne Browne at St Paul, Covent Garden, on 28 May 1836.

Caillot, François ₍*fl.* 1771–1793₎, *pyrotechnist.*

Monsieur François Caillot produced dis-plays of fireworks at Ranelagh Gardens in celebration of the birthday of George III in 1771. Advertised as "firemaker to Ranelagh Gardens," on 13 September 1773 he produced exhibitions at the Star and Garter, Chelsea, in which lighted air balloons played a major part. He served as a fireworks maker at Marylebone Gardens in the summers 1773–76 and at Ranelagh in 1774. On 19 July 1793 he directed a display of fireworks for the benefit of the waiters at Ranelagh.

Cain or **Cane.** *See* ARMSTEAD, MRS.

Caird. *See* D'ARCY, MR.

Cairns, Catherine. *See* ST LEGER, CATHERINE.

Cairns, Mrs William. *See* ACHMET, MRS.

Cajanus, Mynheer ₍*fl.* 1734₎, *actor.*

On 1 April 1734 the role of Captain Bully in *Britannia* at Goodman's Fields was announced to be played by Mynheer Cajanus, Senior, "Brother to the famous Tall Man who lately appeared at Drury Lane." Cajanus Senior, presumably of nor-mal size, repeated the role 13 additional times until 23 May.

Cajanus, Daniel 1703–1749, *giant.*

Daniel Cajanus was, according to The-ophilus Cibber, "a Fellow of an enormous Height" who came to London from Ger-many in 1734 "to be shewn for a Sight" at Drury Lane. Agreeing to "some very ad-vantageous Terms," Cajanus was secretly brought into the theatre and during a per-formance of *Cupid and Psyche* on 5 Febru-ary 1734 was shown, as the character of Gargantua, "arising from a Trap-Door, to the no small Admiration of the Spectators." Cajanus appeared in the afterpiece eighteen times that month. On 22 February the bill announced "this is the last time of Mynheer Cajanus, the Tall Man's, Appearance on the Stage," but on 28 February it was reported that "Mynheer Cajanus is prevail'd upon (at the Request of several Persons of Distinction) to stay a few Days longer in England, and will appear as usual in . . . Cupid and Psyche." He appeared again on 2 March and 5 March for a total of 20 exhibitions.

Cajanus died at Haarlem, Holland, on 28 February 1749, at the age of 46. Reports as to his actual size vary. An obituary in the *London Magazine*, February 1749, claimed he was seven feet eight inches (with a heartbeat of 52 times per minute, according to Dr Bryan Robinson). Egmont, who saw him at Drury Lane on 22 February 1734, described Cajanus in his *Diary* as "the tallest man of all that I have seen. He is seven feet ten inches and half in height, a German by birth." A Dutch newspaper stated he measured eight feet four inches and that his coffin was nine feet seven inches. Despite Cibber's and Egmont's statements that he came from Germany, he was usually called the "Swedish Giant," and, according to some obituary notices, had been born in Finland. A Dutch newspaper, *Algemeen Handelsblad*, however, on 5 May 1860, claimed that he was a native of the Netherlands in its report of the auction sale of a slipper—14½ inches long—which "once had been the property of the Dutch giant Daniel Cajanus." Sold at the same time was the miniature shoe of a dwarf named Simon Jane Paap, whose full height did not exceed 16 inches. Two marble stones on a pillar of the porch of Haarlem Cathedral indicate the contrasting sizes of Cajanus and Paap.

A Mynheer Cajanus Senior, billed as the "Brother to the famous Tall Man who lately appeared at Drury Lane," performed the role of Captain Bully in *Britannia* at Goodman's Fields in the spring of 1734. On 14 March of the same year, for a performance of *The Necromancer*, John Rich capitalized on the Giant's popularity by portraying himself as "Mynheer Cajanus's Sister, the Tall Woman."

"Cajanus's Sister." *See* RICH, JOHN.

Calari. *See* CALORI.

Calcagni, Mr [*fl. 1790*], *singer.*
Mr Calcagni was one of the singers in the concerts organized by J. P. Salomon at the Hanover Square Rooms in March 1790.

Calcot. *See* CALLCOTT.

Caldicot, Jonas [*fl. 1661*], *singer.*
On 16 February 1661, along with the elder Henry Purcell and other Gentlemen of the Chapel Royal, Mr Jonas Caldicot was installed as a Petty Canon of the Chapel. He paid a 5*s.* installation fee. The only other mention of Caldicot in the Westminster Abbey Precentor's Book is that of 30 March 1661 when he was noted as having received 7*s.* 4*d.* for singing at the funeral of the King's eldest sister, Princess Mary.

Calducci, Signor [*fl. 1781–1782*], *singer.*
A manuscript in the Burney papers at the British Museum lists a Signor Calducci as the second man in serious parts in the comic operas at the King's Theatre for 1781–82, but his name is not found in the extant bills.

Cale. *See* GALE.

Calkin, Mr [*fl. 1790–1817*], *gallery doorkeeper.*
Mr Calkin was a gallery doorkeeper at Drury Lane Theatre from about 1790–91 through 1816–17. His salary from 1800–1801 through 1813–14 was £1 10*s.* per week, but in 1815–16 it dropped to 18*s.* He was related to the Calkin family of musicians who were members of the Drury Lane band during this period.

Calkin, Joseph [*fl. 1781–1815*], *musician.*

Joseph Calkin was a musician at London during the last quarter of the eighteenth century and the first quarter of the nineteenth century. He was probably a member of the Drury Lane band before 1801 (in which year his name was in the pay list at £1 15*s.* per week), for his son Joseph was engaged as a musician in the same theatre by 1798. He seems to have continued at Drury Lane at least until 1807.

He was a member of the Royal Society of Musicians (though no record of his admission is extant), for on 1 January 1815 he recommended his son Joseph for admission.

Little else is known of Joseph Calkin's professional life. By his wife Mary he was the progenitor of a large musical family, including four sons:

Joseph Calkin (1781–1846), son of Joseph and Mary Calkin, is entered separately.

James Calkin (1786–1862), son of Joseph and Mary Calkin, was born on 19 September 1786 in the parish of St Giles in the Fields. He was admitted to the Royal Society of Musicians (before his elder brother Joseph) on 6 March 1808, at which time he was engaged in the Drury Lane band and at the Covent Garden oratorios; he performed on the pianoforte, violin, tenor, and violoncello, and was not married. For the details of his nineteenth-century career see Grove or Sainsbury's *Dictionary of Musicians* (1827). In March 1861, at the age of 74, having been obliged to relinquish all his professional engagements for several years "because of frequent attacks of swimming in the head and an asthmatic attack which confines him to the house every winter," James Calkin claimed against the Fund of the Royal Society of Musicians. He was dead by March 1862, for then his "widow," Victoire Calkin, aged 74, claimed against the Fund. Their eldest son, James Joseph Calkin (1813–1868), born in the parish of St Marylebone on 8 April 1813, became a member of the Royal

Society of Musicians in 1835 and was a player on the violin and pianoforte, with engagements at Covent Garden Theatre. James Joseph Calkin married Mary Ann Whiting Batten, of the parish of St Mary Newington, Surrey, on 13 March 1845. He died on 11 October 1868, in Harrington Street, St Pancras, of an embolism. Another son, Joseph Calkin, called "Tennielli" (1816–1874), a singer, studied under Lamperti at Milan and appeared in concerts at London. A third son, John Baptiste Calkin (b. 1827), was organist at Woburn Chapel (1853–57), Camden Road Chapel (1863–68), and St Thomas's, Camden Town (1870–84). A fourth son, George Calkin, born 10 August 1829, became a member of the Royal Society of Musicians in 1852, was a violoncellist and teacher of piano at London, played at the Royal Italian Opera, Drury Lane Theatre, the Philharmonic Society concerts, and then became a professor at the London Academy of Music. He died at London on 13 July 1911, at age 82.

Samuel Calkin, son of Joseph and Mary Calkin, was born in the parish of St Marylebone on 3 September 1792. When recommended to the Royal Society of Musicians by his father, Joseph Calkin, on 1 January 1815, he was described as having been apprenticed for seven years to Mr Cobham, and was engaged as first tenor at Drury Lane (at £2 2*s.* per week) and the Haymarket (at £1 16*s.* per week) and as violist for the Covent Garden oratorios. He taught pianoforte and violin, at the time was married to Eliza Calkin, and had a daughter, Elizabeth Anne, born 11 December 1813. Pierre Jacques Poitry Calkin, the son of Samuel and Eliza Calkin, of William Street, St Pancras, was baptized on 31 August 1831. In the middle of the century Pierre played the violin and pianoforte at Drury Lane and at Vauxhall; on 8 April 1850 he married Elizabeth Braine, of Kensal New Town, in St John's Church, Kensal Green; their daughter Elizabeth Ann was baptized on 4 June 1851 in the Church of St Marylebone. Pierre became a member of the Royal Society of Musicians in 1852.

William Calkin, son of Joseph and Mary Calkin, was born in St James's Parish, Westminster, on 5 September 1796. At the time of his recommendation to the Royal Society of Musicians in May 1819, he had been apprenticed seven years to his father, played the violin, violoncello, and pianoforte, was engaged in the orchestra at Drury Lane, was married, and had one child, William, seven months old. Later he was organist of the parish church at Arundel, Sussex, and received an appointment from the Duke of Richmond as organist for Sussex county.

Calkin, Joseph *1781–1846, violinist, violist, violoncellist, bookseller.*

According to affidavits in the records of the Royal Society of Musicians, Joseph Calkin was born on 10 January 1781 in the parish of St George, Hanover Square, the son of Joseph and Mary Calkin. He was baptized on 17 March 1781. He was one of at least four brothers whose musical careers in London and elsewhere in England have often been confused with each other. The records of the Royal Society of Musicians help to correct some of this confusion.

The elder Joseph Calkin (fl. 1781–1815) was probably the "Calkin Senr" who was on the Drury Lane pay list at £1 15s. per week as a member of the band in 1801 (although this notation may have referred to Joseph, his son, and the "Calkin Jr" to James Calkin).

In any event, Joseph Calkin, the subject of this entry, was apprenticed to Thomas Lyon who taught him to play the violin; he also was instructed by Spagnoletti for two years. Calkin's first engagement in an orchestra was in 1798, at Drury Lane, where he remained for 10 years, at a salary of £1 15s. from 1803–4 through 1807–8. At the time of his recommendation by Thomas Lyon to the Royal Society of Musicians on 5 April 1812 (elected unanimously 5 July 1812), he was performing on the violin at the Pantheon and at the concerts given by Knyeths and Vaughan; he also played the violoncello and first tenor, had "some business" as a piano teacher, and was unmarried. Later he was engaged at the Opera, the Ancient and Vocal Concerts, and at the Philharmonic Society, which he served as librarian at least until 1827.

Active in the Royal Society of Musicians, in 1813 he played at the Society's annual concert at St Paul's for the benefit of the clergy and in 1835 served as a member of the Court of Assistants. No doubt some of the numerous other references in the records of the Society to "Mr Calkin"—without Christian name—pertaining to offices and concerts refer to Joseph. In 1821 he was given the title of Musician in Ordinary to His Majesty and was appointed to the King's state band.

In 1813, Joseph Calkin married the widow of Mr Budd, bookseller of Pall Mall, and took over that business, which included appointment as bookseller to the King. He died at London on 30 December 1846. His issue are unknown. The violinist, James Joseph Calkin (1813–1868), was not (as stated by Grove) his son, but the son of his brother, James Calkin (1784–1862).

Callcott, Augustus Wall *1779–1844, painter, singer.*

Augustus Wall Callcott was born in his father's house in the Mall, Kensington Gravel Pits, on 20 February 1779. He was the son of Thomas Callcott, bricklayer and builder, by his second wife, Charlotte Wall Callcott. Augustus was the younger brother of the musicians Dr John Wall Callcott (1766–1821) and William Callcott (fl. 1790–1800). Arabella Wall Callcott, who married Thomas Buckley at St George, Hanover Square, on 25 August 1803 was probably his sister.

As a child, Augustus showed strong in-

By permission of the Trustees of the British Museum

AUGUSTUS WALL CALLCOTT
by Linnell

clinations both to music and to drawing and spent six years as a chorister in Westminster Abbey, earning each year £7 and three and a half yards of "coarse black baize." In 1794, when Callcott was 15, he was listed in Doane's *Musical Directory* as a performer in the Handelian celebrations at the Abbey and as a singer (no doubt in the choruses of the oratorios) at Drury Lane Theatre. Soon, however, he turned in earnest to the study of painting under the tuition of Hoppner, and by 1799 he had exhibited at the Royal Academy a portrait of a Miss Roberts which was received with enthusiasm. His reputation was, however, to be earned as a landscape painter. Elected an associate of the Royal Academy in 1806 and to a full membership in 1810, Callcott exhibited four pictures between 1805 and 1810, ten in 1811, and six in 1812. From then until 1822, he exhibited his best

works, seascapes such as "The Entrance to the Pool of London" (1816) and "The Mouth of the Tyne" (1818).

In 1827 Callcott married the widow of a Captain Graham, a woman of considerable literary reputation (see Lady Maria Callcott in *The Dictionary of National Biography*). After a visit to Italy, he began to paint Italian scenes. He was knighted by Queen Victoria in 1837. In 1844 he became Conservator of the Royal Pictures. He enjoyed the admiration of Turner and Stothard and is still regarded as one of the early masters of the English school of landscape. Among his portrait work is a painting of his brother John Wall Callcott, engraved by F. C. Lewis and published in 1824.

He died on 25 November 1844 and was buried in Kensal Green Cemetery. Additional information about his artistic career can be found in *The Dictionary of National Biography* and Redgrave's *Dictionary of Artists*. The oil portrait of him by J. Linnell which was exhibited at the Royal Academy in 1832 was engraved and published by the artist that same year. It was later used as the basis for an engraving by J. Guillaume. The painting is now in the Mellon Collection in the National Gallery, Washington, D. C.

Callcott, John Wall *1766–1821, musician, composer, singer, teacher.*

John Wall Callcott was born in a house in the Mall, Kensington Gravel Pits, on 20 November 1766, the son of Thomas Callcott, bricklayer and builder, by his second wife Charlotte Wall. The father's first wife was also named Charlotte, for his previous marriage to Charlotte Urry, of Kensington, is recorded in the register of St George's Chapel, May Fair, for 12 August 1750. At the age of seven, John Callcott became a day boy at a neighborhood school run by William Young, where he studied Latin and Greek and was long considered "the head boy." Family circumstances compelled his withdrawal from the school after five years, and Callcott, having been attracted to the organ during a period when his father was doing repairs to Kensington Church, was introduced in 1778 to Henry Whitney, then organist of that church, from whom he received initial instruction in music.

Originally intended for medicine, he also studied anatomy for about a year, but after witnessing an operation, in the course of which he fainted, he turned toward the serious study of music. He practiced on a spinet bought for him by his father in 1779, but having been delighted with the wind instruments he frequently heard played by the military bands on encampment in Hyde Park, he purchased a clarinet and soon after an oboe. In 1780 he wrote music for a Christmas play at Young's school. He found time to cultivate French and Italian, and it was said that he also studied Hebrew and Syrian, as well as algebra and mathematics. In 1782, by attendance at Westminster Abbey he became acquainted with Arnold, Cooke, and the elder Sale. Sale, according to an early biographer, "quickly became strongly attached to him, in consequence of the peculiar simplicity of his character, the enthusiasm which he displayed for his art, and the astonishing industry, which he exhibited in pursuit of it."

Between 1783 and 1785 Callcott sang in the chorus of the oratorios at Drury Lane. Upon the recommendation of Attwood, he became assistant organist under Reinhold at St George the Martyr, Queen Square, a position he also held from 1783 until 1785. About the same time Cooke introduced him to the Academy of Ancient Music. Callcott was allowed to perform as "a supernumerary hautboy" player in the Academy's concerts at the Crown and Anchor Tavern in the Strand. In the concerts for the 1787–88 season, he was on the pay list as "Tenor Voice" at £6 6s.

Callcott's connections in the Academy turned him to the study and writing of glees. His first glee, composed to the words of Gray's ode "O Sovereign of the Willing Soul," was sent to the Catch Club in 1784. It failed to win a prize, though it was printed in the twenty-third number of Warren's *Collection*; but in 1785 he took three of the four prizes with his glee "Dull repining sons of care," his catch "O beauteous fair," and his canon "Blessed is he." About this time he also composed an instrumental anthem for two double choirs, which was performed for the benefit of Thomson, librarian to the Academy of Ancient Music, a setting for Collins's "Ode to Evening," and another anthem and ode which were performed at the Freemasons' Hall.

On 4 July 1785, at the invitation of Dr Philip Hayes, Professor of Music at Oxford, he took the degree of Bachelor of Music, his exercise for the occasion being a setting of Warton's "Ode to Fancy." His autograph score of a two-act opera, "The Mistakes of a Day," dated 1785, is in the British Museum; there is no record of a performance at London, but a two-act musical entertainment of the same title was played at Norwich in 1787; the anonymous manuscript is in the Larpent Collection at the Huntington Library. An operetta called *The Mistake of a Minute* (Larpent MS 766), never published, was performed at Drury Lane on 23 April 1787. In the autumn of 1785 Callcott composed an ode for the Humane Society, performed at the Freemasons' Hall in February 1786, and in 1786 he obtained two more medals at the Catch Club, for his catch "On a Summer's Morning" and his canon "Bow down thine ear."

By now, at barely 20, Callcott was recognized as a young composer and executant of extraordinary talents. In 1787 he sent in nearly 100 selections to the Catch Club, of which he was now an honorary member, stating he was determined to prove "that, if deficient in genius, I was not deficient in industry." His canon "Thou shalt shew me the path of life" and his glee "Whann Battayle smethynge" took medals, but the society resolved to prohibit more than 12 entries from any one competitor in the future. Taking offense at the rule, Callcott refused to compete for two years but relented in 1789, when he won all four medals. Between 1790 and 1793 he took nine additional medals.

Callcott also had joined with Arnold and others in forming the Glee Club, the first meeting of which occurred on 22 December 1787, in London at the Newcastle Coffee House. On 10 July 1788, he was recommended by Thomas Dupuis for membership in the Royal Society of Musicians, and he was elected on 2 November 1788. He remained active in the Society for a number of years, playing at the annual concerts at St Paul's Cathedral in 1789, 1793, and 1799, serving as a Governor in 1792, 1793, and 1794, and as a member of the Court of Assistants in 1797, 1800, 1803, and 1807.

When Clark, the organist of St Paul, Covent Garden, died in 1789, Callcott competed with Charles Evans for the position; after some sharp canvassing by both parties, a joint appointment was agreed upon, an arrangement which continued until the church was destroyed by fire in 1795. In 1793, Callcott also became organist of the Asylum for Female Orphans, which post he held until 1802, when he resigned it to his son-in-law William Horsley. During some of this period he lived at No 6, James Street, Covent Garden, and later at the Kensington Gravel Pits.

When Haydn visited London in 1791, Callcott, now one of the most successful composers of popular songs but with little experience in orchestration, took some lessons from the master. A symphony, in imitation of Haydn, was still among his manuscripts in 1824.

The popularity of Callcott's catches and glees caused them, of course, to be sung at the theatres. On 17 April 1789, his new

JOHN WALL CALLCOTT
engraving by Lewis, after A. W. Callcott

hunting glee "Tis health that gives birth" was introduced in *The Devil to Pay* at Drury Lane. The catch "When Arthur first in court began" was sung by Incledon, Reeve, and Blanchard at Covent Garden on 17 May 1791 and then became a regular feature of the repertory. "Fa la la" was first sung in the course of *The Irishman in London* at Covent Garden on 5 April 1796. A number of Callcott's songs were sung by Incledon as his specialty numbers at Covent Garden. They included "The New Mariners" on 23 May 1794, "Ye Gentlemen of England" on 28 April 1795, "When Britain first her Flag uprear'd" on 7 October 1799, and "The Red Cross Knight" on 26 April 1800. Callcott also composed the music for *The Battle of Eddington*, a three-act historical drama by John Penn, produced at the Haymarket on 28 March 1796. In 1791 he had been associated with Arnold in the preparation of the airs for *The Psalms of David for the use of Parish Churches*. He was also a member of the Madrigal Society.

During this period Callcott was laying the groundwork for the writing of an extensive dictionary of music. He had purchased from Marmaduke Overend's widow all of that musician's manuscript collection, which included Overend's compositions and those of Dr Boyce as well. With great energy he pursued the study of the theoretical writings of other musicians, and mathematical and philosophical treatises relating to music, devoting much of his days to research at the British Museum and his evenings to the preparation of extracts. At the same time he carried out an exhausting schedule of other duties, including many hours of teaching. In 1797 he issued a prospectus for the dictionary, but his ever-active mind continued to take him along other paths. He had taken a commission in the Kensington Volunteer Corps upon its formation in 1795, and in 1801 he formed a military band for the corps; supported by subscriptions, he bought all the instruments, composed, compiled, and arranged the music, and taught the musicians.

On 18 June 1800 he proceeded to the degree of Doctor of Music at Oxford, presenting the Latin anthem "Propter Sion non tacebo" as his exercise.

In 1801 Callcott anonymously published *The Way to Speak Well, made easy for Youth*, being "the chief words of the English Tongue, classed in Sentences, according to the number of their Syllables: with a short Dictionary at the end of each Book, containing four separate divisions of Substantives, Adjectives, Verbs, and Particles." On 25 October 1802 he wrote an anthem, "I heard a Voice from Heaven," which was sung four days later at Dr Samuel Arnold's funeral. Soon after, Callcott applied for Arnold's post as Composer to the King, but he was unsuccessful. While the compilation of his dictionary went on, and thinking that "the Public would be led

to expect something from him, on the Theory of Music," he published in 1806 his *Musical Grammar* (also 1809, 1817) and in 1807 a *Statement of Earl Stanhope's System of Tuning Keyed Instruments*. In 1806 also he succeeded Dr Crotch as lecturer of music at the Royal Institution and wrote a *scena* on the death of Nelson for the singer James Bartleman.

In 1807, at the age of 41, Callcott's excessive exertions brought him to nervous collapse, and he was confined in an asylum for some five years. His professional colleagues gave a concert for his benefit in 1809 which filled the large King's Theatre with well-wishers. Callcott recovered sufficiently in 1812 to return to public life, but on a strictly reduced schedule. He gave up necessarily the laborious design for his dictionary of music, but he did resume some of his teaching. His mind failed him again in 1816 (he sent thanks to the Royal Society of Music for a benefaction on 4 February 1816) and once more he was compelled to go into an asylum, near Bristol, where he died on 15 May 1821, at the age of 55. His body was brought to London and buried in Kensington Churchyard on 23 May.

Callcott had married Elizabeth Mary Hutchins at St Paul, Covent Garden, on 14 July 1791, and for that occasion wrote the words and music of the glee "Triumphant Love." They had at least three children, probably more. Administration of Callcott's property was granted to his widow on 26 January 1821.

Their eldest daughter Elizabeth Hutchins Callcott married the musician William Horsley (1774–1858) in 1813 and survived him until 20 January 1885. Their son Charles Edward Horsley (1822–1876) was also a musician active in England, Australia, and the United States. It was William Horsley who published *A Selection of Glees from the MSS . . . of the Concentores: being the Compositions of Dr Callcott* in 1824, with a memoir of his

By permission of the Trustees of the British Museum

JOHN WALL CALLCOTT

engraving by Meyer

father-in-law's life, "written from my own recollections; from communications made to me by Dr Callcott's Family and Friends; and, more particularly, from a brief sketch of the principal events of his life, drawn up by the Doctor himself, and now in my possession."

Callcott's other known daughter Sophia became "eminent as a teacher of the pianoforte" and resided near London in 1827. His younger son, William Hutchins Callcott, was born at Kensington Gravel Pits on 28 September 1807, according to a deposition of his uncle Augustus Wall Callcott to the Royal Society of Musicians on 4 April 1830; he was baptized at Kensington Church on 24 October of the same year. He was organist of the new district Chapel in Addison Road, Kensington, and a teacher of music when he was admitted to the Royal Society of Music on 4 July 1830.

Having attained some distinction as a composer and arranger, William Hutchins Callcott died at his home, No 1, Campden House Road, Kensington, on 4 August 1882; execution of his estate of £14,954 5s. 10d. was granted on 14 September 1882 to his son, William Robert Stuart Callcott (1852–1886), also an organist.

John Wall Callcott's brothers, the above-mentioned Augustus Wall Callcott and William Callcott, are noticed separately. An Arabella Wall Callcott, who married a Thomas Buckley, probably a musician, at St George, Hanover Square, on 25 August 1803, was no doubt their sister.

John Wall Callcott was a prolific writer of glees and other pieces of vocal harmony. An extensive list of his published music is found in the *Catalogue of Printed Music in the British Museum*. In addition to dozens of glees and catches, they include anthems and hymns sung at the Asylum Chapel, six sacred trios, six sonatinas for the harpsichord, and two curious musical settings of the multiplication and pence tables. Many of his manuscripts, including his collection for a dictionary of music, are at the British Museum. Numerous other manuscripts, autograph and holograph, are in the Euing Collection, Glasgow University Library. John was painted by his brother, Augustus Wall Callcott; an engraving of the portrait, by F. C. Lewis, was prefaced to the collection of his glees (with a memoir) published by Horsley in 1824. A portrait engraving of him was done by H. Meyer.

Callcott, William [*fl.* 1790–1800], *musician.*

William Callcott was the son of Thomas Callcott, bricklayer and builder, of Kensington. He was a relatively obscure figure in comparison to his more famous brothers, Dr John Wall Callcott (1766–1821) and Sir Augustus Wall Callcott (1779–1844). As legal documents concerning William do not give him the middle name of Wall (the maiden name of his father's second wife Charlotte), his mother probably was Charlotte Urry, his father's first wife, who had married Thomas in 1750. If that is so, then William was the eldest of Thomas Callcott's known sons. He was probably the "William Calcutt," bachelor, who married Mary Bagnall, spinster, at St Paul, Covent Garden, on 23 January 1790.

In 1794 Doane's *Musical Directory* listed William Callcott as a player on the horn and violin, associated with Astley's Theatre and the Apollo Gardens, and then living at No 30, Princes Street, Soho. Either his wife Mary had a second name, Elizabeth, or before 1800 he married again, for when his son—also William Callcott—was recommended for admission to the Royal Society of Musicians on 1 April 1821, the vicar of St Mary Abbots, Kensington, certified that he had been baptized on 7 May 1800, the son of William and Elizabeth Callcott, of Wrights Lane in that parish. Elizabeth Callcott also swore on 27 June 1821 that her "lawful Son William Callcott by her late Husband deceased" had been born on 26 March 1800 at Kensington. The younger William Callcott, who played the pianoforte, violin, and tenor, was doing considerable private teaching and was engaged at Covent Garden Theatre at the time he was elected to the society on 24 June 1821.

Callfield. *See* CAULFIELD.

Calliari. *See* GIRARDEAU.

Callois. *See* CAWLEY.

Calori, Angiola *1732–c. 1790, singer.*
The soprano Signora Angiola Calori was born at Milan in 1732, but "Nothing is known of her career in Italy," according to Grove, before her engagement at the King's Theatre, London, in 1757–58, as the second woman for serious opera and for serious parts in the burlettas. Her first appearance

of record at the King's was as Radamisto in Cocchi's new opera *Zenobia*, given on 10 January 1758, although she may have sung in *Demetrio* which opened on 8 November 1757 and was repeated throughout the season. She sang Osmino in *Solimano* (31 January) and probably had roles in *Issipile* (14 March) and *Creso* (4 April). On 6 April 1758 she sang at a concert for the benefit of the Fund for the Support of Decayed Musicians.

Signora Calori appeared regularly at the King's Theatre over the ensuing three seasons. Her roles (with date of first performance) included: Zomira in *Attalo* (11 November 1758), Arpalice in *Il Ciro riconosciuto* (16 January 1759), Lucilla in *Vologeso* (13 November 1759), Servilia in *La clemenza di Tito* (15 January 1760), Ramise in *Arminio* (1 March 1760), Ermione in *Antigona* (17 April 1760 and for her benefit on 15 May), Ismena in *Erginda regina di Livadia* (31 May 1760), Flaminia in *Il mondo nella luna* (22 November 1760), Laodice in *Arianna e Teseo* (16 December 1760), Eugenia in *Il filosofo di campagna* (6 January 1761), Sabina in *Tito Manlio* (7 February 1761), and Eurilda in *La pescatrice* (28 April 1761). She also sang at various concerts, including performances of *L'isola disabitata* at the Great Room in Dean Street, Soho, on 13 March 1760, at the Haymarket on 27 March 1760, and at Hickford's Room on 29 April 1760. On 5 June 1760 she sang at the Haymarket, and on 28 January 1761 again at the Great Room in Dean Street, for the benefit of Tenducci. Perhaps she sang in the oratorios *Samson* and the *Messiah* in the spring of 1759.

The statement by Grove that Signora Calori did not appear again at London after 1761 is probably correct, despite the listing of her name as a member of the King's Theatre company in 1765–66 by *The London Stage*, which cites a 1765 edition of *La clemenza di Tito* as evidence for including her in the cast of a performance of that opera on 3 December 1765. The cast given in the 1765 edition, however, is the same as that printed in the edition of 1760, in which year she did sing Servilia. No casts are known for the other three operas performed at the King's Theatre in 1765–66.

After singing at Dresden "with great success" in 1770, Signora Calori returned to Italy in 1774, where she appeared at the various opera houses until 1783. She died about 1790. According to Grove, she "had a soprano voice of great extent, a profound knowledge of music and extraordinary rapidity of execution."

Calverley, Thomas [fl. 1665–1667], actor?

Thomas Calverley was a member of the King's Company from at least as early as 8 June 1665, when his name first appeared in the Lord Chamberlain's accounts, through the 1666–67 season. Possibly he was an actor, though no roles are known for him. He may have been related to the dancing master of approximately the same name who ran a dancing school in the early eighteenth century.

Calverly, Joseph [fl. 1794], singer.

Joseph Calverly was listed by Doane's *Musical Directory* in 1794 as an "alto" (i.e., countertenor singer) living at No 26, Market Lane, St James's, and a member of the Choral Fund, the Handelian Society, and a singer in the oratorios at Drury Lane.

Calvert, Mrs [fl. 1772], singer.

A Mrs Calvert sang at Marylebone Gardens in 1772. Perhaps she was related to the Mrs Calvert, a widow in distress who had four children and who received a benefit at Covent Garden Theatre on 9 December 1757.

Calvert, [Charles?] [fl. 1784–1786], actor.

A Mr Calvert, announced as from Smock Alley Theatre, Dublin, made his first appearance on the London stage as Freeport in *The English Merchant* at the Haymarket, out of season, on 22 March 1784. He made two other appearances at the Haymarket, as Richard III on 17 September 1784 and as Tamerlane on 6 March 1786.

He may have been the actor, identified by William Clark as Charles Calvert, who, as a "Young Gentleman," made his first appearance at Smock Alley as Jaffeir in *Venice Preserv'd* on 19 December 1770 and then played Myrtle in *The Conscious Lovers* on 24 January 1771 and also acted at Cork, 1772–74. According to Strictland in the *Dictionary of Irish Artists* (he does not provide a first name) that Irish Calvert did not remain long an actor but started wax-modeling under the tuition of Cunningham. He had been a pupil of the sculptor, James Moore, at London, and in 1767 had exhibited at the Free Society a bas-relief in Portland stone of "The Death of Socrates" and drawings of the head of Scipio Africanus and Democritus. Probably he was the Calvert who advertised in the *Hibernian Journal* on 9 April 1777, from No 64, Dame Street, Dublin, between Crow Street and Temple Bar, that he did "likenesses in miniature profile." In 1783, about a year before the actor Calvert appeared at the Haymarket, a Mr Calvert, living at Mr Crashley's in Long Acre, exhibited six models of colored wax at the Society of Artists, including one of the Covent Garden actor Lewis.

There is also a possibility that the subject of this entry was either Raisley Calvert (d. 1794) (a sculptor who bequeathed £900 to his friend William Wordsworth) or his brother, the elder Charles Calvert. The latter was, according to *The Dictionary of National Biography*, an "amateur artist," who was born in 1754 and died on 13 June 1797 and was buried in St Mary's Churchyard, Manchester. No mention is made of that Calvert's having been an actor. By 1785 he was the agent for the Duke of

Norfolk's estate, Glossop Hall in Derbyshire. That Charles Calvert had four sons: Charles Calvert, the younger (1785–1852), a landscape painter; Frederick Baltimore Calvert (1793–1877), an actor and lecturer on elocution; and Henry Calvert and Michael Pease Calvert, nineteenth-century painters.

Calvesi, Vincenzo [fl. 1786–1788], singer.

Although he may have been with the English Opera as early as 1783, Signor Calvesi made his first noticed appearance at the King's Theatre as Fenicio in *Alceste* on 23 December 1786. In that season he also sang Capitan Francone in *Giannina e Bernardone*, Martufo in *Il tutore burlato*, and a principal character in *Didone abbandonata*. In 1787–88 he sang Teodoro in *Il re Teodoro in Venezia*, Sumers in *La locandiera*, Don Berlicco in *Gli schiava per amore*, Gonzalini in *La cameriera astuta*, Aminta in *L'Olimpiade*, a principal character in *La Frascatana*, and Annio in *Giulio Sabino*, making his last appearance of record in London in this last role on 28 June 1788. He was the husband of the singer Teresa Calvesi. Vincenzo Calvesi was the subject of an engraving by Loeschenkohl after an unknown artist.

Calvesi, Teresa [fl. 1783–1792], singer.

According to her letter to the *Morning Post* on 14 April 1791, Signora Teresa Calvesi had been "one of the many unfortunate performers who were left unpaid in the year of 1783 by Mr Taylor," the manager of the King's Theatre. Her name, however, did not appear in the bills until 1 March 1791, when she sang Vespina in *La bella pescatrice* as a member of the King's Opera at the Pantheon. That season she also sang Donna Eugenia in *La molinarella* and Marinetta in *La locanda*. On 12 April 1791 she was unable to sing her role in *La bella pescatrice* because "De-

prived of resources, she naturally contracted debts," she explained in her letter to the press, "for one of which (yesterday evening going to obey her duty to the Public) she was arrested and so expeditiously and secretly hurried away as to deprive her of the assistance of the Manager or her Friends to liberate her 'till an hour too late for Performance." In the following season she sang Donna Florida in *La pastorella nobile* on 17 December 1791.

When the Pantheon burned down on 14 January 1792, the company moved to the Haymarket, where Signora Calvesi made her first appearance on 14 February as Dorinda in *La trame deluse*. Her other roles there were Cardellina in *La discordia conjugale* and Marinetta again. She made her final London appearance of record at the Haymarket on 9 June 1792 in the role of Vespina. She was the wife of the singer Vincenzo Calvesi. She was the subject of an engraving by Loeschenkohl after an unknown artist.

Camano, Mrs [fl. 1733], actress.

A Mrs Camano acted Glumdalca in *The Opera of Operas* at the Haymarket Theatre on 4 June 1733.

Camargo, [Sophie? or Marie-Anne Charlotte?] Cupis de [fl. 1728?–1770?], dancer.

The "Madam Cupis Camargo" who danced at Drury Lane Theater in 1750–51 and then for another four seasons at Covent Garden, 1751–55, was not, as is commonly believed, the famous "star" ballerina of the Paris Opéra, Marie-Anne Cupis de Camargo (1710–1770), but rather one of her two younger sisters, either Sophie or Marie-Anne Charlotte. Indeed, the great Camargo was dancing in her last month on the stage at the Paris Opéra (before retiring in March 1751) at the very time that the name of the other Camargo was appearing in the Drury Lane bills.

The three dancing sisters were descended

from an illustrious Roman family which included a cardinal and other high dignitaries of the Church. Their father was Ferdinand Joseph de Cupis who had been born in Flanders where his father had migrated in the seventeenth century. The latter died soon after his marriage in Flanders to a well-born Spanish lady by the surname of Camargo, leaving Ferdinand Joseph's mother to see to his education. Widow and child eventually moved to Brussels, where Ferdinand Joseph married and where his first children were born. Adopting the maternal name of Camargo, apparently because it had a better ring than Cupis, Ferdinand styled himself "écuyer, lord of Renoussart and Opperzielen," but in reality he was only a violinist and dancing master. When his eldest daughter, Marie-Anne, showed a promising talent for dancing, he provided her with early training at Brussels and Paris, and about 1725 he found an engagement for her at the new Opéra at Rouen, where he had a position in the band. By May 1726 the family was employed at the Paris Opéra.

Two younger sisters of Marie-Anne Cupis de Camargo are known. Sophie, born in 1715, was dancing, as "Camargo *cadette*," at the age of 13, with Marie-Anne and a brother, at the Paris Opéra. The three Camargo names are found on a bill for the revival of the opera *Bellérophon* there on 8 April 1728. In May of that year, prima ballerina Marie Cupis de Camargo and the young Sophie were carried off by the Comte de Melun to his mansion. Their outraged father, Ferdinand Joseph de Cupis, petitioned the Prime Minister for redress in his "Requète de M. De Camargo à son Eminence Monseigneur le Cardinal de Fleury, à L'Occasion de L'Enlèvement de ses Filles," demanding that the Count marry his elder daughter and provide a dowry for the younger. But it seems that the sensational business was treated lightly by the authorities.

Soon Sophie came home to her father, but Marie-Anne remained with the Comte de Melun, who was merely the earliest in a string of paramours which included the Duc de Richelieu, the Marquis de Sourdis, and the Comte de Clermont. The second younger sister, named Marie-Anne Charlotte, daughter of Ferdinand Joseph de Cupis by (probably his second) wife Marie-Anne de Smeldt, was baptized at the Church of Saint Sauveur, Paris, on 3 February 1731. Among the witnesses' signatures was that of her famous sister Marie-Anne de Cupis, then 21 years old.

The "Madame" Cupis de Camargo who danced at London in the middle of the eighteenth century was either Sophie, who would have been about 35 at the time, or Marie-Anne Charlotte, born 1731, and then about 19. The fact that she was without doubt one of the lesser-known sisters provides the answers to the questions raised by Stanley W. E. Vince's article, "Camargo in London," *Theatre Notebook* (1958), concerning "a curious and largely unexplained episode" in the life of the great Camargo. In a postscript to his article, in *Theatre Notebook* (1959), some further light was cast with the assistance of Lillian Moore, who pointed to the existence of a Camargo *cadette*, sister of the famous dancer of the same name, who was *première danseuse* at the Comédie Française in 1755. "Elle revenoit d'Angleterre" in that year, according to Parfaict's *Dictionnaire des Théâtres de Paris*, and she appeared in at least two ballets at the Théâtre Français, *Le Poirier* on 18 January 1755 and *Les Bergeries* in July. It is still not known whether that Camargo *cadette* was Sophie, who was indeed known to have been a professional dancer, or Marie-Anne Charlotte, about whom little else but her baptism is known. A further confusion is added by the fact that in 1770, the great Camargo mentioned in her will only one sister (perhaps the other had not survived): "demoiselle Anne Cupis, fille majeure, demeurant rue Saint Denis." Anne, of course, was the middle name of the youngest of the known daughters of Ferdinand Joseph Cupis de Camargo, but Anne might also have been one of Sophie's names.

Whether reporting Sophie or Marie-Anne Charlotte, the *General Advertiser* of 19 September 1750 misspelled the last name as "Camarr" in its announcement of the Drury Lane program for the next day, at which the dancer made her inconspicuous debut. But the paper corrected itself on the day of the performance, 20 September, announcing "a Rural Dance by Mons. Grandchamps, Mr. Mathews and Mad. Cupis Camargo (Being the First Time of her appearing in England)." Her name appeared in the Drury Lane bills that season for 62 evenings (by mid-November the "Cupis" was dropped and she was billed as Madame Camargo), including some 30 performances of a "Comic Dance" with such partners as Mathews, M'Neil, and "the little Swiss," a "Rural Dance" with Mathews, and a "Savoyard Dance" with Mathews at his benefit on 26 April 1751.

She also danced in the masquerade scene of *Much Ado About Nothing* (first time on 7 November), in *Comus* on 13 October and 3 May, in several performances of a comic entertainment called *The Bird-Catchers* (first time on 27 November), and with Devisse, Mathews, and Madame Auretti in 15 consecutive performances of Garrick's successful production of *Alfred*, with music by Thomas A. Arne. The *General Advertiser* of 25 February reported the "universal Applause" the piece had received on its opening night, 23 February 1751, but noted that "the Spectators rightly found fault with some Improprieties in the Performance of the inferior Dancers and Actors, which will all be corrected in this Night's Representation." Madame Camargo's first season at London created no great stir, and no attempt seems to have been made to capitalize on the reputation of her more illustrious sister. Her benefit on

13 May 1751 was shared with six other minor figures of the company. Originally it was to occur on 13 April (the printed bill for that date gave her address at the Golden Head, in Broad Street, Covent Garden), but the program was cancelled by the death of the Prince of Wales.

In 1751–52 Madame Camargo transferred to Covent Garden where for three seasons she continued with singular lack of distinction. Her name first appeared in the bills of that theatre on 11 November 1751 as the Scaramouch Woman in Rich's pantomime-ballet *The Necromancer*, which was given 27 performances that season. Perhaps her most important role was as Daphne to Villeneuve's Apollo in Rich's ballet pantomime of *Apollo and Daphne* on 4 December and 16 other times. She also danced in the "Grand Ballet" on the same program. She danced one of the twelve aerial spirits in *Merlin's Cave*, or *Harlequin Skeleton* on 9 January, once with Lalauze in *Pyramus and Thisbe* on 9 December, and for Lalauze's benefit on 15 April in a dance entitled *Le je ne scay quoy*, with Dennison and Settree. Her own benefit on 18 April was shared with Grandchamps and Howard.

In 1752–53 and 1753–54, Madame Camargo filled similar assignments at Covent Garden in such pieces as *The Oracle* (10 March 1753), in which she personified an animated statue, probably *Harlequin Sorcerer* (played regularly in 1752–53), *The Italian Peasants* (20 November 1753 and 27 other times), and as a dancing shepherd in *The Sheep Shearing* (24 April 1754). In her last full season she did not enjoy even a shared benefit status, but on 16 April 1754, when she danced a minuet and louvre with Gardiner, "tickets delivered out by Mad. Camargo and Miss Ferguson" were taken. Her name was on the Covent Garden bill for dancing on 23 November 1754 but, as noted above, by January 1755 "Elle revenoit d'Angleterre" and was dancing at the Théâtre Français. Soon afterward she vanished from the public records.

Madame Camargo also had at least three brothers: Jean-Baptiste de Cupis (1711–1788), violinist and composer and father by his wife Constance Dufour of his namesake (b. 1741), who was also a musician and composer in France; François de Cupis (1719–c. 1764), violinist at the Paris Opéra; and Charles de Cupis, a musician at the L'Académie Royale de Musique. All three were mentioned in the will of Marie-Anne Camargo in 1770; Jean-Baptiste and François are noticed in Grove. According to French sources, the patriarch of the family, Ferdinand Joseph de Cupis, alias Camargo, died at Paris in 1767, in his late seventies.

Cambert, Robert *c. 1628–1677, composer, impresario, band leader.*

Born about 1628 in Paris, Robert Cambert studied under Chambonnières and became, about 1655, organist of Saint-Honoré. Most of his career was devoted to musical composition, and with the Abbé Pierre Perrin he contributed importantly to the development of French opera. Their *Ariane* was written in 1661 but was not performed in public until 1674 in London. In 1666 Cambert became superintendent of music to Anne of Austria, the widow of Louis XIII, and in 1669 he received royal permission to produce operas. On 3 March 1671 Cambert and Perrin's *Pomone* was performed at the converted tennis court that was the first home of the Paris Opéra. After some initial success, Cambert lost his privilege to Lully, in 1672.

Cambert joined his student Louis Grabu in London in September 1673. He formed the Royal Academy of Musick and with Grabu produced his *Ariane* at Drury Lane on 30 March 1674; his *Pomone* was presented at Whitehall in July. A Lord Chamberlain's warrant dated 4 July 1674 ordered 12 of the violinists in the King's Musick to rehearse with Cambert for a musical performance at Windsor scheduled for 11 July. Sainsbury stated that Cambert became master of the band of Charles II, but Burney said that Cambert's post was that of leader of a regimental band.

Robert Cambert died in London about February 1677. The few pieces of music by Cambert which have survived are discussed in *Grove's Dictionary of Music and Musicians.*

Cambray. *See* **FENNELL, JAMES.**

Camel, Tom *[fl. 1785], equestrian.*

On 21 October 1785, a day when Charles Hughes at the Royal Circus took "the liberty to acquaint the Nobility, Gentry, and Public, that he will continue the NEW PERFORMANCES at this Place. . . . assisted by his TROOP from DUBLIN," one "Tom Camel [Campbell?] jun." appeared (in yellow silks) on a horse named Old Lath against five other entries in a "New Jockey Race." Whether Camel, who is not otherwise recorded, was a regular member of Hughes's London company, one of the "Dublin troop," or a professional jockey brought in for the occasion is not known.

Camerford. *See* **COMERFORD.**

Cameron, Mr *[fl. 1797], actor.*

A Mr Cameron played Decius in a single performance of *Cato* given at the Haymarket on 4 December 1797. Other members of the cast included Tate Wilkinson and Mr Bellamy from the York Theatre Royal.

Cameron, Mr *d. 1800, boxkeeper.*

Mr Cameron was a boxkeeper at Drury Lane from 1774–75 through 1799–1800, regularly taking benefits with other house servants. In 1775–76 he was paid 12*s.* per week; by 1789–90 his salary was reduced to 9*s.* per week. On 9 July and 26 July 1800 his widow received payments of £13

2s. 10d. each "for salary due to her late husband."

Camery, Mr [*fl. 1777–1778*], *actor.*
A Mr Camery made his first appearance on the London stage as an unspecified character in a single performance of Robert Hitchcock's comedy, *The Coquette*, at the Haymarket, out of season, on 9 October 1777. No other performances by him are known; however, Camery was paid £1 2s. 6d. by Drury Lane Theatre on 14 October 1777, according to a manuscript in the Folger Library, and on 21 October 1777, according to a manuscript in the British Museum, for "9 days not on list." On 26 May 1778 he shared tickets with Hodges. Presumably he was a supernumerary at Drury Lane at this time.

"Camilla." See **TOFTS, CATHERINE.**

Camille, Master [*fl. 1712*], *dancer.*
"Young Mr Camille"—so billed—danced with Hester Santlow at a benefit concert for Nicolini at the Queen's Theatre in the Haymarket on 22 March 1712.

Camillo, Mary [*fl. 1796–1797*], *posture maker.*
Mary Camillo was one of seven members of a Sicilian troupe of posture makers and tumblers, headed by Signor Saccardi, which performed at Sadler's Wells in the summer of 1796. Probably she accompanied the troupe which Saccardi brought to entertain at the Cambridge Fair in 1797.

Campanini, Barbarina *1721–1799, dancer.*
Barbarina Campanini (known professionally as "La Barbarina") was one of the most celebrated ballet dancers of the eighteenth century. Born at Parma in 1721, by the age of 10 she was a pupil of Rinaldi Fossano, a Neopolitan whom Noverre called "the most charming and witty of comic dancers." At the age of 18, she was

taken to Paris by Fossano and presented at the Académie Royale de Musique (l'Opéra) where she made her debut on 14 July 1739 in Rameau's ballet *Les Fêtes d'Hébé*. Rameau had expressly written four dances for her in the piece—an *entrée vivre*, a louvre, a minuet, and a gavotte—to exhibit her virtuosity. Her debut was a great success, and with Fossano as her dancing partner, La Barbarina enjoyed a continuous run of over 50 performances in *Les Fêtes d'Hébé*. Contemporary reports indicate that she danced in the style of Mlle Camargo. In his *Mémoires*, Réne-Louis Argenson wrote that though she had fat legs she danced with precision; he expressed some fear that her Italian style of dancing would be copied at Paris.

Campanini's other successes in her first season at the Opéra included *Momus*

Harvard Theatre Collection

BARBARINA CAMPANINI
engraving by Eccart, after Pehsne

amoureux and *Zaide*. Mlle Salle, who became very jealous of Barbarina's success, danced with her in the latter piece. Between 29 October and 5 November 1739, La Barbarina danced at Fontainebleau and was presented with a gift by Louis XV. Her tutor and partner Fossano departed for Italy in November of that year, but La Barbarina reappeared at the Opéra with great success in Rameau's ballet *Dardanus* on 3 December and again in *Les Fêtes d'Hébé* on 10 December 1739.

La Barbarina's popularity brought her the attentions of numerous fashionable suitors at Paris. She soon became the mistress of the Prince de Carignan, but the affair was short-lived after he discovered that she was distributing her favors among other noblemen: the Prince di Conti, the Duc de Durfort, Lord Arundel, and others.

Early in 1740 La Barbarina performed at Versailles with a troupe of the Comédie Française. She was then engaged by John Rich at a salary of £2 2s. per day for the ensuing 1740–41 season at Covent Garden. Soon after her arrival in England in July, La Barbarina danced at the *festa teatrale* organized by the Prince of Wales for the birthday of the Princess Augusta of Brunswick in the gardens at Cliveden on 1 August 1740. Several months later, on 25 October, she made her London debut dancing with Denoyer. She continued regularly throughout the season in such pieces as *The Italian Peasants, Mars and Venus*, and *Le Tirolesi*. On 2 February 1741 she danced a garden nymph in *The Royal Chace*. She received a clear benefit on 14 February, taking £240 15s., for which she performed a louvre, a minuet, a new tambourine dance with Denoyer, and *Les Savoyards* with Villeneuve.

In the spring of 1741 the scenographer Giovanni Servandoni was sent to London on a successful mission to persuade Barbarina to return to Paris. She reappeared at the Académie Royale de Musique on 13 June in *Empire de l'amour* and on 4 July danced in *Les Fêtes Grecques et Romaines*. By October of 1741 she was back at Covent Garden. In mid-winter a "violent Feaver" prevented her appearance for some time. In this season of 1741–42, her sister, Signora Domitilla, also danced at Covent Garden. In the middle of June she arrived in Dublin to perform with the Smock Alley company which at this time also included Peg Woffington and the young Garrick, who had made his sensational debut at Goodman's Fields only eight months before. La Barbarina returned to London in the ensuing season to dance, not at Covent Garden (where her sister was still engaged), but at the King's Theatre. At the opening of the opera season there on 2 November 1742 she made her debut. Horace Walpole reported in a letter to Mann an attempt to abduct her as she left the theatre.

By September 1743, La Barbarina had returned to Paris, where the Prussian minister engaged her services for Frederick the Great. But instead of going to Berlin as contracted, she fled to Venice with the intention of marrying James Stuart-Mackenzie. They had met in London, and Mackenzie's infatuation with her became matter for a romantic *cause célèbre*. The indignant Frederick had the Venetian government arrest La Barbarina and had her sent to his frontier under escort. She arrived at Berlin in May 1744, to be followed soon by Mackenzie, who had taken another route. His pursuit was in vain, for with the cooperation of the British ambassador in Berlin Mackenzie was expelled from Prussia, while La Barbarina, virtually under house arrest, was forced to remain. Mackenzie was back in England by July 1744 and for a while continued to write ardent letters to her.

Barbarina made her debut at Berlin on 13 May 1744 with extraordinary success. For four years she continued as a prima ballerina in the operas and *intermezzi* at the Court Opera, appearing in such pieces as *Catone in Utica* (1744), *Artaserse*

(1744), *La Clemenza di Tito* (1744), *Alessandro e Poro* (1744), *Lucio Papiro* (1745), *Adriano in Siria* (1745), *Demofoonte* (1746), *Cajo Fabricio* (1746), *Arminio* (1747), *Le feste galanti* (1747), *Cinna* (1748), *L'Europa galante* (1748). In her apartment in the Behrenstrasse, Barbarina regularly convened a salon of intellectuals and nobility. Frederick himself, it is said, sometime graced her dinner table after performances.

Soon after her debut, Frederick settled on her an emolument of 5000 thalers per year, raised to 7000 after the first year, with a nullifying clause if she should marry. Toward the end of the third year of her engagement she became involved in a scandal which brought about her disgrace at Court. At the conclusion of one of her performances, the Baron Carl Ludwig von Cocceji, son of Frederick's Grand Chancellor, went up on the stage and publicly declared his love for her. Frederick was provoked enough to withdraw permission for her to go to England, where she had kept money, on the pretext that she had large debts in Berlin. She paid the debts, however, and left for London. On 25 July 1748 the *General Advertiser* announced that "On Wednesday last arrived here from Berlin, the Celebrated Signora Barbarini, with her Sister Signiora Domitilla." Her sister had been with her on her first visit to London in the earlier part of the decade,

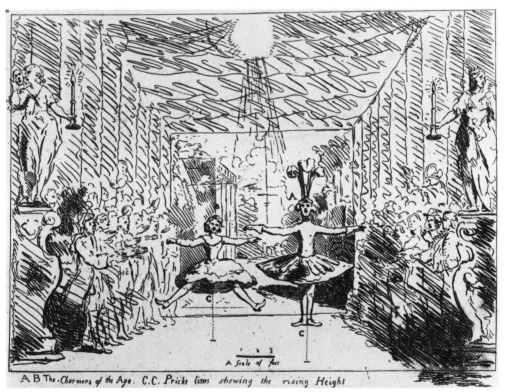

A B The *Charmers of the Age*: C.C. *Prickt lines shewing the rising Height*

By permission of the Trustees of the British Museum

BARBARINA CAMPANINI and MONS DENOYER
"The Charmers of the Age"
engraving by Livesay, after Hogarth

but there is no record that either dancer performed in the London theatres during this second visit in 1748.

In 1749, Barbarina returned to Berlin, whereupon on 6 August Cocceji was arrested. He was released after six months, and the couple then married secretly. Not until the end of 1751 was Frederick informed of the marriage, and upon its discovery Frederick at first vented anger on the priest who had performed the ceremony. Finally accepting the marriage, however, Frederick sent the couple off to Glogau, in remote Silesia, where Cocceji was given a public appointment.

Now a baroness, and retired from professional life, La Barbarina lived with Cocceji for eight years. They separated in 1759. She went to live at her castle of Barschau which she had bought with income from her investments. Soon she obtained from Frederick's successor, Frederick Wilhelm, the title of Gräfin von Barschau and then in 1787 the title of Gräfin von Campanini, on condition that she would leave all her belongings to a home for poor girls of noble origin. Cocceji obtained a divorce from her in 1788, and she is said then to have married "a German Baron of sixteen quarterings." In her last years she gave personal direction to her girls' home. After La Barbarina's death at Barschau on 7 June 1799, at the age of 78, her will was nullified and most of her estate was sold for the benefit of the state. She was buried in the church at Barschau.

Barbarina had two sisters. One, named Miriamne, was the dancer who accompanied her to Austria and who danced in Paris, and in Berlin in January 1747. Probably she was the Signora Domitilla who danced in London in 1741–43. The other sister married a Florentine merchant. Barbarina's mother was living with her at Berlin in the 1740s.

A popular figure in German theatrical history, Barbarina Campanini has been the subject of biographies by W. Roseler, *Die Barbarina* (Berlin, 1890) and J. J. Olivier and W. Norbert, *Barbarina Campanini* (Berlin, 1909), as well as of a German film, *Die tanzezin Barbarina* in 1920 and of a ballet, *Barbarina*, which was performed at the Staatsoper, Berlin, in 1935. Barbarina was painted at least three times by Antonio Pehsne: with a group on a wall screen, with a group of dancers, and alone. All three paintings are in the Potsdam Stadtschlosses. A statue of her as Pygmalion, by Pehsne, is in the Musikzimmer of the Palace of Sansouci. A pastel portrait of her by Rosalba Carriera is in the Royal Gallery at Dresden. A painting of her at the age of 34, with a dog, is at the Palace of Barschau; a miniature by Diemoz (1764) and a painting of her at age 65 by J. Anton Bausewein are also at Barschau. A well-known engraving of her, holding her skirt in her hands, was done by C. B. Glassbach. She is pictured dancing in mid-air in Hogarth's satire on opera dancers, "The Charmers of the Age," engraved by Livesay and published in 1782.

Campbell. *See also* **CAMEL.**

Campbell, Mr [*fl.* 1732–1736], *actor.*

A Mr Campbell attempted London in a pickup company which rented the new Haymarket Theatre on 2 March 1732 to present for the first time *The Blazing Comet: The Mad Lovers; or, the Beauties of the Poets* by the eccentric Samuel Johnson of Cheshire. This astral phenomenon burned out after seven scattered performances, but Campbell was probably in one or more of the other farces given by Johnson and company at the Haymarket that season.

The name "Campbell" was absent from London's theatrical bills until 11 February 1736 when there was a program for the benefit of a Mr De Villiers "At the Desire of several Persons of Quality," in which a Campbell, probably our subject, played Leander in the afterpiece *The Mock Doctor* at the Haymarket.

Campbell, [Mrs? Miss?] [*fl.* 1722–1724], *actress.*

When on 12 April 1722 the managers of Drury Lane and Lincoln's Inn Fields drew up articles agreeing to desist from raiding each others' rosters in the ensuing season and inventoried their players, a woman named Campbell was listed as acting at Drury Lane. The sketchy and infrequent playbills for 1722–23 reveal that she played Dol Mavis in *The Silent Woman* on 14 February, Teresia in *The Squire of Alsatia* for her benefit shared with Mrs Bretton on 24 May, Lady Frances Howard in *Sir Thomas Overbury* on 12, 14, and 19 June, and Queen Margaret in Theophilus Cibber's alteration of *Henry VI* on 5 July 1723.

In the season of 1723–24 she returned to Drury Lane to play Dol on 6 November, Flareit in *Love's Last Shift* on 19 November, Charlot in *Henry V* on 5 December 1723, Doraspe in *The Captives* on 15 January, and Emilia in *The Man of Mode* on 29 April 1724 for her benefit shared with Theophilus Cibber. She did not appear in London after these dates.

Campbell, Mrs [*fl.* 1751], *singer, actress.*

A Mrs Campbell sang the role of Polly in *The Beggar's Opera* for Yeates's benefit performance in his Great Tiled Booth at Southwark Fair on 17 September 1751. She was not heard from again in London.

Campbell, Miss [*fl.* 1779], *actress.*

A Miss Campbell was cast in the role of Emily in the afterpiece *The Students; or, The Humours of St Andrews* at a special performance given at the Haymarket on 11 January 1779 "By Authority of the Lord Chamberlain" for the benefit of two of the other actors, Stewart and M'Donald. Several others of the cast had Caledonian names—Sinclair, Henderson, Hamilton—and some of them, including Miss Campbell, may have been amateurs.

Campbell, Miss, later Mrs J. Gunning [*fl.* 1799–1806?], *actress.*

Miss Campbell seems to have been first introduced to London as from the Theatre Royal, Newcastle, when she played the part of Julia in *The Surrender of Calais* at the Haymarket on 10 September 1799. The *Thespian Dictionary* (1805) in recalling this performance said that the young performer had been very much alarmed at first but that "repeated approbation" had dissipated her fears. The same account asserted that she had played at Margate and had appeared (presumably only once) in the part of Fanny in *The Clandestine Marriage* at Drury Lane the "preceding" season. The extant bills do not confirm the latter assertion but it is possible that she had substituted for Miss Miller, whose part it was.

More probably the writer for the *Thespian Dictionary* was remembering her performance as Fanny when she joined the Drury Lane company on 21 September 1799, again advertised as from Newcastle. Her salary was £3 per week for a season in which she also appeared in the bills as Lady Touchwood in *The Belle's Stratagem*, Angelina in *Love Makes a Man*, and the Marchioness Merida in *The Child of Nature*, with several repetitions in each part.

Miss Campbell continued in this general line of characters at Drury Lane through the 1802–3 season at least, despite the dismissal of her talents as trivial by Thomas Dutton in his *Dramatic Censor* of 1 January 1800.

The O. Smith manuscript history of the stage in the British Museum says that Miss Campbell was "afterwards Mrs Gunning the Novelist." That she married a Mr Gunning is probable, in view of the fact that Ralph Wewitzer, who was with Miss Campbell in the Drury Lane Company, testified in his *Dramatic Chronology* that she was "now Mrs Gunning" in 1817 and the additional fact that a "Mrs J. Gunning" was acting at Drury Lane in 1804–5 and 1805–6. Smith probably took the information about Miss Campbell's marriage from Wewitzer and gratuitously added "the Novelist." She could not possibly have been the novelist Mrs Susannah Gunning (1740?–1800), who was born Susannah Minifie and who in any case died too early to fit. Nor is she likely to have been *Miss Elizabeth Gunning* (1764–1823), Susannah's daughter, employing a stage name up to 1804 and then reverting to her maiden name, for Elizabeth married Major James Plunkett of County Roscommon on 5 November 1803.

Campbell, J. *d. 1802, actor.*

J. Campbell was first noticed in London at Covent Garden Theatre on 18 November 1793 as one of the two Gentlemen in *The Tempest*. He repeated the role on 22 November. What he did to earn his weekly pay of £1 10*s*. between then and his next billed appearance, as Laval in James Boaden's *Fontainville Forest*, is not known. Boaden's melodrama was first performed on 25 March 1794. Campbell also was Dan Duart in *Love Makes a Man* on 14 May, Mercury in *The Speechless Wife* on 22 May, and Vincent in *The Sicilian Romance* on 28 May 1794.

Campbell was then absent from the London bills for over two and a half years. He was added to the pay list at Drury Lane at 6*s*. 8*d*. per day on 5 November 1796, having made his debut on that stage two nights previously as Charles Surface in *The School for Scandal*. He repeated Charles on 14 December and several other times and played such solid secondary parts as Solarino in *The Merchant of Venice* (16 December), Frederick in *The Wonder* (10 January 1797), Don John in *Much Ado About Nothing*, Sanchio in *Rule a Wife and Have a Wife*, Axalla in *Tamerlane*

(3 February, though Charles Kemble replaced him in this on 8 February, and the *Authentic Memoirs of the Green Room* [1799] claimed the substitution was due to his inferior performance), Lenox in *Macbeth* (replacing Whitfield) on 14 March, and Montano in *Othello* on 20 March, each repeated at least twice.

The subject of this entry may have been the Campbell who played at Birmingham in the summer of 1797. He was certainly at Edinburgh at various times the following winter, from 7 January 1798 and also in the season of 1798–99. "Timothy Plain," the severe Edinburgh critic, gave him sundry unkind cuts for "bellowing" and "blubbering":

The part of Douglas [in Home's *Douglas*] was filled up by Mr Campbell, who is one of those that are said to be from "the Theatre Royal, Drury Lane," and therefore I must be more minute as to him. I have witnessed many attempts to make something of this character; but, Mr. Siddons excepted, I have never met with anything on the stage that tortured both my eyes and ears so much as Mr Campbell's Young Norval—his figure is neither manly nor genteel—there is nothing meaning in his countenance, and his voice is made hoarse by attempts at imitation—his conception of the character is erroneous in many places . . .

In 1798–99 he played also at Bristol and was there in 1799–1800, 1800–1801, 1801–2 as well. He died ("a promising young actor") on 3 September 1802 at Bristol Hot Wells.

Campbell, Mrs James Elijah. *See* WALLIS, TRYPHOSA JANE.

Campbell, William [*fl.* 1784–1810?], *violist, violoncellist.*

One William Campbell, a performer on the viola and violoncello, was listed by Doane's *Musical Directory* (1794) as having performed in the Handelian performances in Westminster Abbey. (They were held in May and June of 1784 and in several years subsequently: 1785, 1786, 1787 and 1791.) Campbell lived in Dean Street, Soho, at the time Doane wrote. A file of residents of the Holborn district of London in the Holborn Central Library lists a William Campbell, musician, living at No 37, New Compton Street, about 1810.

"Campioli," stage name of Antonio Gualandi [fl. 1708–1732], singer.

Antonio Gualandi (or Guaxandi), called "Campioli," was born in Germany of Italian parents. After receiving training in Italy he returned to Germany, made his first Berlin appearance in 1708, and sang at Wolfenbüttel in 1720. In 1726 he performed in Hamburg, then toured Germany and Holland, and sang in Dresden in 1731.

Campioli's male contralto voice was heard in London during the 1731–32 season at the King's Theatre. He sang Gandarte in *Poro* on 23 November 1731, Trasimede in *Admeto* on 7 December, Argone in *Sosarme* on 15 February 1732, Azzio Tullio in *Coriolano* on 25 March, possibly Teodata in *Flavio* on 18 April, Cominio in *Lucio Papiro* on 23 May, and Damon in *Acis and Galatea* on 10 June. By the following 25 November Campioli had left the King's Theatre. According to Grove, the singer spent the rest of his life in Italy. He was doubtless related to the performer Margherita Guallandi, called "la Campioli," who was active in Italy in 1725 but never appeared in England.

Campion, Maria Ann. *See* POPE, MRS ALEXANDER THE SECOND.

Campion, Mary Anne *c. 1687–1706, singer, dancer, harpsichordist.*

Born about 1687 of lowly parents, Mary Anne Campion had a brief but sparkling career at Drury Lane and in the concert halls around the turn of the century. The first notice of her was in March 1698 when she was a member of Christopher Rich's company and sang at a performance of *Phaeton*. She was styled "Mrs" Campion, doubtless a misprint, for she was later called Miss and was, at this time, only 11 years old. She was given singing assignments regularly for the next several seasons at Drury Lane, but she also spoke an epilogue in May 1699 and danced an entry with Weaver and Cottin in *The Pilgrim* in July 1700. She continued appearing at the theatre through 1703–4, singing and dancing, but she also performed at York Buildings on occasion. On 22 June 1703, for her benefit at Drury Lane, she displayed nearly all her talents: she sang Purcell and Weldon songs with Leveridge, danced with Du Ruel, and played the harpsichord. She was also fluent in Italian, but she offered no Italian songs on this occasion.

Miss Campion was much in demand and commanded a good fee. For performing Weldon's prize music at Lincoln's Inn Fields for the Duke of Bedford in 1702, for instance, she was paid £3 4s. 6d., a considerable sum for the time. Her last public stage appearance was probably on 14 March 1704, after which she retired.

She had caught the fancy of the Duke of Devonshire, and at his behest she left the stage. He was in his sixties and she in her teens, and though their unmarried relationship was apparently a happy one, it did not last long. In early 1706 she became ill ("a hectic fever"); on 23 April she made her will; and on 19 May 1706 Mary Anne Campion died. Devonshire had her buried in the church of Latimers in Buckinghamshire, his family burial place. In the chancel he erected a monument with a sanctimonious inscription which, along with traditional praises, declared:

Her lovely form with every grace conjoined
Illustrated the virtues of her mind.

*Though meanly born, her morals were
          sincere
And such as the most noble blood might
          wear . . .*

On 5 July 1706 Devonshire proved her will. To her only daughter, "known by the reputed name of Mary Ann Cavendish," she left her house in Bolton Street, St Martin-in-the-Fields—her parish. She directed that all her jewelry, plate, and other valuables be used to create income for her daughter when she should reach 21. Should her daughter die, the Duke of Devonshire was to be given the personal estate except for jewelry and similar items, which were to go to Bridget, daughter of Davenant Sherbourne. She also left £10 to her grandfather and wearing apparel to her servant. The Duke of Devonshire died in 1707, afflicted with dropsy, gout, the stone, and repentance; on 19 October 1710 Davenant Sherbourne, as alternate executor of Mary Ann Campion's will, proved it a second time.

Campioni, Signor ₍fl. 1744–1770?₎, dancer, ballet master.

Although Signor Campioni first danced on the English stage, with his wife, at the King's Theatre on 3 January 1744, his name did not again appear in the bills until 27 November 1749, when he made his debut at Drury Lane as Acis, in the ballet *Acis and Galatea*. (He danced "well" according to the prompter Richard Cross.) He then moved over to Covent Garden in mid-season, being paid by the latter theatre £21 for clothes and £42 10*s.* for 51 days of work, before he was taken off the salary list on 7 April 1750. Evidently he then went to Ireland for four years. He returned to London to become a member of the Drury Lane dancing company in 1754–55, making his first appearance there "in five years" in a new dance, *The Shepherd's Holiday*, with Mademoiselle Auretti, on 8 October. On 5 December he and Mademoi-

selle Auretti performed a new afterpiece, *The Genii* ("an Arabia Nights' Entertainment") which proved very popular and was repeated many times during the season. Campioni's name was not seen again in London until 5 September 1769 when the *Public Advertiser* announced his engagement as ballet master at the King's Theatre for the ensuing season. The Larpent manuscript for *Le contadini bizzarre*, a piece performed at the King's on 7 November 1769, lists him as the director of the dances.

Campioni, Signora ₍fl. 1744–1754?₎, dancer.

Signora Campioni made her first appearance on the English stage at the King's Theatre on 3 January 1744, when she danced with her husband Signor Campioni (fl. 1744–1770?). Perhaps they danced again in the operas for that season but their names appeared in no other bills. In 1744–45 Signora Campioni engaged at Covent Garden where she made her first appearance on 17 November in a dance entertainment which included Cooke and Lalauze and which was repeated throughout the season. She also appeared in *The Rape of Proserpine, Orpheus and Eurydice,* and the masque *Comus.* For her benefit on 18 April 1745 she performed with Picq in a serious dance, a comic allemande, and a minuet. Tickets were available from her at the Black Lion in King Street. She appeared in similar programs at Covent Garden in 1745–46 and 1746–47. Her salary in the latter year was £3 10*s.* per week, and for her benefit on 29 April 1747 (when she lived at a house "at a Green Lamp" in Leicester Fields) she took a small profit of £14 9*s.* Signora Campioni gave her last performance at Covent Garden on 1 May 1747, as a nymph in *Orpheus and Eurydice.*

Perhaps Signora Campioni accompanied her husband to Dublin, where he performed between 1749 and 1754. Her modest salary and career at London would seem to discredit entirely the "Memoirs of the celebrated Campioni," which appeared about 20 years later in the *Town and Country Magazine*, October 1770, where she was alleged to have been the opportunistic mistress of a Count Haslang in the 1740s. In this salacious and imaginative account, it was claimed that she had been "one of the first-rate opera dancers at that time, more celebrated for her charms than her theatrical merit," and that she had enjoyed a "very considerable" salary. Because of her beauty she was persuaded by "an eminent painter . . . to sit for Venus . . . which is very like her and is now in the possession of Count Haslang."

Campo. *See* DEL CAMPO.

Campolini, Signora ₁*fl. 1767–1768*₁, *singer.*

Signora Campolini was the first woman singer for serious opera at the King's Theatre in 1767–68, making her debut in an unspecified role in *Tigrane* on 27 October. Probably she sang in *Sifare* on 8 December and *Ifigenia in Aulide* on 16 January (and four other times), both new serious operas for which no cast lists are known. All these operas were repeated, with her in the bills. She made her last appearance as Artenices in *Sesostri* on 10 March 1768, for her benefit shared with Guglielmi.

Camus, Mynheer. *See* CAJANUS, DANIEL.

Canadina, Mr ₁*fl. 1761–1766*₁, *house servant, constable.*

A Mr Canadina was paid 12 shillings per week by Covent Garden in 1761–62 as a house servant. Doubtless he was the "Mr Canadine" who was a constable at the same theatre in 1766.

Canadine. *See* CANADINA.

Candoni. *See* CORDONI.

"Candour, Mrs." *See* POPE, JANE.

Cane, Elizabeth Bridget. *See* ARMSTEAD, MRS.

Canlets, Master ₁*fl. 1785*₁, *actor.*

Master Canlets walked as Cupid in the procession of *The Jubilee* performed at Drury Lane 12 times between 18 November and 22 December 1785.

Canning, Mrs George, Mary Anne, née Costello, later Mrs Samuel Reddish the second, and Mrs Richard Hunn *1747?–1827, actress.*

The usual claim to historical notice of Mary Anne Canning, a mediocre actress, is the fact that she was the mother of the great orator and statesman, the Rt Hon George Canning (1770–1827). She was born Mary Anne Costello, at Connaught, about 1750, if the report that she married at the age of 18 in 1768 is accurate. One of her son's biographers states that when she died in 1827 she was 78; another says that she was 80. Her year of birth, if the first biographer's testimony is accepted, was 1747, and if the second is believed, it was 1749.

Most accounts relate that Mary Anne was a penniless if beautiful waif, a legend which H. W. V. Temperley denies in his *Life of Canning* (1905), claiming that reports of her low birth were simply slanders concocted by her son's political enemies and that, in point of fact, "her pedigree extended to the conquest and included not only early Irish Kings but, what is of more importance, many later Irish peers." Temperley offers no detailed pedigree, but F. R. Gale, in *Notes and Queries* (1929), states that Mary Anne was the daughter of Jordan Costello, whose father was descended from a patrician Irish family and whose mother was a daughter of Colonel Melchior Guydickens, scion of an aristocratic Worcestershire family. The assertion by Temperley, however—that Mary Anne was "a woman of spotless virtue"—can hardly be supported by what is known of her life and it illustrates that biographer's deplorable zeal for improving the maternal background of his illustrious subject.

By the time Mary Anne married the Irishman George Canning (the father of the statesman), he had already earned a reputation for having an ardent attachment to civil and religious liberty. These extreme liberal views and his liaison with a young girl prior to his association with Mary Anne, had caused his father, Stratford Canning of Garvagh, to turn him off with an allowance of £150 a year. George went to England in 1758 to become a resident of the Middle Temple, a frequenter of Grub Street, and the boon companion of Churchill, Colman, and Whitbread. As a contributor to Dodsley's *Miscellanies* and by his support of Wilkes, he decried the taxation of America and the tyranny of priests and kings, and boasted of his ancestors "who fought, who bled, and . . . who died" for the cause of "pale liberty, when Popery high her standard bore." Such activities finally proved ruinous for him; heavily in debt, he eventually consented in return for the discharge of his bills to give up further claims on his father's estate, which was quickly settled on a younger brother, Paul. On 21 April 1768, at Marylebone, he married the young Mary Anne Costello, of Wigmore Street, became a moderately successful wine merchant, and died on 11 April 1771, a year after the birth of their son George. The plight of the mother and child was soon rendered critical when Stratford Canning withdrew the allowance of £150.

Mrs Canning turned then to the stage, no doubt through the influence of the eccentric actor Samuel Reddish, with whom she began to live soon after the death of her husband. Billed only as "A Gentlewoman," she made her first appearance "on any stage" in the title part of *Jane Shore*, with Garrick as Hastings, at Drury Lane on 6

Courtesy of Notes and Queries

MARY ANNE CANNING (when Mrs Hunn)

artist unknown

November 1773. The prompter Hopkins described her and her reception in his diary: "A Small mean figure very little power (very So, So.) great applause." The *Town and Country Magazine* was compelled to report that "a continued monotony of voice and very little expression in her countenance, are great impediments to her shining at present in the character of Jane Shore." A bit more promise was discerned by the reviewer in the *Covent Garden Magazine*. He found that she

has great sensibility, is pleasing in her figure, and agreeable in her countenance. But she has a bad voice, an unfortunate sameness of tone, and wants a power to vary her features, as well as spirit in her delivery, [but] . . . is not devoid of the grand theatrical requisites; let us therefore candidly hope she will improve those abilities she evidently possesses, and by study and attention to the duties of her new profession, acquire those excellences in which she is now found wanting.

Mrs Canning acted Jane Shore again on 8, 12, and 22 November, and 6 and 17 December. On 20 November 1773 she was paid £10 10s. on account. She did not act again until the latter part of the season, when she played Perdita in *Florizel and Perdita* on 12 April 1774 and Hero in *Much Ado About Nothing* on 18 April. For her benefit on 26 April 1774, playing for the first time Mrs Beverley in *The Gamester*, with Reddish in the title role, she took profits of £65 3s. Two days later on 28 April she acted Octavia to Reddish's Antony, both for the first time, in *All for Love*. Although not on the regular weekly salary list, she was paid £32 10s. "in full of salary" on 7 May 1774.

In 1774–75, Mrs Canning had no engagement at Drury Lane, but she made one appearance on 30 March 1775, when Mrs Yates would not play, though that actress was advertised for the part of Andromache in *The Distrest Mother*. Only after Mrs Hartley of Covent Garden was besought but refused, was Garrick persuaded by Reddish to let Mrs Canning play the role. Billed simply as "A Lady," she was identified by Hopkins who bemoaned in his diary, "Such a performance I think was never seen in Drury Lane Theatre very bad indeed many hisses." This was a time when managers had little say in the matter of who played for the benefits of their actors, so despite the fiasco of *The Distrest Mother*, Mrs Canning returned to the Drury Lane stage on 23 March 1776, in her first and only appearance of that season, as Monimia in *The Orphan*, again for the benefit of Reddish, who played Castalio. Hopkins wrote "So, So."

Reddish, whose instability was now on the gallop, was persistent in the promotion of his mistress. He had put her in leading roles in 1774 and 1775 at Bristol, where he was summer manager, and this impudence brought him to grief in the summer of 1776, when Mrs Canning emerged at Bristol under the name of Mrs Reddish. Hannah More wrote to Garrick on 28 September 1776, "This is the second or third wife he has produced at Bristol: in a short time we have had a whole bundle of Reddishes, and all remarkably unpungent." Reddish's obsession for casting his "wife" in roles which she manifestly was incapable of playing caused a rowdy reception for her first appearance of the season as Elizabeth to Reddish's Richard III. Forewarned, Reddish had tried to pack the house, but the hissing won out, and the manager was reprimanded by the press:

Where we find private affection operating against public satisfaction, and connubial love against the desire of pleasing, we cannot but lament the misfortune of a person who, blinded by tenderness, can suffer the dictates of judgment to be superseded by the call of ambition. . . . I would remind Mr. Reddish that an *Heroine* is full as necessary on the stage as a *Hero*.

Consequently, Mrs Canning's name was withdrawn for Belvidera in *Venice Preserv'd*. She was supposed to play Constance in *King John*, with Reddish in the title role, for Samuel Cautherley's benefit but Cautherley ignored Mrs Reddish's claim on the part and cast Hester Jackson, announcing that he "thought it would have been an Indignity Offer'd to the Public to intrude Mrs Reddish upon them in so principal a Character, so soon after she had been expelled from the Stage on her first appearance by the united Voice of the Audience." Mrs Canning had suspected Cautherley and Mrs Jackson as the instigators of the hissing, and she forced Reddish to counter with a refusal to play for Cautherley's benefit. The affair gave rise to a humorous mock quarrel in *Farley's Bristol Journal*, 24 August, between "R——h" and "Mrs C——g," in which Reddish was shown as a coarse, jealous, and greedy lout, concerned only for his £12 per week. Correspondence between Cautherley, Reddish, and then Mrs Reddish, was carried by an eagerly accommodating press, until finally, on 31 August 1776, *Farley's Bristol Journal* announced that Reddish had withdrawn from the management, leaving the problems at Bristol to Clarke and Quick.

But when Reddish played Oroes in George Ayscough's *Semiramis* (adapted from Voltaire) at Drury Lane on 14 December 1776, under R. B. Sheridan's management, Mrs Reddish was found in the role of Azema. The play was greatly applauded, but "Mrs Reddish, alias Mrs Canning," reported Hopkins, was so very bad that "she was hissed all through, and must never perform again." On 16 December she was replaced in the role by Miss Hopkins, the prompter's daughter, and indeed never again performed in London.

About this time Mary Anne went to play at Dublin with Reddish, but the Canning family there boycotted her benefit and she drew only a small crowd. As Mrs Reddish she acted at Cork in the summer of 1777 and at Liverpool from June through 19 October 1778, at a salary of £1 11s. 6d. per week. At one time she toured with Whitlock's company in Staffordshire and the Midlands and with Wilkinson at Hull.

It cannot be stated with any certainty whether or not Mrs Canning had ever legally married Reddish, although when one of her children by him, Charles, was christened at St Paul, Covent Garden, on 3 January 1779, he was described in the register as the son of "Samuel Reddish by Mary Ann his wife." But, as we have observed, Reddish had a way of picking up and losing "wives," and the first one, the actress Polly Hart, was still known as Mrs Reddish when she died in great poverty in April 1799. The death of Reddish himself came in a lunatic asylum at York in December 1785, almost three years after Mary Anne had married again. Her nuptials with the provincial actor and silk mercer Richard Hunn were celebrated on 11 February 1783 in the parish of St Paul's, Exeter. She signed the license "M. A. Canning," and in the Exeter Diocesan Registry Hunn signed the following statement on 10 February 1783:

Richard Hunn of the parish of St. Paul in the City of Exeter maketh oath that he this deponent and Mary Ann Canning of the same parish widow with whom he prays licence to be married are respectively above the age of twenty one years not related to each other . . . and that the said Mary Ann Canning hath had her usual abode in the same parish of St. Paul for four weeks and upwards immediately preceding the date hereof.

In the file of the Exeter *Flying Post* at the City Library of Exeter is found the record of Mrs Canning's activities during the years after she left Drury Lane in 1776 and played at Liverpool in 1778. (A complete account was given in articles by Fred R. Gale in *Notes and Queries*, 14 September and 21 September 1929.) In the winter of 1781–82, still known as Mrs Reddish, she acted at Exeter under the management of Hughes. Her roles included Lady Sneerwell in *The School for Scandal* and the title role in *Editha*. For her benefit on 7 March 1783, she was billed as Mrs Hunn. On that night Posthumus in *Cymbeline* was acted by a gentleman making his first appearance on any stage, who may have been her new husband Richard Hunn, and the role of Clio in the farce *The Register Office* was taken by a child of five, Miss Reddish, apparently the twin of Charles Reddish, born late in 1778. In May, Mrs Hunn acted Elvira in *The Spanish Fryar*. In the next several seasons at Exeter she performed a variety of featured roles with her new husband, including Miranda in *The Tempest*, Donna Victoria in *A Bold Stroke for a Husband*, the title role in *Jane Shore*,

Angelina in *Robin Hood*, Julia in *The Fatal Falsehood*, Mandane in *The Orphan of China*, and Fanny in *The Clandestine Marriage*.

The Exeter theatre burned down in 1786; another was built and opened in 1787 but with an entirely different company. By now Mrs Hunn was at Chester, where she acted Gertrude in *Hamlet* in 1787, and she was a member of the company at Newcastle when the new theatre opened there on 21 January 1788, playing Elmira in *The Sultan* on the first night and taking a benefit on 14 November 1788. She did not play in the Newcastle company in 1789, obviously confined by a pregnancy which produced her third set of twins, Frederick and Ann Hunn, who were baptized at St Andrew's, Newcastle, on 8 July 1789. By June 1790 she and her husband were under John Bernard's management at Plymouth. The Hunns grew to be close friends of Bernard who spoke of them warmly in his *Retrospections of the Stage*. When Richard Hunn died is not known to us, but he had failed finally as an actor as he formerly had as a businessman. Winston tells a sad story in *The Theatric Tourist* of Hunn having contracted for a half interest in the Plymouth Theatre with a Mr Wolfe, the proprietor, and having deposited £150 as part of the payment, "but being unable to furnish the remainder, Wolfe threw him into prison; and liberated him only on condition of liberating his claim."

According to *The Dictionary of National Biography*, Mrs Hunn retired from the stage in 1801, when her famous son George, now an undersecretary, was said to have caused a pension of £500 a year to be settled on her. But in his *Life of Canning* Temperley claimed the pension was a fable, or at least was "unconfirmed by the pension list." Canning, however, seems to have kept regularly in touch with his mother by letter and he often visited her. Although he did not recognize the Reddish children as his relations, apparently he provided them with

support from time to time. In his journal, the actor George Frederick Cooke noted visits to Mrs Hunn at No 11, Tufton Street, Westminster, in February 1803.

Mrs Hunn retired in her later years to Bath. She no doubt caused some embarrassment to her son's political ambitions, and his enemies often sought to discredit him by reference to her stage career; Lord Grey once demanded with mock indignation whether "the actress's son" was really to become Prime Minister of England. "Peter Pindar" wrote sneering verses about "Mother Hunn and her daughters from the country theatrical barns."

Mrs Hunn maintained her interest in the stage throughout some 26 years of retirement. In 1814 she wrote to a friend about the theatre at Bath: "our theatre is in a state of new and elegant beautification. I do hope I shall have the pleasure of having you many times in my box this coming season." Samuel Clement Hall (1800–1889), whose father knew Mrs Hunn well, remembered her as "Handsome and attractive in old age, chatty, agreeable, fond of going back to remembrances of people she had known, and greatly enjoying a rubber of whist." As an actress, according to Bernard, her efforts were "more characterized by judgment than genius; but Nature had gifted her in several respects to sustain matrons."

Mary Anne died at her residence, No 35, Henrietta Street, Bath, on 10 March 1827, about the age of 80, some five months before the death of her illustrious son. His will, which was not changed by the time of his death, shows that he had intended to leave £2000 to his mother, secured by life annuities of £300 per year.

By George Canning (d. 1771) Mary Anne Canning (Reddish?) Hunn had a daughter who died in infancy and George Canning, born 11 April 1770, baptized at Marylebone Church on 9 May 1770, died 8 August 1827. On 8 July 1800 he married Joan Scott, daughter of Major-General

John Scott. Their son Charles became Earl Canning, and their daughter, Harriet, married the first Marquis and fourteenth Earl of Clanricarde.

For Samuel Reddish (1735–1785) Mary Anne bore twins who died young. A son, Samuel Reddish, was later a collector of the customs at Falmouth, lived in Jamaica, and died insolvent in 1816. He married Dorothy Ashby, by whom he had a daughter, Mary. Another son, Charles Reddish, was born in 1778 and christened at St Paul, Covent Garden, on 3 January 1779. He went as a cadet to Bengal in 1797, arrived in India in August 1799, was promoted captain in the 22nd Bengal Regiment on 22 November 1807. Invalided on 16 January 1809, he died at Chunar on 8 June 1810. He had married Beatrice Caroline Manning at Calcutta on 28 February 1805. They had a son (b. 1807) and a daughter who married a wealthy indigo planter. That Charles Reddish was no doubt the son of Mrs Canning and Reddish referred to incorrectly in a Folger Library manuscript as Master John Reddish, who for some years was supported by the Drury Lane Theatrical Fund. A female, twin of Samuel, whose name is not known, acted at Exeter, as a child of five, in 1783.

By Richard Hunn Mary Anne had five children. A son, Richard Hunn, was mentioned in the will of his father's sister, Martha Hunn of Plymouth, dated 12 September 1792. A daughter, Mary Hunn, was married November 1801 to Richard Thompson of H. M. Customs House, Thames Street. She died at her mother's home in Henrietta Street, Bath, leaving five children. George Frederick Cooke noted in his journal for 5 February 1803 that he had visited Mrs Hunn on that day and had met Mr and Mrs Thompson; he incorrectly identified the latter as Mrs Hunn's eldest "daughter, by the late Mr Reddish." Another daughter, Maria Hunn, married Humphrey Noad at Weymouth about 1807, died at Bath on 10 March 1866. A

third, Ann, died at the age of five, in 1794. She was the twin of Frederick Hunn. They were baptized at St Andrew's, Newcastle, on 8 July 1789. Frederick was a captain in the Royal Navy. On 15 October 1814 at St Martin-in-the-Fields he married Frances Emma, daughter of Vice-Admiral Francis Picture, by whom he had two daughters. Frederick died on 13 October 1852 at Tavistock Place, Plymouth. (A great granddaughter of Captain Hunn provided the notes [*Notes and Queries*, 21 September 1929] for most of the information about Mrs Canning's children.)

A picture of Mrs Canning, when Mrs Hunn, "from a miniature in possession of a descendant," was reproduced in *Notes and Queries* for 14 September 1929.

Cannon, Nicholas [*fl.* 1662–1665], *drummer.*

Nicholas Cannon was admitted a drummer in the King's Musick without fee (waiting for a vacancy) on 28 February 1665. The parish registers of St Andrew, Holborn, identifying him as a drummer, record the birth of his daughter Katherine by his wife Lyddiah in High Holborn on 19 September 1662 and the child's baptism nine days later.

Cantelo, Ann. *See* **HARRISON, MRS SAMUEL.**

Cantelo, H. *d. 1797, musician?*

A Master H. Cantelo, who performed for Philip Astley's troupe, was drowned crossing St George's Channel to play in Ireland in December 1797. He was probably a younger son of Hezekiah and Sarah Cantelo and the brother of Ann and Thomas Cantelo, all prominent musicians of Bath and London.

Cantelo, Hezekiah *d. 1811, instrumentalist.*

When Hezekiah Cantelo was proposed by Robert Shaw, band leader at Drury Lane

Theatre, for membership in the Royal Society of Musicians on 2 January 1785, he had "practised music for a livelihood upwards of 7 yrs." Shaw deposed that Cantelo "plays trumpet, basoon & etc has 6 children." He also belonged to the band of the First Regiment of Foot Guards. Hezekiah was admitted to the Society on 6 March 1785 (14 yeas and a nay) and was designated by the Governors to play trumpet in the annual charity concert at St Paul's Cathedral on 10 and 12 May 1785.

Shaw's statement scarcely did credit to this versatile man, for the "& etc" covered his talents on the flageolet, the oboe, and the pipe, and he had taught most if not all of his six children to be musicians. It seems rather strange that a musician of his abilities should have been old enough to have fathered six children before being proposed as a member of the Society. The procedure usually occurred upon the termination of the apprenticeship coincident with the twenty-first year. (Hezekiah's son Thomas had been born in 1774. One child, Elizabeth, had been buried in the churchyard of St Paul, Covent Garden, on 29 April 1781; another, Henry, would be buried there on 20 May 1785. A daughter Bathsheba or Barbary later married the Bath and Bristol musician John Loder, and another, Ann, later married the tenor singer Samuel Harrison.) The explanation for the tardy proposal may lie in Hezekiah's late arrival in London and his sudden leap into prominence there.

He was already at that time well established with his wife Sarah and their brood in Bath, where his eldest son Thomas had been christened in March 1774. Like the rest of the Cantelos he retained ties with Bath. We find, for instance, a Bath bill of 26 April 1786, containing "Particulars / of the Performance / for Mr Cantelo's / Annual Night," headlined by "A New Song by Miss Cantelo / composed by Mr Rauzzini. / Mr RAUZZINI / Will accompany the Performance on the Piano-Forte." The

singers included the celebrated Incledon, and Wordsworth, Loder, Howell, Russell, Haynes, Mathews, Woolley, Shepperd, a Cantelo, "and Master Shell & Gray." Furthermore, Longman and Broderip published in 1785 *Twenty Four American Country Dances as Danced by the British during their Winter Quarters at Philadelphia, New York, and Charles Town. Collected by Mr Cantelo, Musician at Bath.*

Cantelo had appeared for the first time on the Drury Lane roster in the 1778–79 season, as bassoonist and piper, at £2 per week. Burney listed two Cantelos among the instrumental performers at the Handel Memorial Concerts at Westminster Abbey and the Pantheon on 26, 27, and 29 May and 3 and 5 June 1784, a trumpeter and an "hautbois" player. He received payments on 11 October 1792 ("Cantelo in full for last season") and, in view of the incompleteness of the record, and the allegation of Shaw to the Society, he had probably been of the Drury Lane band during at least some parts of many seasons by 1792.

Cantelo began to play in the Ashleys' spring oratorios at Covent Garden in 1794 and returned in 1795, 1796, and 1797, in the latter year with Thomas and perhaps others of his family. "The Cantelos" remained with the Ashleys through 1799. In 1800 only Hezekiah joined the oratorios.

In 1801–2 "Cantelo" and "Cantelo jun" were earning £2 and £1 15s. respectively each week in the band at Drury Lane. In the years from 1804 through 1807 "H. Cantelo" was present in the band, sometimes acting as paymaster.

In 1794 Doane's *Musical Directory* placed Hezekiah's residence in Stangate Street, Lambeth. In 1799 he was nominated by Dance as a Governor of the Royal Society of Musicians, replacing the recently deceased J. C. Pring. He was entered in the Minute Book among the Governors on 5 January 1800. He was probably in ill health during his latter years, for after his petition to the Society dated 1 October

1809 he was granted four guineas a month. On 6 October 1811 the Governors voted £8 to pay for his funeral.

Cantelo, Thomas *1774–1807, instrumentalist, teacher.*

When Thomas Cantelo was proposed by Jeremiah Parkinson for membership in the Royal Society of Musicians on 4 October 1795, he was certified to be the son of Hezekiah Cantelo and Sarah his wife, "baptized the fourth Day of March" 1774 at St James, Bath. Parkinson's recommendation attested the usual "seven years and upwards" study and practice of music and asserted him to be proficient on "the Organ, violin, tenor, . . . Harpsichord and piano forte" and to be a teacher of the last two instruments named. He was said to be "engaged at Vauxhall Gardens, the Oratorio and private concerts." He was elected unanimously on 3 January 1796.

Doane's *Musical Directory* of 1794 had given his residence as "Bath, Somersetshire," and he evidently practiced his profession in Bath as well as in London, where he performed irregularly through most of the rest of his career. He played with his father under the Ashleys' direction in the spring oratorios at Covent Garden in 1796, 1797, and 1798 and was listed as violinist in the annual May concerts for the benefit of the clergy at St Paul's Cathedral each year from 1796 through 1800, 1802 through 1804, and 1806 (twice entered as "Cantels").

In the latter end of 1806 he fell ill and received from the Society assistance for medical payments on 7 December, supplemented on 4 January, on 1 February 1807 (four guineas), and on 1 March. On 5 April 1807 his widow was granted £8 for his funeral expenses and £2 12*s*. 6*d*. per month "till further orders." She may have been the Mrs Cantelo whose "affidavit was admitted" (Minute Book 5 July 1836) and whose "declaration was admitted" (Minute Book 2 July 1837).

Cantels. *See* CANTELO, THOMAS.

Canter, Mr *₁fl. 1773–1774₁, dancer.*

A Mr Canter was listed as a principal dancer at the Opera for 1773–74 in an advertisement by the management of the King's Theatre on 23 October 1773. His name, however, did not appear for specified parts on any extant bills.

Canter, James *₁fl. 1768–1783₁, scene painter, machinist, landscape painter.*

James Canter, a landscape artist, painted scenes for the King's Theatre and the Haymarket between 1768 and 1774. Opera productions for which his name appeared on the bills as painter were *Gli amanti ridicoli* on 8 November and *Le donne vendicate* on 13 December 1768 (he was also machinist for both), *Le serve rivali* on 3 June 1769, and *Perseo* on 29 January and *Nitteti* on 19 April 1774 (both with Colomba). At the Haymarket he designed a transparency representation of the fleet at Spithead for *A Trip to Portsmouth*, which was performed regularly during August 1773, and painted new scenes for the afterpiece, *The Genius of Nonsense* on 2 September 1780. His landscape paintings were exhibited at the Free Society in 1774–76, 1778, 1780, and 1783, at the Society of Artists in 1771, and at the Royal Academy in 1773 and 1774.

Cantrell, Mrs *₁fl. 1716–1737₁, actress, singer.*

The first notice of Mrs Cantrell (or Chantrell) was as Dolly in the first performance of *The Northern Heiress* at Lincoln's Inn Fields on 27 April 1716. The first edition noted that the opening night was greeted "with only two single Hisses. . . . The one was a Boy, and not worth taking Notice of, the other a Man who came prejudic'd." On 3 August at the same playhouse she acted Sabina in *The Feign'd Curtizans*. Her name disappeared from the bills until 11 November 1718 when she played Betty in *Woman's a Riddle* at Lincoln's Inn Fields. Then she dropped from sight again until 23 March 1724, when she acted Laetitia in *The Old Bachelor*. In the summer of 1724 Mrs Cantrell played Cynthia in *The Double Dealer*, Lucinda in *Love's Contrivance*, and an unnamed role in *The Roman Maid*. At a salary of 6s. 8d. daily she was a member of the Lincoln's Inn Fields troupe in 1724–25, though her name did not appear in the bills. Not until 24 August 1728 at Bartholomew Fair was she mentioned in London again; on that date she acted Queen Elizabeth in *Bateman* at the Hall-Miller booth. After over ten years of erratic activity (which raises the possibility of there having been a Mrs Cantrell and a Mrs Chantrell), the actress's career stabilized.

In the spring of 1729 she was active again at Lincoln's Inn Fields, playing roles of some significance: Flora in *Hob's Opera* (17 April), Polly in *The Beggar's Opera* (5 May, billed as making her first appearance in that character—one of the earliest observations of this sort), and Margery in *The Wedding* (6 May). She finished the summer acting at the Hall-Oates booth at Bartholomew Fair and returned to Rich's theatre in the fall as a singing actress of some importance.

On 19 September 1729 she acted the title role in *Flora*, one of her most popular parts, which she held for several years. During the next four seasons at Lincoln's Inn Fields and then at Covent Garden, she appeared regularly in pantomimes, burlettas, and comedies, and on occasion she offered specialty songs between the acts. Among her parts were the title role in *Sylvia*, Mrs Sealand in *The Conscious Lovers*, Araminta in *The Old Bachelor*, Venus in *The Judgment of Paris*, Lady Wronghead in *The Provok'd Husband*, Salome in *Mariamne* (one of her few roles in serious plays), Widow Lackit in *Oroonoko*, Lady Wishfort in *The Way of the World*, Alithea in *The Country Wife*, Lady Pliant in

The Double Dealer, Widow Blackacre in *The Plain Dealer*, and Mrs Buskin in *The Strollers*. This last she performed on 7 May 1734 at her shared benefit with Salle's widow and in addition "attempted" a new prologue.

Mrs Cantrell joined the Drury Lane company for the 1734–35 and 1735–36 seasons, playing many of her old roles but adding several new ones in spectacular productions: Venus in *Cupid and Psyche*, Aurora in *Cephalus and Procris*, Calliope in *Harlequin Orpheus*, Phillida in *Damon and Phillida*, and Phoebus in *The Fall of Phaeton*. Among her new comedy roles were Valeria in *The Rover*, Ruth in *The Committee*, Constance in *The Twin Rivals*, Lady Betty in *The Careless Husband*, and Mrs Ford in *The Merry Wives of Windsor*. In September 1735 she appeared in two other Shakespearean roles: Calpurnia in *Julius Caesar* and Melissa in *Timon of Athens*. Her forte, however, was comedy

Harvard Theatre Collection

Benefit ticket for MRS CANTRELL

and pantomime roles where her singing talents could be used.

On 9 April 1736 the Drury Lane troupe used the Lincoln's Inn Fields Theatre for a performance of *The London Merchant* and *Damon and Phillida*. In the latter Mrs Cantrell played Phillida, and in the former a Miss Cantrell, very possibly her daughter, acted the ingenue role of Maria. The performance was a benefit for Mrs Cantrell (and Este) and the conclusion of her association with the Drury Lane company. On 23 August at the Hall-Chapman booth at Bartholomew Fair she played Betty in *The Modern Pimp*, her last known appearance there. When the fall season began, Mrs Cantrell returned to Covent Garden, singing in *Macbeth* on 20 October 1736 and acting Mrs Sealand in *The Conscious Lovers* on 22 October. She acted the latter again on 8 January 1737. By 1 February she had been replaced in the *Macbeth* chorus by Mrs James, and her name (except for entries actually pertaining to *Miss* Cantrell) dropped from the bills.

Cantrell, Miss ₁fl. 1736–1739₁, *dancer, actress.*

Miss Cantrell was probably the daughter of the actress-singer Mrs Cantrell, whose career ended about the time Miss Cantrell's began. The young dancer-actress played a follower of Adonis in *The Fall of Phaeton* at Drury Lane on 28 February 1736, a performance in which Mrs Cantrell also participated. On 22 March Miss Cantrell danced at the same theatre, and on 9 April at Lincoln's Inn Fields the Drury Lane troupe performed *The London Merchant* with Miss Cantrell as Maria and *Damon and Phillida* with Mrs Cantrell as Phillida, for Mrs Cantrell's shared benefit.

Miss Cantrell appeared regularly at Covent Garden in 1737–38, her chief assignments being dance specialties, one of which, a comic dance with Richardson, was repeated frequently during the season. She also played the Scaramouch Woman in *The*

Necromancer (billed in error as "Mrs" Cantrell) on 7 October 1737 and Hour in *The Royal Chace*. She continued her dancing chores between the acts and in pantomimes through early 1739, after which her name disappeared from the bills. The singer Miss Cantrell who performed in 1771 may have been a member of the third generation of this family, though no proof has been found.

Cantrell, Miss ₁fl. 1766?–1771₁, *singer.*

Sometime between 1760 and 1769 – probably after 1765, according to Wroth's *The London Pleasure Gardens* – Miss Cantrell sang at Finch's Grotto Gardens. She certainly appeared there on 22 June and 8 and 22 August 1771. On the last date she played an unidentified role in *The Gamester*, perhaps simply offering a song. During 1771 songs by William Bates, which Miss Cantrell and others sang at Finch's, were published.

Capara. *See* CAPORALE.

Capdeville, Miss ₁fl. 1762₁, *dancer.*

Miss Capdeville, a child of eight, made her first appearance on any stage in a "Serious Dance" at Covent Garden on 7 May 1762. It was her only recorded performance at London. Very likely she was the daughter of the dancer Mademoiselle Capdeville, who performed a hornpipe on the same evening.

Capdeville, Mlle ₁fl. 1754–1771₁, *dancer, proprietor.*

Mademoiselle Capdeville made her first appearance on the Covent Garden stage on 26 November 1754 dancing with Poitier Jr in a new pantomime entertainment called *The Italian Bagpiper*. Both dancers were announced as "lately arriv'd from Paris," (but perhaps the lady was really the Hannah Richardson, of St James's, Westminster, who had married John Capdeville at St George's Chapel, Hyde Park Corner, on 7 December 1753). She danced a "Comic Entertainment" with Poitier on 3 December and a comic dance with Granier on 18 April, both of which were repeated a number of times during the remainder of the season. Probably she also appeared in the ballet *Orpheus and Eurydice*, which was given regularly in that and subsequent seasons but for which no cast is known.

Remaining at Covent Garden for another seven seasons as a specialty dancer, by 1760–61 Mlle Capdeville was earning £150 per year (16s. 8d. per day), the highest salary of any female dancer in the company and more than most actresses. Pieces for which her name appeared in the bills included: the new ballet *Les Statues animées* (2 March 1756), *The Lamplighters* (29 April 1757), Venus in *The Judgment of Paris* (7 April 1758), *The Prophetess* (30 November 1759), Water in *The Rape of Proserpine* (16 January 1760), a new comic dance *The Knife Grinders* (17 April 1760), *The Threshers* (18 April 1760), dances incident to the masque in *Comus* (11 December 1760), and a new comic dance, *Les Sabotiers* (19 April 1762). On 22 April 1756, a girl of seven, announced as "a scholar of Mlle Capdeville" and perhaps her daughter, danced a minuet with Guerin and Mrs Rowland at Covent Garden. Another child, Miss Capdeville, age eight, and no doubt her daughter, performed a serious dance, her first appearance on any stage, at Covent Garden on 7 May 1762, when Mademoiselle Capdeville danced a hornpipe.

At the conclusion of the 1760 season, according to James Winston in *The Theatric Tourist*, Mademoiselle Capdeville purchased the theatre at Plymouth from John Arthur for 500 guineas and appointed Mattocks as her manager. In 1761 Mattocks bought half of her interest, and about two years later Mademoiselle Capdeville sold the other half to Anthony Kerly.

She was a member of the dancing company at the King's Theatre in 1764–65, when she performed throughout the season in ballets with Restier, Mademoiselle Auretti, and Larivierre. No more is known of her except Fuchs's statement that she performed at Nantes in 1771.

Cape. *See also* COPE.

Cape, Mr [*fl. 1758–1773*], *dresser.*

Mr Cape was a men's dresser at Drury Lane from as early as 1758–59 through at least 1764–65; in the latter season his salary was 1s. 6d. per day or 9s. per week. He shared benefits with other house servants on 28 May 1759, 12 May 1760, and 20 May 1761.

Cape was the godfather of the actor Edward Cape Everard, who came under his care in London after Edward's father died in 1755. According to Everard's *Memoirs of an Unfortunate Son of Thespis* (1818), Cape was a native of Durham and a relation of Edward's mother, Ann Sowerby Everard. He had a house in the Little Piazza, Covent Garden, in which lodged the actors Charles Holland, Joseph Austin, and Michael Atkins. In the *Memoirs*, Everard fails to write with affection about his guardian, despite the fact that Cape no doubt helped to prepare him for the profession of acting, or at least brought him up in the neighborhood which provided the best opportunities and associations. When Everard, still carrying his adopted surname of Master Cape, was engaged at the Bristol Theatre Royal in 1765, he had an unsatisfactory time, "owing to the imprudence of my godfather, Cape; he would needs go with me down to Bristol, and destroyed every hope." When the young actor determined to use his real name of Everard in the bills and to strike out on his own in 1773, Cape was still alive, having grown "more indolent, more extravagant, and of course more necessitous." Cape's wife, who was Everard's godmother, died in 1773.

Cape, Master and CAPE, MISS. *See* EVERARD, EDWARD CAPE.

Capelletti. *See* CAPPELLETTI.

Caperon, Nicholas [*fl.* 1660–1668],
trumpeter.

On 11 June 1660 Nicholas Caperon (or Chaperone, Shaperoone) and three other "Dutchmen" were appointed trumpeters in ordinary in the King's Musick; curiously, Caperon was noted as being placed on a pension, with John or Thomas Christmas taking his place. This was only a temporary arrangement, however, for later records show that Caperon was regularly employed. His annual salary in 1661 was £60, and in 1666 he was chosen to accompany Prince Rupert and the Duke of Albemarle to sea at a fee of 5s. per day. The last notice of him in the Lord Chamberlain's accounts was in 1668 when he was still listed as a trumpeter serving under Gervase Price.

Capitani, Master [*fl.* 1760], *dancer.*
See CAPITANI, POLLY.

Capitani, [John?] [*fl.* 1743–1763],
singer. See CAPITANI, POLLY.

Capitani, Polly [*fl.* 1759–1766],
dancer.

As a child seven years old Polly Capitani made her first appearance on the London stage dancing in the opera *Farnace* at the King's Theatre on 15 December 1759, but her name was not on the bills. Announced as "Miss Polly (a child of seven years and a Scholar of Sga Asselin), who appeared in the Opera of *Farnace*," she danced with her teacher at the King's on 10 March 1760 and again on 14 April. On 31 May 1760 she appeared in the role of Logide in *Erginda regina di Livadia*, when her age was given as eight. That summer she performed several new dances with Master Tariot at the Haymarket on 2 June 1760, now billed as Miss Polly Capitani, and a

Terzetta at the same theatre on 5 June with Master Tariot and her brother, Master Capitani, a child of six.

Miss Capitani danced on occasion at the King's again in 1760–61 with Gherardi and Tariot, and in the following summer she appeared several times at Drury Lane, in a pantomime dance with Master Rogier on 16 June and again with him in an entertainment of dancing on 2 and 27 July. She was then engaged on a regular basis at Drury Lane for 1761–62, usually appearing with Master Rogier in such pieces as "A Country Dance," a "Comic Dance," or a "New Swiss Dance." At her first appearance of the season on 14 September, she was billed as a scholar to Gallini, the ballet master. On 28 December she danced in *The Genii.* For her benefit with Master Rogier on 11 May 1762, she performed a hornpipe and two comic dances. She gave similar performances at Drury Lane in 1762–63.

On 9 June 1763 she danced with Master Rogier at the Haymarket for the benefit of her father, who was then in the King's Bench prison. In the *Public Advertiser* for that day was an account of Capitani's distresses — the death of his wife after a long illness and the loss of large sums in trade. Here he was identified as having been a singer at the opera "these 20 years." We fail to find his name in any of the opera bills, however, so conclude that he was employed in a very minor capacity as a supernumerary and member of the chorus. A Mr John Capitani of Suffolk Street had been witness to the will of John Baptist Grimaldi, the father of Giuseppe Grimaldi, on 11 March 1760. Beyond these two references, notices of Capitani are not evident.

After the benefit for her father, Polly danced regularly at the Haymarket in the summer of 1763. Her name appeared in no London bills for 1764–65, and her last notice was on 13 March 1766 when she danced a minuet and a louvre with Sodi at the King's Theatre.

Capon, Mr *[fl. 1789]*, *actor.*

A Mr Capon filled an unspecified supernumerary role in *The Island of Saint Marguerite* at Drury Lane on 13 November 1789. This afterpiece was repeated 27 times that season.

Capon, Mary. *See* STEPHENS, MARY.

Capon, William *1757–1827, scene designer, architect, decorative and landscape artist.*

Born at Norwich on 6 October 1757, William Capon was trained as a portrait painter by his father, who was an artist of some ability, but William soon turned to architecture. In 1780, Capon erected a small theatre in a court adjoining Wells Street, Oxford Street. He assisted the scene painter Thomas Greenwood in the redecoration of the Drury Lane house before the opening of the 1782–83 season. With Michael Novosielski, under whom he had studied architecture, he painted scenes for the Royal Circus in 1784 and helped in the decoration of the King's Theatre in 1785. He also assisted Cornelius Dixon with scenery for the Royalty Theatre which opened in 1787. Again with Novosielski, he worked on the building of the new King's Theatre, after the original had burned to the ground in 1789, and helped him with the decorations at Ranelagh Gardens.

Capon designed and painted scenes for a program at the Royal Circus on 12 May 1789 which included the main piece *The What Is It?* and the pantomime *I Don't Know What!* At the Society of Artists in 1790, while he was living at No 68, Lemon St, Goodman's Fields, Capon exhibited a drawing, a view of Kensington Gardens. He was employed by the Earl of Aldborough to paint scenery for a production of *Douglas* at his private theatre at Aldborough (now Stratford) House in 1791 and for *The Revenge* in 1793, and he was also in charge of the removal of the Earl's

Harvard Theatre Collection

WILLIAM CAPON
engraving by Bond, after Bone

theatre from Aldborough to Belan House, Kildare, in 1794. He also seems to have painted scenery for a fantoccini production in a marionette theatre in Saville Row in 1791.

Capon revealed an early bent for antiquarianism, and his interest in English Gothic attracted the attention of John Philip Kemble, who was embarking on his own efforts to produce plays with some effort at historical accuracy. When Kemble opened the new and spacious Drury Lane Theatre on 12 March 1794 with a concert of Handel's sacred music, Capon designed the orchestra section to represent the interior of a Gothic cathedral. For *Macbeth* on 21 April 1794, the first dramatic work offered at the new theatre, Capon was among seven painters who provided the new scenery. (A detailed discussion of this production is provided by Joseph W. Donohue, Jr, in *Theatre Notebook* [1966].) Payments to him recorded in the Drury Lane account books between 19 March and 2 August 1794 totalled £156 19s. 4d.

In the following season at Drury Lane, Capon provided a view of a new settlement for *The Cherokee* on 20 December 1794 (the other scenes were by Greenwood), and with Greenwood he did new scenery for *Jack of Newbury* on 6 May 1795. He also painted in this year the six chamber wings, based on actual ruins, for stock use in the old English plays and the scenes with wings of New Palace Yard and the Old Palace of Westminster, "as it was in 1793," which were described by Boaden. Total payments to him for the season, including one for £141 5s. 3d. on 10 June 1795, were £237 5s. 9d., but a large part of this amount was probably expended on materials and helpers. Capon's sketch for the Bloody Tower in 1795 was probably for a production of *Richard III* on 9 November 1796. He worked with Marinari on three scenes of Westminster Hall for *The Plain Dealer* on 27 February 1796 and then with Greenwood painted the scenery for Colman's *The Iron Chest* on 12 March 1796. Perhaps it was this production, and not the one in 1814, for which he designed a great hall of the times of Edward IV and Henry VI, with music gallery and screen. In the preface to the printed edition of *The Iron Chest*, Colman complained that there was left "a chasm of ten minutes in the action of the play, and that in the middle of an act," to shift two of the ponderous settings on the great stage. Several weeks later, on 2 April 1796, Kemble foisted upon a skeptical public the notorious pseudo-Shakespearean *Vortigern*, a forgery by William Henry Ireland, with scenes by Capon, again with Greenwood. By the end of the season Capon had received £212 17s. He was very likely the William Capon who married Maria Vost at St George, Hanover Square, on 27 February 1797.

Capon seems not to have been employed at Drury Lane in 1796–97 and 1797–98, although in the latter season he received arrears of £151 14s. He designed a church scene for Boaden's *Aurelio and Miranda* on 29 December 1798, and a celebrated "pile of scenery" for Baillie's *De Montfort* on 29 April 1800, which, according to Boaden, was his "crowning achievement," a fourteenth-century cathedral with nave, choir, and side aisles, magnificently decorated, in seven successive planes, and measuring about 56 feet in width, 52 in depth, and 37 in height. On 3 November 1800 Capon was paid £20 for *De Montfort*, but this was no doubt only a partial and final payment for that work. He did scenes with Greenwood for *Cymbeline* on 14 February 1801, and with Banks for *Adelmorn* on 4 May 1801, during which period he lived at No 4, North Street, Westminster. With Greenwood and Marinari he worked on *The Winter's Tale* produced on 29 March 1802. In this last season, Capon was not paid promptly: in the Enthoven Collection is his billing to Drury Lane asking £63 12s. 2d., "to complete my Painting Account for 1801-2," receipted by his wife on 5 July 1805. Sheridan, the manager, was always greatly in arrears for his employees' salaries, including Capon's. He now added insult to injury by nicknaming the complaining painter "Pompous Billy."

Capon left Drury Lane at the end of 1801–2, presumably to devote more time to his landscape painting and to his architectural studies and drawings. About 1803, according to Winston, he added "some very beautiful flats" to the Margate Theatre. In 1804, he was appointed draftsman and painter of architecture to the Duke of York. For the opening of the new Beaufort Street Theatre at Bath on 12 October 1805, he contributed scenes to *Richard III*, which included an ancient antechamber in the old Palace Yard, an entrance to the Tower, the inside of a courtyard and of an ancient fortress, and a plain chamber. For a production of *Jonny Gilpin or the Linen-Drapers Tour* at the Royal Circus on 28 July 1808, he designed a view of the Bell Tavern at Edmonton and a draper's shop.

When Drury Lane Theatre burned 24 February 1809, the scenery which Capon had previously designed for that theatre was lost, no doubt along with his design drafts. Much of the work apparently had not yet been paid for by Sheridan, and the loss to the painter was reported to be £500. During 1808–9, Capon also worked on ancient street scenes based on architectural ruins for the new Covent Garden Theatre, which had also burned, and the six wings of English streets mentioned by Boaden, referred to above, may have been part of these. He created 20 pairs of flats for Covent Garden, which, still in use in 1828,

had stood the test of scrutiny by gaslight, when that was introduced, because they were so finely designed. His designs for Covent Garden also included some scenes for *Henry VIII* on 5 May 1810, for *Harlequin Asmodeus* on 26 December 1810 — for this he did a view near Hanover Square which the *Gentleman's Magazine* stated was never used — and for *Richard III* on 7 January 1811.

With Greenwood, Marinari, Dixon, and others, Capon contributed scenes for *Hamlet*, which opened the new Drury Lane on 10 October 1812. The same group painted scenes that season for *As You Like It, All in the Wrong, Up All Night, The Wonder, Lionel and Clarissa*, and *She Wou'd and She Wou'd Not*. For *Jane Shore* on 8 January 1813, Capon painted a facsimile of the

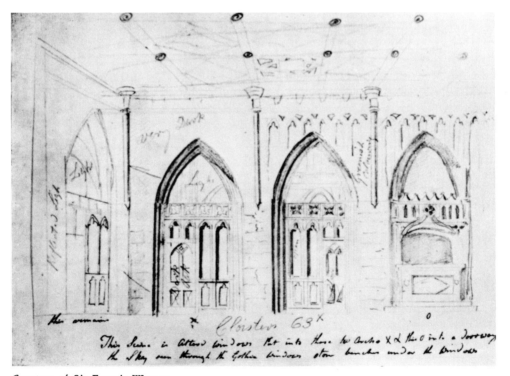

Courtesy of Sir Francis Watson

Scene design by WILLIAM CAPON

from a volume of original designs by Capon belonging to Sir Francis Watson

council chamber of Crosby House, and for *Remorse* two weeks later, a Hall of Armoury and possibly two others. When Kean appeared as Richard III on 12 February 1814, four of Capon's scenes were on the Drury Lane stage; one, a Tudor hall, was a mixture of architecture of the time of Henry VII with painted glass of the time of Henry VI which Capon copied from a church in Kent. In 1814–15, he did scenes for *Macbeth* and *Town and Country*, the latter being his final work for Drury Lane. In 1820, he painted a cloister for *2 Henry IV* at Covent Garden, and an ancient street of Gothic architecture for *Woman's Will*, on 20 July 1820, for the

English Opera Company at the Lyceum.

Extant designs and drawings by Capon include two for ancient streets dated about 1808–9, reproduced by W. J. Lawrence in *The Magazine of Art* (1895) and now in the Shakespeare Memorial Museum at Stratford-upon-Avon; a sketchbook of theatrical drawings and notations, in the possession of Francis Watson, and discussed by Sybil Rosenfeld in *Theatre Notebook*, (1956); his plans of Goodman's Fields Theatre, 1786 and 1802, and a copy of a ceiling painting, at the Folger Library, and discussed by Laetitia Kennedy-Skipton in *Theatre Notebook* (1963); and plans for Covent Garden Theatre as it was in 1791,

Royal Shakespeare Theatre

Scene design by WILLIAM CAPON

which he drew about 1810, owned by Robert Eddison and discussed by him in *Theatre Notebook* (1958).

According to Redgrave, Capon made finished drawings of the interiors of Drury Lane and Covent Garden which were exhibited in 1800 and 1802. He devoted some 30 years to making plans of the old palace of Westminster and the substructure of the Abbey, the former being purchased from him in 1826 for 120 guineas by the Society of Antiquarians, and engraved by Basire. During his leisure time he made an extensive collection of topographical drawings and views of buildings, ruins, and landscapes, some of which were exhibited between 1788 and 1827 at the Society of Artists, the British Institution, the Society of British Artists, and the Royal Academy. Some of these drawings are now in the British Museum. A drawing of a scene of Southwark in the Gardner Collection was copied from one by Capon which had contained the following inscription in his hand:

Part of the dwelling-house of Sir Christopher Wren is seen through the gates of the iron foundry, in which was cast the ironwork of St Paul's Cathedral. From a balcony on top of the house Sir Christopher Wren used to watch the work at St Paul's as it proceeded; it was his constant custom to do so in the morning. I was so informed by a very old gentleman belonging to the foundry, at the time I was making my sketches for the pantomime at the Royal Circus, St George's Fields, in 1789. I have never seen any representative by any hand but my own, and I believe this to be perfectly unique.

By his meticulous care in painting and his vast knowledge of antiquarian architecture, Capon gave impetus and leadership to the movement in romantic scene design which had begun with De Loutherbourg and which became an obsession with Norman and Gothic landscapes at the turn of the century. He was the most significant native scene designer in the English theatre between 1790 and 1825. His influence on later designers such as Planché and Grieve and on producers such as Charles Kemble, William Macready, and Charles Kean, was enormous. A detailed consideration of Capon's work for melodramas and of his achievement in the English theatre is offered by Ralph G. Allen in *Theatre Research* (1966).

Capon died at his house in North Street, Westminster, on 26 September 1827. A portrait of him engraved by W. Bond, after a miniature by W. Bone was published in the *Gentleman's Magazine* in 1828.

Caporale, Andrea Francisca *d. c. 1757, violoncellist, composer.*

Andrea Caporale came to England in 1734 to take the position of first violoncellist in Handel's orchestra for the Opera. He also performed in numerous concerts at London in the 1730s and 1740s. He played solos for his own benefit at Hickford's Room on 22 March 1734. On 13 December of that year he played at Mercers' Hall for the benefit of the organist Young. He also played at musicales sponsored by Percival, Earl of Egmont, on 15 February and 8 March 1735. Other known appearances included concerts at York Buildings on 28 February 1735 (for his benefit), at Hickford's Room on 17 April 1735, at Covent Garden on 19 February 1736, at the Swan Tavern in Cornhill on 11 February 1736 and on 8 March 1737 (for his benefit), and at the Castle Tavern on 2 May 1737.

From December 1740 to May 1741 Caporale was involved in a series of 20 subscription concerts given at Hickford's Room on Fridays, with such musicians as Weideman and Festing and vocalists Andreoni, Mrs Arne, and Reinhold. He was a performer at Ranelagh Gardens during the 1740s. On 10 March 1743 he played for Valentine Snow's benefit at the Haymarket and on 30 March 1743 at the King's and on 10 April 1745 at Covent Garden, the latter two appearances for the benefit of the Fund of the Royal Society of Musicians, of which he was an original subscriber in the Declaration of Trust establishing that organization in 1739, when he was listed as Francisca Caporale. He performed solos at Lincoln's Inn Fields on 11 December 1744, at the Castle Tavern on 14 January 1745, and at the Haymarket on 14 February and 23 March 1745.

In September 1754 Caporale went to Dublin, where he resided until July 1755. He was there again in February 1757. Presumably, he died at London shortly thereafter. "Though no deep musician, nor gifted with a very powerful hand," according to Burney, Caporale was "always heard with great partiality, from the almost single merit, of a full, sweet, and vocal tone." He published 18 solos for the violoncello at London.

One of the labels on the back of a painting of an opera rehearsal by Mario Ricci, now at Castle Howard, identifies "Corporali" as the violoncellist pictured in the musical group. The label was written after 1791 and the picture dates from about 1710; the latter date would seem to dispose of the likelihood that the musician in the painting was really Caporale.

Cappelletti, ₁Petronio? Giuseppe?₁ ₁*fl. 1791–1796?*₁, *singer, composer.*

Signor Cappelletti sang in an entertainment of music and dance which was given at the King's Theatre 12 times between 2 June and 9 July 1791; other vocal parts were filled by Signora Theresa Cappelletti, his wife, Albertarelli, Davide, Tajana, Signora Maffei, and Signora Sestini. Cappelletti's Christian name was given as Petronio on the libretto of *Lo spazzacamino principe*, printed at Venice in 1794. A new ballet, *The Scotch Ghost, or Little Fanny's Love,* devised by Giacomo Gentili, was performed at Drury Lane on 29 October 1796 with music by one Giuseppe Capelletti. The

score was published at London soon afterward by Longman and Broderip.

Cappelletti, Theresa Poggi ₁*fl. 1791*₁, *singer.*

Signora Theresa Poggi Cappelletti, an Italian soprano, was engaged by Salomon to sing at the Salomon-Haydn Concerts at the Hanover Square Rooms in the spring of 1791. She sang the *seconda donna* in the performance of Haydn's *Orfeo.* Her first appearance at the King's Theatre was in an entertainment of music and dance on 26 March 1791, in which she sang a collection of comic songs with Albertarelli, Davide, and Signora Sestini. The program was repeated on 29 and 31 March; between 2 June and 9 July she sang in a similar program of entertainments at the King's with Albertarelli, Davide, Tajana, Signora Maffei, Signora Sestini, and Signor Cappelletti, presumably her husband. Signora Cappelletti's full name was given on the libretto of *Lo spazzacamino principe,* printed in Venice in 1794.

Capper, Miss ₁*fl. 1798–1810?*₁, *singer.*

In the spring of 1798 Miss Capper sang at Ranelagh, and about this time the song "Come follow me my only dear!" was published as sung by her there. Between 8 February and 15 March 1799 she appeared in the Covent Garden oratorios. When she sang in *Ruth* in the Music Room of the King's Theatre on 22 April 1799, the *Monthly Mirror* reported that she "displayed great merit." In the following spring she again sang in the Covent Garden oratorios and was one of the performers who, under the direction of John Ashley, gave the first London rendition of Haydn's *The Creation* at that theatre on 28 March 1800. She continued as a well-known singer during the first years of the nineteenth century.

Capucci. *See* CAPUZZI.

"Capuchino, Signor" [fl. 1746],
dancer.

Signor and Signora "Capuchino," along
with "Mynheer Drollelo," all children lately
arrived from Holland, made their first appearances on any stage at the Lee and
Yeates booth at Southwark Fair on 8 September 1746. In view of the third child's
name, Capuchino was probably a pseudonym.

"Capuchino, Signora" [fl. 1746],
dancer. See "CAPUCHINO, SIGNOR."

Capuzzi, Giuseppe Antonio 1755–
1818, violinist, composer.

Giuseppe Antonio Capuzzi, an Italian
violinist, was born at Brescia on 1 August
1755. Accounted one of the best pupils of

Civiche Raccolte d'Arte ed Incisione, Milan

G. ANTONIO CAPUZZI
engraving by Moretti, after Lorenzini

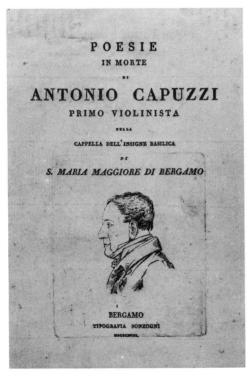

Civiche Raccolte d'Arte ed Incisione, Milan

G. ANTONIO CAPUZZI
artist unknown

Tortini, he studied also under Nazari and
F. Bertoni. He was a violinist at St Mark's,
Venice, and according to Grove and van der
Straeten, he came to London in 1796,
"where he met with great success" and had
a ballet of his composition, *La Villageoise
enlevée, ou les corsaires,* performed. This
ballet, choreographed by Onorati, was produced at the King's Theatre on 12 May
1796; however, Capuzzi's name was not
listed as composer in the bills, nor was there
any other notice of his work in London.
He later was appointed master of the Musical Institute and conductor of the orchestra
at the Church of Santa Maria Maggiore in
Bergamo, a position he retained until his
death in that city on 18 March 1818. According to Fétis, Capuzzi also composed
operatic music, violin concertos, chamber
music, and a *Sinfonia concertante.*

An engraved portrait of Capuzzi served as frontispiece to a collection of verses on his death, published at Bergamo in 1818. Another portrait of him was engraved by Moretti, after Lorenzini. Capuzzi was pictured about 1805 in a painting by L. Scotti of a large group of musicians.

Car. *See* **CARR.**

Carabaldi, Signor ₁*fl.* *1773–1774?*₁, *singer.*

Although Signor Carabaldi was announced to be a singer in the comic operas at the King's Theatre in 1773–74, there is doubt that he ever came to London. On 23 October 1773 the management reported that "The ill health of Sg Carabaldi having prevented his setting out in time," it was impossible for him to appear at the opening performance and that Signor Scheroli would play his part (in *Lucio Vero?*) "until his arrival." Carabaldi's name, however, appeared in no bills for that season. Perhaps this person was Gioacchino Caribaldi (1743–1792), the well-known singer whose career in Italy and France is detailed in the *Enciclopedia dello spettacolo.*

Carabo, Jacques ₁*fl.* *1796–1797*₁, *posture maker.*

Jacques Carabo was "an astonishing little Boy, only 5 years old," who executed "a triple evolution in Posture Work, called the Antipodean March," as a member of a Sicilian troupe of posture makers and tumblers, headed by Signor Saccardi, which performed at Sadler's Wells in the summer of 1796. Probably he accompanied the troupe which Saccardi brought to entertain at the Cambridge Fair in 1797.

Carara, Signora Antonio ₁*fl.* *1768?–1778*₁, *singer.*

Sometime between 1768 and her arrival in England in November 1771, a young Italian singer married Antonio Carara, Garrick's Italian valet, who during his visits to the Continent was used to carry out contract negotiations with foreign performers whom the manager wanted to engage at Drury Lane. Signora Carara was first noticed in the London bills for an unspecified role in *L'Endimione* at the Haymarket on 6 April 1772. She offered several songs in a concert at the King's Theatre on 5 February 1773. Burney found her at this time to be "a young singer, whose voice was naturally drowsy, childish, and insipid"; but, he reported, she was "well received." When she sang in *Nitteti e Perseo* and *Lucio Vero* at the King's Theatre in the spring of 1774, Burney pronounced her to be "not without merit, but it was not of a spirited kind."

By 1775 the Cararas were back on the Continent. On 15 April of that year the husband wrote to Garrick that his wife was to be the "first woman" in serious opera at Florence in the autumn. From Venice on 11 December 1778, in the last of 15 letters from him to Garrick now in the Forster Collection, Carara reported that his wife had been a brilliant success in the first theatres of Italy, but that now, after six years away, they wished to return to England. He solicited Garrick to arrange an engagement for Signora Carara at the King's Theatre or the Pantheon. Apparently Garrick, who died only a month later, could not oblige, and Signora Carara was not seen again at London.

Caratha. *See* **CARATTA.**

Caratta, Mahomet ₁*fl.* *1747–1751*₁, *equilibrist, manager.*

Mahomet Caratta (or Cathata, Charatha), the Turkish equilibrist, was a member of the Nouveau-Spectacle-Pantomime troupe at the Opéra Comique in Paris in the spring of 1747 and made his first appearance in England the following fall. An undated clipping at the Huntington Library which is with another dated in manuscript 26 October 1747 advises that at the Haymarket Theatre "a native Turk, Mahom-

MAHOMET CARATTA .

engraving by Grave

France in the Grande Troupe Étrangère at the Saint-Germain fair. In the fall of 1749 he returned to England with a "numerous company of Turks, men and women" to entertain London with music, dancing, processions, and balancing feats. Caratta balanced a sword on a glass, "put a wooden bar across the rope and [swung] himself to admiration," and danced on the slack rope in wooden shoes. His troupe played at the Haymarket Theatre from 31 October through 3 December 1749 with such great success that John Rich put Caratta on the Covent Garden payroll at £26 5s. weekly through 10 May 1750. The salary included money for the Turk's equipment and attendants.

Caratta sailed for Ireland in the fall of 1750, and from mid-November to February 1751 he dazzled Dublin with his perform-

med CHARATHA, just arriv'd from the Sultan's Court, and the only Master in Europe of his Art, [will perform] the most surprising EQUILIBRES on the Slack Rope Without a Balance." The performance was preceded by "several curious DIVERSIONS" and concluded with Italian fireworks. The second clipping claims that Caratta had appeared before the Royal Family at some point and would give his "surprising Performances" in Southwark at Phillips's booth. About 1747 a picture of Caratta, a copy of which also is to be found at the Huntington, was published showing him on a slack rope balancing a pike on his nose while juggling four balls.

The spring of 1748 found the Turk in

MAHOMET CARATTA

Advertisement, by unknown artist

ances at the opera house in Aungier Street. He toured Cork, Limerick, and Kilkenny, returning to the Smock Alley Theatre in Dublin in late March for his final performances, after which his career cannot be traced. The bill for his 27 November 1750 performance in Aungier Street was probably typical:

[H]e will poize a naked Sword upon the Brim of a Drinking Glass which he holds in his Mouth. At the conclusion he will be put in a Sack, after having been blindfolded with a handkerchief, the mouth of which will be tied over his head, and in this condition he will perform his exercise on the wire. Then he will throw away his ballance pole, charge a gun, and shoot out several candles that shall be presented to him, this to be done upon the Wire, and he blindfolded.

In addition to the c. 1747 picture of Caratta, an engraving was made by R. Grave for Caulfield's *Remarkable Persons*.

Carata Alli, called Young Turk Alli, performed as a ropedancer in Birmingham in 1776 and was probably a descendant of the more famous Mahomet.

Carbonelli, Giovanni Steffano *c. 1700–1772, violinist, band leader, composer.*

Born in Rome about 1700, Giovanni Steffano Carbonelli studied under Corelli before coming to London at the request of the Duke of Rutland in 1719. He lodged at Rutland's house, continuing in the Duke's service until at least 1724, and for his patron he composed a dozen solos for the violin. His first public notice in London was on 13 February 1719 when he played the violin at a concert at Hickford's music room. The following 16 April at Lincoln's Inn Fields, billed as "late from Italy," he played again at a performance of *Camilla*. Thereafter he made frequent appearances at the theatres, sometimes as soloist, sometimes as part of a chamber group; and occasionally he offered his own compositions.

Carbonelli's most interesting solo appearance was on 30 April 1723 at Drury Lane, when he appeared as himself in Act II, Scene i of Steele's *The Conscious Lovers* and performed "a sonata" for Bevil and Indiana. A song had been written for this spot in the play, but no singer was available and the violinist served as a substitute. Into the dialogue Steele had worked a commentary on the social position of musicians: after the musician has left Bevil says to Indiana,

You smile, madam, to see me so complaisant to one whom I pay for his visit. Now I own I think it is not enough barely to pay those whose talents are superior to our own. (I mean such talents as would become our condition if we had them.) Methinks we ought to do something more than barely gratify them for what they do at our command only because their fortune is below us.

Carbonelli's contribution to the performance was apparently well liked, for the bills show him still playing a solo in the play a year later.

In 1720, not long after his arrival and initial success in London, Carbonelli became the leader of the band of the newly instituted Royal Academy of Music, which presented operas at the King's Theatre in the Haymarket, and five years later he was made leader of the Drury Lane band, a post he held until about 1730. After 1730 he continued his appearances at public concerts, played at St Paul's in performances for the benefit of the sons of the clergy, and led the band at Handel's oratorios. On 28 August 1739 he became one of the original subscribers to the Royal Society of Musicians. His musical activities decreased during the 1740s, though he contributed to the benefits "for decayed musicians" at the King's Theatre from 1746 to 21 March 1749—his last recorded appearance.

In his later years Carbonelli turned from music to the importing of continental wines

Fitzwilliam Museum, Cambridge

GIOVANNI CARBONELLI is probably the violinist in this "Music Party" by Laroon

and became purveyor of these potables to the King. His heirs continued the successful business under the anglicized form of his name, Carbonell. Giovanni Steffano Carbonelli had, in fact, earlier given up his native roots: at some point he had renounced his Catholic faith and had married the daughter of Mr Warren, the parish clerk of St James, Westminster (now Piccadilly), and by the time he joined the Royal Society in 1739 he had styled himself John Frederick Carbonell. He died in 1772.

It is doubtless just a coincidence, but on 30 December 1700 (Carbonelli was born about 1700) John, the son of William and Sarah Carbonell, was baptized at St Olave, Hart Street, London.

A pencil sketch by Marcellus Laroon, Carbonelli's musical associate, is now in the Fitzwilliam Museum. Entitled "Music Party," and depicting a violist, harpsichordist, violinist, and singer, it is inscribed in Laroon's hand "made a finished drawing of this for Mr Carbonelli 1731." Very likely Carbonelli is among the musicians shown.

Card, Andrew ⌊*fl. 1683–1707*⌋, *concessionaire.*

On 30 May 1687 Andrew Card and Richard Middlemore bought Dame Mary Davenant's rights of income from fruit-selling at the Dorset Garden Theatre. How long he held an interest in the concession is not known, but his name (unless there was a second Andrew Card) is to be found in several legal documents concerning people with theatrical or musical connections. On 30 April 1683 he alleged the marriage of Martin Folkes and Dorothy Hovell; Folkes was the father of the Martin Folkes who married the performer Lucretia Bradshaw in 1714. On 29 July 1689 Card witnessed the will of Sir John Brownlowe, a sharer in the United Company at Drury Lane and Dorset Garden. On 11 May 1696 he witnessed musician William Clayton's will, and in 1707 he and Drury Lane sharer Nicholas Strawbridge were executors of the will of Mary Davis of Crewkerne, Somerset.

Cardarelli, Signora ⌊*fl. 1775–1776*⌋, *singer.*

Signora Cardarelli (or Cardelli) was the second *buffa* in comic operas at the King's Theatre in 1775–76, making her first appearance on 31 October 1775 in an unspecified role in *La sposa fedele*. In that season she also sang unspecified roles in *La buona figliuola, Il bacio, L'isola d'amore,* and *Alcina.*

Cardelli. *See* **CARDARELLI.**

Cardi, Signora ⌊*fl. 1773–1774*⌋, *singer.*

On 23 October 1773 the managers of the King's Theatre announced that Signora

Cardi had been engaged as one of the women for comic opera and that Mr Gordon had gone to great trouble and expense to put this company together from Italy and France. Signora Cardi sang an unspecified role in *Il puntiglio amoroso* on 7 December 1773 and again on 14, 18, 21, and 23 December and 5 February. Her name appeared on no other opera bills that season.

Cardinale, Mr [*fl.* 1789], *singer.*

Mr Cardinale sang the role of Alcade in the first performances in London of *Il barbiere di Siviglia* at the King's Theatre on 11 and 15 June and 11 July 1789. His name appeared in no other London bills.

Cardon, Louis *1747–1805, harpist.*

Of Italian descent, Louis Cardon was born in 1747 at Paris, where he became an important harpist. Advertised as "late Musician to the Queen of France," Cardon made his first appearance at London on 18 February 1785, when he played a concerto on the French harp at Drury Lane between parts of the oratorio *Acis and Galatea*. In the oratorios at the King's Theatre during the spring of 1785 Cardon was a featured soloist on the harp.

At the outbreak of the French Revolution, Cardon went to Russia, where he died in 1805. According to Grove, his *L'Art de jouer la harpe*, published in the year of his death, was long esteemed. His brother

By permission of the Trustees of the British Museum

ELIZABETH CARELESS, in sedan chair
by Boitard

Pierre Cardon, born at Paris in 1751, was a singer and violoncellist. Louis Cardon was probably also related to the French musicians Jean-Guillain Cardon, Louis-Sanislas Cardon, François Cardon, and J. Cardon, all of whom are noticed in Balteau's *Dictionnaire de Biographie Française*.

Cardoni. *See* CORDONI.

Careless, Elizabeth *d. 1752, actress, singer.*

The name of Mrs (sometimes Miss) Betty Careless first appeared in the extant bills for the role of Polly in *The Beggar's Opera* at the Haymarket on 30 December 1728, although she may have been acting before that time. As a member of various minor companies she played Cherry in *The Stratagem* at the Haymarket on 18 September 1730, at the Lee-Harper booth at Southwark Fair on 24 September 1730, at Goodman's Fields on 26 March 1731, and at the Haymarket again on 1 April 1732. In a booth operated by Cibber, Griffin, Bullock, and Hallam at Bartholomew Fair in August and September 1733, she acted Mariana in *The Miser*, a Lady of Pleasure in *The Ridotto al' Fresco*, and Miss Witless in *The Comical Humours of Sir John Falstaff*.

Although she probably played similar engagements with transient groups during the 1730s, the next notice of Mrs Careless did not occur until 27 October 1741, when she danced a minuet and acted Polly for her own benefit at the small theatre in James Street. At that time she advertised: "Mrs Careless hopes her friends will favour her according to their promise, to relieve her from terrible fits of the vapours, proceeding from bad dreams, tho' the comfort is they generally go by contraries," with tickets available at "Mrs Careless's Coffee House in the Playhouse Passage," presumably in Covent Garden. On 31 March 1743, still "in distress," she performed Cherry at James Street, "Tickets to be had at Mrs

Careless's in Hart St near the back passage of Covent Garden Theatre." Again for her own benefit she appeared at James Street in an unspecified role in *Tunbridge Walks* on 15 April 1743. At Hallam's booth at May Fair in 1744, now billed as "the celebrated Mrs Careless," she performed roles in a number of drolls and plays, including Colombine in *Harlequin Sclavonian* (1 May), Cherry (7 June), and Rose in *The Recruiting Officer* (8 June).

Those theatrical notices for May Fair in 1744 were her last. Mrs Careless, however, had earned also a "celebrated" reputation as an easy woman of the Covent Garden district. Her name was introduced by Hogarth in his last scene of *The Rake's Progress*. The French engraver Louis Pierre Boitard depicted her in a print (1747) of the Covent Garden piazza, which showed her asleep in a chair, attended by the rakes Captain Marcellus Laroon and Captain Montague and their link-boy, Little Cazey —persons regarded by Fielding, when Bow Street magistrate, as "the three most troublesome and difficult to manage of all my Bow Street visitors."

Mrs Careless was buried on 22 April 1752 at St Paul, Covent Garden, having been supported in the poorhouse of that church during her last years. "She had helped the Gay gentlemen of this nation," reported the *Scots Magazine* in that month, "to squander above 50,000£ though at last reduced to live on alms;—almost the certain consequence attending women of her unhappy cast of life." The burial register described her as a widow.

Carestini, Giovanni *1705–1760, singer.*

The male contralto Giovanni Carestini was born at Monte Filottrano, near Ancona, in 1705. At the age of 12 he went to Milan, where he came under the patronage of the noble family of Cusani, thereby acquiring the name of "Cusanino." At first his voice was a powerful and clear soprano, which afterward, by Burney's testimony, "changed into the fullest, finest, and deepest counter-tenor that has perhaps ever been heard." He first appeared at Rome in 1721 in the female role of Costanza in Bononcini's *Griselda*. In 1723 he sang at Prague in Fux's *Costanza e fortezza*, a sumptuous *festa teatrale* produced in the open air with grandiose settings by Giuseppe Galli-Bibiena in honor of the coronation of Karl VI, Hapsburg Emperor, as King of Bo-hemia. The production was one of the truly great musical events of the eighteenth century.

Carestini was at Mantua in 1724 and at Venice in 1725, where he performed in Zaccari's *Seleuco*, and also in 1726, with Farinelli and Paita. He sang in the com-pany at Naples in 1728–29 with Bernacchi, the two of them contending viciously for superiority, and he was also at Rome in 1728 and 1730 where he sang in Vinci's *Alessandro nell' Indie* and *Artaserse*.

In the summer of 1730 George Frederick

Harvard Theatre Collection

GIOVANNI CARESTINI

engraving by J. Faber, Jr, after Knapton

Handel attempted to engage Carestini and another eminent Italian singer, Senesino, for his London opera company. He was pre-pared to offer 1200 guineas to each, but his intermediary in the business, Owen Swiney, formerly a London manager, wrote to Francis Colman from Bologna on 18 July 1730 that Carestini was already contracted for the ensuing season at Milan, as was Senesino at Rome. Senesino, who had been with Handel at London in a previous time, subsequently came to London, but left the manager once more after a stormy season, 1732–33, to join Handel's rival at the "Opera of the Nobility" in Lincoln's Inn Fields Theatre for the next season. In order to arm for the battle for opera audiences, Handel succeeded in bringing Carestini to London, and the singer made his first ap-pearance on 30 October 1733 before the Royal Family as Scitalche in *Semiramis*. He then sang the title role in *Ottone* on 13 November, again before royalty. On 4 December he sang Pyrrhus in Zeno's *Cajo Fabricio* (which Burney mistakenly gave as his debut), with recitatives by Handel. After four representations of the latter piece, spaced a week apart, Carestini appeared as Theseus in Handel's new opera *Arianna in Creta* on 26 January 1734. Handel had expected Carestini to be a soprano and had composed the songs for Theseus accordingly. Finding him to be a countertenor, Handel was obliged to trans-pose a note, sometimes two notes, lower than in the original score. According to Francis Colman's "Opera Register," Carestini sang it "surprising well: a new Eunuch—many times perform'd." (Colman had written the libretto.) Carestini's other roles in that season included Apollo in *Il Parnasso in festa* on 13 March 1734, prob-ably Sisera in *Deborah* on 2 April, the title role in *Sosarme* on 27 April, and Mirtillo in *Il pastor fido* on 18 May.

In the following season Handel had to give up the King's Theatre to Porpora's company which was now greatly strength-ened by the arrival of the popular Farinelli.

Handel's company eventually settled at Covent Garden, where on 9 November 1734 Carestini sang Apollo in *Terpsicore* and Mirtillo in *Il pastor fido*. On 8 January 1735 he appeared in the title role of Handel's *Ariodante* and probably sang the oratorio parts of Ahasuerus in *Esther* on 5 March, Barak in *Deborah* on 28 March, and Joab in *Athalia* on 1 April. His greatest success was with Rogero in *Alcina* on 16 April, which was then played 13 times more in that season. It was reported that when Carestini first received Handel's song "Verdi prali," he sent it back to the composer with the explanation that it was unsuited to him. Handel rushed to Carestini's house to exclaim furiously "You tog! don't I know petter as yourseluf vaat is pest for you to sing? If you vill not sing all de song vaat I give you, I vill not pay you ein stiver!" The startled singer withdrew his objection. The story no doubt was apocryphal, for as Grove points out, Handel spoke Italian.

At the conclusion of the run of *Alcina* on 28 June 1735, Carestini set sail for an engagement at Venice. Subsequently singing at Turin, Milan, and Naples he gained a large reputation which enabled him to command enormous fees. He returned to London in 1739–40, but this time in competition with Handel as a member of Lord Middlesex's concerts at the Haymarket. On 1 December 1739 he sang an unspecified role in *Diana and Endymion*. He participated in the famous "Salve Regina," composed by Hasse, which was sung on 15 December 1739. His other roles were Merode in *Merode e Selinunte* on 22 January, Orlando in *Olimpia in Ebuda* on 15 March, and Busiri in *Busiri, overo, il trionfo d'amore* on 10 and 13 May. His last performance was probably in *Merode* on 31 May 1740.

For another 15 years or so Carestini continued to sing in Europe. He created leading roles in Gluck's *Demofoonte* and *Sofonisba* at Milan, and in 1755 he enjoyed great success in Graun's *Orfeo* at Berlin, though Frederick the Great did not seem impressed. In 1756 he was at St Petersburg, whence he returned to Italy in ill health to retire about 1758. He died at his native Monte Filottrano in 1760.

Quantz said that Carestini had "one of the strongest and most beautiful contralto voices, which extended from d to g." Burney found him to have been in person tall, beautiful, and majestic:

He was a very animated and intelligent actor, and having a considerable portion of enthusiasm in his composition, with a lively and inventive imagination, he rendered every thing he sung interesting by good taste, energy, and judicious embellishments. He manifested great agility in the execution of difficult divisions from the chest in a most articulate and admirable manner. It was the opinion of Hasse, as well as of many other eminent professors, that whoever had not heard Carestini was unacquainted with the most perfect style of singing.

Details of Carestini's continental career are to be found in the *Enciclopedia dello spettacolo*. He was painted by George Knapton; a mezzotint of the portrait was engraved by J. Faber and published at London in 1735. It was believed that Carestini is the singer pictured in Hogarth's Plate IV of *Marriage à La Mode*, but Paulson (*Hogarth's Graphic Works*) makes a convincing case for the view that this person is really Senesino. Carestini, however, is pictured—wittily enough—as the Second Ravisher in Hogarth's "Plate 2d" of *A Rake's Progress*, published on 25 June 1735. Carestini was included in a large group of singers which was painted by Antonio Fedi; an engraving of this group was published in Italy between 1801 and 1807.

Carew, John [fl. 1660–1663], *house servant*.

From 25 June 1660 to 6 August 1663 and possibly later, John Carew served under Sir Henry Herbert as a Yeoman of the Revels, a position which Henry Harris (the player?) held from August 1663 onward. The Lord Chamberlain's accounts for 10 December 1662 indicate the kind of stage-hand and custodial work Carew was given: in preparation for a court performance he was to supply the tiring room at the Cockpit in Court with a mirror, chairs, table, candlesticks, hangings for partitions, coal, shovel, andirons, tongs, bellows, lantern, couch, and a property bed.

Carey, Mr ₍fl. 1714–1716₎, singer.

Though there is a slight possibility that the Mr Carey who sang in London between 1714 and 1716 was Henry Carey the composer and dramatist of later years, proof is lacking. Mr Carey had a benefit recital at Stationers' Hall on 28 January 1714 at which he and two of his scholars, one a gentleman and one a boy, sang. About 1715 was published Daniel Purcell's *Phillis has such charming graces*, and Mr Carey was noted as having sung the work at Drury Lane. On three dates in 1716 Mr Carey is known to have performed at Drury Lane: 25 May (when he sang in English and Italian), and 31 May and 7 August (when he played Aeolus in *The Tempest*). It may be worth noting that Henry Carey had a particular dislike of Italian opera and singers and is not likely to have sung in Italian in public—if, indeed, he was much of a singer at all. Most of Henry Carey's activity dates from the 1730s, and it seems unlikely that he would have appeared as a performer from 1714 to 1716 and then have dropped from sight for more than a decade.

Carey, Mr ₍fl. 1754₎, violinist.

Mr Carey, a violinist in the Drury Lane band, "had his fiddle broke by an apple playing the first music," according to Richard Cross's diary, on 25 February 1754.

Carey, Master. See KEAN, EDMUND.

Carey, Miss ₍fl. 1755–1762₎, actress.

Miss Carey, possibly related to the Drury Lane violinist, was a member of Theophilus Cibber's troupe at the Haymarket Theatre in the late summer of 1755. She was probably the unidentified young woman who played Miranda in *The Busy Body* on 21 August and Kitty Pry in *The Lying Valet* on 25 August. Winston identified her as the young gentlewoman said by the bill to be making her first stage appearance on 28 August as Polly in *The Beggar's Opera*. On 9 September, billed as Miss Cary, she acted Nell in *The Devil to Pay*, and on 11 and 15 September she played Lightning in *The Rehearsal* and Mrs Rist in *Lethe*. The company was silenced after that, and Miss Carey dropped from sight. The *Bath Chronicle* of 30 December 1762 printed a "Prologue to a Play lately acted in a Barn at Chelmsford in Essex, by a Company of Strollers (Spoken by Miss CAREY)."

Carey, George Saville 1743–1807, actor, monologuist, playwright.

George Saville Carey was a son of Henry Carey, the songwriter and author of farces who was himself said to be the illegitimate issue of George Savile, Marquis of Halifax (d. 1695), and a country schoolmistress. George was born probably shortly after his father Henry hanged himself on 4 October 1743 in Warner Street, Coldbath Fields.

On 17 November 1743 Henry Carey's friends at Covent Garden Theatre, led by Kitty Clive, for whom he had written some parts and many songs, gave a benefit for his "Widow and Four Small Children." The bereaved family was then living in Cross Street, Hatton Garden, and were, according to the plea of Mrs Carey in the bill, "left entirely destitute of any provision."

The Dictionary of National Biography states that "About 1763 he resolved to go on the stage" and that he was "encouraged in this course" by Mrs Cibber, Garrick, and others. He played at Covent Garden, where "William Powell did his best for him, but

Harvard Theatre Collection

GEORGE SAVILLE CAREY
engraving by Hall, after Sherlock

he failed to make his way and retired." And so he may have done, but Powell was, of course, then at Drury Lane, and having just come himself to that theatre in 1763 could not have given much help. Moreover, there is no evidence in either the company lists or the playbills of either patent house to show that G. S. Carey was performing before 1773.

He was certainly close to the theatre, in sympathy at least, during the next few years, publishing *The Inoculators*, a comedy in 1766, *The Cottagers*, an opera, *Momus, a poem; or, a Critical Examination of the Merits of the Performers and Comic Pieces at . . . the Haymarket* in 1767, *Liberty Chastised*, a political play (under the pseudonym Paul Tell-Truth), and a masque, *Shakespeare's Jubilee*, in 1769, and *The Old Women Weatherwise*, an "interlude," the burletta *The Magic Girdle*, the pastoral, *Thorney, Laben and Dobin*, and

The Nut-Brown Maid, a comic opera, in 1770. None of these were produced on a London stage (though *The Old Women Weatherwise* was played at Hull in 1825).

Carey's burletta *The Noble Pedlar; or, the Fortune Hunter*, with music by F. H. Barthélemon, came out at Drury Lane on 13 May 1771 as an afterpiece on the benefit night of Evans, the subtreasurer of the theatre. The "Gentleman—first appearance" who took the lead part Florimore was perhaps Carey himself, though this is speculative. (It was repeated with success at Marylebone Gardens that summer.)

The first certain notice extant of Carey's acting was at Covent Garden on 27 April 1773 when, veiled by the conventional (and often mendacious) publicity-device designation "A Gentleman, first appearance [on] any stage," he played King Henry in *1 Henry IV* (identified by a notation on the playbill by John Philip Kemble). The performance was for Mrs Lessingham's benefit. It was evidently Carey's last appearance of the season.

Carey may have played Axalla in *Tamerlane* on 4 November 1773 at Covent Garden, as James Winston suggested, billed as "A Gentleman, his second appearance." Indeed, the *Morning Chronicle* of 13 November identified the representor of Axalla as the actor who had the previous season given imitations at Mrs Lessingham's benefit; and imitations were to be Carey's bread and butter through most of his professional life. Yet the bill of the evening in question does not mention this feature. (He is carried erroneously in the company list printed in *The London Stage* as "Henry" Carey.)

During the summer season of 1774 Carey lectured some half dozen times in the Great Room in Panton Street on the subject "Mimicry." There was a "Dialogue between Mr Patent [Garrick] and Jerry Dowlas" and a "Conversation between Aristophanes [Foote] and Billy Buckraw with the Favourite Cat Scene." He offered the same entertainments at Marylebone Gardens in the summer of 1775.

In 1776 he published this (or another) *Lecture on Mimicry* (they apparently changed in detail from occasion to occasion), with an interesting portrait of him holding a hand mirror (up to nature, doubtless). In 1777 he published *A Rural Ramble, to which is annexed a Poetical Tagg, or Brighthelmstone Guide.* The latter title may furnish some clue as to the infrequency of his name in the London bills of entertainment during the later 1770s and to the end of his career. He was probably traveling in the provinces and entertaining at resorts.

On 2 August 1780 Carey gave "a Variety of *Imitations*" as part of the total performance for the benefit of the New General Lying-In Hospital in Store Street. The *Caledonian Mercury* on 12 February 1783 informed the Edinburgh theatre-goers that

George Saville Carey, from London, will begin his lecture on mimicry at the Lower Room, St Mary's Chapel, on Thursday, at seven o'clock; the whole to conclude with the examination of a stage candidate after the manner of the late Mr Garrick and a dialogue in the Shades between Messrs Foote and Weston. Admittance 2s.

The lecture was repeated several times, both at the Chapel and at the Old Assembly Rooms.

On 17 September 1784 at the Haymarket at the end of the mainpiece

George Saville Carey has voluntarily offered to go through the following *Imitations*: The Examination of a Stage Candidate (in the manner of the immortal Garrick), Juno in her Cups, Etiquette, No Flower that blows, Widow Lovett, the Roundelay (in the manner of a much-lamented Syren [who was certainly Mrs Ann Cargill, who had been drowned, on her return voyage from India, on 12 March 1784]), The Serenade in THE JUBILEE (after the manner of Vernon,

Bannister and Kean.) To conclude with his famous Dialogue, in the manner of Foote and Weston.

As the bill reflects, Carey not only mimicked the voices and actions of famous players of dramatic parts but sang the favorite songs of singers from bass to soprano.

On 28 March 1786 at York and the following 3 and 5 April at Leeds, Carey gave a somewhat different arrangement of the blossoms in the florilegium of imitations:

A Lecture on Mimicry in three Parts, will be delivered by George Saville Carey, as represented at the Theatres-Royal, Covent-Garden and Hay-Market, before their Majesties at Windsor, and at the Universities of Oxford and Cambridge. Characters Imitated. Part I. Dr. Fiddlestick, a Superficial Manager, Dr. Fisher, A Song, Mr Vernon. Othello, Mr Barry. Jane Shore, Mrs Hartley. Waterman, Mr Bannister. Shylock, Mr Henderson. Cymbeline, Mr Hurst. Feignwell, Mr Leoni. Juno in her Cups, Miss Catley. No Flower that Blows, Mrs Baddeley. Etiquette, Mr Edwin. Macbeth, Mr Macklin. Roundelay, Mrs Cargill. The Three King Richards, Barry, Garrick, and Smith. Part II. Mincet, Mrs Bartholemon [*sic*]. Early Horn, Mr Lowe. Amo Amas, Mr Edwin. The Warwickshire Lads, &c. Mr Vernon and Mr Dibdin. Charming Fellow, Mrs Wells. Puck, Mr Woodward. Widow Loveit, Mrs Pitt. Serenade in the Jubilee, Messrs. Vernon, Bannister, and Keane. Part III. Prospero, in the Manner of the late Mr Mossop. The Examination of a Stage Candidate, after the Manner of the immortal Garrick. A New Dialogue in the Shades, between Messrs. Foote and Weston. Doors to be opened at Six, and to begin at Seven o'Clock. Boxes, 2s. 6d.—Pit 1s. 6d.—Galleries 1s. ☞ The above Lecture was delivered on Tuesday last the 28th of March, 1786, to an over-flowing House at York. Great Care will be taken to have the House properly aired.

Carey was also said to have done his imitations at Bath, Buxton, and other pro-

Harvard Theatre Collection

GEORGE SAVILLE CAREY

artist unknown

vincial towns during the 1770s and 1780s. In 1787 he published his *Poetical Efforts*, a miscellany.

In 1792 he tried his hand at another farce, *The Dupes of Fancy*, and after some rebuffs he got it staged—once, at Drury Lane on 29 May. Though such comic talents as those of Baddeley, Suett, and the younger Bannister tried to sustain it, it sank after that night. Carey published it the same year.

By 1797 he had conceived the entirely erroneous notion that his father Harry had been the originator of *God Save the King*, and he fruitlessly petitioned for an audience at court to press his claims to the pension he felt due him on this account.

In April 1799 he was to be found ("never happier in reciting, or more correct in imitation," according to the *Monthly Mirror*) at the New Eidophusikon in Panton Street, between showings of the moving scenes. The same year issued from the press his *Balnea, or History of All the Popular Watering-places of England*, with another portrait. In 1800 he brought out *One Thousand Eight Hundred, or I Wish You a Happy New Year*, a collection of some sixty of his songs. In 1801 he published *The Myrtle and the Vine, or Complete Vocal Library, containing several Thousands of . . . Songs . . . with an Essay on Singing and Song-writing*. Several separately published songs by Carey are also in the collection of the British Museum.

As late as the summer of 1807 he was in London, giving his entertainments. But on 14 July of that year he died suddenly of paralysis, and, like his father, penniless, and was buried by his friends.

In the spring of 1789 Carey had married a Miss Gillo of Salisbury. She seems either already to have been an actress, or then to have become one. She was acting in London by May 1789.

Late in his life Carey, though he had no known connection with the legal profession, was residing in chambers at Gray's Inn. It was there that his daughter Ann Carey, an itinerant actress, was said to have been conveyed from her lodgings in Chancery Lane just before giving birth to Edmund Kean (on either 17 March 1789 or 4 November 1787, according to which of two later reports of a story told by the actress Charlotte Tidswell is accepted). Kean's most authoritative biographers seem to settle on Nancy as Kean's mother, and indeed the soberest and most credible voices of contemporary testimony do seem to offer conclusive evidence for her maternity. It seems also likely that the father was Edmund Kean, clerk to Wilmot the surveyor, rather than either of his brothers, Moses or Aaron. The celebrated actor Edmund Kean was not the only result of Nancy's indiscretions. A writer in the *New Monthly Magazine* for 1834 remembered seeing Nancy accompanied by her son Edmund and another son, named Darnley, sired by a different father. Ann Carey died on 23 May 1833. She did not act in London in the eighteenth century.

J. Hall made an engraving of Carey from an original painting by W. Sherlock. A portrait engraving was published by Terry and Company in 1776.

Carey, Mrs George Saville, née Gillo
[fl. 1789–1798], singer.

A Mrs Carey played a principal character in *The What Is It?*, a musical extravaganza presented at the Royal Circus on 12 May 1789. She was probably the wife of George Saville Carey, though he is not supposed to have been married until a few days before 14 July 1789. She had been Miss Gillo, of Salisbury. About 1796 a song by Carey, *On yonder stile*, was published with the note that it had been sung by Mr and Mrs Carey.

Of Mrs Carey's performing career nothing more is known, but on 17 October 1798 G. S. Carey wrote a lengthy testimonial to a lotion his wife had used:

To Mr Dickinson, No. 55, Long-acre. Sir, I should think myself wanting in gratitude if I did not declare to the world the efficacy of your truly valuable Medicine, called Gowland's Lotion—My wife, who had from her infancy, possessed as good a complexion as most of her sex, was suddenly attacked with a violent surfeit, from eating a glass of ice cream, when she had rather overheated herself with walking, about three years ago, which was a mortification doubly felt, as she was but a young woman, and never had a blemish on her face before. She applied to the Faculty for assistance, she had recourse to the sea-water, making trial also of many other specifics, both internal and external applications, but to no effect; the disorder, as it grew older, became more and more outrageous, disfiguring her so much, that her relatives in the country, to whom she paid a visit last summer, did not know her, until she acquainted them with her name, for it was difficult to discriminate her features. Her

nose became almost twice its natural size; her eyelashes (which were ever remarkably long and handsome) not to be seen; her lips parched and crusted like the outside of the most ordinary kind of bread; her face was exceedingly inflamed, and sometimes of a purple colour, with numerous pustules; but on her forehead and her chin were great abundance of little black spots, interspersed with angry eruptions, that a casual beholder might have supposed she had been shot in the face with large-grained gunpowder, for the black spots, blended with the fiery pimples, produced a hideous effect. I have, however, the satisfaction of telling you now, that her face, from only using one of the quart bottles of your Lotion, is happily restored almost to its pristine hue and natural complexion. I have made this acknowledgment to you from gratitude, and on a general principle of philanthropy to mankind; wishing that all who may happen to labour under so hateful a malady, may meet with the same salutary relief; my wife wishes I should express her grateful acknowledgment for the benefit she has received from your excellent Lotion, while I, feeling myself much gratified at the event, beg leave to subscribe myself, Sir, your most humble and obedient servant, George Saville Carey.

Cargill, Mrs R., Ann, née Brown
c. 1759–1784, actress, singer.

The actress and singer Mrs Ann Cargill was born the daughter of Edward Brown, a London coal merchant, about 1759. Billed only as "A Young Gentlewoman," she made her first appearance on 8 November 1771 as Fanny in *The Maid of the Mill*, at Covent Garden Theatre. A manuscript notation by James Winston, in the Folger Library, identifies her. "A Young Lady" was one of the principal fairies in *The Fairy Prince* on 12 November 1771; and on 23 December the role of Sally in *Man and Wife* was announced as played by the young lady who had performed in *The Maid of the Mill* and *The Fairy Prince*. On 8 June 1772, Miss Brown was paid £31 10*s*. "in full this season."

In the next season, the Covent Garden bill for *Man and Wife* on 29 October 1772 gave "Sally, by Miss Brown who performed last season in the *Fairy Prince* and in *Man and Wife*." She was to remain at Covent Garden through 1779–80, primarily as a singing ingenue. On 20 October 1773 she acted Louisa Dudley in *The West Indian*, followed soon by Venus in *The Golden Pippin* on 26 November, a role she afterwards appeared in regularly. That season, in which her salary was about 10s. per day, she also played Isabella in *The Portrait* on 17 February and Polly in *The Beggar's Opera* on 22 April, both for the first time. In the following season she acted Daphne in *Philaster* for the first time on 20 October 1774, continued in some of the aforementioned roles, and sang in the spring oratorios at the King's Theatre.

Although Miss Brown was called an "inferior" actress by William Hawkins in his *Miscellanies* in early 1775, she had already achieved some success as a delightful singer and by her display of comic talent had become, according to Boaden, "an amazing favorite" with the public. At the same time that she was advancing in her profession, however, her behavior was filling the newspapers with scandalous anecdotes and her talent for attracting dissolute admirers had begun to develop. Reports of her adventures, sometimes confused and contradictory, began in the 1775–76 season, when at Covent Garden she played Leonora in *The Padlock* on 20 September and Fanny in *The Maid of the Mill* on 27 September, both announced as for the first time. On 21 November 1775 she "created" the role of Clara in Sheridan's *The Duenna*, but a few weeks later on 16 December she succeeded in eloping from her watchful father (an earlier attempt on 5 December had failed), and Miss Dayes was substituted in the role. On 31 December 1775, Sheridan wrote to his father-in-law Thomas Linley about losing her from the cast of his comic opera: "however, we have missed her

so little in The Duenna, that the managers have not tried to regain her, which I believe they might have done."

It is not clear whether Miss Brown's truancy was prompted by seduction or a desire to escape from her father's control. On 5 January 1776, the *Morning Post* reported that the youthful "runaway siren" of Covent Garden had been apprehended by her father at her aunt's house in the city. Forcing her into a coach, Brown had driven off with her into the country; however, "she had not been carried above five miles before her cries raised the inhabitants of a village, whom she soon worked to her purpose by declaring that the man (her father) was carrying her away by force, in order to ship her for America." The village folk released her, according to the account, and "she ran to town across the country, and has not since been re-taken by her father."

Still defiant to her father, who objected to her stage career, Miss Brown engaged at Covent Garden in 1776–77 at £6 per week. On 25 September she made her first appearance of the season as Leonora in *The Padlock*. In its review of the performance the *London Magazine* (October 1776) cautioned her not to mistake the applause she had received as anything but that of the encouragement of an audience charitably hoping "to relieve her from that embarass & distress, visible in her countenance & demeanor, & plainly perceivable by the failure of her voice, & her tremulous accents." She next played Polly in *The Beggar's Opera* on 30 September in a manner which drew sour comments from the *London Magazine* (November 1776): "Miss Brown succeeded Catley in Polly, & filled the cells of Newgate with all the affected quavers & warblings of a first serious Signora at the Opera House." Just before she was to play Polly again on 4 October, her father attempted once more to recover her. He seized her from her coach at the end of the playhouse passage in

Bow Street but was foiled by the great outcry of her companion, her aunt, who told the gathering crowd that Mr Brown was mad.

Attracted by the hubbub, actors from the "theatrical garrison sallied out in great numbers . . . to relieve the distressed damsel." Dressed as thieves and culprits ready for the play of the night, they made a formidable spectacle, and the crowd grew so great that the street soon was impassable. At length, reported the *Morning Chronicle* (7 October), "the lady was handed into the Playhouse in triumph," and notwithstanding her unsettled nerves performed Polly "greatly to the satisfaction of a very numerous and brilliant audience, who received her with respected shouts of applause."

That evening Sylas Neville was in the audience and thereafter wrote in his *Diary* that Miss Brown was:

a sweet pretty girl, & I think a good singer. It seems her father is much against her appearing upon the Stage & had her seized this evening just before the play began. This had such an effect upon her that soon after she came on first, before she had spoken three words, she fainted & was obliged to be carried out, but she recovered & did very well.

Brown seems not to have made any more attempts at retrieval of his daughter. During the rest of the 1776–77 season Ann performed Clara in *The Duenna*, Cherry in *The Stratagem*, Harriet in *The Two Misers*, Fanny in *The Maid of the Mill*, Miranda in *The Tempest*, Sabrina in *Comus*, Venus in *The Golden Pippin*, Mandane in *Artaxerxes*, Daphne in *Midas*, and Miss Olive in *The Device*. For her benefit on 29 April she played Diana in *Lionel and Clarissa* and Maria in *The Citizen*, the latter role for the first time. When Mrs Wilson was suddenly taken ill upon the stage in the title role of *The Country Wife* on 10 February 1777, Ann

Harvard Theatre Collection

ANN CARGILL (when Miss Brown) as Miranda and GEORGE MATTOCKS as Ferdinand

engraving by Grignion, after Dighton

went on to read the part for the rest of the performance.

In 1777–78, earning now £7 per week, she made her first appearance as Rosetta in *Love in a Village* on 26 September. She played Mary-Ann in *Love Finds a Way* on 18 November, and throughout the season continued to appear in many of her repertory roles of previous years. On 4 February 1778 she acted both Venus and Maudlin in *Poor Vulcan!*, roles in which she also took her benefit on 25 April, when she received net profits of £83 11s. Tickets could be had of her at No 10, Bow Street, Covent Garden. In 1778–79 she added to her repertory Rose in *Rose and Colin*, Annette in *Annette and Lubin*, Mrs Townly in *The Lady of the Manor* (a new comic opera with music by Hook, on 23 November 1778), Harriet in *The Liverpool Prize* (a new farce by Pilon on 22 February 1779), and the title role in *Calypso*. In that season she also made two appearances at Drury Lane, as Leonora in *The Padlock* on 29 September and as Sylvia in *Cymon* on 23 December. A Covent Garden pay sheet with her signature, now in the Harvard Theatre Collection, indicates that in 1778–79 she received £273 6s. 8d. or £1 6s. 8d. per night, for 178 nights of playing.

In her last season at Covent Garden, 1779–80, when she was paid £10 per week, she played Colombine in *The Touchstone* (on 6 October 1779, with music by Dibdin), Laura in *The Lady of the Manor*, Emilia in *Plymouth in an Uproar* (on 20 October), Nanny in *William and Nanny* (on 12 November), and Colombine in *The Mirror, or Harlequin Everywhere* (on 30 November). Illness prevented her appearance in the latter piece on 10 January 1780, but she was sufficiently recovered to perform Eliza in *The Flitch of Bacon* on 14 January (a role she had played a week earlier). She played Venus in *The Widow of Delphi* on 1 February, Venus again in *The Golden Pippin* on 5 February, Polly in *The Beggar's Opera* on 8 February, Meriel in *The Jovial Crew* on 29 March, and Maudlin in *The Spaniards Dismayed* on 3 April. Her last performance at Covent Garden was as Eliza in *The Flitch of Bacon* on 22 April 1780. (The Miss Brown who shared tickets at the Haymarket on 5 April 1780 was another performer.)

On 24 April 1780 the *Morning Post* rumored that Miss Brown was considering a move from Covent Garden in consequence of that management's attempt to engage Miss Harper (actually Miss Harper did not engage with Covent Garden until 1781–82, a full year later), adding that Miss Brown, "that charming brunette is entirely open to all the feelings of her sex, and full as susceptible of jealousy as she is to the softer sensations of love, in which she is said to participate with a most nice and genuine gusto." In another item in the same issue, the paper reported with some relish that "The little Brunette of Covent Garden eloped on Saturday morning [22 April], with her new Adonis, who has given her the most substantial proof of his affection, by settling £500 per annum upon her previous to their departure." She had, the report continued, returned all her theatrical parts to the manager of Covent Garden, Thomas Hull, informing him that she was going into the country. The information was probably inaccurate, at least as to the date of elopement, for as noted above, Miss Brown's name appeared in the bills as Eliza in *The Flitch of Bacon* for the night of 22 April (although possibly a last-minute unreported substitution was made). "Sir *Jacky John* [an unidentified jilted paramour] employed himself all day in driving himself through the streets," concluded the *Morning Post*, "to convince the world that he was not affected at the loss of his inconstant." "Sir Jacky John's" rival was a certain Mr R. Cargill, whom Ann married about 24 May 1780 at Edinburgh, where Cargill was apparently well known.

The newlyweds were back in London by the end of July. The town delighted in rumors that Cargill was only a fortune-hunting dissolute, but on 8 August 1780, the *Whitehall Evening Post* claimed the public had been "most grossly imposed upon" by previous stories concerning his character and stated he was a young gentleman not yet 21 years of age and of a good family in Jamaica; after Eton he had studied two or three "seasons" at the University of Edinburgh. Having met Miss Brown some six or seven months ago, they soon determined to marry, and accordingly had set off for Edinburgh, where they were wed, remaining a week, "altho' the name and profession of his new married Lady were kept a profound secret." Since their return to London, "Mr Cargill had ex-

Harvard Theatre Collection

ANN CARGILL as Clara

engraving by J. R. Smith, after Peters

perienced some distresses," from which, however, his wife's summer engagement had "luckily relieved him."

Now billed as Mrs Cargill, Ann had joined Colman's company at the Haymarket for the summer of 1780, making her first appearance on 1 August as Euphrosyne and a principal Bacchant in *Comus*, roles she repeated on 3 and 19 August. She acted Louisa in *The Deserter*, for the first time, on 10 August, Isabella in *The Wedding Night* on 12 and 14 August, Eliza in *The Flitch of Bacon* on 21 August, and Diana in *Lionel and Clarissa* on 29 August. The next night she sang Polly in *The Beggar's Opera* and played in *Comus* for her benefit, when tickets were available from her at No 41, Suffolk Street, Charing Cross. On 31 August she played Fanny in *The Maid of the Mill*, and on 2 September "created"

the role of the *Goddess of Health* and the title role in Colman's new afterpiece, *The Genius of Nonsense*, which had ten additional performances through 15 September.

While Mrs Cargill was playing for the summer at the Haymarket, the *Gazetteer* of 19 August 1780 announced that she had been engaged at Drury Lane for the coming season, but upon "the most uncertain terms," for her "expected pregnancy" would allow her to render little service to the manager. She did, indeed, make her first appearance at Drury Lane on 21 September 1780 as Polly in *The Beggar's Opera*, engaged at a salary unknown. On 26 September she played Rosetta in *Love in a Village*, on 28 September Sylvia in *Cymon*, and on 7 October Patty in *The Maid of the Mill*. In her performance as Rosetta, one critic found her, "exclusive of her musical powers . . . extremely just, both in the sprightly and sentimental parts of her character, as strongly evinced abilities, which, by application, could be rendered capital in any line." During the middle months of the season, Mrs Cargill seems to have been semiconfined by the reported pregnancy, her name appearing after 7 October only in the bills for *Comus* on 7 and 30 November, 20 December, (and perhaps on 22 January).

Ann did not play again until 10 March 1781, when she created the role of Miss Uniform in a new comedy, *Dissipation*, by Miles Peter Andrews, with whom, according to the *Monthly Mirror* of April 1797, she had had an affair prior to her marriage to Cargill. Her performances as Louisa in *The Deserter* and Rose in *The Recruiting Officer* brought her £195 13s. 6d. (apparently free of house charges) for her benefit on 18 April 1781. She ended her season's work on 29 May in *Dissipation*.

Mrs Cargill returned to the Haymarket in 1781 for a summer engagement which began on 30 May when she played her roles in *The Genius of Nonsense*. She continued to perform in such familiar pieces as *Lionel and Clarissa* and *The Duenna*. On 22 August 1781 she acted, evidently for the first time, Queen Dollalolla in *Tom Thumb*. On 8 August she had played the role of Macheath in *The Beggar's Opera*, in a transvestite production in which all the male characters were performed by females and the female characters by males. Assisted by her short and thick figure she was said to have acted the highwayman with "singular spirit," moving the audience to tears by her shudders upon hearing the bell toll her impending execution. A notation by James Winston on a playbill (in the Harvard Theatre Collection) for Saturday 8 September 1781, when she again was billed for Macheath, states that "Mrs Cargill run away this day with Colman Jun." The statement is in conflict with other contemporary comment about the affair in two particulars: the precise date of Mrs Cargill's defection and the man who accompanied her. It is not possible to piece out what actually happened from the extensive press coverage of this latest of Mrs Cargill's misadventures. On Tuesday evening, 11 September, she did not play Macheath as advertised. The *Morning Herald* of 13 September reported she had "made an unexpected elopement for Bath in company with a young gentleman somewhat *allied* to the theatre," thereby making it necessary for Mr Wood to perform her part. On the same date, however, the *Morning Chronicle* gave what may be a more accurate account:

Mrs Cargill and her husband took it into their heads to set off suddenly for Bath last week; the consequence was the audience were on Tuesday evening disappointed of their Macheath, and, after an apology, agreed to receive Wood in the character, who played it extremely well, and was much applauded.

Several days later, on 14 September, the role was taken over by Mrs Wells, who wrote in her *Memoirs* in 1811, some 30 years later, that Colman the manager had been agitated because the production was enjoying a run of crowded houses, cut short when Mrs Cargill "eloped with the son of the manager," and that Colman's double distress at the time "can scarcely be conceived."

On 14 September 1781, the *Morning Herald* followed up the gossip with a burlesque "missing person" advertisement, describing the lost party as wearing a Macheath costume and as being about five feet and two inches tall, of a beautiful red and white complexion, "when painted," and "inclined to be fat and has large breasts . . . legs are well shaped . . . is rather prominent behind, and walks with a short step."

On 15 September, the *Morning Chronicle* criticized Mrs Cargill's desertion of the Haymarket before her contract was up, and noted that she and her husband had in several other instances been arrogant with their demands on Colman for money and special concessions related to benefits and, indeed, that she had added insult to injury by running off this time with her theatrical clothing, which belonged to Colman.

On 1 December 1781, the *Public Advertiser* reported that on Thursday, 29 November, was heard at the Court of the King's Bench, Westminster Hall, "the action brought by Mr Colman, as proprietor of the Theatre Royal in the Haymarket, against Mr and Mrs Cargill on account of their elopement to Bath towards the conclusion of the last summer Season." Soon after the jury was sworn the counsel for the Cargills offered a compromise: Mrs Cargill would give up her present articles of engagement at the Haymarket, which were in force for two summers to come, if Colman would drop all proceedings. Colman agreed, especially when the defense counsel declared that if the terms were not accepted, "he would put an end to the matter at once by setting up as a defence the Minority of Both the Defendants at the time of entering into the Engagement." This notice also provides, it seems, the approximate year of Mrs Cargill's birth. If she was still under 21 at the time she engaged with Colman in 1780, her year of birth would have been 1759 or 1760.

In the meantime, Mrs Cargill had run into difficulties with another manager, Palmer, of the Bath Theatre, an engagement with whom during the race week had prompted her "elopement" from the Haymarket in the first place. Palmer snubbed her, said he would not encourage runaway

Harvard Theatre Collection

ANN CARGILL, CHARLES DUBELLAMY, and JOHN PALMER in *The Carnival of Venice*

engraving by Angus, after Dodd

actresses, and wrote Colman of his decision.

Mrs Cargill returned to London to take up her regular season's engagement at Drury Lane. When she appeared on that stage on 27 September 1781 as Euphrosyne in *Comus*, she was chided by the audience for her "late faux pas." In a pretty speech, delivered with appropriate embarrassment, she said she had always hoped to please her public; and English audiences being what they were, she was then received with applause and was encored during the performance. During the 1781–82 season at Drury Lane she played her roles of Macheath, Sylvia in *Cymon*, and Miss Uniform in *Dissipation*, and also acted Patie in Ramsay's *The Gentle Shepherd*, Marinetta in *The Carnival of Venice*, a new comic opera with music by Linley, Senior, Hippolita in *She Wou'd and She Wou'd Not*, and Damon in *The Chaplet*. Her last performance in London was as Patty in *The Maid of the Mill* on 16 May 1782.

At the conclusion of the 1781–82 season at Drury Lane, her summer engagement at the Haymarket now cancelled by the court action taken by Colman, Mrs Cargill went to play for the summer at Liverpool, under the management of Younger and Mattocks. Then followed the oddest, and the final, series of bizarre events in her life. As with the accounts of her previous escapades there is some difficulty in separating fact from sensational journalism. On 26 September 1782, the *Morning Herald* announced that "Mrs Cargill has certainly taken her departure for India, but not with her young and once enamoured Oriental Diamond-Monger, who lately pursuing her to the Isle of Wight, had the mortification to find her a la couche with the Captain of an Indiaman, with whom she has since actually shipped herself." Whether the "once enamoured Oriental Diamond-Monger" was an allusion to her husband or another paramour is not clear. According to an account published some 15 years later in the *Monthly Mirror* (April 1797), some time after her marriage Mrs Cargill had attached herself to a Mr Rumbold, "a thoughtless young man," who soon found himself in the King's Bench prison. His father offered to pay his debts provided he give up Mrs Cargill, but Rumbold would not do so. At length the father determined to send Rumbold off to India, whereupon the young man settled privately with Mrs Cargill that she should follow him there. On 16 April 1783, the *Morning Herald* incorrectly reported that she had died of a fever in passage. She had, in fact, got to India, according to the *Monthly Mirror*, with yet "another hero, to whom she took a fancy in her road" — perhaps the sea captain mentioned by the *Morning Herald*. Apparently she went on the stage in India and acted with success there, not only in her favorite comic characters but in tragedy as well, and a single benefit reportedly brought her the enormous sum of 12,000 rupees. But the directors of the East India Company, "over a dinner at the London Tavern, [had] settled that the pure shores of India should not be invaded by an actress," and Mrs Cargill was required to depart for home.

Ann Brown Cargill's restless life ended at about the age of 24 on the return journey from India, when she perished in the packet *Nancy*, which went down off the rocks of Scilly on 12 March 1784 (some reports state 24 February). Her body was found on the rocks, so it was said, in her shift, with an infant in her arms.

On 28 May 1784, Drury Lane Theatre paid George Colman £14 "for Mrs Cargill's Cloathes." Some months later, the monologuist George Saville Carey gave an imitation called "The Roundelay," in the manner of "a late much-lamented Syren," at the Haymarket on 17 September 1784, which he seems then to have made a permanent part of his act. He offered the same "Roundelay" at Leeds on 3 and 5 April 1786. On 9 May 1789, five years after her death, when she was described as "Ann

Cargill formerly of the Parish of St Mary Lambeth but late of Bengal in the E. India," administration of her unspecified estate and goods was granted to her father, Edward Brown.

Songs published as sung by Miss Brown included Hook's "Beneath a green shade" (1775?), from *The Scheming Lieutenant*; "When sable Night" (1775?), from *The Duenna*; "When first the dear Youth passing by" (1777?), from *Three Weeks After Marriage*; "Ye Fair Ye Lovers at my Call" (1779?), from *Harlequin Touchstone*; "Delightful is a rural Life" (1781), from *The Lady of the Manor*; and (as Mrs Cargill) "Young Lubin was a shepherd boy" (1781), from *The Carnival of Venice*.

Portraits and prints of Ann Cargill include the following:

1. Anonymous engraved portrait (proof before inscription) in the Harvard Theatre Collection.

2. Anonymous engraved portrait published as a plate to the *Town and Country Magazine*, 1776.

3. As Calypso in *Calypso and Telemachus*, an anonymous engraving published as a plate to an edition of the play by Harrison & Co, 1781.

4. As Clara in *The Duenna*, engraved by J. R. Smith, after W. Peters, published by J. Walker, 1777; another engraving by Smith, published by Humphrey, 1778; an engraving by Dunkarton, after J. Russell, published by J. Walker, 1777. The Russell version was also engraved by Sherwin and published by Bradberry, 1787.

5. As Daphne in *Midas*, an anonymous engraving published in 1778.

6. As Louisa in *The Duenna*, engraved by Read, after Russell, published by Walker, 1778.

7. As Marinetta in *The Carnival of Venice*, with Dubellamy as Melvil, and Palmer as Valencio, an engraving by Angus, after Dodd; the performers are shown in the roles they played in the first

performance of this comic opera by Tickell on 13 December 1781.

8. As Miranda in *The Tempest*, with George Mattocks as Ferdinand, engraved by C. Grignion after Dighton and published for T. Wright, 1777.

9. As Polly (when Miss Brown) in Colman's *Polly*, an anonymous engraving after J. Roberts, published in *Bell's British Theatre*, 1777.

10. As Polly in *The Beggar's Opera*, with Mattocks as Macheath, an engraving by Walker, after Dighton, published in Lowndes's *New English Theatre*, 1782.

11. As Rosetta in *Love in a Village*, with Dubellamy as Meadows, an engraving by J. Collyer, after D. Dodd, published in Lowndes's *New English Theatre*, 1784.

Caribaldi. *See* **CARABALDI.**

Caristina or **Caristino.** *See* **CARESTINI.**

Carleton. *See also* **CARLTON** and **CHARLTON.**

Carleton, Mr *d. 1783, house servant.*
Mr Carleton, "Senior," was a passage and lobby keeper and messenger at Drury Lane for at least 17 years between 1765 and 1782. In 1764–65 he was on the pay list for 1s. 6d. per day, or 9s. per week, and by 1776–77 for 18s. per week. Carleton regularly shared benefits with several other house servants. In 1779–80, he shared £137 18s. in benefit receipts with Mortimer, Tomlinson, and Woolams. In May 1776 he lodged at Mr Oudebert's, in Rider's Court, Leicester Fields. His last shared benefit came on 30 May 1782, and he died in the course of the following season. On 29 May 1783 "the Widow of the late Carleton Sen." shared a benefit with Portal, Shade, and Enoe.

His son, "Carleton, Junior," was a house servant at Drury Lane from 1765 through 1790. Perhaps the Miss Carleton who acted at the Haymarket in 1785–86 was his

daughter. A Mrs Carleton who acted at Norwich in January 1791 might possibly have been his widow, but no evidence exists to this effect.

Carleton, Mr [*fl. 1765–1790*], *lobby doorkeeper.*
Mr Carleton, "Junior," was a box lobby doorkeeper at Drury Lane for at least 25 years between 1765 and 1790. In 1764–65 he was on the pay list at 1s. 6d. per day, or 9s. per week. He regularly shared in benefits with other house servants, taking £73 11s. 10d. with Wilson, Shade, and Daglish on 8 June 1787, but unfortunately usually sharing large deficits with them in the later years: £73 18s. on 27 May 1784, £72 18s. on 27 May 1785, £80 13s. 5d. on 2 June 1786, and similar amounts in June 1788, June 1789, and June 1790. After his father, Carleton Senior, also a keeper at Drury Lane, died in 1783 Carleton Junior became known in the bills simply as Carleton.

Carleton, Miss [*fl. 1785*], *actress.*
A Miss Carleton acted Betty in *The School for Wives*, out of season, at the Haymarket on 16 November 1785. She may have been related to the Carletons who were house servants at Drury Lane.

Carleton, John [*fl. 1662–1664*], *actor?*
The Lord Chamberlain's accounts show that on 18 February 1664 John Carleton was a member of the Duke's Company at Lincoln's Inn Fields, and *The London Stage* also lists him as a member in 1662–63. No roles are known for him, and there is no certainty that he was the John Charleton who was buried on 4 December 1664 at St Margaret, Westminster.

Carli, Miss [*fl. 1762–1770*], *singer.*
Miss Carli was an occasional singer at Finch's Grotto Gardens, in St George's Field, Southwark, between 1762 and 1770. The songs *Lads and Lasses, blithe and gay*

and *Sweet summer is coming*, which she sang there with Mr Adams, were published in 1763 and about 1770, respectively.

Carlini, Rosa [*fl. 1758–1759*], *dancer.*

Signora Rosa Carlini was a dancing partner to Giovanni Andrea Gallini, one of Europe's finest dancers, at the King's Theatre during 1758–59. She made her first appearance on 11 November in new dances in *Attalo*, with Gallini, Giuseppe Forti, and Signora Bonomi. For the critic of the *London Chronicle* (18–21 November) there could not be imagined "two more agreeable figures" than Carlini and Gallini, dancing on "a very extensive plain, interspersed with villages." Signora Carlini also appeared in the new dances arranged for Cocchi's *Il Ciro reconosciuto* on 16 January 1759.

Carlino, Sieur [*fl. 1777*], *tumbler, ropedancer.*

The "Sieur" Carlino performed a tumbling act at Astley's Amphitheatre, Westminster Bridge, during May 1777 and perhaps throughout the summer. On 23 September 1777 he and Dawson did stiff-rope dancing and offered a tumbling "Exhibition of Egyptian Pyramids."

Carlisle, Mrs [*fl. 1745*], *actress.*

For a brief period in the spring of 1745 a Mrs Carlisle appeared in leading roles at the Goodman's Fields playhouse and then disappeared from public notice. On 9 March she played Lady Macbeth, on 21 March Desdemona in *Othello*, and on 15 April Amphitrite in *The Tempest*; on 18 April she delivered the epilogue at the premiere of *The Modern Wife*; and on 22 April 1745, her last notice, she acted Lady Outside in *Woman's a Riddle*.

Carlisle, James *d. 1691, actor, playwright.*

James Carlisle was born in Lancashire and had joined one of the two acting companies in London at some time before their union in 1682, for John Downes the prompter observed that by the time that the United Company had formed, Carlisle and Mountfort had "grown to the Maturity of good Actors." Carlisle's first recorded role was Aumale in *The Duke of Guise* on 28 November 1682 at Drury Lane. We know that in 1683–84 he acted Cinna in *Julius Caesar*, Vincent in *The Jovial Crew*, probably Pate in *The Northern Lass*, Lesbino in *The Disappointment*, and Brunetto in *A Duke and No Duke*. No other roles are known for him though he performed with the troupe until 1690–91.

He was mentioned by Christopher Rich and Sir Thomas Skipwith (in their reply to Betterton's complaints in 1694) as being one of the younger actors of about 1687 whom Betterton was allowed by Alexander Davenant to "brow beate and discountenance." This was doubtless an exaggeration, though Betterton is known to have been high-handed in his dealings with his actors at times. Carlisle was one of the many players of the Restoration who tried his hand at writing; his comedy, *The Fortune Hunters*, was produced at Drury Lane about March 1689 and published the same year. When the play was advertised in 1690 in Shadwell's *The Scowrer's*, Carlisle was styled "Captain" and by that year had apparently left the theatre to join King William's army in Ireland. He was killed, along with his brother, at the battle of Aughrim on 12 July 1691.

Carlo, Mr [*fl. 1785–1786*], *singer.*

Mr Carlo sang in the musical spectacles at Astley's Amphitheatre, Westminster Bridge, in the seasons of 1785 and 1786. On 7 April 1785 he was an Aerial Voyager in *The Air Balloon; or, All the World in the Clouds*, and in July he sang the role of Rugby in *The Termagant Mistress*. On 27 September he performed an unspecified vocal part in *Cupid Pilgrim* and on 5 October another part in an untitled burletta. In the following season Carlo played Spades in a new musical piece *The Marriage of the Knave of Hearts* and Clerk in *The Two Nannys*, both on 24 July 1786, Grist the miller in *A Trial of Skill for a Wife* on 4 September, and a part in *A Sale of English Beauties at Grand Cairo* on 17 September 1786; on that last date his name was given as Carlow in the advertisements.

Carlton. *See also* **CARLETON** and **CHARLTON**.

Carlton, Mr (*fl.* 1729), *dancer.*

A Mr Carlton, a dancer, performed the role of Endymion in *Humours of Harlequin* at the Haymarket on 25 February 1729.

Carlton, Peter (*fl.* 1673–1677), *actor.*

Peter Carlton played Abdelcador in Duffett's burlesque, *The Empress of Morocco*, in December 1673 at the Lincoln's Inn Fields Theatre as a member of the King's Company. On 10 May 1675 he acted Jacomo in *Love in the Dark* at Drury Lane, and on 27 August at the same playhouse he was Phillip in another Duffett burlesque, *Psyche Debauch'd*. On 11 December 1676 he was the first Jerry Blackacre in *The Plain Dealer*. He was still with the King's Company on 3 January 1677, when he was ordered arrested for some misbehavior. His name was sometimes spelled Charleton, and Montague Summers in *The Playhouse of Pepys* suggested that he might be identified as William Charleton, who acted in the late 1630s as a boy, but Charleton would have been a bit long in the tooth by 1676 to be playing the 21-year-old Jerry Blackacre. There may well have been a relationship, however, between the earlier and later actors.

Carly. *See* **CARLI**.

Carman. *See* **GARMAN**.

Carmichael, Thomas (*fl.* 1737–1779), *prompter.*

Thomas Carmichael was employed at the Aungier Street Theatre, Dublin, by 1737. On 29 April 1751 and 27 April 1752 he received benefits at the Smock Alley Theatre, Dublin, as prompter under the management of Thomas Sheridan. By 1756–57, Carmichael was prompter at Covent Garden Theatre and he had a benefit on 30 April of that season. Next season he was still prompter at Covent Garden, sharing £119 12s. with Holton, Mrs Stephens, and Mrs Helme at a benefit on 22 April 1758. He was prompter again at Smock Alley in 1772 and later became associated with the Crow Street Theatre. On 24 May 1779 Thomas Carmichael signed his full name to a letter sent by the Crow Street performers and personnel to the *Hibernian Journal*.

On 1 February 1741 Carmichael married at Dublin Miss Furnival, an actress who had made her debut at Smock Alley on 29 May 1740 and who was possibly a daughter of Mr and Mrs Thomas Furnival, actors in Dublin and London in the 1730s and 1740s.

Carmignani, Giovanni (*fl.* 1762–1763), *singer.*

Giovanni Carmignani sang in opera at the King's Theatre in 1762–63. His name was given as "Carrignani" in the bill of 19 February 1763 when he sang Argia in *Orione*, but Burney gave the spelling "Carmignani."

A person billed as Signora Carmignani, according to *The London Stage*, sang with members of the King's Theatre at a concert given at the Haymarket on 9 June 1763 for the benefit of Signor Capitani. She may have been the wife of Giovanni Carmignani, though perhaps an error was made in the bill, resulting in the substitution of "Signora" for "Signor."

Carmignani, Signora Giovanni? (*fl.* 1763), *singer?* See **CARMIGNANI, GIOVANNI.**

Carnaby, James (*fl.* 1701?–1713), *actor.*

In the cast list prefacing the first edition

of *The Virgin Prophetess* (1701), a Carnaby is listed in the role of Hector's young son Astianax. That player seems likely to have been James Carnaby, who was certainly identified as the "Gentleman" who acted Maiden in *Tunbridge Walks* at Drury Lane on 27 September 1705, even though he was then said to be making his first appearance on any stage. His juvenile appearance had perhaps been forgotten or, in the interests of publicity, ignored when he made his adult debut. And though *The London Stage* gives him Drury Lane appearances on 29 March 1705 (as the Nurse in *The Quacks*) and on 12 June 1705 (as a Merchant in *The Royal Merchants*), the casting in each case comes from editions printed long after the performances cited and probably after Carnaby's performance in *Tunbridge Walks* in September 1705.

Carnaby remained with the Drury Lane company, playing such roles as Appletree and Worthy in *The Recruiting Officer*, Charino in *Love Makes a Man*, Roger in *The London Cuckolds*, Leatherhead in *Bartholomew Fair*, Charmante in *The Emperor of the Moon*, Rattle Box in *The Gamester*, and Diocles and Alcander in *Oedipus*. After 1710 he was less frequently cited, but the early years of the eighteenth century are not well documented, and Carnaby may have been acting a full schedule throughout his London career. His last recorded appearance was on 23 February 1713 as Polycletus in *Cinna's Conspiracy* at Drury Lane. Only once, in 1710, did he work at another theatre: at Pinkethman's playhouse in Greenwich. The exact date is not known.

Carnacchini. *See* CORNACCHINI.

Carne. *See also* CARNEY.

Carne Mrs [*fl. 1793–1795*], *actress.*
A Mrs Carne appeared in an unknown piece at Sadler's Wells on 4 October 1793. She was probably the same Mrs Carne who

acted the Countess of Northumberland in a performance of *Chevy Chase, or Douglas and Percy* at the same theatre on 4 August 1795.

Carne, Miss [*fl. 1781–1782*], *actress.*
A Miss Carne acted at the Haymarket, out of season, several times in the spring of 1781 and the winter of 1781–82. She played Lucinda in *Love and a Bottle* on 26 March 1781, acted an unspecified role in *The Spendthrift* on 12 November 1781, and played Lady Flippant in *An Adventure in St James's Park* and Mrs Plotwell in *The Beaux' Duel* on 21 January 1782.

Carne, Miss [*fl. 1799–1802*], *dancer.*
A Miss Carne, sometimes billed as "Mrs," was a minor member of the dancing chorus at Covent Garden between 1799 and 1802. Her name was on the bills for one of the female islanders in *The Death of Captain Cook* and for a dancing lass in *The Deserter of Naples* in 1799–1800. In 1801–2 her salary was £1 10s. per week. She was probably the Mrs Carne who danced in performances of the entertainment *Meadea's [sic] Kettle, or Harlequin Renovated* at Sadler's Wells in 1792.

Carne, John [*fl. 1740–1768*], *house servant.*
John Carne was a house servant at Covent Garden for at least 28 years in the middle of the eighteenth century. Probably he was the Mr Carne who was on the pay list of that theatre as early as the 1740–41 season as stage doorkeeper at 5s. per week. The name (sometimes Carney) is found in Covent Garden lists through 1748–49 at the same salary. In 1744–45, 1747–48, and 1748–49 he shared benefits with other house servants. By 1760–61, John Carne was a boxoffice keeper. In a list of Covent Garden employees in 1767–68 provided by Arthur Murphy, Carne was named as a candleman at 3s. 4d. per day. His wife, Elizabeth Carne, was a housekeeper and

candlewoman at the same theatre at least from 1761–62 through 1782–83.

John Carne was dead by 1778, for a bequest was made to his widow in the will of Priscilla Rich, dated 9 November 1778. He may well have been the dancer named Carney who performed at Drury Lane during the 1730s and later at Goodman's Fields and Lincoln's Inn Fields and whose dancing career was cut short by illness before 1744–45.

Carne, Mrs John, Elizabeth [fl. c. 1762–1783], house servant.

According to testimony given in litigation over George Colman's management of Covent Garden in 1770, Elizabeth Carne had care of the candles and oil at that theatre from about 1762. Her job was to collect tallow drippings and candle ends for resale to various outlets. The proceeds, amounting to some £120 per season, she turned over to Mr Sarjant, the chief housekeeper.

Mrs Carne also was in charge of the charwomen of the house. Her salary in 1768 was £30 a year, and she and her husband, a boxoffice keeper, lived in the theatre. In a will dated 9 November 1778 and proved 12 March 1783, Priscilla Rich, wife of the late manager John Rich, left £5 "unto Elizabeth Carne widow of John Carne and now residing at the Theatre Royal in Covent Garden," thus providing the last item of record about Mrs Carne.

Carnelys. See CORNELYS.

Carnevale, Pietro [fl. 1782?–1791], musician, deputy manager, proprietor.

Pietro Carnevale probably came to England with his wife about 1782. Although Signora Carnevale, a singer, made her debut at the King's Theatre as early as 7 January 1783, her husband's first notice was not until two years later when he was one of the instrumental performers in the Handel Memorial Concerts which were given at Westminster Abbey and the Pantheon in May and June of 1784. By the following season, Signor Carnevale was the deputy manager of the opera company at the King's Theatre, a position which suggests a possible connection with that company before that year. As deputy manager in 1785–86 he received a salary of £100 and a benefit on 1 June 1786. He served in this capacity until 1788–89, when he was replaced by Ravelli, but he remained at the theatre. On 7 February 1789, when the manager Gallini could not be found to answer to the audience which threatened to destroy the house because of their displeasure with the poor dancing, Carnevale was sent forward to appease them. Pressed to answer as to when better dancers could be expected, he replied that "he had not the least concern in the management, and although his name was inserted in the license, yet he had no power to make any engagements."

The King's Theatre was gutted by fire on the evening of 17 June 1789, at a loss of £40,000. One report attributed the sensational and tragic conflagration to a drunken carpenter loose in the scene loft with a lighted candle, but most signs pointed to arson. Some suspected the manager Gallini himself, but according to Brayley, Carnevale, who had a grudge against his replacement Ravelli, confessed on his death bed at Bristol about twelve months later to having set the blaze. Brayley's credibility, however, is suspect on at least two counts: Carnevale may not have died as early as Brayley attested; moreover, Brayley claimed that Carnevale had been leader of the band at the King's Theatre during years when it is known that Cramer held that position.

In January 1790 Carnevale opened a little theatre in Savile Row, in space previously occupied by Squibb's Auction Rooms, for the purpose of exhibiting Italian fantoccini puppet shows. The theatre was "very pretty . . . with a pit and two rows of boxes, beautifully decorated with arabesque paintings" by the Italian artist Biagio Rebecca, then working in England. Carnevale's connections at the Opera assured the tiny playhouse the most fashionable audiences, which included the Prince of Wales, the Duke of Bedford, the Duke of Cumberland, Lord Salisbury, Lord Cadogan, Lord Cholmondeley, and others of similar status and influence. In a three-month season, during which 12 fantoccini pieces were performed twice a week, Carnevale enjoyed full houses by subscriptions of four guineas; some individual seats were sold for performances near the end of the season at the very stiff price of 10s. 6d. each. The season closed on 9 April 1790, with public expressions by Carnevale "for the very kind patronage with which the entertainments had been received" and an announcement that he had sold the enterprise to Lord Barrymore, the eccentric peer who also maintained a private theatre at Wargrave in which to indulge his passion for dramatic activities.

It would seem that Carnevale had done well financially with his Savile Row investment. In early 1791 Carnevale was reported by Horace Walpole (in a letter to the Misses Berry, 5 March 1791) to have won a prize of £20,000 in a lottery, but he did not receive the entire sum, having previously sold two-thirds of his investment in the ticket to others. Little more is known of Carnevale. The date of his death is not known, but on 20 April 1796 a fantoccini show was given at Ranelagh Gardens "as performed under the direction of the late Mr Carnevale." The last known notice of his wife's performing in London was on 3 May 1792.

Carnevale, Signora Pietro [fl. 1783–1792], singer, actress.

Signora Pietro Carnevale made her first appearance on the English stage in the title role of Bertoni's new serious opera *Cimene* at the King's Theatre on 7 January 1783. According to Fanny Burney, who saw the performance, she had "a loud, violent voice, very harsh and unpleasing, and as little manageable or flexible as if she had sung all her life merely by ear, and without any teaching of any sort." After repeating *Cimene* on 16 January and 1 March, Signora Carnevale sang the title role in *Creusa in Delfo* on 28 April and 3 May, a role in *La buona figliuola* on 3 June, and Laurina in *L'avaro* on 14 and 21 June. In the following season she sang the part of the Queen in *La regina di Golconda* 11 times between 18 March and 8 June 1784.

Fanny Burney's judgment that although "She has all the abilities to be a great singer and she is worse than any little one" appears to have been accurate, for, having made little stir, Signora Carnevale did not appear again at the Opera, despite the fact that her husband Pietro Carnevale was an acting manager there between 1785 and 1789. Her only other appearances in London were in the title role of *Zelma*—her first attempt in a speaking part on the English stage. The musical romance was first performed at Covent Garden on 17 April 1792 and once again on 3 May of the same season.

Carney. *See also* CARNE.

Carney, Mr [fl. 1733–1745], dancer, actor.

Mr Carney was a dancer at Drury Lane from 1733 through 1740–41. He was billed as Young Carney for the first time on 24 October 1733, when he danced Pompey in *The Harlot's Progress*. On 5 February 1734 he played Pistolet in *Cupid and Psyche* at Drury Lane, and on 24 May 1734 he acted the leading role of Trueman in *George Barnwell* at the little James Street Theatre. Carney remained a member of the chorus at Drury Lane for eight years, appearing almost always in such parts as a Peasant in *Robin Goodfellow*. In 1741–42 he went over to the Goodman's Fields

Theatre, and according to the *Public Advertiser*, 8 September 1742, he was the person who danced there as David Ap Shenkin in the spring of 1742. Also on these bills was a Winifred Ap Shenkin and their son and daughter (but see the accounts of John Hippisley and Richard Yates).

In the next season he was at Lincoln's Inn Fields Theatre, where he danced comic pieces with Mrs Roland and others until 14 March 1743, when he joined a small company at the New Wells Theatre in Lemon Street, Goodman's Fields. His name, however, is found on the bills of both Lincoln's Inn Fields and the New Wells for 7 April 1743. After this season, he appears to have retired from dancing, and on 4 February 1745 he was given a benefit at Goodman's Fields. The bill stated that tickets were to be had at his lodgings at "Mr Comer's, the bottom of Lemon Street, at the taphouse of the Wells"—but that his "long illness" prevented him from performing or "waiting on his friends."

Carnish. *See* CORNISH.

Carnivalli. *See* CARNEVALE.

Carny. *See* CARNE *and* CARNEY.

Caro. *See* DEL CARO.

"Carolina, Signora." *See* PITROT, CAROLINA.

Carpenter, Mr [*fl.* 1736], *actor.*
A Mr Carpenter acted Blunt in a performance of *The London Merchant* given at York Buildings on 26 April 1736.

Carpenter, Robert 1748–1785, *actor, singer.*
Robert Carpenter made his first appearance on the London stage at the Haymarket on 10 August 1774, when he replaced Courtney in an unspecified role in *The Cozeners*, under Foote's management. During that summer he played in *The Cozeners* ten additional times and also acted a role in *The Bankrupt* on 24 August and 14 September, Lint in *The Mayor of Garratt* on 2 September, Sir Roger Dowlas in *The Patron* on 5 September, Ben Budge in *The Beggar's Opera* on 6 September, and Sullen in *The Beaux' Stratagem* on 19 September. Carpenter then joined Garrick's company at Drury Lane, making his debut there as Spavin in *The Note of Hand* on 20 September 1774 and continuing for five seasons mainly in a line of minor roles and as a bass chorus singer at 5s. per day, or £1 10s. per week.

In 1774–75 he played the Lieutenant in *Richard III*, a role in *The Christmas Tale*, a Soldier in *The Deserter*, Wolf in *The School for Wives*, a role in *The Genii*, one of the mob in *The Alchemist*, a Planter in *Oroonoko*, Verges in *Much Ado About Nothing*, a vocal part in *The Maid of the Oaks*, a role in *Harlequin's Jacket*, a Waiter in *The Male Coquette*, a Sailor in *The Brothers*, a role in *A Peep Behind the Curtain*, Abhorson in *Measure for Measure*, vocal parts in *Timanthes* and *Macbeth*, the Bookseller in *The Committee*, Mump in *Phoebe*, the Clown in *The Elopement*, a Bacchanal in *Comus*, a Countryman in *The Quaker*, and Doodle in *Tom Thumb*. In the latter role on 19 May 1775 he shared benefit receipts of £128 3s. 6d. with Lamash, Griffiths, and Kear.

Over the following four seasons he added to his repertory such roles as the Constable in *Old City Manners*, Tom in *The Jealous Wife*, an Officer in *Twelfth Night*, the Boatswain in *The Tempest*, and Rugby in *The Merry Wives of Windsor*; he also sang regularly in the chorus. For a benefit which they shared on 4 May 1776, Carpenter, Wright, and Butler suffered a total deficit of £30 12s. 6d.

The report by the *Public Advertiser* on 12 September 1776 that Carpenter had died at Liverpool—where he acted during that summer at £1 5s. per week—while playing the Clown in *Harlequin Sorcerer* on 5 September was incorrect. For on 21 September he was back at Drury Lane playing in *New Brooms* and *Twelfth Night* and living at No 11, Little Russell Street. Similarly suspect is the notation in the Jerome papers that Carpenter was dismissed from Drury Lane on 31 December 1778 for forging Mr Linley's ticket orders, for his name continues in the bills during January and February of that season.

Having gone to play at Bristol in March 1779, he was charged in that city on 23 March with the rape of one of Lord Peterborough's serving maids but was discharged a fortnight later for lack of evidence. The remand kept him from returning to his business at Drury Lane until 3 May when he appeared in his usual role of Rugby in *The Merry Wives of Windsor*. His last role at Drury Lane was Verges in *Much Ado About Nothing* on 29 May 1779. According to the Winston fundbook at the Folger Library (in which his Christian name is given as Richard), Carpenter claimed against the fund in November 1780 but in January 1782 was expelled for defrauding it. He then seems to have been employed as a navy agent at Portsmouth. On 2 April 1785 he was hanged at Winchester for forging seamen's wills. Robert Carpenter was buried in the churchyard of Winchester Cathedral on 4 April 1785, aged 37. The Miss Carpenter who acted at Plymouth and died at Bath on 17 December 1804 may have been his daughter.

"Carpentier, Mr" ₁fl. 1754₁, actor?

A "Mr Carpentier" delivered a prologue to *Mrs Midnight's New Carnival Concert* at the Haymarket on 8 and 13 August 1754. The name is probably the pseudonym of one of the unidentified actors in the company of Christopher Smart, who styled himself "Mrs Midnight."

Carporali. *See* CAPORALE.

Carr, Mr d. 1797, actor, equestrian, tumbler.

A Mr Carr played an English adjutant in a spectacular production of *The Siege of Quebec* at Astley's Amphitheatre, Westminster Bridge, in September 1787. Probably he was the same Mr Carr who performed tumbling at Astley's on 27 July 1795, when the advertisements promised he would "stand on his Head, in the center of a GLOBE, and ascend 30 feet high, turning round like a Boy's Top." Earlier that year, on 10 February, a Mr Carr performed feats of "Horsemanship Unrivalled"—with other equestrians—at the Lyceum. On 17 January 1798 the *Hibernian Journal* reported that "Mr Car," had drowned, with some other members of Astley's company, in the Irish Sea in December 1797.

Carr, Mr ₁fl. 1797₁, watchman.

A Mr Carr was on the Drury Lane pay list dated 23 September 1797 at 12 shillings per week as watchman. Perhaps he was the Carr who subscribed 10s. 6d. to the Drury Lane fund in 1797.

Carr, Mrs ₁fl. 1741₁, dancer.

A Mrs Carr performed as one of the chorus of countrywomen in *Harlequin the Man in the Moon* in Lee and Woodward's booth at the Southwark Fair on 14 and 15 September 1741. She may have been the wife of Oliver Carr, who was a provincial manager, an actor at Covent Garden, and a performer at the fairs at this period.

Carr, Benjamin 1768–1831, composer, publisher, musician, singer.

Benjamin Carr was born at London on 12 September 1768 (according to information provided by his niece Mary Jordan Carr Merryman) and not in 1769 as commonly stated. He was the son of the music publisher and composer Joseph Carr (1739–1819). Thoroughly trained in music by Dr Samuel Arnold and Charles Wesley, he was associated with the Concerts of the Academy of Ancient Music, sometimes as conductor, from 1776 to 1793. On 16 October 1792 his pastoral opera *Philander and Silvia, or Love Crown'd at Last* was performed at Sadler's Wells. This piece evidently was not published; nor was the composer's name given in the advertisements, but it was included in a manuscript list of his works in Carr's handwriting which is in the possession of Arthur Billings Hunt, Brooklyn. Carr was listed in Doane's *Musical Directory* (1794) as a principal tenor, a harpsichordist, and a member of the Academy of Ancient Music. In the early 1790s his address was No 5, Middle Row, Holborn, the same as that of his father and of his brother Thomas Carr (1780–1849).

In 1793, Benjamin Carr emigrated to the United States and was followed within several months by his father and his brother Thomas. Another brother, John Carr (1772–1832), remained in England, wrote *The Stranger in Ireland*, the *Caledonian Sketches*, and other travel literature, and was knighted by the Duke of Bedford, Viceroy of Ireland. He had written the words for *Poor Richard*, a song by Benjamin which had been sung "at the principal concerts of England" by 1793. The three Carrs, father and sons, established music shops in three American cities; Joseph and Thomas set up their Musical Repository in Market Street, Baltimore, by 1794; Benjamin opened two businesses, one at No 136, High Street, Philadelphia, and another at No 131, William Street, New York. In his *Bibliography of Secular Music*, Sonneck states that both of Benjamin's operations were opened by July of 1793—the one in New York said to be the first of its kind in that city—but they were not listed in the directories of either city in that year. A listing for "Benjamin Carr, at his musical repository," then at No 122, High Street, appeared in the *Philadelphia Directory* in 1794, but not until 1795 did Carr's name appear (as "Music and Musical Instrument

Seller, 137 William St.") in the *New York Directory*. Over the next 35 years the Carrs were to make enormous contributions to the development of musical life in the young nation through their imprints, and Benjamin especially through his numerous secular and sacred compositions, and by his endeavors on and for the musical stage.

Benjamin Carr made his first appearance on the New York stage as Young Meadows in the comic opera *Love in a Village* at the John Street Theatre on 15 December 1794. William Dunlap, with whom he would soon collaborate, reported that "his deportment was correct, but timid, and he never acquired or deserved reputation as an actor. His voice was mellow and knowledge of music without graces of action made him more acceptable to the scientific than to the vulgar auditor." The overture that he had provided for the evening, however, had "the advantage of being eminently calculated to attract universal approbation," according to the *Theatrical Register*. He remained a performer with Hodgkinson's American Company for a brief period only, playing in Hartford in the summer of 1795, and then devoting his energies to his publishing and composing.

Between 1794 and 1797, especially, Carr busied himself with arranging, adapting, and providing new music for the emerging musical theatre of America. His earlier efforts were concerned with pieces already familiar on the English stage. On 7 July 1794, *The Spanish Barber*, Colman's version of Beaumarchais's *Le Barbier de Seville*, with music by Dr Arnold, was given at the New Theatre, Philadelphia, with accompaniments and additional airs by Carr. He provided accompaniments and additional songs for Arnold's *The Children in the Wood* at the same theatre on 24 November 1794 (later produced in New York and Boston by the American Company). For a new production of *Macbeth* in New York on 14 January 1795 he adapted Locke's earlier music and compiled some

Scotch pieces as entr'acte diversions. Other productions for which he labored included *The Deserter* (New York, 19 May 1795), *The Caledonian Frolic* (Philadelphia, 4 May 1795), and *Poor Jack, or the Sailor's Landlady* (Boston, 21 April 1795).

In 1796 Carr provided a medley overture and some new songs for *The Patriot, or Liberty Obtained,* a piece based on the legend of William Tell and produced with success at the Chestnut Street Theatre, Philadelphia, on 12 February and at Baltimore on 3 September. Several months later, working with the same subject matter, Carr did the entire original music for *The Archers, or The Mountaineers of Switzerland*, to a libretto by William Dunlap. The first performance of *The Archers*, which may be regarded as America's second opera (the first being *Tammany* [1794] with music by James Hewitt, Carr's friend, and book by Ann Kemble Hatton, Mrs Siddon's sister) was given at the John Street Theatre on 18 April 1796 to "unbounded applause." According to Dunlap, Carr was supposed to have played the principal role of Tell, but the surviving bills specify Hodgkinson. The piece was repeated in New York at least on 22 April and 25 November, and it was said to have been performed in Boston twice, though the only date known was 7 October 1796. Extracts of the score of *The Archers* were published in No 7 of Carr's *Musical Miscellany*, these being a section from the overture, the solo "Why Huntress, why, wilt thou life expose?" and the song "There Lived in Altdorf city fair," sung by Mrs Hodgkinson in the New York production.

The Baltimore Carrs, Joseph and Thomas, had the distinction in 1814 of publishing what was probably the first edition of *The Star-Spangled Banner*. In 1794, as part of a medley of patriotic airs compiled by him for *The Federal Overture*, Benjamin first printed the song "Yankee Doodle." He also advertised a pianoforte arrangement of *The Federal Overture*, "as

performed at the Theatre," in the *New York Advertizer* on 9 January 1795. The piece was played in a concert directed by Decker and Graupner at Norfolk on 7 October 1796. In 1798, at Philadelphia, Carr published *The New Federal Song*. It had originally been known as *The President's March*, and perhaps had been composed for Washington's first inauguration in 1789 by Philip Roth or Philip Phile. The tune had been published by Carr earlier in the fifth number of his musical monthly, *The Gentleman's Amusement and Companion to the Flute*. For this music Joseph Hopkinson had written the verses of *Hail Columbia* as a patriotic song to be sung by the actor Fox at his benefit at the New Theatre, Philadelphia, in 1798. The song was encored six times by an exuberant audience, and two days later Carr printed it again. The song continued to attract such spirited response at the theatre that President John Adams came to hear it.

Also vigorously involved in concert life, Carr sang and played in such places as the New Assembly Room in William Street in New York and the Pennsylvania Tea Gardens, Oeller's Tavern, and the City Tavern in Philadelphia. With Cross, Heysfield, Schetky, Taylor, and other musicians, he established a fund "for the relief of and support of decayed musicians and their families, and for the cultivation and diffusion of taste in music" in 1820 under the auspices of his group called The Musical Fund Society of Philadelphia. Concerts to raise the fund included the earliest performances of Beethoven's music in America, in 1821. Haydn's *The Creation* in 1822, with Carr conducting, was heard by an audience of some 2000. In 1824 the Society erected its own concert hall where it became host to the most significant musical activities in the city for many years. Carr edited the *Musical Journal*, founded by his father, and he also provided songs for his father's publication, *Carr's Musical Miscellany in Occasional Numbers*, which began in 1813.

In 1801 Carr became musical director of the new St Augustine's Church, a position he retained for his remaining 30 years of life and in which he wrought many improvements in ecclesiastical music in America and in choir training. He published in 1805 his *Masses, Vespers and Litanies*, with selections by Jomelli, Schetky, Raynor Taylor, and himself. His book of *Lessons in Music*, published about 1814, gave influential direction to church choral training. Carr also wrote the "Dead March and Monody" which was played at George Washington's funeral ceremonies in 1799. An extensive list of his compositions is given in Virginia Larkin Redway's "The Carrs, American Musical Publishers," *Musical Quarterly* (January 1932). Some of Carr's manuscripts are in the New York Public Library and some are in the Library of Congress.

At the age of 62, Benjamin Carr died at Philadelphia on 24 May 1831 (in this year his business address was given in the *Philadelphia City Directory* as No 72, South 5th Street). He was buried on 26 May in St Peter's Churchyard in Philadelphia. Two of his closest friends, the musicians George Schetky and Raynor Taylor, now rest beside him. By his will Carr left his library and a trust fund for "the use and comfort" of his brother Thomas, who survived him by 18 years, dying on 15 April 1849, at the age of 69. His father Joseph Carr had died at Baltimore in October 1819, at the age of 80. No wife or children were mentioned in Benjamin's will. A monument was placed over his grave by the Musical Fund Society, engraved with the epitaph: "A distinguished professor of music, charitable, without ostentation, faithful and true in his friendships. To the intelligence of a man he united the simplicity of a child."

In his will, Carr bequeathed to Schetky "a miniature colored profile of himself." A portrait of him by J. C. Darley, engraved by Sartain, was published in Simpson's *Eminent Philadelphians*, 1859.

Harvard Theatre Collection

BENJAMIN CARR

engraving by Sartain, after Darley

Carr, Oliver [*fl. 1741–1769*], *actor, manager.*

Although probably he had acted previously in the provinces, the first notice of Oliver Carr at London was when he played a witch in the pantomime *Harlequin Sorcerer* on 4 August 1741 in Lee and Woodward's booth at the Tottenham Court Fair. He may have been at Goodman's Fields Theatre in 1741–42, for, according to the *Theatrical Inquisitor* (June 1815), Carr boasted of having taught David Garrick how to act when the young Roscius made his first appearance at Goodman's Fields on 19 October 1741 as Richard the Third. Later, when Carr was a manager of strolling players in the vicinity of London, it was said he dressed his Richard "in the same garments which were worn by Garrick" at his debut, and that this "dress was held, by the strollers of his company, in high estimation; and as their wardrobe was not overstocked, it was frequently used in comedy as well as tragedy." Allowances must be made for such theatrical legends.

While Garrick was attracting large crowds at Goodman's Fields in 1741–42, the only notice the bills took of Carr was when he played Isman in a single performance of *Zara* at the little James Street Theatre on 7 April 1742 for the benefit of "a Tradesman in Distress." In the following season, however, Carr became a member of the company at Covent Garden, making his first appearance as Tyrell in *Richard III* on 14 October 1741. That season he also played Northumberland in *1 Henry IV*, Zama in *Tamerlane*, Cimber in *Julius Caesar*, Lopez in *The Pilgrim*, a Sailor in *The Fair Quaker*, and Frederick in *The Miser*. For his benefit on 2 May 1743, which he shared with Martin, Carr acted Vainlove in *The Old Bachelor*. He also played Drawcansir in a single performance of *The Rehearsal* at Lincoln's Inn Fields on 7 December 1742.

Carr maintained the above roles in the Covent Garden repertory over the next four seasons. His other roles (with season of first performance) included: (1743–44) Marcellus in *Hamlet*, Gayless in *The Lying Valet*, Harry in *The Mock Doctor*, Prince of Tanais in *Tamerlane*, Hastings in *2 Henry IV*, Mat in *The Beggar's Opera*, Alberto in *A Duke and No Duke,* Hemskirk in *The Royal Merchant*; (1744–45) Sergius in *The Siege of Damascus*, Strato in *The Maid's Tragedy*, Rhubarb in *The Double Gallant*, the Governor in *Papal Tyranny*, Morochius in *The Merchant of Venice*; (1745–46) Theodore in *Venice Preserv'd*, Gondi in *The Massacre of Paris*, Seyton in *Macbeth*, Alberto in *Duke and No Duke*, Smith in *The Man of Mode*, Antonio in *Much Ado About Nothing*, and an English Lord in *Cymbeline*; (1746–47) Scales in *The Recruiting Officer*, Philip in *She Wou'd and She Wou'd Not*, and Elder Worthy in *Love's Last Shift*. On 12 May 1747, Carr's share of benefit tickets amounted to £7 6d. His salary that season was 12s. 6d. per week. He also made a single appearance at Drury Lane, on 15 September 1743, as Kite in *The Recruiting Officer*.

After his final season at Covent Garden in 1746–47, Carr appeared only occasionally in central London. He acted Jeptha in *Jeptha's Rash Vow* five times in Yeates and Warner's great booth on the Bowling Green, Southwark, in September 1750, at the time of the fair. In the late summer of 1755 Carr acted four roles at the Haymarket: the Duke in *Othello* on 1, 3, and 6 September, Blunder in *The Honest Yorkshireman* on 3 September, Appletree in *The Recruiting Officer* on 9 September, and Charon in *Lethe* on 11 and 15 September. He turned, in the meanwhile, to the management of strolling players around London, playing at Fulham, Croydon, and other places in Kent and Surrey. It was under his management that John Quick, at the age of 14, began his acting career in 1760.

It is known that Carr acted at Richmond in July 1769, but we have no knowledge of him after that time. The Mrs Carr who acted at Southwark Fair on 14 September 1741 was, perhaps, his wife.

Carr, Richard ₁*fl. 1684₁, musician, music publisher.*

With Henry Playford, Richard Carr in 1684 took over the music publishing business of John Playford at the Middle Temple Gate facing St Dunstan in the West. John Playford described Carr, the son of his friend John Carr, as "one of His Majesty's Musick, and an ingenious person, whom you may rely upon."

Carr, Robert ₁*fl. 1674–1696₁, violist.*

Violist Robert Carr replaced John Hingeston in the King's Musick sometime in 1674, when he was granted an annual livery allowance of £12 2s. 6d. The warrant appointing him was repeated on 22 December 1683, perhaps because his livery was in arrears, and it was noted that his regular salary was £50 per year. Carr continued in the royal service until a warrant dated 9 January 1696 ordered Thomas Tollett to replace him. During his years in the King's Musick, he frequently accompanied the King on trips, as in 1685 when he was paid 3s. per day for attending their Majesties on journeys to Windsor and Hampton Court, or in January 1691 when he was among those chosen to accompany William III to Holland.

Outside the court Carr is known to have participated in the St Cecilia's Day celebrations at Stationers' Hall on 23 November 1691; he was one of the six stewards— four of them being persons of quality and two being chosen from among London's professional musicians.

Like so many court musicians, Carr was sometimes in debt. On 26 April 1692 he was petitioned against by Mr Dardon and Mr Needham for a debt of £32 12s., and by that time poor Carr's annual salary had dropped to £30 per year because of a royal retrenchment in 1689. When Carr was replaced in 1696 by Tollett, the documents implied that he was still living, but of his career after that nothing is known.

Carré, Marie-Thérèse b. 1757, dancer.

According to a manuscript in the Public Record Office, one "Theresa Carre" received a salary of £85 as a performer at the opera at the King's Theatre, London, in the season of 1784–85, but her name appears in no extant bills.

Campardon cites an official record which details how Mlle Marie-Thérèse Carré, born in 1757, a dancer in the Académie Royale de Musique at Paris, had appeared before a magistrate on 29 September 1784 to pour out a complicated complaint about having been swindled of her jewels by a stranger whom she had befriended. Very likely she was the dancer at London.

Carrier. See also CURRER.

Carrier, Mrs [fl. 1743], actress.

On 1 February 1743 at Punch's Theatre in James Street, run by the eccentric Charlotte Charke, "The part of the Queen of Hungary [in Tit for Tat was played] by Mrs Carrier, the celebrated Actress tho' now almost out of date . . ." There is a slim possibility that this was Elizabeth Currer, but she would have been in her nineties by 1743 and had not acted since 1690—more than "almost out of date."

Carrignani. See CARMIGNANI.

Carrington. See CHERINGTON.

Cartell, Mrs. See CASTELLE, MRS.

Carter, [Mr?] [fl. c. 1661–1662], performer.

A manuscript cast in a Folger Library copy of the 1637 edition of Heywood's The Royall King, which was performed by the King's Company at their Vere Street playhouse about 1661–62, includes one Carter. No role is assigned Carter, and it is impossible to tell whether this person was a man or a woman.

Carter, Mr [fl. 1746], actor.

A Mr Carter acted Boniface in a performance of The Beaux' Stratagem on 16 October 1746 at Southwark Fair.

Carter, Mr [fl. 1760–1761], candleman.

A Mr Carter was on the Covent Garden pay list in 1760–61 for 1s. 6d. per day as a candleman.

Carter, Mr [fl. 1800], puppeteer.

A Mr Carter was a puppeteer at Bartholomew Fair in 1800.

Carter, Mrs [fl. 1719–1726], dresser.

A Mrs Carter was in charge of the

women dressers at Lincoln's Inn Fields Theatre from about 1724–25 through 1725–26 and was probably the Mrs Carter who shared a benefit there with three other women on 28 May 1719. In December 1724 she received two payments from the theatre—£2 8s. for 12 days and £3 19s. for six days—but from these amounts, no doubt, she had to pay her helpers.

Carter, Mrs ₁fl. 1728–1736₁, singer, dancer.

A Mrs Carter, "who never sung in Public before," sang English and Italian songs, accompanied by Signor Adamo Schola on the harpsichord, at the Haymarket on 3 April 1728. Probably she was the same Mrs Carter who played a role in The Royal Captives on 27 March 1729, Peg Ambler in Thomas Odell's highly successful new farce The Smugglers on 7 May 1729, and Arab in Charles Coffey's ballad pastiche The Beggar's Wedding on 29 May 1729 (and 32 other times through the summer), all at the Haymarket.

In the three seasons 1730–31 through 1732–33 a Mrs Carter regularly played the featured dancing-and-singing female role in Rich's pantomime Perseus and Andromeda. The Mrs Carter who with others sang Purcell's revived original music in a production of King Arthur on 28 September 1736 and was one of the followers in Harlequin Shipwrecked on 21 October 1736, both at Lincoln's Inn Fields, was perhaps the same person, although she may have been the "Miss Carter" who performed 1741–42.

Carter, Miss. See also WHITFIELD, MRS ROBERT.

Carter, Miss ₁fl. 1741–1742₁, actress, singer.

A Miss Carter acted Roxana in The Rival Queens on 4 August 1741 in Middleton's booth at Tottenham Court Fair. On 9 November 1741 she played Maria in George Barnwell and Elvira in The Spanish Fryar, and sang "Swains I scorn, who is Nice and Fair" at the theatre in James Street, an evening given at the desire of the Honourable Society of Mercurians. At the same theatre on 7 April 1742, Miss Carter played Selima in Zara, Kitty Pry in The Lying Valet, and sang "The Amazon."

Carter, Miss ₁fl. 1759–1765₁, singer.

A Miss Carter sang with Lowe, Mrs Mattocks, and Miss Brent in a performance of Alfred the Great for the benefit of Thomas A. Arne and his son Michael Arne at Drury Lane on 23 March 1759. On 13 November 1765 a Miss Carter, probably the same person, sang with Vernon, Champness and Mrs Vincent in a performance of Acis and Galatea given for the benefit of the widow and numerous children of a Mr Lambe, who had been killed in a fire in Wardour Street.

Carter, Andrew d. 1669, singer.

Andrew Carter, a "Priest" from Salisbury, was sworn a Gentleman of the Chapel Royal on 16 January 1665, but he was not to receive any pay for his services until a tenor or countertenor place became vacant. He succeeded to a position on 1 September 1666 after the death of Thomas Peers. Carter died at Salisbury on 18 October 1669, according to the Old Cheque Book of the Chapel Royal.

Carter, Charles Thomas c. 1735–1804, organist, composer, harpsichordist.

The musician Charles Thomas Carter was born in Dublin about 1735, the elder son of Timothy Carter, who was a member of the choir of Christ Church Cathedral. According to O'Keeffe's Recollections, Charles Thomas, or Thomas as he was usually called, was "brought up in the choir of Christ Church Cathedral and . . . any music he had never seen before, placed before him, upside down, he played it off on the harpsichord." He held the post of organist at St Werburgh's Church from 1751 to about 1769. From this point the facts of his life have often been confused with those of another Thomas Carter, an Irish singer who later lived in London, dying there in 1800, and also with those of a third Thomas Carter, a musician who lived in Dublin at the turn of the century. It has been said of the subject of this entry that after 1769 he traveled in Italy and then went to take up the post of musical director of the theatre at Calcutta, but more likely these events belong to the life of the Thomas Carter who died in 1800.

According to Grove, Carter settled at London about 1772 but he was probably the person of that name who several years earlier played Barthélemon's new concerto on the organ at Marylebone Gardens on 21 August 1770. He soon attracted the attention of the Reverend Henry Bate, who wrote *The Rival Candidates*, a comic opera, "from no motive of literary vanity, but in order to introduce to the world a young musical composer, whose taste he conceived might do honour to his profession." (Grove suggests that Bate's reference to Carter as a young man could "hardly apply to a man of forty" and questions, therefore, the date of about 1735 usually given for his birth.)

In its review of *The Rival Candidates*, which had its first performance at Drury Lane on 1 February 1775, the *Westminster Magazine* of that month found Bate's fable light and trivial indeed but judged that Carter "more than promises to be a composer of taste and genius," who in his first performance "both received and deserved the greatest encouragement and applause." On 18 March 1775 Carter was paid £42 by Garrick's treasurer, "in full," for the music to *The Rival Candidates*.

Carter's next theatrical work was the music for *The Milesian*, a comic opera by Isaac Jackman, which was first performed on 20 March 1777 at Drury Lane. The song "Stand to your guns, my hearts of oak" became a popular favorite and was sung by Bannister on 14 May 1778 and by others through the years. As late as 2 May 1794 it was sung by Bowden at Covent Garden. Carter during one period also wrote songs for Vauxhall. One of them, "Tally Ho!" was sung by Miss Wrighten at Drury Lane on 28 April 1778 as one of her Vauxhall favorites. On 18 May 1782 Carter provided entirely new music and an overture to Frederick Pilon's comic opera *The Fair American* for the author's benefit on 21 May 1782 (the piece had been initially performed when Pilon was acting at the Crow Street Theatre, Dublin, on 20 May 1771). Pilon absconded without paying Carter for the music.

In 1787 Carter took up the post of musical director of Palmer's new Royalty Theatre in Wellclose Square, where in 1787 and 1788 he wrote music for *The Birthday*, *True-Blue* (a new setting of Carey's *Nancy*), *The Constant Couple*, and *The Constant Maid*. About 1790 he was director of music for the Earl of Barrymore's private theatricals at Wargrave and also provided some music for the pantomime *Blue Beard* and a few songs for *The Surrender of Calais*. He wrote the music for Thomas Hurlstone's comic opera *Just in Time*, produced at Covent Garden on 10 May 1792.

Carter, who was accounted "an excellent performer on the harpsichord," also composed 12 "Familiar Sonatinas" and variations on "Carillons de Dunquerque," as well as six sonatas for that instrument. A collection of his Vauxhall songs was published in 1773. It included the popular "O Nanny wilt thou fly from me." Published music by Carter in the British Museum includes *When I was a little Baby*, an epilogue song given by Mrs Mattocks in *A Bold Stroke for a Husband* (1784); *In full cry*, a hunting song, sung by Incledon at Vauxhall (1792?); *Lira Lira La*, an air sung by Mrs Bland in *The Surrender of Calais* (1795?); *The Loyal Tar*, sung by

Sedgwick at the Ad Libitum Club (1796?); *When we're married*, sung first at the Wargrave Theatre and then by Mrs Bland in *The Surrender of Calais* (1792?); *A Third Collection of Favourite Songs sung at Vauxhall* (1780?); and a collection of *Songs, Duos, Trios, Catches, Glees, and Canons* (1801). An improbable story that Carter had forged a Handel manuscript, which he then sold for 20 guineas, was often told after his death.

In 1794 Carter was living at No 51, Edgeware Road, according to Doane's *Musical Directory*. On 9 June 1797 two of his songs, "My dear Molly—oh! what Folly" and "La Verginella," were sung by Delpini at Covent Garden.

Charles Thomas Carter died at London on 12 October 1804. His brother (elder, according to *The Dictionary of National Biography*, and younger, according to Grove) Sampson Carter was a chorister at St Patrick's Cathedral, Dublin, until 1766. Sampson took a doctorate in music at Dublin in 1771, settled in that city as a teacher of music, and became vicar choral of St Patrick's in 1797. Sampson Carter joined the Irish Musical Fund on 1 June 1788 and served that organization in several offices, including that of president, through 1809. The Thomas Carter who was a member of the Irish Musical Fund from 1803 through 1809 may have been related. The singer Thomas Carter (d. 1800) is entered separately.

Carter, Edmund. *See* KEAN, EDMUND.

Carter, J. *ifl. 1794i, singer.*
A Mr J. Carter was listed in 1794 in Doane's *Musical Directory* as a bass singer, then living at Canterbury, and a participant in performances at Westminster Abbey.

Carter, Richard *ifl. 1728–1743i, musician.*
Richard Carter was listed as one of the original members of the Royal Society of Musicians when it was established by a "Declaration of Trust" on 28 August 1739. Probably he was the Mr Carter who received a benefit concert at York Buildings on 12 April 1728 and who shared in benefit tickets at Goodman's Fields on 27 April 1736 and at Drury Lane on 20 April 1742. On 15 March 1743 Carter shared a benefit with the musicians Bosch, T. Collet, and Gair at Lincoln's Inn Fields. Although his name does not appear as a performer at these times, it was customary for a musician to play at his own benefit.

Carter, Thomas *1768–1800, singer.*
The life of the singer Thomas Carter (1768–1800) has been so regularly conflated with biographies of another Irish musician, Charles Thomas Carter (d. 1804) that one cannot now separate the events of their earlier lives with any confidence. The subject of this entry was probably the Thomas Carter who received his musical education in Italy, under the patronage of the Earl of Inchiquin, after having been a chorister at Cloyne Cathedral. Perhaps he was also the Thomas Carter who served as musical director of the theatre at Calcutta.

On 3 March 1786 Thomas Carter sang a vocal part in a performance of the *Messiah* at Drury Lane. When the oratorio was repeated on 10 March, Negus had taken his place. There is no further record of Carter's connection with a London theatre, although he was apparently a member of various musical societies. He died in London on 8 November 1800, at the age of 32. According to the *Gentleman's Magazine* of that month he was "a victim in early life to the fatal ravages of the liver complaint." He left a widow, whom he had married at London in 1793. She was a Miss Wells from Cookham, Berkshire.

Carterett. *See* CARTWRIGHT.

Carthright. *See* CARTWRIGHT.

Cartwright, Mr (fl. 1710), door-keeper.

Mr Cartwright, gallery doorkeeper at Drury Lane, shared a benefit with Mr Martin on 16 May 1710.

Cartwright, Mr (fl. 1740–1751?), actor.

A Mr Cartwright acted the role of Orpheus in the pantomime *Orpheus and the Death of Eurydice* in several of Yeates's fair booths in the summer of 1740: on 23 August at Bartholomew Fair, on 29 August at the Welsh Fair, and on 8 September at Southwark Fair. He was probably the Cartwright who played Sir John in *The Devil to Pay* at Goodman's Fields Theatre on 15 March 1746 and acted the title role in *The Mock Doctor* at Southwark Fair on 17 September 1746. From 31 October through 3 December 1746 Cartwright became a member of the Hallam company at Goodman's Fields Theatre where he acted Gibbet in *The Stratagem*, Vernon in *1 Henry IV*, Haly in *Tamerlane*, Tattle in *Love for Love*, Modelove in *A Bold Stroke for a Wife*, Blunt in *The London Merchant*, Old Gerald in *The Anatomist*, Ginks in *The Royal Merchant*, Basset in *The Provok'd Husband*, Subtleman in *The Twin Rivals*, Bazil in *The Stage Coach*, Pedro in *The Spanish Fryar*, Day in *The Committee*, Ramilie in *The Miser*, Brazen in *The Recruiting Officer*, Charino in *Love Makes a Man*, Rosencrantz in *Hamlet*, and Rakish in *The School Boy*. Perhaps he was the Mr Cartwright who played Richard III at the Orchard Street Theatre, Bath, in August 1751. A Mrs Cartwright, possibly his wife, played Lucy in *The Gamester* at the same theatre on 29 February 1753.

Cartwright, Mr (fl. 1785), actor.

A Mr and Mrs Cartwright performed unspecified roles in a performance of *The Fair Refugee* at the Haymarket on 10 February 1785.

Cartwright, Mrs (fl. 1671), actress.

Mrs Cartwright, possibly the wife of the Restoration actor William Cartwright, played Leonore in *Love in a Wood* at the Bridges Street Theatre in March 1671.

Cartwright, Mrs (fl. 1772), singer.

A Mrs Cartwright sang at Marylebone Gardens in the summer of 1772. On 6 August her name was on the bills for a new musical entertainment (playing "the Fourth Time") called *The Coquet*, which was performed several times afterward. She also sang in *La serva padrona*, *Il dilettante*, and *The Magnet*.

Cartwright, Mrs (fl. 1785), actress. See **CARTWRIGHT, MR** (fl. 1785).

Cartwright, Mrs d. 1792, actress.

A Mrs Cartwright performed the role of Mrs Chat in *The Committee* at Drury Lane on 24 May 1775. In the following season, she was paid £1 per week by the same theatre, but her name appeared in the bills only for Mrs Chat on 15 October 1775 and 21 April and 15 May 1776, so she doubtless performed a number of supernumerary functions. In 1775 she subscribed 10s. 6d. to the Drury Lane Theatrical Fund, against which (according to Winston's "Fundbook") she claimed in 1778. She died in December 1792, that document shows.

Cartwright, Master b. c. 1750, dancer.

A Master Cartwright, "a Child nine years old," danced a hornpipe at Covent Garden on 17 May 1759.

Cartwright, Miss (fl. 1800), player on musical glasses. See **CARTWRIGHT, JOHN.**

Cartwright, John 1756–1824, player on musical glasses.

From time to time in the 1790s John Cartwright took the Lyceum Theatre to give concerts in which he played on musical glasses. In reporting his performances there in February 1800, the *Monthly Mirror* claimed that Cartwright had "brought the science of the musical glasses to a degree of perfection, that we could hardly ever expect to have seen," and that he was enjoying well-deserved patronage.

Cartwright's daughter joined his act in March 1800, when the *Monthly Mirror* stated that "Her performance . . . sola, and in concert with her father, affords an exquisite treat for the amateur of the purest 'concord of sweet sounds' we have ever witnessed." In 1806 Cartwright performed at the New Royal Circus.

By October 1821 he was to be found at Boston, Massachusetts, where his musical exhibitions usually closed "with a display of philosophical fireworks." The *Boston Commercial Gazette* of 15 October 1821 stated that he had been performing in England for "twenty or thirty years past." On 1 December 1824 the *Columbian Centinal* of Boston reported that John Cartwright, "celebrated performer on musical glasses," had recently died at New York at the age of 68. Perhaps he was the John Cartwright who had married Elizabeth Meadows of St George, Hanover Square, on 8 March 1791 at St Marylebone.

Cartwright, William *c. 1606–1686,* actor.

William Cartwright was born about 1606, the son of the Elizabethan actor of the same name, under whom, doubtless, he was trained for the theatre. The younger Cartwright married Elizabeth Cooke on 1 May 1633 at St Giles in the Fields and, after her death, married Andria Robins on 28 April 1636 at the same church. Since Cartwright in later years spoke of his first and last wives, scholars have supposed he married a third time. Andria Cartwright was buried at St Giles on 12 May 1652, and a William Cartwright married Jane Hodgson of St James, Clerkenwell, on 19 November 1654. But identifying the actor in

parish registers is most difficult, for the name was remarkably common. The St Giles registers appear to contain two or more William Cartwrights during the second quarter of the seventeenth century; our William's father was probably the William Cartwright "Player" in the St Giles, Cripplegate, registers, but that parish also contained a second man of that name; there were at least two William Cartwrights in the parish of St Martin-in-the-Fields and one or more in St Andrew Holborn (the parish in which the actor worked for a while).

Of Cartwright's early acting career equally little can be said with certainty. On 10 March 1635 he and his father were performing at Norwich, and since some of the players there were members of the King's Revels in London, perhaps the Cartwrights belonged to that troupe. We know that the younger William acted at the theatre in Salisbury Court at some time before the Commonwealth period.

There is a slight possibility that at some point Cartwright went to France, perhaps in 1646 when a troupe of English players is known to have performed there. In London he engaged in some surreptitious acting during the Commonwealth, one occasion being in 1648 at the Cockpit in Drury Lane. The efforts of the actors were frustrated when soldiers raided the theatre, took away the players' habits, and marched them off to Hatton House. But for a livelihood during the Commonwealth, Cartwright set up as a bookseller at the end of Turnstile Alley. The files at the Holborn Public Library show that between 1640 and 1658 he lived at Great Turnstile. Presumably he printed in 1658 the *Actor's Vindication*, a variant reprint of Heywood's *Apology for Actors*.

When theatrical activity began again before the Restoration, Cartwright became a member of the company playing at the old Red Bull Theatre, possibly as early as May 1659. By October 1660 he was with the

Harvard Theatre Collection

WILLIAM CARTWRIGHT

engraving by Clamp, after S. Harding's copy
of Greenhill's portrait

group acting at the Cockpit in Drury Lane,
and on 5 November he was a member of
the newly formed King's Company under
Thomas Killigrew at the Red Bull. Of
Cartwright's roles during these months very
little is known, but at some point he acted
Van Dunck in *The Beggar's Bush* at the
Red Bull. The King's troupe settled into
their converted tennis court playhouse in
Vere Street, and there on 5 December 1660
Pepys saw a performance of *The Merry
Wives of Windsor* in which Cartwright
may have played Falstaff. The diarist liked
Justice Shallow and Dr Caius, but he found
the acting of "the rest but very poorly, and
Sir J. Falstaffe as bad as any." A few other
assignments are recorded for Cartwright
during the period 1660–63 at Vere Street:
possibly the Duke of Missena in Flecknoe's
Erminia (he was one of two actors the
author intended for the part), Sir Epicure

Mammon in *The Alchemist*, Lygones in *A
King and No King*, an unnamed part in
The Royall King, and Whitebroth in *The
Cheats*.

In addition to serving as one of the important actors in the King's Company, Cartwright was a sharer. When plans for the
new Bridges Street Theatre were drawn
up on 21 December 1661, Cartwright and
others signed an indenture for the plot of
ground, and on 28 January 1662 he purchased two building shares and agreed to
act at the new house when it was finished.
He also bought one acting share in the
company proper, the annual income from
which may have run as high as £280. As a
member of a troupe under royal patronage,
Cartwright received liveries each year, and
his name was frequently included in official
company transactions. On 10 June 1663 he
was involved in another profitable enterprise: he and five other actors rented to a
widow for £24 a year one of three houses
they had built in the parish of St Martin-in-
the-Fields. The other houses may have been
rented in due course. Cartwright's total income is not known, nor is it certain that he
kept his bookshop after he resumed acting,
but he died a very wealthy man.

At the new Bridges Street Theatre, where
the King's Company played from 1663 to
1672, Cartwright acted Baglione in *Love's
Sacrifice*, perhaps Lord Nonsuch in *The
Wild Gallant*, Corbaccio in *Volpone*, the
Priest in *The Indian Emperor*, probably
Bonhomme in *Damoiselles à la Mode*,
Morose in *The Silent Woman*, Grimani in
Flora's Vagaries, Falstaff in *1 Henry IV*,
Lord Latimer in *The Black Prince*, Antonio
in *The Sisters*, the Governor in *The Island
Princess*, a role in *Catiline*, Brabantio in
Othello, Apollonius in *Tyrannick Love*,
Arsenius in *The Roman Empress*, a Ple-
beian in *Julius Caesar*, Abenamar in *The
Conquest of Granada*, Don Bertran in
Generous Enemies, and Thunder and the
Second King of Brentford in *The Re-
hearsal*. His Falstaff drew high praise from

Pepys who, on 2 November 1667, "was pleased in nothing more than in Cartwright's speaking of Falstaffe's speech about 'What is Honour?'"

After their playhouse in Bridges Street burned, the King's Company acted temporarily at Lincoln's Inn Fields. There Cartwright played Hermogenes in *Marriage à la Mode*, Mario in *The Assignation*, and Harman in *Amboyna* (he seems to have been one of Dryden's favorites).

On 17 December 1673 Cartwright and his fellow actors agreed to perform at the new Drury Lane, and when new articles of agreement were drawn up on 20 March 1674, he was listed as still holding a share in the troupe. Money was needed to pay for scenery, costumes, and a new scene house, and Cartwright invested £160. Within two years Cartwright and others in the company were finding little profit in the enterprise, and they threatened to withdraw when Thomas Killigrew failed to abide by the articles signed in 1674. Thomas called in his son Charles to help pacify the players, and the younger Killigrew somehow persuaded Cartwright and the others to enter into new articles on 1 May 1676. These articles cancelled the 1674 agreement by which each sharer received £1 13s. 4d. each acting day until his £160 investment was paid back; instead of that each sharer would be paid 5s. each acting day for life and £100 would go to his executors upon his death.

Thomas and Charles Killigrew wrangled over the managership, Thomas being unwilling to relinquish control completely, and on 9 September 1676 the Lord Chamberlain settled matters by placing Hart, Mohun, Kynaston, and Cartwright in control of the group. Shortly after that the power was given to Hart alone, though Cartwright and the others remained actively involved in company affairs.

While at Drury Lane, Cartwright acted Seneca in *Nero,* Sir Jasper Fidget in *The Country Wife,* Hircano in *Love in the Dark,* Chylax in *Lucina's Rape,* Agrippa in *Gloriana,* Oldfox in *The Plain Dealer,* John in *The Destruction of Jerusalem,* and Spitzaferro in *Scaramouch.*

On 28 September 1677 Charles Killigrew gathered the building sharers together and they made an agreement with the younger members of the King's Company to form a new troupe. Cartwright still held two building shares, but he was not one of the actors under consideration. The new company never materialized, and the King's players struggled on, plagued by debts and internal strife. By 1680–81 Cartwright rarely acted. On 1 June 1681 he testified that he had "been sick and kept his house for almost the whole six months last past, and hath not been amongst the . . . Players . . . above four or five times, as he believes, in all that time." When the amalgamation of the King's and Duke's companies became imminent, Cartwright agreed to the leasing of Drury Lane to Charles Davenant and the rival Duke's players.

Cartwright still held one acting and two building shares in the new United Company when it began operations in late 1682, and his health improved sufficiently to allow him to act again. He played Cacofogo in *Rule a Wife and Have a Wife* on 15 November 1682 at Court and probably Baldwin in *The Bloody Brother* on 20 January 1685 at either Drury Lane or Dorset Garden. But he was nearly eighty, and he hardly needed to act for a living, so after the 1684–85 season he retired.

Cartwright owned, in addition to his shares, part of a house in Playhouse Yard, "a howse Backside and howse of Office with its appurtenances in Clerkenwell Close within the parish of St Johns," ready money amounting to perhaps as much as £490, a number of debts owed him which were secured by bonds, and a great many books, paintings, and valuable household goods. Having had some contact with the actor Edward Alleyn in early Stuart times, Cartwright decided to leave his estate to Dulwich College, which Alleyn had founded. In early December he made the following agreement:

That he will pay into the hands of the most Reverend ffather in God the Lord Arch B͞p͞p of Canterbury or such other person or persons as his Grace shall appoint the Sum̃e of ffoure hundred pounds to purchase Land of Inheritance of twenty pounds per Annum for himselfe for life the remainder for the benefit of Dullwich Colledge founded by M͞r Allen That he will give two guilt silver Tankards one Indian silke Quilt one large damask Table Cloth with other convenient lynnen for the Com̃union Table and the beautifying of the Chappell, and also a large Turky worke Carpett for the dyning Roome and severall pictures of Storyes and Landskips for the beautifying the Dyning Roome and Gallery and also such of his bookes convenient for a library as the Master Warden and Schoolmaster shall approve of for the service of them and the Schollars He is contented to be buryed in the place entring into the Chappell which the Master and Warden have told him of and desires That if it shall please God to enable him to goe sometimes to the said Colledge, he may at such time have a roome in the Colledge for himselfe and a place for his Man paying the Colledge for their Dyett If he finds occasion he may doe more. That the Master and Warden for their care and kindness [shall] have the profitt of the Lands purchased with the said ffoure hundred pounds or the Interest thereof for the first year after his decease to be equally divided That the fower fellows of the said Colledge for their respect and kindnes shall have the profitt of the Lands purchased with the said ffoure hundred pounds or the Interest thereof for the second year after his decease to be equally divided.

What Cartwright did not know was that his servant Francis Johnson and Mrs Johnson were dissatisfied with a promised £16 annuity when the actor died and unhappy with their work under him while he lived. They were contriving to make off with as much of the estate as they could, one of Johnson's tricks being to fail to deliver the above agreement as directed. The aging actor's plans were likewise foiled by the negligence of his solicitor and scrivener, the result being that about 9 December 1686 Cartwright was thrown "into such a passion as overcame his Spiritts" and fell into a coma from which he never recovered. He died on 17 December at the age of 80.

The actor's gift to Dulwich College was the subject of much litigation after his death, chiefly due to the Johnsons' having "absconded themselves" with a fair portion of Cartwright's valuables. As late as 1712, parts of the estates were still trickling into College hands. Of an original inventory of 239 pictures which Cartwright owned, 46 were missing when the College counted what it had received. Also missing were a number of other items and 390 broad pieces of gold. Of the paintings that have survived, two are of Cartwright's wives: one he listed as "My first wife's picture like a shepherdess" and the other as "My last wife's picture with a black veil on her head." Also in Cartwright's own inventory were two pictures of himself: one by Greenhill showing the actor "in a black dress with a great doge" and a second of "Young Mr Cartwright Actour." *The Dictionary of National Biography* reported the second picture lost, but Miss Eleanor Boswell states that the catalogue description and a painting at Dulwich of a young man in a Vandyke collar match and that the painting is of the person shown in the Greenhill work.

Many of Cartwright's books and manuscripts failed to reach Dulwich. Among the known missing items were two Shakespeare plays dated 1647, three of Ben Jonson's works "yᵉ 1ˢᵗ vollum" and one Jonson work "2ᵈ vollum." In time even some of the books the College did receive were sold or traded. It was said that a few of the actor's books formed the nucleus of David Garrick's collection in the eighteenth century, though there seems to be evidence of only one such item ending up in Garrick's hands.

Very little was reported of Cartwright as an actor. Aubrey called him "an Excellent Player" and the prompter John Downes listed him as one of the "good" actors of the King's Company.

S. Harding did a portrtait of Cartwright, after the Greenhill picture at Dulwich College, which was engraved by R. Clamp and published by E. and S. Clamp in 1794; the engraving was also published as a plate to Waldron's *Shakespeare Miscellany*, 1802. An oil painting of Cartwright by John Riley was owned in 1949 by Major General Lord Sackville.

Caruso, Mr ₁fl. 1748–1756₁, *musician*.

A favorite song sung by Reginelli in the first act of *Dido* at the King's Theatre on 26 April 1748 was accompanied by "Caruso on the Saltero, which was never performed in any Concert before." The only other notice of Mr Caruso occurred when he played a solo on the violoncello at Drury Lane, after the regular season, on 12 August 1756.

Carver, Miss. *See* KARVER, MISS.

Carver, Robert *d. 1791, scene painter, landscape artist.*

Robert Carver was born in Dublin, the son of Richard Carver (d. 1754), an historical and landscape painter, known for painting an altarpiece at Waterford. After receiving early training from his father and under Robert West in the George Lane School, young Carver exhibited watercolors at Dublin with some repute. For a while he painted scenery for the theatre at Cork, and in the winter of 1754 succeeded Lewis as a scene painter at Smock Alley, Dublin, under the management of Sowden and Victor. For a ball at Smock Alley on 21 February 1760, he designed and executed paintings "after the manner of the Opera

House in London on Masquerade Nights." In the same month he worked on new scenes for *Creusa*, which was played on 5 March 1760 at the Crow Street Theatre under the management of his friend Spranger Barry. He created an "entire new set of Scenes painted in the true Chinese Taste" for *The Orphan of China* at Crow Street in January 1761, and as "Painter to the Theatre Royal" he was given a benefit (unusual for a scene painter) on 23 April 1761.

Other productions for which Carver executed scenery at Crow Street over the next seven years included: an "Astonishing Effect of the Representation of the Waterfall at Powerscourt" for *A Trip to the Dargle* on 15 December 1762; *Diocletion* (a tapestry scene and enchanted chair), *King Arthur*, *The Indian Emperor*, and *Mercury Harlequin in Ireland* (1763); *Caractacus* and *The Humours of Dublin* (1764); *Love in a Village*, *The Maid of the Mill*, and *The Enchanted Lady* (1766), and a revival of *King Arthur* in March 1766 in which "the sudden Changes of the beautiful Variety of Scenery, seemed to surprise and alarm the Audience, as the Effect of real Magic . . . and not the Invention of theatrical Art." In November 1768 he provided a new prospect of a waterfall for a revival of *A Trip to the Dargle*. An old scene of his painting remained at the Crow Street Theatre for many years; according to O'Keeffe, "the carpenters preserved [it] as a relic; so that, while they could wield a hatchet or handsaw, no painter dared to touch it with his brush." Carver and Thomas Sheridan also converted a barn at Longfield into a theatre for a production of Brooke's *Jack the Giant-Queller*.

Carver's work at Dublin attracted the attention of Garrick, who, it was said, upon the recommendation of Spranger Barry commissioned him to paint a scene for Drury Lane. No doubt this was the well-known "Dublin Drop," which Edward

Dayes stated was Carver's first work at Drury Lane and which he described as

a representation of a storm on a coast, with a fine piece of water dashing against some rocks, and forming a sheet of foam truly terrific; this with the barren appearance of the surrounding country, and an old leafless tree or two, were the materials that composed a picture which would have done honour to the first artist, and will be remembered as the finest painting that ever decorated a theatre.

The date and the production for which the "Dublin Drop" was painted are not known, but Carver did exhibit two landscape paintings at the Free Society of Artists in 1765, when he was said to be "Of Dublin." He then seems to have returned to Dublin for several more years of work at Crow Street. Between 1765 and 1768 he also exhibited at the Society of Artists in that city.

By 1768–69 Carver was back at London, for on 14 July 1768 the author Isaac Bickerstaffe wrote to Garrick of his doubts that Carver would have "any opportunity of displaying his Art in the Scenes" of *The Hypocrite*, a piece which Bickerstaffe was writing for Drury Lane. In December 1770, Carver designed, with French, the scenes for Garrick's *King Arthur*. In the next season, his name was on the Drury Lane salary list at £6 per week. On 11 November 1771 a payment of £3 11s. 4d. was made to him and Messink, the machinist, for "Windsor Bill," this sum reimbursing the expenses for a journey to Windsor in preparation for *The Institution of the Garter* at Drury Lane on 28 October 1771, with new machines, dresses, decorations, and scenes, which the prompter Hopkins thought were "exceedingly fine." Carver did two scenes of Vesuvius for a revival of *The Witches* on 26 December of that year, one depicting the volcano burning at a distance and reflected in the Bay of Naples, the other showing lava overflowing rocks and said to be an exact

representation of an eruption in 1769. The same scenes were used again for *Harlequin's Invasion* on 19 March 1772. In 1772–73 Carver continued at Drury Lane at £6 per week, £188 for the season. He contributed scenes with De Loutherbourg, French, and Royer for a revival of *Alfred* on 9 October 1773.

According to Dayes, Carver was dismissed from Drury Lane after 1773–74 as the result of an intrigue against him. With his good friend Barry, he transferred to Covent Garden Theatre in 1774–75 (he lived in Bow Street at this time), where he was to work until his death in 1791, creating scenes for the various spectacle pieces in collaboration with the other established scene painters, Dahl and Richards, and with his own pupil Hodgins. Payments to him recorded in the Covent Garden account books are irregular, making it difficult to estimate his weekly salary. On 20 July 1776 he received £80 17s; on 18 February 1777 he was paid £105 19s. for 159 nights, about 13s. 4d. per night (but Saxe Wyndham claimed his wages were a guinea a night). In 1779–80 Carver's salary seems to have been £245, and by 1782–83 it was £260.

Productions at Covent Garden with scenes by Carver included: *The Druids*, a new pastoral masque and pantomime (19 November 1774), *The Sirens* (26 February 1776), *The Norwood Gypsies*, which contained a perspective view of Norwood, a farm yard at sunrise, and a cascade (25 November 1777), *The Medley* (14 October 1778), *The Touchstone* (4 January 1779), *The Liverpool Prize* (22 February 1779), *Calypso* (20 March 1779), *The Dockyard*, a new dance (22 September 1779), *The Mirror* (30 November 1779 and revised as *Harlequin Everywhere* on 27 December 1779), *The Siege of Gibraltar*—"The entering of Admiral Rodney's fleet into the Bay of Gibraltar," reported the *London Magazine*, June 1780, was "as beautiful a spectacle as has been seen on the stage for some time"—(25 April 1780), *Harlequin Free-Mason* (29 December 1780), *The Choice of Harlequin* (26 December 1781), *The Castle of Andalusia* (2 November 1782), *Friar Bacon* (23 December 1783), *Harlequin Rambler* (29 January 1784), *All the World's a Stage* (20 September 1784), *The Magic Cavern* (27 December 1784), *Omai*, under the design and supervision of De Loutherbourg (20 December 1785), *The Enchanted Castle* (26 December 1786), *The Dumb Cake* (26 December 1787), *Aladdin* (26 December 1788), and *The Picture of Paris, Taken in the Year 1790* (20 December 1790). A surviving promptbook of *As You Like It* has a scenic notation for "Carver Gar[den]" and one of *The Tempest* for "Carvers Rock & Bank" and "Carvers Rocks." Carver also was scenic artist to the Brighton theatre in the season of 1777.

The last payment to Carver from Covent Garden was on 14 November 1791. He died a few weeks later, on or about 25 November, at his house at No 13, Bow Street, which he rented from the theatre at £60 a year, and was buried at St Paul, Covent Garden, on 4 December 1791. In his will, hastily drawn up on 3 May 1790 without witnesses and apparently without legal assistance, Carver left his unspecified estate to his wife Anne Carver, whose maiden name was Jolly. On 19 December 1791, Michael Hayman, of St Clement Danes, and Henry Hodgins, scene painter, of St Paul, Covent Garden, attested to Carver's handwriting, and administration was granted to the widow on the following day. Carver's only known issue, a son, had died as a child on Lazar's Hill, Dublin, in March 1766.

Carver also enjoyed success as a landscape painter and exhibited many landscapes and watercolors in London between 1765 and 1790. He was elected to the Free Society of Artists in 1771, was made a Director in 1773, and was elected Vice-President in 1776 and President in 1777. His pictures were exhibited regularly at the Society of Artists during the 1770s and at the Royal Academy in 1789 and 1790. His excellence in creating atmospheric effects contributed to the romantic movement in painting and scene design which was emerging at the time. He was known to have "a generous and convivial temperament, [was] a free liver, and [was] fond of society," attributes no doubt contributing to the gout from which he suffered during his mature years. His two Irish pupils, Henry Hodgins and Whitmore, also became scene painters at Drury Lane.

Cary. *See also* **CAREY.**

Cary, Mrs. *See* **LOGAN, MISS J. H.**

Casaia, Miss ⌊*fl. 1766–1767*⌋, *dancer.* Miss Casaia danced with Miss Ferci in a *Variety Show* presented by Signor Placido and his company of tumblers, rope walkers, singers, and dancers at the Haymarket from 27 October 1766 through 14 January 1767. She concluded the program each night with a hornpipe.

Casali, Luigi ⌊*fl. 1791*⌋, *dancer.* Luigi Casali made his first London appearance at the King's Theatre, dancing with Mlle Aimé on 2 June 1791. He performed Tomas in the ballet *La Fête du Seigneur* on 28 June and danced in *Les Folies d'Espagne* on 2 July and a divertissement on 9 July. No subsequent appearances are known.

Casanova, Gaetano Giuseppe Giacomo ⌊*fl. c. 1719–1727*⌋, *actor. See* **CASANOVA, SIGNORA GAETANO GIUSEPPE GIACOMO.**

Casanova, Signora Gaetano Giuseppe Giacomo, Zanetta, née Farusi ⌊*fl. c. 1719–1727*⌋, *actress.* Gaetano Giuseppe Giacomo Casanova and his wife Zanetta, the parents of the famous adventurer Casanova de Seingalt and the battle painter Francesco Casanova, performed in England in 1727. Gaetano had been an actor for some time, having fallen in love with an actress named Fragoletta about 1719. They lived together for five years, and Gaetano served as a dancer and then as an actor in her troupe. The pair parted and Gaetano met and married Zanetta Farusi, the beautiful daughter of a Venetian shoemaker, Jeronimo Farusi, during the summer of 1724. Zanetta's family was against the marriage, for they held actors to be an abomination. But Zanetta took up her husband's profession, and the couple acted in London in 1727. No roles are known for Gaetano, but on 25 April at the King's Theatre in the Haymarket, Zanetta was Silvio in a dance that appears to have been a blending of the faithful shepherd story with a harlequinade. Gaetano may have been in the cast, but the actors were identified only by their character type names: Pantaloon, Harlequin, and Brighella.

On 2 April 1725 the Casanovas brought their first son into the world, Giacomo Girolamo, better known later as Casanova de Seingalt. Francesco the future painter was born in 1727 in London during his parents' engagement at the King's Theatre. A third son, Giovanni Battista, also became a painter.

Casarini, Signora ₁fl. 1746–1748₁, *singer.*

Signora Casarini, an Italian soprano, was a principal singer in the King's Opera company for two seasons 1746–47, 1747–48. In her first season she sang roles in *Annibale in Capua* and *Mitridate* and probably in *Fetonte, Rossane,* and *Bellerofonte,* the five operas which were performed regularly. In 1747–48 she sang Berenice in *Lucio Vero* at the King's and Nerina in three performances of *La ingratitudine punita,* given at the Haymarket on 12 and 26 January and 2 February by some rebellious

singers discontented with the management at the King's. But she was back at the King's Theatre for her benefit on 16 February when she sang some new songs in *Enrico,* which she repeated on 5 March. She also sang in the Covent Garden oratorios that spring: Achsah in *Joshua* on 9 March, Cleopatra in *Alexander Balus* on 23 March, and probably in *Judas Maccabaeus* on 1 April. Signora Casarini's last recorded appearance was singing Handelian selections in a concert at the King's Theatre on 5 April 1748 for the benefit of the Musicians' Fund.

Case, Master ₁fl. 1737–1739₁, *dancer.*

Master Case was one of the "Lilliputian" dancing scholars of Monsieur Leviez who performed as country lads in the pantomime *The Burgomaster Trick'd* at Drury Lane on 19 November 1737, 11 other times that season, and on 4 and 5 December 1739.

Caselli, Signora ₁fl. 1743–1744₁, *singer.*

According to a letter from Lady Hertford to Lord Beauchamp, Signora Caselli sang a role in *Rossane* at the King's Theatre on 15 November 1743, but Deutsch does not list her in a role. *Rossane* was repeated 14 times that season. Signora Caselli was given in the bills, however, as Fernando in *Alfonso* on 3 January 1744 (and seven other times), as Montano in *Roselinda* on 31 January (and eight other times), as Eurito in *Aristodemo* on 3 April (and five other times), and as Mitrane in *Alceste* on 24 April (and 12 other times including her last performance in London on 16 June 1744). She also sang in a musical entertainment at the King's on 28 March 1744.

Casemere. *See* CASIMERE.

Casentini, Anna. *See* BORGHI, SIGNORA LUIGI.

Casey, Mr [fl. 1748], actor.

A Mr Casey acted the character of Squire Allnight in performances of a droll, *The Consequences of Industry and Idleness*, in Yates's great theatrical booth facing the Hospital Gate, on 24, 25, 26, and 27 August 1748, at the time of Bartholomew Fair.

Casey, Mrs [fl. 1783–1785], dresser.

A Mrs Casey was a women's dresser at the King's Theatre from 1783 through 1785, and possibly longer.

Casey, John d. c. 1792, actor.

John Casey acted at Dublin before joining the Norwich company in July 1766. After a season at Norwich, he was engaged at Covent Garden at 5s. per day, making his first appearance there as Wellbred in *Every Man in his Humour* on 24 November 1767. That season, his only one at Covent Garden, Casey also acted the minor roles of Tressell and Ratcliffe in *Richard III*, Harcourt in *The Country Wife*, Sicinius in *Coriolanus*, and Melidor in *Zara*. For his benefit on 31 May 1768, which he shared with Redman, Dumai, and Bates, he took £14 4s. The day prior to this benefit Casey had played an unspecified role in *The Devil Upon Two Sticks* at the Haymarket, where he remained as a member of Foote's 1768 summer company, also acting there Sir Charles Freeman in *The Stratagem*, Loveit in *Miss in her Teens*, Alonzo in *Rule a Wife and Have a Wife* Simon in *The Commissary*, Ben in *The Beggar's Opera*, Harcourt in *The Country Wife*, Alphonso in *The Spanish Fryar*, Arcas in *Damon and Phillida*, a part in *The Oratory*, and Smith in *The Rehearsal*.

Casey never played again at a London Theatre. He acted at Leeds in 1772, at York in July 1772, and at Liverpool in 1773–74. Soon after (it was said by Tate Wilkinson) Casey entered the linen trade, and he died at Chester about 1792.

Casey, Polly [fl. 1741], singer.

Miss Polly Casey sang at Lee and Woodward's great theatrical booth, opposite the Hospital Gate, on 22 August 1741, at the time of Bartholomew Fair, announced as making her first appearance on any stage. No subsequent appearances are known.

Cash. See COYSH.

Cashell, Oliver d. 1747, actor.

According to the testimony of William Chetwood, Oliver Cashell was born in Ireland "of a very antient reputable Family" and received a good education. Little is known of his earlier years as an actor in his native country except that apparently he made slow progress in the profession and that he played Duart in *Love Makes a Man* at the inaugural performance of the new Smock Alley Theatre, Dublin, on 11 December 1735. He continued at that theatre for several years; John Kemble's manuscript notes on the Dublin theatre (in the Harvard Theatre Collection) indicate that he was still at Smock Alley in the spring of 1738.

In the summer of 1739 Cashell played at Bristol with Charles Macklin, his friend, who soon recommended him to the management of Drury Lane. There on 24 September 1739, he made his London debut as Carew in *Sir Walter Raleigh*, a role in which "his good Figure was his best Friend," according to Chetwood, "for Fear had made his Voice not his own." His second role was Cromwell in *Henry VIII* on 20 October, and the rest of the season he was seen in a number of minor supporting roles (probably familiar to him in the provinces) which included Freeman in *A Match in Newgate*, Haly in *Tamerlane*, Freeman in *The Plain Dealer*, the son in *A Hospital for Fools*, Vernon in *1 Henry IV*, Poins in *2 Henry IV*, the second spirit in *Comus*, Messala in *Julius Caesar*, Curio in *The Pilgrim*, Phoenix in *The Distrest Mother*, Heli in *The Mourning*

Bride, and Heartfree in *The Provok'd Wife,* in the last of which performances he shared a benefit with Yates and Green, on 20 May 1740. His most important role that season was Brutus in *Julius Caesar* on 13 March.

During 1740–41, his second season at Drury Lane, Cashell continued in many of the above roles and added to his repertory: Scale in *The Recruiting Officer,* Mat in *The Beggar's Opera,* Bully in *The Provok'd Wife,* Aegeon in *Oedipus,* Horatio in *Hamlet,* Malcolm in *Macbeth,* Decius in *Julius Caesar,* Antonio in *Twelfth Night,* the Moor in *The Merchant of Venice,* Sir William Morley in *The Blind Beggar of Bethnal Green,* and (for his benefit on 13 May 1741) Alcibiades in *Timon of Athens.*

In 1741–42, Cashell went over to Covent Garden, where the increased importance of his roles reflected the "much encouragement" which the manager John Rich reputedly provided him. After his first appearance there on 23 September 1741 as Bertran in *The Spanish Fryar,* that season he acted Don Juan in *Rule a Wife,* Page in *The Merry Wives of Windsor,* Buckingham in *Richard III,* Oliver in *As You Like It,* Smith in *The Rehearsal,* Cinthio in *The Emperor of the Moon,* Dorilant in *The Country Wife,* Zama in *Tamerlane,* Diocles in *The Winter's Tale,* Hemskirk in *The Royal Merchant,* Montano in *Othello,* Garcia in *The Mourning Bride,* Clerimont in *The Double Gallant,* Roverwell in *The Fair Quaker of Deal,* Scandal in *Love for Love,* and Mowbray in *2 Henry IV,* as well as Horatio in *Hamlet* and Curio in *The Pilgrim.* For his benefit on 5 May 1741, which he shared with Marten, Cashell offered Macbeth, his first truly major role.

During his next five years at Covent Garden, Cashell continued in a similar repertory of serviceable roles, occasionally coming on in a major one. On 25 November 1742 he acted Angelo in *Measure for Measure,* and on 27 April 1742, when he lodged at the Dial in Little Wild Street,

near Lincoln's Inn Fields, he acted Jaffeir in *Venice Preserv'd.* He played Pierre in the latter piece on 14 October 1746. Perhaps his greatest success was as Macheath in *The Beggar's Opera,* in which he first appeared on 7 November 1743; his singing and acting in the role, it seems, gave the piece, according to Chetwood, "a large fresh Run in Covent Garden." He gave a command performance in the part before the Prince and Princess of Wales on 9 June 1746. For his benefit on 26 April 1745, when tickets could be had of him at Mr Elwood's, staymaker, in Hunt's Court, St Martin's Lane, Cashell played Hamlet, and for his benefit on 3 April 1746, Othello. In 1745–46, when Garrick played at the end of the season at Covent Garden, Cashell acted the Bastard, Cassio, Aimwell, and Banquo to the great man's Lear (11 June), Othello (20 June), Archer (23 June), and Macbeth (27 June).

Cashell's other roles at Covent Garden included (with season of first performance): (1742–43) Eliot in *Venice Preserv'd,* Seyward in *Macbeth,* Sempronius in *Cato,* Omar in *Tamerlane,* Casca in *Julius Caesar,* Cornwall in *King Lear,* Daran in *The Siege of Damascus,* Vernish in *The Plain Dealer;* (1743–44) Camillo in *The Assignation,* Laertes in *Hamlet,* Norfolk in *Henry VIII,* Truman in *The Squire of Alsatia,* the younger brother in *Comus,* Kisler Aga in *Abramule,* Muley Moluch in *Don Sebastian,* the French King in *Henry V;* (1744–45) Manuel in *The Revenge,* Clermont in *The Miser,* Lysippus in *The Maid's Tragedy,* Raleigh in *The Unhappy Favourite,* Duart in *Love Makes a Man,* Melum in *Papal Tyranny,* the High Priest in *Mariamne,* Sir Friendly Moral in *The Lady's Last Stake,* Dauphin in *The Silent Woman,* Antonio in *The Merchant of Venice,* Manly in *The Provok'd Husband;* (1745–46) Aboan in *Oroonoko,* Colonel Woodvil in *The Nonjuror,* the Admiral of France in *The Massacre at Paris,* Bajazet in *Tamerlane,* the King in both parts of *Henry IV,*

Belguard in *Sir Courtly Nice*, King John in *Papal Tyranny*, Pedro in *Much Ado About Nothing*, the King of France in *All's Well that Ends Well*, the title role in *Cymbeline*, Miramont in *Liberty Asserted*; (1746–47) the Ghost in *Hamlet*, Blunt in *The Committee*, Townley in *The London Cuckolds*, Fainall in *The Way of the World*, and Richmore in *The Twin Rivals*.

He also acted at the Jacob's Wells Theatre, Bristol, in the summers of 1742, 1743, and 1744. In the summer of 1746 he was at Twickenham and Richmond, and when he also came to play at Covent Garden in June he was paid £2 6d. for expenses.

Holding high Tory principles which he did not trouble to conceal, Cashell, according to Davies, was given to throwing out rash notions on government and politics. During the Jacobite Rebellion of 1745, a jealous actor laid secret information against Cashell which resulted in his being taken up by a general warrant. He was released after examination. He went directly to the Bedford Coffee House. There he by chance met the informer, who fled in terror as Cashell, unsuspecting, was about to relate the occurrence. Soon after (Davies's account continues) when the King was advised to show himself at a command performance at Covent Garden, Rich had doubts about the propriety of allowing Cashell to go on as Macbeth, but after inquiries to the King, who assured the manager that he had no objections, Cashell appeared. In 1745–46 Cashell did act Macbeth on 15 November, 21 December, and 14 and 22 January, but the bills do not indicate that any of these were command performances.

Cashell's last benefit at Covent Garden was on 22 April 1747, when he played Myrtle in *The Conscious Lovers* for the first time and took a profit of £76 3s. That season his salary was £2 per week. His last complete performance was as Moral in *The Lady's Last Stake* on 20 May 1747.

A few months later, while acting Frankly in *The Suspicious Husband* at Norwich on 26 August 1747, he was fatally stricken. According to a notation in the Burney papers, he dropped dead immediately on the stage; Chetwood, writing two years after the event, stated that Cashell was carried to his lodgings, where he died a few hours later; another manuscript notation in the British Museum claims that he was struck speechless on the stage and died the next day.

A Mrs Jane Cashell of St Martin-in-the-Fields married a Mr John Brown of St Giles in Norwich at St George's Chapel, Mayfair, on 23 February 1748, about six months after the death of Oliver Cashell.

Cashing. *See* CUSHING.

Casimere, Mons ₁*fl.* 1785–1787₁, *tumbler, ropedancer.*

Monsieur Casimere was a tumbler and ropedancer at Astley's Amphitheatre, Westminster Bridge, from April to October 1785. He was also featured as a trampolinist at Hughes's Royal Circus in April 1787; at this time his son, "Casimere Junior," performed with him on the trampoline, and his wife, Madame Casimere, was a featured dancer. Casimere and his son also performed acrobatics at Bristol in 1785–86.

Casimere, Mme ₁*fl.* 1787₁, *dancer.* *See* CASIMERE, MONS.

Casimere fils ₁*fl.* 1785–1787₁, *tumbler.* *See* CASIMERE, MONS.

Cason, Mr ₁*fl.* 1726?–1761₁, *dresser.*

A person named Cason served as a dresser and wardrobe keeper at Covent Garden from at least 1735–36 through 1760–61. In September 1735 the theatre reimbursed him a total of £7 12s. 9d. for money laid out. On 28 July 1742, the management of the theatre at Richmond, Surrey, paid six shillings to "Caston, Mr Rich's Wardrobe keeper in London." In 1760–61, Cason's salary was two shillings per day. He perhaps was the Mr Caston who was on the free ticket list at Lincoln's Inn Fields Theatre between 1726 and 1729.

Cassani, Giuseppe [fl. 1708–1712], singer.

Giuseppe Cassani came to England at the beginning of 1708. The earliest mention of him occurred in a letter of the musician Haym dated 12 January of that year. Haym noted that "Cassanino" was to be paid all that manager Christopher Rich of Drury Lane had agreed upon. This consisted, we learn from Vice Chamberlain Coke's papers at Harvard University, of £300 salary, £87 10s. for transportation from Italy, and £50 for eight months' lodging and board—including a bottle of wine daily. In addition, Rich gave Cassani an unspecified gift.

Cassani was a *castrato*, and on 7 February 1708, hailed as lately arrived from Italy, he sang the role of Metius in *Camilla* at the Queen's Theatre in the Haymarket. The singer did not satisfy the audience, and Addison on 24 February 1708 noted that the new eunuch had been hissed so severely that he probably would not stay in the company. Cassani sang again, however, but Vanbrugh wrote a letter on 14 May 1708 to Coke saying,

what to do About Cassani I don't well know, thoᵍ something shall: Not that I really think he has a Claim to almost any thing; for take the two Audiences together and they were a great deal short of what has been rec'd on Common Occasions, and there was an Expence of near £30. for his Cloaths: with a Cruell Clamour & Disgust of the Towne against the House for Imposing such a Singer: wᶜʰ gave the Opera a very mischevious shock. I therefore think Charity is his Chief Plea, wᶜʰ is of full as much force to the Lords who seem'd to Patronise him, as to me who am so vast a sufferer by this Years

Adventure. I shall be out of Towne but about ten days; what I am able to do, (either by my self or others for him at my return) I will; and Mʳ Swiny will in the Interim, lend him something to keep him from Distress.

Cassani probably did not stay in England after that failure, though he was at least considered for the role of Demetrio in *Pirro e Demetrio*. But it opened in December 1708 without Cassani in the cast.

The singer was, nevertheless, brought back to the Queen's in early 1710 and sang Gemir in *Almahide* on 10 January and Artaserse in *L'Idaspe fedele* on 23 March. He stayed the next two seasons, to sing Temiso in *Etearco* on 10 January 1711, the Magician in *Rinaldo* on 24 February, Ptolomy in *Antioco* on 12 December 1711, and Siffrido in *Ambleto* on 27 February 1712.

Cassanino. *See* CASSANI.

Cassarini. *See* CASARINI.

Cassimir. *See* CASIMERE.

Casson, Margaret b. c. 1775, harpsichordist.

Margaret Casson, a child six years of age, played the harpsichord at the Pantheon on three days beginning 19 April 1781, the performances being announced as "positively the last time during her stay in London."

"In the Seventh Year of her Age," she composed the song *Attend ye nymphs*, which was published at London. Other songs composed and published by her which are in the British Museum's collection include *The Cuckoo*, with an accompaniment for pianoforte or pedal harp, and *Noon*, a rondo. A pastoral, *Absence*— "Sung at Mr Casson's Concert"—was published at Liverpool about 1785.

Cast. *See* CLOUGH and COYSH.

Castalio. *See* **COSTOLLO.**

Castel. *See* **CASTLE** and **CASTLES.**

Castell, Thomas *d. 1730, doorkeeper.*
The *Daily Journal* on 2 November 1730 reported the death of the Drury Lane stage doorkeeper Thomas Castell on 31 October. Castell, the obituary said, had served the theatre in that capacity for 30 years.

Castelle, Mrs ₁*fl. 1787–1804*₁, *singer.*
Mrs Castelle (sometimes Castelli) made her Irish debut on 26 November 1787 at Smock Alley, Dublin, announced as from the theatre at Norwich. She was engaged at Covent Garden for 1793–94 at £1 per week and in her first season sang in the chorus of the dirge in *Hamlet*, played a villager in *Nina*, and filled vocal parts in *The Woodman* and *The Travellers in Switzerland*. In the following summer she played at the Royalty Theatre. The *Thespian Magazine* (June 1794) found her "a very pleasing actress" who sang the parts allotted to her "with great spirit." Despite this praise, she continued only as a chorus member at Drury Lane at least through 1803–4, singing in works as diverse as *Macbeth*, *Lock and Key*, *The Lad of the Hills*, *Romeo and Juliet*, and *Bantry Bay*. Her salary was raised in 1795–96 to £1 5s. per week and in 1796–97 to £1 10s. per week. In the summers of 1800 and 1801 she sang minor roles at the Haymarket. She had also played at Birmingham in the summer of 1796. The Mr Castello who was a house servant at Covent Garden between 1793 and 1803 may have been her husband.

Castelli, Mr ₁*fl. 1783–1784*₁, *dog trainer.*
Mr Castelli's troupe of performing dogs acted a play called *The Deserter* at Sadler's Wells in 1783. They were in Dublin the next year, and on 16 November 1784 at Smock Alley Castelli was given a benefit. The dogs, in addition to their pantomimic work, danced minuets and cotillions. Castelli's name is given as "Costello" in Wroth's *The London Pleasure Gardens*, but the spelling in W. J. Lawrence's scrapbooks at the National Library of Ireland has been followed here.

There was a Mrs Castelli acting in Ireland from 1787 through 1791, billed as from Norwich, but it is not clear whether or not she was related to the dog trainer.

Castelli, Anna ₁*fl. 1754–1755*₁, *singer.*
Anna Castelli was one of the Italians, including Francesco Baratti and Gaetano Quilici, who were engaged in a burletta company which performed several times at Covent Garden in 1754–55. On 18 November 1754 she made her first appearance singing the part of Mlle Lindora in the first performance in England of Galuppi's *L'Arcadia in Brenta*. It was repeated on 22 November. The company also sang Ciampi's *Bertoldo in corte* five times between 9 December and 3 January. As the company met "with very little attraction or applause," the promoter of the engagement disappeared, leaving the singers with debts and without income. They received a benefit at the Haymarket on 22 January 1755 when they performed *La serva padrona*. Additional benefit performances of that opera were held on 29 January and 7 February.

Castello. *See also* **COSTELLO.**

Castello, Mr ₁*fl. 1793–1803*₁, *doorkeeper.*
A Mr Castello was a doorkeeper at Covent Garden at least between 1793–94 and 1802–3, at a constant salary of 15s. per week. He may have been the husband of the singer Mrs Castelle who was at Covent Garden during this period.

Castelman. *See* CASTLEMAN.

Castephens or Castevens. *See* STE-
VENS, WILLIAM.

Castiglione, Mr [*fl.* 1734–1736], dancer.

Mr Castiglione was a member of the
dancing chorus at Drury Lane in 1734–35.
His name appeared on the bills for dancing with Mademoiselle Roland and Poitier
on 28 October 1734, as a sea god in
Cephalus and Procris on 1 November (repeated a number of times) and in a dance
program on 18 January (repeated throughout the season). On 28 March 1735, for
his own benefit taken at the Haymarket,
he danced seven selections: *Les Warriors,
Les Transfigurations, The Prisoner,* a "Comical Pantomime Dance," *Pierot and
Peraitte,* a "Wooden Shoe Dance," and a
"Pantomime after the Venetian Manner."
On 23 May 1735 he danced at Goodman's
Fields, although when he later performed
a pastoral dance there with Mrs Bullock
on 6 October 1735, he was announced as in
his first appearance on that stage.
Castiglione also performed a *Grand Dance
of Warriors,* a new comic dance called
"The Pastoral," and a "Grand Masquerade
Dance" at the Haymarket on 20 February
1736.

Castiglione, Master [*fl.* 1771], dancer.

Master Castiglione danced in Foote's
summer company at the Haymarket in
1771. On 14 June and 3 July he performed a hornpipe, on 17 June a comic
dance, and on 5 July a piece called *The
Piero.*

Castini. *See* BORGHI, SIGNORA LUIGI.

Castle, Mrs [*fl.* 1734], actress.

Mrs Castle played Mirtilla in *The Provok'd Husband* at the Lincoln's Inn Fields
Theatre on 20 August 1734 and Jenny

Melton in *The Cobler's Opera* two days
later at the Haymarket Theatre. The "Mr
Castles" who worked at Drury Lane about
that time may have been related to her.

Castle, Richard *d.* 1779, actor.

An actor of minor comedy roles in the
London theatres for some 17 years between
1757 and 1774, Richard Castle had begun
his career in the provinces, playing at
Bath from 1750 to 1755. He had played
also at Richmond and Twickenham in the
summer of 1750. On 18 November 1757
Castle made his London debut at Covent
Garden as Jack Meggot in *The Suspicious
Husband,* but when the play was repeated
the role was acted by Cushing. Castle had,
no doubt, returned to the provinces. He
acted at the Jacob's Wells Theatre in
Bristol in the summer of 1758.

Castle did not appear again in a London theatre until he acted John in the
first performance of *The Jealous Wife* at
Drury Lane on 12 February 1761. This
successful piece was repeated 16 times
before the end of the season, during which
Castle also played Sir Brilliant in the first
performance of Reed's *The Register Officer*
on 25 April 1761, Pedro in *The Spanish
Fryar* on 11 May and Guildenstern (with
Garrick as Hamlet) on 3 June. He re-
turned to Drury Lane for 1761–62, taking
on a number of minor roles including a
part in *The Rehearsal,* Canker in *The
Minor,* the Servant in *The Old Maid,* an
Officer in *Cymbeline,* the Steward in *King
Lear,* Talthybius in the first performance of
Hecuba on 11 December 1761, a role in
The Genii, Cleomines in *Florizel and
Perdita,* the Steward in *The School for
Lovers,* an Officer in *Tancred and Sigis-
munda,* a role in *The Reprisal,* Rosen-
crantz in *Hamlet,* Mask in *The Musical
Lady,* and Mortimer in *1 Henry IV.*

Castle continued in these and many
similar roles at Drury Lane for another 11
years, serving regularly as a utility performer without any special distinction.

When he played Count Basset in *The Provok'd Husband* on 3 March 1764 he was hissed, but in his performance as the Apothecary in *Romeo and Juliet* on 3 October 1766 (when he was being paid 4*s.* 2*d.* per day, or £1 5*s.* per week) he was acclaimed by a critic in the *Public Advertiser* as "the best figure I ever saw." That writer thought that he "spoke more sensibly than I ever heard an apothecary speak in my life." Castle had rescued the character from ridicule and had "worked by pity what buffoonery used to run off with—applause."

In summers Castle also played regularly with Foote's company at the Haymarket, where he first appeared on 20 June 1763 in an unspecified role (probably Lint) in *The Mayor of Garratt*. On 6 July he acted a role in *The Diversions of the Morning* and on 11 August the Physician in *The Rehearsal*. At the Haymarket through 1774 he played regularly, as Quildrive in *The Citizen*, Baron and Sir William Wealthy in *The Minor*, Folly in *The Lyar*, a character in *Taste, or, Tragedy à la Mode*, a spouter in *The Apprentice*, Cook in *The Lying Valet*, the Physician in *King Lear*, Corin in *As You Like It*, Paduasoy in *The Commissary*, the Watchman in *The Provok'd Wife*, Puff in *The Castle*, and Sourgrouts in *The Maid of Bath*.

By 1771–72 Castle's usefulness at Drury Lane diminished, for in that season he played only Lint in *The Mayor of Garratt* and Crib in *Harlequin's Invasion* and in 1772–73 only Lint. Perhaps his health was failing (although he played at the Haymarket in the summers), and in 1773–74 he again acted only once, Lint on 5 October 1773. The next summer he played but a few times at the Haymarket: Lint, a committeeman in *The Committee,* and roles in *The Maid of Bath* and *The Nabob,* giving his final London performance in the last piece on 8 August 1774. Later in that year he claimed against the Drury Lane Theatrical Fund—to which he had subscribed £1

1*s.* per year beginning in 1766—and retired to Bath, where he died in late March 1779.

In addition to those characters given above, an incomplete list of Castle's regular roles at Drury Lane includes Claremont in *Philaster*, Valentine in *Twelfth Night*, Heli in *The Mourning Bride*, Flute in *The Fairy Tale*, a Servant in *The Dupe*, Ernesto in *The Orphan*, Thessalus in *The Rival Queens*, the Gravedigger in *Hamlet*, a character in *The Elopement*, a walking role in *The Jubilee*, a Servant in *'Tis Well It's no Worse*, a role in *The Devil Upon Two Sticks*, the Beggar in *The Beggar's Opera*, a Planter in *Oroonoko*, Brush in *All in the Wrong*, a Miser in *The Witches*, a Slave in *Barbarossa*, Ratcliff in *Richard III*, Dizzy in *The Male Coquette*, Mendozo in *Elvira*, Chatilion in *Zara*, Jeremy in *Love for Love*, Clincher Junior in *The Constant Couple*, and Menander in *The Mock Doctor*.

Castleman, Richard *[fl. 1711–1739]*, *treasurer.*

Richard Castleman was first mentioned in London playbills on 12 June 1711 when he was granted a benefit as the Drury Lane treasurer; on 5 May 1739, after 28 years of quiet and faithful service, he had his last benefit and retired. Between those dates there was a virtually unbroken record of annual benefits, at first in the less desirable month of June, then in mid-May, and beginning in 1724, in early May. Beyond that, little is known of Castleman's life, though bits and pieces of information suggest something of the range of his duties.

On 19 January 1714, for instance, Sir Richard Steele wrote to the actor Thomas Doggett and mentioned that the theatre patent was in the safekeeping of Castleman. On 2 June 1716 the treasurer was directed by the managers to discharge some of the members of the Drury Lane band, to acquaint one of the musicians with a new salary arrangement, and to tell the men in the acting company that henceforth they would have to purchase their own gloves for ordinary use on stage.

A note dated 24 July 1716, from a lawyer to Castleman, concerned a new manner of handling payments for Steele's share of the company profits. The managers ordered the treasurer to enter a new actress on the payroll and reduce the salary of another on 28 November 1719. On 9 February 1722 Steele asked Castleman to supply him with a catalogue of "Our Stock of plays," a request that one would suppose the prompter would have taken care of. When Steele and others on 4 September 1725 brought a suit against the Drury Lane company for fraud, Castleman was named along with the managers as a representative defendant. In 1732, when Curll was preparing a book on Robert Wilks, it was Castleman who served as intermediary between the author and the actor's family. In addition to keeping the company books and handling the payroll, then, the treasurer clearly had many other heavy responsibilities.

Only once does the evidence show Castleman in a ticklish situation, and he apparently handled it with aplomb. On 26 September 1733 the Drury Lane bill contained a note to the effect that Castleman had handed over the duties of company treasurer to Samuel Wrexham; on 3 May 1734, however, Castleman was back in his old position and had his annual benefit. We can conjecture what happened. When Theophilus Cibber failed to succeed his father as manager, he withdrew with many of the players to act at the Haymarket; the seceders returned to Drury Lane on 10 March 1734. Castleman either washed his hands of the whole business and temporarily relinquished his job until the squabble for control of Drury Lane was over, or he joined Cibber at the Haymarket and returned in March to assume his old duties.

When Castleman retired, his benefit bill of 5 May 1739 stated that tickets were available from him at his lodgings at Mr Watford's the upholder, beside the Sun Tavern in Russell Street near the theatre—an address he had had for some years. The bill concluded with: "Mr. Castleman *gives many Thanks to all his Friends. . . . This is his Last Benefit.*"

Castles, Mr [*fl.* 1734], *house servant?*
On 21 May 1734 at Drury Lane a Mr Castles (possibly an error for Castle) was among those allowed to sell tickets and keep the proceeds, a form of "benefit." His function in the theatre is not known, though he may have been a house servant. Perhaps he was related to the Mrs Castle who acted at Lincoln's Inn Fields and the Haymarket Theatre later that year.

Caston. *See* CASON.

Castrucci, Pietro 1679–1752, *violinist, composer, band leader.*
Pietro Castrucci was born in Rome in 1679, studied under Corelli, and came to England about July 1715 with Lord Burlington. His first appearance seems to have been at a concert held for his benefit on 23 July of that year at the Great Room in James Street. He quickly established himself as one of the finest violinists in London, became a member of the band at the Queen's Theatre in the Haymarket where virtually all operas were performed, and was much in demand at public concerts.

At the opera, where his (younger?) brother Prospero also worked, Pietro was probably paid a base salary plus a percentage of the nightly income, for his pay varied considerably from night to night. For playing for *Clearte* on 15 December 1716, for instance, he received £2 3s.; for *Pirro e Demetrio* on 2 February 1717 he was paid £10; for *Tito Manlio* on 13 April, £16 2s. 6d.; and for *Rinaldo* on 5 June, £14 18s. Perhaps as early as 1716 but certainly by 1718 Pietro was leader of the opera band, a post he held for about 20 years and which he managed very well. In 1727 when the composer, theorist, and instrumentalist Johann Quantz visited London he heard the band and said they made "an extremely fine effect." Handel was so intrigued with a new instrument which Castrucci invented, the *violetta marina* (a kind of violin with sympathetic strings), that he scored a pair of them into *Orlando* and *Sosarme* for the Castrucci brothers to play in February 1732.

Though his position as leader of the band of the opera was his constant station, Castrucci's roving career as a concert violinist was equally impressive. Soon after his arrival in 1715, he began making appearances. In quick succession on 14, 15, and 21 March 1716, for example, he played at Hickford's music room at benefits for himself, Isabella Aubert, and "The Baroness" Johanna Maria Lindelheim. In 1717 on 13 and 27 March and 10 April he played again at Hickford's, and for the following 15 years he appeared frequently there and at York Buildings, Stationers' Hall, Drury Lane, the Haymarket Theatre, and Lincoln's Inn Fields. He often performed works by Corelli, and he offered London some of his own compositions. Though he wrote no music of great distinction, he turned out a dozen competent solo violin pieces, three books of sonatas for the violin, and 12 violin concertos.

In concert he liked to dazzle his audiences. At Hickford's on 19 March 1725, for instance, he offered several new compositions "in which Mr Castrucci will make you hear two Trumpets on the Violin." And on 26 February 1731 at the same music room, billed (as usual) as the "first violin" of the Opera, he said he would offer a solo work of his own composition in which he would play "*twenty-four* Notes with one bow." This feat was ridiculed the next day when it was advertised that "the *last violin of Goodman's Field's playhouse*" would play "*twenty-five* notes with one bow."

Burney called Castrucci "more than half mad," and it was common knowledge that the violinist was insanely jealous of his rival, Michael Festing, who ultimately replaced him at the opera. Castrucci's friends, the story goes, would greet him with, "How do you do, Mr. Festing—ah—excuse me—Signor Castrucci?" and then watch for the almost apoplectic effect. Perhaps because of this known violence of temper, Hogarth's amusing print called "The Enraged Musician" was thought by many to represent Castrucci, but most Hogarth authorities now feel that the artist intended to ridicule Michael Festing's brother John.

By 1737 Castrucci was past his prime and ready for replacement. The vain and irascible man at first refused to give up his position at the opera, and tradition has it that Handel finally convinced him by writing a piece with equally difficult parts for Castrucci and young John Clegg. Clegg played his part to perfection, Castrucci stumbled through his, and the aging Pietro finally had to admit that his technique was in decline. On 28 August 1739, after he had stepped down from the band leadership, he became one of the original subscribers to the Royal Society of Musicians. Little was heard of him during the 1740s, except for an erroneous report that he had died suddenly in Marylebone Street in December 1746.

He was alive, if not well, however, and on 13 November 1750 he arrived in Dublin. On 21 February 1751 he gave a benefit concert at the Fishamble Street Music Hall. Castrucci died in Dublin—possibly from the effects of malaria, which had plagued him as early as August 1719. Most sources place his death on 29 February 1752, but some give 7 February and others 7 March. He was buried at St Mary's, and though he died poverty-stricken, he was accorded a grand funeral. *Faulkner's Journal* reported that his cortege would be "attended by the whole Band of Musick from the New Gardens in Great Britain St., who will perform the Dead March in Saul, composed by Mr. Handel." A "vast concourse of people" attended, with the violinist Dubourg as chief mourner. A week after his burial it was suggested that a monument be erected to Castrucci's memory, "on which would be engraved the music of Corelli's Jig [probably a favorite of Castrucci's], surmounted by a bust of Corelli." The project was never carried out, and Castrucci's perturbed spirit would never have rested if it had been.

Castrucci, Prospero *d. 1760, violinist.*

Brother of the more famous Pietro and, like him, a violinist, Prospero Castrucci may have studied under Corelli in Rome. Perhaps he came to London with Pietro in 1715. He was certainly there by the end of 1716, playing in the band at the Queen's Theatre in the Haymarket, for the bills and accounts mention a Castrucci "senior" and imply a pair of violinists of the same name. The first clear reference to Prospero in concert hall bills was on 25 February 1729 at Hickford's music room when he played for his own benefit. Like Pietro, he frequently played at Hickford's and at Stationers' Hall as well as at the theatre, though he was overshadowed by his more talented (elder?) brother and the bills often made little effort to clarify which Castrucci was performing.

The Castle Society of Music was founded in 1724—a mixture of professionals and amateurs—and Prospero Castrucci led the band for the group for some years. With his brother he became proficient on the *violetta marina*, which Pietro introduced in 1732, and for the instrument Handel wrote some music in *Orlando* and *Sosarme*. On 28 August 1739 Prospero joined the Royal Society of Musicians as a founding member. Six violin sonatas were published by him in 1739, and it is known that he died in 1760, probably in London.

"Casuist." *See* **"TWANGDILO."**

Cataneo, Signor [*fl. c. 1735–1762*], *musician, teacher.*

There are two references to Signor Cataneo, 27 years apart. On 3 March 1735 select pieces on the violin were played by a youth of 13, who never performed in public before, billed as "A Scholar of Signior Catanio," at Drury Lane; the same boy, evidently, played the violin at Covent Garden several weeks later on 24 March. On 14 April 1762 the management of the King's Theatre gave part of the profits of the evening "towards relieving old Signor Cataneo, who during forty years was useful at the Operas, but is now in extreme Distress." Apparently he passed his long but obscure career as a musician in the band of the King's Theatre and as a teacher of music. Perhaps he was the Joseph Cattani who was listed as one of the original members of the Royal Society of Musicians when it was established on 28 August 1739.

Catchpole, Mr [*fl. 1799*], *puppeteer.*

A Mr Catchpole was listed in the "Pie Powder Court Book" (at the Guildhall Library) as giving puppet shows at Bartholomew Fair in 1799.

Cateley. *See* **CATLEY.**

Catenacci, Maria [*fl. 1783–1786*], *singer.*

Signora Maria Catenacci was a singer at the King's Theatre between 1783 and 1786. Her roles included: (1783–84) Celia in *Silla*, Belinda in *L'albergatrice vivace*, the Countess in *I rivali delusi*, Fedra in *Il trionfo d'Arianna*, Ulania in *L'eroe cinese*, Donna Alba in *Li due gemelle*, and principal parts in *Demofoonte* and *Issipile*; (1784–85) again the Countess in *I rivali delusi*, a part in *Demetrio*, and the title role in *Nitteti*; (1785–86) Selene in *Didone abbandonata*, a part in *Perseo*, and Tullia in *Virginia*. Her Christian name is found on a libretto of *Andromaca*, published in Venice in 1790.

Caterina, Signora [*fl. 1756*], *wire dancer.*

A Signora Caterina entertained at Sadler's Wells on 9 October 1756. Probably she was a wire dancer, as she was billed with Isabella Wilkinson, a known slack-wire performer.

Cates, Mr [*fl.* 1746], *actor.*

A Mr Cates was named in the bills for Gibbet in *The Stratagem* at Covent Garden on 23 June 1746. "Cates" may have been a misprint for "Oates." A Cates, Junior, however, had played Harlequin at Smock Alley, Dublin, on 22 October 1741.

Catesby, Mr [*fl.* 1741], *actor.*

A Mr Catesby acted the role of Truman in a performance of *The London Merchant* given by a transient company at the James Street Theatre on 9 November 1741, for the benefit of Mr Spackman and by desire of the Honourable Society of Mercurians.

"Catgutaneo, Signor." *See* **ABEL, KARL FRIEDRICH.**

"Cat-Harris". *See* **HARRIS, CAT.**

Cathata. *See* **CARATTA.**

Catherly. *See* **CAUTHERLEY.**

Catillion. *See* **CHATILLION.**

Catley, Ann, later Mrs Francis Lascelles *1745–1789, actress, singer, dancer.*

Ann Catley became, even during her lifetime, the subject of numerous memoirs which must be approached with caution because of their mixture of fact and fiction. Even the more dependable ones written shortly after her death (like Miss Ambrose's *The Life and Memoirs of Miss Ann Catley,* which is used extensively throughout this entry) sometimes err gravely.

Ann Catley was said to have been born in lodgings in an alley near Tower Hill in 1745. Her father, Robert Catley, was coachman to a Quaker named Barclay. Her

mother was a laundress, and among her clientele were the military officers on duty at the Tower. By the age of ten, sweet-voiced and a blossoming beauty, Ann sang at various public houses in the neighborhood. Soon she was entertaining the officers garrisoned at the Tower and by the age of 14 reportedly had already been the mistress of numerous soldiers. Her first seducer, however, was a linen-draper's apprentice in the Minories.

Ann suffered "inhuman severity" from her parents, who made her give a strict accounting of her earnings. The contemporary memoirs are replete with salacious accounts of her adventures at "every brothel within a mile of the Tower." Before long she had become one of London's most sought-after higher-class prostitutes.

But at the age of 15, Ann was apprenticed to the musician William Bates, who in return for a £200 bond from her father was to care for her and secure for her a professional engagement. Ann made her first appearance in public singing at Vauxhall in the summer of 1762. She then appeared at Covent Garden on 8 October 1762 as a "pastoral nymph" in *Comus.* The critic of the *Theatrical Review* (1763), identifying her as from Vauxhall Gardens, wrote that she had as yet "given not very glaring proofs of her theatrical abilities; time alone can therefore decide the true merit of this young lady." Her next appearance at Covent Garden was several weeks later, on 22 October, as Rachel in *The Jovial Crew.* On 1 November she was one of the singing witches, with Beard, Miss Davies, and Polly Young, in *Harlequin Sorcerer,* and on 15 November she sang with others the "Solemn Hymn" by Purcell which was introduced in a performance of *The Royal Convert.* Incorrectly billed as "Miss Tatley," she played one of the bridesmaids in a performance of *The Witches* at Drury Lane on 23 November, but by 24 January she played Proserpine in *The Rape of Proserpine.*

In April of 1763 when Ann went to sing at Bath for the benefit of Samuel Derrick, the master of ceremonies there, she became involved in a disagreement between Derrick and John Arthur, the manager of the Bath Theatre. Having been so well received, Ann decided to take a benefit for herself at the Bath Rooms, but Arthur refused to provide Derrick with musicians from his band because Ann had changed the hour to one conflicting with the performance at the Theatre. On 26 April, Ann was again at Covent Garden to perform Sally in *Thomas and Sally*. On that night she introduced with Mattocks a new ode by Bates entitled "A Briton the son of a Briton" and, alone, sang "Nymphs and Shepherds."

About this time Ann became the central figure in a confusing litigation, the outcome of which has been misconceived by various biographers. Her master William Bates had handed her over to Francis Blake Delaval, the profligate son of a baronet, who intended to set her up as a prostitute, a proposal to which Ann seemed unopposed. Reportedly she had persuaded Delaval to pay Bates the £200 forfeiture which her father would have been obliged to suffer when she left the musical profession. Catley, however, brought suit against Bates in the King's Bench in May 1763, and Delaval was served with a writ of habeas corpus obliging him to bring in Ann Catley. According to the account in the memoir by Miss Ambrose, judgment was found against Bates, Delaval, and his attorney, a Mr Frayne, all of whom were fined by Lord Mansfield for their unholy conspiracy. Despite Miss Ambrose's presumed verbatim transcript of the court testimony, the case, it seems, was really settled quite to the contrary and not until July 1764 (according to a clipping in the Burney papers). An undated clipping in the Harvard Theatre Collection also informs us that "On Tuesday last come on in the Court of the King's Bench, Westminster, a trial between Robert Catley, plaintiff (father of the celebrated Miss Catley) and William Bates of College-Street, Westminster, defendant (master of the said Miss Catley), for a breach of articles; when the jury brought in a verdict for the defendant."

Meanwhile Ann had been engaged by Thomas Lowe when he took over the management of Marylebone Gardens in May 1763, and with Lowe and Miss Smith she sang a "Musical Address to the Town" on the opening night. On 28 June 1763 she sang there in Handel's *Alexander's Feast*, for the benefit of Lowe and by the desire of the Society of Free Masons. The song *Now the summer advances*, as sung at Marylebone by Ann, Lowe, Miss Miles and Miss Smith, was published in that year.

By this time, Ann had become a pupil of Charles Macklin, who suggested to Mossop, then the manager at Smock Alley, that the

Harvard Theatre Collection

ANN CATLEY, as Euphrosyne

engraving by Dunkarton, after Lawrenson

controversial actress would strengthen his theater's competition against Spranger Barry at Crow Street. Ann arrived at Dublin in December 1763 and made her debut at Smock Alley as Polly in *The Beggar's Opera* on the twenty-third of the same month. Despite the fact that she was in an advanced state of pregnancy—presumably Delaval was responsible—she was an immediate success. Her performance as Polly, which "pleased beyond expression," was often repeated to crowded houses and brought her a salary, according to the *Thespian Dictionary* of 40 guineas per night, no doubt a gross exaggeration. Her great popularity moved the ladies of Dublin to have their hair "Catleyfied" in imitation of her fashion. The record of her Irish performances is fragmentary, but she is known to have acted at Cork in September 1765; on the ninth of that month she played Rosetta in *Love in a Village* and was "indeed perfection," and for her benefit on the sixteenth, at which she took £160, she displayed her "elegant, fine figure" in men's clothes as Captain Flash in *Miss in Her Teens*. Her last known engagement during this long stay in Ireland was for "a few nights" at Crow Street in February 1770.

While in Ireland Ann had a variety of amorous adventures imaginatively related by her several contemporary biographers. "She received her lovers with ease," wrote the author of the *Brief Narrative . . . of Miss C*tl*y*; "if they did not rise to her price, she dismissed them with apathy, and that price was always proportioned to the idea Nan formed of their fortune." Her vast number of lovers, it was said, led one wag to quip that to secure a majority in either house of government at Dublin "*it was only necessary for C—tl-y to instruct her own member.*" While in Ireland she gave birth to a child reputedly sired by the Duke of York, as well as the child by Delaval.

After an absence of some seven years Ann returned to London in the fall of 1770, making her appearance at Covent Garden as Rosetta in *Love in a Village* on 2 October 1770. The critic of the *Town and Country Magazine* (October 1770) reported that "she acquitted herself greatly to the satisfaction of the audience" and entered into the spirit of the part, particularly as a singer, equal to any one who had ever before attempted it. He noted, however, that she had an ungraceful stoop and that in her dialogue she effected a lisp which, combined with her hurried diction, made her lines unintelligible. Because of the great applause which she earned, a salary of 15 guineas per week was settled upon her for the season. After repeating Rosetta on 4 October, she played Leonora in *The Padlock* on 23 October, also to "great applause." On 8 November she performed Jenny in *Lionel and Clarissa*, on 22 November Isabella in *The Portrait*, and on 13 December Rachel in *The Jovial Crew*. For her benefit on 16 March 1771, she offered Rosetta, with the additional songs "The soldier tir'd of war's alarms," and "Water parted from the sea."

Ann made her last appearance of the 1770–71 season at Covent Garden on 23 March as Leonora, for the benefit of Mrs Mattocks, and then engaged for the summer at Marylebone Gardens, where on 27 June 1771 she played an unspecified part in *The Magnet*, and where she continued regularly through 12 September. She did not return to Covent Garden in the fall of 1771, evidently preferring to pass her time giving private concerts and singing at Vauxhall Gardens. She had met Colonel Francis Lascelles in Dublin in 1768 and by November 1770 had already had two children by him, according to the *Town and Country Magazine*. Before her marriage to Lascelles, which occurred about 1771, Ann had insisted upon legal assurances that her fortune should go to her children (presumably those by Delaval and York), that she should be allowed to continue to play, while her health permitted her to do so, and that the marriage should be kept secret until she retired from the stage.

On 30 September 1772, after an absence of about a year and a half, she returned to Covent Garden to sing Rosetta. That performance was followed by appearances as Polly in *The Beggar's Opera* on 13 October and Euphrosyne in *Comus* on 17 October. No doubt to the amusement of her audience, she sang as one of the chorus of "British Virgins" in *Elfrida* on 21 November. At the rival house on 26 December 1772 Mrs Wrighten gave a ludicrous imitation in *The Pigmy Revels* of Ann's manner of delivering songs, which often were embellished by indecent and vulgar attitudes. When Ann "created' the role of Juno in the new English burletta *The Golden Pippin*, by Kane O'Hara, on 6 February 1773 —a piece which originally had been censored by the licenser on 5 April 1772 but

later was allowed to pass—she was provided with ample opportunity for her indulgences. William Hawkins in *Miscellanies in Prose and Verse* (1775) observed that the author of *The Golden Pippin* had drawn a close resemblance between the character of Juno and the performer's "private and public conduct" and that Miss Catley played the role in a manner "exceedingly low and immodest." The performance brought forth "An Ode to Miss Catley," by the Rev Charles Jenner (original MS in the Huntington Library):

> *Hail vulgar Goddess of the foul mouth'd race!*
> *(If modest Bard may hail without offence)*
> *In whose majestic, blush-disdaining face*
> *The steady hand of Fate wrote Impudence;*
> *Hail to thy dauntless front, and aspect bold;*
> *Thrice hail, magnificent, immortal scold!*
> *Thee, Goddess, from the upper gallery's height*
> *With heedful look the jealous fish-wife eyes,*
> *Tho early train'd to urge the mouthing flight,*
> *She hears thy bellowing powers with surprize.*
> *Returns instructed to the realms that bore her,*
> *Adopts thy tones and carries all before her.*
> . . . .
> *Proceed then, Catley, in thy great career*
> *And nightly let our maidens hear and see*
> *The sweetest voice disgust the listning ear*
> *The fairest face assume deformity!*
> *So shalt thou arm them with their best defense,*
> *And teach them Modesty by Impudence.*

Harvard Theatre Collection

ANN CATLEY

engraving by Jones, after Roberts

In *The Golden Pippin* she introduced a song "Where's the mortal can resist me," to which she danced a hornpipe (and which, in a slightly varied form, became known as the hymn tune "Helmsley"). After singing in *Judith* on 26 February 1773 and then in an oratorio pastiche on 19 March, Ann Catley took her benefit on 27 March, when she played Mandane in *Artaxerxes* and Nell in *The Devil to Pay*. After the farce she sang "The Wanton Girl" from *Comus*. The benefit was reported to have brought her upwards of £271, according to the *Morning Post* of 1 April 1773, but the Covent Garden account books indicate that it was more like £194. Miss Catley took space in the press to thank her public, hastening to do so because she was "informed her life is shortly to be imposed" upon them (probably a reference to the "Memoirs and Anecdotes in the Life of the Celebrated Miss Catley," in *Macaroni Savoir Vivre and Theatrical Magazine*, April 1773), and assured that she would "ever make it her study to please." On 13 April 1773 she played Fanny in *The Maid of the Mill*, for the first time. Her final performance of the 1772–73 season at Covent Garden was as Leonora in *The Padlock* on 28 April. The *Morning Post* reported on 23 April 1773 that at a masquerade she had collected upwards of £32, "which she gave with her own hand to a widow who had six helpless children."

After playing at Crow Street, Dublin, in the summer of 1773, Ann returned to London on 27 September, but the *Morning Post* of 29 September reported that she was not to be engaged at Covent Garden. On 6 October that newspaper advised that since she had cleared £1900 in three months at Dublin she was refusing to engage in London on last year's terms; but then the paper reported on 14 October that she had indeed settled on the same terms. She appeared on 16 October 1773 as Euphrosyne in *Comus*, with the additional song of "Sweet Echo," and then played her usual roles of Polly, Rosetta, Leonora, and Juno. The *Town and Country Magazine* in October 1773 declared her to be no actress but allowed that as a singer she was "at

present, the sweetest warbler on the English stage." In person, the critic found her still "well-made," fair of complexion, with "lascivious and enchanting eyes." On 16 December she sang the role of Thetis in the new comic opera *Achilles in Petticoats*.

For her benefit on 7 January Ann took a profit of £203 16*s.* and then gave what was announced to be her last performance of the season, as Rosetta, on 8 January 1774, after which she went into confinement to await the birth of another child, a daughter Frances, by Lascelles. The child was christened at St Paul, Covent Garden, on 18 April 1774. Ann returned to Covent Garden, however, on 12 May 1774 to play Euphrosyne, for that night only, for the benefit of Joseph Younger the prompter, whose house and belongings had been destroyed on 3 May 1774 by a fire which had taken the lives of his house guests, the actress Mrs Laurence Kennedy and another woman. Several weeks later, on 7 June 1774, Miss Catley sang in a concert given at the Haymarket for the benefit of Mr Light, who had recently been burnt out of his music shop in King Street, Covent Garden.

At Covent Garden again in 1774–75, after opening her season as Rosetta on 28 September and as a British Virgin in *Elfrida* on 3 October, she performed (by desire) for the first time Lucy in *The Beggar's Opera* on 5 October. On 23 December she sang the favorite song of "Guardian Angels" and the duet, with Miss Brown, of "Ellen Aroon." In another new musical entertainment by O'Hara entitled *The Two Misers* she was the first interpreter of the role of Harriet, on 21 January.

After her last performances of the season as Rosetta and Euphrosyne on 25 March 1775, Ann left for Ireland. *Faulkner's Dublin Journal* announced on 20 May 1775, however, that "The report of Miss Catley dying in childbed in Athlone, Ireland, as mentioned in the papers, is void of truth, private letters from that place informing that she is in perfect health."

Ann remained in Ireland through the 1775–76 season to perform in Michael Arne's musical pieces at Crow Street. Her Dublin salary was first reported by the London press to have been an enormous £40 a night. Later, the *Morning Post* (27 January 1776) asserted the salary to be 80 guineas for a three-night week. Mrs. J. Walker wrote to Garrick from Dublin on 4 January 1776 that "I have the utmost contempt for the Theatrical taste here as that wretched being Miss Catley is the only Creature that is followed. She is the sole support of the house & the contention will now be between Foote [who was about to arrive there] and her which brings most." But Ann was soon obliged to give up playing at Dublin, because "she has for some time been in a decline & Dr Jebb has declared that her theatrical exertions would in all probability prove fatal" (*Morning Post*, 2 February 1776).

By the fall of 1776 Ann had recovered sufficiently to engage at Covent Garden at the very large salary of £27 6*s.* per acting night. She made her reappearance there on 27 September 1776 as Polly in *The Beggar's Opera*, which she repeated on 30 September and 4 October. Sylas Neville saw the latter performance and was displeased at her deteriorating physical appearance. "She sings well & gives many of the songs uncommon expression," he wrote in his *Diary*, "but she is vulgar to a degree even beyond what might be expected from the character & has all the appearance of an impudent battered woman of the Town." On 7 and 8 October she played Euphrosyne, on 9 October Rosetta, and on 15 October Juno, a role she repeated throughout the season, including the night of her early benefit on 23 October (when tickets could be had of her at No 12, Cockspur Street) at which she took £297 13*s.*, free of house charges. In November she left London to play to crowded houses at Edinburgh for about a month, and before departing from that city she performed a special benefit for

the Charity Workhouse, which brought her a letter of gratitude from the treasurer of that institution. By 3 January 1777 she was back at Covent Garden to play Lucy in *The Beggar's Opera*. She received a second free benefit, a privilege very unusual for the times, on 10 March 1777, and she took another £302 3*s.* Tickets could be had of her at Wilson's, the watchmaker, at No 150, Drury Lane.

Miss Catley was then absent from Covent Garden for three years. She evidently was at Dublin for part of 1777 ("On Friday last Miss Catley arrived in town from Ireland," clipping in Harvard Theatre Collection, hand-dated 30 December 1777). She returned to Covent Garden in mid-season, 1779–80, to play Juno in *The Golden Pippin* ("with a new *Scotch Air*") on 5 February 1780, after what the *Morning Post* of 7 February described as a "long indisposition" which had impaired her features and figure: "the powers of her voice remain as perfect and enchanting as ever nor has she forgotten the exercise of those little stage wantonesses which made her an object of admiration." Engaged at a salary of £17 5*s.* per night for the remainder of the season, she repeated Juno a number of times and played Euphrosyne in *Comus* regularly. She also acted her role of Rosetta in *Love in a Village* on 11 April 1780, but on 11 May she played the older role of Deborah in that piece (with a song in character), and as the complete old maiden aunt she was able to "look the part so well." For her benefit on 29 March, when she was living at No 115, Jermyn Street, St James's, she received £290 4*s.* 6*d.*, once again free of house charges. A salary sheet, receipted with her signature, now in the Harvard Theatre Collection, indicates a total of £420 for the half-season. In 1780–81 she played at £25 per week, and in addition to her usual roles she acted Clara in *The Duenna* for the first time on 20 September 1780. She was still living at No 115, Jermyn Street, on 26 February 1781,

Harvard Theatre Collection

ANN CATLEY as Rosetta, with JOHN PALMER as Young Meadows

artist unknown

when she took her benefit, playing Queen Dollalolla in *Tom Thumb*, and bringing in £303 7s.

The managers considered her terms too exorbitant to meet for the next season and by 6 October 1781 she had not yet been articled. They agreed, however, to £21 per week, so on 16 October she appeared as Captain Macheath in *The Beggar's Opera*, the first time she had taken that male lead in London although she had performed the part at Smock Alley some years before, in 1764–65. She played infrequently, however, offering Nell in *The Devil to Pay* on 14 February. Her clear benefit receipts amounted to £282 14s., with tickets now available at her house, No 27, Percy Street, Rathbone Place. Her performance of Nell again on 28 May 1782 proved to be her last (and not in 1784 as given by some biographers).

At the age of 37 the celebrated Ann was too ill to continue her professional life. The press reported on 8 November 1782 that though a little recovered in appearance she was "yet so infirm in the lungs, as to make it impossible for her to sing on the stage." With her husband (now a major general) and her children, Ann lived out the rest of her life in a large house at Ealing, near Brentwood, which she had bought out of the handsome fortune her voice and other talents had brought her. One contemporary biographer claimed that she became "a beneficent friend" of the poor in the neighborhood. By 16 September 1789 her health was in so deplorable a state that her death was expected hourly. She died at Ealing on 14 October 1789, at the age of 44, of a consumption which was "probably accelerated by her early indulgencies in dissipation, and great exertion of voice which injured her lungs." She was buried at Ealing Church.

Her will, which was abstracted by Miss Ambrose in *The Life and Memoirs of the Late Miss Ann Catley* (1789) and to which she signed her name as "Ann Cateley," showed her to have died worth at least £5000. Probably her assets were considerably greater. She divided her estate equally among her eight children: William Francis Lascelles (the one who was a cornet of dragoons?), Rowley Lascelles, Frances Lascelles (to whom she also left her wearing apparel and trinkets), Charlotte Lascelles, Jane Lascelles, George Robert Lascelles, Elizabeth Lascelles, and Edward Robert Lascelles. Another child, Hugh, who was christened at St Paul, Covent Garden, on 6 July 1772, had died in infancy and had been buried there on 6 September of the same year.

On 3 June 1800, "A Young Lady" made her first appearance at Covent Garden in the role of Lady Eleanor in *Every One Has His Fault*. She was identified as Miss Lascelles in the *Morning Post* the next morning. She was, according to Thomas Dutton in *The Dramatic Censor* (1800), related "to a well-known family," but we do not know that she was one of Ann Catley's daughters. By a codicil to her will Ann gave £50 to each of her nephews, Robert and William Fox, and £10 for a mourning ring to her husband, whom she appointed executor. She made no mention in the will of her mother and father, who, according to the *Biographical and Imperial Magazine* (October 1789), were still alive and who kept a public house at Norwood "where they were constantly visited by their only daughter." But according to Miss Ambrose's *Life and Memoirs*, Ann had not been an only child; she had a sister named Mary, called Polly, to whom "she did not behave affectionately" and who is said to have become a strolling player in Ireland.

Ann Catley had been, in the words of one journalist, "the favourite of Thalia, the favourite of the Town, and the favourite of Fortune." She was by most reports an exquisite singer and an adequate actress. Her "lively spirits" on stage brought many charges of indecency, especially in *Juno*, a performance which became legendary enough in her own time for George Saville Carey to include the song "Juno in her Cups" in his *Lecture on Mimicry*. Not beautiful, but pleasingly attractive, she had small features, a high forehead, dark hair, dark freckled skin, and a petite thin frame. Evidently she was a good mother and a chaste wife, and generous, too, despite her reputation for avariciousness and the undoubted promiscuity of her earlier years. One obituary in the monthly press evoked in her behalf the extraordinary dictum that the "Morality of Players, like that of Princes, is exempt from the precision of vulgar rules."

Among the songs published as sung by Ann Catley were *Cease Gay Seducers* (1770?), *Down the Bourne and thro' the Mead* (1770?), and *Love's Subtle Poison* (1775) (all three from *Love in a Village*), *Guardian Angels now protect me* (1780?

from *The Golden Pippin*), and *E'er love did first my thoughts employ* (1775), by J. Hook.

Ann Catley was the subject of many portraits:

1. She was identified as the subject of a painting by Sir Joshua Reynolds which was shown in an exhibition of "A Series of Historical Portraits" at the South Kensington Museum (now the Victoria and Albert) in 1867. The painting was shown in a photograph as No 587 in the catalogue of the exhibition, where it was said to be owned by John Rhodes. Subsequently it became the property of Sir Ernest Cassel, Bart, and then of the Countess Mountbatten, in whose hands it still was in 1952. Art experts in London, however, are dubious about the attribution of the painter and the identification of subject.

2. Engraving by J. Jones, after J. Roberts, published by W. Humphrey, 1777.

3. Anonymous engraving of her at the age of 30, published as frontispiece to her *Life and Memoirs* by Miss Ambrose, 1789.

4. Crude portrait engravings published by the *Town and Country Magazine* in November 1770, in 1782, and in December 1788.

5. As Euphrosyne in *Comus*. By W. Lawrenson, engraved by Dunkarton in 1777, by W. Evans in 1807, and by W. Read (n. d.).

6. As Euphrosyne. Engraved by Thornthwaite, after J. Roberts, *Bell's British Theatre*, 1777.

7. As Euphrosyne. Plate in the *Hibernian Magazine*, 1775, by an anonymous engraver.

8. As Euphrosyne. By an anonymous engraver, published by Wenman, 1777.

9. As Euphrosyne, with three other characters. Engraved by W. Walker, after Dighton, for the *New British Theatre*, 1777.

10. As Leonora in *The Padlock*. Engraved by T. Bonnor.

11. As Leonora. By an anonymous engraver.

12. As Rachel in *The Jovial Crew*. Engraved by Thornthwaite, after Roberts, for *Bell's British Theatre*, 1781.

13. As Rachel. By Terry, published by Harrison, 1780.

14. As Rosetta in *Love in a Village*, with Palmer. Anonymous engraver. Plate to the *Lady's Magazine*, 1770.

15. As Kitty (in *The Lying Valet*?). By an anonymous engraver, published by Harrison, 1781.

16. As Polly in *The Beggar's Opera*. Colored drawing by J. Roberts, in the British Museum.

17. A satirical print entitled "The Whimsical Duet or Miss C-tl-Y teaching Her Fat Dane Bitch to Rival Miss Y—G," published in the *Oxford Magazine*, April 1773, depicts Ann seated on a high-backed sofa and a man in regimentals, presumably Delaval, beside her. A Dalmatian dog stands on its hind legs, and a coachman with whip in hand stands behind the dog. The accompanying text reads, "the celebrated Miss C-t-ly on her return home from Drury Lane Theatre, ordered her servant to bring up the fat kitchen bitch and set her on her hind legs; as she was positive she could learn her to sing as well as a certain lady."

Caton, Mr ₁*fl. 1796–1804*₁, *boxkeeper.*

A Mr Caton was on the Drury Lane personnel lists as a boxkeeper from 1796–97 through 1803–4, in which latter season he was paid 9*s.* per week. A Mrs Caton, no doubt his wife, was named as a member of the Drury Lane house personnel on a manuscript list dated June 1802.

Cattani, Joseph ₁*fl. 1739*₁, *musician.*

Joseph Cattani was listed as one of the original members of the Royal Society of Musicians in the "Declaration of Trust" which established the Society on 28 August

1739. It is possible that Joseph Cattani was the Signor Cataneo, musician and teacher who practiced in London from 1735 through 1762.

Catton, Charles *1728–1798, artist, decorator, scene painter?*

The elder Charles Catton was born at Norwich in 1728, one of a family of 35 children. After serving an apprenticeship to a London coach painter and studying at St Martin's Lane Academy, he became known chiefly as a landscape and animal painter and as a decorator. Catton was one of the founding members of the Royal Academy and was coach painter to George III. In 1780 he was paid £667 for decorative wall painting at Somerset House, which he carried out with Reynolds, Cipriani, Angelica Kauffman, Biagio Rebecca, John Rigaud, and C. Beaumont. In 1784 Catton was Master of the Company of Painter-Stainers.

There is no clear evidence that Catton was a scene painter, although his son, also Charles Catton (1756–1819), painted scenes for Covent Garden. On 21 October 1767 the elder Catton was indeed paid £18 by that theatre but probably for decorations to the house or perhaps for stage properties. He may have been the Catton who together with Richards, Carver, Hodgkins, and Cipriani was paid £36 for painting scenery for *The Choice of Harlequin*, which opened at Covent Garden on 26 December 1781, but probably this person was the son. On 6 May 1782, a "Catton painter" was paid £36 by Covent Garden whereas most subsequent payments to any painter of that name were specified for "Mr Catton Junr. Painter." The substantial sum of £320 2*s.* paid by the theatre on 30 June 1783 to "Mr Catton House Painter" was probably to the father.

Catton died at his house in Judd Place, the New Road, on 28 January 1798 and was buried in Bloomsbury Cemetery near Brunswick Square. Information on his career as an artist and decorator is to be found in *The Dictionary of National Biography* and Redgrave's *Dictionary of Artists*. Catton is included in a large group of members of the Royal Academy in 1772 on a canvas painted by Zoffany which now hangs in Windsor Castle. The picture was engraved by R. Earlom and published in 1773 by R. Sayer. He also appears in a similar group painting of "Royal Academicians assembled in their Council Chamber . . . in 1793," by H. Singleton, which belongs to the Royal Academy. The painting was engraved and published by C. Bestland, with a key-plate, in 1802.

Catton, Charles   *1756–1819, artist, scene painter.*

The younger Charles Catton was born in London on 30 December 1756, the son of the painter and decorator, Charles Catton (1728–1798). Trained in painting by his father and at the Royal Academy schools, he then traveled extensively throughout England and Scotland doing sketches, some of which were later engraved and published. Probably he assisted his father in decorative painting, and he also earned a reputation as a topographical draftsman. In 1775 he exhibited two paintings at the Royal Academy: a "View of London from Blackfriars Bridge" and one of "Westminster from Westminster Bridge." Between 1776 and 1800 he exhibited 37 works. With E. F. Burney he exhibited designs for Gay's "Fables" in 1793, which later were published. In 1788 his own engravings of a number of animal drawings were published.

Between 1781 and 1794 Catton was engaged as a scene painter at Covent Garden. His first job there was probably the scenery, painted with others, for *The Choice of Harlequin*, on 26 December 1781, although the Catton mentioned in the bills may have been his father. On 6 May 1782, a "Catton painter" was paid £36; and it is uncertain whether this and some of the subsequent payments in the Covent Garden accounts refer to the son or the father. For *Lord Mayor's Day*, an afterpiece first performed on 18 January 1783, one Catton assisted Smirk and Hodgins in executing designs by Richards. On 6 June 1783, "Mr Catton Junr. Painter" was paid £45. On 4 June 1784 he was paid £4 10*s*. Before the opening of the season 1785–86, the younger Catton helped Richards in the renovation and decoration of the house, which included enlargement of the boxes, embellishment of the pillars, the painting of the faces of the boxes and galleries "warm lilac," and wainscotting the backs of the boxes, which were painted crimson. The cheque for £30 which he received on 28 November 1785 was probably payment for his share in this work.

Catton assisted De Loutherbourg with scenery for the successful afterpiece *Omai*, which was first performed on 20 December 1785. On 8 January 1787, "on account of last season," Catton received £40 10*s*., and on 20 February 1787, another £200. An entry for 8 April 1788, "Paid on Acct of Mr Catton into Court £125," suggests either that Catton had been taken into court for debt or that he had sued for recovery of salary. His name did not again appear in the bills or in the accounts until he and many others painted scenery for Kemble's *Macbeth*, the first dramatic offering in the newly opened Drury Theatre on 24 April 1794.

In 1800, Catton was living at Purley. He emigrated to America in 1804 and lived for some years on a farm on the Hudson, with two daughters and a son, painting only on occasion and dying there on 24 April 1819. It was said that he had "acquired wealth" by his painting.

A scene painted by "Mr Catton" was imported from London in 1795 by the Federal Street Theatre at Boston. No theatrical work executed by Catton when he lived in America is known.

Catzoni. *See* CUZZONI.

Cauley. *See* CAWLEY.

Caulfield, John [*fl. 1794–1819*], *singer.*

In Doane's *Musical Directory* of 1794, John Caulfield was listed as a bass singer at Drury Lane Theatre and as living at No 8, Dartmouth Street, Westminster. Also living at the same address was his brother Thomas Caulfield (1766–1815), a Drury Lane actor, whose entry should be consulted for information about the family.

For some 25 years John Caulfield served as a chorus singer at Drury Lane. While he may have been with the chorus earlier, his name first appeared in the bills on 12 February 1795 when he sang as one of the satraps in *Alexander the Great*. His other chorus duties at Drury Lane included service in such productions as *The Cherokee, The Pirates, The Iron Chest* (1795–96); *The Prisoner, Harlequin Captive, Richard Coeur de Lion, The Honey Moon* (1796–97); and *The Captive of Spilburg* (1798–99). He also sang at the Haymarket from 1797 to 1801 in such pieces as *The Surrender of Calais, The Italian Monks,* and *Obi*. In 1802–3 his Drury Lane salary was £1 5*s.* per week, a figure which remained constant through 1818–19.

Caulfield's wife's name is found in the Drury Lane account books as a chorus singer from 1810–11 through 1818–19, also at £1 5*s.* per week. On 6 July 1813 Caulfield signed his full name to a pay receipt for 8*s.* 14*d.* on behalf of his wife. The Miss Caulfield—"a very pretty singer, and a very pretty modest Girl"—who sang at Sadler's Wells in 1801 and at the Royal Circus in 1802 was probably their daughter. A Samuel Caulfield, who received payments, probably from the Haymarket, in the early nineteenth century was doubtless a brother to John Caulfield.

Caulfield, Thomas *1766–1815, actor.*
The actor Thomas Caulfield was the son of a music engraver of Clerkenwell and the brother of James Caulfield (1764–1826), who was an author, printseller, and publisher of numerous books including *Portraits, Memoirs, and Characters of Remarkable Persons* (2 vols., 1794–95 and 3 vols., 1813). Another brother, Joseph Caulfield, of Camden Town, was also a music engraver and a "most excellent teacher of pianoforte." In manuscripts now at the Folger Library, James Winston noted that Thomas also had two brothers who sang in the chorus at Drury Lane: one was John Caulfield (fl. 1794–1819) and the other was probably the Samuel Caulfield who sang in the theatre in the early part of the nineteenth century. The Susan Caulfield who was the mistress of General John Burgoyne and had four children by him between 1782 and 1788 may have been Thomas's sister, but she was certainly not his mother; nor was Burgoyne, as some biographers have suggested, his father. Caulfield's obituary in the Boston *Columbian Centinel* of 17 May 1815 stated his age at the time of his death to have been 49, thereby placing his birth in 1766.

Thomas Caulfield was probably the Mr Caulfield who was acting in the provinces as early as 1787. In that year, at the Blackburn Theatre between 25 April and 4 July, according to the extant bills, he acted the title role in *Robinson Crusoe*, Canton in *The Clandestine Marriage*, Sir Clement Flint in *The Heiress*, Captain Clement in *Hunt the Slipper*, Sir Oliver Oldflock in *He Would be a Soldier!*, George Barnwell, Iago, the Governor in *The Critic*, Manly in *The Provok'd Husband*, Douglas in *Percy*, and at least six other roles. He acted at York in 1788, at Bath in 1789, and at Derry in 1790. Also acting in the same provincial companies was a Mrs Caulfield, presumably his wife.

Engaged at a salary of £1 per week, Caulfield made his debut as a member of the Drury Lane company, then playing at the King's Theatre while a new theatre was being built, in the role of Trophonius in *The Cave of Trophonius* on 15 October 1791. Next he acted Ismael in *The Siege of Belgrade* on 24 October. His numerous other roles in that season, a repertory which confirms his provincial experience, included: Montjoy in *Henry V*, Valentine in *Twelfth Night*, Carlos in *Don Juan*, Florestan in *Richard Coeur de Lion*, Rimenes in *Artaxerxes*, a vocal part in *Poor Old Drury!*, Don Pedro in *The Pannel*, a Gentleman in *Isabella*, Chusanes in *Huniades*, Mezzano and Spinosa in *Venice Preserv'd*, the Dauphine in *The Englishman in Paris*, Rossano in *The Fair Penitent*, Arcas in *The Grecian Daughter*, Essex in *King John*, the Duke of Burgundy in *King Lear*, Diego in *The Regent*, a Roman Officer in *Coriolanus*, the Duke of Suffolk in *Henry VIII*, William in *No Song, No Supper*, and others.

In the summer of 1792 Caulfield acted at Richmond, Surrey, and at Liverpool. With the Drury Lane Company again at the King's (and sometimes at the Haymarket) in 1792–93, at £2 5s. per week, he performed many of the above roles and also added Manuel in *Love Makes a Man*, Conrade in *Much Ado About Nothing*, the Earl of Oxford in *Richard III*, Charles in *The Haunted Tower*, the Captain in *The Pirates*, a Gentleman in *The Chances*, Selim in *The Mourning Bride*, Don Lewis in *She Wou'd and She Wou'd Not*, Seyton in *Macbeth*, Butler in *The Devil to Pay*, a Gentleman in *The Belle's Stratagem*, Monford in *The First Floor*, and Serjeant Kite in *The Recruiting Officer*. For the last-named play, done at his benefit on 1 June 1793, at the Haymarket—a performance in which he also sang "O! what a charming thing's a battle"—he shared tickets worth £115 15s. with Miss DeCamp and Miss Tidswell. His address at this time was No 8, Dartmouth Street, Westminster; his brother John Caulfield, a bass singer in the Drury Lane chorus, lived at the same address.

Thomas engaged at the Haymarket for the summer of 1793 and stayed on there for most of the following season, since the Drury Lane company had temporarily disbanded while awaiting erection of their new building, and Colman, the Haymarket manager, had rented the patent from Harris for the winter. There he acted his familiar roles and a great number of new ones including Oliver in *The Children in the Wood*, Planter in *Inkle and Yarico*, Leander in *The Mock Doctor*, Eustace in *Love in a Village*, and Gayless in *The Lying Valet*. When the new Drury Lane Theatre opened on 21 April 1794, Caulfield was there as Serjeant in the inaugural production, *Macbeth*. In the following summer of 1794 he was at Liverpool again.

Caulfield continued to be engaged at Drury Lane Theatre regularly every winter and at the Haymarket in the summer until 1805, when he departed for America. In a manuscript now at the Folger Library, James Winston noted that Caulfield had lost an eye in a skirmish during a performance of *The Babes of the Wood* at Drury Lane in 1797, but there is no verification of this incident in any other source.

His salary at Drury Lane in 1795–96 was £2 5s. per week; in 1797–99, £3; in 1799–1800, £4; and by 1802–3, £6. On 27 November 1796 he was admitted as a subscriber to the Drury Lane Actors' Fund. On 6 October 1801 Caulfield signed his full name to a letter authorizing Richard Peake, treasurer of Drury Lane, "to deduct from my salary the sum of two guineas every week [his salary at this time was £6 per week] for the purpose of paying the same to Mr Thos. Drury or his attorney Mr Davis, till the sum of sixty pounds thirteen shillings shall have been paid to Mr Drury . . . for a debt now due from me." As long as he remained a London actor, he seldom rose above the function of a daily journeyman actor who played a variety of inconsequential supporting roles mostly in burlettas, pantomimes, and musical extravaganzas.

In addition to those cited above, which he continued to play in the repertory, he acted dozens of parts. A selection of the roles most regularly associated with him would include Patowmac in *The Cherokee*, Ptolemy in *Alexander the Great*, Adolphus in *Lodoiska*, Ormandine in *Harlequin Captive*, Tybalt in *Romeo and Juliet*, Snake in *The School for Scandal*, Spahis in *Blue Beard*, Almagro in *Pizarro*, Catesby in *Richard III*, Freeman in *A Bold Stroke for a Wife*, Rosencrantz in *Hamlet*, Villers in *The Belle's Stratagem*, Muley in *The Castle Spectre*, and a Robber in *What a Blunder!* He did achieve some popularity with an entertainment of imitations which he introduced during Lent at the Haymarket on 4 March 1794. George Colman was impressed enough to feature the act in the following summer during performances of his prelude *New Hay at the Old Market*. The author of the *Authentic Memoirs of the Green Room* suggested that Caulfield's imitations "saved the Young Manager's piece from damnation" and described the mimic: "having a genteel figure, [he] is tolerable in third-rate characters. He is very seldom perfect, and we are sorry to add, he is not an improving actor." Less temperate, however, was F. G. Waldron's assertion, in *Candid and Impartial Strictures on the Performers . . .* (1795), that Caulfield was "Lately lugged out neck and heels from the shades of obscurity, and excepting his *imitations* we never saw anything about him that would make us much regret were he to return to his old dingy regions again." The imitations were also featured in *Sylvester Daggerwood*, actually another version of *New Hay at the Old Market*, in which Caulfield first played Apewell at the Haymarket on 8 July 1796. One reviewer acknowledged his excellence as a mimic but wondered if the actor did not think to ensure applause by blending the imitations "with a dash of the burlesque?" The *Monthly Mirror* (July 1796) commented that "Caulfield's imitations of Aickin, Suett, King and Dignum are exact even to astonishment—of the rest we do not think much."

Except for his skill at mimicry, Caulfield might well have remained somewhat ob-

scure had it not been for his affair with Maria Teresa Bland (1770–1838), a Drury Lane singer of substantial reputation. By 1795, although married to the actor George Bland (d. 1807), she was living with Caulfield, presumably at No 2, William Street, the Adelphi, and predictably the liaison became matter for the public press and journals. Responding to the rumor that Caulfield intended to whisk Mrs Bland off to America, John Williams (under the pseudonym of Anthony Pasquin) in *A Pin Basket to the Children of Thespis,* regretted that by this "base seduction" London would lose "one of the sweetest singers, and, as a singer, one of the best comic actresses that ever walked the boards." In America, predicted Williams, Caulfield's "boasted love will consequently be seen in its true colors." But the pair remained in London, and it

Harvard Theatre Collection

THOMAS CAULFIELD, as Mirabel
engraving by Leney, after De Wilde

was George Bland who was driven off the London stage by the gossip and who went to America. Caulfield lived with Mrs Bland for some ten years: in William Street in 1796; at No 25, King Street, Covent Garden, by August 1797; at No 8, Cockspur Street, Haymarket, by May 1799; at No 6, Southampton Place, Tottenham Court Road, by May 1800; at No 475, The Strand, corner of Lancaster Court, by May 1801 and until May 1802; at No 25, Great Russell Street by May 1803; and at No 16, Charles Street by May 1804.

Caulfield acted at Derry again in 1798. He made his debut on the Bath stage at the opening of the New Theatre Royal in Beaufort Street on 12 October 1805, as Buckingham in *Richard III*. He should not be confused with Captain Henry Caulfield (d. 1808), an officer in the Guards and amateur actor, who was at Bath in 1804–5 and also was a professional actor at Covent Garden in the first decade of the nineteenth century.

In 1806, recruited by John Bernard for his theatre at Boston, Thomas Caulfield left London and Mrs Bland. In his *Retrospections of America*, Bernard described in a romantic vein a time early in the voyage when the ship was becalmed for several days in the Bay of Biscay:

One beautiful, still, moonlight evening, when we were all on deck enjoying the scene, watching the shores of France in the distance and the white sails here and there dancing in the moonbeams, Caulfield suddenly sprang forward and began that favorite sea-song which took its title from the place where we lay – "The Bay of Biscay." I had heard Incledon and several other celebrities sing it before, but whether it was from the circumstance of the locality and the train of feelings aroused by the scene, or, as I am inclined to believe, far more from the exquisite expression Caulfield threw into the song, I was never before so affected by a piece of music. When he had finished, Mrs Stanley turned to me with a smile and observed: "If Mr Caulfield can speak on the stage as well as he sings here, you have indeed a valuable acquisition."

Caulfield, by Bernard's report, was indeed well received on the American stage. He made his debut at the Federal Street Theatre, Boston, on 31 October 1806 as Rolla in *Pizarro*, a role he had been allowed to play on occasion in London when J. P. Kemble was otherwise occupied. But according to Bernard, "finding money, wine, and amusement abundant, his head grew giddy with pleasure and success," and he soon began to neglect his professional responsibilities. Despite the fact that Bernard had directed him to prepare during the sea voyage for Lord Hastings in *Jane Shore*, when the night for the performance of that play came "he knew little or nothing of the character, and came to a distressing standstill in several passages." In a petty display of temperament, Caulfield refused to play supporting roles to Thomas A. Cooper when that actor engaged at Boston in the winter of 1807.

Proving less and less dependable, Caulfield was replaced at Boston in 1808–9 by John Mills. In the summer of 1809 he played at Providence and then was engaged with the Placide company at Charleston until 1813, and from there joined the Commonwealth Company at the old Southwark Theatre in New York in the summer of 1813. (He had previously appeared in New York on 8 June 1809 for a concert in Mechanics' Hall.) The company went to Philadelphia for a while but returned to New York on 1 November 1813 to play at the converted Circus at Broadway and White Street. In 1815 Caulfield's peregrinations brought him to Turner's company in Cincinnati. In April of the same year his indulgences brought him to death, at the age of 49 according to a report in the Boston *Columbian Centinel* of 17 May 1815. This newspaper and Ireland gave his place of death as Cincinnati, but a manuscript in the O. Smith Collection in the British Museum states: "Incledon in a letter from America dated Aug 28, 1815 said, Poor Caulfield, who for the last five years had been in the habit of taking too much refreshment, fell down in a fit on the Kentucky Stage and expired."

Nothing further is known to us about the Mrs Caulfield who acted with Thomas Caulfield in the provinces in the 1780s. Perhaps the Miss Caulfield who sang at Sadler's Wells in 1801 and at the Royal Circus in June and September 1802 was their daughter, but more likely she was a child of Thomas's brother John. For a discussion of the children Caulfield sired for Anna Maria Bland, see her biography in an earlier volume.

A painting by De Wilde of Caulfield as Mirabel in *The Inconstant* is at the Garrick Club. An engraving of the De Wilde picture, by W. Leney, was published by Cawthorne in *Bell's British Theatre*, 1795. An engraving by Reading, after Graham, of Caulfield as Arviragus in *Caractacus* was published in the same work in 1796. A portrait of him by De Wilde was engraved by W. Ridley for Parson's *Minor Theatre*, 1794.

Caun, Susanna [fl. 1729], *actress.*

Miss Susanna Caun played Molly in a performance of *The Beggar's Opera* given by children ("Lilliputians") at Lincoln's Inn Fields Theatre on 1 January 1729 and repeated 11 times that month.

Causton, Mr [fl. 1720–1746], *house servant?*

A Mr Causton shared a benefit with three others on 7 June 1720 at Lincoln's Inn Fields, and a Mr Caustin, very likely the same person, had his tickets accepted at Sparks's benefit at Drury Lane on 19 May 1746. The bills provided no indication of the man's function in the theatre, though he may have been a house servant.

Cautherby. *See* CAUTHERLEY.

Cautherley, Samuel *d. 1805, actor.*

Samuel Cautherley was persistently rumored to be the illegitimate son of David Garrick. For instance, in its brief biography of the actor Bensley, *Theatrical Biography* (1772) spoke of the "almost *paternal* influence of Mr. Garrick" over Cautherley. The very phrase was repeated by the plagiarizing 1795 edition of *The Secret History of the Green Room*. The *Thespian Dictionary* repeated in successive editions through 1805 that Cautherley "was a supposed natural son of Mr. Garrick." The 1775 edition of *Theatrical Biography* made, however, a puzzling comment in the course of implicating the actress Jane Hippisley Green and Garrick in a liaison:

The very great care and attention this skilful director took in the cultivation of her talents, might very well account for her progress; nor is it to be wondered at, when it is said that there were still stronger reasons for attentions than mere managerical regard. . . . The lady *could* not be . . . cruel; sensible of the mischiefs she had done [to Garrick's heart], she repaired them by good-nature—a chopping boy bore witness to their loves,—whose death is since to be lamented, both on a private and public account; on the former, as it was the *only* child our English Roscius ever had; on the latter, as posterity may possibly be deprived of one day *seeing the father blazoned in the son.*

No other woman seems to have been suggested as Cautherley's mother by anyone who thought him Garrick's son, and we can only suppose that the writer of the passage above had been misinformed about the death of the child—and if he was inaccurate in one circumstance, perhaps he was incorrect in all. Certainly, though, Cautherley was brought up, educated, and trained for the stage under Garrick's anxious care and direction and for a long time lived in the household of the actor-manager.

The introduction of Master Cautherley to the public was in the part of Jasper in *Miss in Her Teens* at Drury Lane on 28

April 1755 in a cast made up of children. Evidently he succeeded well enough so that his patron was persuaded to test him more thoroughly the following season. On 23 October 1755 he played the young Duke of York in *Richard III*, a traditional debut part for youngsters bent seriously on stage careers. Garrick was in the title role. By 17 November Samuel had learned the trifling business for the Page in *The Orphan* when Garrick played Chamont. The boy did not appear again in the bills until 5 May 1756 when with some of the young companions of his first appearance he played in a childrens' production of *Lethe* for the benefit of the Simsons.

Garrick did not overwork his protégé, and (in the light of subsequent statements about Samuel's ability) he may have had a difficult time inducing Samuel to learn his parts. Not to put too fine a point on the matter, Cautherley was handsome but not very bright. During the next three seasons —1756–57, 1757–58, 1758–59—he appeared only five times: on 21 September 1756 as the Duke of York; on 3 December 1756 as Lord Flimnap in *Lilliput*, a children's farce by Garrick (which the *Theatrical Examiner* called a "stupid parcel of rubbish"); on 18 January 1757 as the Page in *The Orphan*; on 13 September 1757 as the Duke of York; and on 22 December 1757 as a Page in *The Gamester*. At this point Garrick evidently decided to withdraw him from the boards entirely and put him to school.

The first reference extant to the connection between Garrick and young Sam Cautherley was in the letter of 7 March 1759 from Garrick to Dr John Hawkesworth, the journalist and playwright who was then keeping a small school for young girls at Bromley in Kent. Garrick wanted Hawkesworth to see Samuel entered in a boys' school near him:

I could not send yᵉ Boy immediately to Bromley, when will be the properest time;

is there any breaking up near? or will it be better to send him before Easter. I shall be directed by you—the boy is a Sweet Lad & of a most insinuating disposition, & his follies are those of Idleness & Indulgence—

and three days later:

I shall send the Boy tomorrow by yᵉ Bromley Stage consigned to you, & I must desire you to give him safe into yᵉ hands of his Master. He is a very pretty Lad but my great fatigues & *Strangeness of Temper* (as Dʳ Hill is pleas'd to call it) make me incapable of attending to his Education as I ought to do—he has fine Parts & good Nature but being too much fondled by yᵉ Ladies, he is a little spoil'd. I hope they will take care of his Religious Principles for he is backward in every thing.

About 20 July 1759 Garrick sent a note to Hawkesworth by the hand of Samuel, who was returning to school:

I shall desire you to speak to his Master to be a little strict with him—he is very deficient in his Reading, & repeats his Catechism very imperfectly—I shall try him at that school another Quarter & then shall determine about him. therefore be so kind to Speak to Mʳ Booth in behalf of yᵉ Lad for I fear he is Idle—is it not strange that he cannot yet read English, & yet has tolerable good Parts?

Hawkesworth kept an eye on the difficult boy. On 7 August 1759 Garrick wrote:

I have sent our house-Taylor (a great Man I assure You, & tho a Taylor a brave one) to inspect the rents and lacerations in Cautherly's Cloaths—he Writes me Word that he is in Woeful Plight, wᶜʰ surprizes Us a little, as he was Set out in good & creditable order—I intend that he shall remain only his half Year at Bromley, having fix'd upon another Course for him.

The course "fix'd upon" was a return to the theatre, where Samuel was to be found on 9 October 1760 playing Edward in *Richard III* for the first appearance at Drury Lane in 16 years by Thomas Sheridan, who played Richard. On 17 December Sam was Prince Henry in *King John*, and on 29 April 1761 Donalbain in *Macbeth*. He shared a benefit with other minor actors on 8 May 1761 but was not named again in the playbills that season. His activities were sparse, or obscure, in 1761–62 and 1762–63. He was Prince Edward again on 26 September 1761 and repeated Donalbain on 31 October, Gloster in 2 *Henry IV* on 3 November 1762, and Donalbain on 17 January 1763. The anonymous author of *The Smithfield Rosciad* (1763) included in his satirical review of the Drury Lane company a player who seems never to have been mentioned in either the playbills or the account books of the time, unless what is intended is a veiled phonetic transcription of some variant pronunciation of the last name of Samuel Cautherley.

> *Behind this motley crew, COTT——L*
> *——came,*
> *As dead to common sense as dead to*
> *   fame.*
> *A formal, stooping, stam'ring, hodge-*
> *   podge thing,*
> *Who Dab-chick like mov'd off on foot,*
> *   on wing.*

There ensued then another hiatus of two years in his acting career. Surely it was due to Garrick's conviction that Samuel needed more polish. Garrick had built up a drawing account with his Paris banker Selwyn of over 70,000 livres as early as 1759, according to G. W. Stone. Professor Stone calls our attention to a document in the Victoria and Albert collection dated 23 September 1763 which lists many payments to Cautherley and to one J. Convert—perhaps Samuel's tutor—e.g., "18 June [1763], 1st quarter a l'academe pour Mr Cautherley Livres 724, plus 240 livres to J. Convert for same: total 964." The bilingual payment

list covers the period from June 1763 to November 1764 inclusive and shows that Garrick expended 22,982 livres on Cautherley for various purposes during that time. In the Folger Library is a receipt signed by Cautherley for £5 received of Selwyn in Paris, dated 14 September 1763.

Samuel Cautherley's rise to man's estate in the London patent theatre did not come until 26 September 1765, when he was sent forward at Drury Lane thinly veiled as "A young gentleman," in the leading role of George Barnwell in the apprentice-tragedy *The London Merchant*.

Perhaps Garrick had provided for his young friend's entry to the regular company by inducing the puff in the *Universal Museum* of September 1765, which unblushingly employed the cliché "with universal applause" about Sam's reception and testified that "The moment he appeared, his interesting figure, so admirably adapted to the Character, spoke for him," that his voice, though not strong, was distinct, and that he played with "great simplicity . . . no unnatural start, no affected tricks." But on 25 November 1765 Cautherley essayed Zaphna in *Mahomet*, specially altered by Garrick for its first performance in 20 years. Tom Davies thought that Garrick had this time pushed Cautherley beyond his depth in forcing instruction in a role which had been one of Garrick's notable ones. Davies believed that Cautherley's natural attributes were too weak for tragedy. The comment seems to have been just. When Cautherley was permitted the part of Dorilas in *Meropé* on 6 January 1766, the judicious prompter Hopkins entered in his diary: "very decent, but wanted spirit." On 20 March 1766 Cautherley was for the first time the Dauphin in *King John*, a part which could not tax his powers.

By this time Samuel had begun to give his guardian uneasiness on other scores. Though laggard in school and deficient in acting talent, he was precocious with women. On 8 March 1766 David Garrick had written from Marlborough to his brother George asking him to

keep a Watch upon our house in Southampton Street—if I suspect any Mortal to be more particularly bewitch'd than any other, it is our house maid, *Molly*—She has all kind of people follow^g her, & I have great fears about her I wish you^d take her by Surprize, & if You find her bad, turn her out, directly—she is a great peeper into papers . . . —as for Cautherly *Mansquibbing* her (wch he certainly does) I don't mind—but I suspect she has all kind of fellows in our Absence & I don't know w^t may be ye consequence—

During the spring of 1766 Garrick endeavored through his minion Hopkins to induce James Love, who had secured the management of the new summer theatre at Richmond, to allow Cautherley to play a few tragedy parts during the coming summer season. Garrick finally applied sufficient persuasion—after all, Love and his wife and most of his players were employed at Drury Lane in the winters—so that Cautherley was assigned both Romeo to Sophia Baddeley's Juliet and Hamlet to her Ophelia at Richmond. The Richmond theatre was convenient to Garrick's house at Hampton where Cautherley was then staying.

The Richmond experience was a warmup for Cautherley's first performance of Hamlet at Drury Lane, on 23 September 1766, again with Mrs Baddeley as his Ophelia. He was also allowed to give Romeo on 30 September, with Mrs Barry attempting Juliet for the first time. The *Public Advertiser* reported: "In the garden scene an unlucky accident happened to Cautherly . . . his nose ran with blood and he was oblig'd to keep his handkerchief to his nose all through, which was a great loss to his audience." The reviewer in the *Public Advertiser* gave him cool approval but concentrated the compliment on his teacher: "Mr Cautherly a pupil of the

greatest master of the art of acting that ever graced the English stage (if not the European) . . . has this summer convinced us that he is susceptible of the refined instructions of his great patron and tutor."

Samuel's other new parts during 1766–67 were: Charles in *The Jealous Wife*, Belville in *The Country Girl*, Clerimont in *The Old Maid*, Felix in *The Wonder*, Lovel in *High Life Below Stairs*, and Tressel in *Richard III*. Somewhat strengthened in confidence, he returned to Richmond in the summer. A local critic saw his Lord Falbridge in *The English Merchant* and thought that he wanted the dignity and deportment necessary to support the man of quality, and that he was still stiff and affected. The critic leveled a prophetic judgment: "This young gentleman, although he has great pains taken of him, by his great master, will never be an ornament to a London theatre."

But his great master continued to take pains and buoyed him up for nine more years at Drury Lane, "trembling for his benefit," throwing good parts his way, puffing in the press, and apparently giving him every protection and consideration. During the period Cautherley added the following roles to his repertory, in order: Lovewell in *The Clandestine Marriage*, Constant in *The Provok'd Wife*, Hamet in *The Orphan of China*, Beverly in *All in the Wrong*, Sidney in *False Delicacy*, Florizel in *Florizel and Perdita*, Welldon in *The Absent Man*, unspecified characters in *The National Prejudice* and *Like Master Like Man*, Lord Hardy in *The Funeral*, Malcolm in *Macbeth*, Bassanio in *The Merchant of Venice*, Claudio in *Much Ado About Nothing*, Charles in *The Hypocrite*, Saville in *Wit's Last Stake*, the original Lord Eustace in Mrs Elizabeth Griffith's *The School for Rakes*, Captain Constant in *The Ghost*, Seyward in *The Hypocrite*, the Prince of Wales in *1* and *2 Henry IV*, Guiderius in *Cymbeline*, Lovemore in *The Way to Keep*

Him, Villars in *A Word to the Wise*, Charles Dudley in *The West Indian*, Lewson in *The Gamester*, Slender in *The Merry Wives of Windsor*, Sebastian in *Twelfth Night*, Cassio in *Othello*, Alwin in *The Countess of Salisbury*, Polydore in *The Orphan*, Plume in *The Recruiting Officer*, Monesses in *Tamerlane*, Lothario in *The Fair Penitent*, Olinthus in *Timoleon*, Don John in *The Chances* ("Don John Mr Cautherly—la! la!" wrote Hopkins the prompter), the Nephew in *The Irish Widow*, Rivers in *The Note of Hand*, Clermont in *The Heroine of the Cave*, Careless in *The Committee*, and Philotas in *The Grecian Daughter*.

But Cautherley had been increasingly restless in the secondary parts to which his meager abilities for the most part confined him; indeed, he seemed not to have perceived that he would never have risen to second rank—much less to an occasional lead—without the powerful hand of Garrick clearing his path. He was married on 4 July 1771 at Richmond to Susanna Blanchard, daughter of the cardmaker to George III, who had grown wealthy through other business interests. Francis Gentleman said she had "several thousand pounds to her fortune." It was enough to make Cautherley grow lordly with Garrick since he no longer needed his weekly £4 from Drury Lane. Correspondence ensued. Its tone and the general situation may be gathered from a letter from Garrick to Cautherley, dated from the Adelphi on 7 October 1773:

Sir, / Some peculiaritys in Your Behaviour of late, demand my Notice, which I shall communicate to you now, & from this time all Correspondence shall cease between us.— You were pleas'd to keep the part of Lelio, *Nine* days & then return it to my Brother.— As the taking Five pounds from you, for your giving up a part (which I most certainly do) is no recompense, or excuse for your Behaviour, I shall tell you my Mind, &

give a Check if I can to a most unjustifiable importance you are pleas'd to assume; which having no foundation but in your own brain, is as insufferable, as it is foolish. You say, that if I desire You to do this, or that, You will condescend—Sir, I will receive no favours from *You*, I cannot, but I will desire you to do your business or to leave it— one or the other you *must*, & *shall* do.—You talk'd to my Brother of being *Just to your self*, a foolish conceited phrase—You had better take care to be Just to other people, & to your Duty; The rank, & Importance you have assum'd I have given you, & for which I have been frequently abus'd publickly & privately.— The Character of Lelio is worthy of as good an Actor; the Character which Mrs Abington plays is much inferior to Lelio, which You have rejected—however it is dispos'd of to one, who will play it with good humour, & agreeably to the Public. I am oblig'd to You for throwing *The Irish Widow in my teeth*; depend upon it, that I shall always think *of Your Condescension with all due Gratitude*.—would Mrs Barry be Satisfy'd I would not let you appear in it again upon any Account. As You are growing too important for Me, and as I shall not Submit to ask favours of You, If You will not do your business as You ought, I would advise You to make the best, & properest retreat You can, *with Justice to yourself, &* I am not displeas'd that you are in such a happy Situation, that You can live without the Stage / Your humble Servt / D Garrick. / Be assur'd that I shall no more hurt your importance by sending You any parts.

Rash Cautherley was brought to heel momentarily and wrote Garrick a terrified letter of obeisance in which he expressed an "earnest desire . . . of retaining the good Opinion of my Benefactor and best friend whose favor shall ever be thought of with Gratitude."

Reformation did not last. Cautherley went back to his secondary parts and was even elected to the Committee of the Drury Lane Actors' Fund in 1774–75, but his resentment smoldered. It burst out again in a complaint of 27 September 1775 and was answered with cold third-person formality in a letter which effectually ended the relationship (and Cautherley's London career) on 2 October 1775. The exchange follows:

I have flatter'd myself till the last Minute with hopes of receiving a favorable Answer to a Letter I did myself the Honor to send you before I left Town and am sorry to find your silence proceeds from a determined resolution not to do anything in my favor. My Situation in the Theatre for these four years past has been worse and worse & the impossibility I find of living on my Salary without involving myself in difficulties obliges me (tho' with the greatest reluctance) to take my leave of Drury Lane begging you will accept my most grateful Thanks for all the favors your bounty formerly bestow'd

Replied Garrick:

When Mr Cautherly's letter, which will be ever memorable, in the annals of a Theatre, came to Mr Garrick he was confin'd with a fit of ye Stone, & could not write: — had not Mr Cautherly's impatient vanity been too strong for his discretion & gratitude, he would have waited at least till the Saturday Morning, when the fullest, & best answer would have been given to his letter by the treasurer — has this Young Man a proper sense of right & wrong? for taking Mr Garrick out of ye Question, should not he, have given Notice *before* the beginning of the Season to any *indifferent* Manager of his intentions of quitting the Theatre? — to begin the Season was misleading the Manager, & not to go on, is not only contrary to ye Establish'd rules of a Theatre, but unjust, illegal, & dishonourable — what would the publick & Mr Cautherly's friends have said, had M^r G: discharg'd M^r C: during the Acting Season? — We shall soon hear what they say upon ye present occasion: perhaps Mr Cautherly thought that his going away at a time when the Manager rely'd upon him, would be more distressing: in this, as in many other things, he is very much mistaken — Mr Garrick said in a former letter, that Mr Cautherly could confer no favour upon him, which he now retracts; for he confesses, Mr Cautherly has found a Way to confer a very great one.

Cautherley's last recorded performance at Drury Lane was as Rivers in *The Note of Hand* on 26 September 1775. The apostate turned up at the Bristol Theatre in 1776 and 1777 playing his usual saccharine young lovers and bloodless villains (he had acted there in the summer of 1775: Michael Edkins had entered a 2s. payment in June "To Gilding a Crown for Mr Cautherly in King Arthur"). He neglected his annual subscription payment to the Drury Lane Fund in 1775 and at Dublin in 1778. He was at Hull and Edinburgh in 1779 and 1780 and also at York in 1780. He was again at Edinburgh in the winter season (beginning in January) of 1784 and perhaps also in 1785 and 1786 and even later.

Cautherley wrote to Mrs Garrick in 1800, over twenty years after his benefactor's death: "The Gratitude I shall ever feel for the many kindnesses confer'd on me, while under your Hospitable Roof (for almost Twenty years) can never be effaced."

He died at his house in Richmond on 15 November 1805. His widow Susanna survived him, dying on 22 March 1820.

The couple had had at least four children, and probably five or more. The parish register of the church in Richmond, Surrey, shows the baptism on 30 August 1772 of "Samuel son of Mr Samuel Cautherley." On 9 December 1776, the entry carried the baptism of

Iohn and ⎱ tweens of Mr Samuel Cautherly
Susanna ⎰   and Susanna his wife.

On 16 July 1778 "Willm son of Mr Saml Cautherley and Susanna his wife" was christened. "John Cautherley a child" was buried at the church on 23 December 1778. The Harriett Cautherley who was buried on 20 June 1777 was probably a child of Samuel and Susanna.

Susanna's will mentioned that by

a certain Indenture of Settlement made previously to my Marriage with my late husband Samuel Cautherley Esq. bearing the date the 3rd July 1771 and made between my said late husband of the first part, myself by my then name of . . . Susanna Blanchard of Richmond Spinster of the second part and Thomas Dyliff, Esq . . . Edward Emily[,] Clerk and George Garrick Esq of the third part

a considerable property consisting of South Sea Annuities, Bank of England stock, "other securities granted by Commissioners for paving the City of Westminster," and several leasehold messuages and tenements had passed to her husband, and at his death back to her. The will provided generously for the three surviving children, Samuel, William, and Susanna.

Cautherley's notices ranged from lukewarm to insulting. He was well enough in a narrow range of young gentlemen in afterpieces, but he persisted in yearning for nobler and more challenging roles, and for a long while his patron encouraged him in his delusion. Was the usually astute Garrick, who had packed off many an insistent aspirant to deserved country exile, blinded by fatherly fondness? The quality that the *Theatrical Biography* of 1772 called Samuel's "constitutional insipidity" was saluted by Downman in *Drama, a Poem* in 1775 in the couplet

Faint as a shadow Cautherley glides by,
And melts without impression on the
eye.

A small crude engraving by an unknown engraver, published for William Tringham at an unknown date, which depicts him and Jane Barry as Romeo and Juliet, is reproduced in Volume 1 (p. 354) of this dictionary.

Cavana, Mr *fl. 1789–1792], singer.*

Mr Cavana was billed as playing a principal character in the musical extravaganza *The What Is It?* at the Royal Circus on 12 May 1789. Cavana played minor roles at Bristol during the 1791–92 season.

Cave, John *d. 1664, singer.*

John Cave was a member of the Chapel Royal at the time of the coronation of Charles II on 23 April 1661 and he continued in the royal service until his death. With other singers, his debts to the crown in 1661 were canceled by royal order in 1663 and he was exempt from subsidies levied by Parliament after the Restoration. Of his musical career nothing is known, but of his death there is a full report.

The Old Cheque Book of the Chapel Royal contains the report that Cave, "goeing home to his lodgeing upon the 30th of January [1664] about 7 or 8 of ye clock in the evening, about the new Exchange, was by one James Elliott, a Scott, run through the body, of which wound he departed this life the 16th day of February following . . ." Samuel Pepys heard of the murder, too: "I hear how two men last night, jostling for the wall about the New Exchange, did kill one another, each thrusting the other through; one of them of the King's Chapel, one Cave, and the other a retayner of my Lord Generall Middleton's."

John Cave was buried in the cloisters of Westminster Abbey on 18 February 1664. The will of a John Cave of Capell, Kent, was proved on 4 March 1670 by his widow Margaret, but unless there was a great deal of litigation because of the murder, this would seem too late a date for the probation to refer to the singer.

Cavell, Will *fl. 1671–1672], performer.*

A warrant was issued on 31 March 1671 to apprehend Will "Cavile" for presenting a dumb show illegally—presumably in London. A similar warrant was issued on 5 September 1672 to arrest Cavell (so spelled) and one Sandys for performing dumb shows without a license from Sir Henry Herbert.

Cavile. *See* **CAVELL.**

Cawbraest, Walter ₁*fl. 1665*₁, *drummer.*

Walter Cawbraest, a drummer in the King's Musick, was paid £4 on 29 June 1665 for a banner.

Cawder, Jo. ₁*fl. 1760–1761*₁, *sweeper.*

The constant charges at Covent Garden in 1760–61 included Jo. Cawder as a sweeper receiving 1*s.* 6*d.* daily.

Cawley, Master ₁*fl. 1757–1759*₁, *dancer, actor.*

A Master Cawley performed with other children in *A Medley Concert and Auction*, an entertainment presented at the Haymarket commencing on 15 June 1757 and continuing through August. On 31 October 1757 he played Harlequin in a performance of *Harlequin Trick'd* given at the Haymarket by children. He acted Glanville in a children's performance of *Cleone* at the same theatre on 18 April and 10 May 1759, and on 6 and 7 September of that year he danced (billed as "Master Callois") with Miss Burn at Marylebone Gardens.

Cawston, Mr ₁*fl. 1789–1797*₁, *house servant.*

The Drury Lane account books first mentioned Mr Cawston on 19 September 1789 when he was paid 9*s.* per week. By 3 December 1796 he was earning 15*s.* weekly; and the last reference to him, on 13 June 1797, grouped him with other house personnel.

Caxton, Mr ₁*fl. 1747*₁, *painter.*

On 8 and 29 August and 19 September 1747 in the Covent Garden account books were listed payments of £10 10*s.* to Mr Caxton, a painter. The payments were toward a total agreement of 50 guineas, probably for scene painting.

Cayford, Mr ₁*fl. 1735*₁, *house servant?*

Mr Cayford was paid by the Covent Garden Theatre for 11 days work at 20*d.* daily in 1735; the account books indicate that he was discharged on 8 October 1735 but make no mention of the service Cayford rendered.

Caygill. *See* **KAYGILL.**

Ceca. *See* **CIECA.**

Ceedo. *See* **SEEDO.**

Cefalo, Pietro ₁*fl. 1670*₁, *musician.*

In the Lord Chamberlain's accounts under the date of 15 March 1670 three names were cited in connection with Italian musicians in the court of Charles II: Pietro Cefalo, Giovanni Sebenico, and Mr Killigrew. The Killigrew referred to was doubtless Thomas, manager of the King's Company at the Bridges Street Theatre; the juxtaposition of his name with those of Cefalo and Sebenico would suggest that the two Italian musicians may have served in the theatre band as well as at court.

Celatti. *See* **CELOTTI.**

"Celebrated Grimacier, The" ₁*fl. c. 1790*₁, *clown.*

Caulfield, in his *Remarkable Persons* (1820), reported that

About thirty years since, Mr. Astley, of the amphitheatre, Westminster-road, engaged an Italian buffoon, who appeared under the title of the celebrated grimacier, and distorted his face into thirty different characters, totally dissimilar one with another; the salary of this man was ten pounds per week.

Celementina, Signora. *See* **CREMONINI, CLEMENTINA.**

"Celeste" or **"Celestina."** *See* **HEMPSON.**

Celestino, Eligio *c. 1737–1812, violinist, composer.*

Eligio Celestino was born at Rome in 1737, according to van der Straeten, about 1739 according to Grove. He studied the violin in his native city, where Burney heard him play at the Duke of Dorset's residence on 21 September 1770, reporting him—through Fanny Burney's *Early Diary*—as "the principal violin here" who played "among other things, one of his own solos, which was very pleasing, though extremely difficult, with great brilliancy, taste, and precision." Celestino was at London in 1772, where he "led the band" for a concert at Burney's house on 5 May, and, reported Fanny, "charmed us all with a solo."

In 1776, Celestino was appointed violinist of the court orchestra at Stuttgart. He gave a concert with his wife at Frankfurt in 1780, and by 1781 he was the concert master to the court chapel of the Duke of Mecklenburg-Ludwigslust, a post he retained for the rest of his life. Van der Straeten states that Celestino returned to London in 1797, at the age of 60, "where he was considered one of the greatest artists of his time." *Six Sonatas for a Violin and Bass* and three *Duos a Violino e Violoncello* composed by him were published by Clementi at London in 1798. Despite the high regard Burney held for him in 1772, he did not mention Celestino in *A General History of Music*, published in 1789, before the violinist's second visit to London. In his *London Notebook* Haydn included "Celestinis" in the lists both of female and male singers at London in 1792, and perhaps the female was Eligio Celestino's wife. *The Dictionary of Music* (1824) states that Celestino resided "for some time" at London (and gives his year of birth as 1755). There seems, however, to be no specific notice of any public performances by either Signor or Signora Celestino at London. Eligio Celestino was back at Ludwigslust by 1800. He died at Rome on 14 January 1812.

Celestino, Signora Eligio ₍*fl. 1780–1792*₎, *singer.* See CELESTINO, ELIGIO.

Cell. *See* SELL.

Celotti, Ziuliana ₍*fl. 1705–1714*₎, *singer.*

Billed as having lately arrived in England, Ziuliana Celotti (or Juliana Cellott) sang in Italian at the Lincoln's Inn Fields Theatre on 9 February 1705. She had a benefit recital at York Buildings on 2 April, another on 13 March 1706, and a third on 22 January 1707. After a gap of five years her name appeared again in the bills. On 13 November 1712 she presented a benefit concert at Hickford's Music Room; she had another benefit at Stationers' Hall on 4 March 1714; and on 19 April 1714 she gave her last recorded performance, again a benefit, at Caverley's Dancing Academy in Chancery Lane.

Celson, Miss ₍*fl. 1798*₎, *singer.*

Miss Celson sang at Covent Garden in the Handel memorial concerts on 14, 23, 28, and 30 March 1798, the first appearance being advertised as her debut. Her songs were "Thou shalt bring them in" from *Israel in Egypt*, "What tho' I trace" from *Solomon*, and "O mirror of our fickle state" from *Samson*.

Cemmitt, Miss ₍*fl. 1785–1791*₎, *singer.*

Between 1785 and 1788, Miss Cemmitt was a vocalist at Bermondsey Spa Gardens. In June and July 1791 she played the role of Nancy in *The Blunt Tar, or True Love Rewarded* at Astley's Amphitheatre, Westminster Bridge.

Centlivre, Joseph ₍*fl. 1715–1739*₎, *organist.*

Joseph Centlivre, not to be confused with the husband of Susanna the playwright, began his musical career as a boy singer in the Chapel Royal. In 1715 he was paid £20, according to the Calendar of Treasury books, as one of the boys whose voices had changed. On July 1726 the Vestry Books for St Margaret, Westminster, showed that Centlivre had auditioned for the position of organist but had lost out to Edward Purcell. At some point he became organist of the Oxford Chapel, Vere Street, a post in which he was succeeded by William Boyce in 1734. On 28 August 1739—the last record of his activities—Centlivre became one of the original subscribers to the newly founded Royal Society of Musicians.

Cerail, Mlle *d. 1723, dancer, singer.*

The Mademoiselle Cerail (or Crail) who performed in England in 1717 was probably the dancer Mlle "Corail" who was with Saint-Edme at the Saint-Germain fair in 1713 and then joined the troupe of Mme Baron. She was advertised as lately arrived from Paris when she danced at the King's Theatre on 16 and 21 March 1717 and at Lincoln's Inn Fields for Moreau's benefit on 23 April. She was probably the Mlle "Coraill" who sang "several New Songs composed by the famous Dominico Scarlatti" at Hickford's Music Room on 26 March 1718. Later that year, back in Paris, she entered the Académie Royale de Musique. Mlle Cerail died of smallpox in November 1723.

Cerespi. *See* **CRESPI.**

Cerestini. *See* **CARESTINI.**

Cervetto, Giacobbe   *1682–1783, violoncellist, composer.*

Giacobbe Cervetto, called Cervetto the Elder, was born in Italy, probably at Venice, in 1682, of Jewish parents with German origins. His original name was Giacomo Basevi; the name "Cervetto," which he later adopted, meaning "a little stag," suggests a translation of the German-Jewish name of Hirschel. As a dealer in Italian musical instruments he came to London in

1728 at the age of 46 but, failing in trade, he became a performer on the violoncello, an instrument for which he obviously had had earlier training. According to Grove, he played for a performance of Arne's *Comus* in 1737; and in 1739 Cervetto, Abaco, Lanzetti, Pasqualini, and Caporale, "brought the violoncello into favour" through their concerts at Hickford's Room in Brewer Street, according to Burney. In his manuscript "Memoirs" (at the British Museum), Burney wrote that Cervetto was a "worthy Hebrew . . . a Venetian & knew the Fingerboard of his instrument, and composition, very well; but he had not that vocal tone for which his son [James Cervetto] became so justly celebrated."

For a number of years Cervetto was a musician in the Drury Lane band and he often gave solo performances on the violoncello. The first such solo noted in the bills was a concerto on 22 November 1742. In that season he played regularly, taking a benefit on 5 May 1743. He played in concerts for the benefit of the Musicians' Fund at the King's Theatre on 14 April 1747 and 12 March 1761. He also performed in the oratorio *Judas Maccabaeus* at the Haymarket on 18 April 1769, in the oratorios at Covent Garden in the spring of 1777, and in the Drury Lane oratorios between 19 February and 26 March 1779, for which he was paid £5 5s. per night. Cervetto was a featured violoncellist at the King's Theatre in the three seasons 1773–76 and in the spring of 1778. His habit of wearing a huge diamond on the forefinger of his bow hand lent sparkle to his performances. At the age of 98, according to the press, Cervetto continued to play every summer at Vauxhall and went "through his business as well as ever, being of a thin habit of body, temperate in his living, and chearful in his disposition."

A concert of vocal and instrumental music, directed by J. C. Bach and Abel, was given for Cervetto's benefit on 24 April 1778, at the New Rooms in Totten-

GIACOBBE CERVETTO

engraving by Picot, after Zoffany

ham Street, Charlotte Street, Rathbone Place, when Cervetto performed with such eminent musicians as Cramer, Fischer, Crosdill, and Stamitz, with songs given by Signor Amantini and Signora Balconi. Tickets, at 10s. 6d., were to be had of Cervetto at No 7, Charles Street, Covent Garden, where he lived for many years. Earlier, at least by 1763, he had lodged "at Mr Marie's, tobacconist, in Compton Street, Soho."

The violoncellist's prominent nose was the inspiration for several amusing incidents and became a standing joke with the upper gallery at Drury Lane, whose habitués frequently hailed him as "Nosey." Garrick came to the musician's defense in a prologue delivered on 20 October 1753:

In like extremes your laughing Humour flows;

Have ye not roar'd from Pit to upper Rows,
And all the Jest was,—what?—a Fiddler's Nose.
Pursue your Mirth; each Night the Joke grows stronger,
For as you fret the Man, *his Nose looks longer.*

Arthur Murphy printed the prologue in the *Gray's Inn Journal* on 27 October 1753, adding that despite Cervetto's long nose "no feature of his Mind is out of Proportion, unless it be that his good Qualities are extraordinary," and chastising the public for its cruelty in rendering the musician "uneasy in the Business, in which he is eminent and by which he must get a Livelihood."

A story is told by Gilliland in the *Dramatic Mirror* of an incident involving Cervetto at Garrick's first appearance, on 14 November 1765 at Drury Lane, after his two-year grand tour. Playing Benedick in *Much Ado About Nothing*, the great actor was in the midst of one of his famous pauses which suspended the audience, including the Royal Family, in an expectant hush, when Cervetto, sitting in the band, yawned loudly. Gales of laughter ensued and it was some time before Garrick could again catch the mood of the audience. Later in the music room, Cervetto explained to Garrick that it was "alvay the vay I go when I haf the greatest *rapture,* Mr Garrick," a wily excuse which the actor, we are told, instantly accepted.

Cervetto died at Friburg's snuff shop in the Haymarket on 14 October 1783 at the age of 101. According to a clipping in the Jerome papers, he had married soon after his arrival in England and by 1777 had grandchildren. In his will dated 1 August 1778 and proved on 16 April 1783, Cervetto, describing himself as of the parish of St Paul, Covent Garden, and expressing his desire to be buried "according to the rites and ceremonies of the Church of England," left all his "ready securities

GIACOBBE CERVETTO

artist unknown

for money plate pictures jewells household goods ffurniture," and all other estate to his "dear natural son James Cervetto," whom he also named executor. No amounts were mentioned in the will, but his fortune at the time of his death was reported to be about £20,000, garnered mostly, it would seem, from a profitable business in music tuition. Presumably he outlived by many years his wife, who seems not to have been the mother of James Cervetto. No other children or grandchildren were mentioned in his will, although people by the name of Basevi were left bequests in the will of James Cervetto.

Burney, at whose home Giacobbe Cervetto and his son used to participate in musical parties, thought highly of the elder musician but found his tone "raw, crude," and uninteresting compared to his contemporary rival Caporale and stated also that the younger Cervetto, even when a child, had a better tone and "played

what he was able to execute, in a manner much more *chantant* than his father."

Cervetto wrote a variety of trio sonatas for cellos, violins, and harpsichord, numerous solos for cello and thoroughbass, solos for German flute and *continuo*, and six lessons or *divertimenti* for two cellos. A list of his compositions may be found in the *Catalogue of Printed Music in the British Museum*.

A fine portrait of Cervetto by Zoffany was published in mezzotint by M. A. Picot in 1771. There is a portrait by an unknown artist in the British Museum. It has often been supposed that Cervetto was the subject of Hogarth's well-known print of "The Enraged Musician," but the testimonies of Thomas A. Arne and John Ireland indicate that that person was John Festing.

Cervetto, James *1749–1837, violoncellist, composer.*

James Cervetto was born at London in 1749, the natural son, by some unknown mother, of Giacobbe Cervetto (1682–1783), from whom he learned to play the violoncello. As a boy he was also the pupil of Abel. Burney thought that when he was quite young and not yet fully acquainted with the gamut, he had a better tone "and played what he was able to execute, in a manner much more *chantant* than his father."

On 23 April 1760, advertised as being 11 years old, James played in a concert of instrumental music presented at the Haymarket Theatre, with "The Solos by young Performers who never appeared in Public." The other young musicians included Master Barron, age 13, on the violin, Esther Burney, age 9, on the harpsichord, and Miss Schmelling (later Madame Mara), age 11, on the violin. According to *The Dictionary of National Biography*, James then traveled abroad, playing at many capital cities of Europe, but he was back at London by 1765 to play with his father in a concert given by Parry, the harpist. Fanny Burney wrote in her diary of a "little concert" held at the Burneys on 15 November 1768, at which the two Cervettos played—"we had two solos on the violincello by young Cerveto, who plays delightfully." James became a member of the Queen's private band in 1771 and of Lord Abingdon's private orchestra in 1780.

At various professional concerts at London, Cervetto earned a reputation as a matchless performer on his instrument. From 1780 he played at the concerts at the Hanover Square Rooms. There in 1784 he performed a cello concerto by Haydn and at about that time was joined by a Chabran, probably Francesco. In November 1782 he was engaged as soloist at the Oxford Music Room, and in May and June of 1784 he was one of the instrumental performers at the Handel Memorial Concerts given at Westminster Abbey and the Pantheon. On 11 June 1789, Cervetto played a trio for pianoforte, violin, and violoncello with Clementi and Cramer at the King's Theatre, and on 29 April 1790, with Clementi and Cramer, he accompanied the singer Marchesi in two songs.

In 1794, Cervetto was listed in Doane's *Musical Directory* as living at No 7, Newport Street, Soho, a member of the Concert of Ancient Music, the Professional Concerts, the band at the Opera, and the Royal Society of Musicians. During the early decades of the nineteenth century, Cervetto seems to have retired on the inheritance, reputed to have been £20,000, left to him by his father's will in 1783. In 1828 he was living at No 65, Warren Street, Fitzroy Square. On 5 June 1836, when he was identified in the Minute Books as the oldest member, he gave the Society £10 "for continued prosperity."

James Cervetto died at London on 5 February 1837, at the age of 88. In his will, dated 15 February 1821 (when he described himself as of the High Street, Marylebone) and proved on 15 February

Collection of Harry R. Beard, Victoria and Albert Museum

Probably JAMES CERVETTO, playing the cello

artist unknown

1837, Cervetto did not specify any of his legatees as relatives. He named, however, his "good friend" George Basevi, of Montague Street, Russell Square, as his executor; Basevi had been the proper surname of his own father, to whom he had been born out of wedlock. To George Basevi, and residually to Basevi's two sons Nathan Basevi and George Elias Basevi, he also left his musical books, instruments, and the remainder of his estate not otherwise bequeathed. To one James Basevi, of Sloane Street, Chelsea, he left £1000 in three percent bank annuities. Separate bequests of £500 each in those bank annuities were also made to Emilia, Emily, Louisa, and Olivia Linto, the four daughters of Ephraim Linto, merchant, of Edmonbury Place, Islington, and to Benjamin Linto, his son; and of £1000 in three percent bank annuities to Maria D'Foradi, wife of Isaac D'Foradi, of Bloomsbury Square. A Jaspar Cervetto, not mentioned in the will, who was a nineteenth-century author of a *divertimento* for two cellos and two books of duets for violin and cello, was no doubt related.

A list of James Cervetto's compositions for violoncello and other instruments can be found in the *Catalogue of Printed Music in the British Museum*.

Probably he is the cellist shown in the humorous prints titled "A Sunday Concert" published on 1 June 1782 and "A Bravura at the Hanover Sq. Concert," published on 27 May 1789.

Cestini. *See* SESTINI.

Chaboud, Pietro [*fl. 1707–1725*], *instrumentalist, composer.*

Pietro Chaboud, often referred to by his first name alone, was proficient on the bassoon, flute, bass viol, and oboe, and composed for most of them. His name first appeared in British documents in 1707 when he bid for a post in the band at the Queen's Theatre in the Haymarket. He asked for £1 10*s.* nightly but settled for 10*s.* He seems to have worked in the band until about 1711, first as bassoonist but then as a bass viol player. By the end of his tenure he was earning 15*s.* nightly.

He augmented his income, as did most theatre musicians, with concert work, his earliest notice being at York Buildings on 23 May 1707 when he played a sonata on the flute. On 25 April 1715 at the Great Room in James Street he played the bass viol and German flute for his benefit, and he performed at Hickford's music room on 27 March and 3 May 1717. About 1717–20 he was in the service of the Duke of Chandos, playing flute and oboe and composing for those instruments for the Cannons concerts. The last concert date known for Chaboud was 18 February 1719 at Hickford's.

About 1725 he published his *Solos for a German Flute Hoboy or Violin with a Thorough Bass for the Harpsichord or Bass Violin . . . being all Choice pieces by y*ᵉ *greatest Authors and fitted to the German Flute.*

Chabran, Charles *b. c. 1723, violinist.*

Charles Chabran, properly Carlo Chiabrano, was a member of an Italian musical family from Piedmont. He has often been confused with other musicians of that family name, apparently all related. He was born at Turin about 1723, was a nephew and student of Somis, and was a member of the Royal Chapel at his native city in 1747. He enjoyed great success at Paris in 1751, publishing six sonatas for violin and *continuo*; these were also published by Welcker of London when Chabran appeared there in 1752–53.

Little is known of Chabran's stay at London except that on 19 March 1753 he played the violin at a concert at the Great Room in Dean Street, Soho, for the benefit of the nine-year-old prodigy on the harpsichord, Miss Davies, and he again played in a concert for the benefit of the Musicians' Fund at the King's Theatre on 30 April 1753.

Chabran's importance, according to Grove, "lies in the fact that, together with other pupils of Somis, he handed the latter's art down to posterity." Gaetano Chabran (fl. 1755–1771), the violoncellist and composer, who seems not to have been at London, was probably his brother (see Grove). Another Chabran, named Francesco, but apparently called Felice or Felix at London, was perhaps the son of either Charles or Gaetano, but probably not, as suggested by van der Straeten, their brother.

Chabran, Francesco [Felice?] *c. 1757–1829, violinist, guitarist?, composer.*

Francesco Chabran, a member of an

Italian musical family, was born about 1757, perhaps at London, where the violinist Charles Chabran (Carlo Chiabrano) had come in 1752–53. The latter, who was about 34 years old when Francesco was born, may well have been his father or uncle, but not his brother as claimed by van der Straeten.

When Francesco Chabran was recommended to the Royal Society of Musicians by William Shield on 6 January 1782, his Christian name was given as Felice; he was described as a single man about 25 years of age, as having studied and practiced music for seven years (the usual apprenticeship), as a performer on the violin and tenor, and as belonging to the band of the Opera at the Pantheon. Probably he was the Chabran who played in the Concerts of Ancient Music in 1784 (and not Gaetano Chabran as suggested by Grove) and at the Handel Memorial Concerts at Westminster Abbey and the Pantheon in May and June 1784. He certainly played at the annual concert for the benefit of the clergy at St Paul's in May 1785 and later in 1791 and 1792. Chabran was a member of the band at the King's opera in 1790 and leader of the band for the ballet at the King's opera between 1791 and 1795. His salary in 1793–94 was £80. In 1794, his address, as "Felix Chabran," was listed in Doane's *Musical Directory* as No 16, Wardour Street. On 5 January of that year he informed the Governors of the Royal Society of Musicians that he had fractured his thumb in a fall and, unable to perform, he asked for relief. He was granted £20. In January 1798 he was serving as a Governor of the Society.

Chabran seems to have retained a position as a second violinist at the King's Theatre through 1818–19, or until he was beset by illness. The Governors of the Royal Society of Musicians granted him £4 13s. 6d. per month for relief on 5 March 1820. On 1 July 1821 he petitioned for additional aid, stating he had received nothing from the opera in 1820–21 and only £21 9s. 6d. in 1819–20. The Governors granted him £5 5s. per month and £9 for future medical aid. He died on 1 March 1829, and on 5 April his widow was granted £12 funeral expenses by the Society. Mrs Chabran died late in 1829 or early in 1830; on 7 February 1830 her niece applied to the Society for a funeral allowance, which was refused because the niece had already received all the effects, including the lease, of the deceased. But when the niece reapplied on 7 March 1830, the sum of £8 to defray expenses for Mrs Chabran's funeral was granted, in consequence of the "embarrassed circumstances of the Deceased."

The Favourite Opera Dances for the Year 1790 . . . Selected and adapted for the Piano-Forte, Flute or Violin by F. Chabran, were published in four books at London about 1795. Two solos for violoncello and bass, "Composed by Sig.r

Civiche Raccolte d'Arte ed Incisione, Milan

FRANCESCO CHABRAN, with Pugnani detail from a large group, engraving by Scotti

Chabran" and published by J. Bland at London about 1785, were probably by Francesco and not by Gaetano Chabran.

Francesco Chabran is pictured in a painting by L. Scotti of a large group of musicians, done about 1805.

Chaffe, Christopher *(fl. 1794), musician.*

Christopher Chaffe was listed in Doane's *Musical Directory* in 1794 as a player on the bassoon and a tenor, a member of the New Musical Fund and of the Titchfield Chapel Society, and a participant in the Handel Memorial Concerts at Westminster Abbey; Chaffe was then living at No 61, Mount Street, Grosvenor Square. A Master Chaffe, his son, of the same address, was listed by Doane as a singer in the Titchfield Chapel Society.

Chaldicot. *See* CALDICOT.

Chaliez. *See* DESCHALLIEZ.

Chalke. *See* CHOCK.

Challoner, Neville Butler *b. 1784, instrumentalist, band leader, teacher, composer, music seller.*

Born in the Parish of St Andrew, Holborn, in 1784, Neville Butler Challoner studied the violin at a very early age under Claude Joseph Dubroeck, a native of Brussels. He gave his first solo recital on the violin at the age of nine (according to Sainsbury's *Dictionary of Musicians*), presumably at London. At the age of 13 he was articled to the musician General Ashley, but "previously to receiving any instruction" he was competent enough to play the violin in the orchestra for the oratorios at Covent Garden (1796?) and in public performances at Ranelagh Gardens. Sainsbury stated that Challoner was engaged to lead the band at the Richmond Theatre, Surrey, in 1799, but the accounts for that theatre in that year list him merely as a member of the band at 15*s.* per week. In the following year he reportedly was the leader of the band at the Birmingham Theatre. Afterwards he studied the harp and pianoforte and in 1803 was leader at Sadler's Wells.

On 6 July 1805, when he was living at No 25, Greek Street, Soho, Challoner became a freeman of the Worshipful Company of Musicians in the City and soon after, on 10 July 1805, received his first apprentice, John Edwards, son of a musician of the same name. Appointed first violist at the Harmonic City concerts in 1807, at which the first performances in England of Mozart's *Don Giovanni* were given, Challoner then was engaged as harpist at the Italian Opera, in which situation he continued (except in 1817 and 1818) at least through 1823. In 1813 he also became principal second tenor at the Philharmonic concerts.

On 1 September 1805 Challoner had been recommended by Skillum for membership in the Royal Society of Musicians, to which he was unanimously elected on 1 December 1805. In 1806 and 1811–13 he played at the Society's annual concerts in St Paul's for benefit of the clergy; he served as a governor of the Society in 1810, and on the Court of Assistants in 1835 and 1836, and was still active in the Society in 1839.

Challoner wrote and published a number of pieces for harp and methods for the violin and various other instruments, which he also distributed as a successful music seller in Regent Street during the early nineteenth century. By 1823 his preceptors for piano (published 1806) had sold nearly 9000 copies and those for violin and harp (1806) between 3000 and 4000 each. These sales, plus tutelage of some 600 private pupils, put him in "a state of easy affluence."

By 1824, when Sainsbury published his *Dictionary*, Challoner had been supporting his parents for 20 years and had brought up eight children of his own, all well provided for. His son Thomas Challoner, who had been bound apprentice to his father by the Worshipful Company of Musicians on 11 January 1823, was elected a member of the Royal Society of Musicians on 5 July 1829. Thomas performed "admirably" on the harp and piano and taught private pupils.

Chalmers, James *d. 1810, actor, dancer.*

James Chalmers was the son of the provincial actors James and Sarah Chalmers, who played at Norwich in the 1760s and 1770s. He acted under Tate Wilkinson's management at the Edinburgh Theatre Royal in 1779–80 and joined the York company in April 1780. By this time he had established himself as a harlequin, and one of the earliest accounts of him at York described his benefit on 17 May 1780. The evening concluded with a leap by Chalmers through a stage door seven feet above the floor. He had an accident of some kind in February 1781 and was unable to play the athletic Harlequin, but by his benefit on 2 April 1782 he was up to his acrobatic feats again with a "flying leap over statue of K. William. Lion's leap over 10 men's heads, leap through picture sc. 14 ft. high . . ." He played at Sheffield during "the races and the week following, in June 1781" says Wilkinson, who found him "of great service."

By the 1781–82 season Chalmers had married Eleanor Mills, a young actress in the York troupe who had, like Chalmers, played at Edinburgh and whom Chalmers may well have met at Norwich where she started her career. The couple stayed at York through the 1782–83 season and then came to London. Chalmers chose Tom in *The Conscious Lovers* for his debut at Covent Garden on 8 October 1783, and the *Theatrical Review* reported on it:

MR. CHALMERS is a neat, well made, proportionate figure. His manner is lively, and his action judicious, characteristic, and unembarassed. But we cannot avoid thinking his Tom very deficient of that chaste, animated, and interesting colouring, which it received last season from the performance of Mr. LEE LEWES. However, as he undoubtedly possesses merit, he has our congratulations for the applause he so deservedly received.

Chalmers went on to play during the 1783–84 season such roles as Sir Thomas Lovell in *Henry VIII*, Harlequin in *Friar Bacon* (later altered into *Harlequin Rambler*), Lovelace in *Three Weeks After Marriage*, and Sir Walter Blount in *1 Henry IV*.

The work of the Chalmers couple sufficiently impressed Thomas Harris to make him include them in the list of a proposed company to play in Paris for eight weeks in the summer of 1784, but it is unclear whether or not the pair actually went to France.

The 1784–85 season for Mr and Mrs Chalmers was very odd, yet indicative of the wanderlust that seemed to possess them. Mrs Chalmers acted only until 4 October 1784 at Covent Garden and then left the company. James played Norfolk in *Richard III* and the lead in *Harlequin Rambler* on 11 October, ran off to Dublin to make a debut at Smock Alley on 20 November, and reappeared at Covent Garden on 8 April 1785 as Lovell in *Henry VIII*. The bills make it clear that his roles at Covent Garden from November onward were taken by others. Still, during his on-and-off season in London he added to his repertory Sylvius in *As You Like It*, Biondello in *Catherine and Petruchio*, and Poins in *1 Henry IV*.

Chalmers must have pleased the Irish, for Daly brought James and Eleanor back to Ireland about 1786, and there they stayed for several seasons, playing at Waterford, Limerick, Cork, Kilkenny, and Belfast. Performing under Atkins at the Rosemary Lane Theatre in Belfast in

1788–89, Chalmers was described as "a hardworking and extremely versatile player" and a "decided acquisition" to the company. In addition to comedy and pantomime roles, he was adding tragedy characters to his list, though his career as a tragedian of some renown was yet to come.

By 20 February 1790 Chalmers and his wife were back in York, for on that date he performed in *Harlequin's Animation* and, "by particular desire," leaped through a beautiful transparency of George III. He was referred to as H. Chalmers, but the reference to H. surely was an error for J. From 1789 to 1791 the couple was in Weymouth, where Chalmers acted before the King and Queen. Typically, he went off to Dublin in May 1791 but was back at Weymouth playing Orlando in *As You Like It* in September. Mrs Chalmers died in Dublin on 22 May 1792 and James continued his career alone, appearing with the Birmingham company in the summer of 1792 before heading for America.

Thomas Wignell engaged Chalmers in May 1793 to act at the new Chestnut Street Theatre in Philadelphia, but before his debut there, if T. A. Brown's *History of the New York Stage* is to be trusted, he appeared with the old American Company at Annapolis. His first recorded and dated American appearance, however, was as Vapid in *The Dramatist* on 21 February 1794 in Philadelphia. The critics by 1795 found him to be a sprightly comedian: "to equal him would be difficult, and to excel him impossible." Such praise apparently turned Chalmers's head, and when the Philadelphia troupe was acting at Baltimore in the summer and fall of 1795, he withdrew temporarily in a fit of pique at some slight. His contentious manner and "consummate egotism" (as Dunlap called it) made him an increasingly difficult person to work with, and the rest of his career gained him a combination of praise for his acting and condemnation of his offstage behavior.

The worst and most public affair came in the spring of 1796. John Sollee brought Chalmers into his company and introduced him to Charleston audiences on 7 January 1796 in *The Suspicious Husband*. Sollee also cast Chalmers as Charles Surface in *The School for Scandal*, Shylock in *The Merchant of Venice*, Horatio in *The Fair Penitent*, and, most importantly, as Romeo, Richard III, and Hamlet. The Charleston critics praised him for the "manly ease, [and] the natural grace, dignity, and feeling which he displays in difficult parts . . ." But behind the scenes Chalmers became more and more intractable and in April 1796 the papers burst forth with everyone's complaints. Chalmers's benefit bill was twice changed and he lost his leading lady, Mrs Pownall, due to illness; that made a shambles of the musical part of his program, and the actor took it out on the musicians. As a result the musicians rebelled at the performance "from their disgust at Mr. Chalmers's demeanor." In a newspaper advertisement they went on to describe what had happened:

On Monday the 18th instant, Mr. Sollee proposed to the musicians that they should take a benefit on Saturday the 23rd, and they, to accommodate Mr. S. accepted the proposal. On Tuesday, Mr. Chalmers's night, they all punctually attended, but before they entered the orchestra, they deputed Messrs. Daguetty and Graupner to inform Mr. Chalmers of their agreement and to solicit his assistance in the Opera of "The Mountaineers:" But that gentleman, listening only to his own pride and self interest peremptorily refused. Retaliation is just—the musicians withdrew their assistance from *his* entertainments and the orchestra was silent, except that the trios, duets, and songs were accompanied by a single violin.

To this indignity Chalmers retorted in the papers with extensive quotations from his contract and accused Sollee of poor management. Sollee then took his turn in the press, contradicting Chalmers and indicating that the problems which had arisen in connection with Chalmers's benefit were due to the other players refusing to "study for him." Chalmers, said Sollee,

had consistently refused to undertake any new parts, even for the Proprietor himself, which has been the cause of the Public having received the same plays repeatedly and it may be added that had Mr. Chalmers behaved with more cordiality and complacency, not only to his fellow performers, but to him also, who has so liberally rewarded him for his services, he never could, with propriety have complained of the extreme disorder and misrule of the theatre which was in a flourishing and orderly state before his admission.

Whereupon Chalmers announced that he was leaving Charleston, though in fact he stayed in town but refused to perform. On 28 April Miss Wrighten's benefit was advertised, and she hoped Chalmers would act in *Fountaineville Forest* with her, but he refused and left town in a huff. (Coincidentally, just after Chalmers departed, the city was ravaged by a disastrous fire that ruined business for Sollee for the rest of the season.)

Chalmers rejoined the Chestnut Street Theatre troupe in Philadelphia on 25 May 1796 and played until 24 June. Among his roles were Puff in *The Critic*, Ranger in *The Suspicious Huband*, Marplot in *The Busy Body*, Mercutio in *Romeo and Juliet*, Petruchio in *Catherine and Petruchio*, Shylock, and Macbeth. At the end of the season the company appeared at Baltimore, and then the constantly moving Chalmers set off for Boston to work under John Brown Williamson at the Federal Street Theatre. He opened there with one of his favorite parts, Vapid, on 19 September 1796. The season ended, unfortunately, with Williamson bankrupt, but Hodgkinson hired Chalmers for a Boston summer season at $25 per week. With Williamson and Barrett, Chalmers gave readings at the

Columbian Museum in Boston in the summer of 1797; after that, in August 1797, Chalmers played briefly in Hartford. Hodgkinson brought the actor to New York for the 1797–98 final season at the John Street Theatre, but there Chalmers proved so difficult that he agreed to leave the company early if the manager would give him his benefit night. It was granted him on 19 March 1798, and he announced a special afterpiece called *Melocosmiotis*. This turned out to be a series of recitations by Chalmers which the audience, anticipating something better, finally drowned out with hisses.

From New York Chalmers headed south to Philadelphia and there spent the summer of 1798 at the Pantheon and the old Southwark Theatre, appearing in variety shows. Hodgkinson let Chalmers return to the American Company fold again for the 1798–99 season in Boston, but his weekly salary was down to $18.66 and, since the Federal Street Theatre troupe was in financial straits, it may have dropped further as the season wore on. Yet, despite his intemperate ways, Chalmers was a good attraction, and his spring benefit in 1799 brought in $1004—the highest in the troupe and almost $100 higher than the amount which Hodgkinson's own benefit drew.

After that season Chalmers returned to Charleston to work with Williamson, Edward Jones, and Alexander Placide, and there he seems to have stayed through 1802–3. But in May 1803 he was back in England, playing at Plymouth and billed as one recently returned from America. His benefit bill on 9 May at the end of his engagement stated that he was living at Mr Saunders's, the confectioner in Market Street. Where he wandered from Plymouth is not known, but on 6 February 1804 he was playing Macbeth in Edinburgh, and on 8 February the Manchester *Townsman* published a letter that suggested he would be arriving there soon. Whether he went to Manchester is doubtful, for James Dibdin's *Annals* place him in Edinburgh for the rest of the season.

Snelling Powell brought Chalmers back to America in the fall of 1804 for a season at the Federal Street Theatre in Boston, but the actor, now in his decline, returned to England in 1805. In 1810 Chalmers, a "comedian of considerable merit and formerly of the Norwich Co. [was] found speechless upon a doorstep of a house in Worcester . . . and died in [the] infirmary," according to the *Norfolk Annals*. Dissipation is said to have ruined him, and his death was recorded as occurring 22 August 1810. Apoplexy was said to have been the cause.

John Bernard in his *Retrospections* called Chalmers "an able comedian, though rather artificial, and more active than humorous. He had been originally a harlequin, but, unlike the great Woodward, had continued his movements to the displacement of character. Lewis was his model, but he had unluckily caught only that great actor's legs."

A painting of a Mr Chalmers as Midas by William Williams, dating c. 1765, has been called James Chalmers the younger, but it must surely be his father.

Chalmers, Mrs James, Eleanor née Mills *d. 1792, actress, singer.*

Eleanor Mills was the daughter of Joseph and Mary Mills and a sister of the Sarah Mills who became Mrs Hugh Sparks. She was also a sister of the Miss Mills who married William Ross and then Mr J. Brown and who became the mother of John Mills Brown, Mrs John Brunton, and Mrs Thomas Shaftoe Robertson. John Mills was Eleanor's brother, and another brother was acting at the Haymarket Theatre in 1786. With theatrical connections in all directions, it is hardly surprising that Eleanor Mills chose acting as a career and married into an acting family.

Eleanor was probably the Miss Mills who played Cupid in *Midas* on 15 June 1775 with the Norwich company at Bungay. In the troupe at that time were Mr and Mrs James Chalmers the elder, and Chalmers had been painted about 1765 as Midas. In time that actor became Eleanor Mills's father-in-law. It is probable also that Eleanor was the Miss Mills at Edinburgh in the autumn of 1775 of whom the *Edinburgh Rosciad* said "[she] is but young; when used to her trade she may be clever in the chambermaid." Miss Mills was apparently back at Norwich in 1776 and 1778, at the Theatre Royal in Edinburgh in late 1778 and 1779, and at York (billed as from Edinburgh) in April 1780. In October 1780 she was at Hull, again hailed as from Edinburgh. Tate Wilkinson approved her as a "clever little woman" and "a very pretty girl, a charming little actress" who "had great merit in the girls; and I am told, at Cheltenham and Worcester [in 1780?] she was much approved in the Second Constantia, Lady Teazle, &c."

By the 1781–82 season she was again at York and married to James Chalmers the younger, son of James and Sarah of the Norwich company. The new Mrs Chalmers and her husband acted at York through 1782–83, after which they headed for London. By that time they had started a family. The parish registers of St Michael Le Belfry, York, show the baptism on 3 April 1782 of Sarah, the second child of James and Eleanor Chalmers, carefully identifying the grandparents on both sides. Information concerning the first child of the Chalmerses has not been found, nor have any records of later additions to the family come to light.

On 19 September 1783 Mrs Chalmers made her London debut as Rose in *The Recruiting Officer* at Covent Garden, sharing the limelight with Bonner from Bath, who played Brazen and gave an introductory address to acquaint the audience with Mrs Chalmers, Miss Scrace (who played

Sylvia), and himself, all newcomers. Mrs Chalmers's weekly salary was £2 10*s*., and her roles during the season were chiefly comic or musical, such as Flora in *She Wou'd and She Wou'd Not*, Ann Page in *The Merry Wives of Windsor*, Dolly Trull in *The Beggar's Opera*, Columbine in *Friar Bacon*, Edging in *The Careless Husband*, Lucetta in *Two Gentlemen from Verona*, and Clarinda in *The Double Gallant*. She also participated in the choral dirge when *Romeo and Juliet* was performed. The 1783 *Theatrical Review* suggested that she would make a good Jenny in *The School for Fathers* and commented that "Mrs. Chalmers has more simplicity of comic humour for such characters, than any actress we have on the stage. So that she could not but perform the character of Jenny with that merit which ranks her one of our foremost comic actresses"—rather extravagant praise for a new actress from the provinces.

Though Eleanor Chalmers began the 1784–85 season at Covent Garden on 17 September 1784 as Emily in *Cross Purposes*, she concluded her contract on 4 October, singing in the *Macbeth* chorus. During the summer of 1785 she and her husband were recruited by Thomas Harris for an eight-week Paris season, but it is not certain that they ever went to France.

To Ireland, however, they did go by 1786–87 for a stay that lasted at least through February 1789. Mrs Chalmers made her Smock Alley debut in Dublin on 22 November 1786, and during her Irish visit she played at Waterford, Limerick, Cork, Kilkenny, and Belfast. She and Chalmers returned to England to play at Weymouth from 1789 to 1791, and it was reported that they were engaged to appear at Drury Lane beginning on 22 October 1791, billed as from Weymouth. They seem not to have returned to London, however. They were in Dublin in May 1791, where Chalmers acted, and since Mrs Chalmers died there a year later,

perhaps she was ill and could not go back to London as planned.

Though several sources are at odds about Eleanor Chalmers's death date, the Dublin *Public Register* of 24 May 1792 was probably correct in reporting that she had died on 22 May. The *Thespian Magazine*, in the August following, said that Mrs Chalmers "was in Mrs. Jordan's and Miss Farren's line—she was very well liked both in Dublin and Exeter."

Chalmers, [Mrs James, Sarah?] [*fl.* 1754–1785?], *actress.*

The "Mrs Chambers" who was advertised at Covent Garden on 15 May 1754 in the part of Dorinda in *The Stratagem* and as then making her first appearance on that stage, was called "Mrs Chalmers" by Isaac Reed in his "Notitia Dramatica." If, as is likely, Reed was correct, there is a further likelihood that she was Mrs James Chalmers, who at a little later date was to begin a long career at Norwich. Whether or not she reappeared at London is uncertain, for there was another Mrs Chambers (the wife of William) in London's bills at this time.

Sarah Chalmers made her Norwich debut as Juliet in the fall of 1756. Her husband, the elder James Chalmers (1725–1775), was with her in Norwich then and until 1770. He was a respected comedy actor, but evidently a thorn in the flesh of management. The Norwich Committee Books show the following notation on 26 May 1770: "Ordd. That Mr. Dewing be desired to prosecute Mr. Chalmers for a Breach of his Articles." On 17 August: "Mr. Chalmers' application to be readmitted into the Company to be determined by the Proprietors Rejected as to Him, But agree to accept his Wife at a Guinea & a Half p week." On 3 January 1771 "Mr. Chalmer's [*sic*] fresh application was refer'd to the Proprs & rejected." He continued to meet his wife at the theatre, and on 6 April it was "Ordd. that Mr. Griffith give Notice to

Mr. Chalmers that he is not to be permitted to go behind the Scenes for the future." Not until 5 December 1771 did the Proprietors agree to readmit him to the company. He was, further, to stay only "so long as he shall behave himself to the Satisfaction of the Proprietors there being deducted out of his Salary the weekly Sum of five shillings & 3d untill the Sum of Five Guineas for which he has given his note to the Proprietors be discharged." He lasted only until 4 March 1773 on which date the Committee Book was peremptory: "Order – That Mr. Chalmers be immediately discharged."

On the same date, 6 April 1771, that Chalmers was made unwelcome behind the scenes it was "Ordered that Mr Griffith give Notice to Mrs Chalmers that if she refuses to take such parts as are allotted to her by the Managers that her Sallary will from thenceforth be discontinued." On 11 May 1775 her salary was "reduced to one Guinea p Week," a particularly hard blow, for her husband was probably very ill. He died on 2 June, according to the *Morning Chronicle*. He had not acted in London, so far as we know. On 30 May 1776 the Book curtly decreed "That Mrs Chalmers be discharged." At what date she re-entered the company is not shown by these fragmentary records, but the last notice they give of her was on 17 May 1781 when it was "ordered that the Sum of Twenty Pounds a piece which had been yearly in the Circuit allowed to Mrs Chalmers & Mrs Pearson be reduced to Ten Pounds each."

The prominent provincial, London, and American actor James Chalmers (d. 1810) was a son of the Norwich couple.

Chalmers, William   *d. c. 1806, scene painter.*

Before working in the theatre William Chalmers was a watercolor painter, one of his earliest exhibited works being a portrait of Mrs Jordan in 1790, which is reproduced with her entry in this dictionary. He exhibited other works in 1791, 1792, and 1793, and then in 1798 he exhibited again, showing one of his last works, Kemble as the Stranger. In the fall of 1797 Chalmers joined the staff of Drury Lane as assistant scene painter at £2 2s. per week, serving with the younger Greenwood and Pugh. The staff was increased in 1798–99 to include Banks, Blackmore, Capon, Demaria, and Marinari, and so it continued in 1799–1800. So Chalmers was in distinguished company and thus seldom received mention in the bills. On 16 January 1798 he was noted as having helped Greenwood with the scenery for *Blue Beard*, and on 19 January 1799 Chalmers and Banks assisted Greenwood on *Feudal Times*. Chalmers seems to have stayed at the same salary throughout the years.

A William Chalmers who was probably the painter drew up his will on 19 February 1784, at which time he described himself as being in perfect health. He left the bulk of his estate to his wife Mary, but to his sister Elizabeth Chapman he bequeathed £20, a bust of his mother, and a miniature of his father. John Greaves and Thomas Pilsbury were appointed executors. The will was not proved until 4 January 1807, and on 21 January William Potts the younger, of Wardour Street, Soho, cabinet maker, and William Woodcock, of Great Queen Street, Lincoln's Inn Fields, glass seller, attested the handwriting in the will to be that of William Chalmers of Brownlow Street, Drury Lane.

Chamberlayne, Mr   [*fl.* 1674], *performer?*

A warrant in the Lord Chamberlain's accounts dated 9 November 1674 lists a Mr Chamberlayne as a member of the King's Company. He could have been the Thomas Chamberlayne, identified as "a gentleman," who charged the actor Robert Shatterel with slander on 23 May 1661, and he could also have been the Mr Chamberlain who, according to Luttrell, fought a duel on 31 January 1693 with Killigrew of the playhouse.

Chambers. *See also* CHALMERS, [MRS JAMES, SARAH?].

Chambers, Mr [*fl.* 1758], *stage-hand?*

In his diary at Drury Lane on 16 September 1758 the prompter Richard Cross noted that Woodward and Barry had entered into a partnership in a new theatre in Ireland and had taken with them, from Rich's company at Covent Garden, a Mr Chambers—along with several others from both patent houses. Chambers's name appeared just before that of Finney, Rich's scene man, so Chambers may have been a backstage worker rather than an actor.

Chambers, Mr *b. 1760 or 1764. See* GROVES, MR.

Chambers, Mr [*fl.* 1777–1779], *actor.*

At a weekly salary of £2 a Mr Chambers worked at Drury Lane for the 1777–78 and 1778–79 seasons and then was discharged. It would seem that he had hoped for a longer tenure, for in 1778 he had subscribed £1 1s. to the company fund. His roles during those two seasons make it apparent, however, that Chambers made little progress and spent most of his time playing small parts. His first role was Pandulpho in *King John* on 29 November 1777 and his last Old Wilding in *The Lyar* on 26 May 1779. In between he acted such parts as Derby in *Jane Shore*, the Lord Mayor in *Richard III*, the Player King in *Hamlet*, and Duncan in *Macbeth*.

The London Chambers may have been the actor of the name who died in Shrewsbury about 1820, "the oldest provincial comedian in the kingdom." That performer had been active at Norwich from 1773 to 1777.

Chambers, A. A. [*fl.* 1785–1797], *actor, singer.*

There were several men named Chambers acting in the last quarter of the eighteenth century, and identifying them accurately is difficult. A. A. Chambers was apparently the unnamed young gentleman who made his first appearance on any stage at the Haymarket Theatre on 12 February 1785 as Frederick in *The Miser*. He may also have been the Mr Chambers who was the Second Player in *Apollo Turned Stroller* at the Royalty Theatre in 1787 and / or the singer Chambers who offered "Crazy Kate" between the acts at the Haymarket on 29 April 1788 and/or the Chambers who acted Axalla in *Tamerlane* and Granger in *Who's the Dupe* at the Haymarket on 22 December 1788.

A Mr Chambers, probably A. A., acted and sang at the Haymarket in the summer of 1789, his named roles being Castruccino in *Ut Pictura Poesis!* on 19 May, Lubin in *The Quaker* on 28 August, and Vizard in *The Constant Couple* on 11 September. He also sang in *The Suicide, The Catch Club* (*The Sons of Anacreon*), and *The Battle of Hexham.* When the younger Colman took over the Haymarket in the fall of 1789, Chambers was one of the performers discharged, and at some point after that he left for America.

The first record of Chambers in America was at the Southwark Theatre in Philadelphia on 24 October 1792 when he played Belville in *Rosina*. Between then and January 1793 he acted Young Meadows in *Love in a Village*, Jemmy Jumps in *The Farmer*, Don Ferdinand in *Don Juan*, and Compton in *The Agreeable Surprise*. In addition to the vocal chores in some of these, he sang in the dirge which was a standard feature of *Romeo and Juliet*. After Philadelphia, Chambers joined the Charleston company, making his debut on 6 March 1793 as Dorincourt in *The Belle's Stratagem*, billed as from the Haymarket, London. In the Charleston troupe was Miss

Charlotte Sully, and on 30 May 1793 she and Chambers were married.

As a member of the American Company, Chambers acted at Hartford in the summer of 1795 and at the Federal Street Theatre in Boston in 1795–96. He then played in Baltimore, one of his known roles being Walter in *Children of the Wood* on 25 July 1796. He spent the 1796–97 season in Philadelphia, playing at the Pantheon with his wife, some of his roles being the title part in *Don Juan*, Clinch in *The Ghost*, Will Steady in *The Purse*, Sharp in *The Lying Valet*, and Daggerwood in *New Hay at the Old Market*. The last notice of his activity was on 14 February 1797 at the Pantheon when he played Jeremy and his wife played Betty in *The Dressing Room*.

Chambers, Charles [fl. 1771], *actor.*

On 23 April 1771 at Covent Garden "a Young Gentleman who never appeared [on] any stage" played the title role in *Oroonoko*. The *Public Advertiser* of 19 April had identified the newcomer as Charles Chambers.

Chambers, Harriet, formerly Mrs William Taplin, née Dyer *d. 1804, actress.*

Mrs Chambers was born Harriet Dyer, the daughter of the performers Michael and Harriet. About 1770 she married William Taplin, an actor, surgeon, and author of a treatise on veterinary surgery. The Taplins acted at Norwich in the early 1770s, the earliest of Harriet's recorded roles being Miss Montague in *A Word to the Wise* on 15 June 1775.

Mrs Taplin made her debut in Dublin at the Smock Alley Theatre on 13 April 1776, billed as from Covent Garden—though she is not known to have appeared there previously. Her husband was with her and probably acted, and on 4 July 1777 he wrote a letter to the *Hibernian Journal* which noted, among other things, that he and his wife had been married "near 7 years." Mrs Taplin, presumably with her husband, returned to England after the 1776–77 season, appeared at Bristol in the spring of 1777, and then joined the York company in 1777–78, hailed as from Dublin. She stayed with the York troupe in 1778–79 but also made appearances at Bristol, playing her usual soubrette roles. After that she and Taplin, whose acting experience seems not to have been as extensive as hers, joined the Theatre Royal, Edinburgh, for the 1780–81 season.

The pair returned to Ireland for the period 1781–84, and Mrs Taplin appeared at Cork in the autumns of 1781, 1782, and 1783 and at Limerick in October 1783. John Bernard in his *Retrospections* recalled a trip from Cork to Dublin in 1782 with Mrs Taplin and others. She had played Gertrude in *Hamlet* on 27 September in Cork and on the trip to Dublin on 15 October the tall, well-formed actress rode at the front of the cart looking as imperious as the Danish Queen herself. On the second day of the journey the players passed her off on the credulous villagers as the Empress of Russia, on her way to her execution in Dublin.

By the fall of 1785 Mrs Taplin was working with Austin and Whitlock's company at Chester, and she continued her association with that group for a number of years, playing some of the towns on their circuit: Chester, Sheffield, Lancaster, Whitehaven, Manchester, and Newcastle-upon-Tyne. She appeared briefly in 1786 at the theatre in Hammersmith, playing Juliet to Hill's Romeo on 12 July for her debut. Her other Hammersmith roles were Victoria in *A Bold Stroke for a Wife*, Lady Grace in *The Provok'd Husband*, and Letitia Hardy in *The Belle's Stratagem*. She and Taplin had perhaps been divorced (he died c. 1807), for at Hammersmith she was billed as Mrs Chambers. Of her new husband (if she had one) nothing is known.

As Mrs Chambers she returned to London in 1793–94 to act at Covent Garden for £2 weekly. Her first role there was Lady Waitfor't in *The Dramatist* on 18 December 1793, after which she acted such parts as Lady Rusport in *The West Indian*, Lady Bull in *Fountainebleau*, Lady Oddly in *Just in Time*, and the Aunt in *The Tender Husband*. Her last appearance at Covent Garden and in London was on 13 June 1794 when she played Lady Rachel Mildew in *The School for Wives*. After that, Mrs Chambers may have left the stage, though perhaps she was the actress of that name who acted at Tunbridge Wells in 1796, in Worcester in 1801, and in Wolverhampton in 1802. Harriet Dyer Taplin Chambers died in Worcester in May 1804 or shortly before.

Chambers, Isabella [*fl.* 1722–1741], singer, actress.

A student of Margherita de l'Épine, Isabella Chambers made her first public appearance singing at Hickford's music room on 8 March 1722 in a program given for her own benefit. On 13 March 1723, again for her benefit, she sang at the Haymarket Theatre, and on 1 April 1723 she made her Drury Lane debut, singing in Italian and English. The following 11 October she performed at the Lincoln's Inn Fields playhouse for the first time.

She had established herself quickly as one of the finest singers in London, and her record of performances at theatres and concert rooms for the following two decades testifies to her popularity. Most of her appearances over the years were as a solo singer, but during her first season at Lincoln's Inn Fields as part of John Rich's troupe she expanded her activity into pantomimes and other musical offerings. Her first named role was St Cecilia in *The Union of the Three Sister Arts* on 22 November 1723, and a month later she had an unspecified part in *The Necromancer*. At her benefit, on 16 March 1724, the total receipts came to £156 8s. 6d. The songs she sang in *The Necromancer* proved popular

enough to warrant the publication of two of them in 1724: *Cease, injurious Maid* and *Cupid, God of pleasing Anguish*. In the 1724–25 season Rich paid her £5 daily, a very handsome sum.

Mrs Chambers continued at Lincoln's Inn Fields through the 1729–30 season, adding to her repertory such roles as a Witch in *Harlequin Sorcerer*, Phyllis in *The Capricious Lovers*, Diana in *Apollo and Daphne*, Selima in *The Sultan*, Lavinia in *Camilla*, and the title part in *The Rape of Proserpine*. She continued offering solo songs, and her benefits usually filled the coffers. During the 1720s and 1730s one of her rivals in song was the quixotic Jane Barbier, and the *Gentleman's Magazine* in January 1777 recalled that Jane was for some time banished from the stage due to Mrs Chambers's enormous popularity, and that on one occasion Isabella's faithful followers hissed *la Barbier* roundly.

Of Mrs Chambers's private life almost nothing is known. From the start of her career she was styled "Mrs," which address at that period did not, of course, necessarily indicate that she was married. The Lincoln's Inn Fields free list for 1726–27 contains references to a Mr Chambers, to a Captain Chambers, to Mrs Chambers's mother, and to a brother and a sister.

Isabella's name disappeared from the bills in June 1730, and not until 20 November 1732 was she mentioned again. On that date she sang Ardelia in *Teraminta* at Lincoln's Inn Fields for Arne, John Rich's company having removed to the new Covent Garden Theatre. In the spring of 1733 she sang in two works, the oratorio *Judith* on 16 February and the opera *Rosamond* on 7 March. In both cases the bills styled her, apparently in error, "Miss" Chambers. In *Judith* she took the title part, substituting for Cecilia Young, who "pretended Sickness"; in *Rosamond* she was Grideline.

Mrs Chambers reappeared at Drury Lane on 15 April 1734 as Venus in *Cupid and*

Psyche, but she was apparently not a regular member of the company there. She joined Giffard's troupe at Goodman's Fields in 1734–35, making her first appearance as a singing soloist on 16 September 1734. During the season, in addition to many specialty offerings, she sang the title role in *Britannia*, a Spirit in *The Necromancer*, and Io in *Jupiter and Io*. She remained with Giffard through 1736–37, taking such new parts as Oenone in *Harlequin Shipwrecked*, a Priestess in *Hymen's Triumph*, Arabella in *The Honest Yorkshireman*, and Polly in *The Beggar's Opera*. It was under Giffard's management on 6 April 1736 that she acted Cherry in *The Stratagem*, the "first Time of her appearing in the Dramatick Way" – and the last.

One of the few commentaries we have on Isabella Chambers comes from the period in her career when she was, perhaps, past her prime. On 3 January 1736 Thomas Gray wrote to Horace Walpole that he had seen *King Arthur*, with Purcell's music, at Goodman's Fields. In "every one of the Choruses Mrs CHAMBERS sung ye chief part, accompanied with Roarings, Squawlings and Squeakatons dire." He especially enjoyed, however, the frost scene with its fine scenery and the "singers, viz: Mrs Chambers, &c: and dancers all rubbing their hands and chattering with cold with fur gowns and worsted gloves in abundance."

Mrs Chambers sang again with Giffard's troupe at Lincoln's Inn Fields in 1736–37, but the Licensing Act curtailed the activity of the minor theatres the following season, and in 1737–38 she made no recorded appearances. In 1738–39 she rejoined Rich's company and performed at Covent Garden, but not as frequently as in earlier years. During that season and the following two, she sang several of her old pantomime roles and added Andromeda in *Perseus and Andromeda*, a Villager in *Orpheus and Eurydice*, and Diana in *The Royal Chace*. On 8 April 1741 she shared a benefit with

Roberts, her last one on record; the accounts showed receipts of £169 13s. On 24 April she sang Andromeda, and on 29 April she was one of the Villagers in *Orpheus and Eurydice*, after which her name disappeared from the bills.

The *Gentleman's Magazine* of January 1777 reported that Mrs Chambers had married the Master of the Hummums Bagnio; if true, perhaps that ceremony was after the conclusion of her stage career. Hummums was owned by Dr John Colbatch from 1704 to 1723, by William Boen from 1723 to about 1739, by John Rigg from 1739 until after 1748, and finally by John Henry Rigg who was proprietor at the time it burned down in 1769. One of these men may have married Isabella Chambers.

Chambers, John [*fl.* 1702], *mountebank.*

On 3 October 1702 the *Post Man* listed a number of strollers who were required to pay 2s. daily to town constables, and among those named was John Chambers. The men named were also called "mountebanks." Since the paper was published in London, they presumably performed there.

Chambers, Mrs William, Elizabeth, [née Davis?] *d. 1792, singer, actress.*

Billed as a gentlewoman who never appeared on any stage before, Elizabeth Chambers began her career as Polly in *The Beggar's Opera* at Covent Garden on 27 September 1751. *The Present State of the Stage* (1753) commented that "Mrs. Chambers [has] great Merit in Polly Peachum. . . . Her Voice is weak, but very sweet; and she would render her Figure much more pleasing, and it is very agreeable, could she shake off a Particularity in her Gait, which is very hurtful to her Person." Perhaps she improved in time, though the criticism came too late to be of help her first season, during which she played Jessica "(with songs adapted to the

Harvard Theatre Collection

ELIZABETH CHAMBERS and THOMAS LOWE, in *The Beggar's Opera*

engraving by McArdell, after Pine

character)" in *The Merchant of Venice*, sang the "Sheep Shearing" song in *The Country Lasses* in a new setting by Arne, acted Philadelphia in *The Amorous Widow*, and (for her benefit, shared with two others on 25 April 1752) sang "If Love's a Sweet Passion" after Act IV of *The Refusal*.

In the seasons that followed, Mrs Chambers advanced but slowly at Covent Gar-den. She added to her repertory only Har-riot in *The Lover His Own Rival*, Chloe in *The Lottery*, Nell in *The Devil to Pay*, Manto (with a song) in *Oedipus*, a Pas-toral Nymph in *Comus*, Mrs Modish in *The Tanner of York*, Arbella in *The Honest Yorkshireman*, Laura in *The Chaplet*, and, most importantly, Ophelia in *Hamlet* (on 2 November 1754). Some of these roles perhaps should be assigned to the Mrs

Chambers (or Chalmers?) who first appeared at Covent Garden in May 1754, but it is likely that all belong to Mrs William Chambers.

In addition to her named roles in plays, Mrs Chambers sang in performances of *Romeo and Juliet, Macbeth, Theodosius, The Prophetess,* and *The Sheepshearing,* and she contributed songs in entr'acte entertainments. In 1753 she also sang at Marylebone Gardens.

The 1757–58 season appears to have been her last at Covent Garden. On 24 April 1758 she shared a benefit with two others. She played Laura in *The Chaplet* and Ophelia, and though she sold £42 18s. in tickets, the performance showed a deficit of £4 3s. 6d. for each beneficiary.

Folger Shakespeare Library

Pastoral song, sung by ELIZABETH CHAMBERS at Ranelagh

Elizabeth Chambers is said to have re-tired to Chiswick after leaving the stage and to have died in 1792. It is probable that a will of an Elizabeth Chambers, drawn on 23 August 1788 and proved on 22 October 1792, was hers. At the time the will was made Elizabeth's husband William was still living, apparently in Edmonton, just north of London. By an indenture dated 22 December 1770, William allowed Elizabeth to make her own will and dispose of property which, by law, belonged to him. The arrangement suggests that the pair were separated but amicable. Using the indenture, Elizabeth bequeathed £200 to William Chambers, the son of her husband (but not by her, inferentially). To her brother John Davis she gave another £200. These legacies were to be paid out of money due to Elizabeth on a £1000 bond from the Shakespearean scholar Edmond Malone. To Malone's brother Richard, Lord Sunderlin of Ireland, she left a ring and 10 guineas; to Malone she left five guineas; to John and Sybilla Walker of Harley Street she left a total of 15 guineas; to Elinor Stephens of Barbados she left a watch; to John Norris of Coventry Street, instrument-maker, she left five guineas; and to Norris's four sisters she left five guineas each.

She asked Lord Sunderlin and Daniel Beaumont, of Lyde Street, Bloomsbury, to collect the £1000 from Malone. The interest on £400 of this sum was to go to the younger William Chambers and John Davis until the principal was paid. The interest on the other £600 was to go to Francis Dudley Fitzmaurice in a similar fashion. The will explained that Fitzmaurice was born in Frederick Street, Dublin, the son of the Earl of Derry, that he was educated by Elizabeth as her own son and that he was living with her in 1788. Fitzmaurice and Beaumont were to be her executors.

Elizabeth Chambers and Thomas Lowe, as Polly and Macheath, were painted in 1752 by R. E. Pine in one of his earliest works. J. McArdell made an engraving in mezzotint of the Pine painting.

Chamless. *See* CHAMPNESS.

Chamness or Chamnys. *See* CHAMPNESS and CHAMPNEYS.

"Champion, Mr" [*fl. 1738*], *actor.*
At Southwark Fair on 5 September 1738 a "Mr Champion" played St George in *Merlin*—but the actor's name was doubtless a pseudonym, for the cast listed "Signior Furioso" as the Spanish Giant and "Old-man" as Merlin.

Champness. *See also* CHAMPNEYS.

Champness, the Masters [*fl. 1794*], *singers. See* CHAMPNESS, THOMAS WELDON.

Champness, Samuel Thomas *d. 1803, singer, actor.*
Samuel Thomas Champness, according to his obituary in the *Gentleman's Magazine* (October 1803), sang as a boy under the direction of Handel. The great composer apparently wrote several songs expressly for the young Champness in the part of Benjamin in the oratorio of *Joseph and his Brethren*, which was performed at Covent Garden on 2 March 1744. Champness devoted most of his long professional career to singing in the oratorios at the London theatres and in various professional and charity concerts.

Champness's oratorio singing was mainly associated with Handel's works and included many performances of the *Messiah*, which he sang at the Chapel of the Foundling Hospital on 15 May 1754 (when he was paid 10s. 6d.), on 27 April 1758 (when he was paid £1 11s. 6d.), in May 1759 (for the same fee), and in March 1774. His other appearances in the *Messiah* included 13 May 1767 at the Chapel of the Lock Hospital, 10 December 1768 at Haberdasher's Hall, and 18 February 1774 at the Haymarket. He sang in *Acis and Galatea* at the Great Room in Dean Street on 1 April 1758 and at the Haymarket on 13 November 1765; in *Alexander's Feast* at Ranelagh on 1 June 1767; in *The Cure of Saul* at Drury Lane on 27 April 1763 and at the King's on 5 February 1768; in *Judas Maccabaeus* at the Dean Street Room in 1760, at the Haymarket in April of 1769, 1770, and 1771, and at Covent Garden on 23 February 1776; in *Judith* at the Lock Hospital on 29 February 1764 and at the Stratford Jubilee in September 1769; in *Ruth* at the Lock Hospital on 25 May 1768 and 3 April 1776; and in *Omnipotence* and *Samson* at the Haymarket in February 1774. His frequent oratorio appearances in the provinces included those at Bath in 1755, Oxford in 1759, and the Three Choirs Festival in 1760 and 1763.

Between 1748 and 1774, Champness also was a featured bass singer at Drury Lane, where his career coincided with that of Garrick, with whom evidently he was on friendly terms. Champness's first theatrical role, so far as is known, was as Friar John in *Romeo and Juliet* on 29 November 1748. He shared net benefit receipts of £85 with Mars, Gray, and Harrison on 9 May 1749 and about £150 with Dickenson and Harrison on 6 May 1751. At the Haymarket on 29 May 1754, he sang with Mrs Arne and the Misses Scott in Thomas A. Arne's new English opera, *Eliza*. He performed at Marylebone Gardens in 1757 and at Ranelagh in 1762 and 1764.

Champness's usual roles at Drury Lane included Hecate in *Macbeth*—a part in which, strangely, he established a considerable reputation—the Demon of Revenge in the very popular *Cymon*, and vocal performances in *Romeo and Juliet*, *Theodosius*, *King Arthur*, *Timoleon*, *Alfred*, *A Christmas Tale*, and *The Heroine of the Cave*. On 31 December 1759, he introduced Boyce's "Hearts of Oak" in *Harlequin's Invasion*, and in the same season regularly

sang Michael Arne's "New Sailor's Song" and Boyce's "Bacchanalian Song." On 2 November 1765, while earning £4 per week, he sang in *Almena*, a new serious opera by Michael Arne, which, though it met with a favorable reception on opening night, was performed only five other nights to thin houses. In 1766–67 his salary was still at £4 per week. He played Caliban (with songs) for the first time on 5 May 1767, and in the following season acted the title role of *The Cunning Man*, on 10 February 1768. In 1769–70, with Vernon, Mrs Baddeley, Miss Radley, and others, he sang in Garrick's production of the *Jubilee Ode*, which ran for 90 performances at Drury Lane that season and allowed Garrick to recover his expenses for the financial disaster he had suffered at Stratford and to turn a handsome profit as well. Champness sang a selection of catches and glees with Mrs Scott on 27 April 1771, and at the end of the following season, on 6 May 1772, he shared net benefit receipts of £88 1*s.* with her; again on 10 May 1773 he shared net receipts of £55 2*s.* 6*d.* with Mrs Scott, and in that season introduced an interlude of singing, in which he personified Wit in *Amphitryon*.

At the end of 1773–74, Champness retired from the stage. Garrick played in *Zara* for his benefit on 13 May 1774, at which time Champness took £58 7*s.* 6*d.* He continued, however, to keep up his reputation as an eminent bass singer by appearing in concerts for a number of years, including the oratorios at Drury Lane in 1777, at the Haymarket in 1779, and at Covent Garden in 1789, 1790, and 1792. Champness was among the vocal performers in the Handel Memorial Concerts at Westminster Abbey and the Pantheon in May and June of 1784. He returned to the theatres occasionally to sing in the programs of the Catch Club, such as those sung at Covent Garden on 17 April 1779, 18 April 1780, and 6 May 1783.

Between 1763 and 1794, Champness

lived in Tothill Street, Westminster. He was a member of the Royal Society of Musicians and served that Society on its Court of Assistants in 1798. He was also a member of the Chapel Royal, his place there taken by Sale on 19 January 1803, by which time Champness's health had apparently faded. He died at the end of September or in early October of 1803. On 17 October 1803, administration of his estate, valued under £600, was granted to Ann Champness, spinster, and Thomas Weldon Champness, his daughter and son. At the time he was described as Samuel Thomas Champnes [*sic*], widower, of the parish of St Margaret, Westminster. Thomas Weldon Champness was no doubt one of the two singers, Master Champness and Master Champness, Junior, listed in Doane's *Musical Directory* as living at Samuel Thomas Champness's address in 1794. The Rev Weldon Champness, vicar of St Pancras, Middlesex, and also an oratorio singer, was the brother of Samuel.

Samuel Champness, according to a press clipping at the British Museum, though not a remarkably good general singer, had a voice peculiarly fitted for oratorios — "full, deep, and majestic." Champness was pictured as Nigromant with Thomas Weston as Tycho in a scene from *A Christmas Tale* painted by De Loutherbourg which was exhibited at the Royal Academy in 1774 but is now lost. Engravings of the work by Charles Phillips are in the Harvard Theatre Collection and the British Museum. Presumably Champness is shown in the same character in a pen and pencil water color, "Floridor fighting Nigromant and the Demons," which is in the Musée des Beaux-Arts, Strasbourg.

Champness, Thomas Weldon ₍fl. 1794–1803₎, *singer.*

In 1794, Doane's *Musical Directory* listed a Master Champness and a Master Champness, Junior, both living at Tothill Street, Westminster, the address of their father, Samuel Champness. Both were described as members of St Peter's Choir and as singers at Drury Lane Theatre and in the oratorios at Covent Garden. Their names, however, appear in no theatrical records we have seen. One of them was no doubt Thomas Weldon Champness, who with a sister, Ann Champness, was granted administration of Samuel Champness's estate on 17 October 1803.

Champness, Weldon ₍fl. 1758–1798₎, *singer.*

Weldon Champness was, no doubt, the Champness whose name was found in the list of singers, at 10s. 6d., for performances of the *Messiah* at the Chapel of the Foundling Hospital in April 1758 and May 1759. The other Champness in the same list (at £1 11s. 6d.) was Samuel, the well-known bass, presumably his brother. Both were cited by Burney as vocal performers in the Handel Memorial Concerts at Westminster Abbey and the Pantheon in May and June, 1784. In 1794, Doane's *Musical Directory* listed the Reverend Weldon Champness, "alto tenor" (countertenor), as living at No 1, St Paul's College, a minor canon of St Paul's, a member of the New Musical Fund, participant in the Handelian Memorial performances at Westminster Abbey, and a member of the choirs of St Peter's, Windsor, and Eton. Weldon Champness witnessed the will of the musician Thomas Aylward on 13 February 1798, at which time he was identified as vicar of St Pancras, Middlesex.

Champneys. *See also* CHAMPNESS.

Champnouveau. *See* CHANNOUVEAU.

Champville, Gabriel-Léonard Hervé du Bus de ₍fl. 1749–1789₎, *actor.*

Gabriel-Léonard Hervé du Bus, called Champville (or de Champville), and sometimes Soli (Soly), was a member of the French company brought to London by

Jean Louis Monnet in November 1749. Their appearance at the Haymarket in *Les amans reunis* on 14 November prompted a disturbance by anti-French factions, and the rest of their engagement, consisting of only three other performances, was beset by troubles. On 22 May 1750, Garrick gave Monnet and his company a benefit at Drury Lane. In a manuscript account of disbursements made by Monnet, now in the Forster Collection at the Victoria and Albert Museum, Champville's salary for his London engagement was stated as £87 10*s*., of which he received only £52 10*s*.

In May 1749, having returned from London, Champville made his debut at the Comédie-Italienne at Paris as an *amoureux* in *Surprise de la haine*. By 1754 he was a "*simple pensionnaire*" in that company and, on 21 April 1759, was appointed as a *sociétaire* at 3000 livres. His specialties were the roles of *amoureux* and parodies of peasants and old women. He left the Comédie-Italienne in 1769 with a pension of 3000 livres, and was still alive, according to Campardon, at the beginning of 1789.

Champville's portrait in the character of Colas was engraved by J. B. de Lorraine after De Lorme.

Chanlue. *See* DESHALN.

Channel, Luke   [*fl.* 1653–1691?], dancing master.

Luke Channel (or Cheynell), probably of French extraction, organized a private performance of Shirley's masque, *Cupid and Death*, for presentation before the Portuguese ambassador on 26 March 1653. By 24 September 1660 Channel was running a dancing school in Broad Street which Pepys described as "the house that was formerly the glass-house . . . where I saw good dancing, but it growing late, and the room very full of people and so very hot, I went home." Channel was mentioned that same year in *Select City Queries* as a "hop-

merchant"—the cant term for dancing master.

By 1664–65 Channel had joined the Duke's Company at their Lincoln's Inn Fields playhouse, and it is probable that he served the troupe as dancing master and perhaps a performer for at least the following ten years. His name appeared occasionally in the Lord Chamberlain's accounts, usually in connection with his membership in the Duke's Company, but once, on 23 February 1665, in relation to a suit between Channel and a William Carpenter. The dancing master's greatest claim to fame came in 1673 when he and Josias Priest created the dances for the new operatic version of *Macbeth*, done at Dorset Garden on 18 February with music by Locke.

Nothing more is known of Channel's activity after that, though two later references may concern him. On 4 September 1678 Joseph Prince of Greenwich married Judith Channell, spinster, age 20, daughter of Luke Channel, Gentleman, also of Greenwich. Interestingly, there was a Joseph Prince who was born about 1657 who became dancing master at Drury Lane. A Luke Channell, described as "Aged," was buried on 1 January 1691 at St Bride, Fleet Street, but there is no way of determining whether or not that was the dancing master.

Channouveau, Jean   [*fl.* 1661–1667], manager, actor.

Jean Godart, Sieur de Channouveau (or Champnouveau), led a troupe of French players to London in 1661–62, apparently at the request, or at least with the blessing, of Charles II. On 10 December 1661, according to the State Papers, he was granted £300, probably a gift from the King. The company had arrived in the summer of 1661 and had established themselves at the Cockpit in Drury Lane. There Pepys saw them on 30 August. They acted at Whitehall on 16 December, witnessed by Evelyn, and they were probably the troupe seen by a Danish student on 30 January 1662 performing *Andromède*. It is likely that during their stay the company also acted *Le Mariage d'Orphée et d'Eurydice*.

Channouveau was at the Hague in November 1663, leading a troupe in partnership with de la Granière, and in March 1664 he was in the Troupe de Mademoiselle in Brussels. He joined the company at the Marais Theatre in Paris in 1665, and from that company he retired in 1667.

Chantrell or **Chantrill**. *See* CANTRELL.

Chanu. *See* PIELTAIN.

Chanville. *See* "CHAMPVILLE."

Chapelle. *See* DE LA CHAPELLE.

Chaperone. *See* CAPERON.

Chaplain. *See* CHAPLIN.

Chaplin, Henry *d. 1789, actor, singer.*
Before appearing at London, Henry Chaplin acted at the Crow Street Theatre in Dublin, between 1770 and 1774, and at Cork in 1774. On 3 March 1773 he was one of several Crow Street actors agreeing to perform regularly with Charles Macklin. Chaplin made his London debut as Ratcliff in *Richard III* on 22 October 1774 at Covent Garden. During the remainder of the season he acted similar minor roles, such as the lieutenant in *Jane Gray*, an officer in *Phaedra and Hippolitus*, and Philario in *Cymbeline*. As a member of Foote's summer company at the Haymarket in 1775 he acted Quaver in *The Virgin Unmask'd*, Francis in *Cross Purposes*, Alphonso in *The Spanish Fryar*, Sir Charles in *The Beaux' Stratagem*, Knowlife in *The Tobacconist*, Mat in *The Beggar's Opera*, and roles in *Eldred*, *The Orators*, and *A Trip to Portsmouth*. He returned to Foote's company in the summer of 1776, adding Alberto in *A Duke and No Duke* to his modest repertory.

Chaplin joined Drury Lane in 1776–77, at £1 10s. per week, as a utility actor and tenor in the chorus. He made his first appearance there as Oswald in *Matilda* on 28 September 1775. That season he acted a soldier in *The Roman Father* and sang in the funeral procession of Juliet in *Romeo and Juliet* and as a spirit in *The Tempest*. In this journeyman capacity he passed a total of 13 consecutive seasons, serving as Dorilas in *Cymon*, Reginald in *The Battle of Hastings*, Perdiccas in *Alexander the Great*, the Justice in *The Provok'd Wife*, Balthazar in *Romeo and Juliet*, Douglas in *1 Henry IV*, Stanley in *Richard III*, a captain in *King Lear*, the Player King in *Hamlet*, the Duke in *Othello*, and an officer in *Tancred and Sigismunda*, and singing in such pieces as *The Devil to Pay*, *The First Floor*, and *The Triumph of Mirth*. On 8 May 1777 he appeared in a minor, unspecified part in the first performance of *The School for Scandal*. The Drury Lane account books indicate his financial hard luck for three consecutive years, 1783, 1784, and 1785, when his benefits, shared with several other actors, resulted in successive deficits, of £81 10s. 1d., £80 7s. 10d., and £76 19s. For his benefit on 18 May 1779 he shared profits of £146 16s. with Griffith, Holcroft, and Miss Field.

Chaplin's last performances were as Duke Frederick in *As You Like It* and a footman in *The Devil to Pay* on 13 June 1789. Several weeks later (on 27 June according to Winston's Drury Lane "Fund Book," and on 29 June according to the Jerome papers) he died. Charles Chaplin, stage manager at Liverpool and Manchester and also of Drury Lane in the nineteenth century, may have been his son. The latter's son, also named Charles Chaplin, and who was also stage manager at Liverpool, died at that city on 18 October 1841, aged 26.

Chapman, Mr [fl. 1674], *actor*.
Mr Chapman was a member of the King's Company and acted Buggio in *The*

Amorous Old Woman in March 1674, probably at the new Drury Lane Theatre but possibly at Lincoln's Inn Fields, where the troupe played while their new house was being built.

Chapman, Mr [*fl.* 1756–1762], *musician.*

Though his position in the Covent Garden band is not known, Mr Chapman must have been one of the more prominent members, for he received benefits (or tickets he sold were accepted at benefit time) from 1756–57 through 1761–62, and on two occasions the accounts show that he received twice as much money as the next-highest-paid person listed. On 12 April 1760, for instance, his share came to £21 4*s.*, and on 17 April 1761 it was £24. Yet a company account dated 22 September 1760 listed him as one of the musicians earning a nightly fee of only 3*s.* 4*d.* When benefit time came, he apparently spared no effort of advertisement to augment his income.

Chapman, Mr [*fl.* 1775], *actor.*

A Mr Chapman played Sprightly in *The Author* for Mrs Gardner's benefit at the Haymarket Theatre on 20 August 1775.

Chapman, Mr [*fl.* 1776–1817?], *house servant.*

A Drury Lane doorkeeper named Chapman was entered in the account books at 9*s.* weekly for the 1776–77 season. A Mr Chapman, possibly the same person, was earning the same salary as checktaker in 1803–4, and from 1812 through 1817 a Chapman was working as a boxkeeper at the same theatre.

Chapman, Mr [*fl.* 1794], *violinist.*

According to Doane's *Musical Directory* of 1794, a violinist named Chapman, of Shoemaker Row, Houndsditch, played for the Handelian Society.

Chapman, Mr [*fl.* 1799–1804?], *dancer?*

On 13 April 1799 and several dates following, a Mr Chapman played one of the Domestics in *Raymond and Agnes*. He was probably a dancer. He or another Chapman acted at Covent Garden in 1800–1801 and again in 1803–4.

Chapman, Charlotte Jane, formerly Mrs MORTON 1762–1805, *actress, singer.*

Charlotte Jane Chapman was born in America in 1762 but spent most of her life in England. Her father was ruined by the Revolutionary War and sent his daughter to Yorkshire to live with a relative. Miss Chapman acted with Suett at York before 1780, and it may have been there that she met and eloped with a strolling actor named Morton. Her hubsand took her to his home town of Shrewsbury where he entered business and, according to *The Secret History of the Green Room* (1790), treated his bride inhumanly. Charlotte left Morton, resumed her maiden name, and joined a troupe of players at Chester. There she came under Hodgkinson's management, and with him she toured to Cheltenham and on to Margate, where she was acting by the summer of 1788, just prior to her London debut.

Harris brought Miss Chapman from Margate at a cost of £5 5*s.* and hired her at a weekly salary of £4 for the 1788–89 season at Covent Garden. She made her first appearance there as Yarico in *Inkle and Yarico* on 22 October 1788 and followed that role with Lady Betty in *The Careless Husband*, Angelina in *Love Makes a Man*, Ann Lovely in *A Bold Stroke for a Wife*, and Araminta in *The Old Bachelor*. After her successful first season in London she returned to Margate in August 1789, one of her parts there being Charlotte in *He Would Be a Soldier*. Then she returned to Covent Garden for the 1789–90 season and received a £1 raise. Among her new roles were Lady Lurewell in *The Constant Couple*, Nerissa in *The Merchant of Venice*, Caelia in *As You Like It*, Lavinia in *The Fair Penitent*, Mrs Fainall in *The Way of the World*, and the Abbess in *A Comedy of Errors*.

Miss Chapman continued at Covent Garden at £6 weekly through the 1803–4 season as a major member of the troupe, gradually adding over the years a sizeable number of significant roles, most of them in comedies but a few in tragedies. Among them were, in chronological order, Selima in *Tamerlane*, Elvira in *Love Makes a Man*, the first Constantia in *The Chances*, Parisatis in *Alexander the Great*, Catherine in *Catherine and Petruchio*, Mrs Strickland in *The Suspicious Husband*, Melinda in *The*

Harvard Theatre Collection

CHARLOTTE JANE CHAPMAN, as Augusta Aubrey

engraving by Thornthwaite, after De Wilde

Recruiting Officer, the Lady in *Comus*, Hero in *Much Ado About Nothing*, Lady Anne (and later Queen Elizabeth) in *Richard III*, Mrs Ford in *The Merry Wives of Windsor*, Clarinda in *The Double Gallant*, Angelica in *Love for Love*, Alithea in *The Country Girl*, Lady Sneerwell in *The School for Scandal*, Gertrude in *Hamlet*, Lady Grace in *The Provok'd Husband*, Anne Bullen in *Henry VIII*, and Lady Percy in *1 Henry IV*.

During the 1790s Charlotte also made other appearances. She was one of the professionals in the Earl of Barrymore's Wargrave theatricals in 1790–92; she acted at Margate in the summer of 1792; she appeared for the first time in Birmingham on 8 July 1795; she went to Ireland and played at Cork on 5 October 1797; and, beginning in the summer of 1799, she acted with the summer company at the Haymarket Theatre in London.

Critical compliment to Miss Chapman was not extravagant, especially considering the importance of many of her roles. The *Biographical and Imperial Magazine* in November 1790 said "Miss Chapman (a tall, *comely* breeches figure) is only tolerable in a part which requires much exertion to make the Piece at all bearable." But on 16 January 1792, after she had substituted for Mrs Esten as Honoria in *Notoriety*, the *Morning Herald* felt she had "sustained the part with . . . good sense, delicacy and feeling." John Williams's *A Pin Basket to the Children of Thespis* in 1797 described Miss Chapman's quiet style in verse:

She's so humble her soul scarcely asks
       for a meed
. . . .
In those trim walking ladies whom
       Decency guides,
She can steer her neat bark through Probation's rough tides;
Though her tones are too sombrous for
       Fashion's vagary,
And she's somewhat too tall to be flippant and airy . . .

And the *Authentic Memoirs of the Green Room* (1799) reported that "Her figure is prepossessing, her expression good, but her musical powers indifferent [she was a soprano]; she performs those characters where *person*, more than power, is required."

Miss Chapman lived at No 16, Henrietta Street, Covent Garden, in 1791, but by the spring of 1794 she had moved to No 33, Norfolk Street, the Strand. Her sister, Mrs Beverly, made her first appearance at Covent Garden on 30 September 1801, shortly before Charlotte's career ended. Miss Chapman was buried at St Paul, Covent Garden on 14 February 1805.

De Wilde painted her as Augusta Aubrey in *The Fashionable Lover*, and Thornthwaite engraved the painting for *Bell's British Theatre*, 1793. De Wilde also pictured her as Celia in *The School for Lovers*, and P. Audinet engraved this likeness for Bell.

Chapman, Christopher *d. 1681,* singer.

Christopher Chapman was a member of the Chapel Royal from at least as early as 30 March 1661 when the Westminster Abbey Precentor's Book mentioned his being paid 7s. 4d. for singing at Princess Mary's funeral. On 23 April 1669 a Christopher Chapman was involved in a suit against Henry Killigrew; perhaps Christopher the singer was in some way connected with the Bridges Street Theatre which the Killigrew family operated.

Though nothing more is known of Chapman's career, his will, the will of his daughter Ann Chapman Clayton, and the Westminster Abbey registers provide us with information concerning his personal life. Chapman wrote his will on 29 May 1681 and was buried on 17 June. His will was proved by his wife Melior on 28 July. He left his widow three parcels of freehold land in Buckinghamshire and, in trust, two houses near Dean Yard, Westminster.

Upon Mrs Chapman's death the country property was to go to Christopher's daughter Ann, who had married John Clayton. Melior Chapman died on 6 July 1707 and was buried four days later in the Cloisters of Westminster Abbey where her husband lay. Ann Chapman Clayton died in January 1718.

Christopher and Melior Chapman had at least four other children, all of whom died before the singer. William was baptized on 26 November 1662 and buried on 21 March 1663. Peter, a minor son, died on 1 February 1673 and was buried three days later. Christopher, who received his Cambridge A.B. in 1667 and A.M. in 1671, died in Cambridge (apparently) on 25 March 1675 and was buried at Westminster Abbey two days later. Elizabeth died on 11 March 1681 and was buried four days later at the Abbey.

Chapman, [George?] [fl. 1792–1804?], exhibitor, treasurer.

The Mr Chapman who exhibited De Loutherbourg's *Eidophusikon* in the 1790s was said to have been married to a Covent Garden actress. The Mrs Chapman who performed at that theatre in 1800 was reported by the *Gentleman's Magazine* of May 1804 to have been the wife of a hosier in Pool Lane; she was also mentioned on 13 May 1796 in the *Hibernian Journal* as having married George Chapman, the treasurer of the Crow Street Theatre in Dublin. No certain identification can be made, but it is possible that all the above references were to the same man.

After De Loutherbourg's *Eidophusikon* had been on exhibition under the designer's aegis for a few years, the scenes and machines were purchased by Mr Chapman. He exhibited the *Eidophusikon* in February 1792 at Davis's Great Room, No 60, Great George's Street, Dublin. Later, in April 1799, he exhibited at the small theatre in Panton Street, off the Haymarket, in London. Chapman made some additions to the scenery and augmented the show to include a monologue by John Britton, musical glasses by Mr Wilkinson, and a learned dog "whose sagacious tricks were . . . much admired." Britton remembered in his *Autobiography* that the night of his first appearance was disturbed by "a noted roué lord, who was in the habit of frequenting the minor theatres for the express purpose of annoying performers, and disturbing audiences, by vulgar and disgusting conduct."

Chapman's theatre and its contents burned in March 1800 in a fire which started in a brothel opposite the tennis court in James Street. Chapman lost between £600 and £700, for the property was not insured.

Chapman, Mrs George, Frances R., née Brett *d. 1804, actress, singer.*

Frances R. Brett was called by the *Thespian Dictionary* (1805) the daughter of a musician (apparently not William Brett the singer-actor, though possibly she was related to him) who performed in Ireland until at least 1792. William Brett's daughter, also named Frances, became the second Mrs John Hodgkinson, and has sometimes been confused with our subject.

Frances R. Brett's theatrical career began in Ireland. The earliest mention of her activities was in 1788 when she acted at Dublin's Crow Street Theatre. In 1789 she performed at Cork and Waterford; in 1791 she appeared in Drogheda; she was at Kilkenny, Waterford, Galway, and Wexford in 1792 and at Wexford, Limerick, and Cork in 1793. Some of her roles during those years are known. In June 1792 at Kilkenny she sang Rosetta in *Love in a Village*; in July of the same year at Waterford the repertory was built around her singing talent and consisted chiefly of operettas; at her benefit in Galway in September 1792 she sang a part in *The Haunted Tower* and played Jack Rover in *Wild Oats*; and in July 1793 in Limerick she

played Maria in *The School for Scandal* at Mrs Abington's benefit and Young Hob in *Hob in the Well* at her own. For her benefit she surprised everyone by being on hand at the theatre from ten to three selling tickets before donning her male attire to play Young Hob.

Miss Brett was at Cork again in 1794 and at Carrick-On-Suir and Cork in 1795. When she acted at Carrick-On-Suir in October 1795 she was billed, according to Clark, as Mrs Chapman, though the public records in Dublin date her marriage license 1796 and the *Hibernian Journal* of 13 May of that year reported her as having lately married the Crow Street Theatre treasurer, George Chapman. Since she had signed herself Frances R. Brett on 30 March in the same journal, her marriage probably took place in April 1796. She seems to have masqueraded as Mrs Chapman in the provinces a few months before her marriage (unless Clark's "1795" should read "1796").

Mrs Chapman acted at Cork again in the fall of 1797, stayed in Ireland for the 1797–98 season, and then sailed for England. After a brief engagement at Liverpool she was hired by Harris at £3 weekly for the 1798–99 Covent Garden season. Her debut there was as Moggy M'Gilpin in *The Highland Reel* on 1 November 1798; she was billed as from the Theatre Royal, Dublin. The *Monthly Mirror* commended Mrs Chapman as "Combining the talents of an actress with no inconsiderable musical ability" and felt she would be "extremely serviceable to the interests of the Theatre." She went on to play during that season such roles as Wowski in *Inkle and Yarico*, Barbara in *The Iron Chest*, a Witch in *Harlequin Chaplet*, and Clara in *Hartford Bridge*. Her benefit on 28 May 1799, shared with two others, presented her as Augusta in *Life's Vagaries*, her first appearance in that role.

After playing at Liverpool in the summer of 1799 Mrs Chapman returned to

Covent Garden for the 1799–1800 season, starting off with another new part, Jacintha in *The Suspicious Husband*, on 20 September 1799. During the season she also acted Philippo in *The Castle of Andalusia*, Mariana in *The Miser*, Mrs Dangle in *The Critic*, and Jane in *Wild Oats*. She also sang in the performances of *Macbeth* and *Romeo and Juliet*. One of her appearances during the season provoked a comment from Thomas Dutton in *The Dramatic Censor*: "We know not, whether it may be owing to the form of Mrs. CHAPMAN'S headdress, and the uncouth diadem she wears, as the princess Almina [in *Ramah Droog*], but her face exhibits the exact archtype of a *beef-eater*."

Mrs Chapman left the stage temporarily after that season but not in a huff over Dutton's criticism: on 14 November 1800 her son was born. Though Mrs Chapman had built a good career in Ireland, she was making little headway in London. She appeared at Birmingham in the summer of 1802, but after that she seems to have given up the stage.

Mrs Chapman died at Liverpool in April 1804, described in the papers as formerly of Covent Garden and now the wife of a hosier in Pool Lane. George Chapman, after his fling at exhibiting De Loutherbourg's *Eidophusikon* in London about 1800, seems to have taken up a new trade.

Chapman, Richard ₍fl. *1787–c. 1795?*₎, *instrumentalist, composer.*

In 1787–88 Richard Chapman was paid £6 as a violinist for participation in concerts presented by the Academy of Ancient Music. Doane's *Musical Directory* of 1794 indicated that Chapman was proficient on the viola, violoncello, and organ as well, and that he served as organist at the Paddington Church and played in concerts presented by the New Musical Fund. His address was No 7, Winchester Row, Lisson Green. Chapman also composed, mostly songs. Some of his airs were used in a pro-

duction of *The What Is It?* at the Royal Circus on 12 May 1789. His published works included some songs for *The Feast of Apollo* (1788), *The Overture & Favorite Airs, selected from the popular Entertainments of the Bastille, and Naval Review* (1789), and *Six Favorite New Songs* (c. 1795).

Chapman, Robert ₍fl. *1794*₎, *violinist.*

Doane's *Musical Directory* of 1794 listed Robert Chapman as a violinist living in Duke Street, Aldgate. He performed for the Cecilian Society.

Chapman, Thomas *c. 1683–1747, actor.*

Thomas Chapman may have been born about 1683, but clear evidence has not been found. His supposed descendant, George Ford, wrote a fictionalized biography of the Chapmans and Drakes (*These Were Actors*, 1955) in which he suggested 1683 as an approximate birthdate for Chapman, but as with most information in his book, Ford provided no proof.

Chapman's first notice in theatrical records was on 14 May 1723 when he shared a benefit with two others at Lincoln's Inn Fields. The Drury Lane managers must have tried to lure him to their fold, for on 23 May the Lincoln's Inn Fields manager, John Rich, wrote to Wilks, Booth, and Cibber at Drury Lane telling them "to take notice that Mʳ Chapman & Mʳ Merrival are entertain'd as Actors at the Theatre Royal in Lincoln's Inn Fields. . . ." Some accommodation may have been made, for the first edition of *The Impertinent Lovers* (presented at Drury Lane on 16 August 1723) listed Chapman as Meanwell. In September at Pinkethman's Southwark Fair booth Chapman acted Sir Robert Brackenbury in the droll *Jane Shore* and Rakish in *The Blind Beggar of Bethnal Green*.

Chapman insisted on trying serious roles, but Davies in his *Dramatic Miscellanies* said the actor turned "dissonant and un-harmonious" in tragedies. His first recorded role of the tragic sort was Albany in *King Lear* which he acted for his shared benefit with Hulett on 15 May 1724 at Lincoln's Inn Fields. (That was, incidentally, his first billed role for the 1723–24 season.) In the summer of 1724, from 27 June to 18 July, Chapman played lighter roles at Pinkethman's theatre in Richmond. There he acted Fantome in *The Drummer*, Aimwell in *The Stratagem*, Alberto in *A Duke and No Duke*, and Raymond in *The Spanish Fryar*. On 21 July he returned to Lincoln's Inn Fields to play Orbellan in *The Indian Emperor*. Rich was apparently keeping track of Chapman's activity, for in his account books he recorded that Chapman had acted 18 times between 23 June and 20 August, presumably including his stint at Richmond. The actor finished the summer at Southwark Fair in September 1724, playing Aurelius in *Merlin*.

At Lincoln's Inn Fields from 1724–25 through 1726–27 Chapman's activity was mentioned rarely in the bills. He was a regular member of the troupe, working at a salary of 5s. daily plus a shared benefit in the spring, but he restricted his acting to the late months in the season. It is possible that he was also serving Rich in some administrative or managerial capacity. Among the few roles he played these seasons were Blandford in *Oroonoko*, Peppo in *Massaniello*, and the Mad Priest in *The Pilgrim*.

His 1727–28 season was altogether different. If he had previously helped Rich behind the scenes, he could hardly have done so that season and also have sustained the heavy acting schedule that is on record. A list of his roles that season, with the dates on which he first appeared in them, indicates how busy he was as well as the kinds of parts that were typical for him during his career: Stanmore in *Oroonoko* on 20 September 1727, Cogdie in *The Gamester* on 17 October, Cornwall in *King Lear* on

19 October, Dorilant in *The Country Wife* on 25 October, Aegeon in *Oedipus* on 31 October, Peregrine in *Volpone* on 16 November, Osric in *Hamlet* on 8 December, Brazen in *The Recruiting Officer* on 15 December, Renault in *Venice Preserv'd* on 16 December, Shamwell in *The Squire of Alsatia* on 8 January 1728, Dion in *Sesostris* on 17 January, the Beggar in *The Beggar's Opera* on 29 January, Littlegad in *The Fortune Hunters* on 9 March, Pandar in *Bath Unmask'd* on 21 March, Clodio in *Love Makes a Man* on 28 March, Brisk in *The Double Dealer* on 4 April, the Beggar in *Love and a Bottle* on 6 April, Sir Philip in *A Bold Stroke for a Wife* on 23 April, Cardenio in *2 Don Quixote* on 24 April, the Lieutenant in *The Cobler's Opera* on 26 April, Gibbet in *The Stratagem* on 29 April, Brass in *The Confederacy* on 6 May, Prig in *The Royal Merchant* for his shared benefit with Morgan on 16 May, Razor in *The Provok'd Wife* on 18 May, Pamphlet in *Love and a Bottle* on 22 May, and Sparkish in *The Country Wife* on 30 May. Chapman may have learned nearly all these roles in the 1727–28 season (only Cogdie was an old part, it seems), but it is more likely that he had done far more acting, perhaps in the provinces, than is known.

By 1728 Chapman was married. Ford claimed the actor's wife was the former Nora Lynch, but he offered no proof. As will be seen, Chapman's wife in his later years was named Hannah. The Lincoln's Inn Fields free list for 27 December 1728 cited "Mr. Chapman's Wife and Sister" but gave no first names. Mrs Chapman's acting career seems to have begun in 1729.

Chapman's performing pattern remained much the same in the dozen years that followed. He acted heavy schedules yearly at Lincoln's Inn Fields and (beginning in 1732) at Covent Garden, and he continued appearing at the late summer fairs. Among the many new roles he essayed were Roderigo in *Othello*, Fenton in *The Merry Wives of Windsor*, Setter in *The Old*

Bachelor, Lucio in *Measure for Measure*, Malcolm in *Macbeth*, Marplot in *The Busy Body*, the Ghost in *Hamlet*, Diagoras in *The Maid's Tragedy*, Sealand in *The Conscious Lovers*, Sir Politic in *Volpone*, George Barnwell and the Uncle in *The London Merchant*, Poins, Glendower, and Winchester in *1 Henry IV*, Dervise and Stratocles in *Tamerlane*, Abel in *The Committee*, Laertes in *Hamlet*, Kent in *King Lear*, Witwoud in *The Way of the World*, Novel in *The Plain Dealer*, Sciolto in *The Fair Penitent*, the Poet in *Timon of Athens*, Sir Novelty in *Love's Last Shift*, Diomedes in *Troilus and Cressida*, Syphax in *Cato*, Foppington in *The Careless Husband*, the title role in *The Squire of Alsatia*, Gratiano in *The Merchant of Venice*, the title role in *The Gamester*, Cloten in *Cymbeline*, Pandulph in *King John*, Benedick in *Much Ado About Nothing*, and Canterbury in *Henry V*.

But his schedule with Rich left him with time on his hands in the summers. As early as 1725, when Pinkethman had died, Chapman had apparently thought of a playhouse of his own, but not until 1730 did his hope become a reality. On 4 June 1730 the *Daily Journal* reported:

There is building, and almost finish'd here [in Richmond], a small, but very neat and regular THEATRE, a little higher on the Hill than where the late Mr Penkethman's stood. We hear it will be open'd next week by a Company of Comedians from the Theatre Royal in Lincoln's-Inn-Fields and that their first Play will be the Recruiting Officer . . . and that they design to perform three or four Times a Week during the Summer Season, which we expect will be a very good one.

On 24 June Chapman made his first appearance at his own house as Sir George Airy in *The Busy Body*, after which he acted Lord Townly in *The Provok'd Husband* and the Beggar in *The Beggar's Opera*. The opening season met with "universal Approbation and Encouragement"

and Chapman's venture flourished well into the 1740s. Not all the bills for his summer seasons have survived, but we know that, during the 1730s, in addition to managing his playhouse, he acted such parts as Sir Harry Wildair in *The Constant Couple*, Shallow in *The Merry Wives of Windsor*, Prince Hal in *1 Henry IV*, and some of his earlier roles.

When his season at Richmond concluded each summer (usually at the end of July, but later as the years went on) Chapman appeared at Bartholomew Fair. During the 1730s he turned exclusively to management and operated booths with Ryan, Laguerre, and Hall in August 1734, with Hallam in 1736, and with Hippisley and "Legar" (probably Laguerre) in 1739.

Chapman's benefit bills at Lincoln's Inn Fields during the 1730s exhibit the player's facetious manner and tell us something of his personal life. On 24 April 1731, for instance, his benefit on 26 April was puffed:

We hear that on Monday next the Ancient & Honorable Company of Lumber Troopers will perform a fine exercise in New St Square & thence proceed in a Body to the Theatre in Lincoln's Inn Fields to see the play called The Busy Body with the Opera of Flora which will be acted there that night for the benefit of Mr Chapman belonging to the said Troop.

Chapman presumably wrote the puff and organized the procession. A few years later, on 10 March 1737, his benefit bill noted that he was living in Clare Street, near Clare Market, but by 27 March 1739 he had moved to the corner of Bow Street, Covent Garden. On the latter date he told the public of an affliction which may have been plaguing him for some time: "N. B. I being in danger of losing one of my eyes am advised to keep it from the air, therefore stir not out but to attend to my business at the theatre."

The actor's association with John Rich came to an end after the 1738–39 season.

He and Rich appear to have worked well together, however. In 1735 when Rich had founded the Sublime Society of Beefsteaks, Chapman had become one of the 24 original members; and the actor's pay, at least in 1735–36, was 16s. 8d. nightly, a good salary for that period. Rich had clearly valued Chapman's services, typically using him in performances 153 nights during a season. Why the actor chose to leave Covent Garden, therefore, is not clear. But in 1739–40 and 1740–41 he played at Drury Lane.

On 3 October 1739 he began his new winter engagement with one of his most popular roles: Marplot in *The Busy Body*. During his two seasons at Drury Lane he appeared in such new parts as Cutbeard in *The Silent Woman*, Tattle in *Love for Love*, Vizard in *The Match at Newgate*, Surrey in *Henry VIII*, Snap in *Love's Last Shift*, Abel Drugger in *The Alchemist*, Touchstone in *As You Like It*, Feste in *Twelfth Night*, and Launcelot in *The Merchant of Venice*. To puff his benefit night on 8 April 1741 Chapman wrote to the *Daily Post* the day before, calling himself "an unlucky puppy" and asking the editor to "help a lame dog over the stile." The problem facing him was a Handel performance of *L'Allegro ed il Penseroso* at Lincoln's Inn Fields on the same night as his benefit. He said he heartily wished Handel success and hoped that "at least 20,000 persons . . . would flock to that Theatre." But: ". . . as that house could not hold above 20 hundred, if but a tithe of those who were turned back would be so good as to call en passant at Drury Lane Theatre they would be very kindly received."

In 1741–42 Chapman returned to Covent Garden, and there he spent the rest of his winter seasons. Though ill from time to time, he tried such new roles as Bayes in *The Rehearsal*, Autolycus in *The Winter's Tale*, Ramilie in *The Miser*, Foppington in *The Careless Husband*, Mustapha in *Don Sebastian*, the Clown (presumably Parolles) in *All's Well that Ends Well*, Richmond in *Richard III*, Dr Wolf in *The Non-Juror*, Puff in *Miss in Her Teens*, and (replacing the ailing Garrick) Ranger in *The Suspicious Husband*. By 1746–47 he was earning £2 10s. weekly.

Despite illnesses which sometimes kept him from soliciting his patrons in person at benefit time, Chapman kept remarkably active and in good humor. On 2 April 1743, for example, he sent a letter to the *Daily Post* noting that he had heard

that a certain person being possess'd of a great quantity of my tickets, has some thoughts of getting them up to a considerable premium, I out of meer Friendship, not at all with regard to my own interest (if you'll believe me) do privately and secretly, in this public manner, advise you, to send away to my house, the corner of Bow St. near the said theatre, where I will oblige you with what number of tickets you please, at Par, to within an Hour of the Play's beginning.

During the 1740s, as earlier, Chapman was busy during the summers. Indeed, at some point he kept billiard tables in Bow Street and hired the young Ned Shuter as an apprentice marker, giving him acting lessons on the side. But his main activity when he was not performing for Rich was managing his theatre at Richmond and helping to operate booths at Bartholomew Fair. The latter activity continued only until 1743, his partner for that year and the previous three having been Hippisley. His Richmond venture occupied him until his death in 1747. In the 1740s he acted there, among other roles, Peachum in *The Beggar's Opera*, the title role in *The Lying Valet*, Richard III ("to empty benches" said Davies; Chapman refused to the end to give up his pretensions to tragedy), Witwoud in *The Way of the World*, Toyman in *The Toy Shop*, and Crispin in *The Anatomist*. He extended the Richmond operation to include performances at nearby Twickenham in the mid-1740s, and his season gradually stretched into September.

Chapman completed the 1746–47 season at Covent Garden, his last appearance there being on 29 May 1747 when he played Puff in *Miss in Her Teens*. On the following 14 July he died at Richmond of a fever. He was buried at Richmond on 17 July, and on 29 July administration of his estate was granted to his wife Hannah. The *General Advertiser* two days after his death regretted the loss of "a very excellent Comedian."

In his fictionalized biography Ford claimed that Chapman had two sons (by Nora Lynch Chapman), one of whom went to America and was killed in Braddock's retreat and one of whom married early but was lost at sea. Ford also said that a William Chapman Senior, called "Covent Garden Chapman," was a grandson of Thomas Chapman and the son of Thomas's younger son, the one who died at sea. Ford made no mention of Hannah Chapman who, the records show, managed Thomas's Richmond theatre after his death.

Years after his death Chapman was remembered by Davies as a "most excellent actor in various parts, but especially in all Shakespeare's clowns, in petulant would-be wits, fops and fantastics." Brass in *The Confederacy*, Marplot in *The Busy Body*, and Lucio in *Measure for Measure* Davies thought to be Chapman's most celebrated roles, and he believed that only King equalled his dry and voluble Touchstone. The highest praise came from William "Gentleman" Smith, who wrote to his friend Coutts that Thomas Chapman was "a perfect genuine genius — the real Essence of the Histrionic art."

Chapman, Mrs Thomas, Hannah *d. c. 1756, actress, dancer.*

Hannah Chapman, the wife of the more famous Thomas, was first mentioned in the bills as playing Faunia in *Dorastus and Faunia* at Bullock's Bartholomew Fair booth on 25 August 1729. A year later she acted with the company from Lincoln's Inn Fields which her husband had gathered to play at his new theatre in Richmond. Not many of the summer seasons there were well documented, and frequently the casts were not publicized, but we know that during the first summer, in 1730, Mrs Chapman played Myrtilla in *The Provok'd Husband*. She was with John Rich at Lincoln's Inn Fields in 1730–31, though only one role is known for her: a Country Lass in *The Rape of Proserpine* on 30 November 1730, replacing Miss Holliday. The following July 1731 she played again at Richmond, taking the roles of a Maid in *Love's Last Shift* and Lucinda in *The Conscious Lovers,* and in August she acted Lucy in *The London Merchant* at Bullock's booth at Bartholomew Fair.

Mrs Chapman danced in Rich's company in 1731–32, but, again, her only billed role was the small part in *The Rape of Proserpine*. In the summer of 1732 she reappeared at Richmond and at Bartholomew Fair. Her 1732–33 season followed the same pattern, though the bills mentioned her a bit more frequently: she played a Woman Peasant in *Apollo and Daphne* and Scentwell in *The Busy Body* at Lincoln's Inn Fields and Euphrosyne in *The Gardens of Venus* at Bartholomew Fair. She acted Scentwell again at Covent Garden on 27 September 1733, after which her name disappeared from the bills for over 12 years. She apparently continued working with her husband at Richmond but as the "Office Keeper" next door to the playhouse. She was mentioned again in the summer of 1746 at Twickenham, where the Richmond troupe played, and on 22 August she shared a benefit with young Edward Shuter.

Her husband Thomas died on 14 July 1747, and Mrs Chapman was given benefit nights at Twickenham on 22 September, at Richmond on 26 September, and at Covent Garden on 29 March 1748. In the summers of 1748 through 1753 at Richmond or

Twickenham (and sometimes at both) she was granted benefits, but after the one at Richmond on 28 July 1753 they ceased. After that date the rate books mentioned the theatre as Mrs Chapman's "Music Room," but in 1756 she was referred to as the late Mrs Chapman, and it is probable that she died that year or the year before. But a "Widow Chapman" was buried at Richmond on 5 July 1763, and perhaps that person was Hannah.

Chapman, [**William?**] [*fl.* 1770?–1820?], *actor, singer.*

William Chapman—if that was actually his name—may have been a descendant of the comedian Thomas Chapman (c. 1683–1747) who had a considerable career earlier in the eighteenth century. According to George Ford's *These Were Actors*, a fictionalized and undocumented biography of the Chapmans and the Drakes, a William Chapman, called by Ford "Covent Garden Chapman," was the grandson of Thomas and married Penelope Britt. By Miss Britt, William had six children: William, Samuel, Bernard, George, Teresa, and Sarah. Possibly the Mr Chapman who is our subject was indeed William, but the identification needs further proof.

Our man may have been the "Mr Chapman" who began his career on 17 November 1770 at the Capel Street Theatre in Dublin, billed as "A Gentleman." But that identification seems unlikely, for when our Mr Chapman made his Drury Lane debut on 3 October 1782 as Hawthorn in *Love in a Village* he was styled "a young gentleman." During the 1782–83 season Chapman went on to play Giles in *The Maid of the Mill* on 26 October, Lieutenant Bumper in *Too Civil by Half* on 5 November, Boreas in *The Fair American* on 7 February 1783, Wheatear in *Belphagor* on 26 April for his shared benefit with Suett, and a Strolling Player in *Imitation* and a Beggar in *The Ladies' Frolick* on 12 May. His address in London that season was No

49, Carey Street, Lincoln's Inn Fields.

Some of his parts during the 1783–84 season, in addition to his old roles, were Subtle in *The Englishman in Paris*, Rashly in *The Lord of the Manor*, and Simon in *The Metamorphosis*. For his shared benefit on 12 May 1784 he replaced Kenny in *Harlequin Junior* and sang a "new Hunting Song." Still at Drury Lane in 1784–85 and 1785–86, Chapman repeated a good many of his earlier roles, added a few new ones, and sang in musical productions more frequently. By his benefit night on 9 May 1786, he had moved to No 5, Prince's Street, Drury Lane. His name did not appear in the bills of the patent houses in 1786–87, but he joined the company at the Haymarket Theatre in the summer of 1787, offering songs and playing such new roles as Pedro in *The Spanish Fryar*, Antonio in *Much Ado About Nothing*, Tubal in *The Merchant of Venice*, and Sileno in *Midas*. On 31 October 1787 he was one of the principals in *The Birthday* at the Royalty Theatre. Peripatetic Chapman was back at the Haymarket in the summers of 1788 and 1789, singing and acting; some of his parts were Mat o'th' Mint in *The Beggar's Opera*, Mate in *Inkle and Yarico*, Rosencrantz in *Hamlet*, and Tom Errand in *The Constant Couple*.

Drury Lane engaged him in the fall of 1789 at 4s. 6 d. (per day, presumably), but his only recorded appearance was as Nimming Ned in *The Beggar's Opera* on 24 September. He popped up at the Haymarket again in the summer of 1790 and returned to Drury Lane for at least the first half of the 1790–91 season, acting and serving as a tenor in the chorus. His parts were again small ones, such as Scroop in *Henry V* and a member of the mob in *The Island of St Marguerite*. His notices in the Drury Lane bills ceased after December 1790. The pattern the following year was similar: he summered at the Haymarket in 1791 and appeared at Drury Lane in September and October. A Kemble note tells us that during the 1791–92 season "Chapman went away—Cooke engaged in his place."

The Secret History of the Green Room in 1792 summarized Chapman's erratic career up to that point: he was "Sometimes engaged with the Drury-Lane Company; sometimes with the Summer . . . Haymarket; at another at the Royalty Theatre; and frequently disengaged from all of them." His vocal talents were only tolerable, the report went, and he frequently played old men in farces, but he was willing to appear "anytime . . . in any thing" and was a "useful" player.

The Chapman who turned up at Covent Garden in 1801 was probably not our man, but rather the dancer of the same name. The actor-singer was engaged by Colman to take Murray's place in 1803. "Though not equal to his predecessor," said the *Thespian Dictionary* in 1805, "he ranks in the list of respectable performers. In 1804, he procured a situation at Covent Garden Theatre." Chapman had lately "applied himself to the study of old sentimental gentlemen. . . ." He was back at the Haymarket in the summers of 1804 and 1808, and he may have been the Chapman referred to by Oxberry in his *Dramatic Biography* as still at Covent Garden about 1819–20. Oxberry said he was Miss Chester's tutor, "a good speaker, and a sound judge of acting; one who has seen all the best artists of his day, and is therefore well fitted to be a guide to a juvenile aspirant."

Chappell, Mr ₁fl. 1690–1691₁, *actor.*
A manuscript cast in a 1682 edition of *Madam Fickle* at the British Museum shows a Mr Chappell playing Flaile. The cast probably dates about 1690–91 at Drury Lane. Chappell is otherwise unknown.

Chappiell, Richard *1774–1830, musician.*
The musician Richard Chappiell was born on 6 August 1774, the son of Richard and Ann Chappiell, of the parish of St

George, Hanover Square, where he was baptized on 5 September 1774. When he was recommended by John Howles on 5 May 1805 for membership in the Royal Society of Musicians, the usual testimony was given that Chappiell had been a professional musician for upward of seven years. He was a performer on the violin, clarinet, and trumpet. At the time Chappiell was said to be single, to be a member of the New Musical Fund, to teach music students, and to be engaged at the Circus. On 4 August 1805 he was elected to the Society by a ballot of 13 yeas and two nays.

Little else is known of Chappiell's professional life. He was on the list of musicians appointed to play for the Royal Society of Musicians' annual concerts at St Paul's, for benefit of the clergy, in 1806, 1811 (when he was allowed a deputy in his place), 1812, and 1813. In 1815 and 1816 he served the Society on the Committee of Accounts.

Chappiell died in February or early March 1830; on 7 March of that year his widow, Mrs Ann Chappiell, was granted a full allowance by the Society for herself and her daughter, who had been born on 2 November 1818. On 4 November 1832, her fourteenth birthday, the Society placed the child out for an apprenticeship with "a respectable person at Uxbridge." A year later, on 3 November 1833, Miss Chappiell was granted £8 for her mother's funeral and another £10 for clothing for herself.

Chappington, Mr ₁fl. 1735–1736₁, *constable.*
The Covent Garden accounts for 1735–36 listed Mr Chappington as constable at 2s. daily for a total of £17 3s. for 172 acting days and one opera performance.

Charatha. *See* CARATTA.

Chardin, Mr ₁fl. 1729₁, *actor.*
Mr Chardin played Adonis in *The Humours of Harlequin* on 25 February and

26 May 1729 and Chaunter in *The Beggar's Wedding* on 29 May and 6 June 1729. On the last date the performance was billed as a benefit for "King Chanter" —presumably Chardin.

Charini, Mr [fl. 1786], equestrian?

On 28 and 31 October 1786 at the Royal Circus the "Troops" of Charini and Nicolini performed interludes, assisted by the equestrian Hughes and his pupils. Charini was probably an equestrian himself and the leader of a group of riders.

Charke, Catharine Maria, later Mrs Harman 1730–1773, actress.

Born about the latter half of 1730, Catharine Maria Charke was the daughter of the eccentric Charlotte Charke and her fiddling husband Richard. Miss Charke was first noticed in the bills on 22 November 1742 as Nell in *The Devil to Pay* at the theatre in James Street where her widowed mother was playing. Catharine Maria acted Lucia in *The Royal Hero* at May Fair on 1 May 1744, another production which involved her mother. Two days later she played the Prince in *The Captive Prince*; on 7 June she acted Gipsey in *The Beaux' Stratagem*; and on 27 June she was Edging in *The Careless Husband*. At the Haymarket Theatre the following 29 September she played a Page in *Romeo and Juliet*, and she probably acted the Fool in *The Prodigal* on 11 October and Balthazar in *Romeo and Juliet* on 17 December.

About 1750 at Lymington Catharine Maria Charke married an actor named Harman, and under his name she performed for the rest of her career. The couple acted in and around Bath and on the Isle of Wight at some point. On 3 September 1756 at the Swan Inn in London with Hallam's troupe the Harmans played Sir Politick and Lady Tagg in *Adventures of Half an Hour*. At Southwark Fair on 20 September Mrs Harman acted the Landlady in *The Intriguing Captain* with Bence's company.

By 1758 Mrs Harman was in America with her husband, playing at Cruger's Wharf in New York in the company of David Douglass, specializing in duenna roles. After that she spent much of her career in Philadelphia, playing there from 25 June to 28 December 1759, from 14 November 1766 to 6 July 1767, from 4 October 1768 to 6 January 1769, and from 8 November 1769 to 1 June 1770. In America Mr Harman shared roles with young Lewis Hallam, and Mrs Harman took on many of Mrs Adcock's parts. In Philadelphia Mrs Harman acted Lady Anne in *Richard III* and Lady Grace and Miss Jenny in *The Provok'd Husband*, among others. After Harman's death about 1759 Mrs Harman stayed with Douglass's company and acted in Charleston in 1763 and helped open the new playhouse in John Street, New York, on 7 December 1767. One of her parts there was Lady Bountiful in *The Beaux' Stratagem*.

Mrs Harman died in New York on 27 May 1773 at the age of 43 and was buried in Trinity Churchyard. The New York *Mercury* of 7 June reported that "Her little fortune she has left to [the actress] Miss Cheer; and her obsequies were attended, on Saturday night, by a very genteel procession." Mrs Harman had been second only to Mrs Douglass in the company and was remembered as "a just actress and an exemplary woman—sensible, humane, and benevolent." The eccentricities of her parents apparently did not descend to her.

Charke, Fisher Tench. See TENCH, FISHER.

Charke, Richard d. c. 1738, violinist, singer, composer, actor, dancer.

The earliest mention of Richard Charke in theatre documents—unless the reference was to Fisher Tench (Charke)—seems to have been about 1720 when the song *Without affections, gay, youthful & pretty* was published, as sung by Mr Charke. Richard Charke was next heard from on 10 June

1729 when the *Daily Post* carried a quaint puff for his forthcoming performance on 17 June of Harry Hunter in *The Beggar's Wedding*: "the Part of Hunter, in particular, is perform'd by a Person, who, altho his Voice is but indifferent, sings, in the Opinion of all Judges, with a Manner almost as agreeable as Senesino."

After that benefit Charke moved to Drury Lane to play Rovewell in *The Contrivances* and to offer a specialty song, on 20 June 1729. On the following 18 July he was Rake in *The Country Wedding and Skimmington*, and on 29 July he played a violin solo with Magnes at the harpsichord. He was apparently in conflict with Bartholomew Fair managers over his contract for an August performance in which he never appeared. The controversy elicited a letter from him in the *Daily Post* of 11 August 1729 which at least provided posterity with his Christian name.

In the fall of 1729 Charke became a regular member of the Drury Lane company, playing his earlier role of Hunter, plus Edgar in *The Lover's Opera*, Countryman in *The Comical Distresses of Pierrot*, and Death in *Harlequin Dr Faustus*. Halfway through the season, on 4 February 1730 at St Martin-in-the-Fields, Richard Charke married Charlotte Cibber, the daughter of Colley and Katherine. Cibber, as his modern biographers have surmised, may have been happy to get rid of his odd daughter, but hardly could he have chosen (if, indeed, he had any choice in the matter) a less suitable mate for her. Charke was a sponger with a roving eye who quickly tired of married life and had to be hunted "through the Hundreds of Drury," Charlotte later wrote. The marriage bore fruit, however; before the end of 1730 a daughter, Catharine Maria Charke, appeared on the scene.

After his wedding Charke finished out the season at Drury Lane offering violin solos, and for his shared benefit with Miss Raftor (later Kitty Clive) on 28 April

1730 he played his old and appropriately named character Rovewell in *The Contrivances*. At that performance *The Provok'd Wife* was also presented, with Charlotte Charke making her second stage appearance as Mademoiselle and Anne Oldfield making her last as Lady Brute.

Charke busied himself in the 1730–31 season singing, fiddling in the Drury Lane band, playing violin solos on stage, accompanying Miss Raftor, and acting a number of roles which provided him with opportunities to sing and dance. Among his new parts were Hilliard in *The Jovial Crew*, Sycorax in *The Tempest*, Damon in *Damon and Phillida*, Octavio in *Don John*, and Harry in *The Amours of Billingsgate*. In the summer of 1731 he added Tragedo in *Bayes's Opera*, Ananias in *The Devil to Pay*, and Nettle in *The What D'Ye Call It*. By that time Charke had also turned his hand to composing. Several of his theatre songs were published about 1730, including *Come, come let us drink* and *The Provident Damsel*, both used in *The Humours of Oxford*. He later wrote *Sweet Linnets on every Spray*, published about 1735, some violin pieces, and *Six Medley or Comic Overtures in Seven Parts*, published posthumously about 1760. His medley overtures are said to have been the first of that genre, still standard in musical comedies today.

After the 1730–31 season Charke concentrated on music, though he kept acting through 1733, taking such roles as a Mandarin Gormogon in *Cephalus and Procris*, a Triton and Medusa in *Perseus and Andromeda*, Tom Thimble in *The Rehearsal*, and, at the Haymarket Theatre during Theophilus Cibber's brief stay there in the fall of 1733, Osric in *Hamlet*. Charke's chief occupation, however, was playing the violin, occasionally offering specialty songs —once "(in the Italian Stile)"—and providing medley overtures, some of which he composed for his wife's benefits. He also found time for teaching, two of his violin students being Master and Miss Oates, both of whom performed at Drury Lane in May and June of 1736. The last mention of Charke in the theatre bills was on 27 October 1737 when one of his overtures was played, but by that time he had left England.

Wright's *Revels in Jamaica* places Charke on the island in 1735, but he was certainly in London as late as the summer of 1736 and probably sailed for Jamaica after that. It was at the invitation of Henry Moore that Charke went off to the island, borrowing £100 from Moore's London agents before departing, in order to pay off the debts of a "Mrs Sally K——g, one of the Ladies of the Highest Irreputable Reputation at that time in or about Covent Garden"—according to Charlotte Charke. The fiddler planned to have his whore follow him to Jamaica, but she never left London, and Charke, according to Wright, died about a year and a half after his arrival in the Caribbean. If he left England in the latter half of 1736, perhaps his death should be placed about 1738.

Charke, Mrs Richard, Charlotte, née Cibber, later Mrs John Sacheverell
1713–1760, actress, manager, puppeteer, author.

Charlotte Cibber was born on 13 January 1713, the last of seven children of Colley and Katherine Cibber. She was baptized at St Martin-in-the-Fields the following 8 February. According to the *Narrative Life* which she wrote in later years, Charlotte was "not only an unexpected, but an unwelcome Guest" in the family and "regarded as an impertinent Intruder."

By the time she was four Charlotte manifested a liking for male attire, "that by Dint of a Wig and a Waistcoat, I should be the perfect Representative of my Sire." When her sire saw her riding down the street on a mule, led by a ragamuffin sawing away on a fiddle and followed by a bedraggled entourage of children, he cried, "Gad demme! An Ass upon an Ass!" Char-

lotte's eldest sister, Catherine, was apparently given the task of disciplining her, and consequently the relationship between the two was never friendly. Charlotte called Catherine a "cruel Monitor" with a "rancorous Disposition." To learn Latin, French, Italian, geography, music, and dancing, Charlotte was sent off at the age of eight to Mrs Draper's school in Park Street, Westminster, but though the girl gained from this exposure to formal education, she lost none of her interest in more vigorous pursuits. At Hillingdon, near Uxbridge, Colley had a country house where Charlotte taught herself riding, grooming horses, and shooting. She loved to hunt "from Morn to Eve," and when a genteel neighbor of the Cibbers protested this masculine activity Charlotte got even by taking pot shots at the lady's chimney. Once she almost killed a child with a runaway horse and chaise. After spending some time in the home of Dr Hales learning household chores, Charlotte took to nursing the old women of her neighborhood, dressed as a man, spouting Latin, and dispensing her home-brewed medicines.

On 4 February 1730 at St Martin-in-the-Fields Charlotte married Richard Charke, a Drury Lane Theatre jack-of-all-trades. If Colley Cibber, then one of the managers of Drury Lane, thought the marriage might get Charlotte off his hands for a while he was much mistaken, for she soon decided to make her theatrical debut. Billed as a "young gentlewoman" making her first attempt on any stage, she appeared at Drury Lane on 8 April 1730 as Mademoiselle in *The Provok'd Wife*. She repeated the role on 28 April when Anne Oldfield, with perceptive timing, made her farewell appearance. On 1 May Charlotte acted Mustacha in *Tom Thumb*, after which she took time off to engage in the exclusively feminine activity of having a baby. Catharine Maria Charke, Charlotte's daughter, was probably born in late 1730.

Charlotte was back at Drury Lane again

An exact Representation of M.rs Charke walking in the Ditch at four Years of Age, as described by herself in the first Number of the Narrative of her own Life, lately published.

F. Garden Sculp.

Published According to Act of Parliament Sep.r 9.th 1755.

CHARLOTTE CHARKE, at the age of four
engraving by Garden

on 11 January 1731 playing Mademoiselle, and she followed that with Aurora in *Cephalus and Procris*, Flora in *Don John*, Lucy in *The London Merchant*, and Thalia in *The Triumphs of Love and Honour*. Despite her eccentricity in her early years, she seems to have taken her acting seriously, and when she returned to Drury Lane for the 1731–32 season she was given such roles as Trusty in *The Provok'd Husband*, Mrs Raison in *Greenwich Park*, Cloris in *The Rehearsal*, Clarinda in *The Double Gallant*, Andromache in *The Distrest Mother*, Mrs Slammekin in *The Beggar's Opera*, and Alicia in *Jane Shore*. Occasional breeches parts were not enough for Charlotte, however, and on 17 August 1732 she played Roderigo in *Othello*, an omen for the future. On 23 August at the Miller-Oates-Mills Bartholomew Fair booth, on the other hand, she consented to play Lucy in the droll *Henry VIII*.

Again at Drury Lane for the 1732–33 season Charlotte Charke repeated most of her previous roles but moved up to Procris in *Cephalus and Procris* and acted Mrs Lupine in *Caelia*, Fainlove in *The Tender Husband*, Molly in *The Boarding School*, Hoyden in *The Relapse*, and Damon in *Damon and Daphne* (for her benefit on 7 May 1733). She said that she acted with her brother Theophilus Cibber at the Haymarket Theatre in the summer of 1733 for 30s. weekly, but no records of her performances have been found. At the Cibber-Griffin-Bullock-Hallam booth at Bartholomew Fair on 23 August she added another male role to her growing transvestite repertoire: Haly in *Tamerlane*.

When her brother bolted Drury Lane and led a company of malcontents to the Haymarket Theatre in the fall of 1733, Charlotte joined him and attempted such new roles as Louisa in *Love Makes a Man*, Sylvia in *The Recruiting Officer*, Lady Pride in *The Amorous Widow*, Charlotte in *Oroonoko*, Marcia in *Cato*, Abigail in *The Scornful Lady*, Isabella in *Wit Without Money*, Lady Politick in *Volpone*, Doll Common in *The Alchemist*, Mrs Otter in *The Silent Woman*, and Douglass in *The Albion Queens*. When a peace was made and the rebels returned to Drury Lane in March 1734, Charlotte played Lucilla in *The Fair Penitent*, Colombine's Maid in *Cupid and Psyche*, and Primrose in *The Mother-in-Law*. For her benefit on 13 May 1734 she chose Roderigo in *Othello*, and her husband, perhaps in recompense for sponging on her regularly, wrote a new medley overture for the occasion.

The *Daily Journal* of 21 May reported: "We hear that the Mad Company at the Haymarket [last winter] design to keep up that Character, by performing the Beggar's Opera in Roman Dresses, and exhibiting Hurlothrumbo, in which Mrs Charke attempts the Character of Lord Flame." The facetious comment was not too far from correct for at least Charlotte displayed in the summer of 1734 a variety of new male roles: Macheath in *The Beggar's Opera*,

Pistol in *The Humours of Sir John Falstaff*, the title role in *The Mock Doctor*, Sir John in *The Devil to Pay*, Townly in *The Provok'd Husband*, George Barnwell in *The London Merchant*, Lothario in *The Fair Penitent*, Jack Stocks and Lovemore in *The Lottery*, Rovewell (her husband's pet role) in *The Contrivances*, and Sir Charles in *The Beaux' Stratagem*. She also managed a few female parts, such as Minerva in *Penelope*, Polly in *The Beggar's Opera*, and Charlotte in *Oroonoko*. All these and others she performed in the space of a month and a half, a tribute to the mad girl's energy and memory if nothing else.

After that exhausting summer Mrs Charke added little to her repertory at Drury Lane in 1734–35, but there and at Lincoln's Inn Fields (apparently as her own manager) during the summer of 1735 she tried Millwood in *The London Merchant*, Archer in *Squire Basinghall*, Mrs Haughty in *The Stage Mutineers*, Grizzle in *The Tragedy of Tragedies* (which she may have played the previous summer), Marius Junior in *Caius Marius*, Pickle Herring in *Bartholomew Fair*, Charles in *Love Makes a Man*, and the French Harlequin in her own "The Carnival" (never published), with a new overture by Mr Charke. Her medley triumph of the summer came on 19 June 1735 when she acted Lord Foppington in *The Careless Husband* and Sir John Loverule in *The Devil to Pay* and danced a minuet and the *Black Joak* with Miss Brett for the entertainment of visiting "Chinese Mandarins" and for the benefit of a family in distress—possibly her own.

From 1735–36 forward, Charlotte's performing activity became increasingly erratic. She played now here, now there, sometimes with a patent company but often with a pick-up troupe of her own. She began in the fall of 1735 at the Haymarket, acting Alicia in *Jane Shore* and the French Harlequin in "The Carnival" on 17 September. Then she took her young company to York Buildings. She appeared as Polly in

The Beggar's Opera and Mrs Tragic in her own satire on the Drury Lane patentees called *The Art of Management* on 24 September and Millwood in *The London Merchant* and Mrs Tragic again on 1 October. The bill for 24 September noted that the troupe she had gathered had to move from the Haymarket to York Buildings because they were "too young a sett of people to venture at great expence, without first having merited the favour of the town to support them in it." On 26 September the *Daily Advertiser* reported that

Mrs Charke . . . drew tears from the whole audience in her prologue [on the twenty-fourth], which she spoke very pathetically; and the new farce . . . was very much applauded, notwithstanding the impotent attempts of several young clerks to raise a riot, who were for that purpose properly marshall'd by the cunning lawyer their master [Fleetwood, the Drury Lane manager, presumably]. Their rude behaviour was so extraordinary, that several gentlemen were provok'd to threaten them with the discipline of their canes, upon which they [desisted].

Fleetwood had tried to burn all the copies of Charlotte's *The Art of Management*, but he missed a few. In her preface to the farce Mrs Charke reviewed her unhappy relationship with the Drury Lane manager, noting that he had once commended her but had dismissed her on the grounds of weak finances. There was, Charlotte said, "a Motion . . . for my being recall'd," but she was refused, even though she had "at a Quarter of an Hour's Warning, twice read two capital Parts, *viz.* The Queen in Essex, and another Night Cleopatra which, I believe, I did not appear scandalous in." As for "my private Misconduct . . . I'll allow private Virtues heighten publick Merits, but then the Want of those private Virtues wont affect an Actors Performances."

Though Fleetwood threatened to sue her,

Charlotte was reconciled to him by Colley Cibber and returned to Drury Lane on 18 November 1735 to play Doll Common in *The Alchemist*. She acted some of her other old roles through the end of the year, but on 5 March 1736 she was back at the Haymarket again, acting Lord Place in *Pasquin* for four guineas weekly as a member of Fielding's "Great Mogul's Company of Comedians." She followed that role with Tim in *The Female Rake*, Clymene the oyster woman in *Tumble Down Dick*, Gaylove in *The Honest Yorkshireman*, Agnes in *Guilt Its Own Punishment*, Leander in *The Mock Doctor*, and a few of her earlier parts. While working with Fielding, she and her daughter lived, despite her good salary, in wretched rooms in Oxendon Street; she attacked her landlord, writing some dreadful verses about his accommodations. In August and September of 1736 she performed at both Bartholomew and Southwark fairs.

Charlotte's marriage with Richard Charke had been troubled from the beginning by Charke's interest in other women and his appropriation of his wife's money. According to Charlotte, she spent much of her spare time trying to track Richard down among the shady denizens of Drury Lane.

It may have been that situation or Charlotte's breaking with Fleetwood soon after Colley Cibber reconciled the two that prompted the following letter from Cibber to his daughter. It was dated only 27 March, from Tavistock Street, Covent Garden, but perhaps it belongs to 1736 and concerns Richard Charke:

Dear Charlotte—

I am sorry I am not in a position to assist you further. You have made your own bed, and therein you must lie. Why do you not disassociate yourself from that worthless scoundrel, and *then* your relatives *might* try and aid you. You will never be any good while you adhere to him, and you most certainly will not receive what otherwise you might from your Father.

                                        Colley Cibber

About 1736, probably in the last half of the year, Richard Charke went off to Jamaica never to return, but Colley remained estranged from his daughter for many years afterward.

Mrs Charke joined Henry Giffard's company at Lincoln's Inn Fields in the fall of 1736 and there she was assigned such new parts as Flora in *The Wonder*, Tattle in *Love for Love*, Clodio in *Love Makes a Man*, Mrs Peachum in *The Beggar's Opera*, and Alibech in *The Indian Emperor*. On 14 March 1737 she was back at the Haymarket and there played Don Resinando in *A Rehearsal of Kings*, Hen in *The Historical Register*, Spatter in *Eurydice Hissed*, and Kitty Cable in *The Sailor's Opera*. On 3 May 1737 she was granted a benefit, after which her name disappeared from the bills for almost a year.

For the rest of 1737 Mrs Charke occupied herself by setting up as a grocer and oil woman in Longacre, but she was unskilled in business matters, suffered robbery, and finally gave up the trade. On 10 March 1738 she was granted a license by the Lord Chamberlain to run a puppet show, a venture which she went at with a vengeance, laying out nearly £500 on string puppets, elegant scenery, fancy costumes, and a proper theatre. She fitted up the tennis court in James Street which served as a playhouse off and on during the eighteenth century. Billing her enterprise as "Punch's Theatre," she operated from March to May 1738, offering the public such attractions as *Henry VIII* (with additions from *Damon and Phillida*), *The Mock Doctor*, *The Covent Garden Tragedy*, *The Old Debauchees*, *The Unhappy Favorite*, *Henry IV*, *Richard III*, *The Miller of Mansfield*, and *The Beggar's Wedding*. In these works Punch appeared in a variety of guises: as the Mock Doctor, the madame of a Covent Garden brothel, Father Girard, and Falstaff. The plays were augmented by such divertissements as dancing by Mr and Mrs Punch, odes written by Mrs Charke, instrumental music by "an eminent hand," and Job Baker's performances on the kettle drums.

By mid-May Charlotte had exhausted herself physically and had acquired, she said, "a violent Fever, which had like to have carried me off, and consequently gave a Damp to the Run I should otherwise have had" at Punch's Theatre. But from all surviving evidence it appears that she had done a remarkable job, making effective and witty use of Punch and providing her customers with lively entertainment. *The Usefulness of the Stage* (1738) liked her traditional use of squeakers for Punch: " 'Tis said she intends, by their artificial voices to cut out the Italians [at the opera]; for it has been found that Punch can hold his breath and quiver much better and longer than Farinelli [the eminent *castrato*] I wish this may be true, for then we may expect to have Italian songs at a moderate rate, without the use of a knife." Charlotte nursed herself back to health in a house she took in Marsham Street, Westminster. In the summer of 1739 she took her puppets to Tunbridge Wells, but there she encountered competition with the well-established Lacon, so she acted "in *Propria Persona*, at Ashley's Great Room" and returned to London.

She resolved "to make the best Use I could of my Figures, without fatiguing myself any farther, and lett my Comedians out for Hire to a Man, who was principally concerned in the Formation of them [Fawkes?]: but Business not answering his Ends and my Expectations, I sold, for twenty Guineas, what cost me near five hundred Pounds." She finally sold her puppets to either Yeates or Fawkes. After being exhibited at Bartholomew Fair in 1740, the figures seem to have been carried

Harvard Theatre Collection

CHARLOTTE CHARKE
engraving by Boitard, after Dandridge

to America. Charlotte did not give up her interest in puppets, however, for she worked under Mr Russel at Hickford's rooms, probably in 1745, moving "*Punch in particular*" for a guinea a day.

What Mrs Charke was up to from 1740 to 1742 is uncertain, but perhaps it was during this period that she worked at the King's Head in Marylebone dressed, of course, in male attire. Her job there ended when one of the female customers fell in love with the "young man."

On 26 August 1742 at the Fawkes-Pinchbeck booth at Bartholomew Fair, Charlotte appeared as Lovegirlo in *Humours of Covent Garden*. The after-piece that day was a puppet show "by Punch's Company of comical Tragedians from the Haymarket," but the bill did not indicate that Mrs Charke had anything to

do with it. After her stint at the fair she busied herself with preparations for a new venture at the James Street playhouse. On 22 November 1742 she advertised:

For the *Benefit of a Person*, who has a mind to get Money; At the new *Theatre in James Street, near the Haymarket*, on *Monday* next, will be perform'd a *Concert of Vocal and Instrumental Musick:* divided into two Parts. Boxes 3*s* Pit 2*s* Gallery 1*s*. Between the two Parts of the Concert will be perform'd a Tragedy, call'd The Fatal Curiosity, written by the late Mr Lillo, Author of George Barnwell. The Part of Mrs Wilmott, by *Mrs Charke*, who originally perform'd it at the Haymarket: The rest of the Parts by a set of People, who will perform as well as they can, if not as well as they wou'd, and the best can do no more.

With variety of Entertainments, viz: Act 1. a Preamble, on the Kettle-Drums by Mr Job Baker, particularly, Larry Grovy, accompanied with French Horns. Act 2d. a new Peasant-Dance, by *Mons Chemont*, and *Madame Peran*, just arriv'd piping hot from the Opera at Paris. To which will be added a Ballad Opera, call'd The Devil to Pay: the Part of Nell by *Miss Charke*, who perform'd Princess Elizabeth, at Southwark. Servants will be allow'd to keep places on the Stage—particular care will be taken to perform with the utmost decency, and to prevent mistakes. the bills for the day will be blue and black.

Other performances at James Street under Charlotte's management in 1742–43 included *The Miser, The London Merchant, The Honest Yorkshireman, Love Makes a Man, The Lying Valet, Don Sebastian, The Constant Couple, Chrononhotonthologos, Aureng-Zebe, The Stratagem, The Committee, Tunbridge Walks*, and *The Recruiting Officer*. Mrs Charke also presented a new piece of her own on 1 February 1743, a puppet show, apparently: "A Whimsical Comical Farcical Operatical Allegorical Emblematical Pistolatical Impromptu Medley called Tit for Tat or Comedy and Tragedy at War."

This rather impressive season might

suggest that Charlotte had made a successful comeback, but her name dropped from
the London playbills again until March
1744. Perhaps during the interim she
busied herself with one or more of the
following activities, all of which she reported but did not date carefully in her
Narrative: playing suitor in men's clothes
to an heiress worth £60,000 who did not
know Charlotte's sex, serving as valet to
an Irish lord who did, or decking herself
out as a highwayman and waylaying her
father in Epping Forest. Though she vehe-
mently denied the truth of the last esca-
pade, her *Narrative* reports its essence: she
threatened to "blow his Brains out that
Moment if he did not deliver." He delivered, begging the thief to mend his ways,
to which Charlotte reportedly replied, "I've
a wicked hunks of a father, who rolls in
money, yet denies me a guinea. And so
a worthy gentleman like you, sir, has to
pay for it!"

On 28 March 1744 Mrs Charke held a
benefit at James Street, tickets for which
could be had of her at her "Stake and Soup
House" in Drury Lane, near Stuart's Rents.
For that occasion she took time off from
her new business to act Lothario in *The
Fair Penitent*. The following May and
June she appeared regularly at Hallam's
new playhouse at May Fair, playing
Eumenes in *The Royal Hero*, Antient
Pistol in *The Captive Prince*, George Barn-
well, Archer in *The Beaux' Stratagem*,
Plume in *The Recruiting Officer*, Lothario
again, Lord Foppington in *The Careless
Husband*, and the King in *The King and
the Miller of Mansfield*. The casts usually
included her daughter. In the fall of 1744
Charlotte joined her brother Theophilus
and his rag-tag troupe at the Haymarket
Theatre, and she stayed on there with her
own "Queen of Hungary's Company of
Comedians" to act Macheath on 26 Sep-
tember 1744. On 4 March 1745 at the
Haymarket she unsuccessfully played Pope
John VIII ("otherwise Pope Joan"),

prompting the *Daily Advertiser* to thank
her for the opportunity of seeing her appear as a woman.

For the month of November 1745
Charlotte joined the company at Goodman's Fields, making her first appearance
there on 4 November as Lady Townly in
The Provok'd Husband. She went on to
play a few of her earlier roles, but the most
remarkable bill was that of 8 November
when she acted Belvidera in *Venice Preserv'd*—but then she would obviously try
anything, and it is not unlikely that she
did the part rather well.

By the end of November Charlotte had
disappeared from public record again, not
to be heard of until 2 May 1745 when she
married John Sacheverell of the parish of
St Andrew, Holborn, at St George's Chapel,
Hyde Park Corner. In the register Charlotte
identified herself only as "of Kensington."
The wedding was clandestine, and when
she reflected on it ten years later she said
"I had better have let [it] alone." In her
Narrative she refused to divulge the name
of her second husband, though about June
1746, soon after the nuptials, she advertised "An Occasional Epilogue written and
spoke by Mrs Sacheverell late Mrs Charke"
to be given, apparently, at the New Wells,
Clerkenwell, where she acted under the
management of Yeates. Sacheverell died
soon after the wedding, leaving Charlotte
destitute. She ended up in prison for debt
but was bailed out by a disreputable woman
who frequented the Drury Lane area;
Charlotte, left jail disguised as a man and
wearing the hat of the arresting officer.

From 1746 to 1755 Mrs Charke spent
much of her time touring the provinces,
but it was probably during this period also
that she worked for a while as a conjurer's
assistant in Petticoat Lane, spent some time
in a sponging house (from which some of
her Covent Garden girl friends rescued
her), set up as a pastry cook and farmer
in Chepstow (but her sow was barren and
her crops wouldn't grow), sold sausages on

A

NARRATIVE of the LIFE

OF

Mrs. CHARLOTTE CHARKE,

(Youngest Daughter of COLLEY CIBBER, *Esq;)*

CONTAINING,

I. An Account of her Birth, Education, and mad Pranks committed in her Youth.

II. Her coming on the Stage; Success there; and sundry Theatrical Anecdotes.

III. Her Marriage to Mr. *Charke*, and its Consequences.

IV. Her Adventures in Mens Cloaths, and being belov'd by a Lady of great For-tune, who intended to marry her.

V. Her being Gentle-man to a certain Peer.

VI. Her commencing Strolling - Player; with various and sur-prizing Vicissitudes of Fortune, during nine Years Peregrination.

VII. Her turning Pastry Cook, &c. in *Wales*. With several extreme-ly humourous and in-teresting Occurrences.

Written by HERSELF.

This Tragic Story, *or this* Comic Jest,
May make you laugh, *or cry——As you like best.*

Prologue to The What d'ye Call It.

LONDON:

Printed for *W. Reeve*, in *Fleet Street*; *A. Dodd*, in the *Strand*; and *E. Cook*, at the *Royal-Exchange*.

M. DCC. LV.

From the collection of Edward A. Langhans

Title page of CHARLOTTE CHARKE's *Narrative*

the streets of London, worked in a printing shop in Bristol, and served as a pastry cook in Wales.

Perhaps Charlotte picked up those odd jobs during her touring years because she disliked strolling so much. She likened it to "engaging in a little dirty Kind of War." She was

not only sick, but heartily ashamed of it, as I have had nine Years Experience of its being a very contemptible Life; rendred so, through the impudent and ignorant Behaviour of the Generality of those who pursue it; and I think it would be more reputable to earn a Groat a Day in Cinder-sifting at *Tottenham-Court*, than to be concerned with them.

She complained that the profession was being invaded by "Barbers 'Prentices, Taylors and Journeyman Weavers" who impudently styled themselves players but had no talent or training. They had, she wrote, "a Dissonancy of Voice which conveyed to me a strong Idea of a Cat in Labour." That did not stop her, however, from spending nearly ten years in the unholy trade. Part of the time she toured under the name "Mr Brown," and while she was strolling, we know, she acted Pyrrhus, Lorenzo, Scrub, and, when the actress cast as Sylvia in *The Recruiting Officer* couldn't perform, a composite of Sylvia and her own role of Plume. She suffered with the rest of her fraternity, once being jailed for strolling. For a time she acted with the company of Linnett, and she both played in Richard Elrington's troupe and managed it during his absence. In 1753–54 she served as Simpson's prompter at Bath, but the company was dissolved because of poor management. Perhaps her most noteworthy role while on tour was the one that sooner or later one would have expected her to try: Hamlet.

Some of Charlotte's time during the early 1750s was spent in writing *A Narrative of the Life of Mrs Charlotte Charke*, which was published in 1775, first in parts and then in book form. In it she tried to reconcile herself to her father. She had been disowned by Colley Cibber and by her sisters some years earlier. Some sources say she had offended him by playing his role of Sir Fopling Flutter, and others suggest that the offense had been her presentation of Fopling Fribble in *The Battle of the Poets*, which had satirized the laureateship. It seems more likely that the break had come in 1736 when Colley persuaded the Drury Lane management to employ her again, only to have her bolt the company. In any case, on 8 March 1755 she attempted to get back into her father's good graces.

The letter she wrote to Cibber on that date he either never read or did not deign to acknowledge:

Saturday, Mar. 8, 1755.
HONOUR'D SIR,
I Doubt not but you are sensible I last Saturday *published the First Number of a Narrative of my Life, in which I made a proper Concession in regard to those unhappy Miscarriages which have for many Years justly deprived me of a Father's Fondness. As I am conscious of my Errors, I thought I could not be too publick in suing for your Blessing and Pardon; and only blush to think my youthful Follies should draw so strong a Compunction on my Mind in the Meridian of my Days, which I might so easily have avoided.*

Be assured, Sir, I am perfectly convinced I was more than much to blame, and that the Hours of Anguish I have felt have bitterly repaid me for the Commission of every Indiscretion, which was the unhappy Motive of being so many Years estranged from that Happiness I now, as in Duty bound, most earnestly implore.

I shall with your Permission, Sir, send again, to know if I may be admitted to throw myself at your Feet; and with sincere and filial Transport, endeavour to convince you that I am,

HONOUR'D SIR,
Your truly penitent
And dutiful daughter,
CHARLOTTE CHARKE.

Charlotte suspected that the letter was intercepted by her sister Catherine Brown. It was returned unopened. But Mrs Charke published it—or rather a version of it for public consumption, as above—in her *Narrative*, and it is doubtful that Colley Cibber was totally unaware of her effort at reconciliation. But he spurned her to the end, leaving her in his will (proved in 1757) £5 "and no more" and making his eldest daughter Catherine his residuary legatee. Perhaps Charlotte deserved no more, for she had, after all, waited a long time to show her filial piety.

With income from her lively autobiography Mrs Charke must have made enough to pay some of her debts, feed her daughter, and keep body and soul together, yet her situation in 1755 was still destitute. Samuel Whyte of Dublin and a bookseller friend became interested in a novel Mrs Charke was writing, *The History of Henry Dumont*, and their visit to her in connection with it was reported by Whyte in the *Monthly Mirror*:

Her habitation was a wretched thatched hovel, situated on the way to Islington in the purlieus of Clerkenwell Bridewell, not very distant from the New River Head, where at that time it was usual for the scavengers to leave the cleansings of the streets, and the priests of Cloacina to deposit the offerings from the temples of that all-worshipped Power. . . . [A ragged maid] with a torpid voice and hungry smile desired us to walk in.—The first object that presented itself was a dresser, clean, it must be confessed, and furnished with three or four coarse delf plates, two brown platters, and underneath an earthen pipkin, and a black pitcher with a snip out of it. To the right we perceived and bowed to the mistress of the mansion sitting on a maimed chair under the mantle piece, by a fire, merely sufficient to put us in mind of starving. On one hob sat a monkey, which by way of welcome chattered at our going in; on the other a tabby cat, of melancholy aspect! and at our author's feet on the flounce of her dingy petticoat reclined a dog, almost

a skeleton! he raised his shagged head and eagerly staring with his bleared eyes, saluted us with a snarl. "Have done, Fidele! these are friends." The tone of her voice was not harsh; it had something in it humbled and disconsolate; a mingled effort of authority and pleasure—Poor soul! few were her visitors of that description—no wonder the creature barked!—A magpie perched on the top ring of her chair, not an uncomely ornament! and on her lap was placed a mutilated pair of bellows—the pipe was gone—an advantage in their present office, they served as a succedaneum for a writing desk, on which lay displayed her hopes and treasure, the manuscript of her novel. Her ink-stand was a broken tea-cup, the pen worn to a stump; she had but one! A rough deal board with three hobbling supporters was brought for our convenience, on which without farther ceremony we contrived to sit down and enter upon business:—The work was read, remarks made, alterations agreed to, and thirty guineas demanded for the copy. The squalid handmaiden, who had been an attentive listener, stretched forward her tawny length of neck with an eye of anxious expectation!—The bookseller offered five!—Our authoress did not appear hurt; disappointments had rendered her mind callous; however some altercation ensued. This was [this] writer's first initiation into the mysteries of bibliopolism and the state of authorcraft. He, seeing both sides pertinacious, at length interposed, and at his instance the wary haberdasher of literature doubled his first proposal with this saving proviso, that his friend present would pay a moiety and run one half the risk; which was agreed to. Thus matters were accomodated, seemingly to the satisfaction of all parties; the lady's original stipulation of fifty copies for herself being previously acceded to.

The number of Charlotte's theatrical appearances dwindled. In September of 1755 she was at the Haymarket Theatre playing Mrs Wilmott in *The Fatal Curiosity* for her benefit on the fourth and Volscius in *The Rehearsal* on the eleventh, with a company led by her brother Theophilus Cibber. She and King had a troupe at

Harvard Theatre Collection

CHARLOTTE CHARKE (?) and COLLEY CIBBER

engraving by Fisher, after Van Loo

Bartholomew Fair on 3 September 1756 and produced *England Triumphant* and *The Merry Beggars,* after which she probably engaged in one or more of the many activities she described in her *Narrative* and for which we have no dates.

On 7 August 1759, having gained little financially by the death of her father in 1757, Charlotte applied to the Duke of Devonshire, then Lord Chamberlain, for permission to act at the Haymarket Theatre for 10 nights:

May it please your Grace

I must confess this Liberty may be deem'd a piece of presumption which wou'd Stand a terrible Chance of being render'd Innexcuseable from many others of An Equal Rank with your Grace, and might naturally have prevented my making so bold an attempt in Intruding on your Grace's Retirement, but as your Humanity is too well known to admit of a Doubt of being forgiven when prompted by necessity, I have ventur'd to Earnest Implore your Graces permission in this vacant Season of the year to perform for ten nights only at the Haymarket Theatre And humbly hope for Sake of the Memory of my Late Father Colley Cibber you will permit the Daughter who was bred to the Stage to take an honest Chance for those few nights of establishing her Self in a way of Business which will make her happy and greatly add to the numerous Blessings Heaven has Inspired your Grace to bestow on many others, An ill State of health obliges me to decline my profession in the winter, And as the [patent] Houses are both Shut up it can be no detriment to those whose happier Fortunes receive the general advantage of that season of the year which renders me incapable of Striving for a Support, if you[r] Graces wonted tenderness to the Distress'd will extend it Self to me in this case, I beg you'll give an Immediate order to any of yr. Servants to write your pleasure, directed to Mrs. Charke at Mrs. Hinds in Leicester Street near Swallow Street piccadilly if yr. Grace conceiv'd how happy I may be made by yr. favourable Compliance I dare believe you'd both pity and forgive this trouble from your Graces most Devoted and obedt. Servt.

Charlotte Charke formerly Cibber please yr. Grace in case tis necessary I shall call at Devonshire house to know yr. Graces commands

The Duke granted her desperate plea, but instead of her projected 10 performances Charlotte was able to give only one: on 28 September 1759 she played Marplot in *The Busy Body* for her benefit, advertising that "as I am entirely dependent on chance for a subsistence . . . I humbly hope the Town will favor me." It was her last stage appearance. On 6 April 1760 Charlotte Cibber Charke died at her lodgings in the Haymarket. The *British Chronicle* of 16 April said only that she was "a gentlewoman remarkable for her adventures and misfortunes."

Though Mrs Charke's "The Carnival" and "Tit for Tat" were never printed, *The Art of Management* was published in 1735. Her *Narrative* and *The History of Henry Dumont* saw print, and she also published two novelettes: *The Mercer* (about 1755) and *The Lover's Treat* (1758).

The Van Loo painting of Colley Cibber with a little girl beside him may depict Charlotte; an engraving of it was made by Edward Fisher in 1758. A plumbago drawing of Charlotte with her father Colley Cibber and her brother Theophilus, by William Robins, is in the collection of Her Majesty the Queen. A painting of Charlotte by Dandridge is at the British Museum; L. P. Boitard made an engraving of it. At the Garrick Club is a wash drawing of Charlotte by an unknown artist. She was pictured in an engraving by F. Garden, showing her in a greatcoat and tricorn hat at the age of four. The scene in Charlotte's hovel was turned into an engraving by an unknown artist in the nineteenth century. The *Catalogue of Engraved Dramatic Portraits* in the Harvard Theatre Collection lists a print of Mrs Charke playing Scrub, but the pictured actress is not her but Mrs Abington.

"Charlatano." *See* CROZA.

Charles, Mons [*fl. 1733–1756*], *French horn player, clarinetist, "sharlarno" player, trumpeter?*

The "Third Musick" at the performance of *The Relapse* by Cibber's company of seceders from Drury Lane at the Haymarket on 6 October 1733 was distinguished by "I: Concerto for French Horns, the French Horns by Charle and Giay, lately arriv'd from Paris" and "III. Solo for French Horn by Charle."

On 29 April, after the reunion of the companies at Drury Lane, for the benefit of the Arnes he was again featured: "By particular Desire Mons Charle will perform a Solo on the French Horn, the first time of his Appearance on this Stage, and the last of his Performance in Publick during his Stay in England."

On the opening night of the following season, 9 September 1734, one of the divertissements at Goodman's Fields Theatre was a *"Concerto on the French Horn by Mr Charles, his first time on this Stage."* He repeated on 11 and 13 September. He performed for De Fesch's benefit at the Haymarket on 26 March 1735. On 1 April 1735 Charles, "Master of the French-Horn," gave a concert at the Swan Tavern for his own benefit, performing "several new Pieces on the French Horn and Clarinet," probably the first public performance on the clarinet by a named player in the British Isles. At Goodman's Fields on 15 May he proffered "A Piece of Hunting-Musick on the French Horn." At that theatre on 10 October 1735 for the benefit of the playwright Carey he teamed with Buchinger, who played the German flute, in *Se larco.* He was back at the Swan Tavern, wringing another benefit from the public on 26 November, where he played on his favorite instrument, the French horn, and had the assistance not only of "several songs and duets by the two Miss Youngs" but of Pelicour, playing the German flute, "lately arrived from abroad, being the first time of his performing in England." On 11 February 1736 Charles was at Mercers' Hall, performing with the flutist Balicourt and the kettledrummer Benjamin Baker and Cecilia, Isabella, and Esther Young, for the benefit of the girls' father, Charles Young, organist of Allhallows, Barking.

On 11 March 1737 for five shillings the town could be admitted to Stationers' Hall for a concert of Music "By the best Hands. With a Solo, and several new Pieces on the French Horn, Clarinette, and Sharlarno by Mr Charles. Also several pieces on the French Horn by an English Gentlewoman, and a Negro Boy of ten Years old, both Scholars of Mr Charles."

"Two little Negro-Boys, Scholars to Mr Charles, who never perform'd before" kindly assisted the benefit of their colleague, young Master Ferg "Scholar to Mons Livier," at Drury Lane on 3 March 1738.

Nothing of Charles's activities was given by the bills or public prints from the spring of 1738 until that of 1740. He may have been touring in the provinces. On 21 May 1740 he assisted a benefit of several of Drury Lane's backstage personnel and then faded again from London accounts. In March of 1742 or earlier he was in Ireland, playing in the pit band at Aungier Street Theatre and advertising for pupils. *Faulkner's Dublin Journal* called him "the Hungarian," though the probability is that he was French.

His reputation for usefulness to benefit-seekers evidently preceded him to Ireland where, on 17 May 1742 in Smock Alley Theatre "For the Benefit of Mr Will. and Bar. Manwaring, at the Request of the Charitable Musical Society on College-green," he played, from Walsh's parts, sections of Handel's *Water Music*, accompanied on the kettledrum by Kounty. (He also gave a concert for his own benefit on 12 May playing on the *hautbois d'amour* and the "sholarno.") His "late Concert having given such general Satisfaction" he advertised that on 19 May he would play "once more before he leaves this Kingdom." He postponed the appearance until 2 June, and he also postponed his departure from Ireland, since he seems to have taken over for awhile the music room which had been abandoned by Francesco Geminiani in 1740, and on 12 February 1743, according to the *Dublin Journal*, he projected still another benefit, at Aungier Street.

By the fall he was in England again, advertising in November to perform *en trio* upon horns with his wife and sons, also on clarinet, *hautbois d'amour* and

"Shalmo, being instruments never heard here before."

In the winter he was still in London, being heard on 20 February 1744 ("first time of his performing since his arrival") in Macklin's illegal project at the Haymarket, playing a horn concerto after *Othello*.

A person named Charles appeared as clarinetist at Edinburgh in 1755. He probably was the Charles who composed "Twelve Duettos for two French Horns or Two German Flutes" which are appended to *Apollo's Cabinet*, published by John Sadler at Liverpool in 1756. There are in manuscript at King's College, Cambridge, a "Solo" for French horn and two "Solos for Spinnet" by "Mr Charles." One or all of those references may be to the Charles of this entry.

Charles, Mr [fl. 1740–1741], *dancer*.

One Charles, a dancer, appeared in the tiny part of the Porter in the pantomime afterpiece *The Imprisonment, Release, Adventures, and Marriage of Harlequin* at Goodman's Fields on 15 December 1740. He may have been present in the company throughout the season from October 1740 through May 1741, for the manager Giffard often did not advertise full casts.

Charles, Mr [fl. 1744–1755], *actor*.

On 22 September 1744 a Mr Charles played Roderigo in *Othello* with the young company assembled by Theophilus Cibber at the Haymarket. He may have performed in other pieces earlier in the summer but he is not cited in the bills. He repeated the part on 1, 3, and 6 September 1755 and played Sir John in the afterpiece *The Devil to Pay* on 9 September.

Charles, Mr [fl. 1784–1785], *stage doorkeeper*.

One Charles is listed as a stage doorkeeper at the King's Theatre for the season

1784–85 in a document of the Lord Chamberlain's office.

Charles, Master [fl. 1748]. See **POITIER, CHARLES.**

Charles, Master [fl. 1780], actor.
A Master Charles played the small part of Boy in *The Detection; or, A Sketch of the Times* in a special performance at the Haymarket on 13 November 1780. There was no regular company at the house that winter and he does not seem to have acted elsewhere.

Charles, John [fl. 1671–1672], scenekeeper.
John Charles was a scenekeeper in the King's Company in 1671–72, according to a Lord Chamberlain's warrant dated 20 March 1672.

"Charles the Merry Trumpeter," [fl. 1729–1733?], horn player, dancer, actor.
One "Charles the Merry Trumpeter," further identified only as "a Batchelor, who used to sound with Mr Bullock," was the beneficiary of a special performance at Lee's Booth on the Bowling Green, Southwark, on 14 October 1729. Charles danced "Countryman" in *A Comic Dance between Scaramouch and a Countryman.* (Charles performing this dance was portrayed by Hogarth as a detail of his famous engraving "Southwark Fair" in 1733.)
At the same booth on 8 October 1730 he was again benefited and was then called "the Merry Trumpeter of Oxford," a sobriquet retained in the bill for a third benefit at Fielding's booth at Southwark on 28 September 1731. On the latter occasion he gave entertainments between the acts of *A Bold Stroke for a Wife*, "particularly the *Black and White Joak*, to be sounded by Charles, and also a Joak of his own." At Lee's Great Booth on 12 October 1732 "persons from the Theatres" were

advertised in *Love Makes a Man*, "but the principal part [was] to be perform'd by Charles the Merry Trumpeter, that is to take the Money." Charles also danced during the performance. The bill ends with the doggerel: "And 'tis well if it takes / If not, the Trumpet breaks; / And they that are my Friends, that come to see my Play, / If it happens to rain, shall have a Coach to carry 'em away." He was given a benefit performance of *Oroonoko*, also at Lee's booth, on 18 October 1733. The presumption must be that he performed more than once at these booths in each of these seasons.

Charleton, Mrs Charles. See **GLASSINGTON, ELIZABETH.**

Charlotte, Miss. See **CLOUGH, MISS.**

Charlton. See also **CARLTON.**

Charlton, Mr [fl. 1729–1731], boxkeeper.
A Mr Charlton, boxkeeper at Goodman's Fields in 1729–30 and 1730–31, shared benefits on 18 June 1730 and 11 May 1731.

Charlton, Mr [fl. 1794–1798], violinist.
A violinist named Charlton was living at No 21, Artillery Lane, Bishopsgate Street, about 1794. He played for the concerts of the Academy of Ancient Music and the meetings of the Cecilian Society. He was a member of the considerable band of musicians under Barthélemon's leadership which supported leading singers in a performance of the *Messiah* organized by Dr Arnold for the benefit of the "Choral Fund, instituted for the Relief of their decayed Members, their Widows, and Orphans," at the Haymarket on 15 January 1798.
Charlton, possibly a relative of Charles Charlton, a well-known provincial manager of the time, does not appear to have be-

longed to the Royal Society of Musicians. He was perhaps the Cuthbert Charlton whose son Michael was buried on 20 November 1782 at St Paul, Covent Garden. On 19 August 1777 was baptized "Margaret Daughter of Culbert [*sic*] Charlton by Mabel his Wife."

"Charmante." *See* "LA CHARMANTE."

Charole. *See* SHAROLE.

Charon, Mme ₁*fl. 1755–1756*₁, *dancer.*

A Mme Charon was among the handful of French dancers in Garrick's company in 1755–56, the season of the "Chinese Festival" riots, when the interior of the theatre was demolished by mobs. How many times she danced—or attempted to dance—is not known. She was named in the bills only once, on 8 November 1755.

Charpentier, Mme ₁*fl. 1734–1735*₁, *dancer?*

A Madame Charpentier was a member of Francisque Moylin's French company at the Haymarket in 1734–35, the first foreign company to play in London for seven years. They opened on 26 October and carried a repertoire of comedies and farces, with a few tragedies, through 3 June. They also played twice at Goodman's Fields, were patronized by the gentry, and gave several command performances. It is not known what parts Madame Charpentier essayed. She may have been a dancer.

Charrier. *See* CHERRIER.

Chart, Mr ₁*fl. 1794–1795*₁, *carpenter.*

A Mr Chart was a carpenter during the 1794–95 season at Covent Garden at an unspecified salary.

Chateauneuf, Mons ₁*fl. 1748–1749*₁, *dancer, manager.*

A Monsieur Chateauneuf was a dancer in the company assembled at Rich's behest by Jean Louis Monnet and brought to England in 1748–49. (Max Fuchs observes that "Chateauneuf" was a banal "pseudonyme, fut porté par de nombreux comédiens"). Rich, for fear of censure by the xenophobic public, withdrew at the last moment, leaving the financial burdens on Monnet.

Monnet attempted at the Haymarket on 14 and 15 November 1749 to present performances but they were interrupted not only by riotous superpatriots among the English but by angry Huguenots who had jammed into the pit. Subsequent performances were postponed for prudential reasons because of strung-out elections. The upshot was a kind of bankruptcy for Monnet, who returned to France, leaving only partly paid the salaries of his company. Chateauneuf received only £15 17s. of his contracted £43 15s. for the season.

At some point in his career before coming to England Chateauneuf had adopted a female orphan, had given her his name, and had taught her to dance, according to W. R. Chetwood. He later married her. At some time after leaving England the pair organized their own company and played, reportedly, at Bordeaux.

Chateauneuf, Marie *b. 1721, dancer, singer, manager.*

According to the testimony of W. R. Chetwood, Marie Chateauneuf was born in France on 15 April 1721, was early orphaned, and was adopted and brought up by a dancer named Chateauneuf who later married her.

Marie Chateauneuf first appeared in London as "Mlle" Chateauneuf dancing in the French company managed by Francisque Moylin which played at the Little Theatre in the Haymarket about 116 times from 26 October 1734 through 3 June 1735. How many times Mlle Chateauneuf danced that season is not recorded.

She was next seen in the London bills in 1738 as a part of the company which arrived in England on 25 September under the management of Jean Baptiste Lesage and the younger brother of Francisque Moylin. Their attempt to play at the Haymarket on 9 October was met with a violent anti-French riot. Troops and magistrates were called but to no avail. The rioters won their point and no further performances were given that season.

Mlle Chateauneuf may have returned to France for a time, but she was in Drury Lane's corps of dancers for the 1739–40 season. Though she was not particularly noticed in the bills, she was in public demand, as was violently demonstrated on 23 January 1740 when she was ill and could not dance. Through error her name was in the bills, and when she did not appear "several Gentlemen in the Boxes pull'd up the Seats and Flooring of the same, tore down the Hangings, broke down the partitions, all the Glasses and sconces, the King's Arms over the middle front Box was pull'd down and broke to Pieces; they also destroy'd the Harpsichord, Bass Viol, and other Instruments . . ." and so on, damaging the house to the amount of perhaps £400. During the next season, Marie headed the female dancers and her name appeared in the bills some 100 times, reflecting her continuing popularity. She often danced solo but more frequently with the accomplished dancer Muilment. At the time of her benefit, 1 April 1741, she lodged at Mr Farnel's in Bridges Street.

She was soon afterward in Ireland. The *Dublin Journal* announced in mid-April 1741 that the proprietors of the Aungier Street Theatre had contracted with her to play there during the ensuing winter and that she was "already on her journey thither." She was also announced to dance at the theatre on 8 June.

There is no trace of Mlle Chateauneuf in the London bills for 1742–43. The *Dublin Journal* of 16 June 1743 announced her as dancing at Aungier Street on that date and added that she had "just arrived from England along with Mons Mullemont [*recte* Muilment] and Mons Picq." Neither one of these dancers was in London enterprises in 1742–43, and it may be supposed that all three had been either obscurely in the provinces or in France. Mlle Chateauneuf remained in Dublin where, during 1743–44, she was engaged at Smock Alley for (according to the *Journal*) "100 pounds certain for that season and a benefit."

According to the vague account of W. R. Chetwood, he had (by about 1748) been told by a "gentleman from Bordeaux" that Marie was lately married to her foster-father. Chetwood had also heard that, after leaving England, she and Mons Chateauneuf had headed a troupe of comedians of their own, playing in Bordeaux, where "Madem Chateauneuf" was heard to sing "several English songs by Desire of the Audience, particularly the Song of Rosy Wine from the Masque of Comus." That she did sing on occasion seems clear, for Chetwood claims that he had instructed her in the part of Polly in *The Beggar's Opera*.

Chatillion, Mons (*fl. 1735*), *dancer.*
Monsieur Chatillion made his first, and evidently his only, appearance on the London stage in a dance called *Two Pierrots* with Le Blond at the Haymarket on 17 September 1735.

Chatin. *See* CHATEAUNEUF, MARIE.

Chatterley, Miss (*fl. 1791–1798*), *actress, singer.*
The Miss Chatterley who made her theatrical debut at the Haymarket on 26 September 1791 was probably the daughter of the instrument maker turned theatrical call-boy "Bob" Chatterley. Her first part was that of Miss Summerville in the after-

piece *The Double Amour*. She was Nerissa in *The Merchant of Venice* at a special benefit performance for Wilkinson at the Haymarket on 20 February 1792. She next played Peggy in *The Gentle Shepherd* in Walker's benefit at the Haymarket on 22 October 1792 and during part of the year was employed in Duckworth's company at the New Theatre, Parson's Green, Fulham. From February through March 1794 she was at the Manchester Theatre Royal.

Probably through the interest of her father (who collected her 16s. 8d. each week) she came to Drury Lane on 21 April 1794 to assist in the opulent production of Kemble's revision of *Macbeth* by singing in a *"Chorus* of Witches and Spirits."

During the 1794–95 season Miss Chatterly was constantly employed at Drury Lane from 27 September through 6 June. As one of numerous female "Captives" of the Tartar horde in *Lodoiska* and as an Indian in *The Cherokee*, she sang in various choruses but was never plucked from such anonymity for a speaking part. She returned to Drury Lane in 1796–97 from 19 October through 28 March, again always submerged in the choruses supporting extravaganzas. She was not seen again in the bills until 5 June 1798 when she played some unspecified small part in the afterpiece *The Eleventh of June*. After a repetition of this piece on 13 June 1798 she was seen no more.

Chatterley, J. [fl. 1795?–1803?], dancer, actor.

A "Master Chatterley" danced at Richmond, Surrey, in the summer of 1795. A "Master J. Chatterley" was at Drury Lane on 5 February 1799 dancing, along with his brother "Master W. Chatterley," (William Simmonds Chatterley) as one of the anonymous peasants in a dance called *Moggy and Jemmy*. He danced Sauny in *The Scotch Ghost* on 2 December 1799, repeated several times that season. He re-

turned to the company in similar but infrequent dances in 1800, 1801, and 1802.

We believe Master J. to have been the elder brother of William Simmonds Chatterley inasmuch as several Drury Lane bills (for instance 22 December 1800, placing them among the "Pantomimick Characters") cite "Masters Chatterley and W. Chatterley," and in such cases the initial letter of the younger brother's first name was nearly always furnished in the bills. Master J. was probably a son of the performers Mr and Mrs Robert E. Chatterley.

Chatterley, Robert E. [fl. 1792–1818], messenger, prompter, actor.

The father of William Simmonds Chatterley the actor (1787–1821) was, according to several accounts of the life of the younger man, a surgical instrument maker of Cannon Street who was first employed at Drury Lane Theatre in 1791 and who remained there through 1817–18. A manuscript note by John Philip Kemble calls the elder Chatterley "porter" to the theatre. We believe that he is to be identified as the Chatterley of the Folger Library's Drury Lane account books: 5 July 1799, "Bob Chatterley, messenger," and 23 November 1799, "Robert Chatterley." He appears in salary receipts of 1813 now in the Harvard Theatre Collection as "R. E. Chatterley."

Bob Chatterley was by turns termed "caller" and "messenger" and seems to have done many small tasks for a theatre which rewarded him with £1 5s. for a six-day week in 1812–13. He was pressed into service also as an actor at least once before 1800. A Chatterley was actors' caller in the Drury Lane accounts of 1796–97 at 18s. a week. Kemble noted in a memorandum of 11 February 1799: *"Hamlet—*Mr Wewitzer never came to act Lucianus so the Prompter's call-boy acted it." Under "Powell-Prompter" in the next week's pay list a Chatterley is listed as "Call-Boy." By 1813–14 Bob Chatterley was deputy prompter at £1 10s. per week, and he was listed as prompter in 1816–17 and 1817–18.

An undated ledger in the Folger Library containing the habitual roles of dozens of Drury Lane actors at the turn of the century lists the parts played by "Mr. Chatterley." They were too small for, and not in the exact line of, W. S. Chatterley, and though they could conceivably be assigned to his brother "J. Chatterley," we are inclined to give them to Bob Chatterley, particularly inasmuch as he and his wife were constantly present at Drury Lane throughout the early years of the nineteenth century.

The parts were: First Sailor in *Hamlet*, Fidler in *The Devil to Pay*, Lewis in *The Duenna*, Dubbs in *The Review*, Joe in *Bee Hive*, Simon in *Turn Out*, Matthias in *Midnight Hour*, Dennis in *As You Like It*, Smuggler in *Up All Night*, Servant in *The Wonder*, Rugby in *The Merry Wives of Windsor*, Thomas in *No Song, No Supper*, Page in *Honey Moon*, Gypsy in *Maid of the Mill*, Tapster in *The Beaux' Stratagem*, Rapine in *The Castle of Andalusia*, the Carrier in *1 Henry IV*, Sentinel in *Matrimony*, Post Boy in *She Wou'd and She Wou'd Not*, a Servant in *The Inconstant*, Quill in *Hit or Miss*, Vasques in *Rule a Wife and Have a Wife*, Jeffery in *Netley Abbey*, Jessamine in *The Confederacy*, Richard in *Raising the Wind*, Mob in *The Mayor of Garratt*, Simon in *The Suspicious Husband*, Tom in *The Jealous Wife*, Samson in *Romeo and Juliet*, Jacob in *False Alarms*, Moresco in *Remorse*, Antonio in *Othello*, Tamuri in *Lodoiska*, Wolf in *The School for Wives*, Cook in *Love in a Village*, Conrad in *Ella Rosenberg*, First Servant in *The Peasant Boy*, First Frenchman in *The Russian*, Robin in *Fontainebleau*, Perequille in *The Mountaineers*, Robber in *The Maniac*, Jeffery in *The Way to Get Married*, Porter in *Seeing's Believing*, John in *Speed the Plough*, Stockbroker in *Bold Stroke for a Wife*, Diggory in *First Impressions*, Napkin in *Modern Antiques*, Selim in *Illusion*, the Clown in *Fortune's Frolic*, the Watchman in *The Apprentice*, an Officer in *The Siege of Belgrade*, Dangerfeldt in *The Woodman's Hut*, Dick in *The Belle's Stratagem*, Bailiff in *Riches*, Corporal Squib in *The Rival Soldiers*, the Second Murderer in *Macbeth*, the Serjeant in *The Ninth Statue*, the Groom in *Richard II*, Peasant in *Ira*, an Officer in *The Wheel of Fortune*, an Irishman in *Rosina*, a Highlander in *Family Legend*, Marker in *The Road to Ruin*, a Robber in *Honesty's the Best Policy*, Maurice in *The English Fleet*, a Countryman in *The London Hermit*, the Master of the Horse in *The Critick*, and a Fidler in *Chrononhotonthologos*. His most frequent parts were waiters (in *Three and the Deuce*, *Ways and Means*, *Cure for the Heart Ache*, *Inkle and Yarico*, *Two Strings to Your Bow*, *The Farmer*, *Past Ten O'Clock*, *Town and Country*, *The World*) and bailiffs (*The Honest Thieves*, *The School for Prejudice*, *Wild Oats*, *Lose No Time*, *Riches*).

Robert Chatterley and his wife, who also acted, are sometimes liable to confusion with the better-known Mr and Mrs William Simmonds Chatterley, who were at Drury Lane during some of the periods when the Robert Chatterleys were employed there. Bob Chatterley was apparently the paterfamilias of the Chatterleys and had at least two more offspring besides William Simmonds Chatterley on the British boards during the eighteenth and / or early nineteenth century: Master J. Chatterley the dancer and a Miss Chatterley who was an actress.

Chatterley, Mrs Robert E. [*fl. 1795–1819*], *actress*.

Mrs Robert E. Chatterley was carried in the Drury Lane accounts in the season of 1795–96 and after 1807–8, remaining in the company until at least 1818–19. When she was paid separately she was named in the pay lists among the actresses, though on most Saturdays "Mr and Mrs R Chatterley" were paid together. Curiously, though, she was never in the playbills before 1800.

A Drury Lane ledger of the early nineteenth century, now in the Folger Library, gives a list of her habitual parts: Lucy in *The Devil to Pay*, Betty in *The Hypocrite*, Gypsy in *The Maid of the Mill*, Isabel in *Rule a Wife and Have a Wife*, the Housekeeper in *The West Indian*, Fanny in *The Way to Get Married*, Hibernia in *The Orange Boven*, Selina in *Lock and Key*, the Attendant in *Jean de Paris*, a Witch in *Macbeth*, Iris in *Bold Stroke for a Husband*, and a Milliner in *The Road to Ruin*. But she was often pushed into parts even smaller than most of these (usually as a maid, a type she played in *The Rivals*, *The Duenna*, *Lionel and Clarissa*, *The Suspicious Husband*, *The Jealous Wife*, *Love in a Village*, and *The Wheel of Fortune*).

Mrs Chatterley also played at Brighton in 1809.

Chatterley, William Simmonds
1787–1821, actor, dancer.

William Simmonds Chatterley was born in London on 21 March 1787, probably the son of an instrument maker, Robert E. Chatterley, who secured menial employment at Drury Lane theatre and was later to become an actor and prompter there. William's mother was an actress and singer at Drury Lane, and he had a brother and a sister on the stage.

William was said in an early account to have been acting from midway of his third year, in the fall of 1789, playing Cupid in *Arthur and Emmeline* and the King of the Fairies in *The Jubilee*. The parts are not to be found in the bills; however, on 26 December 1789 a "Master Chatterley" was listed at Drury Lane as an unnamed character in the popular pantomime *Harlequin's Frolics*.

William was doubtless the Master Chatterley who was given the part of Young Marcius in *Coriolanus* at Drury Lane on 31 March 1792, repeated on 21 April. He was not otherwise noticed that season at Drury Lane, but he danced at the Haymarket the following summer. He was very likely the Master Chatterley listed as a dancer at Drury Lane from 27 December 1792 through 21 May 1793, but he never performed solo parts.

In fact, Chatterley was brought along very slowly in his profession, probably by his father, and in 1793–94 the bills showed him at Drury Lane for a week only, earning £1 as the apparition of the Crowned Child in Kemble's production of *Macbeth*. He danced anonymously that season also. He enjoyed a full season both dancing and acting at Drury Lane from 23 September 1794 through 14 April 1795, helping to fill up mob scenes and choruses, dancing in specialties with other children, but also becoming somewhat less anonymous, as the Boy in *Henry V*, the Crowned Child again, and the Child in *Isabella*.

William was in the female role of Juliana in *The Prisoner* on 18 May 1797, one of the children in *The Children in the Wood* on 19 September 1797, was promoted from the Crowned Child to Fleance in *Macbeth* on 18 September 1798, was the Duke of York in *Richard III* on 25 September 1798, the Child in *The Outlaws* on 16 October 1798, Lilly in *The Son-in-Law* on 21 December, (acting along with his brother J. Chatterley), danced as a peasant in *Moggy and Jemmy* on 5 February 1799, and was the Boy in the first performances of R. B. Sheridan's *Pizarro* on 24 May 1799 and afterward.

By 1799–1800 William was earning 15s. weekly. He had also been noticed by John Bannister, who, according to Oxberry, took him to Birmingham to play juvenile parts, and soon "By the friendship of [the actor] Captain [George] Wathen, he was introduced to the patronage of Mr Maddox, M. P. and a society of his friends, who employed him in their private performances, during which he experienced considerable kindness from the Margravine of Anspach." Chatterley was fortunate to find such friends and such employments during his awkward years of adolescence. After the season of 1803–4, when he was 17 years old, he left Drury Lane for a provincial experience in Birmingham, Sheffield, and Leicester. He then joined itinerants near London, then Thornton's company at Gosport, and went thence to Watson's company at Cheltenham, going meanwhile up the ladder from small parts to larger ones in genteel comedy. When he was 21 years old he discovered, apparently quite suddenly, that despite his youth he was best suited for old eccentrics like Sir Peter Teazle, Ogleby, and Sir Francis Gripe. He underwent further seasoning at Birmingham and Brighton in the winter of 1809. Palmer and Dimond hired him for Bath in 1810–11 to take Lovegrove's place, and he was an immediate success there in such parts as Sir Luke Tremor in *Such Things Are*, Verdun in *Lover's Vows*, Coupee in *The Virgin Unmask'd*, and Lingo in *The Agreeable Surprise*. Genest much later remembered that, though William Chatterley was "not above 24 or 25 [actually he was 23] – yet he played the *very* old men so well – that he might be said to have been almost another Spiller."

While he was in Bath William met a young woman, Louisa Simeon by name, "blue-eyed and above the common height," according to Oxberry, the daughter of a fashionable French milliner of St James's Street, Piccadilly. Louisa is said to have been placed at age three in a convent near Liverpool where she had remained for four years and then to have been sent to the boarding school conducted by Mrs Habersham at Bath. Chatterley married her on 11 August 1813 and brought her onto the stage, where she demonstrated both native talent and aptness to learn. Her first ap-

pearance was as Juliet in *Romeo and Juliet* at Bath in November, 1814.

The Chatterleys went in 1816 to London and were engaged at the Lyceum. William appeared for the first time as an adult, and for only one performance, at Drury Lane on 2 June 1817 as Lord Ogleby in *The Clandestine Marriage* and was "received with great applause" according to the theatre's account book.

But William Chatterley had always been more than a little bibulous, and convivial gatherings began to seem more attractive to him than rehearsals. Soon he was reduced to accepting temporary engagements at the less fashionable London houses – the Adelphi, the Surrey, the Olympic – and in the provinces. The latter years of his life are obscure. He died at Lynn, Norfolk, in April 1821. In May administration of property worth only £40 was recorded to Marie Louise Antoinette Florence Chatterley "late of Craven Buildings in the Parish of St Clement Danes, Middx."

Genest remembers that Chatterley "had one great fault – like Shuter he did not care whether he put in or left out nonsense – he never kept the stage waiting, but having a general notion of what he was to say, he went on with something or other – Stanley used to say . . . that if Chatterley gave him the right cue he was all astonishment."

Mrs Chatterley had, in her husband's final years, much surpassed him in activity and publicity. Oxberry, who managed the pair at the Olympic, says that it was there that she finally made her fame in the interlude called *Twelve Precisely*, in which, as Amelia Wildlove, she revealed her versatility in a series of disguises: an Irish chambermaid, a French marchioness, a military officer, and a French husband. William Hazlitt called her a "delectable victim" when she acted in the gothic horror play *The Vampyre* in 1820. On 6 November 1821 she appeared for the first time at Covent Garden, playing Kate Hardcastle in *She Stoops to Conquer*. There she remained,

Harvard Theatre Collection

WILLIAM S. CHATTERLEY, as Justice
Woodcock

engraving by Thomson, after Chater

at 12 guineas a week through at least
1825–26. An unattributed manuscript in
the Folger Library claims: "Since Mr Chatterley's decease this lady has married Mr
Place, a tailor, residing at Charing Cross."

A stipple engraving by J. Thomson,
after Chater, for the *Theatrical Inquisitor*
of 1 October 1817 depicts Chatterley as
Justice Woodcock in *Love in a Village*. He
was pictured by an anonymous engraver as
Miss Abigail Antique in *The White Cat*
in a "tuppence coloured" print published by
West in 1812. W. Heath drew and engraved him as Columbine in *The White
Cat*, with James Kirby as Clown, in another
print (penny plain or tuppence coloured)
published by West, 1812.

Chaundler, George [*fl. 1669*], *manager?*

On 18 June 1669 a warrant was issued
to apprehend George Chaundler and others
"for keeping playhouses and sounding
trumpets, drums and fifes at dumb shows
and modells" without first having paid the
usual fee to the royal sergeant trumpeter.

Chavigny. *See also* CHEVIGNY.

Chavigny, Mons [*fl. 1720–1721*],
actor.

Monsieur and Madame Chavigny were
members of de Grimbergue's troupe of
French comedians who played a total of 51
performances in London between 29 December 1720 and 4 May 1721 at the new
Haymarket Theatre. Though the company
suffered financial reverses at first through
lack of audience response, they finally drew
crowds large enough to warrant staying the
whole winter. But when the French group
left in July 1721 the *London Journal* felt
that it was "good Riddance of those Apish
Impertinents."

The Chavignys were probably the unnamed pair mentioned in the 16 January
1721 playbill for *Le joueur*: Gamester was
acted by a player newly arrived from the
King's Theatre in Paris, and a new actress
making her first appearance in England was
also in the cast. Most of the bills were
similarly vague about the performers'
names, but the Chavignys were mentioned
specifically on 28 April 1721 at their benefit: "De le Colle des Femmes" of Molière
was the play, and the bill said "The two
greatest Parts [were] by Clauigney [*sic*]
and his Wife." The performance was for
the "Benefit [of] Mons Clauigney, who acts
the Part of the Burgaway Gentilhomme,
and his Wife the little Actress." *The London Stage*, in error apparently, cites Madame Chavigny as "Mlle" in the company
roster.

Chavigny, Mme [*fl. 1720–1721*],
actress. See CHAVIGNY, MONS.

Chaville. *See* CHEVALIER.

Chazal. *See* DE GAMBARINI.

Checa. *See* CIECA.

"Checo Torinese." *See* TORINESE, CHECO.

Cheese, Mr [*fl. 1784*], *singer.*
A Mr Cheese, said to be from Manchester, was listed by Burney among the tenor singers at the Handel Memorial Concerts at Westminster Abbey and the Pantheon on 26, 27 and 29 May and 3 and 5 June 1784. (He may have been related to Miss Cheese, a singer whose name appears under date of 26 February 1815 in the Minute Books of the Governors of the Irish Musical Fund on her appointment by the Governors to sing that year in the Dublin commemoration concert.)

Chelleri, Signor [*fl. 1725*], *bass viol player.*
A Signor Chelleri played a solo on the bass viol on the occasion of the benefit of the Italian opera singer Gaetano Philippo Rochetti, on 12 April 1725. It was for Chelleri "the first Time of his appearing on the English Stage." We have no record of other performances by him, but there is a possibility that he was Fortunato Chelleri (1690–1757) the composer, who was in England, according to Grove, for 10 months in 1726.

Chelsum, James *c. 1700–1743, singer.*
James Chelsum was born about 1700 and sworn a Gentleman of the Chapel Royal replacing James Hart on 12 June 1718. On 21 June 1731 he married Mary Ward. Their first son, James, was born on 13 April and baptized on 15 May 1738 at, apparently, both Westminster Abbey and St John the Evangelist, Westminster. A second son, Robert, was born on 19 June 1740 and buried on 26 September 1744.

The elder James Chelsum died on 3 August 1743 at the age of 43, and administration of his estate was granted his widow Mary on 18 August 1743.

Chembini, Mr [*fl. 1784–1785*], *singer?*
The Lord Chamberlain's accounts listed an opera performer named Chembini, possibly a singer, who was at the King's Theatre in the Haymarket in 1784–85 at a season salary of £200.

Chementi. *See* CHIMENTI.

Chemont, Mons [*fl. 1742*], *dancer.*
At the playhouse in James Street on 22 November 1742 a benefit was held for "a Person who has a mind to get money" (probably Charlotte Charke), and Monsieur Chemont entertained with a new *Peasant Dance.*

Chene. *See* CHENEY and CHEYNE.

Cheney, Master [*fl. 1770*], *singer.*
A Master Cheney sang in concert at Marylebone Gardens some half dozen times from 16 June to 11 September 1770 in programs which also included comic opera, instrumental solos, and fireworks. His name appeared opposite the character Cupid on the dramatis personae list accompanying the 1795 publication of Thomas Chatterton's burletta *The Revenge,* which has been reported as having been put on at Marylebone Gardens in 1770. It was probably not then performed, however.

Cheney, Sarah. *See* GARDNER, MRS WILLIAM.

Chenu. *See* PIELTAIN, CHARA.

Cherington. *See also* CHERRINGTON.

Cherington, Richard [*fl. 1678–1685*], *singer.*
On 8 April 1679 a Richard Carrington

was listed in the Lord Chamberlain's accounts as one of the singing Chapel boys serving under John Blow. On that date he was paid 3s. per day for having attended the King at Windsor from 14 August to 26 September 1678. At the coronation of James II on 23 April 1685 a Richard Cherington marched as clerk of the choir at Westminster. Which is the correct spelling of the name is uncertain, and two different people could be involved, but there was another Chapel boy serving under Blow, one John Cherrington, in 1676, so perhaps something like the spelling used here is correct.

Cheriton, David c. 1707–1758, singer.

David Cheriton was born about 1707. Nothing is known of his early life or musical education. He was a member of the choirs of Westminster Abbey and St Paul's Cathedral and a Gentleman of the Chapel Royal. He was on the list of the performers of the *Messiah* at the Foundling Hospital in May 1754, being paid 10s. 6d. His first wife Frances died (age 21) on 13 April 1739 and was buried in the North Cloister of Westminster Abbey on 19 April. His daughter Arabella died on 4 March 1738 and was buried on 6 March in the West Cloister. A David Cheriton, perhaps his father, was buried at St Margaret, Westminster, on 28 January 1750. According to the Funeral Book of Westminster Abbey the singer died on 6 January 1758 and was buried on 11 January in the West Cloister of the Abbey. His second wife and relict Elizabeth proved his will (signed 2 January 1758) on 13 January. It left all his estate, unspecified, to her.

Cherrier, Miss [fl. 1708], dancer.

On 20 and 24 January 1708 at the Queen's Theatre in the Haymarket Miss Cherrier danced with her father, the dancing master and choreographer René Cherrier, and she may have appeared there

regularly, unsung, throughout the spring of the year.

Cherrier, René [fl. 1699–1708], dancer, choreographer.

René Cherrier and his wife, Ann de la Croix, were performing at the opera in Metz from February to May 1699, and Cherrier was spoken of as the head of the opera troupe there on 21 August 1699. But Cherrier's wife had either retired or died before he began his English career.

Cherrier's earliest noticed dancing in London was on 14 December 1703 at a Drury Lane concert with Du Ruel, l'Abbé, and others. From that time forward he was much in demand at the theatres, providing entr'acte specialty dances, often of his own composing. Most of the dancing he did was described in little detail in the bills: "A new *Entry*," "a new *Chacone*," "Punchanello," "Spanish Dance," and the like. Once, however, on 21 June 1704 at Drury Lane, he was cited as dancing the Cyclops dance in *Psyche,* "in which Monsieur Cherrier perform'd the part of Vulcan with great Applause." On 24 April 1704 when *The Merry Wives of Windsor* was performed by Betterton's troupe at St James's, Cherrier and the Du Ruels provided the dancing. When Walsh published *A Collection of the most celebrated Jigs, etc.* in 1705, included were a number of "new Stage Dances" by Cherrier and others.

The dancer's most famous pupil was Hester Santlow, who made her debut at Drury Lane on 28 February 1706 dancing with her master. The two had signed an agreement by which Cherrier received half of what Miss Santlow made for her appearances for a period of five years. The agreement, in the Coke papers at Harvard, indicated that Cherrier had trained her for two years "before she went upon ye stage." She became in time one of the favorite actress-dancers of the day and wife of the tragedian Barton Booth.

By early 1708, Cherrier was a member

of the opera company at the Queen's Theatre in the Haymarket, and there he was paid £1 10s. daily, second only to Desbarques, who received £1 more. With him in the troupe were his daughter, who made a few appearances in early 1708, and Hester Santlow; but gone were the popular Du Ruels and l'Abbé. Gone, too, after the season ended on 20 May 1708, was René Cherrier.

Cherrier seems to have been skilled at both serious and, as it was called, "grotesque" dancing, but of his style we know little. In 1734 Kellom Tomlinson published *The Art of Dancing* and said he *"had . . . the good Fortune to be . . . instructed in the Theatrical Way, by that great Performer Mr.* Cherrier, *once contemporary with the inimitable Mr.* L'Abbe *. . . Mr.* Cherrier's *great Merit, after he quitted the Stage, was supported a long Time by the late Mr.* John Shaw."

Cherrington. *See also* CHERINGTON.

Cherrington, John ₁*fl. 1676*₁, *singer.*

John Cherrington was one of the Chapel boys under the care of John Blow. On 8 November 1676, according to the Chapel records, Blow was to be paid for expenses involved in teaching and caring for the boys, and part of the money was to go for a nurse for Cherrington, who was "sick of spotted fever."

"Cheshire Boy." *See* SANT, MR.

Chettle, Mr ₁*fl. 1740–1748?*₁, *actor, dancer, singer.*

Mr Chettle was first seen in London as a member of Giffard's company at Goodman's Fields in the season of 1740–41. He danced *The Drunken Peasant* on 23 and 24 October, 19, 20, 22, and 24 November 1740, 19 March, 6, 13, 15, 16, 20, and 22 April 1741, but otherwise figured only in a comic ballet with four other dancers on 29

October. He offered his chef d'oeuvre again for a benefit at James Street on 16 June and several times at Turbut and Yates's Great Theatrical Booth during the time of Bartholomew Fair in late August 1741.

Chettle was not seen again in London so far as theatrical news or announcements show, until he joined Hallam's Company at Goodman's Fields on 3 December 1744, playing Filch "(with a Hornpipe)" in *The Beggar's Opera.* By 10 December he was again doing his specialty dance *The Drunken Peasant.* On 26 December he and a fellow dancer, Daniel, played the two Recruits in *The Recruiting Officer*, and it is to be suspected that the parts involved dancing, as perhaps also did the added part of Death in the Dryden-Davenant musical version of *The Tempest* which the Goodman's Fields company presented first on 14 February 1745 and repeated several times. On 20 February Chettle had been promoted to the role of Stephano, and on 15 April he played Setebos.

Chettle seems to have performed but once in 1745–46, although his lowly condition and the incomplete state of the bills leave open the possibility that he was there during most of the season. But he assuredly danced his *Drunken Peasant* on 17 February 1746, the occasion of the benefit of Mr and Mrs Dove.

He managed his own "Great Theatrical Booth opposite Greyhound Inn" at Bartholomew Fair in 1747. The bills of 22, 25, and 26 August show a company composed partly of Chettle, Smith, and Miss Moreau performing *Miss in Her Teens* and the pantomime *Frolicksome Lasses*, in which Chettle was Harlequin and also did a hornpipe. "Italian Fireworks" were also set off just as the show began at noon.

The Chettle who was singing at Sadler's Wells on or around 14 March 1748 was probably our man. (A Mrs Chettle, a timber merchant, was paid occasional large sums by Drury Lane Theatre from 1783 through 1787.)

Chetwood, Richabella, later Mrs Tobias Gemea (fl. 1738–1771), actress.

Richabella Chetwood was the daughter of William Rufus Chetwood, the Drury Lane prompter, by his first wife. Her debut was on 17 May 1738 at Drury Lane as Lucy in *The Squire of Alsatia* at her father's benefit shared with his fiancée, Anne Brett. Miss Brett and Chetwood married in June 1738, and for a time the bills did not carefully distinguish between Mrs and Miss Chetwood. It is probable, however, that Richabella played Kate in *The King and the Miller of Mansfield* on 25 May 1738 and Sukey in *The Beggar's Opera* on 28 May 1739. She acted Sukey again on 6 September 1739 but either did not stay for the rest of the season or assumed roles too small to be noted in the bills. She was next mentioned on 29 September 1744 as Charlotte in *The Mock Doctor* at the Haymarket Theatre, where Theophilus Cibber was holding forth. After that she went to Ireland to pursue the rest of her career as Mrs Tobias Gemea, wife of a provincial Irish actor.

She played at Smock Alley in Dublin in 1746, and she and her father were in Dublin at the end of February 1747 when they both signed a plea to the Lord Lieutenant to reopen the playhouses. Then she headed north, where she spent most of the next two decades. In 1751–52 she and her husband were at Belfast under Love's management, two of her parts being Mistress Quickly in *The Merry Wives of Windsor* and Combrush in *The Honest Yorkshireman*. The following season found the Gemeas again at Belfast, where they were joined by Richabella's father, who served as prompter. The Gemeas were in the Drogheda company playing at the Vaults in Belfast under Sheriffe in early 1758. They acted in September 1759 at Ballymena Market House and by 2 December were playing at the Town Hall, Coleraine. On 27 December Mrs Gemea played Angelica in *Love for Love* at a performance sponsored by the Masons. The summer of 1761 found the couple again at Belfast, after which they dropped from sight until the summer of 1770. Richabella, apparently without her husband, acted at Belfast again in 1771, her last known appearance being on 16 August. Her husband was still acting in 1773 at Waterford and Kilkenny, after which his name also disappeared from the bills. So far as is known, Tobias Gemea never appeared in London.

Chetwood, William Rufus d. 1766, prompter, playwright, actor.

According to his *General History of the Stage* (1749), William Rufus Chetwood traveled a great deal, perhaps as a sailor, before he began his long career in the theatre about 1715. "I have been in most Parts of the World in my Youth," he wrote, and he was delighted to see Irishmen in charge of things in so many places he "touch'd at (as the Sailors term it)." "Even the distant Chinese have very fine Theatre," he said—despite the lack of Irish help, one supposes. "I saw, in my Youth, a Chinese Performance at Canton, where the Scenes, Machines, and Habits, were surprising and magnificent," but, he confessed, not understanding the language he could make little sense of it. His interest in theatre, at any rate, was stimulated by his travels, and when he was first mentioned in the London playbills he may well have had some practical experience behind him.

On 10 June 1715 at Drury Lane Chetwood was given a benefit as prompter, shared with King the boxeeper. He continued at Drury Lane through the 1720–21 season, sharing annual benefits with one other person. *The London Stage* lists him as the Lincoln's Inn Fields prompter in 1718–19, but his benefit at Drury Lane on 2 May 1719 would seem to deny this. He did move to Lincoln's Inn Fields in 1721–22, however, and was granted a solo benefit on 4 April 1722 which brought in £94

2s. He worked under John Rich that one season only, and on 15 September 1722 received an indulgence discharging him and giving him freedom to work for another playhouse if he wished. In the following season he returned to Drury Lane.

From 1722–23 through 1740–41 Chetwood served as prompter for Drury Lane, usually getting individual benefits in the spring but occasionally sharing with others. His shared benefits, however, seem to have been special ones, such as that shared with the actor Bowen's widow one year, with a family in distress another, or (after his marriage to Anne Brett) with his wife. Of his job as prompter we hear little, though we know that in that position he was able to help actors learn their trade. He and Theophilus Cibber, Chetwood said later, recognized Kitty Clive's talent when she was still Miss Raftor and recommended her to the elder Cibber; Spranger Barry "received the first Rudiments" from the prompter; and Mlle Chateauneuf was instructed by Chetwood when she was preparing for the role of Polly in *The Beggar's Opera*. Playwrights, too, addressed themselves to Chetwood for opinions on their work.

Chetwood spent some of his summers dabbling in acting and managing. He prompted for Pinkethman at his playhouse in Richmond in the summer of 1724, receiving a benefit there on 3 August, and a month later he operated a Southwark Fair booth with Norris, Orfeur, and Oates. His one attempt at acting was apparently on 2 September 1724 when he played Bussle Head in *Merlin the British Enchanter* at that booth.

Soon after he began working in the theatre in London, Chetwood went into the bookselling business. Before opening his own shop he was an apprentice to Curll, but by the fall of 1719 Southerne's *The Spartan Dame* was "printed for W. Chetwood at Cato's Head under Tom's Coffee House in Russell Street, Covent Garden.

. . . ." In the spring of 1720, now located at "the Post-House in Covent-Garden," Chetwood joined four other booksellers to print *The Half Pay Officers*, a Lincoln's Inn Fields play. Publications printed for or by Chetwood continued into the 1750s (though Plomer's *A Dictionary of Printers and Booksellers* oddly excludes his activity). In August or September 1739 Dr Johnson wrote his wife of his play *Irene*, then unproduced and unpublished, which "Chetwood the Prompter is desirous of bargaining for . . . and offers fifty Guineas for the right of printing after it shall be played." The proposal never came to anything, and not until ten years later was *Irene* presented to the world.

Chetwood also found time for a considerable amount of writing during his years at Drury Lane, some of it dramatic. Two of his earliest plays, published in 1720, were satires on the South Sea project and not intended for the stage: *South-Sea; or, the Biters Bit* and *The Stock-Jobbers, or, The Humours of Exchange Alley*. *The Lover's Opera*, performed at Drury Lane on 14 May 1729 as the afterpiece to *The Country Wife*, was printed in 1729–30. *The Generous Free-Mason*, a ballad opera, was published in 1731 and perhaps became *The Mock Mason* (unpublished) which was performed at Goodman's Fields on 13 April 1733. Two other Chetwood dramatic works, *The Emperor of China, Grand Volgi, or The Constant Couple and Virtue Rewarded* (produced at Bartholomew Fair on 24 September 1731) and *The Stage Coach Opera* (given at Goodman's Fields on 17 July 1730), were not printed. The prompter's considerable number of non-dramatic works are included in the list appended to this entry.

Of Chetwood's early personal life little is known. He married, perhaps in the 1720s, but the name of his first wife has not been discovered. Richabella, his daughter by this marriage, made her first appearance on stage in 1738 when Chetwood was living at the Blue Door in Maiden Lane, Covent Garden. By that time the first Mrs Chetwood had died (apparently), for on 15 June 1738 the prompter married Anne Brett at St Benet, Paul's Wharf. She was the daughter of Dawson Brett and his wife Elizabeth, née Cibber; like her father Colley, Elizabeth was a performer, and her daughter Anne, by 1738, had ten years of acting experience. The Chetwoods set up housekeeping at No 11, Wild Court, but by the spring of 1741 they were living at the Golden Ball in May's Buildings.

During his last season at Drury Lane (1740–41) Chetwood ran himself into debt. To his rescue came, not his own company but John Rich of Covent Garden, which suggests a friendship between the two of some years standing and a clue to the odd name of Chetwood's daughter Richabella. On 12 January 1741 a benefit was given at Covent Garden for the relief of Chetwood, "now a Prisoner in the King's Bench." By the following 5 May when the prompter's regular Drury Lane benefit came up, he was apparently out of trouble. His own *The Lover's Opera* was performed with his wife playing Lucy, and no mention was made of his financial troubles.

On 10 December 1741 Chetwood received a benefit at the Smock Alley Theatre in Dublin, billed as "an utter Stranger in the Country." He told of his Irish experience in his *General History*:

Harvard Theatre Collection

WILLIAM R. CHETWOOD

artist unknown

When I came first from England, in the Year 1741, I brought over an experienc'd Machinist, who alter'd the [cramped Smock Alley] Stage after the Manner of the Theatres in France and England, and formed a Machine to move the Scenes regularly all together; but since laid aside, as well as the Flies above, which were made as convenient as the Theatre would admit.

What else he did at Smock Alley is not known, but it would appear that he was brought there not as a prompter but as a technical consultant. Mrs Chetwood acted with the troupe during their stay in Dublin.

The couple returned to London about the fall of 1742. On 2 December at St Martin-in-the-Fields they buried a child, Elizabeth-Peggy, shortly after which Mrs Chetwood began an engagement at the Lincoln's Inn Fields Theatre under Giffard. She was active in the London theatre through the end of 1744. On 12 February of that year the Chetwoods buried another daughter, Colley-Elizabeth. The character of Chetwood's activity during those two years is not known; he was presumably in London and

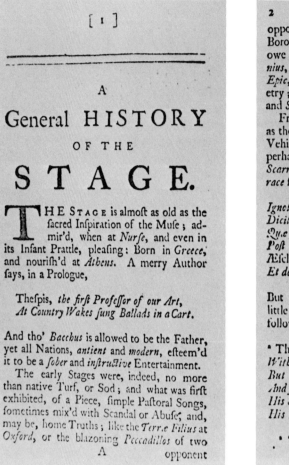

From the collection of Edward A. Langhans

Opening pages of WILLIAM R. CHETWOOD's *A General History of the Stage* (1749)

perhaps spending his time writing. On the other hand, we know something of Chetwood's life from 1744 to 1755, but almost nothing of his wife's.

By February 1747 Chetwood was back in Ireland with his daughter, now Mrs Tobias Gemea. In that month they signed a petition to the Lord Lieutenant to have the Dublin theatres reopened. Possibly Chetwood had returned to Dublin before then —if, indeed, he had ever left. The records of burials of his two daughters in London would perhaps indicate that he was there from 1742 to 1744, but the *Cambridge*

Bibliography of English Literature suggests that perhaps Chetwood was the author of *The Medler* (26 numbers), published in Dublin from 4 January to 28 June 1744. In any case, he was certainly there in 1747, and Dublin publications by him suggest his presence also in 1748 and 1750. His *General History*, by far his most important contribution to the theatre, was printed in London in 1749, but where he was at that time is unknown.

Chetwood was with his daughter at Belfast from May to September 1753, and he was given a benefit there as prompter on 31 August. His wife reappeared briefly on the London stage in 1755, but Chetwood's Dublin publications about that time suggest that he may not have been with her. By 1760 he was in debtor's prison in Dublin, and a benefit performance was given to alleviate his circumstances. If the pitiful letter from his wife to an unnamed nobleman (quoted in her entry) belongs to this period, it is noteworthy that in beseeching assistance she made no mention of her husband. William Rufus Chetwood died poverty-stricken on 3 March 1766, presumably in the Marshalsea Prison of the Four Courts in Dublin.

The kindest description of Chetwood was written by himself for his *British Theatre* (1750): "for twenty Years Prompter to Drury Lane Theatre, and accounted very excellent in that Business; he was for some time an eminent Bookseller in Covent Garden . . ." George Steevens called Chetwood "a blockhead and a measureless and bungling liar." More valid was Edmond Malone's warning in his own copy of Chetwood's *British Theatre*:

[I]t is not to be depended upon, for he certainly has forged dates for early quarto editions of Shakespeare's plays, sixteen of which never appeared in print till the year 1623, when they were published by Hemming & Condell in folio—As we have almost certain proof of Chetwood's infidelity *in this instance* . . . he is not to be trusted in *any* of his dates.

Malone was talking about Chetwood's scholarship, of course, but there seems to be enough evidence in what we know of the prompter's life to suggest that in many things he was somewhat irresponsible.

He admitted in his *General History* that he had made enemies, and he thanked an unnamed friendly lawyer who "has made my Cause his own" and Barrington and Miss Bellamy of the Covent Garden Theatre who "often eas'd an aching Heart." "Tho' my enemies have beat me to the Pit (as Brutus said), yet, thank Heaven!

some few friends have interpos'd, and prevented my falling in . . ." But they were not on hand, it seems, when the end came.

William Rufus Chetwood's portrait served as a plate to his *General History.* From a variety of sources it is possible to make up a tentative list of his writings and of works published by or for him:

The Voyages, Dangerous Adventures & Imminent Escapes of Capt. Richard Falconer. London, 1720. Novel published by and presumably written by Chetwood.

South-Sea; or, the Biters Bit. London, 1720. Play, not intended for the stage, by Chetwood.

The Stock-Jobbers, or, The Humours of Exchange Alley. London, 1720. Play, not intended for the stage, by Chetwood.

Ildegerte, Queen of Norway. London, 1721. By Eustache Lenoble, printed for Chetwood.

Voyages & Adventures of Capt. Robert Boyle. London, 1726. Novel by Chetwood? or Victor? Advertised as Chetwood's in 1741.

The Lover's Opera. London, 1729–30. Ballad opera by Chetwood.

The Generous Free-Mason. London, 1731. Ballad opera by Chetwood.

The Voyages, Travels, and Adventures of William Owen Vaughan Esq. London, 1736; Dublin, 1754. Novel by Chetwood; Dublin edition published by Chetwood.

Five New Novels (The Twins; or The Female Traveller. The Stepmother, or Good Luck at Last. The Inhuman Uncle; or the Repentant Villain. The Virgin Widow. Adrastus and Olinda; or Love's Champion.) London, 1741. By Chetwood and available "at the Author's Lodgings, the Golden Ball in May's Buildings, St. Martin's Lane." The advertisement identified Chetwood as the Drury Lane prompter and author of the Falconer, Boyle, and Vaughan novels. According to the preface, dated 20

February 1741, the *Five New Novels*, like other works by Chetwood, were written in prison. *The Twins* was published separately in 1742–43, and all five novels were reprinted in *Six Historical Relations*, Dublin, 1755.

The Dramatic Congress. London, 1743. By Chetwood.

The Medler. 26 numbers, Dublin, 4 January to 28 June 1744. Possibly by Chetwood.

A Tour through Ireland. London, 1748. By Chetwood.

Kilkenny: or the Old Man's Wish. Dublin, 1748. Printed for and written by Chetwood.

A General History of the Stage. London, 1749. By Chetwood.

The British Theatre. Dublin, 1750. By Chetwood. Written in prison.

A Select Collection of Old Plays . . . Dublin, 1750. Edited and printed by Chetwood.

St. Patrick for Ireland. London, 1751. By James Shirley, with an account of the author by Chetwood.

Theatrical Records. London, 1756. By Chetwood. An abridgment of *The British Theatre* of 1750.

Memoirs of the Life and Writings of Ben Jonson. Dublin, 1756. Printed by Chetwood.

"The Emperor of China, Grand Volgi, or The Constant Couple and Virtue Rewarded." Unpublished. By Chetwood.

"The Stage Coach Opera." Unpublished. By Chetwood.

On 21 August 1753 Chetwood issued proposals through the Belfast *Newsletter* for the printing by subscription of a book of voyages of two brothers, but apparently nothing came of it.

Chetwood, Mrs William Rufus the second, Anne, née Brett *b. 1720, dancer, actress.*

Anne Brett, the granddaughter of Colley Cibber and daughter of Dawson and Eliza-beth Cibber Brett, was christened at St Paul, Covent Garden, on 8 May 1720. Elizabeth Brett danced and acted at Drury Lane from 1722 to 1730, and young Anne began her career there on 9 November 1727. On that date the "young Son of Mr Lally's and a little Girl, who have never appear'd upon any Stage before" danced between the acts of *The Provok'd Wife*. Anne had been trained by the dancing master Boval, and on 21 November 1727 she first appeared by name. She spoke the epilogue to *The Provok'd Husband* on 11 April 1728—her "first Performance in that Capacity"—and on 3 May she danced and shared her first benefit with Miss Lindar. Anne's mother reduced her activity at Drury Lane the following season, and by 1730 she had left the stage clear for her daughter.

Anne Brett seems to have been an instant success. She danced frequently during the 1728–29 season, usually taking such appropriate roles as the Child of Love in *Harlequin Happy*. On 8 April 1729 she attempted her first role in a drama, playing the Page in *The Orphan*, and on 7 May she acted Falstaff's Boy in *2 Henry IV*. By 7 June 1731 at the age of 11, she was considered skilled enough to be cast as Ariel in *The Tempest*. Though her specialty remained dancing, over the years she slowly added to her dramatic repertory, so that by the summer of 1735 when she played at Lincoln's Inn Fields, the bulk of her assignments were in acting. Among her parts were Maria in *The London Merchant*, Jenny in *The Provok'd Husband*, and Tom Thumb in *The Tragedy of Tragedies*.

On 29 June 1736 with a Lilliputian company at the Haymarket Theatre she played Lady Townly in *The Provok'd Husband* for her benefit; on 23 September at Drury Lane she was Lucy in *The Squire of Alsatia*; on 23 October she acted Dol Mavis in *The Silent Woman*; on 27 December she played Chloe in *Timon of Athens*; and on 26 May 1737 she was

Rose in *The Recruiting Officer*. Other roles which she attempted indicate her preference for comedy: Sylvia in *The Old Bachelor*, Doll Tearsheet in *2 Henry IV*, Anne Page in *The Merry Wives of Windsor*, Mincing in *The Way of the World*, and Belinda in *The Man of Mode*.

Still only a miss in her teens, on 15 June 1738 at St Benet, Paul's Wharf, Anne Brett became the second wife of William Rufus Chetwood, author, bookseller, and Drury Lane prompter. To the marriage Chetwood brought a daughter, Richabella, and on the 15 May preceding the wedding, *The Squire of Alsatia* was performed for the benefit of Chetwood and Anne Brett, with Miss Brett playing Teresia and young Richabella making her debut in Lucy, Anne's old role. During the 1738–39 season, when the Chetwoods were living at No 11, Wild Court, the Drury Lane bills featured both Mrs Chetwood and Miss Chetwood, and the printers were not always careful about the ascriptions. It is likely, though, that Anne Brett Chetwood's parts that season included a Grace in *Mars and Venus*, Mademoiselle in *The Provok'd Wife*, the second Colombine in *Robin Goodfellow*, Coriane in *The Confederacy*, a Milkmaid in *Harlequin Restored*, and Clara in *Rule a Wife and Have a Wife*.

During the next two seasons Mrs Chetwood much reduced the frequency of her appearances; in 1740–41, for instance, she performed only during May and June. On 5 May 1741 she acted Lucy in Chetwood's *The Lover's Opera* for his benefit only, tickets being available at Chetwood's lodgings at the Golden Ball in May Buildings; she had no benefit for herself. Her last appearance at Drury Lane (until 1744) was on 4 June 1741 when she played Lucy in *The London Merchant* and Lucy in *The Virgin Unmask'd* for the benefit of a family under misfortune. The family may well have been her own, for in 1741 Chetwood was in prison for debt.

By the fall of 1741 the Chetwoods were

in Ireland. Mrs Chetwood played Colombine (probably in *Robin Goodfellow*) at Smock Alley on 22 October 1741, and she doubtless appeared in other Dublin productions. She, and presumably W. R. Chetwood as well, was back in London for the 1742–43 season. By that time the Chetwoods had had at least one child, Elizabeth-Peggy; this infant was buried at St Martin-in-the-Fields on 2 December 1742, just before Mrs Chetwood returned to the London stage. They had a second daughter but all we know of her is that she was named Colley-Elizabeth and was buried at St Martin's on 12 February 1744. The use of Elizabeth in her name would suggest that she was born after Elizabeth-Peggy died in 1742.

Mrs Chetwood joined Giffard's company at Lincoln's Inn Fields in late 1742, and on 28 December, billed as "from the Theatre Royal in Dublin," she acted Cherry in *The Stratagem*. Then, in addition to some of her old roles, she played Edging in *The Careless Husband*, Flippanta in *The Confederacy* (for her benefit with two others on 14 March 1743), Angelica in *The Constant Couple*, and Lady Grace in *The Provok'd Husband*. Her address on her benefit bill was given as the Castle Tavern, Drury Lane, but no mention was made of her husband. After a period of silence, she returned to Drury Lane on 13 January 1744 to act Mademoiselle in *The Provok'd Wife*. She followed that with some of her earlier parts plus Harlequin's Wife in *The Amorous Goddess*, Rachel in *The Jovial Crew*, Mrs Foresight in *Love for Love*, and Mrs Fainall in *The Way of the World*. In the midst of that activity, she buried her daughter Colley-Elizabeth on 12 February.

In the fall of 1744 Mrs Chetwood joined Theophilus Cibber's troupe at the Haymarket, acting several new roles: Jenny in *Love in Low Life*, Harriot in *The Prodigal*, Margery in *The Gardener's Wedding*, Cephisa in *The Distrest Mother*, and Mrs

Slammekin in *The Beggar's Opera*. She may have returned to Ireland after that (Chetwood was there in 1747 and perhaps earlier), but the next mention of her in the records was not until September 1755 when she again worked with her uncle Theophilus at the Haymarket. She played Lucy in *The Recruiting Officer* on 9 September and Parthenope in *The Rehearsal* on 11 and 15 September 1755, after which her name disappeared from the bills.

At some time after her grandfather's death in 1757, possibly in 1760 when W. R. Chetwood was languishing in prison in Dublin, Anne Chetwood applied for assistance to some unnamed nobleman:

May it please your Grace I am an unfortunate grand daughter of the Late Colley Cibber whose unhappines was never to feell for the distress of his own family otherwise then by a Partiall Judgement the aflictions of his Children was greatly owing to his unfeelingnes my Mother My Lord never Commited She Could Say it on her Death Bed an Act of Disobeadeince: to her and my Aunt Charke [i.e., Charlotte Charke] he Left but five pound Each to there Children nothing but the bulk of his fortune my Aunt [Catherine] Brown had and my uncle Theophilus Daughters [Jenny and Betty] had a thousand pound Each Worn down by Affliction and growing years not brought up to Earn my Bread by Servile Business a wrong Judgement in Parents who flatters us with Hopes we never Tast the old Nobility all dead who usd thro pity to Aleavate the Distresses of my family inforces me to plead to your pity in this hope that my Aunt Charke Shard [i.e., shared] in your Compassion I never and please your grace Intreated your Assistance before but as I am informed your Benevolence at this to be in the Number as my distress is great and all I am Capable to do is with my Needle and there is no imploy all Publick Charity. taking it in that Heaven with its Choisest Blessings may await you Shalle ever be the fervent wish Wish [sic] and Prayer of your Most Obeadant Ser^t

ANA CHEETWOOD

If Anne Brett Chetwood deserved such a heartbreaking end, the evidence does not show it.

Chevalier, Mons [*fl. 1784*], *exhibitor*.

A Monsieur Chevalier exhibited the Montgolfier air balloon in February 1784 in "the Grand Apartment called the Lyceum, three doors above Exeter 'change." The balloon, overlaid with gold, was 40 feet in diameter. It was said to be on its way to exhibition at Oxford.

Chevalier, Pierre [*fl. 1780–1788*], *dancer, choreographer*.

Pierre Chevalier, according to Campardon in *Les Spectacles de la Foire* an "acteur du théâtre des Grands-Danseurs du Roi" at Paris, had a role in a ballet called *Grosse Merveilleuse* on 30 January 1780, and danced again in the ballet-pantomime *Glycère et Alexis* on 19 February. He was at Milan in 1784 under the appellation "Pietro Le Chevalier" and turned up at London dancing in the opera ballet at the King's Theatre in 1787–88.

On the opening night of the opera, 8 December, he shared attention with the ballet master, the eminent Noverre, as each one produced a new dance. Chevalier presented at the end of Act I of *Il re Tedoro in Venezia* a divertissement, in which he danced the principal part, assisted by Vestris, Coulon and Miss Coulon (her debut), the Misses Simonet, and Sga Bedini. It was repeated in eight successive performances until 12 January 1788, when Chevalier substituted another effort of his own composition, *The Military Dance*, in which he also took a leading part. This was repeated in five performances. One or another of these compositions was frequently in the bills throughout the rest of the season. Chevalier also danced an occasional *pas seul*, and principal parts in ballets by Noverre. He disappeared from the London bills after 28 June, probably returning to the Continent.

Chevalier, Thomas [fl. 1694–1699], oboist.

On 10 June 1695 a Thomas "Chaville" and other oboists were to be paid £6 10s. each for playing at the King's birthday ball on 4 November 1694 and at six rehearsals that preceded it. A similar warrant dated 23 October 1699 listed Thomas "Chevalier" and others as musicians of Princess Anne of Denmark who were to be paid a total of £22 11s. 6d. for performing at two balls and a play. Both documents must refer to the same musician, but the correct spelling of his name is not known.

Chevigny. *See also* CHAVIGNY.

Chevigny, Mr [fl. 1797–1798], dancer?

Mr Chevigny joined the opera company at the King's Theatre in the Haymarket in 1797–98 but seems not to have remained in London after the season ended. He may have been related to the dancer Mlle Sophie Genevieve Chevigny (c. 1775–1818) who is not known to have performed in London before the end of the eighteenth century.

Chevrier, [Mons?] [fl. 1726–1727], dancer.

A dancer named Chevrier was a member of the Italian troupe which was in England by 21 September 1726 and which began performing at the King's Theatre in the Haymarket on 28 September. During the 1726–27 season the company performed at the King's on nights when no opera was being presented.

Cheyne, Mr [fl. 1794–1806], carpenter, machinist.

A Mr Cheyne (often "Chene" in the theatrical account books) was employed at Drury Lane Theatre at least twice in the

fall of 1794 and often from the fall of 1795 until at least the end of the season 1805–6.

The first notations in the manuscript account books which involved his name appear to be those of 7 and 18 October 1794: "Chene and Roberts work^g. Air Machine 2s. each Pr. day 9 days to 4th Instant 1.16.0," and "Cheney and Roberts 8 nts. air Machine." The meaning of the entries is baffling. They may have been operating a bellows to ventilate the theatre.

It is difficult to decide, on the basis of the payments made at nearly weekly intervals for the next several months, whether Cheyne was at this period a bona fide member of the staff at Drury Lane or a master carpenter from outside the theatre being paid large sums to disburse to his journeymen. At any rate, the entries show him to have been very busy from before 17 October 1795 until February 1796: 17 October "Cheny carpenters bill 2 wks. in full 69.0.0"; 24 October "Cheyne for Carps. bill to this date 42.17.10," and so on, some £325 in all, including on 5 December "Cheyne . . . paid for Liquopodium 3.18.0," 8 December "Liquopodium 4.5.8"; 15 December 1795 "Liquopodium by Cheyne 4.16.0"; 25 January 1796 "Liquopodium etc by Cheyne 7.11.1," 2 February "for Liquopodium etc 6.1.7," and other entries employing the same term.

We suppose that the enormous expenditures for carpenters are all connected with the construction of the "Liquopodium," which we conjecture must have been a term for the huge tank employed in the new afterpiece presented on 14 October 1794, *The Glorious First of June*. The bills for that evening promised "End of Act 1" of the afterpiece "an exact Representation of the Engagement between the British and French Fleets on the First of June [1794]." There are occasional payments to Cheyne as carpenter in 1796–97, 1797–98, and 1798–99, but one entry (of 1797) reads: "Cheyne for goats."

From 1802–3 through 1805–6 Cheyne seems to have been regularly employed as a carpenter at Drury Lane.

Cheyney. *See* CHENEY.

Chiabrano. *See* CHABRAN.

Chianti, Margaret. *See* CHIMENTI, MARGHERITA.

Chiaretta. *See* AQUILANTI.

"Chiaro Oscuro" *See* COLMAN, GEORGE *1732–1794.*

"Chichester Boy." *See* MOUNTIER, THOMAS.

Chickingham, Mr [*fl.* 1799], *actor.*
Fitzgerald, in his *New History of the English Stage*, reported that a Mr Chickingham burst a blood vessel while acting Osman in *The Castle Spectre* in 1799. No actor of that name is known to have played the role at Drury Lane, where the play was done that year, so Chickingham may have suffered the accident in the provinces.

Chico or **Chicoo.** *See* TORINESE, CHECO.

Child, Mr [*fl.* 1732], *actor.*
A Mr Child played Corydon in *Damon and Phillida* at the "Great Booth on Windmill Hill" on 27 May 1732 and "During the Holidays."

Child, Mr [*fl.* 1794–1795], *dresser.*
A Mr Child is listed as a men's dresser on a surviving manuscript pay list now in the British Museum, relating to the 1794–95 season at Covent Garden Theatre.

Child, Mrs [*fl.* 1773?–1782], *actress.*
A Mrs Child played in two specially licensed performances in the fall and winter of 1781–82 at the Haymarket

Theatre, usually dark at those times of the year. The first, on 16 October, was for the benefit of the actor Walker. Mrs Child played Olivia in a revival of Mrs Centlivre's *The Artifice*. On 14 January 1782 she acted Lady Lurewell in *The Constant Couple* for the benefit of the actors Mrs Greville and Mr Williams. A Mrs Child appeared for her own benefit at York on 26 March 1773, playing Arpasia in *Tamerlane*, and was advertised to be appearing for the first time in the character and the fourth "on any stage." Conceivably she was the same as the London actress.

Child, Miss. *See* WEBB, MRS.

Child, Anne [*fl.* 1666–1668], *actress?*
Anne Child was included in a livery warrant dated 30 June 1666 (during the plague) as a member of the King's Company. *The London Stage* lists her as a member again in 1666–67, and her name appeared once more on a livery warrant dated 8 February 1668, indicating her membership in the troupe in 1667–68. In the 1668 warrant, however, her name was written in the margin and then deleted, so she had probably died or left the company in mid-season. No roles are known for her, and it is only a guess that she was an actress.

Child, Thomas [*fl.* 1714], *actor.*
Drury Lane managers Cibber, Wilks, and Booth issued a pay slip for 5s. on 24 April 1714 for Thomas Child for performing in *Richard III*. Since no actor of that name is otherwise known, it could be that the player in question was a boy whose last name was Thomas, playing one of the children's roles.

Child, William *1606–1697, singer, composer, instrumentalist.*
Born in Bristol in 1606, William Child served as a chorister under the organist Elway Bevin before taking his Bachelor of

Music degree at Christ Church, Oxford, on
8 July 1631. Even before his degree was
granted, on 19 April 1630, Child had been
appointed a countertenor lay clerk at St
George's Chapel, Windsor. On 26 July
1632 he advanced to the positions of organist and master of the choristers and was
concurrently appointed one of the organists
of the Chapel Royal in London. He had
married and started a family by that time,
and by 4 October 1638 his increasing
brood and commendable work at Windsor
led to the enlargement of his living quarters at the Castle. Sons of his were baptized
at Windsor in 1636 and 1638. His gradua-
tion exercise at Oxford was published in
1639. It is said that with the dissolution
of the royal musical establishment in 1643
Child retired to a farm near Windsor and
spent the Interregnum composing.

At the Restoration he returned to his
organist's post at Windsor and was reappointed a Gentleman of the Chapel Royal
and a member of the King's private music
in London. He received (not always on
schedule) an annual livery allowance of
£16 2s. 6d. plus an unspecified salary. On
23 April 1661 Child was one of the royal
musicians who participated in the coronation of Charles II. In London he was given
multiple duties: as one of the musicians for
the wind instruments he replaced Clement
Lanier on cornet, and he took Alphonso
Ferrabosco's place as composer for the
winds. In addition, it seems that he also
served as the private organist to Lord
Sandwich from about 1660 to 1663. Back
at Windsor the authorities became concerned that Child was spending too much
time in London, and on 1 September 1662
the Chapter ordered that an assistant be
searched for unless "Mr. Child shall give
assurance for better attendance in his office." Child apparently gave them no such
assurance, and an assistant was hired to
permit him to devote more of his energies
to musical affairs in London.

Child had become a friend of Samuel

Courtesy of the Curators of the Bodleian Library

WILLIAM CHILD
by Kneller

Pepys in 1660, and the *Diary* contains
several references to the musician. In
November 1660 Pepys thrice found Child
at Lord Sandwich's, playing the organ, and
for the diarist Child set the base to the
theorbo for two songs by Henry Lawes.
On 30 December of the same year Pepys
dined with Child, and the musician spent
some time playing the lute and writing out
some theorbo lessons for Pepys. The diarist
was pleased to note on 25 June 1663 that
his friend was to receive his D. Mus. from
Oxford that year, and on 8 July the honor
was granted. Child performed his gradua-
tion exercise anthem at St Mary's Church
on 13 July. Carried away with Child's ac-
complishment, Pepys thought he might try

for a doctorate in music too, but of course the dream came to nothing.

In late February 1666 Pepys visited Windsor and was given a tour of St George's Chapel and the towns of Windsor and Eton by Dr Child, who had an anthem and a great service performed for his visitor. In return, Child visited Pepys on 15 April 1667 and spent the morning "making me bases and inward parts to several songs that I desired of him, to my great content."

By 1668 Dr Child, in addition to his livery allowance, was being paid £46 10s. 10d. as a member of the wind instruments at court. His livery payments were badly in arrears, however; in 1666, for example, he still had not received his fees for 1663, 1664, and 1665, and in time his inability to collect led him into financial difficulties.

On 1 August 1668 Matthew Green, Dr Child's lay clerk and master of the choristers at Windsor, assaulted his superior. Green "did hastily and irreverently goe out of the Chappell in tyme of Divine service and gave Dr. Child uncivill and rude language while he was doeing his duty in playing upon the organ, and after the ending of the said Divine service did trip up his heeles and when down did inhumanly beat him." Green's punishment was astonishingly mild. He was made to apologize and post a £5 bond as security that he would not attack the 62-year-old Dr Child again.

In 1669 King Charles had to retrench. Some of the activities of the court musicians were curtailed and their pay, presumably, was reduced. Though Child, perhaps because of his long years of service, was exempt from the retrenchment, he was hurt by the effect it had on his colleagues. Many of the musicians borrowed heavily or contrived devious ways to get money, and Child may have been the victim of one such scheme. On 4 May 1670 he petitioned against his fellow musicians "for deteyning six years and a half of board wages upon the pretence of his not attending the

service." With his duties divided between London and Windsor, Child was, indeed, frequently absent, and his fellows were within their rights to withold part of his board money, yet Child was legally supposed to receive it in full whether he was in residence in London or not.

By 1671 Child was in financial trouble. In October of that year he and others petitioned to have their arrears from 1669, 1670, and 1671 paid to their colleague Humphrey Madge, who had lent them money. On 28 October 1673 Benjamin Rogers, who had been hired by Child to serve as a substitute when Child was away from London, testified that Child owed him money, so on 14 April 1674, £5 was deducted from Child's salary and given to Rogers. On 8 November 1675 Child had to order his livery payments turned over to his attorney, Thomas Haines, to whom he was also indebted. By the end of October 1676 Child was still to be paid his livery allowances for 1672 and 1673 – and had they been paid, of course, Haines would have been the ultimate recipient. Under such circumstances Child must have been pleased on 26 May 1675 when he was given his house (in Windsor, presumably) rent-free in return for his duties, especially since most of his duties by then were performed by his eventual successor at Windsor, John Golding.

At the coronation of James II on 23 April 1685, Dr Child marched among the bass singers and was noted by contemporaries as the eldest Gentleman of the Chapel Royal. King James, to his credit, tried to pay some of the debts King Charles had accumulated, and on 21 September 1686 Child received £161 5s. in arrears. Under Charles, Child claimed he had been £500 in arrears and "would be glad if anybody would give him £5 and some bottles of wine in trade for the money owed him" – which his fellow canons gave him, half in jest. When King James paid the arrears, the canons agreed to release Child from his bargain if he would pave the floor of the choir in St George's Chapel, which he accordingly did.

Child participated as organist at the coronation of William and Mary on 11 April 1689, but by then he was too old for much activity, and the bulk of his considerable career as a composer (documented in Grove) was behind him. Yet he lived on at Windsor for several years longer and on 9 February 1697 made his will. On 23 March he died, and on 26 March he was buried in St George's Chapel. His will was proved before the Dean and Chapter of Windsor on 6 April 1697. Dr Child had previously given £20 toward the building of the Windsor Town Hall, and his will bequeathed £50 to the Corporation to be used for charitable purposes. He left to the Oxford Music School a painting of him done in 1663 after he had received his doctorate. James Caldwall engraved the head of this full-length portrait for Hawkins's *General History of Music*.

"Child of Promise, The." *See* HANDY, MISS.

Chiliby ₍fl. 1783₎, *performing horse.*
In 1783, and perhaps before and after, a "wonderful horse" named Chiliby performed tricks of various sorts at Charles Hughes's Royal Circus. For instance, on 21 October 1783 it was announced that Chiliby would "dress and undress a Lady's Head, jump on and off the Stage, take off the Lady's Cap, &c." He was, however, only one of a number of "Sagacious Horses" to be exhibited that year to the equiphilic English. Most are not named in bills.

Chimenti, Margherita ₍fl. 1736–1738₎, *singer.*
In the fall of 1736 Margherita Chimenti, also known as "La Droghierina," joined the so-called Opera of the Nobility, which was organized at the King's Theatre in the Haymarket to oppose Handel's opera company at Covent Garden. Apparently she first sang in London before the Royal Family at Kensington on 15 November 1736. She made her public debut in the secondary role of Medarse in *Siroe* on 23 November 1736, an opera which was repeated 12 times during the season. She was Trasimede in *Merope*, introduced on 8 January 1737, Olinto in *Demetrio* on 12 February, Annius in *Tito* on 12 April, and Matthusius in *Demofoonte* (she was listed as "Mrs Marg Chianti, called Droghierina" in the edition of 1737). She quite probably also sustained some part in *Sabrina*, for which no performers' names are available, on 26 April. Mrs Pendarves wrote to Mary Delany that she was "a tolerable good woman with a pretty voice."

Handel and Heidegger took over the King's Theatre for the ensuing season. Margherita doubtless sang her part in *Sabrina* when the theatre opened on 19 December 1737, though no cast was given in the bill. On 3 January 1738 a new opera, *Faramondo*, with music by Handel opened before "a splendid audience," and she sang Adolfo. She was Absirto in *La Conquista del vello d'oro* when it was first performed at the King's on 28 January 1738, Doralbo in *Partenio*, on 14 March, and Atalanta in *Serse*, a new Handel opera which opened on 15 April 1738. She may also have been in *Alessandro severo*, for which we have no cast, on 25 February. Very likely she was one of the singers in Handel's benefit "Oratorio, With a Concert on the Organ" of 28 March. After the failure of Heidegger in the spring of 1738 to raise a sufficient amount by subscription to continue the opera in the season of 1738–39 she, with a number of her compatriots, disappeared from England.

China, Mr ₍fl. 1724₎, *horn player.*
A Mr China played a sonata on the

"German-Horn" during a concert at Hickford's Great Room on 26 February 1724.

Chinnall, Mr [fl. 1764–1775], doorkeeper, checktaker.

A Mr Chinnall (sometimes Chinnaw, Chinneau) shared a benefit with other house servants at Drury Lane on 22 May 1764. He was said to be a doorkeeper, earning 9s. per week in a surviving pay list of 9 February 1765. He was given partial benefits on 21 May 1765, 16 May 1766, and 30 May 1767, probably on 26 May 1768, and on 17 May 1769, 28 May 1770, 25 May 1771, and 3 June 1772. He was again (or still) at the theatre as of 5 October 1775, when he was mentioned in a letter of Garrick's as a checktaker.

Chippendale, Thomas 1782–1799, callboy.

Thomas Chippendale, who was callboy to Drury Lane Theatre in the 1793–94 season, died, aged 17, at Liverpool on Christmas Day, 1799, according to *The Oracle* of 3 January 1800.

Chippendale, William [fl. 1793–1835?], actor.

William Chippendale first broke into London theatricals as an anonymous Passenger in the new pantomime *Harlequin Peasant*, afterpiece to a performance of *The Tempest*, in a specially licensed bill presented at the Haymarket Theatre on 26 and 27 December 1793. He turned up as a regular member of the Haymarket's summer company in 1796, playing a number of small parts from 22 June through 15 September. On 22 June he filled some unspecified part in *Alfred; or, The Magic Banner*, a new afterpiece by O'Keeffe. He was the servant Peter in *Catherine and Petruchio* on 29 June, a servant in *The Children in the Wood* on 5 July, a countryman in *The Quaker* on 11 July, a servant in *The Provok'd Wife* on 8 August, Malachi

in *The Young Quaker* on 10 August, Gadshill in *1 Henry IV* on 18 August, and Simon in *The Iron Chest* on 29 September.

Chippendale was absent from the London bills until an appearance at Drury Lane on 10 June 1797, when he was pressed into service in the important comic eccentric role of Aminadab in *A Bold Stroke for a Wife*, which had been Grimaldi's character. He rejoined the Haymarket troupe from 13 June through 16 September 1797, playing Cudden in *The Agreeable Surprise* on the former date and following with a Coachman in *A Quarter of an Hour Before Dinner* on 17 June, a Servant in *She Stoops to Conquer* on 19 June, a Waiter in *Inkle and Yarico* on 21 June (also a Waiter in the afterpiece that night, *Two Strings to Your Bow*), a Stockbroker in *A Bold Stroke for a Wife* on 24 June, a Servant in *The Dead Alive* on 27 June, a Servant in *The Recruiting Officer* on 3 July, Pedro in *Love Makes a Man* on 10 July, a Waiter in the first presentation of George Colman's *The Heir at Law* on 15 July, and a Guard in the first performance of James Boaden's *The Italian Monk* on 15 August.

He was again employed by Drury Lane, but for one night only, on 19 May 1798, in some part unspecified in the premier performance of O'Keeffe's *She's Eloped!* He rejoined the Haymarket Company on 13 June and acted regularly through 13 September, playing first Wat Dreary in *The Beggar's Opera*, then his inevitable Waiter in *The Heir at Law* on 14 June, and, on 16 June, in both *Inkle and Yarico* and *Two Strings to Your Bow*, repeating Cudden in *The Agreeable Surprise* on 18 June, Wat Dreary on 19 and 27 June, a Servant in *The Mountaineers* on 20 June, Guard in *The Italian Monk* on 30 June and 9 and 13 July, a Citizen in *The Surrender of Calais* on 14 July and 1 August, an Assassin in *False and True* on 11 August, Oatcake in *Much Ado about Nothing* on 21 August, and a Messenger in *Hamlet* on 3 September, as well as several repetitions of characters from former summers.

Chippendale finally found himself on the pay list of a winter patent theatre in the season of 1798–99 when he signed at Drury Lane for £1 per week. He played from 27 September through 5 July exactly the same line of parts as he had done at the Haymarket (peasants, servants, soldiers, citizens, robbers, minor eccentrics), opening with Cudden in *The Agreeable Surprise* and closing with Robin of Bagshot in *The Beggar's Opera*. From 18 June through 14 September 1799 he was again an underling at the Haymarket. Back at Drury Lane in the fall, he was paid £1 5s. for his walk-ons from 17 September through 12 June and revolved dependably back to Colman's summer theatre from 13 June through 15 September.

He evidently continued this comfortable seasonal alternation at London until at least 1802–3, never earning more than £2 per week. The author of the *Authentic Memoirs of the Green Room* (1799) deprecated his efforts: "Though from a theatrical family, this gentleman aspires no higher than an humble messenger." Thomas Dutton in *The Dramatic Censor* (1800) dismissed him as "a walking character."

Chippendale's wife began to appear sporadically as a singer at Drury Lane from 8 November 1797 and was there in minor roles until at least 1802–3. The Chippendales were acting at Edinburgh from 1813–14 through at least 1819–20. William Chippendale was still on the stage in the early 1830s, playing Polonius at the Victoria Theatre.

The Chippendales' son, William Henry (born in Somers Town, London, on 14 August 1801, died in London on 3 January 1888) had a notable British and American stage career and, by his three wives, 23 children.

Chippendale, Mrs William [fl. 1797–1820?], singer.

Mrs William Chippendale began to appear occasionally as a singer at Drury lane, where her husband was a performer, from 8 November 1797, when she was one of a "Chorus of Peasants" in *Richard Coeur de Lion* (repeated 25 November). She was paid at the rate of £1 per week, but does not seem to have been regularly of the company in that 1797–98 season. On 6 October 1798 she sang as one of a numerous band of melodic peasants in *Blue-Beard* and from that point on until 27 June 1799 when she ended the season by singing (for the twenty-sixth time) in the chorus accompanying Sheridan's spectacular *Pizarro,* she was on the regular pay list of the company. She returned, with a salary of £1 5s. per week, on 14 October 1799 and performed through 28 May 1800 principally, as before, as a member of the chorus. She was seldom in a named role during the time of her humble service at Drury Lane, which extended at least through 1802–3.

Chippendales, man and wife, were at Edinburgh from 1813–14 through at least 1819–20.

Chiri. *See* CIRRI.

Chiringhelli, Signora [fl. 1774], dancer.

At the end of the performance of *The Clandestine Marriage* at Drury Lane on 22 April 1774, a Signora Chiringhelli danced, in "her first appearance in England . . . A New Ballet, call'd The Pirates" with Signor Como and Signora Crespi. There is no further record of Signora Chiringhelli's dancing in London.

Chise, Mme [fl. 1757], dancer.

On all but one of 21 successive performance days, 15 June through 31 August 1757, Theophilus Cibber's company at the Haymarket presented, after their *Medley Concert,* a pantomime called *Harlequin's Frolic; or, a Voyage to Prussia* in which a Madame Chise danced the part of Mother

Demdike. She was not seen again in London, so far as the playbills show.

Chittle, Samuel ɪ*fl.* 1715–1720ɪ, *singer.*

Samuel Chittle, singer, was one of four men sworn as Gentlemen in Ordinary of the Chapel Royal on 8 August 1715. He was one of 24 members subscribing to an agreement concerning rules governing the Chapel Royal on 23 April 1720.

Chitty, Elizabeth. *See* NORRIS, ELIZABETH.

Choak. *See* CHOCK.

Choca, Mrs ɪ*fl.* 1734ɪ, *actress.*

A Mrs Choca made her first and last professional appearance in London in a booth at Mile End Green ("during the time of the fair") on 30 October 1734 as Margery's Mother in the comedy *The Gardener's Wedding; or, The Waterman Defeated.*

Chock, Alexander ɪ*fl.* 1666–1667ɪ, *scenekeeper.*

Alexander Chock was a member of the Duke's Company in 1666–67 and possibly before and after, his function as one of the scenekeepers being recorded on 16 May 1667 in the Lord Chamberlain's accounts. During the season he was sued by Clement and Anne Scudamore, possibly for debt. An Alexander Chock wrote the lyrics for several songs published about 1705 and about 1715, but he was probably another person, though possibly related to the scenekeeper.

Chock, Dennis *b. c. 1689, actress.*

Miss "Dennychock" made her first appearance at the age of six in September 1695 at Drury Lane, when she spoke the epilogue to George Powell's *Bonduca*. She may have been related to Alexander Chock, the Duke's Company scenekeeper of the 1660s and / or the Mrs Chock who acted

with John Coysh's strolling company in the early 1670s. Miss Chock, billed as seven years of age, spoke the epilogue to *The Cornish Comedy*, another play by Powell, in June 1696 at Dorset Garden. And so her career continued in Rich's company for the next two seasons: speaking epilogues or prologues for *The World in the Moon, Phaeton,* and *The Revengeful Queen.* Finally, in late December 1699 at Drury Lane, she played the Duke of York in *Richard III,* her first appearance in a dramatic role and her last notice in the bills.

Chocke, George ɪ*fl.* 1698–1699ɪ, *musician.*

On 3 June 1698 George Chocke was admitted to the King's Musick as a musician extraordinary, that is, without fee until a position was vacated. A document in the Lord Chamberlain's accounts dating 1699 showed him in the same category among the instrumentalists, but as "Choke." The annual salary, if he ever achieved ordinary status, would have been £40.

Chollet, Constance ɪ*fl.* 1771ɪ, *dancer.*

Announcement was made on the opera bill for *Le pazzie di Orlando* at the King's Theatre on 11 March 1771 that "Mlle Constance Chollet, a principal dancer will make her first appearance this Evening." She danced again on 12 March. If she danced in London after that the bills do not show it.

Cholmondeley, Mrs Robert. *See* WOFFINGTON, MARY.

Chori. *See* CORRI.

Chose, Mr ɪ*fl.* 1734–1735ɪ, *dancer.*

A male dancer named Chose was among the 11 executants who presented "I: *The Black Joke.* II: *Revellers.* III: *Pierots.* IV: *Les Bergeries*" at a performance of *The Alchemist* and *The Burgomaster Trick'd* at

Drury Lane on 19 September 1734. It was his first appearance in London, so far as is known. He and his fellows repeated the program on 24 September and he and seven others danced *Les Bergeries* on the night of 26 September. On 3 October the entire dance corps gave an entertainment oddly heralded by the playbill "*La Follette s'cest ravisee. Revellers. Pierots. Les Bergeries.*" On 5 October he was one of three "Swains" who supported the principals of the harlequinade *Cupid and Psyche; or, Colombine Courtezan.* He figured as one of "*Les Bergeries*" on 8 October, he was in the background dancing for the *Sleepy Dutchman and his Frow* on 10 October; and he danced as another "Swain" in "A new *Grand Ballet*" on 17 October.

Though Chose doubtless remained in the theatre, his name did not achieve the bills again until 22 January 1735, when he was Monsieur Harlequin in the pantomime afterpiece called *The Plot.* He dropped from the record thereafter.

Chrispion. *See* CRESPION.

Christian, Mr *(fl.* 1750–1753), dancer.

A Mr Christian was one of the Infernals in the pantomime *Perseus and Andromeda* at Covent Garden on 3 October 1750. He danced the "Brighella" pantomime part, Hercules, in *Merlin's Cave* on 21 December and then either danced no more there that season or settled into the anonymity of mass dances not reported in the bills. His career was singularly obscure in the 1751–52 and 1753–54 seasons, in each of which he achieved printed notice only once or twice, and then only in the autumn half of each campaign: on 30 September 1751 an Infernal and 28 October an Aerial Spirit in *Merlin's Cave,* and a Demon in the character of Scaramouch in *Harlequin Dr Faustus* on 11 November. He was either absent from all theatres in 1752–53 or never noticed in the bills. At Drury Lane

on 12 and 13 October 1753 he figured with others in "A New Dance call'd the *Gipsey Tambourine,*" and, on 26 November with four others, in Act IV of *The Man of Mode,* he danced "a Masquerade Dance proper to the play."

Christian, Mrs, née Vaughan *(fl. 1730–1733), actress.*

Mrs Christian's first name is not known, but she was very likely the daughter of a boxkeeper at Drury Lane Theatre named Vaughan, and she was certainly the sister of the actor Henry Vaughan and the actresses Hannah Vaughan (Mrs William Pritchard) and Martha (or Patty) Vaughan, who became Mrs Nelson. She was evidently close kin to other theatrical Vaughans of the mid-century and later.

She made her debut at Goodman's Fields Theatre under her patronymic on 1 June 1730 as Araminta in *The Old Bachelor* ("first on any stage"). On 5 June she reappeared as Bellaria in *The Temple Beau,* replacing the absent Mrs Purden, with her younger sister Martha playing Clarissa, replacing Mrs Seal. She was next Arabella in the new play by John Mottley, *The Widow Bewitched,* on 8, 10, and 15 June. On 9 June she was Laura in *The Man's Bewitched.* On 19 June she played Advocate in *The Fair Quaker of Deal,* on 6 July Myrtilla in *The Provok'd Husband,* and on 17 July Mrs Topknot in *The Gamester.* This was an arduous regimen for a young player and perhaps suggests some previous experience despite the claim which had been made when she played on 1 June.

The sisters transferred their talents to Drury Lane for part of the next season, 1730–31, but were not much employed in named roles. Martha played Jenny in *Patie and Peggy* on 25 and 30 November. Our subject played Iris (listed as *Mrs Vaughan*) in the first performance of Charles Johnson's *Medea* on 11 December, was Jeany in *The Highland Fair; or, Union of the Clans,* "A New Scot's Opera" by Joseph Mitchell on 20 March, and was Susan in *The Sailor's Opera* afterpiece on 12 May.

The season of 1731–32 was, so far as the playbills show, barren of performance by our Miss Vaughan, and when she and her sister Martha turned up at Goodman's Fields in the season of 1732–33, the older girl had become Mrs Christian. Who her husband was is not known, but evidently he did not act. It is scarcely likely that he was the dancer named Christian who first appeared for a few performances at each of the patent theatres 19 years later.

Mrs Christian first acted under her new name when she played Araminta in *The Old Bachelor* on 6 October 1732. Her other parts that season were Leonora in *The Mourning Bride*, Dorcas in *The Mock Doctor*, Teresa in *The Spanish Fryar*, Situp in *The Double Gallant*, both Myrtilla and Lady Wronghead (on separate nights) in *The Provok'd Husband*, Lady Percy in *1 Henry IV*, Lamorce in *The Inconstant*, Betty in *A Bold Stroke for a Wife*, Clara in *The Lover's Opera*, Mrs Vixen in *The Beggar's Opera*, Gypsy in *The Stratagem*, and Mrs Fulmore in *The Decoy*. For her older sister's benefit on 30 May 1733 Martha ("Mrs Nelson, formerly Miss M. Vaughan") played Clara in the afterpiece, *The Lover's Opera*, and Mrs Christian ("formerly Miss Vaughan") was Mrs Cleriment in the mainpiece, *The Tender Husband*. Tickets were to be had "at Christian's House, No 23, Prescott Street." One Christian was given a benefit concert at Hampstead on 11 September 1734, with airs on the violin by a Captain Dupas, a scholar of Corelli.

Though her relatives, the Vaughans and Mrs Pritchard, continued to be active in London's theatres, seemingly Mrs Christian abandoned the stage after the 1732–33 season.

Christian, Miss (fl. 1784), *actress.*

A young woman, her "first time on any stage," tried a brief flight under the customary anonymous shelter of billing as "A Young Lady," playing Miss Hoyden in *The Man of Quality* at the summer theatre in the Haymarket on 6 August 1784. She was identified by the *Public Advertiser* of 9 August as a Miss Christian. She does not seem to have succeeded, for she never appeared again.

Christian, Benjamin (fl. 1794), *violinist.*

Benjamin Christian was a violinist residing at Buckingham House about 1794, according to Doane's *Musical Directory* of that year. He belonged to the King's Band of Music and played frequently in the Concerts of Ancient Music.

Christian, Charles (fl. c. 1700), *singer.*

According to the British Museum's *Catalogue of Printed Music* Charles Christian, otherwise unknown, sang *Ye envious Winds forbear to blow* at the Lincoln's Inn Fields playhouse. The song was published about 1700.

Christian, Edward (fl. 1784?–1794), *singer.*

Edward Christian, of No 218, High Holborn, was listed by Doane's *Musical Directory* of 1794 as "Alto," which means either that he was a countertenor singer or that he played on the viola or tenor horn. He belonged to the New Musical Fund. He is probably to be identified with the Mr Christian whom Burney lists among the tenor singers at the Handel Memorial Concerts at Westminster Abbey and the Pantheon on 26, 27, and 29 May and 3 and 5 June 1784.

Christian, Thomas. *See* CHRISTMAS, THOMAS (fl. 1692–1696).

Christian, William d. 1699, *singer.*

William Christian was one of the boy singers in the Choir of Westminster at the coronation of James II on 23 April 1685, and he became a regular member at some later date. Identified as "one of the Choir," he was buried in the North Cloister of Westminster Abbey on 14 February 1699. He had a daughter who died in infancy and was buried on 6 August 1697.

Christmas, Mrs [fl. c. 1673–1675], actress?

Though not listed in *The London Stage*, Mrs Christmas was a member of the King's Company about 1673–75, according to the Lord Chamberlain's accounts.

Christmas, John d. c. 1677, trumpeter.

A Mr Christmas, probably John, was given what seems to have been a temporary appointment as trumpeter in the King's Musick, in place of the pensioned Nicholas Caperon. A warrant dated 23 May 1663 appointed John a trumpeter extraordinary (without fee until a position became vacant), but that may well have been a repetition of the earlier order, for, presumably, had Caperon received a pension, no fee would have been available for his position. Somehow Christmas managed to survive by taking interim jobs or doing special work which brought stipends. It may have been because of his "extraordinary" position that he spent some of his career traveling.

On 25 August 1671, for instance, he was paid £20 in advance for attending the English ambassador to Sweden from 26 August 1671 to 1 July 1672; he was also provided sea livery and was later paid 5s. daily for his service. On 18 November 1672 he accepted an appointment to attend the Duke of Monmouth in Sir Philip Howard's troop, and in the spring of 1673 he was off to the Netherlands with Sir Leoline Jenkins and Sir Joseph Williamson. The following January he was back with the troop of Guards, and finally, on 18 May 1674, he was given a permanent appointment in the King's

Musick as a replacement for Nicholas Caperon.

Either John or Thomas Christmas, who may have been brothers, played trumpet in the court masque *Calisto* on 15 February 1675, but John was soon off again, attending Lawrence Hyde, who was in Poland from 9 June 1676 to 12 February 1677. During this Polish journey John Christmas was killed. On 19 July 1677 a new trumpet was ordered for Gervase Price, the master trumpeter, to replace the silver one which had belonged to John Christmas. And Price, on 20 October, was granted £200 to give to Sarah Christmas, John's widow, as a present from the King.

Since we know that Mrs Christmas was named Sarah, it is likely that the following concerns our subject: on 21 September 1669 at St Mary le Bone a John Christmas had married Sarah Dickenson, and on 31 March 1673, a month before the trumpeter went to the Netherlands, John and Sarah Christmas had baptized a daughter Ann (born on 21 March) at St Martin-in-the-Fields.

Christmas, Thomas [fl. 1663], trumpeter.

Thomas Christmas was appointed a trumpeter extraordinary (without fee until a vacancy occurred) on 1 June 1663. The Lord Chamberlain's accounts made no further mention of him, though on 20 September 1665 the will of a Thomas Christmas of St Bride, Fleet Street, who had been buried on 5 September, was proved by a Mary Curtis; and the will of musician Simon Beale, written on 25 September 1691 and proved on 11 February 1695, contained a bequest of 10s. for a mourning ring for a Thomas Christmas whose parish was either St Katherine Coleman or St Katherine Cree. Either or neither of those references may have been to the trumpeter.

Christmas, Thomas [fl. 1692–1696], singer.

Thomas Christmas was a boy singer in the Chapel Royal whose voice changed about 1692. On 9 November of that year he was granted £20 and a suit of clothes as a former Chapel boy. He was probably the Thomas "Christian" still being provided with clothing in January 1696.

Chudleigh, John [fl. 1669–1674], actor?

The Lord Chamberlain's accounts listed John Chudleigh as a member of the King's Company in 1669–70 and again in 1673–74, and it is probable that he also served in the seasons not accounted for. His function in the company was not mentioned, though he may have been a minor actor.

Chumbley, Mr [fl. 1797–1802], box-keeper.

A Mr Chumbley was one of the box-keepers at Drury Lane Theatre in the seasons 1797–98 through 1801–2.

Church. *See also* CHURCHMAN.

Church, Mr [fl. 1744], house servant?

A Mr Church shared a benefit at Drury Lane on 22 May 1744 with seven others, and since some of the beneficiaries were house servants, perhaps Church was too.

Church, Mr [fl. 1752–1753], musician.

When *The Old Woman's Oratory* was produced for Mr Church's benefit at the Haymarket by "Mrs Midnight" on 17 March 1752, Church played the Jew's harp. He repeated that offering, again for his benefit, on 29 March 1753 at the same playhouse. His name sounds actual enough but since those were antic productions by Christopher Smart ("Mrs Midnight"), perhaps "Church" was a pseudonym.

Church, Mr [fl. 1770], actor, singer.

On 1 October 1770 at the Haymarket Theatre a Mr Church sang a song in which were introduced several imitations (unspecified), and on 29 October at the same playhouse he acted Don Diego in *The Padlock*.

Church, John 1675–1741, singer, composer.

Though there may have been two musicians named John Church, the probability is that the one who sang at the Dorset Garden Theatre in 1695 and 1696 was the same as a member of the Chapel Royal in the years immediately following.

John Church was born at Windsor in 1675 and trained as a chorister at St John's College, Oxford. He came to London soon enough to become a friend of Henry Purcell before the great composer died in 1695. Purcell gave a portrait of himself to Church, and in later years it passed from Church's granddaughter, Mrs Strutt, to Joah Bates, who recorded its history. The painting, by an unknown artist, now hangs in the National Portrait Gallery.

By mid-April 1695 Church was singing in *The Indian Queen* at the Dorset Garden Theatre as a member of Christopher Rich's company; in October 1696, at the same house, he sang in *Brutus of Alba*. He was sworn a Gentleman of the Chapel Royal extraordinary (without fee until a vacancy occurred) on 31 January 1697. After the death of James Cobb, a tenor, Church was given a full position with pay on 1 August 1697. Once in the Chapel, Church gave up his theatre singing, but he remained interested in popular music and published in 1699, 1700, and 1719 a number of songs, such as *From that one glance, From all uneasie Passions free, A Beggar, a Beggar, Ho Boy, hey Boy,* and *Ye brave boys* ("the Duke of Ormonde's march"). He also composed several religious anthems and services, wrote an *Introduction to Psalmody*, published in 1723, and edited *Divine Harmony*, a collection of anthems published in 1712. In 1704 he was made lay vicar and master of the choristers of Westminster, an appointment which ran concurrently with that in the Chapel Royal. The Mr Church who sang at a concert in the Inner Temple on 2 February 1726 was probably John.

John Church had a wife named Elizabeth by whom he had several children who were baptized and buried at Westminster Abbey: Elizabeth, baptized on 28 December 1701 and buried on 9 February 1702; Anne, baptized on 5 January 1704 and buried on 19 June 1708; Mary, baptized on 14 February 1706 and buried sometime before 1734; Charles, baptized on 3 June 1709 and buried on 4 July 1719; and Robert, who died in infancy and was buried on 13 December 1711. John and Elizabeth Church had two other sons, John and Ralph, whose baptismal records have not been found.

John Church the musician made his will on 3 July 1734. By that time he was a widower, his wife having been buried on 22 December 1732. He requested a frugal, private burial near his wife and children and left his estate to his sons John and Ralph equally. Church died on 6 January 1741 and was buried on 10 January in the South Cloister of the Abbey. His surviving sons proved his will three days later.

Church, Samuel ₍fl. 1792₎, performer.

An entry of 11 October 1792 in the Folger Library's manuscript account book of Drury Lane Theatre reads: "Samuel Church for his performances in Cymon [£]9." Church was an "extra," for he was not in the regular pay list. He does not appear in the Drury Lane company lists for the seasons of 1791–92 or 1792–93 printed in *The London Stage*. Garrick's *Cymon*, with new music and elaborate scenery and machinery, concluding with "a Grand Procession of the Hundred Knights of Chivalry," troops of "Arcadian Shepherds," mock battles, dwarfs, giants, Turks, and Scythians, had been revived on 31 December 1791,

and had been played many times in the spring and fall of 1792. What character, action, or instrument Church performed as, in, or on, and when exactly he performed are not known.

Church, William ₍fl. 1666–1670₎, scenekeeper.

William Church was one of the scenekeepers in the King's Company at the Bridges Street playhouse from 1666–67 through 1669–70, and since records are so scanty for that period it may well be that he served the company before and after those seasons.

Churchill, Miss ₍fl. 1782₎, actress.

A Miss Churchill performed an unspecified part in *The Fashionable Wife; or, The Female Gallant* on 6 May 1782 at the Haymarket Theatre, usually dark at that time of year. The players, minor folk of the patent houses and novices, were evidently playing for their own benefit, with special license: "By Permission of the Lord Chamberlain." Miss Churchill was not heard from again.

Churchill, John ₍fl. 1699–1700₎, carpenter.

John Churchill was a carpenter in the royal employ at Kensington where, among other duties, he was charged with building a stage (in June 1699, according to the Works accounts) and providing a "convenance for yᵉ Kings musick upon his birth day" in November 1700.

Churchill, William 1760?–1812, violinist, violoncellist, harpsichordist.

When the 23-year-old William Churchill was proposed for Membership in the Royal Society of Musicians by Charles Lintone on 7 December 1783, he was introduced by the usual formula, "Studied and practiced Musick for a livelihood for Seven years and Upwards." The encomium continues informatively: "Plays on the

Violin, Violincello and Harpsichord. A very worthy member of Covent Garden Orchestra. Author of a set of Trios Son[ata]s &c. A single man."

He was the "Mr Churchill" whom Charles Burney listed among the second violins performing at the Handel Memorial Concerts at Westminster Abbey and the Pantheon on 26, 27, 29 May and 3 and 5 June 1784, for Doane's *Musical Directory* in 1794 credited William with these performances. He was on the list dated 6 March 1785 of appointees by the Royal Society's Governors to play the violin at the annual concerts for the benefit of the clergy of St Paul's Cathedral, held that year on 10 and 12 May.

On 2 April 1797 the Minute Books of the Society recorded a petition from him stating that he could no longer follow his profession because of a ruptured blood vessel. He was granted £3 3s. per month until further orders. But by 3 December of that year he had informed the Governors that his health was restored and he no longer needed relief.

On 2 February 1812, pursuant to a letter pleading poor health, the Society granted him 10 guineas, and note was taken of his letter of gratitude at the meeting of 1 March. At some time between that date and 2 August William Churchill died. The Society paid £7 13s. 6d. for funeral costs and "Mr Pilbrow was asked to send a certificate of Mr Churchill's marriage and births of the children." This done, on 6 September 1812 they were placed in a pensionary status, retroactive to 1 July (placing William's death probably in late May).

On 7 March 1813 the Minute Books took note of the granting to "Churchill's children" the "usual allowance for schooling from midsummer and £10 for clothing to be spent at Mr Pilbrow's discretion." Miss C. A. Churchill, "willing to be bound," attended for the drawing up of indenture papers on 6 March 1814, and on 5 March 1815 a grant of £15 was made to

the children for clothing. By 7 January 1816 "Mrs Churchill's 3 children" had been granted an increase in allowance of four guineas a month. A "Son of Mr Churchill" was bound apprentice to Pilbrow on 4 May 1817 and it was ordered that "the allowance be reduced in proportion." By the meeting of 1 April 1821 Miss Churchill was "granted £10 for Serving her apprenticeship with Mr Pilbrow." On 4 May 1823 Pilbrow asked for permission to apprentice the "daughter of [the] late Mr Churchill" and "to use the premium to pay for Mr Churchill's Son's education." The proposition was "Against laws of the Society and regretfully refused."

At the meeting of 5 September 1824 Mr Pilbrow observed that W. H. Churchill, William's son, would soon be 14 years old and, since he loved the sea, should be apprenticed for three years. The Governors asked for further information. C. Churchill was "granted £10 for faithful apprenticing under Mr Pilbrow." The last entry relative to the Churchills is the cryptic "Mr Pilbrow was not granted the apprenticeship fee for Wm. C."

In the British Museum's collection are the following published compositions by William Churchill: *A Favorite Sonata for the Harpsichord or Piano Forte, with an Accompanyment for a Violin*. London: W. Campbell (1785?); *Six Trios four for a Violin, Tenor and Violoncello-obligato . . . Op. prima* (separate parts). London: J. Preston (1785?); *Ten Progressive Lessons for the Piano Forte or Harpsichord . . . Opera 5*. London: R. Birchall (1790?); *and Three Sonatas for the Grand or Square Piano Forte, with or without the Additional Keys, & with an Accompaniment for the Violin . . . op. IV* (separate parts). London: Lewis, Houston & Hyde (1795?).

Churchman, Mr [fl. 1715], actor.

At Lincoln's Inn Fields on 2 June 1715 a Mr Churchman played the Second Whore in *The City Ramble* (according to the 1715 first edition of the work), and on the following 23 June at the same playhouse a Mr Church played Haircut in the premier of *The Doating Lovers* (again according to the 1715 first edition of the play). It is likely that only one performer was involved here, but whether his name was Churchman or Church is a pretty question.

Churton, Mr ₁*fl. 1796*₁, *manager? actor? See* **CHURTON, MRS.**

Churton, Mrs ₁*fl. 1792*₁, *actress.*

A Mrs Churton appeared at the Haymarket in a specially licensed performance for her own benefit on 6 February 1792, playing Desdemona in *Othello* and Miss Biddy in *Miss in Her Teens* the comic afterpiece. Tickets were to be had of her at No 33, New Bond Street. In another such performance, on 20 February, for Wilkinson's benefit, she played Isabinda in the afterpiece *The Busy Body*. She did not act in London thereafter.

(The Lord Chamberlain's records in the Public Record Office cite a license given to a Mr Churton for a program of "plays & entertainments" at the Haymarket on 12 May 1796.)

Ciabrano. *See* **CHABRAN.**

Ciacchi, Signor ₁*fl. 1746–1748*₁, *singer.*

Signor Ciacchi sang at the King's Theatre in London for three seasons, 1746 to 1748, making his first appearance on 7 January 1746 in an unspecified role in *La caduta de' giganti*. His other roles (with dates of first performances) included Scipio in *Il trionfo della continenza* (28 January 1746), the title role in *Antigono* (13 May 1746), a role in *Annibale in Capua* (4 November 1746), Anicetus in *Lucio Vero* (14 November 1747), and Idreno in *La ingratitudine punita* (12 January 1748). He also sang at concerts for the benefit of

the musicians' fund on 25 March 1746, 14 April 1747, and 5 April 1748. According to Dr Burney, Ciacchi did not possess "the powers of pleasing."

Ciardini, Domenico ₁*fl. 1763*₁, *singer.*

Domenico Ciardini was one of several singers announced in the bills as specially engaged for a command performance, a revival of the opera *Orione, ossia Diana vendicata* at the King's Theatre on 19 February 1763. He sang the part of Orion. The opera was a success and was repeated four times. His only other appearance in London seems to have been at the King's in a "Concert of Vocal and Instrumental Music" on 5 April 1763, when he sang two excerpts from opera.

"Ciavartino, Signor" ₁*fl. 1754*₁, *musical performer?*

The play bill for one of Christopher Smart's comic effusions at the Haymarket, *Mrs Midnight's New Carnival Concert* presented on the evening of 13 September 1754, contained the company's usual list of ludicrous pseudonyms, including "Sig Ciavartino." The performers promised to play music "Set for a Smoking Pipe, a Tankard, a Bassoon, a Pair of Tongs, two Wooden Spoons, A Salt Box, and a Pair of Slippers, by the best Italian Masters." Which "instrument" was Signor Ciavartino's and whom the pseudonym hid are facts not known.

Cibber, Colley *1671–1757, actor, manager, playwright.*

Colley Cibber, the first offspring of the sculptor Caius Gabriel Cibber and his second wife, was born on 6 November 1671. He was baptized on the twentieth at St Giles in the Fields, the clerk recording his name phonetically as "Colly Sibber."

The elder Cibber, the son of a cabinetmaker, was born in Flensborg, Slesvig, in 1630 (or, according to his declaration at his second marriage, about 1637). The Danish king sent him to study in Italy, after which, by way of the Netherlands, he came to England. By his first wife, Elizabeth, he had a son Gabriel, who was baptized at St Giles on 29 September 1668; perhaps both Elizabeth and the child died soon afterwards, for there seem to be no later records of them, and Caius Gabriel Cibber married for a second time on 24 November 1670 at his parish church. His bride was Jane Colley, a spinster about 33 years old from Glaston, Rutlandshire. Jane's family was old, royalist, and wealthy, and she brought her husband a dowry of £6000. After their son Colley was born, Caius Gabriel and Jane had two more children: Veronica, baptized at St Giles on 14 May 1674, and Lewis, baptized at St Margaret, Westminster, on 17 August 1680. Caius Gabriel, after a distinguished career as a sculptor, died in 1700; his son Lewis died in 1711. The death dates of Jane Colley Cibber and her daughter Veronica have not been discovered.

Colley Cibber was born in Southampton Street, then a fashionable area, but in 1673 his father lost his fortune gambling and until 1678 was in debtors' prison—albeit at first with freedom to leave daily to cut the bas-relief on the Monument. For the first seven years of his life, therefore, Colley was virtually without a father, and an estrangement developed which never quite healed. The family finances were better by 1682, and Colley was sent off to his mother's part of the country, to the free school of Grantham in Lincolnshire, near Glaston. At school bright young Colley learned the advantages of flattery, which put him on the right side of his teachers and the wrong side of his fellow students. "I was so jeered, laughed at, and hated as a pragmatical bastard (schoolboys' language) who had betrayed the whole form," he wrote years later in his *Apology*," that scarce any of 'em would keep me company."

Caius Gabriel hoped Colley would become a man of the cloth and wanted to enter him in Winchester College, the founder of which, William of Wykham, was said to have been an ancestor of Jane Cibber. But Colley's "naked merit and a pompous pedigree" were insufficient, and he was not preferred. (His brother Lewis later had no trouble gaining entrance—after Caius Gabriel presented the college with a statue of its founder.) Religion's dubious loss became the theatre's certain gain, for in 1687 Colley came to London and "imbibed an inclination, which I durst not [then] reveal, for the stage." His stay in London was brief, for he was summoned to Chatsworth, where the elder Cibber was working on a sculpture. Colley's journey was interrupted by the Revolution, and father and son met at Nottingham, where Caius Gabriel was under arms. Rather than proceed to Cambridge, where his father now had hopes of entering him, Colley took the elder Cibber's place in the army, serving under the Earl of Devonshire.

When the campaign was over, Colley went to Chatsworth, petitioned Devonshire for preferment, received encouragement, and returned to London as part of the Earl's household. While waiting for an expected vacancy in the office of the Secretary of State, Colley renewed his interest in the theatre. Against his parents' wishes, he joined the United Company at Drury Lane. He was 19, had no training, and was meagre in voice and body, but he had a good ear, a "chearful" manner, and boundless ambition.

For nine months, a longer than usual probationary period, he worked for nothing, serving in what capacity we know not. A story later told by Thomas Davies suggests that Cibber's first appearance before an audience coincided with his first salary receipt. Colley, said Davies, was playing a messenger who was to carry a note onstage to the troupe's leading performer, Thomas Betterton, but when Cibber saw the audience he became so nervous he botched the scene. Afterward Betterton asked Downes the prompter who the youngster was who had blundered so. "Master Colley," said Downes. "Master Colley! Then forfeit him." "Why, sir," came the reply, "he has no salary." "No? Why then put him down ten shillings a week and forfeit him five." The story is pleasant but of doubtful authenticity.

Cibber's first recorded role was Sir Gentle's servant in *Sir Anthony Love* at Drury Lane in late September 1690. After that, and probably before it, he doubtless appeared in walk-ons and bit parts that were never cited in cast lists. His other known roles for the 1690–91 season were Sigismond in *Alphonso* in December 1690 and Pyrot in D'Urfey's version of *Bussy D'Ambois* in March 1691. The following season he acted Splutter in *The Marriage-Hater Match'd* in January 1692, Albimer in *The Rape* in February, the Chaplain in *The Orphan* on 9 February, and Pisano in *The Traitor* in March. His role in *The Orphan* was the beginning of his success. He was applauded by the audience, and the actor Cardell Goodman predicted that *"If he does not make a good Actor, I'll be d——'d!"*

In 1692–93 Cibber may have played more than Aminadab in *A Very Good Wife* in late April 1693, but the records show no other roles for him. Poor, at odds with his parents, and entering the theatrical world at a time when players were losing their power to businessmen-managers, Cibber nevertheless decided to marry and raise a family. He had made the acquaintance of John Shore, the trumpeter son of His Majesty's Sergeant Trumpeter, Matthias. While visiting the Shores one day Colley heard the daughter in the family, Katherine, singing and accompanying herself on the harpsichord. She was a student of Henry Purcell and, according to the later account of her daughter Charlotte (Charke), had a "fund of perfection with which art and nature had equally endowed her." To Katherine, Colley seemed a sprightly wit, and though Matthias Shore was against the match, Colley

wooed and won her. On 6 May 1693 the pair were married at St James, Duke's Place, Aldgate, whereupon the disgruntled Matthias spent his daughter's dowry on a floating place of amusement on the Thames which wits dubbed Shore's Folly. Matthias partly relented later; in his will in 1696 he left a third of his property to Katherine, but he called her "Shore," not "Cibber" — a calculated insult to Colley.

Katherine took to the stage to augment the family income, yet before the end of the century she became the mother of two children: Catherine (*sic*), born in 1694, and Anne, born on 1 October and baptized on 15 October at St Martin-in-the-Fields. Catherine grew up to marry Colonel James Brown, after whose death she stayed with her father and inherited the bulk of his estate; she was, according to Charlotte Charke, a she-dragon with a rancorous disposition. Anne in later years ran a shop where she sold china, tea, and other items, and between 1727 and 1734 she married John Boultby. Mrs Cibber's modest stage career was curtailed not only by the birth of her children but also by asthma attacks. By the end of the century Colley had rented a place for her in Uxbridge, near Hillington, where she lived in retirement for some time and raised the Cibber family.

At the time of his marriage in 1693 Colley was earning 15*s*. weekly at the theatre and enjoying £20 annually from the estate of his uncle Edward Colley. Cibber played such small parts in 1693–94 as Amorin in *The Ambitious Slave* and Perez in the first part and Duke Ricardo in the second part of *Don Quixote*. But a real opportunity came in 1694 when he substituted for Edward Kynaston as Lord Touchwood in Congreve's *The Double Dealer*. The author gave Colley the role at the last minute when Kynaston was too ill to perform, and the event was made greater by the presence of the Queen in the audience. Perhaps it took place on 13 January 1694, on which date Her Majesty and her maids of honor are known to have seen the play. Congreve was delighted with Cibber's performance, put in a good word for him with the Drury Lane managers Christopher Rich and Sir Thomas Skipwith, and Colley was granted a five-shilling raise.

When Thomas Betterton and some of the older players at Drury Lane rebelled against the managers and formed a new troupe, Cibber wisely stayed with Rich and Skipwith, where the competition was less keen. In late May 1695 George Powell, the manager of acting, gave Colley a role he had wanted to try, Fondlewife in *The Old Bachelor*, Thomas Doggett's old part. "*If the fool has a mind to blow himself up at once*," Powell said, "*let us e'en give him a clear stage for it.*" Powell cast himself in Betterton's role of Heartwell and planned to mimic the veteran. Taking that as a cue, Cibber imitated Doggett as Fondlewife: ". . . I had laid the Tint of forty Years more than my real Age upon my Features, and to the most minute placing of an Hair, was dressed exactly like [Doggett]: When I spoke, the Surprize was still greater, as if I had not only borrow'd his Cloaths, but his Voice too." Three surges of applause came after Cibber's exit in his first scene, and even Doggett, sitting in the audience, was pleased. The author of *The Laureat* in 1740 did not remember the characterization so kindly: "in my Opinion, on the whole, he over-does it much. The Character appears too vigorous and robust in some Places, which *Dogget* kept under a lower Key, and stuck much closer to *Nature*."

The managers offered Cibber no more such parts, but that did not deter Colley. If they would not give him roles suited to his growing talent for playing fops, he would write such parts for himself. That he did in *Love's Last Shift* in 1696, a remarkable first play combining the crispness of Restoration comedy with the bourgeois moral sentiments that the audiences of the late 1690s preferred. It was the first sentimental comedy, and it set a trend for the ensuing cen-

tury; further, it displayed Cibber's fine sense of what would please an audience, an instinct that abetted him throughout his career in acting, writing, and management.

For himself in *Love's Last Shift* he created the role of the foppish Sir Novelty Fashion, or perhaps it would be truer to say he wrote himself into the play, for it is difficult to distinguish Cibber the actor from the parts he played so well. He gave the script to the established playwright Southerne, who in turn recommended it to the Drury Lane managers. "*Young Man!*" Southerne said to Colley (according to Colley), "*I pronounce thy Play a good one; I will answer for its Success, if thou dost not spoil it by thy own Action.*" Cibber certainly did not spoil it. The Lord Chamberlain called it "*the best First Play that any Author in his Memory had produc'd; and that for a young Fellow to shew himself such an Actor and such a Writer in one Day, was something extraordinary.*" *Love's Last Shift* was first performed at Drury Lane in January 1696. Again the managers, though pleased with the success, gave Colley no special preferment; they probably realized that the vain Cibber would continue doing well for them whether encouraged or not, and Rich and Skipwith were not ones to spend money needlessly. But Colley may have given them second thoughts when, for a brief period in 1696, he transferred to Betterton's company at Lincoln's Inn Fields.

It seems probable that Cibber's move was calculated. He is not known to have acted any roles while at Lincoln's Inn Fields, though he began writing his second play, *Woman's Wit*, for that troupe. In the preface to the printed work in 1697 Cibber said, "In the Middle of my Writing the Third Act, not liking my Station there, I returned to the Theatre Royal." The scanty records of performances of the time would suggest that his stay with Betterton took place during the summer of 1696. In the fall he was back with Rich and Skipwith, and on 29 October he signed a contract with them for his new play. The agreement provided him with a clear benefit the third day, detailed plans covering the continuation of the run if it should prove profitable, and a guarantee to Cibber that he could enjoy all the profits from the published work. The contract concluded with an agreement that Cibber would, as long as he remained an actor at Drury Lane, sell his new plays only to that theatre.

Woman's Wit was performed at Drury Lane in January 1697 with the author as Longville; publication followed in March. But the work was hastily written and rehearsed, the production was not a success, and Cibber did not even deign to mention the play in his *Apology* years later.

Though his second play was not worth remembering, other aspects of the 1696–97 season were. He played a number of roles, the most important of which was Lord Foppington in *The Relapse*, a part written especially for him by Vanbrugh in a play designed as a sequel to *Love's Last Shift*. *The Relapse* was presented on 21 November 1696, and Vanbrugh followed it with the second part of *Aesop*, in which Cibber acted the desirable title role. Cibber was quite willing to admit his deficiencies as a writer, and one might suppose that once better playwrights began tailoring parts to his talent he would give up writing and concentrate on acting, but, as will be seen, Colley's itch to write afflicted him to the end of his life.

During the last years of the seventeenth century Colley's finances were shaky at best. He loved the town and enjoyed gambling at the Groom Porter's. Perhaps it was in connection with his gambling that Jane Lucas, probably the actress of that name, had Cibber imprisoned. Between 19 April and 26 December 1697 (when the Earl of Sunderland was Lord Chamberlain) Colley wrote a plea to be released from durance. How long he was in prison, and why, remain a mystery.

His next play was *Xerxes*, a work in which Christopher Rich sensibly expressed no interest. Cibber took it to Betterton's company. They foolishly accepted it, and it opened and closed on the same afternoon in February 1699. More successful was Cibber's version of *Richard III*, which was produced in late December 1699 at Drury Lane with Cibber in the title role. He had good material to begin with, and, to give him credit, he did not butcher Shakespeare as badly as some adapters did. But his version was mangled by Charles Killigrew, the Master of the Revels and censor of plays, who deleted the first act, into which Cibber had introduced a portion of *3 Henry VI*. Consequently, the audience was puzzled, the first run was short, and Cibber netted less than £5 at his third-day benefit. But, as he wrote later, "for several Years since, it has seldom, or never fail'd of a crowded audience." Cibber's version of the play has remained popular down to the present day.

The critics of the eighteenth century were less interested in Cibber's adaptation of the text than in his portrayal of Richard. Vanbrugh found Colley effective, but virtually everyone else of sense who ever saw Cibber play the part thought he was dreadful. In 1734 the *Grub Street Journal* said:

When [Cibber] makes love to Lady Anne, he looks like a pickpocket, with his shrugs and grimaces, that has more a design on her purse than her heart; and his utterance is in the same cast with his action. In Bosworth Field he appears no more like King Richard than King Richard was like Falstaff: he foams, struts, and bellows with the voice and cadence of a watchman rather than a hero and a prince.

The same year Aaron Hill in *The Prompter* criticized Cibber's "comic shruggings" and "low, mincing curtails of magnanimity." Cibber played Richard with "the distorted heavings of an unjointed caterpillar," said Hill. The author of *The Laureat* in 1740 was even more withering:

[H]e screamed thro' four Acts without Dignity or Decency. The Audience, ill-pleas'd with the Farce, accompany'd him with a Smile of Contempt; but in the fifth Act he degenerated all at once into Sir *Novelty*; and when in the heat of the Battle at *Bosworth Field*, the King is dismounted, our Comic-Tragedian came on the Stage, really breathless, and in a seeming Panick, screaming out this Line thus—"*A Harse, a Harse, my Kingdom for a Harse.*" This highly delighted some, and disgusted others of his Auditors; and when he was kill'd by *Richmond*, one might plainly perceive that the good People were not better pleas'd that so *execrable a Tyrant* was destroy'd, than that so *execrable an Actor* was silent.

Despite harsh criticism throughout his career of his acting in tragedy, Cibber insisted on attempting serious roles for which he was hopelessly ill-suited.

His next play was *Love Makes a Man*, cribbed from two plays by Fletcher. For himself he created the role of the fop Clodio. The play was an inconsequential work, as Cibber later admitted: "The *Fop's Fortune* [the play's subtitle] lagg'd on the Fourth Day, and only held up its Head by the Heels of the *French Tumblers*, who it seems had so much Wit in their Limbs, that they forc'd the town to see it, till it laugh'd it self into their good Graces." It stayed in the good graces of audiences deep into the eighteenth century. During the 1700–1701 season Cibber also acted the Marquis in *Sir Harry Wildair* and, for his benefit on 19 June 1701, the title role in *Volpone*. The players at both theatres came under heavy attack for "uttering several blasphemous expressions" in plays during the summer and winter of 1701. Cibber was among those from Drury Lane who were arraigned, and he who took such care not to be offensive must have been chagrined to find himself under attack. The players were acquitted, but the pressure to reform the drama was strong, and Cibber was especially sensitive to the changing mood. It may not have

been a coincidence that in 1701 Cibber was appointed an adviser to Christopher Rich in the management of Drury Lane.

Less important to Cibber, to judge by his later indifference to her and her offspring, was the birth in 1701 of his third daughter, Elizabeth. She was baptized at St Paul, Covent Garden, on 16 March. She eventually went on the stage and then married Dawson Brett; their child, Anne, also acted and became the second wife of the Drury Lane prompter W. R. Chetwood.

In 1701–2 Cibber acted Lord Hardy in *The Funeral* and Don John in *The False Friend*. The next season saw him as Young Woudbe in *The Twin Rivals* and (on 26 November 1702) Don Manuel in his own *She Wou'd and She Wou'd Not*. His new play was not immediately popular: it "did not pay the Charges on the Sixth Day, tho' it has brought me, as a Sharer, more than I was then disappointed of as Author."

Cibber's ambition and his jealousy of those more successful than he was did not set well with his colleagues. *A Comparison Between the Two Stages* in 1702 included a dig at Cibber's vanity:

RAMB[LE]. But prithee look o' this side: there's *Cibber*, a Poet and a fine Actor.
CRIT[ICK]. And one that's always repining at the Success of others, and upon the Stage makes all his fellow Actors uneasy.

There was truth in that; in his *Apology* he either ignored or was unfairly critical of such successful performers as John Verbruggen, George Powell, and Richard Estcourt, but he seldom missed an opportunity to show himself in the best light. To disarm critics of his vanity Cibber frequently and unashamedly confessed his own weaknesses. For example, one of his important parts in 1703–4 was the title role in *Sir Courtly Nice*, which he acted on 30 October 1703 for his benefit. The role had been William Mountfort's in earlier years, and the prompter Downes said that of later actors only Cibber equalled him in the part. In his *Apology* Cibber admitted his debt to Mountfort and then wallowed in self-pity: ". . . I, alas! could only struggle thro' with the faint Excuses and real Confidence of a fine Singer under the Imperfection of a feign'd and screaming Trebble, which at best could only shew you what I would have done had nature been more favourable to me."

On 25 November 1703, in the midst of a great storm, Colley's son Theophilus was born. He was baptized at St Martin-in-the-Fields on 19 December. Theophilus was destined to become as famous and perhaps almost as good an actor as his father, and, like Colley, he was to be a playwright. He was also to be an embarrassment to the elder Cibber because of his scandalous and outrageous private life.

In November 1704, Colley signed a five-year contract with Christopher Rich to act at a weekly wage of £3 10s. A separate verbal agreement gave him an additional 10s. weekly for casting parts, reading plays, and "other services," plus 20s. weekly for assisting in the management of the theatre. That made Cibber the highest paid actor in the troupe and certainly the most influential.

A month later, on 7 December, his next play, *The Careless Husband*, came out. For himself he wrote the role of Lord Foppington. He originally intended Lady Betty Modish for Mrs Verbruggen, but after her death in 1703 he refashioned the part for Anne Oldfield. For Robert Wilks he created Sir Charles Easy. With such a combination success should have been assured, for the play was probably the best thing he had written, but Cibber later said, " 'Twas at first a moot Point whether the *Careless Husband* should live or die; but the Houses it has since fill'd have reproach'd the former Coldness of its Auditors."

Cibber had put himself in an awkward position by accepting a share in the management, and his critics were quick to ac-

Harvard Theatre Collection

COLLEY CIBBER, as Lord Foppington
engraving by Simon, after Grisoni

cuse him of a conflict of interests. In 1704 *Visits from the Shades* (possibly by Defoe, though it smacks of Tom Brown's humor) contained an imaginary conversation between Cibber and the dead playwright Nathaniel Lee:

CIBBER. The town has a [good] opinion of my parts, and my plays have raised me to a sort of viceroy in the theatres: for I try, acquit, or condemn; and there's nought to be represented but what is stamped by my approbation and tried by the touchstone of my own sense.

NAT LEE. Why the truth on't is, you are a very pretty deputy under Apollo [Rich], and the poets must need have a fine time on't, to be governed by such a quack of Parnassus, a stage tartar, that graze for your dialogues from the poets of the last age (for thank Heaven the ancients are far enough out of reach of your plagiarism). In short, your plays and your judgment are monstrous and defective.

CIBBER. Mr R[ic]h and Mr S[kipwit]h think otherwise, and I value no one's opinion beside.

The satire criticized Cibber for turning down the script of *The Ambitious Step-mother*, which the author of *Visits* considered worthy—though we should note to Cibber's credit that he accepted a number of good plays, including pieces by Steele and Farquhar, which proved lasting.

In 1705–6 Cibber turned out another new play, sired another child, and devised another new characterization. The play was *Perolla and Izadora*, a tragedy in every sense of the word, which was performed late in 1705. Dennis later paired it off with Cibber's *Ximena* and called both of them "full of Nonsense and False *English* . . . stiff, awkward, affected Stuff, and Lines that make as hideous a Noise, as if they were compos'd in an Itinerant Wheel-Barrow." Cibber's new child was James, born on 25 July 1706 and baptized on 7 August at St Martin's; of him nothing else is known (perhaps he died in infancy), and he has not hitherto been noticed by Cibber biographers. Cibber's new role was a gem: Brazen in *The Recruiting Officer*, which he first performed on 8 April 1706.

In the years immediately following 1706 the state of the theatre in London was one of confusion. The new Queen's Theatre in the Haymarket had opened in 1705, and the players found themselves, because of shifts among the adventurer-managers, now at the Queen's and now at Drury Lane. Cibber performed at the Queen's Theatre in 1706–7 with a fine group of players and a good stock of plays, and his season there, unlike some earlier ones, was quite fully recorded. On 7 November 1706 he played Lord Foppington in *The Careless Husband*, after which he was seen as Sir Fopling Flutter in *The Man of Mode*, Brazen, Sir Courtly, Sharper in *The Platonick Lady*,

Corvino in *Volpone*, Humphrey Gubbin in *The Tender Husband*, Sir John Daw in *The Silent Woman*, Howdee in *The Northern Lass*, Surrey in *Henry VIII*, a citizen in *Caius Marius*, the Chaplain in *The Orphan*, Gibbet in *The Beaux' Stratagem*, a plebeian in *Julius Caesar*, the Mad Englishman in *The Pilgrim*, and Renault in *Venice Preserv'd*. Perhaps some of his managerial tasks continued at the Queen's, but there he served under Owen Swiney and was only indirectly connected with Rich, so he may have gone back onto a straight salary as an actor only. For the Queen's he wrote a new play, *The Comical Lovers; or Marriage à la Mode*, based on Dryden. It was first presented on 4 February 1707 with the author as Celadon.

Cibber had been a friend of Colonel Henry Brett since the turn of the century, and Brett in 1707 found himself a sharer in the Drury Lane patent. Skipwith, having gained little from his share, gave it to Brett, and Brett turned to Cibber for advice on what to do with it. Cibber, probably with an eye to his own future, told Brett to confront Rich, demand his share of control over Drury Lane, and insist upon a union of the Drury Lane and Queen's companies. Brett and Rich reached an agreement and effected a union which placed the opera singers under Swiney at the Queen's and brought the actors to Drury Lane from January to April 1708. Following Cibber's advice, Brett at first took an active part in the management, but in March 1708 he about-faced and delegated his powers to Cibber and the actors Wilks and Estcourt. That turn of events alienated Rich, who allied himself with the minor investors in the patent, reduced actors' salaries, and took a third of the profits of each actor's benefit. When the actors complained, Rich told them they could quit the company if they pleased— but with the opera troupe performing at the Queen's and Lincoln's Inn Fields no longer serving as a playhouse, there was no place for them to go.

In 1708–9 Cibber, Wilks, Doggett, and Anne Oldfield petitioned the Lord Chamberlain to silence Rich if the manager should refuse to give them their full benefit profits. They also began negotiations with Swiney at the Queen's Theatre, and Cibber, Wilks, and Doggett signed an agreement with him on 10 March 1709 for the following season. Cibber's share was to be £200 yearly plus a clear benefit; the trio of actors agreed to take half of any profit and share half of any losses at the end of the season; Swiney agreed to accept £300 annually and share the other half of the profits or losses. When benefit time came in the spring of 1709 at Drury Lane, Rich insisted on taking his share of each benefit. The players, as planned, appealed to the Lord Chamberlain. On 6 June 1709 Drury Lane was ordered closed, and Rich found himself without a theatre. Secure in their arrangement with Swiney, the players looked forward to acting the following season at the Queen's.

On the defensive, Rich published the probable income of the leading players, to demonstrate to the public that the actors were well off. Cibber was said to have received a salary of £111 10*s*., plus £51 10*d*. at his benefit, plus about £50 in gifts, for a total of £212 10*s*. 10*d*. for acting 71 times during the 1708–9 season. But Rich's stratagem was too late. His employment gone, he started laying plans for a new theatre in Lincoln's Inn Fields, a project he did not live to see completed.

During the 1707–8 and 1708–9 seasons Cibber continued to busy himself with playwriting, acting, and procreation. He wrote *The Double Gallant*, which opened at the Queen's Theatre on 1 November 1707 with Colley as Atall, and *The Lady's Last Stake*, which opened there on 13 December of the same year with the author as Sir George Brilliant. Neither play was immediately successful, though *The Double Gallant* later gained acceptance and held the stage into the nineteenth century. The best part

of *The Lady's Last Stake* was Cibber's epilogue, a mockery of the operas at Drury Lane in which Cibber piped in Italian and English, ending with "But if you can't allow my voice inviting, / E'en let me live by acting and by writing"—which audiences, despite carping critics, did for many years.

At the Queen's in 1707–8 Cibber acted such new roles as Busy in *Bartholomew Fair* and Worcester in *1 Henry IV* in addition to the parts in his own new plays. During the early months of 1708 when the players worked at Drury Lane, he attempted Hilliard in *The Jovial Crew*, Osric in *Hamlet*, Ben in *Love for Love*, Roger in *The Scornful Lady*, Trim in *Bury Fair*, and Frederick in *The Rover*—among other new roles. The following season saw him as Gloucester in *King Lear*, Tiresias in *Oedipus*, Glendower in *1 Henry IV*, Subtle in *The Alchemist*, Iago in *Othello*, Sparkish in *The Country Wife*, and Samuel Simple (on 11 January 1709) in his next new play, *The Rival Fools*.

The addition to the Cibber family during these years was in the fall of 1707: Colley's namesake was born on 29 October and baptized at St Martin-in-the-Fields on the following 23 October. Perhaps he died in infancy, for we know of no further record of him, and he has been unnoticed by previous biographers.

With Christopher Rich silenced, the actors at the Queen's Theatre under Swiney should have fared well, but they did not. Cibber in 1709–10 wrote no new play, and he acted hardly any new parts—perhaps because he was busy with managerial duties. The season ended with a deficit of £206; Swiney left for Ireland; and the leading players ran a series of benefits which brought them little profit. The trio of actor-managers helped themselves from the till, Cibber and Doggett taking £100 each for their season's pains, and Wilks £150, since he had overseen rehearsals. Swiney, they felt, had mismanaged the company and had overcharged them for costumes and scenery.

(Perhaps it was no consolation for them, but the feeble troupe at Drury Lane under William Collier did not do well either.)

Swiney returned in the fall of 1710, furious at what he thought was irresponsible behavior on the part of his fellow managers. He opened and closed the Queen's in early October, fearful that with current elections and small houses he could not meet the payroll. New negotiations were begun between Collier at Drury Lane and the troupe at the Queen's, the result being an agreement dated 20 November 1710 which put Collier in command of the opera at the Queen's and Cibber, Wilks, and Doggett in charge of the actors at Drury Lane. Swiney was squeezed out of control and given a reduced salary, and though he took the matter to court and precipitated litigation which lasted for two years, the shifting of companies between Drury Lane and the Queen's ceased. Ultimately, Swiney fled to the Continent to avoid his creditors, and Collier settled for a yearly stipend of £700 for staying idle so the actors could govern themselves.

The triumvirate of Cibber, Wilks, and Doggett, despite differences in temperament, ran Drury Lane effectively. They paid their bills promptly, were generous in salaries to valuable actors, and were sensitive to the taste of the town. Wilks the extravagant was balanced by Doggett the parsimonious, and serving as mediator was the conciliatory Cibber. Wilks looked after rehearsals, Cibber took care of the correspondence, legal matters, and the choice of repertoire, and Doggett seems to have spent most of his time acting and guarding the purse strings. Wilks acted a remarkably heavy schedule, but Cibber's managerial tasks prevented him from acting as frequently as he might have wished. He did, however, find time in 1712 to write *Ximena*, a bad adaptation of Corneille's *Le Cid*; he did not publish it until 1719.

On 13 January 1713 Cibber's daughter Charlotte (later Mrs Charke) was born. She was baptized at St Martin-in-the-Fields on 8 February and grew up to be Colley's folly, the most eccentric of his children and a frequent embarrassment to him. In 1713 Katherine Cibber inherited some money from the Shores, earmarked for her and her children, but by going to court and claiming that he was a poor man, Colley managed to get control of the bequest.

Nor was Cibber's acting in the 1712–13 season anything to be proud of. His interpretation of Syphax in *Cato* was remembered by the author of *The Laureat* with disdain:

I have seen the Original *Syphax* in *Cato*, use many ridiculous Distortions, crack in his Voice, and wreathe his Muscles and his Limbs, which created not a Smile of Approbation, but a loud Laugh of Contempt and Ridicule on the Actor. This must be very disadvantageous to the warm and beautiful Lines of the Poet. . . . Mr *Addison* was the most tender Author in these Points, that ever trusted a Play on the Stage. When he found it could not be help'd, and that *Syphax* must be *Cibber*, and *Cibber Syphax*, he was obliged to acquiesce, but he cou'd never take that for a Mark of Approbation, which was always a Mark of Disapprobation. . . . In my Opinion, the Part of *Syphax*, as it was originally play'd, was the only Part in *Cato* not tolerably executed.

Colley also played Edmund in *King Lear* in 1712–13, but (perhaps mercifully) we do not know what the critics thought of his portrayal.

After his success in *Cato* Barton Booth pressed to join in the management of Drury Lane. By 11 November 1713, after much bickering and against Doggett's will, Booth was granted a share. Doggett stomped out in indignation, refusing to act, but demanding his portion of the profits; the matter was not finally settled until 1716 when Doggett accepted over £600 as indemnity and left the troupe. During the lengthy negotiations Cibber played the mediator, and it is likely that he was responsible for Drury Lane's remaining stable during a period of dissension among the managers which might have wrecked the company. Instead, Drury Lane prospered, and each manager enjoyed no less than £1000 annually through 1714.

During this period Cibber did not attempt very many new roles. In 1713–14 he played the Duke of Gloster in the first production of *Jane Shore*; in 1714–15 he added Abel in *The Committee* to his list of parts; in 1715–16 he tried Pharamond in *Philaster* and Tinsel in *The Drummer*; and in 1716–17 he acted Plotwell, a satire on himself, in *Three Hours After Marriage*. The last-named work brought on a quarrel with Alexander Pope, who, with Gay and Arbuthnot, had had a hand in the writing of the play. The work was hissed, and at a performance of *The Rehearsal*, probably on 7 February 1717, Cibber in his role of Bayes ad-libbed a jibe at the Gay-Pope-Arbuthnot flop. Pope, Cibber reported later, was livid. He "came behind the scenes, with his lips pale and his voice trembling, to call me to account for the insult, and accordingly fell upon me with all the foul language that a wit out of his senses could be capable of . . ." Cibber vowed to repeat his ad-lib at every subsequent performance, and at the next one Gay came backstage to cane Colley. Cibber "fairly gave him a fillip on the nose, which made them both roar," according to Paston's biography of Pope. "The guards came and parted them, and carried away Gay, and so ended this poetical scuffle." It did not end the enmity, for thereafter Pope grasped every opportunity he could to lampoon Cibber, finally making him in 1742 the King of Dunces in *The New Dunciad*.

Cibber's first new play in several years, *The Non-Juror* (an adaptation of *Tartuffe*) opened at Drury Lane on 6 December 1717 with the author playing Dr Wolf, the hypocrite. The work was pure propaganda against the Jacobites, which pleased all

Hanoverians immensely but drew sharp criticism from some quarters. George I gave £200 to Cibber, Lintot paid him £100 for the copyright, and Drury Lane enjoyed its first real success since John Rich opened the rival Lincoln's Inn Fields playhouse in 1714. Pope ridiculed *The Non-Juror*, as might have been expected, and Charles Johnson wrote to *Mist's Weekly Journal* on 20 February 1718, calling the play a heap of "malice, nonsense, and Obscenity." Johnson went on to say that he understood Cibber had made over £1000 on the work, which he was "decently stripped of at the Groom Porter's," gambling. Even more personal was Johnson's statement that

the other masters of the playhouse, seeing [Cibber's] daughter very bare in clothes, kindly offered him a private benefit for her; and I am credibly informed that it amounted to fourscore pounds, which this inhuman father, rather than let his child have necessaries, made away with also.

Which daughter that was (if, indeed, there was any truth to the story) was not mentioned, but in light of other facts we have about Cibber's family, it could well have been little Charlotte, who had already taken to odd habits of dress.

Between 1717–18 and his first retirement from the stage in 1733, Cibber played such new roles as Alexas in *All for Love*, Witwoud in *The Way of the World*, À la Mode in *Chit Chat*, Dufoy in *The Comical Revenge*, Burleigh in *The Unhappy Favourite*, Shallow in *2 Henry IV* (one of his best roles), Witling in his own *The Refusal* on 14 February 1721, Wolsey in *Henry VIII* (*The Laureat* said that "his Action and his Voice carry it into Ridicule and Farce"), Novel in *The Plain Dealer*, Tom in *The Conscious Lovers*, Achoreus in his own *Caesar in Egypt* on 9 December 1724, Sir Francis in *The Provok'd Husband*, Philautus in his own *Love is a Riddle* on 7 January 1729, Scrub in *The Stratagem*,

Grinly in *The Modish Couple*, and Lord Richly in *The Modern Husband*. Victor, writing of *Caesar in Egypt* when it opened in 1724, said:

But alas! I can remember being of the merry Party in the Pit the first Night of Cibber's CAESAR IN EGYPT, in which he performed the Part of Achoreus; and we then laught at his quavering Tragedy Tones, as much as we did at his Pasteboard Swans which the Carpenters pulled along the Nile.

But criticism of Cibber's acting during those years was mild compared to the resistance he encountered as a manager. He was a shrewd manager, to be sure, and he helped bring stability and prosperity to Drury Lane after years of split loyalties and shifting control. Yet Cibber made blunders. In 1715 he offended the Lord Chamberlain by writing him an unnecessarily curt letter; he provoked the actor John Bickerstaff to a challenge by cutting his salary in half—and then turned coward, refused to fight, and restored the salary; he regularly made enemies of playwrights whose works he rejected as the company's reader, for he was apparently blunt in his criticisms; he often altered other writers' scripts without consulting them; he was imperious with underlings; and he was a social snob.

On the other hand, Cibber was one of the best critics of acting of his day or any other; he had a remarkable sense of what was theatrical; he had, as James Ralph wrote in *The Case of Our Present Theatrical Disputes* in 1743, "a fund of good Nature, which made him unwilling to see any Breaches, and he had so friendly and facetious a Way of shewing People their own Foibles, that he seldom failed of putting an end to Disputes, by convincing both Parties, that they were ridiculous"; his judgment of scripts was usually sound; he rewarded merit when he saw it; he was the first to admit his own failings; and his notions of good management were eminently sensible.

But his faults were more apparent to his enemies than his virtues were, and he came in for criticism so harsh that a weaker spirit would have withered under it. During the 1720s his chief opponents were the critic John Dennis and the journalist Nathaniel Mist. Mist can perhaps be taken lightly, for he merely made sport of a fop who kept inviting ridicule. Dennis, however, was a respectable, though highly emotional, critic-playwright writing for posterity.

The conflict between Dennis and Cibber began in 1718 when Dennis's *The Invader of His Country*, based on *Coriolanus*, was offered to Drury Lane. It was accepted for production the following season but then postponed when the rival troupe produced Shakespeare's original play and effectively undercut Dennis's work. "I am almost overwhelmed both with sickness and grief," Dennis wrote Steele, who had become a sharer in the Drury Lane patent at the death of Queen Anne. When rehearsals finally went forward in the fall of 1719, nothing satisfied Dennis. He objected to alterations that had been made in the script, to the date of the opening (for the King would be out of town), and to the frivolity of the epilogue Cibber had prepared. He was convinced that everyone was against him, and when the play was withdrawn after the third night because of insufficient income at the box office, Dennis was furious. He published the play with a complaining dedication to the Lord Chamberlain, who at the time was peeved at Cibber and looking for a reason to punish him. (Cibber had spurned the Lord Chamberlain when he tried to interfere with casting, and Steele had irritated him by opposing the Peerage Bill.)

On 19 December 1719 the Lord Chamberlain wrote the managers:

These are to require you immediately to Dismiss Mr Colley Cibber from Acting at the Theatre in Drury Lane, and from being any ways concern'd in the management of the said Playhouse: And you Colley Cibber One of the Managers and Players at the said Theatre are hereby requir'd to cease and forbear Acting, or any ways concerning your self in the Management of the said Theatre, as you will Answer the Contrary to your Peril.

On 23 January 1720 Drury Lane was silenced, and on 27 January the Lord Chamberlain forced the managers to take a new license which deprived Steele of a share. He made the surviving managers swear allegiance to the Lord Chamberlain, the Vice Chamberlain, and the Gentleman Usher in Waiting.

The delighted Dennis quickly published *The Character and Conduct of Sir John Edgar* (i.e., Steele), which contained a scathing attack on Cibber. He accused Cibber of inhumanity, atheism, blasphemy ("It is credibly reported that he spit on the face of our Savior's picture at the Bath"), and reckless gambling ("in the compass of two years [he] squandered away £6000 at the Groom Porter's without making the least provision for either his wife or his children"). Cibber may indeed have been running up debts: a letter from him dated December 1721, now in the Garrick Club, requested Mr Lockyer of the South Sea Company to "Pay to M͏ʳ Tho͏ˢ Robinson the Dividend [sic] on one Thousand Pounds being all my Stock in the South Sea Company's Books for half a year due Midsummer last."

Dennis attacked Cibber again in *The Decay and Defects of Dramatick Poetry* in 1725. Cibber had been reinstated at Drury Lane, of course, and Dennis described him as "Their oracle of wit . . . [A]n Amphibious creature, Half Player, Half Poetaster, like the Leathern wingd animal, that takes its groveling flight in the Dusk, and passes for a singing Bird only with Beasts, and for a Beast with all the Tunefull choir."

Mist was far less vicious and limited his attack to Colley's failings as a writer. When

Cibber's *The Refusal* opened to hisses on 14 February 1721, Mist reported that

On Tuesday night last at the theatre in Drury Lane was acted a comedy called The Refusal, or the Ladies' Philosophy, which was stolen from a comedy lately acted in Lincoln's Inn Fields called No Fools like Wits, which was stolen from a comedy called The Female Vertuosoes, which was stolen from a comedy of Molière called Les Femmes Savantes. Such authors as this Mr D[enni]s says are fed like hogs in Westphalia; one is tied to the tail of another and the last feeds only upon the excrements of the rest and therefore is generally when full grown no bigger than a pig.

On 2 January 1725 after seeing Cibber's *Caesar in Egypt* Mist wrote that Colley "seems to have a great aversion to the English tongue and mangles it without the least mercy."

Even when the successful comedy *The Provok'd Husband* came out on 10 January 1728 Mist complained:

On Wednesday last a most horrid, barbarous, and cruel Murder was committed at The Theatre-Royal in Drury Lane upon a posthumous Child [i.e. the incomplete *A Journey to London*] of the late Sir John Vanbroog, by one who, for some Time past, has gone by the Name of Keyber. It was a fine Child born, and would certainly have lived long, had it not fallen into such cruel hands.

There was no murder so far as most playgoers were concerned, however; the play ran a month and made more money for Drury Lane than any work produced there over the previous 50 years.

One of Cibber's worst blunders as a manager was turning down Gay's *The Beggar's Opera* (though his rival John Rich almost refused it too). James Ralph later wrote:

. . . Gay, under [Cibber's] Dictatorship, was driven from Drury-Lane to Lincoln's-Inn-

Fields and had it not been for an uncommon Confederacy of Men of Rank and Parts in support of his Pretensions, his excellent Opera . . . had been rejected at *both* Houses alike.

Chagrined, Cibber tried to make up for his mistake and committed another: he attempted a ballad opera himself. *Love is a Riddle* opened in January 1729, and, except for introducing Miss Raftor, the future Kitty Clive, it was a failure. The audience howled so much that Colley had to beg their pardon and promise never to perform the work again. But he salvaged from it the comic subplot and in 1729 created the popular afterpiece, *Damon and Phillida*. After the 1720s Cibber did little playwriting, though he doubtless had a hand in the work of others from time to time and wrote occasional epilogues (as, for instance, the one for his son's *The Lover* in 1731).

In 1730 Colley cast his eyes on the laureateship. Having been a staunch supporter of the Hanoverians (witness *The Non-Juror* of 1717), Cibber would certainly have been among those poets to be considered for the post when Eusden died. He was no better but no worse than such other versifiers of his day as Theobald, Philips, and Dennis, but Stephen Duck was the popular choice. (Pope, a Catholic, could not have been considered.) Duck had the necessary court connections and was announced in the *Daily Post* on 30 October 1730 as the certain successor to Eusden. But Cibber had the advantage of the Duke of Grafton's friendship, and Grafton was to make the final decision. In November, when the deadline came, Duck was out of town because of the death of his wife, and Cibber was on hand, campaigning for himself. Pope ridiculed the whole business in the *Grub Street Journal* on 12 November:

> *Shall royal praise be rimed by such a ribald,*
> *As fopling C[ibbe]r or attorney T[heobal]d?*

> *Let's rather wait one year for better luck;*
> *One year may make a singing swan of Duck.*
> *Great G——! such servants since thou well canst lack,*
> *Oh! save the salary and drink the sack!*

In the same journal on 19 November Pope urged that the new laureate should enter town in triumph on a mule or an ass, "unless Mr C[ibbe]r be the man, who may with great propriety and beauty ride on a dragon if he goes by land, or, if he choose the water, upon one of his own swans from Caesar in Egypt."

Within a week Grafton had chosen Cibber. The *Grub Street Journal* on 31 December could not believe the choice:

> *But guessing who would have the luck*
> *To be the b[irth]day fibber,*
> *I thought of Dennis, Theobald, Duck,*
> *But never dreampt of Cibber.*

A scene was added to *Tom Thumb* poking fun at Cibber in the character of Fopling Fribble; Mist ridiculed the choice by casting aspersions on Colley's parts of speech; Pope stated in print that Grafton had made "a laureate of an ass"; and Swift felt that if the Queen had been responsible for the choice, the verses she would get from Cibber would be exactly what she deserved.

The new laureate dutifully wrote the traditional ode, which the Chapel Royal sang on 1 January 1731. It was a typical piece of work, no worse than the verses which the previous line of laureates back through Shadwell had turned out. The appointment brought Cibber permanently into the courtly circle he had aspired to, and, to give him his due, he apparently worked hard at his verses even if the results were seldom impressive.

All the while Cibber kept up a heavy schedule of acting and managing at Drury Lane. His last full season as a regular member of the troupe was 1732–33, and his roles are worth recording in full, for the season was for him a résumé of most of the parts he had played over the years. He began the season as Bayes in *The Rehearsal* on 8 September 1732, after which he appeared as Foppington in *The Relapse*, Fondlewife in *The Old Bachelor*, Richard III, Shallow in *2 Henry IV*, Young Reveller in *Greenwich Park*, Ben in *Love for Love*, Subtle in *The Alchemist*, Wolsey in *Henry VIII*, Sir Fopling in *The Man of Mode*, Sir John in *The Provok'd Wife*, Atall in *The Double Gallant*, Witwoud in *The Way of the World*, Sir Courtly Nice, Clodio in *Love Makes a Man*, Tattle in *Love for Love*, Sir Roger in *The Scornful Lady*, Sir Francis in *The Provok'd Husband*, Tom in *The Conscious Lovers*, Foppington in *The Careless Husband*, and the Chaplain in *The Orphan*. It was a remarkable schedule for a man of 62, especially when one considers that there were multiple performances of most of the plays he was in. Just as noteworthy was the tenacity with which Cibber clung to roles he had first acted many years before, even those for which he was unsuited.

With Cibber's retirement in 1733 the era of the triumvirate at Drury Lane ended. Wilks had died in 1732, and Booth, ill and inactive for several years, died in 1733. The trio had not prepared themselves for the time when their power would pass on to others, and as a result there were no properly qualified people to take their places, save Colley's wayward son Theophilus. In July 1732 Booth had sold half of his share to the would-be actor John Highmore, and after Booth's death his widow sold the other half to the Goodman's Fields manager Henry Giffard, apparently with the stipulation that it not be resold to any Drury Lane actors. Wilks's widow made the painter John Ellis her representative. On 29 October 1732, at the beginning of his last season, Cibber had rented his share to his son for £442 and gone on salary at 12 guineas weekly. The stage was set for a battle over the control of Drury Lane. Remarkably, Cibber seems not to have been much concerned over the fate of the theatre to which he had devoted his life.

In 1733 *Do You Know What You Are About?* summarized what happened:

After the Death of Mr. Wilks, Co-Monarch of Drury-Lane Theatre, there arose an universal Discontent among the great Men of the Empire of Drury; our Laureat forseeing nothing but War and Bloodshed, wisely slip'd his Neck out of the Collar, sold his Share, pocketed the Pence, and left 'em to fight it out among themselves.

Behind the back of Theophilus Cibber, Highmore and Ellis bought Colley's share for 3000 guineas. Theophilus eventually fought his way back into control—but that is a part of his story.

Concerning his retirement Colley later said:

If those particular Gentlemen [the critics] have sometimes made me the humbled Object of their Wit and Humour, their Triumph at least has done me this involuntary Service, that it has driven me a Year or two sooner into a quiet Life than otherwise my own want of Judgment might have led me to: I left the Stage before my Strength left me, and tho' I came to it again for some few Days a Year or two after, my Reception there not only turn'd to my Account, but seem'd a fair Invitation that I would make my Visits more frequent . . .

Indeed, in the 1734–35 season Cibber agreed to play (apparently for 50 guineas nightly) his favorite parts: Bayes, Lord Foppington, Sir John Brute, Sir Courtly Nice, Sir Fopling Flutter, and Fondlewife. And he returned again for a few performances in 1735–36.

Colley waited until 1738–39 before making another return engagement. He acted Richard III and Shallow. Richard, as before, was well out of his range, and he told Victor in the third act that he wished he was home by his fire. His Shallow, on the other hand, was splendid. Tom Davies remembered his performance:

Whether he was a copy or an original Shallow it is certain that no audience was ever more fixed in deep attention at his first appearance or more shaken with laughter in the progress of the scene than at Colley Cibber's exhibition of this ridiculous justice of peace. . . . Whether it was owing to the pleasure the spectators felt on seeing their old friend return to them again, though for that night only, after an absence of some years, I know not, but surely no actor or audience were better pleased with each other. His manner was so perfectly simple, his look so vacant when he questioned his cousin Silence about the price of ewes and lamented in the same breath with silly surprise the death of old Double, that it will be impossible for any surviving spectator not to smile at the remembrance of it. The want of ideas occasions Shallow to repeat almost everything he says. Cibber's transition from asking the price of bullocks to trite but grave reflections on mortality was so natural and attended with such an unmeaning roll of his small pig's eyes, accompanied with an important utterance of tick, tick, tick not much louder than the balance of a watch's pendulum, that I question if any actor was ever superior in the conception or expression of such solemn insignificancy.

Cibber's literary output in the 1730s consisted of birthday odes and other verses expected of him as laureate, but he also tried his hand (though unsuccessfully) at writing an opera libretto for *Polifemo* in 1735 for the King's Theatre. Far more important was his *An Apology for the Life of Mr Colley Cibber*, published in 1740. With all its vanity and faults of grammar, style, and organization, it is one of the most important theatrical books ever written and Cibber's greatest contribution to arts and letters. The *Apology* needs no apology; if Cibber had not written it, our understanding of the theatre of his time and the people in it would be very dim indeed. Many of

Harvard Theatre Collection

COLLEY CIBBER, at the age of 67

engraving by Van der Gucht, after Van Loo

his sketches of actors are perceptively written, and in some cases Cibber is our only source of information. His candid, though slanted, story of the management of Drury Lane reveals the inner workings of the early eighteenth century theatre as no other source does. The portrait of Colley himself—who was the most important figure in the London theatre between Betterton and Garrick—is invaluable. And much of the *Apology* is not only informative but makes delightful reading.

The work was an immediate success. Two editions came out in 1740; there was an attempt to pirate it; four editions appeared before Cibber died in 1757; there were five reprintings in the 1800s; and it has been reprinted four times in the present century.

The *Apology* did not silence Colley's critics, one of whom quipped that Cibber had lived his life only so that he might apologize for it. Indeed, if Dennis and Mist had been sharp in their attacks on Cibber in the 1720s, they were nothing compared to Colley's critics of the following two decades. His most formidable and important foe was Alexander Pope. Following the *Three Hours After Marriage* incident in 1717, Pope carried on a running attack on Cibber: he ridiculed *The Non-Juror* in 1718, poked fun at Colley in his *Art of Sinking in Poetry* and the first *Dunciad* in 1728, satirized his laureateship in 1730, and criticized his odes in the *First Satire of the Second Book of Horace* in 1733. Then came the *Arbuthnot* epistle in 1735 and the beginning of a more vicious attack: "And has not Colley still his lord and whore? / His butchers Henley, his freemasons Moore?" Colley's only response was a general one in the *Apology*: "I have always had the comfort to think, whenever [my critics] designed me a disfavor, it generally flew back into their own faces, as it happens to children when they squirt at their playfellows against the wind."

Pope must have been disconcerted when Colley refused to bite back, but the *New Dunciad* of 1742, with Cibber as King of Dunces, finally provoked a response. Cibber began in a conciliatory and reasonable tone in *A Letter from Mr Cibber to Mr Pope* (1742), but when he came to Pope's lines in the *Arbuthnot* epistle about Colley's whore he struck back smartly: "I believe I know more of *your* whoring than you do of *mine*; because I don't recollect that ever I made you the least confidence of *my* amours, though I have been very near an eyewitness of *yours*." Whereupon he related a deliciously vulgar story of how England's greatest poet was saved from the clap. A late young nobleman

one evening slyly seduced the celebrated Mr Pope as a wit and myself as a laugher to a certain house of carnal recreation near the Haymarket, where his lordship's frolic proposed . . . to slip his little Homer, as he called him, at a girl of the game, that he might see what sort of figure a man of his size, sobriety, and vigor (in verse) would make when the frail fit of love had got into him; in which he so far succeeded that the smirking damsel who served us with tea happened to have charms sufficient to tempt the little-tiny manhood of Mr Pope into the next room with her: at which you may imagine his lordship was in as much joy as what might happen within as our small friend could probably be in possession of it. But I (forgive me all ye mortified mortals whom his fell satire has since fallen upon) observing he had stayed as long as without hazard of his health he might, I,

Pricked to it by foolish honesty and love,

as Shakespeare says, without ceremony threw open the door upon him, where I found this little hasty hero, like a terrible tomtit, pertly perching upon the mount of love! But such was my surprise that I fairly laid hold of his heels and actually drew him down safe and sound from his danger. My lord, who stayed tittering without in hopes the sweet mischief he came for would have been completed, upon my giving an account of the action within, began to curse and call me an hundred silly puppies for my impertinently spoiling the sport; to which with great gravity I replied, "Pray, my lord, consider what I have done was in regard to the honor of our nation! For would you have had so glorious a work as that of making Homer speak elegant English cut short by laying up our little gentleman of a malady which his thin body might never have been cured of? No, my lord! Homer would have been too serious a sacrifice to our evening merriment." Now as his Homer has since been so happily completed, who can say that the world may not have been obliged to the kindly care of Colley that so great a work ever came to perfection?

Cibber had repaid Pope in kind, and the wits of the town made much of it—including satirical prints of Colley saving "Homer" for posterity.

The infuriated Pope went to work on a final version of *The Dunciad* while Cibber rehashed matters in *The Egotist, or Colley* upon *Cibber* (January 1743) and *A Second Letter from Mr Cibber to Mr Pope* (February 1743). The final *Dunciad* (October 1743), flawed because Pope tried to force ridicule of Cibber into a framework not originally designed for him, still summed up Pope's criticism of Colley:

> Next o'er his books his eyes began to roll,
> In pleasing memory of all he stole,
> How here he sipped, how there he plundered snug,
> And sucked all o'er, like an industrious bug.
> Here lay poor Fletcher's half-eat scenes, and here
> The frippery of crucified Molière;
> There hapless Shakespeare, yet of Theobald sore,
> Wished he had blotted for himself before.
> . . . .
> "Some demon stole my pen (forgive the offense)
> And once betrayed me into common sense:
> Else all my prose and verse were much the same;
> This prose on stilts, that poetry fallen lame.
> Did on the stage my fops appear confined?
> My life gave ampler lessons to mankind.
> . . . .
> What can I now? my Fletcher cast aside,
> Take up the Bible, once my better guide?
> Or tread the path by venturous heroes trod,
> This box my thunder, this right hand my God?
> Or chaired at White's amidst the doctors sit,
> Teach oaths to gamesters, and to nobles wit?
> Or bidst thou rather Party to embrace?
> (A friend to Party thou, and all her race).
> . . . .
> What then remains? Ourself. Still, still remain

> Cibberian forehead and Cibberian brain.
> This brazen brightness, to the squire so dear;
> This polished hardness, that reflects the peer:
> This arch absurd, that wit and fool delights;
> This mess tossed up of Hockley-hole and White's;
> Where dukes and butchers join to wreathe my crown,
> At once the bear and fiddle of the town."

Cibber replied with a third *Letter* in January 1744, but during Pope's last illness he generously advised everyone to let the matter drop. In May Pope died, and the feud was ended. Though no match for Pope's wit and bite, Cibber had come off remarkably well in the engagement by remaining cool when Pope turned hot.

Colley's other opponent in the 1730s and 1740s was Henry Fielding, who playfully nipped at both Colley and his son Theophilus. In *The Author's Farce* in 1730 Cibber was satirized in the character of the theatre manager Marplay Senior, who says to his son, "The art of writing, boy, is the art of stealing old plays, by changing the name of the play, and new ones, by changing the name of the author." In 1736 in *Pasquin* Fielding ridiculed Cibber's inability to write odes, and the same year, in *The Historical Register*, he had Ground-Ivy (Cibber) say, "It was a maxim of mine when I was at the head of theatrical affairs, that no play, though ever so good, would do without alteration." As usual, Cibber took the jibes lying down. An author in *Common Sense* (possibly Lord Chesterfield) wrote on 11 June 1737:

Of all the Comedians who have ever appeared upon the Stage within my Memory, no one has taking [*sic*] a Kicking with so much Humour as our present most excellent Laureat, and I am inform'd his Son does not fall much short of him in this Excellence; I am very glad of it, for as I have a Kindness for the young Man, I hope to see him as well kick'd as his Father was before him.

In 1739 in his journal *The Champion*, Fielding took a lick at Cibber's lack of learning:

I know it may be objected that the English Apollo, the prince of poets, the great laureate abounds with such a redundancy of Greek and Latin that, not contented with the vulgar affectation of a motto to a play, he hath prefixed a Latin motto to every act of his *Caesar in Egypt*. . . . Nay, his learning is thought to extend to the Oriental tongues, and I myself heard a gentleman reading one of his odes cry out, "Why, this is all Hebrew!"

In his paper in 1740 Fielding wrote a delightful burlesque in which Cibber was put to trial:

for that you, not having the Fear of Grammar before your Eyes, on the   of   at a certain Place, called the *Bath*, in the County of *Somerset* [and] in *Knights-Bridge*, in the County of *Middlesex*, in and upon the *English* Language an Assault did make, and then and there, with a certain Weapon called a Goose-quill, value one Farthing, which you in your left Hand then held, several very broad Wounds but of no Depth at all, on the said *English* Language did make, and so you the said Col. *Apol.* the said *English* Language did murder.

To which Fielding had Cibber respond:

Sir, I am as innocent as the child which hath not yet entered into human nature of the fact laid to my charge. This accusation is the forward spring of envy of my laurel. It is impossible I should have any enmity to the *English* language, with which I am so little acquainted; if, therefore, I have struck any wounds into it, they have rolled from accident only.

Fielding had fun with Colley's mangling of the language, but some of the sting was taken off by Cibber's frank admission of his errors, as in the *Apology* when he pleaded guilty to an absurdity in his preface to *The Provok'd Husband*:

[M]y words ran thus, viz: "It is not enough to say that here [Mrs Oldfield] outdid her usual outdoing." A most vile jingle, I grant it! You may well ask me, how could I possibly commit such a wantonness to paper. And I owe myself the shame of confessing I have no excuse for it but that, like a lover in the fullness of his content, by endeavouring to be floridly grateful I talked nonsense.

Cibber found time in the early 1740s to return to the stage and to write one last play. In January 1741 he appeared as Fondlewife at Chetwood's benefit and then at his own, at Drury Lane. He wrote and delivered a special "Epilogue upon Himself:"

Now worn with Years, and yet in Folly
　　strong,
Now to act Parts, your Grandsires saw
　　when Young!
What could provoke me!—I was always
　　wrong.
To hope, with Age, I could advance in
　　Merit!
Even Age well acted, asks a youthful
　　Spirit:
To feel my Wants, yet shew 'em thus
　　detected,
Is living to the Dotage, I have acted!
T'have acted only Once excus'd might be,
When I but play'd the Fool for Charity!
But fondly to repeat it!—Senseless
　　Ninny!
—No—now—as Doctors do—I touch the
　　Guinea!
And while I find my Doses can affect
　　you,
'Twere greater Folly still, should I neg-
　　lect you.
Though this Excuse, at White's *they'll*
　　not allow me;
The Railliers There, in Diff'rent Lights
　　will shew me.
They'll tell you There: I only act—sly
　　Rogue!

To play with Cocky [Mrs Woffington]!
—O! the doting Dog!
And howsoe'er an Audience might re-
gard me,
One—tiss ye Nykin [Cibber], amply
might reward me!
Let them enjoy the Jest, with Laugh
incessant!
For True, or False, or Right, or Wrong,
'tis pleasant!
Mixt, in the wisest Heads, we find some
Folly;
Yet I find few such happy Fools—as
Colley!
So long t'have liv'd the daily Satire's
Stroke,
Unmov'd by Blows, that might have
fell'd an Oak,
And yet have laugh'd the labour'd Libel
to a Joke.
Suppose such want of Feeling prove me
dull!
What's my Aggressor than—a peevish
Fool!
The strongest Satire's on a Blockhead
lost;
For none but Fools or Madmen strike a
Post.
If for my Folly's larger List you call,
My Life has lump'd 'em! There you'll
read 'em all.
There you'll find Vanity, wild Hopes
pursuing;
A wide Attempt: to save the Stage from
Ruin!
There I confess, I have out-done *my* own
out-doing!
As for what's left of Life, if it still 'twill
do;
'Tis at your Service, pleas'd while pleas-
ing you:
But then, mistake me not! when you've
enough;
One slender House declares both Parties
off:
Or Truth in homely Proverb to advance,
I pipe no longer than you care to dance.

During the 1741–42 season Cibber appeared at both Drury Lane and Covent
Garden, playing Sir John Brute, Lord Foppington (in *The Relapse*), Shallow, and

Sir Novelty Fashion. In February 1745 he
brought out his version of *King John*,
called *Papal Tyranny*. He should not have
tried to act, for he had just lost his teeth,
and the theatre, Covent Garden, was larger
than his voice could fill in the character of
Pandulph. Davies found his performance
extravagant, studied, and more like Lord
Foppington than a man of the cloth, but
the play had a fairly successful opening on
15 February and ran for ten performances.
Cibber's last stage appearance was on 26
February 1745 at the age of 73. It is unfortunate that he did not choose to end his
stage career in a more appropriate part; a
Shallow without teeth, for instance, might
have been delightful.

Cibber was so active in the 1730s and
1740s following his initial retirement that
he almost forgot his family. Of his wife
Katherine he said practically nothing in
his *Apology*. His usual address from 1721
to 1740 in London was No 3, Charles
Street, but his wife died on 17 January
1734 at Knightsbridge—which suggests a
possible estrangement. Colley was left with
a sizeable family, though by 1734 his
surviving children were grown up and on
their own. Catherine was 40 and by 1734
had probably married Colonel James
Brown; Anne had married John Boultby
at some time during the previous seven
years and was 35; Elizabeth, aged 33, was
married to Dawson Brett and had recently
concluded her own stage career and
initiated that of her daughter Anne;
Theophilus was 31, and in 1734 he married
for a second time, to Susanna Maria Arne;
James and Colley had apparently died when
young; and Charlotte, 21, had married the
musician Richard Charke in 1730.

Charlotte kept dunning her father for
money, which he seems to have refused as
steadfastly to give her as she refused to
accept his fatherly advice. Her antics were
notorious: she took to men's clothes and
masculine sports at an early age; she
married a ne'er-do-well; she dabbled in

(among other things) puppetry, conjuring, acting, and tavern keeping; and she supposedly waylaid her father in Epping Forest and robbed him. Colley wrote her from Tavistock Street (on 27 March, year unknown):

Dear Charlotte—
I am sorry I am not in a position to assist you further. You have made your own bed, and therein you must lie. Why do you not disassociate yourself from that worthless scoundrel [Charke?], and *then* your relatives *might* try and aid you. You will never be any good while you adhere to him, and you most certainly will not receive what otherwise you might from your Father.
                                        Colley Cibber

Cibber finally disowned her, as did her sisters. Colley refused to forgive her and tried to forget her, even when she made a public apology at the publication of her autobiography in 1755.

If Charlotte was an embarrassment, Theophilus was a disgrace. His offstage conduct toward his second wife excited London with two court trials, at one of which, in 1738, Colley was called to testify. Colley, fortuitously or purposely, was in France during part of the hullabaloo, but he was on hand in December 1738 to testify that he had, indeed, instructed Theophilus's second wife, Susanna Maria, and had found her a most promising actress. She also turned out to be a most promising adultress—though Theophilus arranged his own cuckolding, and the town was as willing to forgive her as it was to ridicule him.

Cibber kept up his writing in the 1740s —especially when he was involved in polemics with Pope—but after his last play in 1745 his literary output tapered off. He published, in addition to occasional small pieces, *The Character and Conduct of Cicero* in 1747, *The Lady's Lecture* in 1748, and *A Rhapsody upon the Marvellous* in 1751.

He retained an interest in the new generation of actors, but from a distance. Of Spranger Barry in 1746, for instance, he wrote to Victor:

I am not a little pleased with the character you give me of Barry, particularly of his discretion in not picquing himself into any sort of rivalship. . . . If he comes over [from Ireland], I should wish him to stand upon his own legs; for if he leans upon another's merit he may be dropped when he is to make a new bargain, and if he has the merit you seem to allow him he will need no better friend to support him. But what's Hecuba to me, or I to Hecuba? I love to speak my mind in matters indifferent to me.

Cibber's attitude toward David Garrick vascillated. On 9 December 1741 Garrick had written his brother Peter that "old Cibber has spoke with ye Greatest Commendation of my Acting." On 8 August 1749, on the other hand, Garrick wrote to the Countess of Burlington:

. . . Your Lady^p must know, that Notwithstanding the great Nonchalance that Cibber boasts of, he has as much Envy, as Vanity & as little Benevolence, as Judgment: My Success in Life & in his own Profession, has given him visible uneasiness, he can't bear to think of my obtaining that in a few Years, which he & his Brother Patentees were labouring thirty or forty Years; I have been told by some Gentlemen of White's Club, that any Praises they bestow'd upon Me, were Death to him, & he always Endeavour'd as much as in him lay, to hurt Me in their Opinions, & to Criticise Me in my Characters; his Behaviour to Me was always the reverse, which is so certain an indication of a mean contemptible Mind, that I have never cultivated his Acquaintance, by not offering that incense to his vanity, which he has so often receiv'd, & Which He expects from Every Young Actor—

Only reluctantly, according to Walpole, did Cibber one day admit to Anne Brace-

Courtesy of Mr Robert Eddison

Called COLLEY CIBBER
by Worlidge

girdle that Garrick did, indeed, have some merit.

But Cibber's views on the new generation of players were those of an elder statesman who had little real concern beyond that awe he might inspire by offering an opinion. His attention in the 1740s and 1750s turned more toward pleasure. He was remarkably fit. In *Common Sense* in 1739 Thomas Earl wrote that Colley was "return'd from Tunbridge, where he went to drink the Waters—for a little Immortality, I suppose:—Health and Spirits I am sure he does not want (for he looks but Forty, 'tho he is, I believe, Sixty-nine)." Ten years later Chetwood described Cibber as "strait, and well made; of an open Countenance, even free from the conspicuous Marks of old Age. Meet or follow him, and no Person would imagine he ever bore the Burden of above two Thirds of his Years."

Cibber had his faults, but he was good company. *The Laureat* found

he had humor and a kind of wit, but not conducted by any judgment or reflection, nor seasoned with any tincture of letters. He affected to know much; and as it must often happen to those who would be thought knowing when they are ignorant, he frequently got out of his depth and exposed himself to ridicule and contempt. But the gentlemen who condescended to be his companions were contented to be diverted with him as he could divert them. They would delight to hear him squeak in an eunuch's treble, or mimic Roscius, or rehearse the little histories of his scenical amours, or invent new oaths at play. . . . He could be noisy or silent, saucy or well-bred, obscene or modest, the joker or the jest, the pleasure or contempt of the company, just as he found they required it.

As a consequence, he found himself accepted, if sometimes reluctantly, into high society.

Horace Walpole wrote in 1741 of seeing him at an elegant affair at Sir Thomas Robinson's; there were "none but people of the first fashion," Walpole commented, "except Mr Kent, Mr Cibber, Mr Swiney, and the Parsons family, and you know all these have an alloy." For a while in the 1740s Colley enjoyed being part of Samuel Richardson's literary circle, though Cibber was too liberal in his views to remain acceptable for long. When he suggested to Richardson that his Sir Charles Grandison should have had a mistress, the ladies of the circle hid behind their fans until Colley left their company. More fun for him was the companionship of his old friends Owen Swiney and Beau Nash. With them he could chase pretty young things at the spas in summer. One of Colley's *tendres* was for the fashionable Miss Chudleigh. He also developed heart flutters for Peg Woffington (so did Swiney), but she dallied for a while with Garrick, after which

Swiney won her by spiriting her off to France.

Cibber had better luck with the poetess Mrs Letitia Pilkington, since the competition for her was not so keen and since she needed money, which he had. He helped her get some of her verses published; he introduced her to people of wealth who might aid her; he gave her money and contrived to get her out of debtors' prison; and for these favors he received we know not what: some poems, flattery, and the knowledge that, like Swift, he had helped the lady—perhaps little more.

Finally the years began to take their toll. In late 1750 Cibber was, he thought, on his deathbed. On Christmas day he wrote a letter:

Sr. Tho' Death has been cooling his his [*sic*] heels at my door these Three weeks, I have not had time to see him. The Dayley conversation of my friends have kept me so agreeably alive, that I have not passed my time better a great while. If you have a mind to [visit?] us, I will order Death to come another day—to be serious I long to see you, and hope you will take the first opportunity. And so wish as merry a Christmas, as many New Years as your heart can hope for . . .

To the Duke of Grafton Colley recommended that after his death the laurel should go to Henry Jones, the promising bricklayer-poet. Lord Chesterfield's comment was that "A better poet would not take the post, and a worse ought not to have it." But no matter; Jones ruined his chances by dissipation, and Cibber made a remarkable recovery.

Colley's escape from death was due not just to his good humor but also to Dr James's Fever Powders, or so Cibber said in a glowing testimonial dated 1 February 1751:

Sir

On the 6th of December last I was seized with a Fever which in 24 hours was so violent that I became extremely Delirious, insomuch that I obstinately refused all manner of Medicines. This Continued till about Decr the 16th when all my friends thought me near Expiring, and the more because I was then in the 80th year of my age, at this time my Relations gave me a Dose of Dr James's Fever Powders in some Tamarinds, unknown to me, which, as it had no Taste, I did not Discover. This gave me one Stool, & the next morning I was much better. From that [time?] my Relations gave me the same Medicine, without my Knowledge, in small Beer, Tea & every thing I took. This was attended with so good an Effect that in three days the Fever, with all its Simptoms, entirely left me, insomuch that I am now Perfectly recovered.—This I Esteem my Duty to the Publick to Communicate for the General Advantage of Mankind.

I am Sir, Your Humble S^t
Colley Cibber.

On 24 October 1753 he made his will. To Jane and Elizabeth Cibber, the daughters of Theophilus by his first wife, Colley left £1000 each. To his daughter Anne and son Theophilus he left £50 each; to Elizabeth Cibber Marples (she having remarried after Dawson Brett's death) he left £5 "and no more"; and to Charlotte, who had lost her husband Richard Charke and, in 1746, married John Sacheverell, Colley also left £5 "and no more." To his eldest daughter, Catherine Brown, then a widow and looking after him, Cibber bequeathed the rest of what was probably a considerable estate. He remained impervious to the plight of his destitute granddaughter Anne Brett Chetwood, and he left nothing to his other grandchild, Catherine Maria Charke Harman.

On 11 December 1757 Colley Cibber died quietly in his bed at the age of 86. His funeral was apparently on 18 December, though there is uncertainty as to whether he was buried in Grosvenor Chapel, South Audley Street, Grosvenor Square, or in the Cibber vault at the Danish Church, Wellclose Square. His burial was

recorded in the sexton's book at St George, Hanover Square. The newspapers were curiously uninterested in the passing of so famous a man, and there was not the usual flutter of verses eulogizing the dead. His daughter Catherine certainly settled things in a hurry after Colley's death: his will was proved the day after he died, and on 12 January 1758 his elegantly furnished house in Berkeley Square at the corner of Bruton Street was advertised to be let.

Aaron Hill in *The Prompter* on 19 November 1734 had anticipated the day when Cibber would be no more and had written a facetious obituary:

[H]is shape was finely proportioned, yet not graceful; easy, but not striking. . . . [H]is features were narrowly earnest and attentively insignificant. There was a peeping pertness in his eye, which would have been spirit, had his heart been warmed with humanity or his brain been stored with ideas. In his face was a contracted kind of passive, yet protruded, sharpness, like a pig, half-roasted. And a voice, not unlike his own, might have been borrowed from the same suffering animal, while in a condition less desperate. With all these comic accomplishments of person, he had an air and a mind which completed the risible talent, insomuch that, when he represented a ridiculous humour he had a mouth in every nerve and became eloquent without speaking. His attitudes were pointed and exquisite, and his expression was stronger than painting. He was beautifully absorbed by the character and demanded and monopolized attention. His very extravagancies were coloured with propriety, and affectation sat so easy about him that it was in danger of appearing amiable. It had been in nobody's power but his own to demonstrate him incapable of some parts he ought never to have appeared in. But while he forgot his own limits, he trespassed in the enclosures of others, and, carrying his fool's coat into the council chamber, made it observed there, to his disadvantage, that he was unlike the rest of the company and had mistaken the place he was dressed for.

Signature of COLLEY CIBBER, on Articles of Agreement with CHRISTOPHER RICH, 29 October 1696

Had Cibber ever been able to see himself objectively, he might have described himself so. But doubtless he would have preferred as an epitaph James Ralph's breezy statement in *The Case of Authors Stated* in 1758: "Cibber was Player, Writer, and Manager too, and, over and above, a Bottle of as pert small Beer, as ever whizz'd in any Man's Face."

A number of works have been attributed to Colley Cibber which he probably did not write. Defoe said Cibber wrote *Cinna's Conspiracy* (1713); the *Biographia Dramatica*, in addition to reporting that attribution, made Cibber the author of the opera *Chuck* (1736); *The Contre Temps; or, Rival Queans* (1727) was included in Cibber's *Dramatic Works* in 1777; *Hob*, by Doggett, has been assigned to Cibber by some authorities; *The Temple of Dul-*ness (1745) and a piece based on it, *Capochio and Dorinna*, have been called Cibber's. A book list at the back of Thomas Parnell's *Poems* (1726) contains "The Tell-Tale; or, The Invisible Mistress . . . By Mr Cibber" and "The Secret History of Arlus and Odolphus . . . By Mr Cibber." The first is a love story and the second a pamphlet with a Tory bias.

Colley Cibber has been treated to a fine study by Richard Barker (1939) which is still definitive. A newer work by Leonard R. N. Ashley (1965) adds some useful new material and helpful notes on the times in which Cibber lived. Barker and Ashley provide bibliographies which include Cibber's nondramatic writings. Less scholarly is Dorothy Senior's 1928 study. The May and November 1967 issues of *Restoration and 18th Century Theatre Re-*

search contain an extensive bibliography of articles and books dealing with Cibber.

Portraits of Colley Cibber include:

1. Painting by J. B. Van Loo showing Cibber with a little girl. Engraved by Edward Fisher, G. Van der Gucht, J. S. Miller, A. Bannerman, J. Hopwood, J. Baker, C. W. Sherborn, N. Parr, R. B. Parkes, H. R. Cook, S. Freeman, Rhodes, and at least two anonymous engravers.

2. Painting by George Beare.

3. Plumbago drawing by William Robins in the collection of Her Majesty the Queen, showing Cibber with his son Theophilus and daughter Charlotte.

4. Drawing by Thomas Worlidge called Colley Cibber, in the collection of Robert Eddison. The subject may have been Henry Brett.

5. Another drawing by Worlidge called Colley Cibber, in the collection of Robert Eddison. The subject, again, may have been Henry Brett.

6. Colored bust, presumably by Roubiliac, formerly at Strawberry Hill and now at the National Portrait Gallery. See frontispiece.

7. Etching by Gravelot. Engraved by T. Priscott.

8. As Lord Foppington in *The Relapse*. Painting by G. Grisoni at the Garrick Club. Engraved by G. Clint and J. H. Robinson, J. Simon, S. Freeman, and R. B. Parkes.

9. Anonymous engraving showing Cibber with Mary Porter and John Mills.

10. Engraving by N. Roberts showing Cibber listening to a blind boy sing.

11. Satirical print in Hogarth's style entitled "A Just View of the British Stage," 1721, showing Cibber, Wilks, and Booth, the managers of Drury Lane.

12. Satirical print by John Laguerre entitled "The Stage Mutiny," 1733, showing Theophilus Cibber leading his dissident players and Colley Cibber gloating over his bags of gold.

The British Museum *Catalogue of Engraved British Portraits* lists two anonymous engravings of Colley Cibber as Ancient Pistol, but that character belonged to Theophilus Cibber.

Cibber, Mrs Colley, Katherine, née Shore *c. 1669–1734, singer, actress.*

Katherine Shore was born about 1669, the daughter of His Majesty's Sergeant Trumpeter, Matthias Shore. The Shore family was decidedly musical, with the sons William and John following their father as trumpeters and Katherine being placed with Henry Purcell to study voice and harpsichord. According to Charlotte Charke, the eccentric youngest daughter of Katherine and Colley Cibber, Katherine first met Cibber in the early 1690s when he was visiting the Shores and heard her singing to her own accompaniment. Colley married Katherine on 6 May 1693 at St James, Duke's Place, Aldgate, against the wishes of her father, who probably did not see young Cibber as much of a prospect. To show his resistance, Matthias spent Katherine's dowry on a Thames showboat which came to be dubbed Shore's Folly, but he eventually relented and left her a third of his estate.

Katherine and Colley Cibber wasted no time starting a family, dowry or not. First came Catherine, born in 1694, a "cruel monitor" according to her younger sister, Charlotte Charke; young Catherine in time married Colonel James Brown, stayed close to her father Colley in his last years, and inherited the bulk of his estate. The next child was Anne, born on 1 October 1699 and baptized on 15 October at St Martin-in-the-Fields; after a career as a shopkeeper, Anne married John Boultby, sometime between 1727 and 1734. Elizabeth was the third child, baptized at St Paul, Covent Garden, on 16 March 1701; she married first Dawson Brett, by whom she had a daughter Anne who became Mrs William Rufus Chetwood, and second Joseph Marples; both Elizabeth and her daughter Anne had stage careers, and Anne's husband was for many years the Drury Lane prompter.

The fourth Cibber offspring was the wayward Theophilus, born on 25 November and baptized on 19 December 1703 at St Martin-in-the-Fields; Theophilus married first the actress Jane Johnson (by whom he had two actress-children, Jane and Elizabeth) and second the talented singer-actress Susanna Maria Arne (by whom he had two more children, Susanna and Caius Gabriel, both of whom died in infancy). Theophilus, of course, had a notorious career as an actor-manager.

James Cibber was the next child of Colley and Katherine. He was born on 25 July and baptized at St Martin's on 7 August 1706. He is otherwise unrecorded by historians. A third son, Colley, was born on 29 October and baptized on 23 November 1707 at St Martin's, and he, too, has hitherto escaped notice. It is probable that both James and Colley the younger died young.

The last of Colley and Katherine's children was the oddest: Charlotte, born on 13 January 1713 and baptized the following 8 February at St Martin's; she married first Richard Charke the violinist, by whom she had a daughter Catherine Maria who became an actress and married a Mr Harman, and, second, John Sacheverell; Charlotte led a bizarre life acting, managing, puppeteering, strolling, writing, and dabbling in numerous non-theatrical activities.

Because Cibber was an underling at the Drury Lane Theatre and his salary was meagre under the tight-fisted manager Christopher Rich, Mrs Cibber took to the stage to supplement the family income. In the winter of 1693–94 at Dorset Garden, Katherine Cibber played Aglaura in *The Rape of Europa*. In February 1694 at Drury Lane (for the United Company operated two theatres) she sang at a performance of *The Fatal Marriage*, and she was billed as singing Purcell's "The Genius of England"

in 2 *Don Quixote*, with her brother John playing the trumpet *obligato*, in late May 1694 at Dorset Garden. In the 1694–95 season she sang in *Don Carlos*.

The Cibbers stayed with Christopher Rich at Drury Lane when Betterton and the older players formed a separate company at Lincoln's Inn Fields. This loyalty provided more opportunities for both Colley and Katherine, and in 1695 Katherine was noted as playing three roles: Galatea in Settle's *Philaster*, Hillaria in Cibber's first play, *Love's Last Shift*, and Orinda in *The Lost Lover*. In January 1697 she sang and acted in Colley's *Woman's Wit*, one of her songs being Leveridge's "Tell me Belinda, prithee do." She was a member of Rich's troupe in 1698–99, though no roles are known for her. Indeed, the information we have for the last years of the seventeenth century is slim, and the few appearances that were recorded for Katherine Cibber may represent only a small portion of her theatrical activity. We know, for instance, that she sang "Damon if you will believe me" in *A Duke and No Duke*, for it was published with her name attached in *Wit and Mirth* in 1719, long after she left the stage, but there is no record to tell us when she participated in a performance of that work.

Mrs Cibber retired from the stage at the end of the seventeenth century, for she had asthma, and the London fogs forced her to move to a house Colley had rented in Uxbridge, near Hillington. She may also have left the stage because Colley no longer needed her theatrical income. By the end of the century his double career in acting and playwriting was well begun, and in 1700 the couple came into some money, first from Edward Colley on Cibber's side of the family and then from Matthias Shore. Later, in 1713, William Shore and his wife Rose also left the Cibbers legacies. William bequeathed money to his widow, and after her death the sum was to go to Katherine Cibber and her children; £30 annually was earmarked for Mrs Cibber's "own separate use." This and other terms of the wills of William and Rose Shore were not carried out, for Colley wanted all the money himself, including that designated for his children. Katherine took the matter to court, Cibber pleaded poverty (which was perjury, for by then he was earning about £1000 annually), and yet at the hearing on 13 July 1714 the court sided with the husband and let him spend his children's money during their minority.

How much all this may have disrupted the family peace may never be known, and in his *Apology* in later years Colley said as little as possible about Katherine and the family. Perhaps, with all her children born and with Colley busying himself at the theatre, Katherine lived happily enough, though obscurely and not always in the best of health. She died at Knightsbridge on 17 January 1734, after an asthma attack, at the age of 65.

Cibber, Elizabeth. *See* BRETT, MRS DAWSON.

Cibber, Jane *b. 1730, actress.*

Jane Cibber was the first child of Theophilus Cibber and his wife Jane. Jenny, as she was called, was probably born sometime in the spring or summer of 1730, to be followed in January 1733 by her sister Betty, giving birth to whom Mrs Cibber died. The two little girls shared a benefit at Covent Garden Theatre on ˅2 August 1739 when their father played Lord Foppington in *The Relapse* to raise money for their support (and, probably, for his complicated pleasures). By that time Theophilus had remarried, and the bill was careful to note that Jenny and Betty were the children of his first wife.

On 19 December 1741 Jenny made her debut at Drury Lane playing a traditional child's role, the Duke of York in *Richard*

Courtesy of Mr Robert Eddison

JANE CIBBER (?)
by Worlidge

III; she also delivered an epilogue written for the occasion. At her father's benefit on 20 March 1742 she spoke another epilogue, as "un Petit-Maître" — just as her mother had done years before. On the following 28 April Jenny and Betty shared a benefit again, the tickets for which were available through their aunt, Mrs Dawson Brett of Berwick Street, near Soho — where perhaps the girls were living. By then Theophilus had made a shambles of his second marriage, was constantly in debt, and was so frequently on the move that it is not likely that he concerned himself much with his daughters except when he could exploit them to gain public sympathy.

At Drury Lane in October 1742 Jenny Cibber played the Page in *The Orphan*, a role in *The Rehearsal*, the Duke of York again, and the Page in *Love Makes a Man*. She was likely the Miss Cibber who acted

Edward v in *Richard III* on 27 December 1742 and Corinna in *The Conspiracy* on 14 March 1743 with Giffard's troupe at Lincoln's Inn Fields.

Jenny's big opportunity came on 11 September 1744 when she played Juliet to her father's Romeo at the Haymarket Theatre. An anonymous admirer burst forth with verses in the press: "Where Innocence and ripening Beauty meet, / A solid Judgment and a Piercing Wit . . ." Impressed with her work, "Mr Neitherside" in *An Impartial Examen* (1744) recommended that she attempt Jenny in *The Provok'd Husband* and Miss Notable in *The Lady's Stake*—roles Jenny's mother had once played. Theophilus, exaggerating as usual, compared her with Anne Bracegirdle and said later in his *A Serio-Comic Apology* (1748) that "She shew'd a happy Genius: The uncommon Applause of her Spectators manifested their thorough Approbation of her young Attempts. She was then but barely Juliet's Age, *viz.*—not quite Fifteen." A more sober judgment was made in Hill's *The Actor* in 1750:

We remember a little Juliet, of very considerable merit, at the Hay-Market; and nothing is more certain, than that she would have appear'd, even with the same share of genius and accomplishments, much more pleasing than she did, if there had been some gay young fellow for her lover, instead of a person whom we could not but remember, at every sentence she deliver'd concerning him, to be too old for her choice, too little handsome to be in love with, and, into the bargain, her father.

But Theophilus Cibber was eager to exploit the young talent he had trained, and on 22 September 1744 at the Haymarket he brought Jenny out as Desdemona to his Othello. Then she attempted Rose in *The Recruiting Officer*, Indiana in *The Conscious Lovers*, Hermione in *The Distrest Mother*, and Imogene in *Cymbeline*—quite a repertoire for a youngster, and again

reminiscent of her mother's first full season. On 15 February 1745 after Cibber's Haymarket venture had closed, Jenny moved to Covent Garden and played Arthur in *King John*, a role more within her range. She was apparently cast in March 1745 as Angeline in *Pope Joan*, otherwise *Pope John VIII*, at the Haymarket under her aunt Charlotte Charke's management. But Colley Cibber interfered, Theophilus withdrew Jenny from the cast, and the project collapsed.

Colley Cibber took quite an interest in Jenny, and, to judge by his will written in later years, which left £1000 to each of his granddaughters, he had a great fondness for both Jenny and her sister. He gave Jenny some coaching before her return to the stage, as appears from David Garrick's 18 October 1750 letter to the Countess of Burlington:

[T]o Morrow a Grand Daughter of Mr Cibber plays ye Part of Alicia in Jane Shore— She has been instructed by him for some time; the Young Lady may have Genius for ought I know, but if she has, it is so eclips'd by the Manner of Speaking ye Laureat has taught her, that I am affraid it will not do— We differ greatly in our Notions of Acting (in Tragedy I mean) & If he is right I am, & ever shall be in ye wrong road . . .

Garrick was right, of course, and one wonders what Jenny's career might have been like had she not come under the guidance of the elder Cibber, who tried to teach her a style of tragic acting which was out of style and at which he himself had failed.

At any rate, on 19 October 1750 at Drury Lane, Jenny "attempted" Alicia, and Richard Cross the prompter noted in his diary: "quite in old style, not liked at all, tho' not hiss'd—given out again and great hiss'd & so not done." One critic liked her, however; "Mary Midnight" (Christopher Smart's pseudonym) in *The Midwife* in 1751 said, "she play'd the Part much better than cou'd be expected from one of her Years and Practise; and if a proper Regard is paid to her Modesty and Merit, I make no Doubt she will become an exceeding good Player." But Smart was an odd fellow who produced a variety of ludicrous entertainments which suggest eccentric tastes, and the opinion of Garrick prevailed. Jenny Cibber seems never to have acted again.

In Robert Eddison's collection is a drawing by Worlidge called Jane Cibber, wife of Colley. But Colley's wife was named Katherine, and Worlidge did not begin making such portraits until after 1740, long after Katherine Cibber and Theophilus Cibber's first wife, Jane, died. The Worlidge drawing, then, is probably of Theophilus's daughter Jane, though she would have been in her 'teens in the 1740s, and the picture shows a mature woman.

Cibber, Theophilus   *1703–1758, actor, dancer, playwright, manager.*

Theophilus, the fourth child and first son of Colley and Katherine Cibber, was born on 25 November 1703 during the great storm (an omen?) that raged over much of Europe and was particularly destructive in England. Theophilus was baptized at St Martin-in-the-Fields on 19 December. In time he was sent to Winchester College, the hope apparently being that he might become a lawyer or doctor, but at the age of 16 Theophilus left school to join the Drury Lane company which his father co-managed.

He was paid 35*s.* weekly at first, but his pay rose to 40*s.* before he was even cited in a cast list. His first notice was in the 1720 edition of *2 Henry IV*, where he was assigned Clarence; the work was performed on 17 December of that year. He must have shown some promise during the season even if he was not noticed in the bills, for on 20 May 1721 he shared a benefit with Rogers. A year later, on 14 May 1722, he was granted a solo benefit when *Richard III* was played, but no cast was listed, and

again Theophilus's name had not appeared in any of the season's bills.

In 1722–23, when Cibber was not yet 20, he began receiving frequent good parts. On 15 September 1722 he acted Osric in *Hamlet*, on 13 October Young Bellair in *The Man of Mode*, on 22 October Hardy in *The Funeral*, on 7 November Daniel in *The Conscious Lovers*, on 11 December Abel in *The Committee*, on 7 January 1723 Hippolito in *The Tempest*, on 9 January LeBeau in *Love in a Forest*, on 12 June the Earl of Somerset in *Sir Thomas Overbury*, and on 5 July Prince Edward in his own alteration of *Henry VI*. "Signior Ciberini," probably Theophilus rather than his father, played Harlequin in *The Tricks of Harlequin* on 9 July. The younger Cibber was very likely Toywell in *A Wife to Be Let* on 12 August 1723 when there was also presented "A new Dramatic Entertainment" called *Apollo and Daphne,* "design'd by Mr Theo. Cibber, with new Music compos'd and adapt'd by Mr Jones." On 16 August Cibber played Pert in *The Impertinent Lovers* to conclude a remarkable season.

Precocious and, apparently, appealing to audiences despite his physical unattractiveness, Theophilus went on in 1723–24 and 1724–25 to add a number of good new roles to his list: Dapper in *The Alchemist*, Petit in *The Instant*, Buskin in *The Strollers*, the Gentleman Usher in *King Lear*, Snap in *Love's Last Shift*, Lory in *The Relapse*, Ptolomey in *Caesar in Egypt*, Jerry in *The Plain Dealer*, Jonas in *The What D'Ye Call It*, and the Poet in *Timon of Athens*. He sometimes took roles Colley had played, and it is likely that he received instruction from his father. In 1723 he was also made manager of the Drury Lane summer company, replacing Mills; by 1727 he became assistant to Wilks, the manager of acting at Drury Lane during the winter season.

Theophilus was attracted to a promising young actress in the troupe, Jane Johnson, and on 21 May 1725 they were granted a license to marry. Theophilus described himself as from the parish of St Paul, Covent Garden, and a bachelor "above 21"; Jane identified herself as from St Martin-in-the-Fields, a spinster 19 years old, marrying with the consent of her guardian Richard Savage, her parents being dead. The couple were married at St Benet, Paul's Wharf, on 22 May 1725.

After acting Alexis in *Semiramis* at Bartholomew Fair on 23 August 1725, Cibber returned to Drury Lane, where for the following eight years he busied himself expanding his repertory, occasionally turning out a play, and learning the business of management. His annual schedules were heavy, and he received yearly benefits, shared with his wife through 1730 and thereafter solo. Among his many new parts during these years might be mentioned Young Fashion in *The Relapse*, Daniel in *Oroonoko*, the Statue in *Harlequin Dr Faustus*, Pantaloon in *Apollo and Daphne*, the title role in *The Miser*, Pistol in *2 Henry IV* (his most famous part, first played on 21 February 1727), Octavio and Manuel in *She Wou'd and She Wou'd Not*, Lenox in *Macbeth*, Carlos in *The Fatal Marriage*, Basset in *The Provok'd Husband*, Tressel in *Richard III*, Don Cleophas Leandro in *Perseus and Andromeda*, Sir Joseph in *The Old Bachelor*, Beau Clincher and Sir Harry in *The Constant Couple*, Roderigo in *Othello*, Fountain in *Wit Without Money*, the title part in *The School Boy*, Robin in *The Contrivances*, Young Indolent in *Whig and Tory*, Omar and Axalla in *Tamerlane*, Rakehell in *She Wou'd If She Cou'd*, Moody in *The Lover's Opera*, Roger in *Patie and Peggy* (his own adaptation of *The Gentle Shepherd*), Mizen in *The Fair Quaker of Deal*, the Squire, the Noble Venetian, Pierrot and Cephalus in *Cephalus and Procris*, Marplot in *The Busy Body*, Razor in *The Provok'd Wife*, Captain Smart in his own comedy *The Lover* (on 21 January 1731), Crack

in *Sir Courtly Nice*, Foigard in *The Stratagem*, Shorthose in *Wit Without Money*, Peter Nettle and Sir Roger in *The What D'Ye Call It*, the title role in *Hob*, Surrey in *Henry VIII*, Springlove in *The Jovial Crew*, George Barnwell in the premiere of *The London Merchant*, Bayes in *Bayes's Opera*, Abel Drugger in *The Alchemist*, Sir Amorous in *The Silent Woman*, Pearmain in *The Recruiting Officer*, Cokes in *Bartholomew Fair*, Mustachio in *The Tempest*, Syphax in *Cato*, Trim in *The Funeral*, Teague in *The Committee*, Volscius in *The Rehearsal*, Humphrey in *The Tender Husband*, Grizzle in *The Tragedy of Tragedies*, Lovegirlo in *Covent Garden Tragedy*, Orestes in *The Distrest Mother*, Glendower in *1 Henry IV*, Tattle in *Love for Love*, Iago in *Othello,* Sparkish in *The Country Wife*, and Atall in *The Double Gallant*.

Like his father, Theophilus tried a wide range of characters, and his popularity in foppish parts and as Pistol has perhaps overshadowed his talents as a pantomime performer. He was not the equal of John Rich at Lincoln's Inn Fields, but when Drury Lane took to pantomimes in self-defense, the younger Cibber became a valuable asset. He danced with great vigor, and on 19 February 1726 the journalist Mist noted that "Yesterday, as young Mr Cibber was performing the Part of Harlequin in Apollo and Daphne, his Foot slipp'd, and he fell down the Stage and broke his Nose."

Critical attention to Cibber, once it began, however, seldom focused on his pantomime parts. In 1732 *The Comedian*, possibly by T. Cooke, praised Theophilus as Pistol, Abel Drugger, and Father Martin in *The Old Debauchees*, and noted that "the Success of the *Mock-doctor* is more own't to the extraordinary good Action of him and Miss *Raftor* [later Mrs Clive] than to the Merit of the Writer . . ." The same year *The Players*, probably by Edward Phillips, lauded Cibber:

A Reputation by a Father won,
Young C[ibbe]r knows, descends not to
*   the Son;*
He sees his Father's Honour fully grown,
Yet wisely labours to advance his
*   own . . .*

It was probably Fielding who wrote the satirical *An Apology for the Life of T......* *C......* *in* 1740 and there observed that Theophilus in his early years tried to get all the little, sprightly parts, the first of which was the country footboy in *The Conscious Lovers,* in which he received much applause. As he gained experience, the author said, he succeeded to some of Jubilee Dicky Norris's roles. Davies, writing later, commented on Cibber's "effronterie" on stage and the "ridiculous squinting and vile grimace" with which Theophilus sometimes overemphasized roles—qualities that were perfect for Pistol but hardly suitable for all characters. As Pistol, Davies wrote, Cibber had a "peculiar kind of false spirit," "uncommon blustering," "long unmeasurable strides," and "loud and grotesque vociferation" which made his characterization a favorite with audiences and won him "Pistol" as a nickname. Some of these same qualities clearly seem to have been part of Cibber's offstage personality.

Though Cibber's *Patie and Peggy* of 1730 had little literary merit, it went through two editions in two years and pleased audiences. His comedy *The Lover,* of 1731, ran into difficulties on opening night. Colley Cibber's denigrators tried to blame the piece on him and cried it down on 21 January when it opened, though the elder Cibber's only contribution was a clever epilogue-dialogue between Theophilus and his wife. The (Fielding?) *Apology* has Theophilus describe the dialogue:

[S]he told me I was a blockhead to write, and that I was my Father's own son; all which were strong Jokes with the Audience. I put on a pitiful Face, told her I wrote to pay my Debts, and that I would, for the future, prove a good and loving Husband, if she would save my Play: The Audience being won by her Entreaty . . . The Play liv'd nine Nights.

The jibe at Cibber's personal life was not without warrant. It was said that he led a dissolute life from the start of his stage career and was as often in bagnios and taverns as on the stage. He did have two children by his wife—Jane in 1730 and Elizabeth in 1733—but Mrs Cibber died in giving birth to the latter and was buried at St Paul, Covent Garden, on 28 January 1733. Much later Cibber lamented his loss in his own *Serio-Comic Apology:* "My dear, dear faithful Wife—I might have been Happy! possessed of a Treasure I knew not the real Value of, 'till it was snatch'd from me. / Yet, I wrong'd this Angelic Woman! threw all my Hours away in sullied dear purchased Pleasures . . ."

The death of his wife came at about the same time as the death of his hopes to succeed his father at Drury Lane. Though Colley Cibber apparently advanced Theophilus's career and must have encouraged Wilks to take him on as an assistant, when the time came for the Drury Lane managership to pass on to others, Colley spurned his son. According to Pilkington in his *Real Story,* "Old Cibber frequently declared to my mother, that he would never have believed Theophilus was his son, but that he knew the mother of him was too proud to be a whore." Colley certainly had reasons for wondering whether Theophilus should succeed him, yet the way he went about disinheriting his son from the Drury Lane empire was rather underhanded.

For his part, Theophilus had a legitimate claim to a share in the management. He had learned the trade, had worked hard as a player, and was popular with the audience. The reign of the triumvirate that had brought many years of prosperity and stability to Drury Lane ended in the early 1730s. Robert Wilks died in 1732 and Barton Booth in 1733. Their shares went partly to two gentlemen amateurs, John Highmore and John Ellis, the former a would-be actor, the latter a painter, and neither very familiar with theatre management. Theophilus, of course, hoped to inherit Colley's share.

In 1732–33 Colley rented his share to Theophilus for £442 and went on straight salary, which act made the younger Cibber a co-manager, but not in his own right. Nevertheless, he plunged into the operation of Drury Lane with a vengeance and made a number of expensive yet sensible adjustments with which Highmore and Ellis went along. He raised some of the actors' salaries, brought Joe Miller back into the company, mounted new productions, gave Kitty Clive a gift following a good performance, and worked up his own *The Harlot's Progress*. He was apparently difficult and demanding, but he knew more about theatre than his partners and usually got his way. But then double misfortune struck him. An undated newspaper clipping copied by Latreille that must date about January 1733 reported: "We hear Mr Cibber Junr of the Theatre Royal in Drury Lane is gone out of Town for the recovery of his health, having had a violent cold, attended with a fever & an inflammation in his stomach & Mrs Cibber lies dangerously ill of a fever." The combination of his own illness and the death of his wife kept Theophilus away from the theatre in early 1733. (The calendar shows that he did not act during most of January and February.)

During his absence, Highmore and Ellis substituted a pantomime by Ellis for Cibber's *The Harlot's Progress*. Though Theophilus got his work put back in the schedule and saw it produced on 31 March 1733, the incident created much ill will and made Cibber suspicious of his partners, who had

earlier been rather submissive to his will. Then the *Daily Post* on 27 March 1733 carried the small but important item: "Colley Cibber Esq. one of the Patentees of His Majesty's Company of Comedians has sold his intire Share of the Cloaths, scenes & Patent to John Highmore Esq. At the end of this season he quits the stage altogether." Later, on 2 June, the *St James's Evening Post* printed a letter saying that "the reason which he gave for such conduct was, that he chose to convert it into ready money, that he might make a proportionable division of what fortune he may happen to have among all his children." How much of the 3000 guineas that Colley received ever reached any of his children is not certain.

Left out in the cold, Theophilus gathered about him a number of the Drury Lane actors who did not like Highmore and Ellis and so revolted. The anonymous *Do You Know What You are About?* in 1733 neatly summed up what ensued:

Thus divided, Ancient Pistol heads the Malcontents, and leads his Troops cross the Plains of Covent-Garden, over the Fields of Leicester, and at last encamps himself in the Haymarket, where he gives defiance to the Patentees, who keep their intrenchments and defend themselves with equal bravery.

The secession was pictured by John Laguerre in a satirical print, "The Stage Mutiny," in which was shown the bold and brash Theophilus, decked out as Pistol, leading his dissident players, and Colley, seated in the corner, counting out his wealth. In July 1733 Covent Garden produced a topical satire, *The Stage Mutineers*, to commemorate and capitalize on the disruption of the rival patent house. The newspapers were full of news about the theatrical melodrama. Cibber's *The Harlot's Progress* was advertised for 28 May at Drury Lane but dismissed; Highmore and Ellis closed the theatre doors against The-

ophilus; "Pistol" and his followers petitioned the Lord Chamberlain for a license
to act at the Haymarket (and Colley, in an
odd reversal, supported their proposal); on
4 June Highmore and his colleagues stated
their case in the papers; and on 9 June the
papers said the whole town was waiting for
a counterstatement from Theophilus. Cibber had the upper hand, for with only a few
exceptions (Mrs Clive, Mrs Horton, Bridg-
water) the best of the Drury Lane performers had joined him in his rebellion.

As promised, Theophilus published *A
Letter from Theophilus Cibber, Comedian,
To John Highmore, Esq.* (1733), a windy
but explicit answer to the state of the case
the patentees had made. As expected, Cibber whitewashed himself, shamelessly used
the plight of his late wife during her last
months as proof of the patentee's unfeeling
and evil managerial methods, pointed out
(again and again) the lack of theatrical experience of Highmore and Ellis, claimed
control of Drury Lane as his "Birthright,"
lamented his own distresses—but managed
also to make a good case for the mutiny.
A license to play at the Haymarket was
granted Cibber for the 1733–34 season,
and, knowing he had the better of the two
acting companies under his command, on
10 September 1733 he casually went to
Richmond and played the title role in *The
Mock Doctor* for Chapman's benefit and
"his own diversion." On 26 September with
his dissenting players he opened at the Haymarket with *Love for Love*, playing Tattle.
The new Theophilus Cibber, brash, commanding, full of energy, and only 30,
opened a new and turbulent chapter in his
career.

Highmore and Ellis stood firm, but Cibber and his crew drew good and sympathetic audiences while Drury Lane's customers dropped in number. It appeared that
all the rebels had to do was bide their time
until Highmore and Ellis acceded to their
demands to turn over Drury Lane to them.
Moreover, Highmore and Ellis exacerbated

their difficulties by perpetrating a malicious
act which turned out to be a serious psy-
chological blunder. They had one of Cibber's best actors, Harper, arrested as a va-
grant, as an example to others. But their
case did not stand up in court, the town
turned against them, and by the end of
1733 the case of the patentees collapsed.
Highmore sold his share to another businessman, John Fleetwood, and left the
theatre. Ironically, the patentees might have
won. After the seceders' initial success at
the Haymarket, their audiences diminished.
John Rich at Covent Garden saw an opportunity to unite his theatre with Drury
Lane and talked his friend Fleetwood into
buying out Highmore. Had a union of
Covent Garden and Drury Lane been effected, Cibber and his band would have
been ruined, but Rich and Fleetwood had a
falling-out, Fleetwood was left to face Cibber alone, and on 12 March 1734 Theophilus led his troupe back to Drury Lane
in triumph.

Considering how busy Cibber must have
been in 1733–34 managing his splinter
group at the Haymarket and carrying on his
battle with the patentees, it is astonishing
how much performing he did and how
many new parts he essayed. He began on 5
October 1733 by playing Clodio in *Love
Makes a Man*. Between then and 12 February 1734 he played Foppington in *The
Relapse* and *The Careless Husband*, Glendower in *1 Henry IV*, the title role in *The
Mock Doctor*, Brazen in *The Recruiting Officer*, Renault in *Venice Preserv'd*, Hotspur
in *1 Henry IV* (with book in hand, replacing the arrested Harper), the Old Woman
in *Rule a Wife and Have a Wife*, Witwoud
in *The Way of the World*, Sir John in *The
Silent Woman*, the Servant in *The Burgomaster Trick'd*, Gloster in *Jane Shore*,
Looby Headpiece in *The Mother-in-Law*,
and some of his other old parts. He had, according to the *Biographia Dramatica*, "an
apparent good understanding and quickness of parts; a perfect knowledge of what

he ought to represent; together with a vivacity in his manner" and, obviously, a great capacity for work.

On 12 March 1734, back at Drury Lane, Cibber started his presentations with Head-piece again and went on to act Lothario in *The Fair Penitent*, Janno in *The Country House*, Tom in *The Conscious Lovers*, and Othello ("attempted by Cibber," with Kitty Clive as Desdemona, on 13 May 1734). Not yet exhausted after a season so full of incident, Theophilus and other players from Drury Lane performed *The Lottery* at Lincoln's Inn Fields on 29 June (he acted Jack Stocks and delivered the Epilogue on an Ass); then for Milward's benefit at Richmond, Cibber played in *The Stage Coach* and *The Fair Penitent*.

The spring of 1734 also saw a change in Cibber's personal life. He married Susanna Maria Arne, the talented sister of the musician Thomas Augustine Arne; the wedding was performed by a Catholic priest, probably in an embassy chapel, on 21 April 1734. The couple had two children, both of whom died in infancy. Their first child was Susanna, buried at St Paul, Covent Garden, on 14 February 1735; their second, Caius Gabriel, was buried on 17 April 1736 at the same church, though by that date Theophilus described himself as of the parish of St Giles in the Fields. Theophilus had been living in Playhouse Passage on 5 April 1733, but by the time of his marriage he was lodged at the Cocoa Tree, opposite Tom's Coffee House in Russell Street.

In 1734-35 some of Cibber's new roles were Cassio in *Othello*, Garcia in *The Mourning Bride*, Richmond in *Richard III*, Casca in *Julius Caesar*, Messala in *Junius Brutus*, Slender in *The Merry Wives of Windsor*, the Italian Lady in *Merlin*, Alexas in *All for Love*, Amasie in *The Christian Hero*, Carlos in *The Fatal Marriage*, Captain Spark in *The Universal Gallant*, Martin in *The Man of Taste*, Daran in *The Siege of Damascus*, Blunt in *The Rover*, and Scrub in *The Stratagem*. The season

was marked by an altercation in the Drury Lane scene room when Charles Macklin killed Thomas Hallam; Cibber, who one might suppose would have done something rash or irresponsible under the circumstances, was the one who called for a surgeon. By the end of the season (to keep ahead of his creditors?) he had moved again. His benefit tickets for 29 March 1735 were available at Newton's Warehouse (the Crown and Scepter) in Tavistock Street.

Greatly affecting the theatre world in the spring of 1735 was Barnard's new Licensing Act. In March many players petitioned against the bill, for they saw financial disaster ahead if it passed. Cibber was one of ten players who claimed to be paying £900 annually (some reports said £920) to Fleetwood to lease Drury Lane; actually, their plan to lease the theatre for 15 years had been contemplated at the end of the 1734-35 season but had not been carried out. Ultimately, the Licensing Act had less effect on the players at the patent houses than they had anticipated.

By 1735-36 Cibber's participation in pantomimes had decreased, and he concentrated more and more on foppish and braggadocio roles, prologues and epilogues, and, like his father before him, tragic parts for which he was unsuited. In that season he added to his repertoire such new roles as Brisk in *The Double Dealer*, Nerestan in *Zara*, Lord Modely in *The Connoisseur*, Sir Novelty in *Love's Last Shift*, the King in *1 Henry IV*, and Flash in *Harlequin Restored*. By the time of his benefit on 23 March 1736 he had moved again, to a house in Great Queen Street. The following season he essayed the title role in *The Squire of Alsatia*, Spitfire in *The Wife's Relief*, Polyperchon in *The Rival Queens*, Laertes in *Hamlet*, Cassander in *The Rival Queens*, the King in *The King and the Miller of Mansfield*, Joculo in *The Universal Passion*, and Pylades in *The Distrest Mother*.

The season of 1736–37 was enlivened by a controversy that delighted the town: a battle between Kitty Clive and Mrs Cibber over who should play Polly in *The Beggar's Opera*. Theophilus, of course, in his position as co-manager, was involved in the fray on his wife's side. *The Beggar's Pantomime; or, The Cotending Colombines*, a satire on the petty squabble, was produced by the rival Lincoln's Inn Fields players. The prologue was a song set to the tune of *Chevy Chase* which went, in part:

At length bold Pistol *thus did say,*
As One in doleful Dumps,
My Wife shall have the Part, or I'll
My Pen write to the Stumps.

O then he writ at such a rate,
That in each dreadful Page,
Truth, Sense, and English all did fall
The victims of his Rage.

Now cry'd the Manager so Wise,
Whom Actors all obey;
Pathetick Cibber, Lucy *you,*
Pert Clive *shall* Polly *play.*

O heavy News then Pistol *cry'd,*
With that he wept full sore;
O heavy News his Wife reply'd
Then fainted on the Floor.

Fielding poked fun at the controversy in his *Historical Register for the Year 1736*, in which Pistol gathers a mob and asks:

Say then, Oh Town, is it your royal will
That my great consort represent the part
Of Polly Peachum in the Beggar's
Opera?
                              [*Mob* hiss
Thanks to the town, that hiss speaks
their assent;
Such was the hiss that spoke the great
applause
Our mighty father met with, when he
brought
His riddle [Love in a Riddle] *on the*
stage; such was the hiss

Welcomed his Caesar to th' Egyptian
shore;
Such was the hiss in which John should
have expired;
But, wherefore do I try in vain to
number
Those glorious hisses, which from age to
age
Our family has bourne triumphant from
the stage?

But the bickerings of 1736–37 over whether or not Mrs Cibber should be allowed to play Polly were nothing compared to the scandal that was brewing in Cibber's home. The domestic tremors did not, however, disrupt Theophilus's career, at first. He began the 1737–38 season in ill health at Kingston, whence he had moved his household; on 13 September Macklin had to read Cibber's part of Tom in *The Conscious Lovers*. But Cibber was back in the theatre on 8 October to play Dick in *The Confederacy*, and he went on to act Lucio in *Measure for Measure*, Sir Polidorus in *Aesop*, Novel in *The Plain Dealer*, himself in *The Coffee House*, Julio in *Art and Nature*, the King in *Sir John Cockle at Court*, a Brother in *Comus*, Sir Fopling Flutter in *The Man of Mode*, and Melisander in *Agamemnon*—quite a number of new roles. By the spring of 1738 he had another address: No 12, Wild Court, Great Wild Street. He began the 1738–39 season on 26 September 1738 as Roderigo in *Othello* and then acted Tinsel in *The Haunted House*, Gardiner in *Lady Jane Gray*, and Sir Joseph in *The Old Bachelor*. On 5 December he took time off to go to court, for he had charged his wife with adultery and had sued her paramour for £5000 damages.

For some time Theophilus had been robbing his wife to pay his debts. In 1735 he had taken half her salary; in 1736 he took a present of £50 which Fleetwood had given her for her appearances in *Zara*; and in 1737 he collected most of what she made at Drury Lane and stripped her wardrobe of dresses and her closets of linen. He also had himself "colorably" arrested in order to seize the rest of her belongings and sell them to raise needed money to pay for his loose pleasures about the town. His most despicable and notorious action, however, was pushing his wife into the arms of a lover in order to sue her paramour for adultery. If it was true, as Fielding (?) charged in his satirical *Apology*, that on the night of Cibber's first wife's funeral he had had "a Brace of *Drurian* Doxies vile in the same house," Theophilus was running true to form.

William Sloper, a country squire of some wealth, had become acquainted with the Cibbers in 1736–37. He visited their house at Kingston and, with Cibber's encouragement, spent a good deal of time with Susanna Maria. Cibber occasionally borrowed money of Sloper and went off to spend it in town, leaving Sloper and his wife together. Theophilus and William decided that the latter should have a pseudonym, so Sloper was known to the servants as "Thompson," Theophilus's "cousin." Cibber called him, according to testimony offered in the trial later, "a *Romp*, and a *good-natured Boy*" and sometimes referred to his guest as "Mr Benefit." Sloper's visits to Kingston appear to have started about March 1737. Anne Hopson the housekeeper said, "Mr *Cibber* was then very bare of Money, and afraid of his Creditors. I was very sorry for it; for he owed me a good deal of Money, and does so still. But one Day he told me: *Anne*, says he, I shall have a good deal of Money soon, and you shall have some. And I know he soon after had a good deal of Money, and he paid me five Guineas."

Susanna Maria and Sloper did not at first take advantage of the situation into which Cibber had thrust them, though they had grown fond of one another. At some point, it was said, when Theophilus's scheme seemed not to be working, he took Susanna to Sloper's room, drew a pistol, and

Courtesy of Mr Robert Eddison

THEOPHILUS CIBBER (?), in his marriage dress

by Worlidge

told his wife she would stay with Sloper or he would shoot her through the head. Given such encouragement, Mrs Cibber apparently felt that indiscretion would be the better part of valor, and she and Sloper became lovers. With the aid of Anne Hopson, Sloper and Mrs Cibber arranged for lodgings in Blue Cross Street, Leicester Fields, on 5 December 1737, and there they met and engaged in what the court later proved to its satisfaction was criminal conversation. Though the details of their amours are part of Susanna Maria's story, it was clear that Theophilus knew about and encouraged the affair.

On 16 April 1738 Theophilus went to France to escape his creditors, and from Calais on 21 May (new style) he wrote to his wife a wild, rambling, repetitious letter:

Thou Dearest best of Women, My Angel Tina where where are words to express my

Fondness! my high Opinion of you? — I have wept your Letter all over! Be not angry?, Love they were Tears of Joy of Gratitude to my Dear sweet Preserver If in ye Agonys of my Mind I have said one word, to give you Pain, Remember, I this instant recall 'em. The letter I wrote last & wch. youl Receive much about ye time I write this, I hope will not make you uneasy I tremble for your health, for that & your happiness is my [chief?] Prayer to God & [indeed?] Dear I do Pray sincerely: I never will lie or disguise a Thought but one (Little sweet Naughty Child) & when I [Fib?] there Ill cut any Rascalls Throat yt shall dare to Contradict me — And dost thou thank me for my Diligence? God bless thee, my Child — Oh thou art a Dear Good Girl Yes Dear I will be easy & you shall be easy, 'Tis my Duty to make you so, and if ever you see me have a Grave Look, think, 'tis only a Reproach [upon?] myself. You shall wake me from ye thought, and to Entertain thee, I'll laugh like a Frenchman. We'll be very nonsensical — yes you shall be Mistress of yourself, Your dear Heart shall feel no Pang, God forgive me for ever having given it one. — But Miss Rantipole, I'll be master of your Conduct. Youre a Little Simple Child & not to be left quite without a Leading String. And has my Sweet Numps thought coolly? When she does I'm sure she'll think right and does it leave to my Determination our living in a House together? Why, then, I declare — May the Great God whom I adore give me up to Eternal Perdition if I think I could Reconcile myself to living under a different Roof from you, to be firmly fixed on ye Throne of France, or any Nation whatever! what! lose ye Pleasure of your Society! then I were lost indeed . . . My Dear 'tis now 3 weeks & upwards since I parted from you, if I have had one night's rest since may I never know rest again The Melancholly of my Countenance has drawn Tears from ye Eyes of Men; I am certain I have never slept Ten Minutes at a Time, & have been in one Continued Fever. . . .

Oh Dear I own you have great Power over Men I cant express with what generosity I would willingly act towards you; — yes Numps shall be fat and fair & saucy & I'll

abuse her abundantly — I Purpose with this sending a Letter to Fleetwood which you may carry to him, at your Leisure; when you think most proper and I will act determinately towards him; He's all Counterfeit, Dear I'll make him know, or I'll eat Bread alone & drink water, whom he ought to set a value on: any importunate Air he may affect, I shall laugh at while I know my Numps approves of my Conduct, and that there's no Black Guard, at a Door to lay his stinking Paws upon my Shoulder. — I'll behave like a Gentleman towards him, but by God I'll behave like a Man of spirit The Letter I send him, shew to Quin and Milward (shew it privately to our Friend [Sloper?]. I think he has Honour (Ay and very good Sense and therefore should be glad of his opinions). Remember me to Quin and Milward. . . . Let me but live to see your little Countenance Smile and have a chearfull friendly Social Meal, with Saucy Tina, and I'll think every Fortune overpaid. — Yes Tina will do all she can, to make him Easy who would do so much for her. — Oh Jewell shall I live to see my little Actress (The little Actress for there's none like you) shine again, and her Poor Theo: assistant to her, in her Business — I'll set down by & by Numps, & draw a [schedule?] of what Demands to make on Fleetwood and be very Civil, and Stately my little Dame; 'tis ye only way to Deal with him. And if he's obstinate and Blockhead enough, not to comply, be certain I have farther thoughts to your advantage, tho I know he'l come to it if we have Resolution. I have reminded Finch in my Letter, that comes by a Vessel, not to word any thing, in my Letter of License, that may at all tie me down to Fleetwood; for I will be free: I know (however he or any other of his Dirty Trenchard Counsellors may Chatter) that my Articles have been long made void by him in the Strictest Sense of ye Law and Justice.

And my Creditors seem by Finch's Letter to be good naturedly inclined, I will inspite of Fleetwood's tooth shew myself on a Theatre, I warrant you, were it to be but a few times sufficient to get a Morsel of Bread for myself (to vex him) and give a proper Quota to my Creditors — Yes Dear believe me, I have Resolution Enough to go thro' more than People Imagine; and I can think yet, ay and act to—and while my Spirit is supported by your kind Opinion Tina—I'll not flinch. Yes Tina, while you can convince me that you have Still such an esteem and regard for me (and that ye World thinks no less of me than Finch says they do) I will support myself with a Becoming Pride. . . . I must not be to Grave, no, my dear wife Tina bids me not, my beautiful Tina, my Sensible Tina, my worthy Tina—how greatly relieved how Joyous I am, to hear you're Better. Naught's ever in Danger you say,—I am afraid Dear I have had to great a right to Protection, according to that [Rule?] but why dont I talk a little of Business? Because you little Baggage I can talk of nothing but thee. Pray let Finch get my Paper from Capt. Gilby, as soon as possible . . . Let me but live once more to breath my Native Air with Liberty, & convince you, how much I love you how highly I esteem you, how tenderly I feel for you, and how greatly I prefer your quiet to all Considerations; I shall think my follies & Crimes expiated, and ever be ready to resign my Last Breath to him who gave it. How may we Extract Comfort from Misery? Nothing but thy self could have wakened me to thought sure I never thought before: But I'll think chiefly now for thee. But we'l not think to gravely neither Dear.

If that thing Fleetwood gives out I owe him anything (His Damned bond excepted) say I declare 'tis a Lie, for upon my Honour by Ballance he's indebted to me: and I laugh at him.—But he will Lie! Good Gods! How he will Lie? The Devil never made a greater Liar—He is in reality more Contemptable than his lowest Creature round his filthy Table who daily gobble down his ill drest Meat and Stumd Wine . . . May God Almighty Eternally bless and Comfort you!—and believe me, my Angel Tina, I am most Cordially, most Sincerely your fond affectionate Husband

The Cibber

God love you, God bless you my Sweet Dear Dear Tina—I wil Seal this now by God—God bless—Yet let me stop to say if I live to unload [part?] of my poor mind to you and one more you both will still honour &

Pitty your unhappy Theo: God bless you thou [worthy?] Angel—I may make you laugh yet—God bless.

Directed . . . To Mrs Cibber at Mr Carler's a Gardner in Church Lane in Islington near London.

When this outrageous, or perhaps unbalanced, man returned to London in the summer of 1738 he dropped by the lodgings Sloper and Mrs Cibber had used in Blue Cross Street, asked the landlady if Anne Hopson had had lodgings there and if visitors used them, received a description of the visitors which satisfied him, and "so he said no more," according to the landlady, "and went away."

Anne Hopson testified later that Cibber "was at a Bagnio in Goodman's Fields" while Mrs Cibber and Sloper carried on their affair at lodgings they had in Kensington. Cibber then moved to Blue Green and finally to his wife's Kensington house.

During the summer of 1738 the trio shared a house at Burnham. Mrs Hopson reported that Theophilus and Susanna Maria occupied a room adjoining Sloper's.

Mrs *Cibber* used to undress herself in my Master's Room, and leave her Clothes there, and put on a Bedgown, and take away one of the Pillows from my Master's Bed, and go away to Mr *Sloper's* Room; my Master used to shut the Door after her, and say, *Good Night my Dear* . . .

While enjoying this amicable arrangement, the trio discussed a divorce (and Theophilus's letter hints that perhaps they had talked of the matter earlier). Cibber, in a letter he made public later, claimed he had no interest in a financial settlement. "I think money dirt, sir," he wrote Sloper. Upon further reflection he decided he really should have Mrs Cibber's earnings, and since she made £400 per year whenever she acted and had cost Cibber easily that much to support, and since his debts were her debts, perhaps he should get something out of a divorce. "And so," he wrote to Susanna Maria (in still another letter he made public later), "thou weakest and most worthless of thy sex, farewell for ever."

Then Cibber changed his mind and retrieved his wife by force. In September 1738 she and Sloper were still at Burnham but Cibber had returned to London. He hired three men, one (a Mr Fife) a sergeant in the Guards, and went with them to Burnham by coach to confiscate his wife. Upon their arrival they found Sloper in his slippers and Mrs Cibber in her nightgown, having tea. After some harsh words between Sloper and Cibber, Susanna Maria was conveyed to the carriage, and Theophilus carted her off toward London. In passionate pursuit, Sloper caught up with them at an inn in Slough, where more hot words were exchanged. Mrs Cibber admitted she was with child by Sloper and called her husband "a great many Villains"; Sloper fired off a pistol into the air; Cibber made speeches; and finally the three quieted down. The pregnant Mrs Cibber was put to bed, with a woman servant to guard her; Theophilus sat up all night like an expectant father; and Sloper slipped off into the darkness.

Once back in London with his prize, Theophilus provided for her handsomely in his house in Wild Court, Great Wild Street. He took the precaution, however, to keep her under lock and key, with a guard named Stint (a candlesnuffer at the theatre) watching over her. Soon to Mrs Cibber's rescue came her brother Thomas Arne and a mob. Theophilus had Arne committed to Bridewell; in retaliation Mrs Cibber, who had again escaped to Sloper's arms, swore the peace against her husband; and Cibber sued Sloper for adultery and £5000 damages. In yet another letter he made public later Cibber claimed that Susanna Maria "did, on September the 7th, 1738, elope from her Husband (by the Contrivance of that ungreateful bad

Harvard Theatre Collection

THEOPHILUS CIBBER, as the Mock Doctor

by Powell?

Woman, her Mother, her villainous Brothers, and Others) . . ."

The trial, at which most of the information above was presented in complete detail, took place on 5 December 1738. Criminal conversation was established without question, but the defense made it abundantly clear that Cibber had connived at the whole affair and virtually sold his wife to her lover. The jury took only half an hour to decide that Sloper was guilty, but they awarded Theophilus only £10 in damages.

On 6 January 1739 Cibber came once again before his public at Drury Lane, as Lord Foppington in *The Relapse* and the title role in *The Mock Doctor*, but his adversaries were ready for him. Lady Stafford wrote to Lord Wentworth just before the event, "I hear there will be a vast riot to night at the Play, for young Cibber is to act and the Templars are resolved to hiss him off the stage." They came close to succeeding. Said Lady Stafford in a later note, "Young Cibber was vastly hiss'd a Thursday, but his old friend Impudence kept him from being either out of countenance or in the least disturb'd at the noise . . ."

A more complete account was printed in the *Apology for T...... C......:*

[T]he harmonious discordant concert of catcalls, whistles, etc., etc., began to play before the curtain drew up. Well, though the actors were all frightened, the play began with calmness and applause; but this was only a prelude to the battle. When the scene came in which he was to appear, there was a dead silence, till he popped his poor head from behind the scenes; then at once the hurly-burly began, volleys of apples and potatoes and such vile trash flew about his ears. He retired, the storm subsided; he advanced, it began again. In the most humble gesture and address he made a motion to be heard; it was all in vain and he was once more pelted off. . . . But determined to go through the play, he went through it amidst the greatest uproar that ever was heard so long a space in a theatre, and by a confident heart he surmounted what many of less resolution would have sunk under.

Another report stated that "At the end of the entertain^t he in a speech thanked the audience for their indulgence to him." Cibber finished out the season, braving his way, but his days at Drury Lane were then ended for a time. His benefit bill of 26 March 1739 indicated that he was living at Mrs Holt's in Bow Street, Covent Garden.

On 27 June Mrs Cibber again made life interesting for Theophilus by having him arrested. Divorce proceedings were apparently being bogged down by Cibber's reluctance to settle for nothing. To defend himself he took to the press again. He re-

Harvard Theatre Collection

THEOPHILUS CIBBER
benefit ticket for *The Mock Doctor*

by Hogarth?

minded the public that Mrs Cibber had long since been convicted of adultery. She had eloped from her husband

and still continues to abscond from him; and has also caus'd that scandalous Wretch, formerly his unfaithful Servant Anne Hopson (who has been her Convenient, or Procuress, a long Time) secretly and fraudently to convey away, without his knowledge, and contrary to his express Commands, several Effects of his, such as Table-Linen, Sheeting; great Quantities of Wearing-Apparel, as Gowns, Petticoats, Riding-Habits, Linen, fine Laces, and many other Things of considerable Value; and as no base Endeavours have been omitted (not even Perjury) by several of the Confederates of the said Susanna Maria, Unjustly, Falsly, Scandalously, and Maliciously, to Asperse and Villify her Husband's character, distress his Circumstances, and ruin his Fortune;—and as the said Susanna Maria has endeavour'd to carry on a scandallus and malicious Prosecution, in the Commons, against her Husband, to the manifest Injury of his present Circumstances, his whole Salary

being assign'd, and paid, to the Use of his and her former Creditors; and whereas, at present, she has no visible Way of getting her Livelyhood: This is to forewarn all Persons whatsoever (at their Peril) to harbour, countenance, or trust the said Susanna Maria, —her Husband being resolv'd not to pay any Debts she shall contract, or may have contracted; as also, to prosecute (with the utmost severity of the Law) any Person that shall give her any Harbour or Assistance, she having declared, she will endeavour to ruin her Husband by Law, who is too well convinc'd she must be privately supported by one whose Name need not be mentioned, and is omitted only in Respect to his Relations, &c. And whereas a base Lie was artfully spread Abroad, and villainously asserted, That her Husband had received a Sum of Money for a Consideration too infamous to mention: Now, this is to certify, The Said Theophilus Cibber was, on June the 27th, 1739, arrested for a Debt due on his Bond (to which action he gave Bail) merely because he would not sign such an Article of Separation to his Wife, as would have left her at Liberty to have pursued her infamous Practices with her vain, insolent Paramour with Impunity.
THEOPHILUS CIBBER

If that did not wring the hearts of Londoners, perhaps the benefit at Covent Garden on 2 August 1739 for Cibber's two daughters by his first marriage (Jenny and Betty) did. Theophilus was not above such things: four days before the adultery trial he had rather belatedly erected a tablet to the memory of his first wife, and he had made sure the public should hear about his gesture.

Cibber acted in August 1739 at Covent Garden, among other parts, Mat (in the character of Pistol) in *The Beggar's Opera*. For the following two seasons he made Covent Garden his theatrical home. The manager, John Rich, was doubtless responsible for Cibber's election to the Sublime Society of Beefsteaks, a club Rich had founded, on 22 September. By that time the furor over the adultery case had subsided,

but Cibber was so deeply in debt that he had assigned his salary to his creditors. To get needed money (and more publicity?) he initiated a new suit against Sloper, now for £10,000. With consummate effrontery he accused Sloper of depriving him of his wife's financial help by "assaulting, beating, &c., the plaintiff's Wife, whereby he lost her Assistance to his damage." At the second trial, on 4 December 1739, it was proved only that Sloper and Mrs Cibber had continued to co-habit and that by Sloper she had had a child (Maria Susanna or Susanna Maria—official documents vary) on 26 February 1739. The jury again found for the plaintiff and this time awarded Cibber £500 damages.

Cibber acted a heavy schedule (for his creditors) at Covent Garden in 1739–40, playing many of his old roles, some of them "new dressed." Among his parts during the season were Buskin in *The Strollers*, the title role in *The Double Gallant*, Beau Clincher in *The Constant Couple*, Bayes in *The Rehearsal*, Young Gubbins in *The Tender Husband*, Pistol in *Henry V*, Teague in *The Committee*, the title role in *The School Boy*, Trueman in *The Twin Rivals*, and Blunt in *The Rover*. By his benefit on 10 March 1740 he was living at Mr Bolney's in the Great Piazza, Covent Garden. The trial hardly interrupted his schedule (he acted on 1 and 6 December and sandwiched the trial in on the fourth), so to keep himself in mischief Theophilus fought a duel with his erstwhile friend James Quin.

Animosity between the two had developed in recent years. The *Apology for T......* *C......* said that the pair had quarrelled in 1737 or 1738. "In this Contest," Cibber is made to say, "I valued nothing so much as his Contempt of *Me*; for on my smart cutting Repartees on him, he cry'd with a Laugh, Quarrelling with such a Fellow is like sh——t——g on a T——d, walking off as cool as a Cucumber." The argument on 9 March 1740 started at the Bedford

THEOPHILUS CIBBER, as Pistol;
detail from "The Stage Mutiny"
engraving, after Laguerre

Coffee House. Cibber refused to act at
Quin's benefit, used some words at which
Quin took umbrage, and when the argument grew heated the pair went out into
the Piazza of Covent Garden and duelled
with Swords. Cibber was slightly wounded
on the arm and Quin on the fingers, and
after their wounds were dressed the two
went back into the coffee house and started
quarreling all over again, "but the Company prevented any further Mischief."

Theophilus returned to Covent Garden
in 1740–41 at £1 daily but hardly earned
his keep. The season got off to a bad start
for him, for Rich had to deny in the papers
"the Report of Mr Cibber and Mrs Horton
being engag'd to another Theatre." Theophilus acted infrequently during the season, was ill for a while in December, and

appeared in no new roles. At his benefit on
30 March 1741, however, he made a tidy
profit of £192 15*s*. 6*d*. He had moved yet
again, for his benefit bill stated that tickets
could be had of him at Shell House in
Spring Gardens. At the end of the season he
and Rich parted company.

In emulation of his celebrated (and by
then thoroughly embarrassed) father, and
to make some money, Theophilus announced that he would publish his true
memoirs. As has been said, it was probably
Fielding who anticipated him with the half-
satirical *An Apology for the Life of Mr.
T...... C......, Comedian . . . Supposed to be
written by Himself.* The work came out in
1740, was reprinted the same year in Dublin, and effectively scotched Cibber's plans
to bring out his own apology.

Perhaps it was in hopes of returning to
the good graces of his father that Theophilus returned to Drury Lane for the
1741–42 season, for Colley came out of
retirement to act a few of his old parts, and
Theophilus appeared with him. On 3 December 1741, for instance, Colley played
Sir John Brute and Theophilus Razor in
The Provok'd Wife. The season also saw
the younger Cibber as Tattle in *Love for
Love,* Jaques in *As You Like It,* and
Parolles in *All's Well that Ends Well.*
Though some modern historians have taken
Theophilus to task for having the gall to
play Hamlet, the fact is that on 26 January
1742 Milward was unable to perform the
role and "his part was read by Cibber Jun,"
according to the prompter Cross. After acting in *The Man of Mode* on 6 April, "Cibber elop'd," and for the remainder of the
season his parts were taken by others. What
caused his fresh unhappiness is not known,
but he may well have been fleeing his
creditors again.

He was back on the boards in 1742–43,
but with Giffard's troupe at Lincoln's Inn
Fields. With them he attempted such new
parts as Richard III (on 27 November
1742), Gloucester in *King Lear,* the title

role in *The Non-Juror*, Moneytrap in *The Confederacy*, and Crack in *Sir Courtly Nice* before Giffard's venture foundered. Theophilus then went to Dublin, where he made his first appearance at the Smock Alley Theatre on 12 May 1743 playing Foppington in *The Careless Husband*. He was warmly received by Dubliners and proved (at first) to be a gentleman rather than a comedian. Or so said Pilkington in his *Real Story* in 1760. The good character did not last, and the true Theophilus soon showed his colors by getting into difficulties with the popular Irish actor Thomas Sheridan.

The difficulties began over a robe Sheridan needed for his part in *Cato* on 14 July 1743. Arriving at the playhouse, Sheridan found that the robe was gone and refused to act without it. He apparently accused Cibber of locking up the garment in an attempt to undermine him. On 21 July a riotous group of student supporters of Sheridan broke up Cibber's performance and, according to Pilkington, Theophilus had to make his escape through a window. Cibber may well have intended a *coup*, for the Smock Alley company was badly managed and neither the visiting English actors nor the regular members of the troupe were getting their pay.

After his brief stay with the Irish, Cibber returned to Drury Lane for the 1743–44 season. He appears to have attempted only one new part—Manly in *The Provok'd Husband*—and he missed performances in the early part of the season because of a bad cold. Yet Cibber had not lost his appeal. "Mr Neither-side" in *An Impartial Examen* in 1744 asked, "Have we so good a *Foppington*, a *Brazen*, a *Clodio*, an *Attall*, a *Parolles*, &c. as Mr Cibber on any stage?" To that critic and others, Theophilus was the "best now living" comedian.

On 11 September 1744, armed with a rather shaky license, Cibber opened a season under his own management at the old Haymarket Theatre. The first offering was grotesque: *Romeo and Juliet* with Theophilus and his 14-year-old daughter Jenny. The critics were quick to point out that the age difference between the two (quite apart from their known relationship), made the performance incredible. Undaunted, Cibber then offered Jenny as Desdemona to his Othello, after which he played a few of his old roles and tried Sir Nicholas Spottey in *The Prodigal*. At the request of Fleetwood, the Lord Chamberlain stopped the Haymarket performances on 22 October, but Theophilus got around that by restyling his organization an "Academy" and offering musical concerts followed by free "rehearsals" of plays. He was closed again on 10 November and had to return to Covent Garden. There he finished out the season acting (and being hissed as) the Dauphin in his father's last play, *Papal Tyranny in the Reign of King John*. He also tried Antonio in *Don Sebastian*, Pistol in *2 Henry IV* (for the first time in a good while), and Timothy in *The What D'Ye Call It*.

A perfectly normal season for Cibber would have been a novelty in itself. But 1745–46 was no such thing. He was engaged once more at Covent Garden but could not start the season because he was languishing in Fleet Prison for debt. According to his own *Serio-Comic Apology* of 1748, he was "close confined upwards of six months." He must have felt quite at home, for he had been there before, following "suits in the Commons and Chancery" with which his wife had pestered him. Aaron Hill tried to rescue him, but his offer was ironic: he would let Cibber take the author's benefit nights at Hill's new play, *Meropé*, and Hill tried to get Mrs Cibber to act in it. She, of course, refused, and the play was not presented until 1749. But Cibber was released in time to play some roles at Covent Garden: Lord George in *The Lady's Last Stake*, Sir Courtly Nice, and Gratiano in *The Merchant of Venice*.

Then, as he confessed later, "About Easter in 1746,—I, in a foolish Pet, precipitately (consequently imprudently) left Covent Garden Theatre, and went to Drury-Lane." His imprudence had to do with his wife. She had an agreement with the patent houses that they would never let Theophilus act at a theatre where she was playing. In the spring of 1746 it happened that a benefit had been scheduled for her brother on 12 April at Drury Lane, and though she had not been a member of the company that season, she performed for it. She was understandably alarmed when Theophilus turned up there, and she quickly registered a complaint.

This provided Theophilus with an opportunity to display some more dirty linen. He published a letter to the town, assuring everyone that he had no desire to revive the animosity between himself and his wife and that it was perfectly all right with him if she kept her £700 but that he did not think it cricket of her to persuade the managers of the patent houses to block him from acting.

But low as she has reduced my fortune (and that she has been the source of my calamities I will presently and concisely make appear), my mind has never sunk low enough to seek a mean revenge, even against the most faithless, artful, and ungrateful woman that ever imposed on a good-natured world or disturbed the heart of a weak man . . .

—and so on in his usual vein.

Cibber was in the Drury Lane company during the summer of 1746 and in the 1746–47 season. In 1747–48 he was at Covent Garden playing such parts as Jack Meggot in *The Suspicious Husband*, Abel in *The Committee*, Flash in *Miss in Her Teens*, Sir Amorous in *Woman's a Riddle*, Captain Squib in *Tunbridge Walks*, Luckless (the author) and a Foundling in *The Author's Farce*, Beau Mizen in *The Fair Quaker of Deal*, and the Stuttering Cook in *The Pilgrim*. He was also featured on 6 November 1747 in a song called "The Sailor's Rendezvous at Portsmouth."

In 1748 Cibber's version of *Romeo and Juliet*, which he had used at the Haymarket with his daughter, was published, and Cibber spent a rather busy season at Covent Garden playing, for the most part, his old roles. He participated in a number of benefits for other actors, and at his own on 27 February 1749 he ridiculed the hordes of foreign performers who had appeared in London during the season: "Il Signor Pistolini Cibberini Foppingtonini, detto The Cibber, alias the Mock Doctor, who did not bring into England any one Foreigner, now performing at any Theatre" hoped the town would believe he was obliged to the English "even to the Honour of being born and bred among 'em."

On 25 September 1750 Cibber arrived again in Dublin, where he acted for two seasons before reappearing, on 6 February 1753, at Drury Lane for a special benefit. He played Dr Wolf in *The Non-Juror* and offered his popular "Epilogue by Nobody" in hopes of raising money to help get him out of jail. He was a prisoner in the King's Bench and advertised to one and all that it was a vicious rumor that he was receiving an annual allowance from his wife. The receipts from the benefit were £220, showing that he was still an attraction, but Theophilus was totally incapable of managing his finances, so that it may have done him little good. His performance, on the other hand, was lauded in *The Present State of the Stage* in 1753, where he was ranked among the first actors of the age. All "will lament the evil Fortune which confines to a Prison a Man whom it was once the fashion to follow and encourage."

But encouragement for Cibber was getting harder and harder to come by. From No 4, Falcon Court, Southwark, on 14 June 1753 he wrote to Aaron Hill:

Sir
At the request of some good natured friends I shall in the Term venture at a Benefit—

They flatter me the Town wish to see me; and after some cessation of Plays, A Comedy, and a Farce, will not be unacceptable tho yᵉ Gardens are all open; which, perhaps, numbers may begin to be cloy'd with . . .

He proposed doing *The Careless Husband* and asked Hill if he would supply a special prologue honoring the author, Colley Cibber. Most of the letter was an effusive (but perhaps sincere) puff for his father: "Belov'd by most, admir'd by all; and in unruffled old age, enjoys the spirit of youth—nay, can Laugh with them too; When his Passions Subside, The Vigour of Sense remains." If this was an indirect attempt to curry favor with the elder Cibber, it seems to have done little good. The proposed benefit, lacking encouragement, did not take place, and Colley's will (written coincidentally that year) provided £1000 each for Theophilus's children but only £50 for Theophilus himself.

In 1753–54 Theophilus was again attached to no company, but he held special benefits for himself at Covent Garden on 12 February 1754 and at Drury Lane on the following 2 July. The latter brought in £206 and displayed a new piece by Cibber called *The Humorists*—a potpourri of scenes from *2 Henry IV* in which he played Pistol. The 1754–55 season found Cibber back on the Covent Garden roster playing old parts, and in the early fall of 1755 he was at the Haymarket Theatre acting Othello, and the Player in *The Beggar's Opera*. The Haymarket venture was under Cibber's management.

Much of 1755–56 was for Theophilus a struggle to contrive ways of making public appearances. On 14 January 1756 he had a benefit at the Haymarket, offering a "Dissertation" touching on patentees, acting, theatres, and public diversions. On 28 January he offered the same entertainment at the Lecture Room in the Robin Hood (Macklin's coffee house) near Temple Bar. On 18 March he called his dissertation a "Lecture" and gave it at the New Wells, Goodman's Fields.

Having failed in his earlier attempt to set up an Academy at the Haymarket, where, he had said, he had hoped to train young players, Cibber tried again in December 1756 at his Histrionic Academy on the Bowling Green. He announced plans to present *The Busy Body* and *The Mock Doctor* in rehearsal format with his "assistants, Pupils, Etc." on 15 December, and he bragged that "Cephalick Snuff" would be available. On 14 December, however, he had to state in the *Public Advertiser* that "Some sudden Disappointments (as unexpected as unforeseen) compel me to defer opening my Histrionic Academy." Defeated, Cibber managed to arrange for a benefit for himself at Covent Garden on 25 May at which he played Sir Francis Wronghead in *The Provok'd Husband* and the Fine Gentleman in *Lethe*. A poem appeared ridiculing his playbill:

> 'Mongst the wits and the writings there
>   happen'd of late
> Pro and Con upon Cibber a learned debate
> His play bill was read that ended the
>   strife
> All agreed that a Wronghead he'd act to
>   the life.

Cibber spent the summer of 1757 offering a series of medley concerts at the Haymarket. His first was on 15 June, a mixed bag of entertainments apparently organized by himself. On 5 July he appeared simply as the auctioneer in a similar medley that concluded with an auction of odds and ends. On 11 August his contribution was somewhat larger: he presented an address, two comic lectures, and an auction of "choice curiosities." Subsequent medleys on 22 and 31 August omitted the address. "Mother Midnight" was in some way involved in these offerings, and it is perhaps appropriate that before the end of his career

Theophilus Cibber should have worked with the eccentric poet-manager Christopher Smart who masqueraded under that odd pseudonym. But what a falling off was here! On 2 and 8 September Cibber shared the bill with such pseudonymous performers as Mynheer Von Poop-Poop Broomstickado, the bassoonist. "For the sake of OLD COLL," cried a poem of the time, "let Theophilus eat." The *Impromptu Faragolio* sequel to the medleys, in which Theophilus appeared, though unimportantly, throughout September 1757 apparently brought him a subsistence.

Colley Cibber died on 11 December 1757, and perhaps in charity Theophilus was granted a license to present ten performances at Haymarket Theatre between 1 January and 7 February 1758. (The license was given five days after his father's death.) On a subscription basis he played Manuel in *She Wou'd and She Wou'd Not*, Numps in *Numps' Courtship*, Renault in *Venice Preserv'd*, and Marplot in *The Busy Body*. He stretched his license somehow, for on 6 March, dressed in mourning he offered a maudlin prologue on the death of his father. Theophilus made one more appearance on the stage, though precisely what he did is not known. For one night only at Covent Garden on 6 July 1758 *Madrigal and Truletta* was offered, with "Characters by Mr Cibber & Co."

Though most of Cibber's consorting with women seems to have been at bagnios, at some point he became acquainted with Margaret Pockrich, the wife of the inventor of, and virtuoso performer on, musical glasses. In October 1758 Cibber, Maddox the wire dancer, and other performers were engaged to perform in Dublin. Mrs Pockrich, by then presumably Theophilus's mistress, joined Cibber for the trip. Three sailors and 60 passengers boarded the *Dublin Trader* (the Digges-Ward correspondence called it the *Dublin Merchant*) and sailed from Parkgate on 27 October 1758. The ship struck a sand bar the same day,

and, according to the *Daily Advertiser*, some of the passengers, not liking the crowded conditions, abandoned ship. Not, apparently, Theophilus. The ship was driven north past the Isle of Man and sank with all hands off the Scottish coast, probably the same day, though perhaps the next.

In addition to the works already mentioned, Cibber may have had a hand in *The Beggar's Wedding* in 1731; the work came out in a Dublin edition in 1729 by Charles Coffey, and the work performed at Drury Lane in 1731 seems to have been either Cibber's adaptation of Coffey's work or a collaboration between the two. The *Lives of the Poets* (1753) ascribed to Cibber was mainly compiled by Robert Shields. *The Auction*, listed as Cibber's in Nicoll's *History of English Drama*, consists of scenes from Fielding's *The Historical Register*.

Portraits of Theophilus Cibber include:

1. Drawing by Thomas Worlidge, inscribed "Theophilus Cibber eldest son of Colley Cibber" and "Born 1703." In the collection of Robert Eddison.

2. Another drawing by Worlidge. In the collection of Robert Eddison.

3. A third drawing by Worlidge, probably of Cibber, though the subject looks very like Thomas Augustine Arne. In the collection of Robert Eddison.

4. A plumbago drawing on vellum by Worlidge, dated 1735. In the collection of Her Majesty the Queen.

5. A plumbago drawing by William Robins, showing Cibber with his father Colley and his sister Charlotte. In the collection of Her Majesty the Queen.

6. Engraving by Van der Gucht, showing Cibber writing at a table. Frontispiece to *An Epistle from Mr Theophilus Cibber to David Garrick*, 1756.

7. As the Fine Gentleman in *Lethe*. By R. Clamp after Worlidge.

8. As Flash in *Miss in Her Teens*, in a bravado fencing stance.

9. As Foppington (?) in *The Careless*

Husband. By I. Faber after P. Mercier. Published 1739.

10. As Hannibal, sitting in front of a booth in Goodman's Fields. Satirical print entitled "The Player's Last Refuge," 1735. The print also shows Cibber as Pistol being borne away on a bier.

11. As the Mock Doctor. Drawing, probably by Powell but perhaps by Hogarth.

12. As Nerestan in *Zara*. Engraved by Van der Gucht for the 1736 edition of the play.

13. As Nerestan (presumably) in *Zara*, with Mrs Cibber. Drawing in the collection of Robert Eddison.

14. As Pistol, leading his dissident players. Satirical print by John Laguerre entitled "The Stage Mutiny."

15. As Pistol. Satirical print of 1733 used as a frontispiece to *Theophilus Cibber, to David Garrick, Esq.; with Dissertations on Theatrical Subjects*, 1759.

16. As Pistol. Satirical print of 1733 in the Burney Collection of Theatrical Portraits.

Cibber, Mrs Theophilus the first, Jane, née Johnson   *1706–1733, actress, singer.*

Jane Johnson was born in 1706. She was undoubtedly the Miss Johnson who played Serina in *The Orphan* on 6 April 1723 at Drury Lane. On 24 January 1724 she was Hour in *The Loves of Mars and Venus* and probably played during the season other small parts not mentioned in the bills. In 1724–25 she was more frequently noted, playing Dol Mavis in *The Silent Woman*, Philadelphia in *The Amorous Widow*, Diana in *Virtue Betray'd*, Serina again, Belinda in *The Man of Mode*, Lucy in *Oroonoko*, and Galatea in *Acis and Galatea*. Once, on 9 January 1725, she was incorrectly billed as Mrs Johnson.

On 24 May 1725 at St Benet, Paul's Wharf, Jane married Theophilus Cibber. She was described in the register as a spin-

ster aged 19 from the parish of St Martin-in-the-Fields who was marrying with the consent of her guardian Richard Savage, her parents being dead.

As Mrs Cibber, Jane played a busy season at Drury Lane in 1725–26, acting such new roles as Margery in *The Country Wife*, Silvia in *The Double Gallant*, the first Constantia in *The Chances*, Lady Fanciful in *The Provok'd Wife*, Miss Notable in *The Lady's Last Stake*, Polyxena in *Hecuba*, and Flora in *She Wou'd and She Wou'd Not*. She shared a benefit with her husband on 15 April 1726, playing Belinda in *The Man of Mode*. The anonymous *Reflections upon Reflections* (1726) especially commended Mrs Cibber in *Hecuba*: "I can't help expressing the Satisfaction I receiv'd from the young Lady that plays *Polyxena*; she enters so justly into her Character, and feels so sensibly the Passions at parting from her Mother, that that tender Scene is really heighten'd by her manner of performing it." She seemed to the critic to be a young Barry, Bracegirdle, Oldfield, Porter, and Booth rolled into one—extravagant praise to a beginner, but certainly partly justified, as the rest of her career attests.

In 1726–27 she tried, among other new parts, Valeria in *The Rover*, Amelia in *The Comical Revenge*, Ismena in *Phaedra and Hippolitus*, Prue in *Love for Love*, and Melesinda in *Aureng-Zebe*. Thomas Davies later remembered how effective she was as Melesinda and spoke of her as a pleasing actress, in person agreeable and in private life unblemished—which was a great deal more than could be said for her profligate husband who, by his own later admission, treated her shabbily from the start.

Jane Cibber went on in 1727–28 to attempt Mrs Millicent in *The Feign'd Innocence*, Lucilla in *The Fair Penitent*, Monimia in *Mithridates*, Edward v in *Richard III*, and, for her shared benefit with Theophilus on 11 April 1728, Jenny in *The Provok'd Husband*, in which she sang a new ballad, "The Fine Lady's Life." The following season she added such parts as Hippolita in *The Tempest*, Ianthe in *Love is a Riddle*, Angelina in *Love Makes a Man*, Martha in *The Scornful Lady*, Sylvia in *The Old Bachelor*, Dorinda in *The Stratagem*, Victoria in *The Fatal Marriage*, Hellena in *The Rover*, Lady Harriet in *The Funeral*, Clara in *The Lover's Opera*, and Aura in *The Country Lasses*.

She acted until early May in the 1729–30 season, playing most of her old roles and trying Selima in *Tamerlane*, Phillis in *The Conscious Lovers*, Cyndaria in *The Indian Emperor*, and Ariana in *She Wou'd If She Cou'd*. Her first child, Jane (or Jenny), was probably born in the summer of 1730, since Jenny was nearly 15 in September 1744. By 17 September 1730 Mrs Cibber was back at Drury Lane, offering during the season Isabella in *Wit Without Money*, the title role in *The Fair Quaker of Deal*, Colombine in *Cephalus and Procris*, the Epilogue ("Dress'd like a Petit Maître") to *Patie and Peggy*, Ianthe in *The Lover* (and the Epilogue, with Theophilus, whose play it was), Meriel in *The Jovial Crew*, and Isabinda in *The Busy Body*. She continued into the summer of 1731, playing two Marias: in *Don John* and in *The London Merchant*. Her 1731–32 season brought her such new parts as Rose in *The Recruiting Officer*, Lady Grace in *The Provok'd Husband*, Ethelinda in *Athenwold*, Clarissa (and the Epilogue) in *The Modish Couple*, Edging in *The Careless Husband*, Amanda in *The Relapse*, Lucia in *Cato*, and Charlo in *The Funeral*.

When Mrs Cibber began the 1732–33 season she was carrying another child, yet she acted a full schedule of her old parts in September, October, and November and even took the title role in a new play, *Caelia*, in December. On 14 December 1732 at Drury Lane Jane Cibber acted Angelina in *Love Makes a Man*, shortly after which she went into confinement. On 25 January 1733 she died in childbirth. She had, according to the *Daily Post*, been ill

for some time: "She was brought to bed about a week ago & appeared very much mended but her Fever returning violently carried her off. She is truly lamented by all who knew her, to whom her virtues in private life rendered her very amiable. Young Mr Cibber is very much indisposed." The *Craftsman* said her "Loss is no less regretted by the Stage than by all other Persons who had the Happiness of her Conversation."

Jane's employer at Drury Lane, John Highmore, was so callous as to complain in June 1733 that he had had to pay her whole salary though she had not acted the greater part of the winter—which was as incorrect as cruel. Theophilus Cibber countered in the public press with a lengthy letter concerning Highmore's management, which included the following comments about his late wife:

Mrs *Cibber*, to the Hazard of her Life, play'd the laborious Part of *CAELIA*, In the Perjured Lover, not a Month before Her Death: and in the last tender melancholy Conversation I had with her, she told me, she found her Spirits had made her venture to undertake more Fatigue in her Business than her Constitution was able to bear, and she was certain she could not recover it—'Tis too true, she did not. What her Merits were, as an Actress, the Good-nature of the Town has often declared, and her Merits, as a good Woman, I know, and shall ever heartily Regret the Loss of; under which Calamity my only Consolation is, she is past the painful Apprehension of seeing my Livelihood, and the Support of our Infants, dependant on the Humour and Caprice of some whom I have little Reason to confide in, as I shall endeavour to make appear. 'Tis also well known by the whole Company, Mrs *Cibber*, tho' in a very bad State of Health, big with Child, and near her Time, did attend her Business, both in Acting and Rehearsing, until the 15th of *December* last, when she play'd Angelina in *The Fop's Fortune* [*Love Makes a Man*], which was acted by HIS ROYAL HIGHNESS'S COMMAND. She was brought to Bed on the 18th of *Janu-*

ary following, and died on the 25th: So that Mrs *Cibber* (who always received, and had the sole Disposal of her own Salary) had Twenty Pounds from her Acting to her Death, a most especial Consideration, and worthy the Knowledge of the Publick.

The second child of Jane and Theophilus Cibber was Elizabeth (Betty), baptized at St Paul, Covent Garden, on 24 January 1733, the day before her mother died. Mrs Cibber was buried at the same church on 28 January. The declared desolation of Theophilus may have been sincere, though what is known of his character may raise doubts. He seems to have had in Jane an amiable wife who had given great promise in both comedy and tragedy, could handle parts in pantomimes, and was a determined worker and faithful spouse. It was not until 1 December 1738, however, when Theophilus was plagued with other problems and needed public sympathy, he announced that he would erect a monument to Jane's memory in the St Paul, Covent Garden, churchyard. And in his *A Serio-Comic Apology* Theophilus wallowed in remorse: "My dear, dear faithful Wife—I might have been Happy! possessed of a Treasure I knew not the real Value of, 'till it was snatch'd for ever from me. Yet I wrong'd this Angelic Woman! threw all my Hours away in sullied dear purchased Pleasures . . ."

Cibber, Mrs Theophilus the second, Susanna Maria, née Arne *1714–1766, actress, singer, playwright.*

Susanna Maria Arne was baptized at St Paul, Covent Garden, on 28 February 1714, the daughter of Thomas and Anne Arne. Thomas Arne was an upholsterer at No 34, King Street, and had earlier been a numberer at the Drury Lane Theatre. He had married Anne Wheeler, his second wife, in 1707 and by her had had a daughter Elizabeth who had died in infancy in 1708, a son Thomas Augustine who was born in 1710

and who became one of England's most important musicians, and a daughter Sarah who died in infancy in 1712. After Susanna Maria, came Anne, who died in infancy in 1715, a second Anne, who died in infancy in 1716, and Richard, who was born in 1719. Though never wealthy, the Arnes managed to give their children good educations, and they fostered the musical talent of Thomas Augustine and Susanna Maria. A full discussion of the Arne family history may be found in Thomas Arne's entry in this dictionary.

The *European Magazine* later claimed that Miss Arne's introduction to the world of the theatre was as Tom Thumb in *The Opera of Operas*, when she was 14, a venture to which her talented brother contributed the music. But her first official notice came on 13 March 1732 when she sang the title role in Carey and Lampe's *Amelia* at the Haymarket Theatre. The performers had never appeared in public be-

National Portrait Gallery

SUSANNA MARIA CIBBER
ivory relief, artist unknown

fore, and they were ignored by the critics. The performance of *Amelia* on 24 March was for Miss Arne's benefit. On 17 May she attempted her second role at the Haymarket, Galatea in the production of Handel's *Acis and Galatea* pirated by her father and brother.

In 1732–33 she turned up at Lincoln's Inn Fields to sing the title roles in *Teraminta* on 20 November 1732 and her brother's *Rosamond* on 7 March 1733. On 17 March she sang in *Deborah* at the King's Theatre in the Haymarket. Susanna Maria joined Theophilus Cibber's rebel players at the Haymarket Theatre in the fall of 1733 and there offered *entr'acte* songs ("Rise Glory Rise" accompanied by French horns was one, on 6 October), played Venus in *The Impromptu Revel Masque* (later retitled *The Festival*), sang Dido in *Dido and Aeneas*, and was the Princess in *The Opera of Operas*. After Cibber's group returned to Drury Lane in the spring of 1734 she was Venus in *Love and Glory* (*Britannia*) and Psyche in *Cupid and Psyche*, and she also presented specialty songs. On 28 March she was granted a benefit, and on the following 5 April she made her first recorded appearance at Hickford's Music Room. Though she did not perform often during her first two seasons, she started at the top, singing title roles and receiving solo benefits, and it is apparent that her talent was immediately recognized.

Theophilus Cibber, the scapegrace son of Colley, and a widower since January 1733, was one of those who admired the petite Miss Arne's talent, and on 21 April 1734 he married her, probably at a Catholic embassy chapel. As Mrs Cibber, Susanna Maria sang at Drury Lane in April and May, taking the role of Venus in *Britannia*, offering "Quanto dolce, quanto care" and "Amelia wishes when she dies" as solos between the acts, singing "A teneri affeti" with Mrs Barbier, and appearing as a singer in *The Conscious Lovers*.

Though Colley Cibber had opposed the marriage of his son and Miss Arne (because she had little money) he was won over by her talent. In testimony offered in 1738 he said:

MR CIBBER.   When they married she was a singer, but there were better voices. I thought her voice not the best; and if not the best, 'tis nothing. I thought it might possibly do better for speaking. I asked her husband if he had ever heard her attempt to speak a part; he said he had and that she did it very prettily. I tried her and was much surprised to find her do it so very well.

QUESTION.   Did not the husband take pains to instruct her?

MR CIBBER.   I believe I was the person who chiefly instructed her; I spent a good deal of time and took great delight in it, for she was very capable of receiving instruction. In forty years' experience that I have known the stage, I never knew a woman at the beginning so capable of the business or improve so fast.

Colley's arrogation of the whole credit for Susanna Maria's success is doubly dubious considering the disastrous effects his teaching later had upon his granddaughter Jenny. It is clear that Susanna Maria was a born actress who had the advantage of the stronge discipline of musical training as well.

Perhaps it was during the 1734–35 season, when she appeared infrequently at Drury Lane, that she came under Cibber's tutelage. At the theatre she was billed as playing Psyche again, sang "Was ever Nymph like Rosamond," and was a Spirit in *Merlin*. But she was also pregnant at the time, and her season was cut short by the birth and loss of her first child, Susanna. The baby was buried at St Paul, Covent Garden, on 14 February 1735. Despite the rarity of her appearances at Drury Lane and the brevity of her season, she was apparently receiving a salary of £100 plus a benefit; the *European Magazine* later reported that Mrs Cibber was paid that sum in her first season, was raised to £200 for her second and third seasons, and afterward demanded a salary equal to any other woman in the company plus the first benefit, (which the manager, Fleetwood, refused to give her, and so she resigned).

Mrs Cibber's first appearance in the 1735–36 season was on 12 November, when she played Chloe, Kitty Clive's old part, in *The Lottery*. But greater things were in store for her. On 12 January 1736 she made her debut as a dramatic actress, playing the title role in Aaron Hill's *Zara*, with her husband as Nerestan. Colley Cibber blessed the occasion by writing and speaking a prologue begging the indulgence of the audience toward the novice. But the helping hand was not needed, for the prompter Chetwood wrote that she played Zara "to the Admiration of every Spectator that had their auricular Faculties" and proved herself "the Daughter of Nature in Perfection." The *Daily Journal* of 27 January said she had, "during the run of Zara, shewn her natural Genius by never in any one Night varying in either Tone of Voice or Action from the Way she was taught." Her instructor in this instance, according to Elizabeth Inchbald in *The British Theatre*, was the author Hill, who "received abundant praise for having encouraged Mrs. Cibber's attempt of this part: for having instructed her in it, and even foretold her extraordinary success . . ." (But Hill also instructed the anonymous "Gentleman" who played Osman in *Zara*—Hill's nephew, said the *Gentleman's Magazine*—and he was so bad he was replaced by Mills from 19 January onward.) The play ran 15 consecutive nights, however, and perhaps part of the attraction was a striking gown Susanna Maria wore (her wedding dress, altered to make it more sumptuous), which, according to a drawing in the Robert Eddison collection, had an exceptionally low neckline.

Drury Lane brought her out as Indiana in *The Conscious Lovers* on 9 February

1736, Amanda in *Love's Last Shift* on 13 March, and Andromache in *The Distrest Mother* on 23 March. How she managed to keep acting deep into March is a wonder, for she was pregnant again, and a distressed mother she was to be once more. On her benefit night on 13 April she advertised from her house in Great Queen Street that her condition prevented her from performing as planned in *The Conscious Lovers*. On 6 April the *Daily Post* said, "We hear Mrs Cibber wife of Mr T Cibber, Comedian, was yesterday safely delivered of a son." The child, named Caius Gabriel, after Colley Cibber's father, was buried at St Paul, Covent Garden, on 17 April. Despite the tragic loss of her second child, Mrs Cibber was back on the boards in the summer of 1736 playing Indiana on 26 August.

Though Theophilus Cibber apparently had a Bottom-compulsion to play everything and anything, his wife systematically built up a relatively small repertory which in time included virtually all the great tragic roles written for women in the English dramatic canon. She took occasional roles in comedy, though her talent was best suited for tragedy, especially those roles in which pathos dominated. Her voice, originally soprano, mellowed in time to contralto and never lost its musical quality. Though she continued singing to the end of her career, in acting she had found her métier. It is not surprising to find that, in 1736–37, she added to her repertory Desdemona in *Othello*, Statira in *The Rival Queens*, Eudocia in *The Siege of Damascus*, Isabella in *Measure for Measure*, and Monimia in *The Orphan*.

Writing in *The Actor* in 1750, Hill said it was impossible to describe the "manner in which Mrs. Cibber engages our affection, our tears, in the character of Monimia (in which she seems inspir'd with the very genius of the author who wrote the part, and with the very soul of the heroine whom she represents)." Mrs Cibber's reliance on a handkerchief as a tragic prop, however, bothered some critics. Samuel Foote, who found her Monimia extremely moving, wrote in *The Roman and English Comedy Considered*, in 1747:

Though it may perhaps be deemed hypercritical to observe on trifling Faults, where there are so many glaring Beauties, yet as these Trifles are easily mended, and are, besides, apparent to the most superficial Spectator, I hope I shall have Mrs *Cibber's* Pardon, if I desire her (unless she has an absolute Occasion for it) to put the Handkerchief in her Pocket: And if she would not shake her Head quite so much, and pat her Hands together quite so often, she would infinitely oblige me, and many more of her Admirers.

A Guide to the Stage in 1751, dubbing Mrs Cibber "Monimia," indicated that she had not paid much attention to her critics:

Monimia, taught by nature to lay every tumultuous passion, has the skill to attack the heart in the milder forms of pity, grief, and distress. But are these ever inexpressible without the handkerchief? Must we then always veil the face of Sorrow? I am apt to think that in other particulars, as well as this, Monimia relies so much on an establish'd reputation, as to neglect the most effectual arts she is mistress of to gratify her audience.

The Drury Lane manager, Fleetwood, cast Mrs Cibber as Polly in *The Beggar's Opera* and put the work into rehearsal in early November 1736. The role had belonged to Kitty Clive, who naturally objected to being relegated to the role of Lucy. Rumors had been circulating in the town as early as the previous 27 January that because of Mrs Cibber's triumph as Zara she would be brought on as Polly. As it turned out, when *The Beggar's Opera* was presented on 31 December, Mrs Clive had her old part back. All this might have occurred without creating a disturbance, but Fleetwood was something of a theatrical blockhead, Kitty Clive was not a good one to cross, Theophilus Cibber was spoiling for

a scrap, and the London papers would not keep quiet.

The dissension in the ranks at Drury Lane over the casting was commented on in the *Daily Gazette* on 4 November 1736; the writer spoke of "that Self-conceit and Vanity, that inward Consciousness of their own Abilities, which makes Actors contest parts in Plays with each other," and that journal made it clear that Polly belonged to Mrs Clive and that no one had the right to take the role from her. The *Grub Street Journal* on 25 November argued that the town should not have one of its favorite shows put off and urged giving Mrs Cibber a chance to try Polly. Not to be kept quiet, Theophilus Cibber broke into print in the same paper on 9 December in his usual stormy fashion, declaring that it was "a *dispute* between Mrs. Clive's *Will* and the MANAGER'S *Right*."

Over at Lincoln's Inn Fields Henry Giffard's troupe whipped up a piece called *The Beggar's Pantomime* and performed it on 7 December while the topic was still hot. The prologue, set to the tune of *Chevy Chase*, went:

Cibber, *The Syren of the Stage,*
 A Vow to Heav'n did make,
Full Twenty Nights in Polly's *Part,*
 She'd make the Play-house shake.

When as these Tidings came to Clive,
 Fierce Amazonian Dame;
Who is it thus, in Rage she cries,
 Dares rob me of my Claim.

I, who have charm'd the Pit so low,
 And eke the Gallery high,
Shall I be rivall'd thus? Ye Gods!
 O rather let me die.

With that she to the Green-Room flew,
 Where Cibber *meek she found;*
And sure if Friends had not been by,
 She had fell'd her to the Ground.

O had these Rival Nymphs engag'd,
 How scratch'd had been each Face;
What Slaughter there had been to see
 Of Silks, and eke Bone-Lace.

From the Collection of Mr and Mrs Paul Mellon

SUSANNA MARIA CIBBER, as Cordelia

by Van Bleeck

The spouses of the actresses got into the fray, according to the prologue, but the manager settled things by casting Kitty as Polly and Mrs Cibber as Lucy.

> *O heavy news then* Pistol [Theophilus]
> *cry'd,*
> *With that he wept full sore;*
> *O heavy News his Wife reply'd*
> *Then fainted on the Floor.*

> *God save the King, and bless the Land*
> *With Plenty, Joy, and Peace,*

> *And grant henceforth that foul Debates,*
> *'Twixt Actresses may cease.*

The farce then went on to satirize Fleetwood, Cibber, Mrs Cibber, and Mrs Clive in a similar fashion.

On 1 September 1737, when the next season began, the play had to be changed from *Cato* to *The Orphan* because Mrs Cibber was not ready in her role of Marcia. On 17 September she refused to appear as Ophelia in *Hamlet.* On 6 October, according to a British Museum manuscript, there was "A Quarrel betwixt Mr Quin and Mrs Cibber about dressing in ye Green Room." It was a bad start, though Susanna Maria finally did play Marcia and also appeared as Arpasia in *Tamerlane*, Belvidera in *Venice Preserv'd*, the Lady in *Comus*, Cleopatra in *All for Love*, Loveit in *The Man of Mode*, and Cassandra in *Agamemnon*. Of her Belvidera, Samuel Derrick wrote in *The Dramatic Censor* in 1752 that Mrs Cibber was the "*best* actress in her cast of playing I *ever* saw." "I dare say, Mrs. CIBBER in her *performance* of BEL-VIDERA, would have shewn Mr. OTWAY, were he now living, some beauties in it, which he could scarcely have *imagined* an *actress* capable of delivering to an *audience* . . ." Derrick said "the harmony of her *voice* joined to her vast skill in *music* has often *charmed* the *age*." But in 1737–38 it was a wonder she was able to get through any of her roles with equanimity, and she had good reason for being testy at the opening of the season.

Theophilus Cibber had, apparently from the beginning of his second marriage, paid

Permission of the Manchester Art Galleries, Thomas Greg Collection

SUSANNA MARIA CIBBER, as Monimia, on a delftware tile

after Thornthwaite

little attention to his vows. He was noted for carousing at bagnios; he had a reputation for being constantly in debt; and he fleeced his wife of practically everything she had—clothes, linen, half her salary, and a £50 gift Fleetwood had given her after *Zara*. Cibber's most outrageous act, however, was virtually selling his wife to a well-to-do friend, William Sloper, and then suing for adultery.

Sloper had become acquainted with the Cibbers in 1736–37, had loaned money to Theophilus, had visited the couple at their country home in Kingston, and had developed a fondness for Susanna Maria. Theophilus frequently contrived to leave the pair together, but they apparently did nothing censurable until Cibber threatened his wife at gunpoint and insisted she stay with Sloper. By the end of 1737 an affair between Sloper and Mrs Cibber was in full bloom; and the pair, in December, arranged meetings in a lodging house in Blue Cross Street which Cibber's maid, Anne Hopson, rented for their amours. Mrs Hopson made herself scarce whenever the couple came to use her lodgings "to converse together," as Anne said at the trial a year later.

The owners of the lodging house, Mr and Mrs Hayes, had somewhat different notions about the visits of Mrs Cibber and Sloper. Mrs Hayes did not approve of what she saw going on and later testified,

One Day after I gave Warning, Mr *Sloper* was in a great Passion above Stairs at something, and Mrs *Hopson* came to me, *You have made a fine Kettle of Fish of it,* says she. I did not know what she meant by her Kettle of Fish. *What Fish do you mean?* says I. *Why there,* says she, *you have been talking of Matters, and he's stark mad at it above Stairs.*

Mr Hayes, on the other hand, was playing peeping Tom. He had a closet adjoining the room in which Mrs Cibber and Sloper had their conversations.

I bored Holes through the Wainscoat an could see them very plain. He used to kiss her, and take her on his Lap. On the 22d Day of *December* [1738] I was looking through; he took her on his knee, lifted her Clothes, and took down his Breeches, and took his privy Member and put it in his Hand, and put it between her Legs.

On 12 January Mr Hayes put in quite a day in his little closet, since Mrs Cibber was delayed in her arrival; he was apparently immured from one o'clock in the afternoon to five or six in the evening. The *voyeur* would have told the court more of what he observed, but the trial judge said, "*there is no occasion to be more particular; we are not trying a Rape.*" Mr Hayes was a foreigner, later reports said, and "express'd himself as much by Gestures, as by Words." He was convinced that criminal conversation had taken place, and so was the court.

Mrs Hayes brought her husband's spying to an end by renting the rooms to another party. By the spring of 1738 Mrs Cibber was staying at Mr Carter's, a gardener in Church Lane, Islington, where she received from her husband, who had fled to France to avoid his creditors, extravagant letters declaring his undying love for her. By the time Theophilus returned in the summer, Sloper and Mrs Cibber were carrying on their affair at her house in Kensington, where Cibber finally settled. Then all three took a house at Burnham. There Mrs Cibber was escorted nightly from Cibber's master bedroom to Sloper's adjoining room, and Theophilus would hand her to her lover, go to bed alone, and rouse the pair the next day for breakfast.

A divorce was discussed by the three, though Mrs Cibber's religion would have prevented her marrying Sloper. Cibber claimed, at first, that he had no interest in a financial settlement, but he later changed his mind, and when he found that Sloper was becoming reluctant to lend him any more money, he decided to play the righteous husband and retrieve his wife. With the help of three henchmen he surprised Sloper and Mrs Cibber at tea (she in her

nightgown) and forced his wife into a carriage for a trip back to London. Sloper caught up with the kidnappers at an inn in Slough where he shot off a gun in the air, Theophilus shot off his mouth, and Mrs Cibber announced that she was pregnant. That quieted the men down; Sloper left in the middle of the night, and Theophilus arranged for a woman to stay with his wife while he sat up all night by the fire, contemplating, perhaps, his next mad move.

When Cibber got his wife back to London he put her under guard in his house in Wild Court, Great Wild Street. The guard was Mr Stint, a candlesnuffer from the theatre, who later testified:

Mr *Cibber* employed me to take care of his Wife when he brought her to Town, that she might not be taken away again, and he used her, and provided for her very honourably, and gave Orders at the Tavern, the *Bull-head*, near *Clare-Market*, that she should want for nothing; Meat was dressed there for her, and brought to her, and Wine, a Pint of White and a Pint of Red. She complained it was cold Weather, and I made her a Fire, and locked her up in the Room, but she knocked and called, and begged for God's Sake I would let her out, or else she should be Stifled, for the Chimney Smoaked. So I let her out, and put out the Fire. Mr *Thomas Arne*, her Brother, came there, and he begged and prayed that I would let her go along with him; but I would not break my Trust, I could not do it: He came several times, and finding I would not do it, began to break open the House, and at the same time bid her cry out Murder; she cried out Murder, and I believe there was an hundred Mob assisting him to break open the House. I had a Case of Pistols, and laid my Back against the Door; but they were too strong for me, and took my Pistols out of each Hand, and held me fast by each Arm; and beat me severely, and tore all the Clothes off my Back, and took Mrs *Cibber* away with them.

This dramatic event took place, apparently, on 9 September 1738; a note in Griffin's diary at the British Museum reads: "Mrs

Cibber taken this night out of Wild Court
& he, [Theophilus] hiss'd [at the Theatre]."
Theophilus retaliated by having Thomas
Augustine Arne thrown into Bridewell,
and Mrs Cibber, back with Sloper, swore
the peace against her husband. The time
was ripe for Cibber's next move: he sued
Sloper for adultery and asked £5000 damages.

The trial was held on 5 December 1738,
and the details of the whole affair were
presented. Sergeant Eyre, Sloper's attorney,
argued that Mrs Cibber's susceptibility
partly derived from the fact that as an actress she was always playing scenes of high
passion and was thus affected by the loose
morals owned by characters in plays. Cato,
he noted, "had very free Notions of Love
and Matrimony; . . . he lent his Wife to
a Friend to breed out of her, and when they
had done, he took her back again, very well
contented." Since the last thing Mrs Cibber
wanted was to be taken back by Theophilus, it is perhaps as well that Sergeant
Eyre did not pursue that quaint line of
defense further.

But he did picture for the court the
defenseless position of actresses trained to
please audiences:

That Players are a people who act, and enter
into all manner of Characters; that their
Men and Women are made to fall in Love
with each other every Day, this Day with
one, Tomorrow with another; that this Practice in variety must give them an uncommon
Propensity to Love, without any Confinement of the Passion to a particular Subject;
that 'tis very likely this enters into their
common Course of Life. That their Women
learn all the Allurements that can engage
the Eye and Ear, and strike the Imagination
of young Gentlemen; they dress, chat, sing,
dance, and every way charm unguarded young
Gentlemen, who are not aware of any ill
Consequences.

After painting this erotic picture of the
lives of players, Eyre finally got to the
point: "if there was a Suspicion of any
thing amiss in the Acquaintance between

Harvard Theatre Collection

SUSANNA MARIA CIBBER
engraving by Marchand, after Hudson

Mr *Sloper* and Mrs *Cibber*, that the Plaintiff must thank himself for it; that the
Plaintiff had taken Pains to bring them
acquainted, to live under the same Roof,
and used to leave them together to improve
their Acquaintance . . ."

In the summation, the Solicitor General
urged "the ill Consequence of letting it pass
for a Law that Men might sell their Wives,
which would be the Consequence of giving
a Verdict for the Defendant." This comic-
opera trial, right down to the absurdities
uttered by the lawyers, was settled by the
jury in 30 minutes. They decided that
Sloper was guilty, but they also felt that
Cibber's behavior in the whole wretched
business was despicable, and instead of
awarding him the grand prize he hoped for,
gave him a booby prize of £10. Cibber
returned to the stage, where he was greeted
by catcalls and thrown vegetables, but Mrs
Cibber was more discreet and stayed in
seclusion with Sloper.

Cibber sued again in 1739, for £10,000, claiming that Sloper had deprived him of the money Mrs Cibber would have earned for him had Sloper not absconded with her. Cibber also said that Sloper had assaulted and beat Susanna Maria and continued to cohabit with her. On 4 December 1739 the second trial took place. It was easy to establish that the illicit relationship had continued, part of the evidence being the birth of Mrs Cibber's first child by Sloper, Maria Susanna (or, in other official sources, Susanna Maria) on 26 February 1739. This time the jury awarded Cibber £500 damages.

By December 1741 the ugly events of the past had been sufficiently forgotten by the public, and Mrs Cibber picked up the pieces of her stage career. She accepted an engagement in Dublin for £300 to act with Quin in *The Conscious Lovers* (her first appearance, on 12 December), *The Orphan, Comus, Measure for Measure, The Spanish Fryar,* and *The Fair Penitent.* She also sang in the *Messiah* on 13 April 1742, was probably a participant in Handel's other oratorios, and with Mrs Arne gave concerts of Thomas Augustine Arne's music on 21 and 28 July 1742. According to Burney, Handel "was very fond of Mrs Cibber, whose voice and manners had softened his severity for her want of musical knowledge." "He was despised," in the *Messiah*, was written for her, and Burney said it was never sung so touchingly by anyone else. Handel also transposed for her voice "He shall feed His flock," "Come unto Him," "If God be for us," and "How beautiful." Her voice, Burney said, was "a mere thread, and [her] knowledge of music inconsiderable; Yet, by a natural pathos, and perfect conception of the words, she often penetrated the heart, when others, with infinitely greater voice and skill, could only reach the ear."

Thomas Sheridan, the Dublin actor-manager, wrote of her in *British Education* in 1756:

What then must [the mighty force of oratorical expression] be, when conveyed to the heart with all the superadded powers and charms of musick? No person of sensibility, who has had the good fortune to hear Mrs Cibber sing in the oratorio of the Messiah, will find it very difficult to give credit to accounts of the most wonderful effects produced from so powerful an union. And yet it was not to any extraordinary powers of voice (whereof she has but a very moderate share) nor to a greater degree of skill in musick (wherein many of the Italians must be allowed to exceed her) that she owed her excellencies, but to expression only; her acknowledged superiority in which could proceed from nothing but skill in her profession.

The Festival of Wit (1806) told a story about the first Dublin performance of the *Messiah*: "A certain Bishop [Dr Patrick Delaney, supposedly] was so struck with the extreme sensibility of her manner, that he could not refrain from saying, loud enough to be heard by numbers round him: 'Woman! thy sins be forgiven thee!' "

After her Dublin triumph, Mrs Cibber returned to the London stage, joining the company at Covent Garden in the fall of 1742. She began her engagement on 22 September with Desdemona, revived a number of her other old roles, and added during the season Laetitia in *The Old Bachelor*, Lady Anne in *Richard III*, Lady Brute in *The Provok'd Wife*, Imoinda in *Oroonoko*, Margery Pinchwife in *The Country Wife*, and two parts she had played in Dublin, Elvira in *The Spanish Fryar* and Calista in *The Fair Penitent*. Her Calista did not satisfy Samuel Foote, who in 1747 wrote:

That Mrs. *Cibber* is now and then languid in the Part of *Calista* may, I am afraid, be attributed to the natural Weakness of her Constitution. The Character is of an unusual Length, and the Passions of Rage, Scorn, Grief, and Disappointment, so frequently and forcibly repeated, that it requires more than a common stock of Health and Spirits, to do equal Justice to the whole Part. I cannot presume, that Mrs. Cibber's Judgment is detective [*sic*]; nor is it less obvious, that she is happy in the possession of all the natural Powers required in this Character: To what then can we attribute the little Use she here makes of those Powers, but to the Consciousness of weak Lungs, and a bad Constitution.

Though his statement seems cruel, Foote was quite correct in his judgment of Mrs Cibber's physical condition; as the years went on she was plagued more and more frequently by illness. The strenuous roles she chose to play must have taken their toll.

At Covent Garden in 1742–43 Mrs Cibber sang in Handel's oratorios. She sang Micah in *Samson* and was the contralto soloist in the first London performance of the *Messiah*. Horace Walpole wrote to Horace Mann on 24 February 1743 about the *Samson* performance the day before; Handel, he said, had hired "all the goddesses from the farces [Kitty Clive] and the singers of *Roast Beef* [Reinhold] from between the acts at both theatres, with a man with one note in his voice [Beard], and a girl without ever a one [Mrs Cibber]; and so they sing and make brave hallelujahs." The *Messiah* was not the success in London that it had been in Dublin, and the performance of *Samson* was marred by thieves who filtered through the theatre (even into the royal box) and robbed the ladies of their jewels. Dean, in *Handel's Dramatic Oratorios and Masques*, guesses that Mrs Cibber probably sang in all of Handel's oratorios: in *Acis and Galatea*, possibly Ahasuerus in *Esther*, and possibly David in *Saul*—all in 1742. By her benefit on 14 March 1743 Mrs Cibber was resident (presumably with Sloper with whom she lived for the rest of her life), at Mr Salt's in Henrietta Street, Covent Garden.

Susanna Maria stayed away from the stage in 1743–44 but returned in 1744–45 to sing in oratorios at the King's Theatre in the Haymarket and to act at Drury Lane. She sang Jael in *Deborah* and Lichas

in *Hercules* and acted, in addition to several old roles, Constance in *King John*, Lady Townly in *The Provok'd Husband,* and Sigismunda in *Tancred and Sigismunda.* Davies found her Constance a perfect role, noting that when she made her exit on the line, "O Lord! my boy . . ." she gave "an emphatical scream of agony as will never be forgotten by those who heard it."

To avoid embarrassing encounters at the theatres, Mrs Cibber had arranged with the managers of both patent houses that they would not engage Theophilus to play when she was in the company. This elicited from "Mr Neither-side" in *The Impartial Examen* in 1744 the following:

Mr. *Cibber* (who never exacted unreasonable Salary) before the Season began, by several Letters to the Manager [presumably Fleetwood of Drury Lane], offer'd himself; so far from demanding a large Salary, he left the Terms wholly to the Manager: But the Manager did not even answer his Letters. Why did he not? because at that time he, (the Manager) was in Treaty with Mrs. *Cibber*; and truly she is so very nice, that she won't play on the same Stage with her Husband. So, if that Treaty did not go on, he [the manager] was sure of having the Husband at least; but Mrs. *Cibber* being something more *Novelle* than her Husband, would bring him, at least for one Year, the most Money: That little Cunning soon prevail'd on him, not only to sacrifice Mr. Cibber and his Children: but totally to hinder the Town the Pleasure of seeing these two excellent Performers playing together; for I conclude * Mrs. Cibber's Salary is too considerable an Income for her to live without, since she cannot draw any considerable Subsistence from her Husband, whose Circumstances according to his Management, or some other Reasons, may be very trifling: And by her affecting to play for her Benefit The FAIR PENITENT, &c. &c. nobody can be so ill-natur'd to imagine she has any other Resource than the Play-house.

*This lady's Salary, I am credibly inform'd, is 600 Guineas for playing three times a

Week only part of the Season with Mr. F[leetwood], besides a Benefit clear of Charges; and between 3 and 400*l*. more for singing about twenty times with Mr. H[andel]; so that her Income (without reckoning any Presents, or Gratuities, from any Particular Friends, for her Extraordinary Performances) may, by a moderate Computation, be reckon'd at 1200*l*. for less than six Months Labour; while her Husband (who made her an Actress) and his Daughters (her Children in Law) have yearly—o*l*. o*s*. o*d*.

The criticism seems not to have had much effect. But Fleetwood was soon replaced by James Lacy.

On 18 July 1745 Mrs Cibber wrote to David Garrick from Sloper's country place at Woodhay:

I have often heard that the only way to make a coward fight, is to make him believe you think he has courage; but when you say I have wit, or something better, I suspect you are trying if flattery will have the same effect in this light; but I am sorry to tell you it won't do. If I attempt anything in that style, I shall only be some degrees stupider; so that it is your interest to let me go on my old way; and if you are contented with my usual folly, you are welcome to my letters. . . .

I hear we are both to be turned out of Drury Lane Play-house, to breathe our faithful souls out where we please. But as Mr. Lacy suspects you are so great a favourite with the ladies that they will resent it, he has enlisted two swinging Irishmen of six feet high to silence that battery. As to me, I am to be brought to capitulate another way, and he is to send a certain hussar of our acquaintance [Cibber, apparently] to plunder me.

In this melancholy situation, what think you of setting up a strolling company? Had you given me timely notice of your going to Buxton, I am sure the landlord of the Hall Place would have lent us a barn, and with the advantage of your little wife's first appearance in the character of Lady Townley, I don't doubt but we could have picked up some odd pence: this might have given a great turn to affairs, and when Lacy found

we could get our bread without him, it might possibly have altered their terrifying revolutions.

Garrick mentioned in a letter to Draper on 10 October 1745 that "Mrs Cibber writes me word, that she is turned out of Drury-Lane, and that the schemers intend to send Theophilus to her to force her compliance . . ."

She was not completely turned out. In 1745–46 Mrs Cibber played at both Drury Lane and Covent Garden, though she was not a permanent member of either company. On 14, 16, and 17 December 1745 at Covent Garden she played, at long last, Polly in *The Beggar's Opera* for the benefit of the Veteran's Scheme at Guildhall and made £602 7*s*. for that charity; and on 12 April 1746 she acted Monimia in *The Orphan* for her brother's benefit at Drury Lane. But the season was fraught with difficulties. Mrs Cibber had proposed *The Beggar's Opera* benefits to both patent houses, and John Rich at Covent Garden accepted the plan. On 9 December an anonymous letter in the *General Advertiser* called the benefits "a Jesuitical stroke of a Papist Actress in pursuit of Protestant Popularity," and he noted that Mrs Cibber's "whole Family are, in the strict sense of the phrase, Roman Catholicks" from whom "our Cause" needs no assistance. Mrs Cibber replied with a letter on 10 November admitting to having had a Catholic education, but claiming loyalty to the reigning royal family. On 11 December she wrote Garrick all about it:

The advertisements against me have been found to be sent to the printers by Mr. Lacy's porter, and, as I am assured, are the united works of Lacy, Macklin, and Giffard; so much wit, honesty, and good-nature can scarce be the product of a single person. The morning my first advertisement came out, I wrote Lacy a very civil letter, desiring to know if he consented to my proposal [for the benefits], repeating what I had advertised, and that I

begged an answer in writing if he agreed to
it; also that he would acquaint me with
the charge of his house, that I might lodge
the money in the treasurer's hands. He told
my servant he was too busy to send an answer;
but at half an hour after ten at night a dirty
fellow came to my house, and left word I
might do it, but it must be put off a day
longer than I proposed. I heard that night
that the green-room was in an uproar. I was
cursed with all the elegance of phrase that
reigns behind the scenes, and Mrs Clive
swore she would not play the part of Lucy.
The next morning Mr. Rich sent me an offer
of his house [Covent Garden], that he would
give the whole receipts to the Veteran
scheme, and that he should always esteem it
a great obligation done to him; that he had
sent to Mr. Cibber [who was in the com-
pany], who promised he would never come
near the house during the rehearsal or performances, and that Mr. Rich would answer
with his life he should keep his word; so I
concluded it the same day, which was Sunday.
The next morning came out the Advertisement of my being a rigid Roman Catholic
etc. The answer I made might have been
much better wrote, but I had nobody to con-
sult but myself . . .

The winter benefits, then, turned sour
even if they made money for the charity.
The spring benefit for Arne was marred by
Theophilus Cibber's transferring to Drury
Lane, a move that Mrs Cibber took to be an
attempt to ruin her brother's benefit. Typically, Theophilus took to the press to defend himself. On 10 April, two days
before Arne's benefit, he assured the public
that he had not come to Drury Lane "to
impede Mrs Cibber in her performance
there" and that his wife was most unfair
and ungrateful and made £700 yearly and
wouldn't bail him out of Fleet Prison where
he had languished for six months.

During the season Mrs Cibber kept up a
correspondence with Garrick, who was in
Dublin during part of the season, telling of
her problems in London, chatting playfully,
and talking business. On 24 October 1745

she wrote him from Craven Street saying
that Lacy probably would not be able to
come to terms with his actors at Drury
Lane and that she, Garrick, and Quin
should gather a troupe and play at the
Haymarket Theatre. She had already persuaded the impresario Heidegger to finance
the scheme, and suggested that the trio of
performers should act without salary and
give their profits to help enlist men in
St Martin's parish regiment to fight the
rebellion. Nothing came of that idea, but
she had another in mind.

On 9 November she began her letter
banteringly: "I had a thousand pretty
things to say to you, but you go to Ireland
without seeing me, and to stop my mouth
from complaining you artfully tell me I
am one of the number you don't care to
take leave of. And I tell you I am not to be
flammed in that manner." Then she went
on:

You assure me also that you want sadly
to make love to me; and I assure you, very
seriously, I will never engage upon the same
theatre again with you, without you make
more love to me than you did last year. I am
ashamed that the audience should see me
break the least rule of decency (even upon
the stage) for the wretched lovers I had last
winter. I desire you always to be my lover
upon the stage, and my friend off it.

I have given over all thoughts of playing
this season [she changed her mind a month
later]; nor is it in the power of Mr. Lacy,
with all his eloquence, to enlist me in his
ragged regiment. I should be very glad to
command a body of regular troops, but I
have no ambition to head the Drury Lane
Militia. What I wanted to speak to you about
was a letter, sent me a fortnight ago. The
purport of it was, supposing the remainder
of the [Drury Lane] Patent was to be sold,
would you [i.e., Mrs Cibber] and Mr. Garrick buy it, provided you got a promise of its
being renewed for ten or twenty years? As I
was desired to keep this a strict secret, I did
not care to trust it in a letter; but your going
to Ireland obliges me to it.

The possibility of joining with Garrick on the purchase of a part of the Drury Lane patent occupied her mind for over a year, but Garrick put her off, and the matter was apparently dropped.

Mrs Cibber thought of going to Ireland in 1746–47, though she confessed to Garrick on 26 February 1746 that she could not "muster up courage enough to think of crossing the sea." Instead, she joined the Covent Garden company under John Rich and acted with Garrick, Quin, and Mrs Pritchard—"the best company that perhaps ever was together," as Walpole said. She opened her season playing with Garrick in *The Orphan* on 11 November 1746. During the following months she revived several other old parts and added two significant new ones, Cordelia in *King Lear* on 4 December and Alicia in *Jane Shore* on 2 January 1747. Her Alicia was greatly praised. The *London Chronicle* said of her mad scene: "There is such a wildness of exertion in her powers, and such lively description in her countenance, as almost makes the audience afraid the roof is coming down, and still seems to shrink lower to avoid the beam which her distracted imagination makes her think is falling upon her." In *A General View of the Stage* (1759) Wilkes was quite carried away:

What variety and force of expression are in her Alicia. In the character she shews her unlimited genius, and gives the different passions their proper force. Rage and scorn are painted by her in the strongest light in the first scene of the second act . . . [and in] the last scene of the fourth, act [*sic*] how beautiful is her transition from rage to grief! . . .

When she finds the fatal effects her jealousy produced, she rises into all the extremities of rage, grief, and despair, which terminate in madness. The last scene is allowed to be her master-piece. Her face, her looks, every attitude, are strongly expressive of her inward conflicts.

Yet some critics found qualities in Mrs Cibber's readings of Rowe's lines defective. Cumberland in his *Memoirs* in 1806 must have been thinking of her Calista or her Alicia when he wrote that

Mrs. Cibber in a key, high-pitched but sweet withal, sung or rather recitatived Rowe's harmonious strain, something in the manner of the Improvisatories: it was so extremely wanting in contrast, that, though it did not wound the ear, it wearied it; when she had once recited two or three speeches, I could anticipate the manner of every succeeding one; it was like a long old legendary ballad of innumerable stanzas, every one of which is sung to the same tune, eternally chiming in the ear without variation or relief.

The difference of opinion may have been a matter of the individual taste of the critics or one of variations in Mrs Cibber's performances from one year to another, but, as will be seen, many critics found a sameness in her while others were struck by her variety.

On one point the critics seemed to agree: Mrs Cibber's ability to wring tears from an audience. "When Mrs. Cibber weeps," wrote Aaron Hill to Garrick on 20 January 1749, "who won't weep with her?" Samuel Foote, in *The Roman and English Comedy Considered* (1747), wrote:

This Lady, though by much the youngest Actress (I mean in point of Experience) on the Stage, has almost all her Time reign'd unrival'd in the Hearts of the People. There is a Delicacy in her Deportment, and a sensible Innocence in her Countenance, that never fails to prejudice the Spectator in her favour, even before she speaks. Nor does Mrs. *Cibber's* subsequent Behaviour eraze these first Impressions. Her Expressions of the Passion of Grief, surpass every thing of the sort I have seen. There is a melancholly Plaintiveness in her Voice, and such a Dejection of Countenance, (without Distortion,) that I defy any Man, who has the least Drop of the Milk of Human Nature about him, to sit out the dis-

Harvard Theatre Collection

SUSANNA MARIA CIBBER as Belvidera with DAVID GARRICK as Jaffeir
engraving by McArdell, after Zoffany

tresses of *Monimia* and *Belvidera*, when represented by this Lady, without giving the most
tender and affecting Testimonies of his Humanity.

Or, as Quin put it to Garrick (according to
Davies), "that woman has a heart, and can
do any thing where passion is required."
But such acting was a great strain on Mrs
Cibber's frail body and nerves; in 1746–
47 she was again ill, and her spring benefit
had to be postponed.

Garrick and Lacy bought the Drury Lane
patent, leaving Mrs Cibber out of the
negotiations, but they engaged her for the
1747–48 season, at a handsome annual
salary of £315, to play Belvidera, Desdemona, Cordelia, Arpasia, Indiana, Lady
Brute, the Lady in *Comus*, Monimia, Polly
(with Mrs Clive as Lucy), Alicia, Calista,
Andromache, and one new role: Fidelia in

The Foundling. The *Dramatic Censor* commented that "the softness and pathos, which
distinguished Fidelia sat with much ease on
Mrs Cibber." *The Orphan* that season must
have been something to see: Garrick as
Chamont, Spranger Barry as Castalio,
Dennis Delane as Polydore, and Mrs Cibber
as Monimia. The *Morning Chronicle* of
8–10 March 1757 (when Garrick and
Mrs Cibber were still playing in the work)
said, "They seemed to warm and animate
each other to such a Degree, that they were
both carried beyond themselves." If the
foursome of the 1747–48 season did the
same the results must have been stunning.

Mrs Cibber's 1748–49 Drury Lane season was marked by four important new
parts for her: Mrs Sullen in *The Stratagem*
on 11 November 1748, Juliet on 29
November (not noted as her first appearance in that character, but she seems

not to have played in *Romeo and Juliet* before), Aspasia in *Mahomet and Irene* on 6 February 1749, and Ophelia (finally) on 29 March. Of all her roles during her career, Juliet was perhaps her best. Hill in *The Actor* (1750) wrote:

What is the reason that no body ever play'd Juliet so well as Mrs. Cibber, but that Mrs. Cibber has a heart better form'd for tenderness than any other woman who ever attempted it; and perhaps, in real life, more deserves the name of a lover than any body of her sex ever did? It is easy to see that in all that tenderness Shakespear has put into the mouth of this favourite character, this actress is, as she delivers it, glorying in the opportunity of expressing her own sentiments in such elegant language; and 'tis for this reason that no body after her will ever be endur'd on the same stage in that passionate speech, where she tells Romeo from her window, Thou know'st the mask of night is on my face . . .

Henry Jones, the author of *The Earl of Essex*, wrote an effusive poem which was quoted in *The Present State of the Stage* (1753):

Amazement, Sorrow, Silence best can
    show,
What our Hearts feel for Juliet's des-
    p'rate Woe,
Oh! see she drinks, the Draught fore-
    stalls her Doom,
Distracted paints the Terrors of the
    Tomb;
She wakes, she wakes; here all Descrip-
    tion fails,
Words can't express what Pang the Soul
    assails.

And West Digges, writing to Mrs Ward on 16 July 1753, stated very simply: "Juliet cannot be played better." And perhaps she never has been.

Again Mrs Cibber became ill before the season ended. In early April 1749 she had to miss several performances, and she de-

cided not to act at all in 1749–50. On 4 October 1749 it was reported that she had left her house in New Street, Spring Garden, and had gone to Bath, where she lay so ill that her life was despaired of. The information was called false in the newspapers of the next day.

From 1750–51 through 1752–53 she acted under John Rich at Covent Garden. Her partner was often Spranger Barry, especially during the *Romeo and Juliet* "war" of 1750, and though they worked well together at times, Mrs Cibber seems not have had found him the kind of stage lover she preferred. William "Gentleman" Smith wrote to his friend Coutts of "the resplendent prowess of Barry and Mrs Cibber," yet on 12 October 1750 *Romeo and Juliet* was dropped from the Covent Garden schedule because Mrs Cibber vowed she would act Juliet no longer. She and Barry both refused to act on 7 December; Mrs Cibber was ill later that month and again in late February; and on 30 April 1751 she was reported "perfectly recovered" and ready to play Juliet that night; but she did not. In the summer of 1751 Rich sent her to France to recruit dancers. Garrick wrote to Draper on 17 August, "Have you not heard whether Cibber is engaged or not? — Is she gone to France for some time? — or what is the mystery of her leaving us at this time? — *Quere* — does she want to get rid of Barry, and takes this method of doing it delicately?"

But she was back at Covent Garden in the fall, and during the season played Lady Macbeth for the first time (17 March 1752) and at the same performance acted Cinthia in her own one-act entertainment *The Oracle*, which was published the next day. The masque was an adaptation of *L'Oracle* by St Foix and was reprinted in 1763 and 1778. She also added Athenais in *Theodosius* to her repertory and suffered her annual illness in the spring of the season. In 1752–53 she was seen as Rutland in *The Earl of Essex* and a number of her standard roles. And the critics were as taken with her as ever. *The Present State of the Stage* in 1753 was aglow:

'Tis not in Language to speak the Excellencies of Mrs. Cibber; there is something so affecting in her Look, so harmonious and plaintive in her Voice, that her Distress never fails to affect in the highest Degree. What unspeakable Tenderness and Rapture is there in her Belvidera and her Juliet? what Power, what Variety of Passion in her Alicia?

In 1753–54 Mrs Cibber returned to Drury Lane, and there she remained for the rest of her career. Her new roles over the years between then and the end of 1765 included Venusian in *Boadicea*, the title role in *Virginia*, the second Constantia in *The Chances*, Zaphira in *Barbarosso*, Perdita in *The Winter's Tale*, Thyra in *Athelstan*, Estifania in *Rule a Wife and Have a Wife*, Mrs Wilding in *The Gamester*, Evanthe in *Agis*, the title roles in *Isabella* and *Eurydice*, Amestris in *The Ambitious Step-Mother*, Lady Sadlife in *The Double Gallant*, Cornelia in *The Siege of Aquileia*, Widow Bellmour in *The Way to Keep Him*, Violante in *The Wonder*, Perdita in *Florizel and Perdita* (with a song in character), Celia (a girl of 16) in *The School for Lovers*, and the title role in *Elvira*.

During these seasons Mrs Cibber was frequently absent from the theatre, to the great distress of her managers, Garrick and Lacy. She was ill in late November and early December of 1755 and in April 1756 (she struggled through the first two acts of *Jane Shore* on 6 April, but could not finish the play, and by the end of the month she had left for Bath). By 17 December 1756 her illnesses had so often prevented her from playing that she refused to accept further salary payments. She was ill again in February 1758 and on 23 April she lost her son, her second child by William Sloper (Richard Cross wrote harshly in his diary on 25 April: "Mrs Cibber's son dy'd two

Days ago & she never came to play for Holland, Mrs Yates, or me [at our benefits] ye old Game at this season"). On 13 July 1759 Garrick wrote Dr Edward Barry that Mrs Cibber had attended only a third of her business the previous winter. She was ill in early March and part of April 1760; in 1760–61 she did not begin acting until the end of December when the season was well begun; in early March 1765 she was reported "sick nigh unto death"; and on 28 March 1765 she was reported dead, but the rumor was contradicted the next day.

Such recurrent absence from the theatre because of illness by any other actress might have been ascribed to temperament, and there was an element of the prima donna about Mrs Cibber certainly, but it is clear that she was, during the last 15 years of her life, in serious physical trouble which her doctor could not diagnose accurately. That she managed to act as much as she did, and to continuing critical approval, is most remarkable. On 7 April 1763 Archibald Dalziel wrote to his brother Andrew,

I am particularly charmed wi[th] *Mrs.* Cibber, but you must have known long ere now that her merit much exceeds anything I can say. What is amazing, tho' I am credibly informed she is about the age of sixty [she was 49], she can very well do the part of a girl of five and twenty. I know nobody here that could fill her place was she to die.

In 1759 Wilkes had written in *A General View of the Stage* that the loss of Mary Porter and Anne Oldfield was much lamented, but

since Mrs. Cibber's appearance, those fears are removed, and all the excellencies of each are revived in her. The great sensibility she has derived from nature, her exquisite art and judgment, directs her to give to every passion its full colouring and expressiveness, even beyond our idea. Would she charm us into the most affecting distress, with the woes of a Juliet, or Belvidera, then

Her looks——
Draw audience and attention still as
    night,
Or summer's noon-tide air.

MILTON

'till our hearts have catched the pleasing in-fection, and our eyes confess it in tears.

Were she to confine herself barely to such tender scenes as these, we could not even then sufficiently admire her; but how are we surprised at the wild exertion of her powers in the sudden transitions she makes from love and grief to the extremeties of rage and despair! and how different is her Juliet from her Alicia! and yet how justly does she feel in both, without exceeding the bounds of nature, or infringing upon female delicacy in either?

The musically plaintive tone of her voice gives a surprising softness to her love-char-acters; and her great skill in the passions never fails to direct her in the application of that, and her commanding features to be every way expressive of the poet's idea.

The writer was most impressed with the naturalness and tenderness of her Juliet, the artless grief of her Ophelia, the fresh strength and affecting melancholy of her Belvidera, and the maternal tenderness of her Andromache.

Churchill, in *The Rosciad* (1761), noted Mrs Cibber's deficiencies in comedy but, like others, he was swept away by her talent in tragedy:

*Form'd for the tragic scene, to grace the
    stage
With rival excellence of love and rage,
Mistress of each soft art, with matchless
    skill,
To turn and wind the passions as she
    will;
To melt the heart with sympathetic woe,
Awake the sigh and teach the tear to
    flow;
To put on Phrenzy's wild distracted glare
And freeze the soul with horror and de-
    spair.*

A talent like that, afflicted with frequent ailments of the flesh, was a constant prob-lem for Garrick and Lacy. In 1755–56 they had paid her a full-season salary of £700 and allowed her a benefit, yet she had been able to act only 13 times. The irritated Garrick complained in his journal that she had had "Every thing but ye garniture of her head found her by ye Managers." In 1756–57 she had honorably helped solve the managers' problem by refusing to accept any further salary on 17 December until "her health was estab-lish'd & she cou'd do her business as she ought." Yet the following 9 January 1757 she wrote to Garrick and Lacy:

Gentlemen:

. . . You will please to remember, Your Engagement with me for this Season was for seven hundred pounds, & the first Benefit clear of all Charges. Being call'd Upon to play the first of December, I was so ill, I was forced to refuse; but having recover'd My health will be ready to play the 17th of this Month, which will be near Seven Weeks from the time of my being taken ill. I am there-fore willing to deduct Seven Weeks out of my Salary, according to the number of weeks your House will play this Season. This Gentle-men is what I am ready to agree to, and that no time may be lost I beg your positive and immediate answer. Am I of your Company, or am I not . . . [?]

Davies in his *Life of Garrick* said that Mrs Cibber's physician misunderstood her ailments and treated her improperly. She had (he said) stomach worms, though the doctor diagnosed the case as bilious colic and forced her, much against her will, to bathe in sea water. The treatment over the years did little good, and Mrs Cibber's repeated relapses may well have frightened her into preparing a will many years before it would be needed. The will, written on 18 June 1757 (and proved by William Sloper on 15 February 1766), made it clear that Theophilus Cibber, by virtue of a deed of separation, was to have no control over his wife's estate, all of which she left to Sloper in trust for her two children, Charles and Maria Susanna. Charles died before his mother, and by 1766 Maria Susanna was of age and supposedly received her inheritance. (She married James Burton in 1767 and died on 2 July 1786.) William Sloper was made residuary legatee of Mrs Cibber's estate, which must have been of considerable value. (He died in 1789, leaving property in Southampton, Hampshire, and Wiltshire.)

In 1758–59 Garrick complained that Mrs Cibber had attended only a third of her business, to which she responded that her rehearsals counted toward her pay. The managers pointed out that they supported their property not by rehearsals but by performances. It is apparent that at this period the friendship between Garrick and Mrs Cibber had cooled considerably, and she was more his rival than his artistic partner. A revealing example of the antagonism that had developed concerned Joseph Reed's *Dido*, which was submitted to Garrick for consideration in 1760. Mrs Cibber, according to Reed, liked the script but told the author he would have to alter it to Garrick's taste and make the actor's part of Aeneas shine more brightly than Mrs Cibber's part of Dido. She said, "when Dido makes her appearance, I hope to humble the pride of the theatrical idol. I doubt not of gaining more applause in Dido than he can in Aneas." As it turned out, the work was not produced until after Mrs Cibber's death, but her interest in outshining Garrick may well have manifested itself on stage in other productions.

Mrs Cibber was adept at currying favor with the "quality" in her audiences, and the Drury Lane managers could hardly have been pleased with the following letter (signed CHURCHILLIUS) in *The Volunteer Manager* on 24 April 1763:

I went to Hamlet, on Easter Monday, and was never more astonished in my life, then at an action of Mrs. Cibber's. As that Lady sat upon the Stage, with Hamlet at her feet, in the third Act, she rose up three several times, and made as many courtesies, and those very low ones, to some ladies in the boxes. Pray, good Sir, ask her in what part of the Play it is Said, that the Danish Ophelia (for she was then Ophelia, and not Mrs. Cibber) is acquainted with so many British ladies?— but to be serious—Pray tell Mrs Cibber, that though her parading-it to the whole house, that she was honoured with the acquaintance of some persons of fashion, might be food for her pride, it was neither a proof of her understanding, nor a mark of her respect for the rest of the audience.

Perhaps Garrick can be excused for saying after her death that "she was the greatest female plague belonging to my house. I could easily parry the artless thrusts and despise the coarse language of some of my other heroines; but whatever was Cibber's object, a new part or a new dress, she was always sure to carry her point by the acuteness of her invective and the steadiness of her perseverance."

Critics were candid about her failings as an actress. *The Theatrical Review* of 1757–58 noted that

Nature had bestowed on her an agreeable figure, a bewitching voice, and above all, an exquisite feeling; all which she has improved to a prodigious degree, by her application and good sense; and could she but add to these charms, a more majestic gait, and a little variety in her tones, my notions of tragedy-acting could not reach beyond her; for although she cannot boast that particular justness of speaking, which consists in giving, by proper and well-chosen tones, the meaning of each word in the pronunciation, her feeling of the import of the speeches and situations, upon the whole is such, as throws a general justness on her delivery, and more than balances every trifling defect. It has been objected to her, that her action is not rich in descriptive gestures; but in return, when passions are to be expressed, then she speaks to the eye, as well as to the ear, and through both to the heart.

She seldom appears in comedy, which makes me imagine she lays but little stress on her talents in that branch; I will therefore so far make free with them, as to say, that her humour has never struck me; but as far as justness, decency, and an easy carriage will go, I know no actress who can claim the superiority; however, the public cannot encourage her too much in her attempts that way, since they are to reap the benefit of their indulgence, by the pleasure they will receive from her as a tragedian; which pleasure will grow incessantly in proportion as she improves as a comedian. The connexion between the sock and the buskin is much more intimate than people are aware of.

And, indeed, it is odd that the good humor of Mrs Cibber's letters seems not to have been part of her public or business personality.

Her correspondence with Garrick (some of it may have been lost to us) seems to have picked up again after Garrick's return from the Continent in the 1760s. "[Y]ou have actually starved us," she wrote him about August 1765 from Woodhay, "and prevented our having a morsel of venison the whole summer! for Mr. Sloper has positively declared he will not write for a buck unless you and sweet Mrs Garrick compensate him by your company . . ." In October she again urged Garrick to visit her: "My very parrot is the wonder of the time! equally excellent in the *sock* or *buskin*, and when you come, shall cut a joke, and tip you a tragedy stiffle that will make your very foretop stand on end."

Mrs Cibber's last full season was 1764–65, when, incidentally, Garrick was on the Continent. Absent from the stage in 1763–64, she came to Drury Lane in the fall of 1764 and embarked on a remarkable schedule. She opened with Monimia in *The Orphan* on 23 October. She acted Alicia in *Jane Shore* on 26 October, Belvidera in *Venice Preserv'd* on 31 October, Widow

Bellmour in *The Way to Keep Him* on 8 November, Calista in *The Fair Penitent* on 17 November, Andromache in *The Distrest Mother* on 8 December, Ophelia in *Hamlet* on 12 December, Violante in *The Wonder* on 13 December, Sigismunda in *Tancred and Sigismunda* on 19 December, Cordelia in *King Lear* on 2 January 1765, Indiana in *The Conscious Lovers* on 14 January, Lady Brute in *The Provok'd Wife* on 23 January, the title role in *Zara* on 6 February, and then, after an illness in March that produced false reports of her death, she repeated Andromache on 25 April for her benefit.

Mrs Cibber was paid, according to a

Harvard Theatre Collection

SUSANNA MARIA CIBBER, as Imoinda
artist unknown

Drury Lane salary schedule dated 9 February 1765, £15 weekly, the highest salary among the actresses and only 5s. 6d. less than Garrick and Lacy paid themselves. Kitty Clive complained to Garrick the following fall that he had paid Mrs Cibber £600 for playing 60 nights but had given Kitty only £300 for 180 nights.

Garrick was not sure whether he would have Mrs Cibber's services in 1765–66 or not. She wrote him on 15 November:

I still hold my resolution of being in town on the 30th, though my nerves are plaguy ones as well as yours! I have been ill these two or three days past, but I hope I am getting better. This cold damp weather plays the vengeance with my delicacy; and if it was not for the stage, I should wish, with Lady Townshend, that my nerves were made of cart-ropes.

Soon after that she wrote Garrick again, using an equestrian image to suggest that she would like to play *Venice Preserv'd* soon. Speaking of herself as Belvidera, her favorite mare, she said, "She is an old one, but I believe she will still beat the fillies, and she is sound, wind and limb, has never yet flung her rider, and will take care not to come in on the wrong side of the field." She did not play Belvidera after all. On 5 December 1765 she acted Lady Brute in *The Provok'd Wife* and on 13 December repeated it. She never appeared on the stage again. Susanna Maria Arne Cibber died at her house in Scotland Yard on 30 January 1766 and was buried in the North Cloister of Westminster Abbey on the following 6 February. On the day of her death, Drury Lane closed its doors to pay homage to the greatest of its actresses.

Though some critics had reservations about Mrs Cibber—lack of variety in her intonation, traces of the "old manner of singing and squeezing out their tragical notes," as Victor put it—most of them agreed with what Thomas Davies said in his *Life of Garrick*. She had

that simplicity which needed no ornament; . . . that sensibility which despised all art. There was in her countenance a small share of beauty; but nature had given her such symmetry of form and fine expression of feature, that she preserved all the appearance of youth long after she had reached to middle life. The harmony of her voice was as powerful as the animation of her look. In grief or tenderness her eyes looked as if they were in tears; in rage and despair they seemed to dart flashes of fire.

Upon hearing of her death, Garrick is reported to have said, "Then tragedy expired with her . . ."

The unreliable 1887 biography of Mrs Cibber by an anonymous author will soon be replaced by a new work, *Lady Brute*, by Mary Nash, who kindly provided helpful information for this entry.

Portraits of Mrs Cibber include:

1. Painting by Thomas Hudson. At the Garrick Club. Engraved by J. Faber, junior, J. Marchand, R. B. Parkes, and an anonymous engraver.

2. Painting by R. E. Pine. At the British Museum. Engraved by W. Humphrey.

3. Painting by Thomas Woollaston. In the Book Room at Stapleford Park, Melton Mowbray, Leicestershire.

4. Painting by William Hoare. At Cairnbulg Castle.

5. Painting by Orchard. Engraved by Fairn.

6. Painting by George Beare.

7. Painting by either Reynolds or Zoffany.

8. Plumbago drawing by Thomas Worlidge.

9. Ivory relief, artist unknown. At the National Portrait Gallery.

10. As Belvidera in *Venice Preserv'd*, with Garrick as Jaffeir. Painting by Zoffany at the Garrick Club; other versions in the Somerset Maugham and Earl of Durham collections. Engraved by J. McArdell in mezzotint.

11. As Cordelia in *King Lear*. Painting by Van Bleeck. In the collection of Mr and Mrs Paul Mellon. Engraved by Van Bleeck and by R. B. Parkes.

12. As Cordelia. Painting by Thomas Hudson.

13. As Imoinda in *Oroonoko*. Anonymously engraved for the *Lady's Magazine*.

14. As Monimia in *The Orphan*. Engraved by Thornthwaite for Bell's *British Theatre*, 1776.

15. As Monimia. Delftware tile, after Thornthwaite. In the City of Manchester Art Gallery.

16. As Zara. In the collection of Robert Eddison.

Ciceri, Charles [*fl. 1793–1800*], *scene painter, machinist.*

Almost all that is known of the earlier part of Charles Ciceri's life is in the narrative by his contemporary William Dunlap in his *History of the American Theatre*. Born at Milan, Ciceri was sent to live with his uncle at Paris at the age of seven, soon after the death of his father. At Paris he was taught "the rudiments of science" and some landscape drawing. Several times the boy attempted to run away from his uncle, who was very strict with him, and on one occasion, according to Dunlap, finding himself destitute in Flanders, young Charles begged his way back to Paris. Ciceri then served three months in a cavalry troop, until his friends purchased his discharge. At about the age of 17, he enlisted in a regiment which went to Cape François in Santo Domingo. There he supplemented his soldier's pay by acting as scene painter to the theatre. He "made himself sufficiently master of managing colours in *size*, and with his little knowledge of landscape, and greater proficiency in mathematics, he became invaluable." Within six months he earned enough money to buy a second discharge but remained with the theatre at S. Domingo for five years, accumulating "a little fortune." When S. Domingo became

unsafe—for reasons not explained by Dunlap—Ciceri returned to Paris, where he worked as an assistant scene painter. He was employed also at the theatre in Bordeaux.

The reign of terror drove Ciceri to London, where reportedly he was engaged at the King's Theatre as a machinist in the early 1790s. No record (save Dunlap's assertion) exists of Ciceri's theatrical employment in London. In 1793 Ciceri sailed back to S. Domingo, via Jamaica, and then set off for Philadelphia. A shipwreck off the Bahamas claimed all his property, and "after remaining seventeen days on a desert island," he was rescued by a fisherman who took him to Providence, Rhode Island. There for a while he earned his sustenance as a miniature painter—"though he never could draw a face that might not pass for an owl as [well as] a man"—and then left for Philadelphia, where he worked as an assistant to Charles Milbourne preparing scenery for the new Chestnut Street Theatre prior to its opening in 1793.

After a brief time with the Chestnut Street Theatre, Ciceri went to New York in the employ of Lewis Hallam and John Hodgkinson at the John Street Theatre. He is known to have designed the scenery there for *Tammany*, presented on 3 March 1794. These scenes, according to Dunlap, "were gaudy and unnatural, but had a brilliancy of colouring, reds and yellows being abundant." Ciceri continued with the New York company for six years as "a most valuable auxiliary to the *corps dramatique*, and a faithful friend" to Dunlap, for whose play *Fontainville Abbey* he had done the scenery. By 1798–99 his salary was about $60 per week. Retiring from the American theatre in 1800, and possessed of sufficient money to establish himself in trade, Ciceri went with a partner again to S. Domingo, "where Ciceri lost the goods, and the partner his head." Despite this setback, Ciceri managed to build up a trade between Paris and New York and eventually retired "with a competence to his native country."

Ciceri was always a fine machinist, and his talent at scene painting improved considerably with his experience in America. Edwin Duerr, in *Theatre Arts Monthly* (1932), credits him with making stage effects an important element of the theatre in America:

Ciceri, and his aides, often made use of the new transparent scenery, perfected in England by de Loutherbourg in 1780. From him, also, they had learned to build up their stages with scaffolding or carpentry for such elaborate spectacles that required practicable stairways, doors, windows, mountain passes, bridges. The New Yorkers probably experimented with dioramic, or moving scenery; and perhaps Dunlap and Ciceri knew side walls on their stage.

Although his quickness of temper and imperfect English often led to misunderstandings and tensions with fellow workers, Ciceri was, in the words of Dunlap, "a man of exemplary habits, active mind, quick discernment, fertile in resources, and firm in purpose."

Cieca, Signor *[fl. 1710], singer. See* CIECA, Io.

Cieca, Io *[fl. 1710–1711], singer.*
Signora Io Cieca and her husband were paid £215 by the manager Owen Swiney for singing in *L'Idaspe fedele* and *Pirro e Demetrio* at the Queen's Theatre in the Haymarket from 22 November to 22 December 1710. Their annual salary was £700. A receipt covering performances from 6 March through 2 May in Vice Chamberlain Coke's papers at Harvard makes no mention of Signor Cieca but gives Signora Cieca's first name as Io and lists payment to her of £193.

"Ciface," or "Ciffeccio." *See* "SIFACE."

Cimador, Giovanni Battista *1761–1805, violinist, pianist, composer, teacher.*
Giovanni Battista Cimador was born in 1761 at Venice where he taught music for some time. He was apparently of noble birth, and the *Theatre Almanach de Gotha* styled him "Count" Cimador. The Accademia dei Rinnovati at Venice performed his *Ati e Cibele* in 1789 and *Pimmalione* and *Il ratto di Proserpina* in 1790. About 1791 he settled at London as a teacher of singing. His pupils included William Knyvett and Sophia Corri Dussek. Haydn recorded in his diary for 2 August 1794 a visit to Bath with "Mr Cimandor, a young violin virtuoso and composer."

Cimador's *Ati e Cibele* was performed by Anna Morichelli for her benefit at the King's Theatre on 14 May 1795, when the piece was billed as "An Heroic Entertainment in one act, consisting of Songs and Dances with Chorusses, and never performed upon any public Stage, but composed for the private theatre of a Nobleman at Venice [in 1789]." On 8 June 1797 at the King's Theatre, Viganoni sang Cimador's interlude set piece, *Pimmalione*. When Cimador had composed the piece in 1790, he reportedly had been so dissatisfied that he "had burnt the score and renounced composition for the future." Fétis saw the manuscript score at the Paris Conservatoire Library and pronounced it a mediocre thing; yet it was published at London in 1797 by Corri, Dussek & Co. and proved to be very successful as a concert piece for both male and female singers well into the nineteenth century.

The only known public performance by Cimador was when he played the grand pianoforte in duet, with Mrs Dussek on the harp, at the end of the second part of the *Messiah* at Covent Garden on 7 March 1800.

According to van der Straeten, when the orchestra of the King's Theatre found the symphonies of Mozart too difficult to play,

Cimador arranged six of them for flutes and strings, but that music is not extant. He did compose accompaniments for several vocal numbers from Mozart's operas, which were published at London, along with several sets of duos for two violins and for violin and viola. A manuscript score of a concerto for double bass is at the British Museum.

In the early years of the nineteenth century, Cimador was associated with Monzani as music publisher in London. He died at Bath on 27 February 1805. Additional information on his continental career may be found in the *Enciclopedia dello spettacolo*.

Cimadori, Giovanni Andrea *d. c. 1684, actor.*

Giovanni Andrea Cimadori was born in Ferrara and became a *Commedia dell'arte zanni* with the character name of Finocchio. He served the Dukes of Mantua and Modena, played in Bologna about 1672 and Naples about 1674, and as a member of the Duke of Modena's troupe visited London in 1678–79. The company performed at court six times between November 1678 and mid-February 1679 but was not very successful. Cimadori died at Lione about 1684.

"Cinthio". *See* ROMAGNESI.

"Cintio." *See* COSTANTINI, GIOVANNI BATTISTA.

Ciocchi. *See* CIACCHI.

"Ciperini, Signor" *[fl. 1759], singer.*

A person called "Signor Ciperini" (probably a pseudonym) sang a duet entitled "the Humours of Bartholomew Fair," with one "Alley Croaker," on 3 September 1759 as part of the entertainment at Shuter's New Booth, George Inn Yard, West Smithfield, during Bartholomew Fair.

Ciprandi, Ercole *[fl. 1754–1791?], singer.*

The tenor Ercole Ciprandi was one of six singers in the opera company at the King's Theatre in the 1754–55 season. He sang Danaus in *L'Ipermestra* on 9 November. For the "Fund to Support Decay'd Musicians," benefitted at the King's Theatre on 17 March 1755, he sang a solo. Very likely he also sang leading parts in the operas *Penelope, Siroe, Ricimero,* and *Ezio,* for which no casts are listed.

He was on the roster at the opera for the next season, 1755–56, also, but no casts were presented in the bill. It is nevertheless probable that he sang Danaus in *L'Ipermestra* and roles in *Andromaca, Ezio, Demofoonte, L'Olimpiade, Ricimero, Tito Manlio,* and *Siroe.*

Ciprandi's name was not found in the company lists and bills of the King's Theatre in the Haymarket from 1755–56 until the 1765–66 season. The assertion of the *Dictionary of Musicians* of 1824 that this "good Italian tenor singer . . . sang at the opera in London from 1755 to 1765" appears to be in error. Nor does he seem to have been elsewhere in the British Isles during these years.

Ciprandi returned to the London opera in 1764–65 in an expanded company whose great attraction was the *castrato* Giovanni Manzola. Ciprandi sang Massimo in *Ezio,* which opened the season on 24 November. It was greatly patronized by the fashionable. Burney said that he waited two hours to get his seat for the performance. *Ezio* was repeated 17 times that season.

Ciprandi also sang Osroa in *Adriano in Syria,* Antigono in *Antigono,* and was probably seen in *Il re pastore, Demofoonte, L'Olimpiade, Berenice,* and *Solimano.* He perhaps figured in Handel's oratorio *Israel in Babylon* for the musicians' benefit on 25 January 1765. He was briefly in Paris during 1765, singing at the Opéra. The Duchess of Northumberland judged him in her diary "a most exceeding good tenor," and Burney, in his *History,* praised his "taste and feeling."

In 1765–66 he was named to a company collected at London's opera house by

Gordon, Crawford, and Vincent which included the fine soprano Angiola Calori, Colomba Mattei, Ferdinando Tenducci, and others. He was commended for his acting as well as his singing in a puff by "Musidorus" in the *Public Advertiser*, but what he sang cannot be determined. He was not listed in the 1765 edition of *La clemenza di Tito*, and the other six operas—*Eumene, Sofonisba, Artaserse, Demofoonte, L'eroe Cinese*, and *Pelopida*—either have incomplete cast lists or lack them altogether. He sang several tunes at the musicians' benefit concert on 10 April 1766. After May of that year his name disappeared finally from London. Burney praised his singing at Milan in 1770. Grove places his death date tentatively "after 1790."

Cipriani, Giovanni Battista 1727–1785, *scene painter, historical painter, engraver.*

Giovanni Battista Cipriani, son of a family from Pistoia, was born in 1727 at Florence, where he received early instruction from the English painter Ignazio Hugford and then from Antonio Gabbiani. His earliest public works were two pictures, representing St Tesauro and St Gregory IV, respectively, for the Abbey of St Michael-on-the-Sea at Pelago. Cipriani lived in Rome from 1750, and there developed friendships with Sir William Chambers the architect and Joseph Wilton the sculptor, with whom he went to London upon their return in 1755.

In 1758, Cipriani took up the management of the department of drawing at the school of design opened by the Duke of Richmond in his gallery in the Privy Garden, Whitehall, but the venture shortly ended. In 1763 he was listed by *Mortimer's London Directory* as a history painter and a member of the Imperial Academy of Polite Arts at Florence and as living at the house of Mr Burgess, a carpenter, in Warwick Street, Golden Square.

After being elected a member of St Martin's Lane Academy, Cipriani was named in

Harvard Theatre Collection

GIOVANNI B. CIPRIANI
engraving by Bovi, after Bartolozzi

1768 by George III as one of the founding members of the Royal Academy, where he exhibited regularly between 1769 and 1783. He designed the diploma of the Academy, engraved by Francesco Bartolozzi, and in 1769 was presented with a silver cup—stolen from his son's home on 25 February 1795—in acknowledgment of "the assistance the academy has received from his great abilities in his profession." The original drawing for the diploma plate, presented by his eldest son to the Marquis of Lansdowne, was owned by George Baker in 1806. Not a particularly successful painter of pictures in oil, of which he executed only a few, his reputation was achieved mainly from his pen-and-ink drawings, sometimes colored, done for publishers and mostly engraved by Bartolozzi.

With Dall, Cipriani painted scenes for *The Fairy Prince*, presented at Covent Garden on 12 November 1771. To this was added *The Installation of the Knights of*

Courtesy of Mr Robert Eddison

Design for stage frontispiece, Covent Garden Theatre, 1777
by G. B. CIPRIANI

the Garter, a spectacle which included settings of the exterior and interior of St George's Hall and views of Windsor Park and Castle. (The scene for St George's Hall was used, after Cipriani's death, for a new afterpiece, *Windsor Castle*, at Covent Garden on 6 April 1795.) Several months later (on 20 January 1772) Covent Garden presented *The Fairy Prince* with an additional scene by Cipriani of "the taking of the Bohemian Standard at the Battle of Cressy," which the *Theatrical Review* thought "pleasingly executed," with a "very good effect." (The scene was employed again at Covent Garden for *Phusimimesis* on 7 May 1781.) For his work at Covent Garden in 1771–72 Cipriani was paid £63 on 4 January 1772 and £42 on 1 December 1772.

In the summer of 1777 he planned the redecorating of Covent Garden Theatre and with assistants repainted the entire ceiling, which was described by the *Westminster Magazine* (September 1770) as a representation of Apollo being crowned by Mercury after his victory over Marsyas: "He is attended by three principal Muses, Clio, Calliope, and Euterpe: and beneath is the Genius of Reward offering the laurel to superior merit." He also painted a new proscenium frame depicting Tragedy and Comedy "in characteristic attitudes, whilst their attending Genii are adorning it with festoons of flowers: beneath the Tragic Muse are two emblematic figures representing the consequences of the tragic passions: Thalia is accompanied by a group descriptive of the purposes and effects of Comedy." This decoration of the proscenium drew criticism for interfering with the illusion of the stage scenery behind it. (The original frontispiece drawing, reproduced in Ifan Kyrle Fletcher's "Sales Catalogue No. 207"

A. Carlini, F. Bartolozzi, and GIOVANNI B. CIPRIANI
engraving by Smith

[1963], is now in the possession of Robert Eddison of London.) Cipriani was paid £50 for the redecorating on 26 August 1777.

With Carver, Hodgins, and Richards, he contributed scenes to *The Mirrour, or, Harlequin Everywhere* at Covent Garden on 30 November 1779. The scene of Tartarus, as exhibited in the Pantheon and engraved from a drawing taken on the spot, was published in *London Magazine*, February 1780, as a "wonderful fine painting." On 26 December 1781 he worked with Carver, Catton, Hodgins, and Richards on Messink's new pantomime *The Choice of Harlequin*, which concluded with "an exact Representation of the Procession at an Eastern Marriage" and was repeated regularly in 1782–83 and 1783–84.

Cipriani lived for many years at Royal Mews Gate, Hedge Lane, near Charing Cross, but later in life he moved to Hammersmith, where he died of rheumatic fever on 14 December 1785. He was buried in Chelsea burial ground in a grave marked by a monument erected by his friend Bartolozzi. In 1761 he had married a "lady of moderate fortune" by whom he had two sons and a daughter. His wife having died before him, administration of his estate was granted, on 25 August 1786, to the elder son, Philip Cipriani, to whom on the same date was granted the administration of the estate of Charlotte Cipriani, the daughter (John Baptiste Cipriani having died "without having taken upon him letters of Admon of the goods of the deceased Charlotte"). Philip Cipriani died in 1820, in his house in Harley Street, Cavendish Square, leaving his estate to his widow Maria, who died in 1836. In her will, proved on 23 April 1836, Maria Cipriani bequeathed a substantial estate to friends and relatives, including her daughter Mary. John Baptist Cipriani's younger son, Sir Henry Cipriani, a captain in the Huntingdon Militia, received from this will of his sister-in-law a leasehold estate at No 41, Norfolk Street, the Strand.

Among Giovanni Battista Cipriani's many commissions were allegorical designs on panels of George III's stagecoach, repairs to Antonio Verrio's painting at Windsor, and repairs to the Reubens ceiling in Whitehall in 1788. Some rooms at Somerset House, occupied by the Royal Academy prior to its move to the National Gallery in 1836, have ceiling panels painted by him. From a design by Joshua Reynolds, Cipriani made a watercolor drawing of the gold medallion presented to David Garrick by the Theatrical Fund upon the actor's retirement in 1776. Cipriani also made copies of portraits of Algernon Sidney, Edmund Ludlow, and John Locke. He engraved plates of "The Death of Cleopatra," after Cellini, and "The Descent of the Holy Ghost," after Gabbiani. *A Collection of Prints after the Sketches and Drawings of the late celebrated G. B. C., Esq., R. A.* was engraved by Richard Earlom and published at London in 1789. On 14 March 1786, and for three days following, about 1100 of his drawings were sold at Hutchins's: on 22 March 1786, his picture of "Cephalus and Procris" brought 80 guineas at Christie's; and on 3 May 1821 a collection of his drawings, owned by W. Lock of Norbury Park, Surrey, was sold at Sotheby's. Several of his drawings and many prints are in the British Museum. At his estate at Belmont, the manager Thomas Harris had "two large and beautiful figures of Melpomene and Thalia, painted by Cipriani;" according to Thomas Dibdin (*Reminiscences*, 1827), "they were ingeniously let into the wainscot of his picture gallery, at some distance from each other."

A portrait of Cipriani by F. Bartolozzi painted in 1783 was engraved by Mariano Bovi and published by him in 1792. Nathaniel Dawe's portrait of Cipriani was exhibited at the South Kensington Museum (now the Victoria and Albert) in 1867. An engraving by J. R. Smith, after J. F. Rigaud, of Cipriani with A. Carlini and F. Bartolozzi was published by Boydell in 1778. A detail from Rigaud's painting showing only Cipriani was published by Boydell in an engraving by R. Earlom in 1789. Cipriani is included in a painting by Zoffany of a large group of the members of the Royal Academy in 1772 which now hangs at Windsor Castle; it was published as engraved by Earlom in 1773 by Sayer.

Cipriani, Lorenzo Angelo ₁*fl.* 1791–1796₁, *singer*.

Lorenzo Angelo Cipriani, an Italian *buffo*, made his first appearance at London on 1 March 1791 (and not 22 September 1791 as stated by Grove) at the Pantheon singing Don Alfonso in *La bella pescatrice*, a role he sang another 21 times that season. On 16 June 1792 he sang Valerio in *La locanda*, which he played another seven times that season and 22 times in the next. On 17 December 1791 he sang Don Calloandro in *La pastorella nobile*. When the Pantheon burned to the ground in January 1792 the Opera moved to the Haymarket where Cipriani appeared as Don Artabano in *La trame deluse* on 14 February (and six other times) and as Don Trifone in *La discordia conjugale* on 31 March (and four other times). For a revival of *La bella pescatrice* (12 April and nine other times) Cipriani, impersonating a Frenchman, appeared on the night of 15 May 1792 with a national cockade in his hat, setting off violent hissing in the audience, "and the actor was obliged to cast down his hat," reported the *Morning Herald* of the next day, "which a gentleman behind the scenes took up, and tearing out the offensive *ensign of sedition*, threw it away—the audience warmly applauding."

Cipriani returned to London for the opera season of 1794–95 at the King's Theatre to sing Scevola in *I zingari in*

LORENZO CIPRIANI, as Don Alfonso
engraving by Guisan, after Violet

fiera on 10 January, Fiuta in *La scola de'
maritati* on 27 January, Mitrane in *Semiramide* on 7 February, and an unspecified
role in *L'isola del piacere* on 26 May. In
the last-named piece he gave his final
performance on 9 June 1796 (and not on
31 March 1792 as stated by Grove). His
full name is found in the libretto of *I
fratelli rivali* published at Venice in 1793.

A sketch by P. Violet of Cipriani in the
role of Don Alfonso in *La bella pescatrice*
was engraved by C. Guisan and published
by J. F. Tomkins in 1791.

L. A. Cipriani may have been related to
John Cipriani, a successful clown at Sadler's
Wells and Manchester from 1803 to 1806,
who, with his wife and daughter, played
also at places as far away from England as
Boston, Massachusetts and Louisville, at
least until 1811.

"Circe and Sultana of Soho." *See*
CORNELYS, THERESA.

Cirri, Giovanni Battista *b. c. 1740,
violoncellist, composer.*

Giovanni Battista Cirri was born about
1740 at Forli, the son of Ignazio Cirri,
maestro di cappella at that city. After an
obscure professional life in Italy, he moved
to England to serve for some time as music
master to the Duke of Gloucester, brother
of George III. The first professional notice
of Signor Cirri at London was on 5 June
1764, when he performed a violoncello
concerto in a program of vocal and instrumental music given at Spring Garden for
the benefit of those "Prodigies of Nature,"
young Miss and Master Mozart, who also
played on the program. Cirri played at the
Haymarket on 13 November 1764 for the
benefit of a distressed family, and again
for the benefit of the Mozarts on 13 May
1765 at Hickford's Room in Brewer Street.
His other public performances included
violoncello selections at the King's Theatre on 2 February 1770 for the benefit of
the Musicians' Fund, and again on 12 June
1770 and 21 March 1771. He played solos
at the end of the first part of the oratorios
at the Haymarket on 23 February and
9 March 1774.

Cirri returned to Italy "sometime before
his death," according to Grove. His compositions included cello concertos, string
quartets, quartets for flute, violin, and
continuo, trio sonatas, string trios, and
duets for two cellos.

Cizo, Mr *[fl. 1790], singer.*

Mr Cizo sang in the Drury Lane oratorios
in 1790. On 24 February he delivered
"Pleasures my former ways resigning"
from *Time and Truth* in a concert of
selections from the works of Handel,

which was repeated on 10, 17, and 26 March.

Clabburn, Mr {fl. 1794}, singer.

Mr Clabburn was listed in 1794 in Doane's *Musical Directory* as an alto (countertenor) living at Cambridge and a performer in the performances commemorative of Handel in Westminster Abbey. There had been several of these since the first in 1784.

Clagget, Charles {fl. 1762–1793}, violinist, inventor, composer.

Charles Clagget, Irish violinist and inventor of musical apparatus, was born at Waterford in 1740 according to Grove or about 1755 according to van der Straeten. The fact that his brother, Walter Clagget, was born in 1742 makes 1740 the more probable date. Probably it was he, but perhaps it was his brother Walter, who was leader of the band at Smock Alley, Dublin, from 1762 to 1764 and at Crow Street, from 1764 through 1768. About that time, a Clagget was co-manager with Mahon and Dawson at the Capel Street Theatre there and had a company at Chester in 1771. Charles Clagget led the band of theatres at Liverpool, 1771–73, at Manchester, 1773–75, and at Newry, Ireland, 1778–79. The *Newry Chronicle* of 30 November 1778 described him as a musician of "distinguished abilities," who had come from Dublin to direct the band and the operas as he had done at Kilkenny and Waterford.

In 1776, Clagget went to London to devote most of his energies to the invention and improvement of musical instruments and the exhibition of musical apparatus. He took out a patent in December 1776 for "Improvements on the violin and other instruments played on finger boards," which he claimed made it "almost impossible to stop or play out of tune." Another patent in August 1788 was issued for "Methods of constructing and tuning

musical instruments which will be perfect in their kind and much easier to be performed on than any hitherto discovered." He also invented the "Aiution, or, Evertuned Organ, an instrument without pipes, strings, glasses, or bells, which will never require to be retuned in any climate," which he described along with other apparatus of his invention in his publication called *Musical Phenomena.* He built a "teliochordon" stop for the royal harpsichord at Buckingham Palace in 1790, about which he published a treatise in 1791. Other inventions, mostly to do with the tuning of instruments, are listed in Grove. His collection was kept at his house at No 16, Greek Street, Soho, which he styled "The Musical Museum." During the 1780s, Clagget exhibited some of his inventions at the Pantheon in Oxford Street. He also put them on display at the Hanover Square Rooms about 1791.

At the King's Arms Tavern, Cornhill, on 31 October 1793, Clagget presented an "Attic-Concert," of pieces played on instruments of his design or improvement. Accompanying the performance with "A Discourse on Musick," which was a discourse concerning his contributions to refining the harmony of keyed instruments, he read a letter from Haydn praising Clagget's improvements on the pianoforte and harpsichord. The "Discourse" was published, prefaced by an engraved portrait of Clagget, with the caption, "Harmonizer of Musical Instruments." His published music included *Fidelity, a favorite Canzonett* (1795?), the song *I've rifl'd Flora's painted bower,* as sung by Master Brett (1768), and the song *Nature's magic skill* (1780?). With his brother Walter Clagget, he published at Edinburgh about 1760 *Six Duets for Two Violins, intended to improve and Entertain Practitioners.*

Charles Clagget died about 1795 according to Grove, and in 1820 according to van der Straeten. His wife, Susannah Elizabeth Clagget, acted at Wakefield in

1774, and she was probably the Mrs Clagget who performed at Edinburgh in 1776 and 1777. The provincial actress Miss Clagget, who married the actor D'Arcy at Stamford in 1799, was perhaps their daughter.

Clagget, Walter *1742–1798, instrumentalist, composer, proprietor.*

Walter Clagget was born in 1742, probably at Waterford, Ireland. He seems to have passed some of his early years at Edinburgh with his brother Charles Clagget (fl. 1762–1793), where they published, about 1760, *Six Duets for Two Violins, intended to Improve and Entertain Practitioners*. About this time Walter moved to London, lodging in Great Hart Street in Covent Garden and engaging as a theatrical musician. No doubt he was the "Cloggett" who played a solo concerto on the violoncello at a concert program presented by "Madam Midnight" (Christopher Smart) at the Haymarket on 8 September 1760. Some months later, on 26 February 1761, he again played a violoncello solo at the Haymarket, now billed as "Clagit." He was probably the "Claggit" who shared tickets with the Drury Lane house servants Humphreys and Denny on 30 May 1768. In May 1767 a comic opera, with his music, entitled *The Power of Sympathy, or, The Innocent Lovers* was given at Dublin, and in December 1770 a revival of *Cymon*, with new accompaniments by him, played in the same city. Grove credits him with providing the music for G. A. Stevens's entertainment, *The Cabinet of Fancy*, at the Haymarket on 30 October 1780, but *The London Stage* states that this music was by Charles Clagget, his brother.

When Walter Clagget was recommended for admission to the Royal Society of Musicians by Robert Munro on 1 February 1784, he was said to be 42 years old, one who had been a musician since the age of seven and who played a great variety of instruments including "the Violin, Violon-cello, Tennor, Double Bass, Oboe, German flute, Clarinet, & etc." At this time he was married but had no children. The recommendation also stated that Clagget played at Covent Garden in the winter at a salary of £2 per week and at the Haymarket in the summer at £2 8s. per week. In 1785, 1790, and 1791, Clagget played the double bass at the annual May concerts by the Royal Society of Musicians given at St Paul's for the benefit of the clergy. On 26 December 1787, he provided music for Wewitzer's pantomime, *The Dumb Cake*, at Covent Garden.

In October 1788, Clagget opened the Apollo Gardens (or "Temple of Apollo") on Westminster Road, where he produced musical entertainments in a concert room. It was described by Wroth as a fine building with "a kind of orrery in the dome, displaying a pallid moon between two brilliant transparencies." The opening concert, given by 70 instrumental and vocal performers, with Jonathan Battishill at the organ, was attended by some 1300 people. In the following summers Clagget provided such second-rate vocalists as Binley, Mrs Iliff, Mrs Leaver, and Miss Wingfield, and the organist Costello with new musical offerings "composed by Messrs. Haydn and Pleyel since their arrival in this Kingdom." By 1792, however, the Apollo Gardens had gained an unsavory reputation for attracting cheats and pickpockets. The place was suppressed by the magistrates and the proprietor went bankrupt. At about this time, Clagget rebuilt the Pantheon in Oxford Street, which had burned in January 1792, and he gave concerts and masquerades there for a while.

Clagget died in July or early August of 1798; on 5 August 1798 the governors of the Royal Society of Musicians granted £8 for his burial to his widow Anne, the usual allowance in such circumstances. Several entries in the baptismal registers of St Paul, Covent Garden, may refer to him or to his family. On 8 April 1762,

Charlotte, the daughter of Walter Clagget by Amelia his wife, was christened. Thomas Christian Walter, son of Walter Clagget by Mary his wife, was christened on 20 January 1788. At the time of his death, the musician's wife's name was Anne, so if these entries referred to his children, he was married several times, and the child Charlotte, born in 1762, must have died by 1784, when Clagget stated to the Royal Society of Musicians that he had no children. Walter Clagget may have been related to the Mrs Clagget who acted at Edinburgh in 1776 and 1777, to the Miss Clagget, provincial actress, who married the actor D'Arcy at Stamford in 1799, and to the Irish musician, Theophilus Clagget. The person last-named, who may have been one of Walter Clagget's brothers, was expelled from membership in the Irish Musical Fund on 1 May 1791 for not paying his subscription. He was readmitted on 1 July 1792 and thereafter paid 13s. per year. His last payment was made on 23 March 1795, after which date he died. His widow was granted £5 5s. per week from 23 June 1799 until her death in February 1800 by the Irish Musical Fund, whose accounts also record the support of his children, Eliza and Charles.

In addition to the compositions cited above, Walter Clagget wrote *Six Solos and Six Scot Airs with Variations for the Violon or Violoncello with a Thorough Bass for the Harpsichord*, published at London, 1763; a song *If Fortune when smiling could make us amends*, (London, c. 1783), *A Set of Twenty-four Duetts for two German Flutes, Oboes, or Violins, made from the most celebrated airs in the English Operas, and Haydn's Works* (London, c. 1790), and *A New Medley Overture Consisting entirely of Scots Tunes and Thirty Six of the most Favorite Scots Airs* (Edinburgh, c. 1795).

Claggett, Crispus [fl. 1795–1797], *impresario, licensee.*

According to documents in the Public Record Office, a license was granted on 9 April 1795 to one Crispus Claggett for a masquerade at the Pantheon, which had been destroyed by fire in January 1792 but had now been rebuilt. The *Morning Herald* of 9 April 1795 announced that the Pantheon would reopen that night with a masquerade, the "usual licenses being now fully renewed and established." Additional licenses were granted to Crispus Claggett for a masquerade on 21 January 1796, for 12 nights of concerts between 18 February and 3 May 1796, for additional masquerades in 1796 (period not stated), and on 17 April 1797.

Clamakin, Mrs [fl. 1731], *dancer.*

A Mrs Clamakin, announced as making her first appearance on the stage, danced a *Pastoral* at Lincoln's Inn Fields Theatre on 22 April 1731. No other performance by her is known.

Clanfield, Mr [fl. 1775–1776], *boxkeeper.*

A Mr Clanfield was listed in the Drury Lane account book for 1775–76 as an upper boxkeeper, with no salary stated. On 20 May 1776, he was allowed to sell tickets, at which time he advertised for "the kind Assistance of his Friends on this present Occasion, and humbly hopes they will be punctual in having his Tickets, as the only Method to render him Essential Service."

Clanfield, Mr [fl. 1794], *singer?, musician.*

A Mr Clanfield was listed in 1794 by Doane's *Musical Directory* as a "Tenor" at Sadler's Wells Theatre living at No 98, Holborn Hill. No doubt he was related to the pyrotechnist, Samuel Clanfield, who was living at No 93, Holborn Hill in 1793.

Clanfield, Samuel [fl. 1750–1800], *pyrotechnist, proprietor.*

The name of Samuel Clanfield was associated with fireworks displays at London throughout the second half of the eighteenth century. Because of the long period involved it is possible that there were two pyrotechnists by this name, father and son.

With Clitherow, Clanfield provided "new and splendid" fireworks at the seasonal opening of Cuper's Gardens, Lambeth, on 30 April 1750. Clanfield became the proprietor of Mulberry Gardens for the summer of 1752 and each evening provided vocal and instrumental music from six o'clock and fireworks at nine. During the 1760s and from 1772 to 1774, he frequently engineered displays at Marylebone Gardens. On 19 November 1773, Drury Lane Theatre paid him £3 5s. for fireworks, and that management called upon him frequently during the last two decades of the century to create pyrotechnics for the various pantomime spectacles. In 1784–85, the theatre paid him a total of £28 18s. 2d. as a fireworker, probably in connection with the "Repulse of the Spaniards before the Rock of Gibraltar," an episode introduced into *Harlequin Junior* on 7 January 1784 and then included in all subsequent performances. He received at least £14 4s. 8d. in 1785–86, £35 2s. 4d. in 1787–88, £5 2s. 10d. in 1789–90, and £ 3 14s. in 1790–91. Largest known payments, £40 4s. 6d., came to him in 1795–96. Clanfield also provided fireworks at Covent Garden Theatre in October 1800.

In October 1793, he was showing fireworks at Sadler's Wells Theatre and living at No 93, Holborn Hill. Doubtless he was related to the Mr Clanfield, a musician at Sadler's Wells in 1794, who lived at No 98, Holborn Hill, and to the Mr Clanfield who was a boxkeeper at Drury Lane in 1775–76.

Clapham, Mrs [fl. 1786], actress.

Mrs Clapham, advertised as from the Theatre Royal at York, played Selima in a single performance of *Tamerlane* given at the Haymarket Theatre on 6 March 1786 by a group of provincial actors for the benefit of Griffiths, formerly of Drury Lane.

"Clara, Signora." See DIXON, CLARA ANN.

Claremont, William d. 1832, actor.

William Claremont was born William Cleaver, the son of a shop assistant and delivery man in the City, according to the *Authentic Memoirs of the Green Room.* He was apprenticed early to a linen draper, but "having performed in a private play at the Lyceum, was so captivated with the sock and buskin" and so convinced of his attractiveness to ladies that he determined to go upon the stage. Changing his name to one he considered more genteel, he went to act at Margate in 1792, where in his "provincial drill" of 14 months he played a number of "topping characters."

Claremont was engaged at Covent Garden in 1793–94 at £2 per week. After his debut on 18 September 1793 as Conrade in *Much Ado About Nothing,* he was kept busy in a number of small and middling supporting roles, including Montano in *Othello,* Courtall in *The Belle's Stratagem,* Cabinet in *Grief-à-la Mode, or the Funeral,* Midge in *Wild Oats,* a Turk in *A Day in Turkey,* Corporal Squib in *The Sprigs of Laurel,* a Brother in *Comus,* Charles in *Netley Abbey,* a French Commandant in *British Fortitude,* the Lord of the Manor in *Annette and Lubin,* Hedgeworth in *The World in a Village,* and Albert in *The Widow of Malabar.* In the next season, now earning £3 per week, he expanded his repertory with a role in *The Rival Queens,* Sir Charles in *The Beaux' Stratagem,* Jaques in *Fontaineville Forest,* a Lord in *Cymbeline,* an Officer in *The Count of Narbonne,* and the Duke of Somerset in *The Battle of Hexham.*

Claremont continued as the "stock-nonentity of Covent Garden Theatre" through 1804–5, at a constant salary of £3 per week or 10 shillings per day. He also played summers at Richmond, Surrey, and at Birmingham in 1795 and 1797 and at Birmingham again in 1798. In the summer of 1804 he acted at the Haymarket for Colman, taking more than £116 as his share of a benefit with Waddy on 14 June.

Some of his detractors claimed that Claremont retained his situation at Covent Garden merely through the compassion of the managers, and in 1797 John Williams, in *A Pin Basket to the Chidren of Thespis*, was contemptuous of his talents:

He has carried bad acting as far as 'twill go:
How he tortures hard words—how adroitly he'll mar!
How he jumbles the V, and cross-buttocks the R!

Criticizing Claremont's performance of Charles Stanley in *A Cure for the Heart-Ache* on 13 January 1800, Thomas Dutton in his *Dramatic Censor* wished that "this gentleman would suffer the austerity of his features to relax, when he acts the lover. A continual frown ill accords with the soft workings of the tender passion." Some critics made much of Claremont's affecting of a "hairy and Esau-like appearance," and others mentioned a studied gallantry which became sufficiently notorious in the theatre for his fellows to dub him "Beau Claremont." As late as 1844, Mrs Charles Mathews remembered his inoffensively narcissistic manners and "his convinced mind, that no earthly woman could look upon him without admiration."

Some of Claremont's other roles at Covent Garden included: (1795–96) one of the Murderers and one of the Witches in *Macbeth*, Paris in *Romeo and Juliet*, Guildenstern in *Hamlet* (evidently a role which he acted with great credit), Catesby in *Richard III*, Amble in *A New Way to Pay Old Debts*, Poins in *1 Henry IV*; (1797–98) Willoughby in *The Dramatist*, Viscount de Beaumont in *England Pre-*

served, Marshal Ferbelin in *Love in a Camp*; (1799–1800) Henry Paddington in *The Beggar's Opera*, Albany in *King Lear*, Sir Richard Chances in *The Wise Man of the East*, Raleigh in *The Earl of Essex*, Bellamy in *The Suspicious Husband*, Snare in *Abroad and at Home*, a Mountaineer in *Joanna*, Count Louis in *Peeping Tom*, Clement in *The Deserted Daughter*, Charles in *The West Indian*, Sir Fred Faintly in *Speculation*, Captain Harcourt in *The Chapter of Accidents*, Young O'Donnovan in *The Lie of the Day*; (1800–1801) Captain Clifford in *The Irish Mimic*, Solarino in *The Merchant of Venice*, a character in *Il Bondocani*; (1802–3) a character in *A Tale of Mystery*, Laertes in *Hamlet*, Valentine in *The Intriguing Chambermaid*; (1803–4) Sebastian in *Paul and Virginia*, Donald in *Douglas*, Belford in *Isabella*, a character in *The English Fleet*, and Spinosa in *Venice Preserv'd*.

In 1805–6 Claremont transferred to Drury Lane where he remained for at least 16 years, through 1821–22, regularly sharing very considerable annual benefits: £406 10s., £339 9s. 6d., and £328 12s. 6d., with King on 10 June 1807, 10 June 1808, and 25 May 1809, respectively; £385 5s. with Waddy on 29 June 1810; and £634 9s. with Shaw on 9 July 1812 (all less house charges of about £105). On 15 July 1813 his share of benefit receipts was £268 7s.; on 8 July 1814 it was £255 18s.

William Claremont died on 28 August 1832. Perhaps he was the William Cleaver whose estate, worth less than £20, was granted to the widow Hermina Cleaver by the Consistory Court on 28 October 1834.

As Gilliland wrote, it "would certainly be ridiculous to apply the term great" to Claremont's professional efforts, yet equally wrong "to call them contemptible." His voice, despite early criticism to the contrary, was not unfavorable to the roles he played. He was, according to Mrs Mathews, "never once anything but friendly and gentlemanly. . . . Who . . . ever witnessed Claremont's Guildenstern," she asked, "without feeling satisfied that he ought to have performed Hamlet?"

Clarendon, Miss *[fl. 1742]*, *actress.*
A Miss Clarendon played Maria in a single performance of *The London Merchant* at the James Street Theatre on 8 November 1742.

Claridge, John *[fl. 1766–1790]*, *lobby doorkeeper, supernumerary.*
John Claridge was a lobby doorkeeper at Covent Garden from at latest 1766–67 through 1789–90. His salary in 1767–68 was 2*s.* per day, or 12*s.* per week. Each year he shared a trifling income from benefit tickets with other house servants, his share being £2 5*s.* 6*d.* in 1767–68, £4 6*d.* in 1768–69, £5 6*d.* in 1769–70, £5 1*s.* 6*d.* in 1771–72 and £4 7*s.* in 1772–73. During 1771–72, Claridge was also paid a total of £3 12*s.* 6*d.* for playing in "the Ass and Hog"—animated properties—in 29 performances of *Mother Shipton*. In the following fall, on 3 November 1773, he was paid 12*s.* 6*d.* for another five nights of the same. His name did not appear in the benefit bills after 1789–90.

Clark. *See also* CLARKE.

Clark, Mr *[fl. 1731]*, *actor.*
An actor named Clark played Tipple in the farce *The Banish'd General* at Southwark Fair on 8 September 1731 in the Mills-Miller-Oates booth. He does not seem to have been at the patent theatres.

Clark, Mr *[fl. 1792–1819?]*, *singer.*
A male singer named Clark was employed in choruses at Covent Garden Theatre in the spring of 1792. He was named in the bills of 28 February and 13 March as among 15 "Shepherds, Furies and Shades of Departed Heroes" in Gluck's *Orpheus and Eurydice*.

Clark reappeared in the choruses for the oratorios given under the auspices of Drury Lane at the King's Theatre in the Haymarket in February and March of 1793. This Clark or another turned up in the chorus of soldiers in *Feudal Times* at Drury Lane on 4 February 1799. That popular piece was repeated some 21 times during the season. The same singer was in the original large chorus for R. B. Sheridan's splendidly produced *Pizarro* at Drury Lane on 24 May 1799 and the 24 repetitions that season. In October 1799 he was one of the janizaries in *Blue Beard*. He was paid £1 1*s.* per week in 1799–1800. He may have been employed by the theatre again in the nineteenth century, for a "Clarke," identified as in "the chorus," rose from £1 5*s.* per week in 1812–13 to £2 per week from 1815–16 through at least 1818–19.

Clark, Mr *[fl. 1800]*, *puppeteer.*
A Mr Clark manipulated puppets at Bartholomew Fair in August 1800.

Clark, Mr *[fl. 1800–1806]*, *scene painter.*
A Mr Clark was first noticed in theatrical bills as an assistant to the younger Thomas Greenwood at Cross's Royal Circus on 23 June 1800 when he helped Greenwood and four others to paint the scenes for *The Magic Flute; or, Harlequin Champion*. He may have been with the circus somewhat earlier. The surviving newspaper advertisements and bills credit him in the same capacity as an assistant executant for the new pantomimes *The Golden Farmer; or, Harlequin Ploughboy* which opened on 28 June 1802, *Gonsalvo de Cordova* (16 August), *The Jubilee of 1802* (20 September), *The Rival Statues* (11 April 1803), and "A New Grand Serious Spectacle, which has been a long time in preparation, called LOUISA of LOMBARDY; Or, The Secret Nuptials" (25 April). He was among seven executants of scenery designed

by Whitmore of Covent Garden and Signor Latilla of the Opera House for *Abelline; or, The Bravo's Bride* (15 April 1805) and one of five of Marchbanks's assistants executing that designer's *Cloud King; or, The Magic Rose* (23 June 1806).

Clark, Mr   *d. 1812, waxworks exhibitor.*

A surgeon of Chancery Lane named Clark bought Mrs Salmon's waxworks at her death in 1760. The establishment was located at the sign of the Golden Salmon near the Horn Tavern in Fleet Street. Clark and his wife operated the exhibit there until 1788 when they removed to No 189, Fleet Street. In 1795 they were to be found at the Fountain Tavern, No 17, Fleet Street.

Their waxworks exhibited famous and notorious figures, royal personages, and criminals: George III and Queen Charlotte, Dr Samuel Johnson, the hanged forger Dr Dodd, John Philip Kemble, Mrs Siddons, Dick Turpin the highwayman, and John Wilkes the politician.

Clark died in 1812, his widow operated the place alone for awhile, and then the figures were sold to James Templeman, who removed them to Water Lane, where they were exhibited until 1831.

Clark, Mrs   [*fl. 1695–1723?*], *actress, singer, dancer.*

A Mrs Clark played Alice in *The Mock Marriage* at Drury Lane in September 1695. Perhaps she was the Mrs Clarke who danced and sang at Lincoln's Inn Fields occasionally from 11 June 1703 through 25 January 1705. A Mrs Clarke played Giddy in *The Doating Lovers* when it was first performed at Lincoln's Inn Fields on 23 June 1715; a Mrs Clark acted Alicia in *Jane Shore* at the Haymarket Theatre on 28 June 1722; and a Mrs Clark sang at a concert at Buckingham House on 11 January 1723. There is insufficient evidence to prove that all these appearances were by

the same woman, but neither is there any certainty that three or four different women are referred to.

Clark Mrs   [*fl. 1760–1814?*], *waxworks exhibitor. See* **CLARK, MR** *d. 1812.*

Clark, Mrs   [*fl. 1789*], *singer.*

A Mrs Clark appeared at Hughes's Royal Circus on 12 May 1789 and following, singing a "principal character" in a musical entertainment called *The What Is It.*

Clark, Master   [*fl. 1724–1730*], *dancer.*

A lowly member of the Lincoln's Inn Fields company in 1724–25, "Young Clark," received a daily salary of 2*s.* according to an entry in the account books on 25 September 1724. *The London Stage* reports that at some point he was down to 1*s.* per acting day. He seems to have remained with the troupe at least through the 1726–27 season. He appeared at the Oates-Fielding booth at Southwark Fair on 9 September 1730 as a dancer—the only indication of his specialty in the records. Clark was obviously called Young Clark or Clark Junior to distinguish him from some elder Clark, but which one he may have been related to, if any, is not known; the best guess would be Clarke the house servant, whose name first appeared about the same time.

Clark, Miss   [*fl. 1736*], *actress, singer.*

Miss Clark, the younger of two girls of that name, played Myrtilla in *The Provok'd Husband* at the Haymarket Theatre on 29 June and 7 July 1736, and on the latter date she and her sister (?) sang a dialogue. They were members of a company of Lilliputians.

Clark, Miss   [*fl. 1736–1747?*], *actress, singer.*

Miss Clark played the Page in *The*

Contrivances on 6 April 1736 at Covent Garden. On 29 June and 7 July 1736 she acted Manly in *The Provok'd Husband* as a member of a company of Lilliputians, and on the latter date she and Miss Clark Junior—probably her sister—sang a dialogue. The elder girl appeared at Southwark Fair on 7 September 1736 playing Peggy in *The Innocent Wife*. She appeared once again at Covent Garden on 26 April 1737 repeating her role in *The Contrivances*, after which her name disappeared from the bills until 1742. On 8 November of that year she acted Lucy in *The London Merchant* and also sang, this time at the theatre in James Street. At the Godwin-Adams booth at Bartholomew Fair on 23 August 1743 she played the Queen in *The Triumphant Queen of Hungary*. After this no other activity is recorded for her, unless the *Mrs* Clarke who played the title role in *Jane Shore* at Southwark Fair on 24 September 1747 was she.

Clark, Miss (fl. 1787), actress.

A Miss Clark ("Clerk" in the cast given by *The London Stage*) played only once in *London*—as Lucy in *The West Indian* in a special benefit for Griffiths at the Haymarket Theatre on 12 March 1787.

Clark, D. (fl. 1784?–1794), violinist.

Mr D. Clark, violinist resident in Little Pultney Street in 1794, played in the public performances of the Academy of Ancient Music and was concerned in at least one of the grand performances commemorative of Handel in Westminster Abbey in 1784, 1785, 1786, and 1791.

Clark, Edward d. 1789, singer, organist.

A "Mr Ed. Clark" was listed by Charles Burney as among the tenor singers at the Handel Memorial Concerts, alternately at Westminster Abbey and the Pantheon on 26, 27, and 29 May and 3 and 5 June 1784. He was likely the Edward Clark who was entered in the Minute Books of the Royal Society of Musicians on 7 June 1789 as applying "for present relief, being rendered incapable of earning anything towards his and family's sustenance by long and severe illness." He was at that time granted two guineas.

The burial register of St Paul, Covent Garden, identifies him as the church's organist; he was buried "in ye vault under [the] Charity School" on 1 August 1789. Musgrave's *Obituary* gives his death date as 27 July. On 2 August his widow Jemima signed an application to the Royal Society of Musicians for relief for herself and her children, "she being in very distrest circumstances." She was allowed two and a half guineas for herself and 15s. for each child each month. An entry of 4 October concerns an attempt by Mrs Clark to collect an apprentice fee for her daughter Mary. The Society refused to pay, "it appearing that she exceeded the age of fourteen at the death of her father." On 1 August 1790 it was reported that, since Jemina "had acted with duplicity with respect to her son Edward and had endeavored to impose on the society, it was resolved that the allowance for her said son cease."

Entries of 4 November 1798 and 7 April, 6 October, and 3 November 1799 concern the placing of the "second daughter" Millicent with Mrs E. Richardson, shopkeeper of 19 Bedford Street, Covent Garden, with the society paying the premium of £20. On 2 February 1800 Mrs Clark informed the Governors that she "had placed her daughter Harriet on approval with Mrs Mills, mantua-maker and milliner, opposite the Rope Walk, Woolwich." On 6 April the Secretary reported that "he had bound Harriet Clark to Mrs Mills" and had paid the premium of £20.

On 1 September 1811 Mrs Clarke was granted five guineas for medical aid. On 6 October 1811 her son-in-law Mr Sharp deposed that she had died on 4 September and asked for money to pay her funeral expenses. He was refused on the grounds that the Society had paid her "usual allowance" plus medical aid as of 1 September. Her daughter Millicent, Mrs Sharp, appealed the decision but the Board was adamant.

Clark, Elizabeth. *See* STORER, MRS CHARLES.

Clark, Jerman *d. 1705, dancing master.*

The *Post Man* of 25 February 1703 advertised "a very fine Consort, by several eminent Masters" to be held at Clark's Dancing School, Petty Cannon, St Paul's Alley. Clark was probably the Jerman Clark, "a Dancing Master," who was buried on 1 May 1705 at St Clement Danes.

Clark, John [*fl.* 1793–1803], *scene painter.*

John Clark was an assistant scene painter at Covent Garden Theatre from before September 1793 until after 28 October 1794, apparently earning 7s. 6d. per day. He was again at the theatre in September and October 1799 (when his five days' salary was £2 10s.) and in the seasons 1800–1801 and 1802–3.

Clark, John [*fl.* 1794], *violinist.*

Doane's *Musical Directory* (1794) listed a professional violinist named John Clark who belonged to the New Musical Fund and resided in Windmill Street, Rathbone Place.

Clark, Joseph *d. 1696?, posture maker.*

In 1667 Evelyn wrote in his *Numismata* of "our late *Proteus Clark*, who tho' gross enough of Body, was of so flexible and subtile a Texture, as to contort his Members into several disfigurations, and to put out of joynt almost any Bone or *Vertebra*

of his Body, and to re-place it again." From this one would suppose that Joseph Clark died sometime before 1667, but he is reported to have appeared in Paris in the train of the Duke of Buckingham in 1678, and most sources suggest 1696 or near the end of the seventeenth century as the year of his death. The *Guardian* No 102 reported that Clark was the despair of tailors, for he would be fitted for clothes in one posture and then appear in another when the clothes were delivered. James Moleyns the surgeon was deceived by Clark when the contortionist came to him as a pretended patient with his body thrown out

Harvard Theatre Collection

JOSEPH CLARK

engraving by Taylor, after Laroon

of shape; Moleyns refused even to attempt a cure. Clark regularly played practical jokes on friends, for he had such control over his facial muscles that he could make himself unrecognizable to people with whom he had been moments before. There is no certain evidence that Clark ever exhibited himself for a living, but the sources suggest no other livelihood.

Two drawings of Clark by Marcellus Laroon appeared in Tempest's *Cryes and Habits of London* in 1688. In one drawing, Clark is shown holding his foot against his head, with a monkey imitating him; in the other, which was published again in 1792 by Caulfield in an engraving by Taylor, Clark is shown in a grotesque attitude.

Clark, Richard *b. 1780, singer, pianist, violinist.*

Richard Clark was proposed for membership in the Royal Society of Musicians by John Sale the younger on 5 March 1814. His sponsor gave to the Minute Books a brief history of Clark's career to that point which makes it seem likely that he had played in public for pay long before the century's turn.

He was said by the deposition to be a performer on the piano and violin, 34 years old in 1814, married, and with six children. A certificate in the Minute Books attests that he was born on 5 April 1780 and that he and Jane Wright (born 25 April 1780) had married on 14 March 1803) in St Bride's Church, London. Their children were (with baptismal dates furnished from the register of St George's Chapel, Windsor Castle) Caroline Francis (11 July 1804), Emma Jane (23 May 1806), Harriett (27 November 1809), Susanna (15 June 1812), Richard Spencer (11 January 1814 – and baptized again, for some reason, at St John the Evangelist, Westminster). Sophia Louise, their second child, was baptized on 19 July 1805 at New Windsor, Berkshire.

JOSEPH CLARK
engraving, after Laroon

Sales's recommendation gave testimony that Clark had been "educated as a chorister in the choirs of Windsor and Eton under the late Dr Aylward, he is engaged as a deputy for Mr Bartleman at the Chapel Royal, Mr Sale at St Paul's and Mr J. B. Sale at Westminster Abbey, he is also engaged at the Antient, Vocal, and Ladies Concerts &c. . . ." Clark lived in 1814 at No 13, Barton Street, Westminster. He was elected a member of the Society on 5 June 1814, with 15 ayes and one nay.

Clark, Thomas *[fl. 1670–1691?]*, *actor.*

Thomas Clark was a member of the King's Company at the Bridges Street Theatre by the 1670–71 season, and it may have been about this time that he played

Metellus Cimber in *Julius Caesar*. He was perhaps the Thomas Clarke cited on Lacy's 1673 map of Covent Garden who had a 120' by 30' property on Half Moon Street and Maiden Lane, on the southwest corner of the intersection formed by these streets and Bedford and Chandois Streets.

At Drury Lane on 16 May 1674 Clark played Drusillus in *Nero*; on 30 April 1675 he acted Massina in *Sophonisba*; and on 27 August 1675 he played Woossat (Venus) in *Psyche Debauch'd*. His other known roles during the late 1670s include Novel in *The Plain Dealer*, Dolabella in *All for Love*, and Swiftspur in *The Man of Newmarket*. Internal dissension in the King's troupe in 1678–79 caused Clark, Cardell Goodman, Joe Haines, and others to head for Edinburgh and better opportunities. But Thomas, along with Goodman and James Gray, was lured back to London in February 1680 by assurances that the troubles in the King's Company were settled and that the returning men would be paid travel expenses. On 30 July new articles were drawn up and Clark was granted a single share in the troupe.

In the early 1680s Clark acted the Earl of Essex in *The Unhappy Favourite*, Wilding in *Sir Barnaby Whigg,* and Gayland in *The Heir of Morocco,* and it was becoming evident that he had the talent to carry leading roles. As the union of the King's and Duke's companies drew near, Clark became, according to Cibber's *Apology*, intractable, "Being impatient to get into Parts." He apparently hoped that the line of Charles Hart would come his way when the older actor retired, but at the union Hart's roles fell to Betterton, Smith, and Mountfort. Still, Clark served with the new company in 1682–83 before disappearing temporarily from notice. The Mr Clark who acted Brackenbury in *Richard III* at Drury Lane in 1690–91 was probably Thomas, back for one last try.

Perhaps the following entry in the registers of St. Olave, Hart Street, concerns our subject: on 6 December 1691 Mary, the wife of Mr Thomas Clarke, was buried at St Saviour, Southwark.

Clark, William [fl. 1784–1788], singer.

William Clark was listed by Charles Burney as among the tenor singers performing in the Handel Memorial Concerts alternately at Westminster Abbey and the Pantheon on 26, 27, and 29 May and 3 and 5 June 1784. He was doubtless the W. Clark who was named in a surviving manuscript account of the Academy of Ancient Music: he was paid £3 for singing in some of the Academy's concerts of 1787–88.

Clark, William [fl. 1794], singer.

The Reverend William Clark, a minor canon of St Paul's Cathedral and a member of the Windsor Choir, was listed in Doane's *Musical Directory* (1794) as a "Tenor [singer]" and "Alto" (i.e., countertenor). He lived at No 6, Old Bailey.

Clarke. *See also* CHARKE and CLARK.

Clarke, Mr [fl. 1675], dancer.

A Mr Clarke was listed among the French dancers in the court masque *Calisto* when it was performed on 15 February 1675. The name is probably an anglicized version of the dancer's correct one, but one can only guess that perhaps he was a Monsieur LeClerc. No dancer of that name is otherwise known for this period.

Clarke, Mr [fl. 1724–1726], dancer?

A Mr Clarke shared benefits with three other persons at Lincoln's Inn Fields on 22 May 1725 and 26 May 1726; no indication of his function in the company was given. *The London Stage* lists Clarke as a dancer in the company in 1725–26, but his name does not appear in the bills except for the benefit noted above.

Clarke, Mr ₁*fl. 1726–1728*₁, *dancer.*

At the Lincoln's Inn Fields Theatre on 19 July 1726 a Mr Clarke played Harlequin in *The Jealous Doctor.* He was presumably the same Clarke who joined the Drury Lane company on 9 September 1726 at 13s. 4d. nightly and acted the title role in *Harlequin Doctor Faustus* on 1 October, billed, slightly erroneously, as making his first public appearance. Following that, he was Harlequin in *Apollo and Daphne,* Wagner (in the character of Harlequin) in *The Miser,* and Harlequin again in *Harlequin's Triumph.* On 13 April 1727 he was granted a solo benefit.

Clarke remained at Drury Lane for the 1727–28 season, repeating his old roles and adding yet another Harlequin part in *Harlequin Happy and Poor Pierrot Married.* After this season his name seems to have dropped from the London bills. Though his line was similar to that of Nathaniel Clarke, he was clearly a different person, for the bills show both Clarkes active simultaneously at different theatres.

Clarke, Mr ₁*fl. 1729*₁, *singer.*

A Mr Clarke sang at Mrs Turner Robinson's benefit concert at Drury Lane on 26 March 1729, offering two solos, "*Ti con solo*" and "*No non Temer,*" and two duets with Mrs Robinson, "When Myra Sings" and "*Al Trionfo-Duetto.*"

Clarke, Mr ₁*fl. 1743*₁, *actor.*

A Mr Clarke made his first appearance on any stage at Drury Lane on 27 January 1743 playing Clytus in *The Rival Queens.* He repeated his performance on 2 February and was not heard from again.

Clarke, Mr ₁*fl. 1760–1762*₁, *house servant.*

On 19 May 1760 a Clarke, a male house servant, shared in tickets at Covent Garden Theatre on the benefit night of five doorkeepers. In the season of 1761–62 a house servant named Clarke received 10s. per

week at Covent Garden for some function undisclosed by the account book.

Clarke, Mr ₁*fl. 1765*₁, *singer.*

A Mr and Mrs Clarke sang at Finch's Grotto Gardens in the summer of 1765.

Clarke, Mrs ₁*fl. 1765*₁, *singer. See* **CLARKE, MR** ₁*fl. 1765*₁.

Clarke, Mr ₁*fl. 1778–1779*₁, *actor.*

A Mr Clarke played Leathersides in *The Macaroni Adventurer* at a specially licensed performance at the Haymarket on 28 December 1778 and, at another such performance at the Haymarket on 22 February 1779, he was Villiard in *The Foundling.*

Clarke, Mr ₁*fl. 1786–1790?*₁, *actor.*

A company probably led by Godolphin Waldron assembled at the little Hammersmith Theatre in June 1786 for a short season which, so far as the few surviving bills show, presented 17 nights of plays from 5 June through 8 August.

On the opening night a Mr Clarke played Hardcastle in *She Stoops to Conquer.* He did not play again that season, apparently. A Mrs Clarke, presumably his wife, came on as Lucy in *The Country Girl,* advertised as her first appearance, on 28 June 1786. Her next appearance was as Theodosia in *The Maid of the Mill* on 7 July 1786, was Minette in *A Bold Stroke for a Husband* on 19 July, for a joint benefit, and was both Myrtilla in *The Provok'd Husband* and Columbine in *Harlequin's Gambles* on 24 July. She concluded her service to the company on what was probably the last night of the season, 26 July, by playing parts in three pieces: Miss Ogle in *The Belle's Stratagem,* Malapert in *The Fool,* and Columbine in *Hurly-Burly.*

Mr Clarke may have been the underling who was one of the slaves in *The Gnome* at the Haymarket on 5 August 1788 and after. This Clarke was Barnacle in *The Romp,* played in a pick-up company, by special permission of the Lord Chamberlain at the Haymarket on 29 October 1790.

Clarke, Mrs ₁*fl. 1786*₁, *actress. See* CLARKE, MR ₁*fl. 1786–1790?*₁.

Clarke, Mr ₁*fl. 1793–1795*₁, *doorkeeper.*

A Mr Clarke was a doorkeeper for Covent Garden Theatre at a salary of 15*s.* per week during the 1793–94 and 1794–95 theatrical seasons.

Clarke, Mr ₁*fl. 1797*₁, *actor.*

On 25 November 1797 "A Gentleman," who was said to be making his initial bow on the stage, was allowed to play Falstaff in *1 Henry IV* at Drury Lane Theatre, with John Philip Kemble playing Hotspur, Charles Kemble playing Prince Hal, and the manager Wroughton representing the King. The *European Magazine* (December 1797) identified the gentleman as a Mr Longley. The *Monthly Visitor* (January 1798) called him Mr Clarke. He was not "inferior to some Falstaffs we have seen upon the London stage," thought the critic of the *True Briton* (29 November 1797). This faint praise was evidently part of a critical consensus which damned him. He did not reappear in London.

Clarke, Master ₁*fl. 1781–1783*₁, *dancer.*

A Master Clarke first appeared, dancing with another child, in the pantomime *Medea and Jason* at the summer theatre in the Haymarket on 8 August and 15 times thereafter through 15 September 1781. He did not reappear until 5 June 1783 when he was again at the Haymarket in the same pantomime, repeated on 9 June and 6 August. He did not dance again, so far as the bills show.

Clarke, Edward. *See* CLARKE, NATHANIEL.

Clarke, Isaac ₁*fl. 1660–1664*₁, *musician.*

The parish registers of St Andrew, Holborn, contain three entries pertaining to Isaac Clarke, "musitioner." He and his wife Thomazin had a son Zackary who was born on 25 October 1660 and baptized three days later; their daughter Mary was born on 26 October 1662 and baptized the next day; and their daughter Elizabeth was born on 14 May 1664 and baptized on 22 May. All of the entries describe Clarke as living in Lamb Alley, Saffron Hill.

Clarke, J. L. ₁*fl. 1784?–1811?*₁, *horn player, violinist.*

A Mr J. L. Clarke was described as a player of "bass" (probably bass horn or upright serpent) and violin by Doane's *Musical Directory* of 1794. He had played in some of the Handelian celebrations at Westminster Abbey (which began in May and June 1784, but were revived in 1785, 1786, 1787, and 1791), in the concerts of the Academy of Ancient Music and the Covent Garden oratorios. He was a member of the New Musical Fund. In 1794 he lived in Bow Street, Westminster. He may have been the J. Clarke, instrumentalist, who is entered in the Minute Books of the Irish Musical Fund as appointed on 6 March 1809 by the Governors of the Fund to play Handel's music at the annual Commemoration concert in Dublin. That Clarke was admitted as a professional member to the Irish society in 1811 and lived in Dawson Street, Dublin.

Clarke, Jeremiah 1673?–1707, *singer, organist, composer.*

There is no certainty about Jeremiah Clarke's birth date, but most evidence points to 1673 or possibly 1674, and he was probably related to the musical Clarke family at Windsor. Jeremiah was one of the children of the Chapel Royal under John Blow singing at the coronation of James II on 23 April 1685, and it is likely that by that time he had already been under Blow's tutelage for two or three years. By 26 April 1691 his voice had broken and he was granted livery as a former Chapel boy, and for a while he turned from singing to playing the organ. He was appointed organist of Winchester College in 1692, and three years later he left that post to accept a similar one at St Paul's in London.

During the 1690s he did much of his composing, some of it for the theatre. Grove, as part of an extensive catalogue of Clarke's works, lists 19 songs written for plays, most of which date between 1696 and 1705. He composed incidental music, overtures, or songs for *The Cornish Comedy* (1696), *Love's a Jest* (1696), *Antony and Cleopatra* (Sedley's version, c. 1696), *The World in the Moon* (1697), *The Fond Husband* (1697), *The Campaigners* (1698), *The Island Princess* (in which he also sang a prologue with Leveridge, 1698), *The Bath* (1701), *Love at First Sight* (1704), *The Amorous Miser* (1705), and *The Committee* (c. 1700–1705). His music was also used in productions of *The Comical Mistakes*, *The Sea Voyage*, *Titus Andronicus*, *The Virtuous Wife*, and *A Wife for Any Man*. Clarke's other secular music became popular at the concert rooms about London, especially his setting of Dryden's St Cecilia's Day ode, "Alexander's Feast," first performed at Stationers' Hall on 22 November 1697. The music has not survived.

After assuming his post at St Paul's in 1695, Clarke set up a school, one of his pupils being Charles King, who married Clarke's sister and later succeeded Clarke as organist at the cathedral. The earliest reference to the school seems to have been in the *Post Boy* of 29–31 March 1698: "To morrow being the First of April, in Paul's Alley, near St Paul's Church-Yard, at Mr Clarke's School, will be perform'd a new Consort of Vocal and Instrumental Musick, compos'd by Mr Henry Simsons, beginning at Seven of the Clock exactly. Price of coming in 2s. 6d." On 6 June 1699 Clarke was made vicar-choral of St Paul's; on 7 July 1700 he and William Crofts were sworn Gentlemen of the Chapel Royal extraordinary (without fee until a joint position became vacant); on 11 January 1703 Clarke succeeded Blow as almoner and master of the choristers of St Paul's; and on 25 May 1704 he and Crofts were sworn jointly as ordinary members of the Chapel Royal and succeeded to Francis Piggot's place as organists.

In the early years of the new century Clarke's works were very popular at concerts as well as at the theatres. The newspapers frequently advertised his music as played at York Buildings, at Court before the Monarch, at Mr Hickes's, at Holt's Dancing School, and at the Lincoln's Inn Fields Theatre. Many of his secular works were separately published, and even in 1719 when *Wit and Mirth* came out, many of his pieces were included. One of his songs ended up in *The Beggar's Opera* in 1728. Ironically, his best-known piece today is probably the trumpet voluntary called the Prince of Denmark's March, a work which for many years was erroneously attributed to Purcell. During Clarke's active years in the 1690s and early 1700s he also turned out a great number of anthems, services, choral works, and airs and lessons for the harpsichord.

On 1 December 1707 Jeremiah Clarke shot himself to death in a fit of madness at his house in St Paul's churchyard. He had always been of a melancholy disposition, and the traditional story has it that because of unrequited love he had earlier considered suicide and had flipped a coin to decide whether it should be by hanging or drowning—and the coin ended up stuck in the mud on edge, deterring him from any action. He was buried at St Paul's on 3 December 1707, unmarried and intestate.

Clarke, John [fl. 1671–1701], *theatre keeper.*

John Clarke was a groom in the Office of the Revels from 24 October 1671 to 1701 or later, and from 24 April 1678 he also served as the Court theatre keeper, succeeding Philip Johnson.

Clarke, [John?] [fl. 1770–1836?], singer.

A Master Clarke was a featured singer in a musical entertainment called *The Sons of Anacreon* ("In which [are] several *Catches* and *Glees* selected from the most Eminent Masters") on the bill at Drury Lane Theatre before the acting of the mainpiece on 18 April 1785. The offering was repeated on 16 and 19 May.

Young Clarke was heard on six further occasions in London's public theatres when he sang, with Dignum, Williames, Danby, and others, "Hark! the Lark at Heaven's Gate Sings" in Act II of the altered *Cymbeline* at Drury Lane on 1 February and five other times in 1785–86 and again on 3 November 1787. There is a good chance that those may have been youthful episodes in the career of the well-known musician John Clarke—later known as Clark-Whitfield (1770–1836), organist, master of choristers at Hereford Cathedral, and Professor of Music at Cambridge University.

Clarke, John Woodruff [fl. 1794–1800], actor.

John Woodruff Clarke was probably the Clarke who was on the Edinburgh Theatre's roster in 1794. He was at Manchester on 27 November 1795 as "from Edinburgh," and he came to the Richmond company under Haymes's management in the summer of 1797.

Clarke was introduced to the Covent Garden audience as "from the Theatre Royal, Edinburgh," and making his first appearance "on this stage" in the part of Ferdinand in *The Duenna* on 21 June 1797 in a special benefit performance for the General Lying-in Hospital, Bayswater, after the season was over. He was signed onto the regular roster at Covent Garden the next season, and he acted from 18 September 1797 through 11 June 1798 at a salary of £3 per week. He was put to work at once sustaining a full calendar and wide range of secondary and tertiary parts: young bucks, eccentrics, supporting noblemen, small villains, exotics, and blunt men. On the first night of the season he was Westmoreland in *1 Henry IV*, beginning a season certainly unsurpassed by any other young actor of the period for multiplicity of roles. They were:

Rosencrantz in *Hamlet*, Mr Page in *The Merry Wives of Windsor*, Buckingham in *Richard III*, Charles Gripe in *The Busy Body*, Don Pedro in *Much Ado About Nothing*, the Duke in *Rule a Wife and Have a Wife*, Polydore in *The Orphan*, Lord Randolph in *Douglas*, Snare in *Abroad and at Home*, Serjeant Jack in *The Highland Reel*, the Prince in *Romeo and Juliet*, Lorenzo in *The Merchant of Venice*, Eugene in *The Agreeable Surprise*, Fabio in *An Escape into Prison*, Eustace in *Love in a Village*, Solyman in *The Sultan*, Cornwall in *King Lear*, Frederick in *The Miser*, Erox in *Merope*, Fernando in *The Castle of Andalusia*, William in *The Way to Keep Him*, Bernardo in *The Mysteries of the Castle*, Aladin in *Barbarossa*, Phocion in *The Grecian Daughter*, the English Squire in *England Preserved*, Williams in *He's Much to Blame*, Harold in *Peeping Tom*, Midge in *Wild Oats*, Careless in *The School for Scandal*, the Duke in *The Comedy of Errors*, Olmutz in *Love in a Camp*, Young O'Donovan in *The Lie of the Day*, the Mate in *Inkle and Yarico*, Lenox in *The Rival Soldiers*, Hosier in *The Road to Ruin*, Frank in *Retaliation*, Plywell in *Matrimony*, Freeman in *High Life Below Stairs*, Merlin in *Cymon*, Harman in *Lionel and Clarissa*, Young Knowell in *Every Man in his Humour*, George Bevil in *Cross Purposes*, Meanright in *Such Things Are*, Bellario in *Disinterested Love*, Valentine in *The Farmer*, and Count Valentia in *The Child of Nature*.

The prediction of the *Monthly Mirror* in October 1797 that "In similar parts he will be found eminently useful" was borne out in successive seasons. The versatility of his study continued into 1798–99, when the management rewarded his toil with £4 per week. (He was this season identified by signed receipts as "J. W. Clarke".) He was at Covent Garden through the season (and played at the Haymarket during the summer), and then he transferred to Drury Lane for the 1799–1800 season. There his salary was only £3 per week.

Among other characters which Clarke played were: The Mogul in *A Mogul Tale*, Degagee in *The Dead Alive*, Fripon in *The Prisoner at Large*, Poz in *The London Hermit*, Charles in *The Jealous Wife*, Dick in *The Lying Valet*, Ribbemont in *The Surrender of Calais*, the Bard in *Cambro-Britons*, La Varenne in *The Battle of Hexham*, Rawbold in *The Iron Chest*, Wat Dreary in *The Beggar's Opera*, Guzman in *The Red Cross Knights*, Father Luke in *The Poor Soldier*, Montano in *Othello*, Malcolm in *Macbeth*, Count Hugo von Werdenberg in *The Count of Burgundy*, Muley in *The Castle Spectre*, Woodville in *The Wheel of Fortune*, Russet in *The Deserter*, Sir Rowland in *Children in the Wood*, Oliver in *As You Like It*, and Ithirak in *Lodoiska*.

Clarke, Matthew *d. 1786, actor.*

Matthew Clarke stepped directly from the obscurity of a City tradesman's shop into leading roles in one of the great patent theatres of London, a unique occurrence in the annals of British theatricals. He made his debut under a favorite protective formula ("a gentleman who never appeared on any Stage") in the part of Osman in *Zara* at Covent Garden Theatre on 30 October 1755. He was resplendent in a costume of lace, linen, silk, "Blue stuff," and white flannel, which cost the substantial sum of £2 7s. 2d., according to the theatre's account books. His identity was revealed to the public when he appeared in *The Re-*venge on 26 November: "Zanga—Clarke (whose first appearance was in the character of Osman in *Zara*)." Clarke was thereafter Theseus in *Phaedra and Hippolytus* on 5 February 1756, Byron in *The Fatal Marriage* on 19 February, Ulysses in *Ulysses* on 23 March, and, for his benefit on 29 April, Zamor in *Alzira*.

In 1756–57 Clarke did not appear until 2 November when again he took a leading role, as Theseus in *Hippolyta and Theseus*. He was Byron in *The Fatal Marriage* on 17 November and made his first appearance in comedy—as the bills emphasized—when he assumed Young Woud'be in *The Twin Rivals* on 9 February 1757. He dropped to a secondary part, that of Frederick in *The Rover*, when it was revived for the first time in 20 years on 18 February. He was in the

Harvard Theatre Collection

MATTHEW CLARKE, as Procles
engraving by Pollard, after Roberts

lead again when he took his benefit on 25 April as Chamont in *The Orphan*. (Tickets could "be had of Clarke at Mr Settree's Cap Warehouse, Catherine St.")

Clarke was a mainbrace of Covent Garden through fair weather and foul for over 30 years; and although he did not live quite up to the heroic promise of his youth, he fell back honorably enough into second-line characters in tragedy and eccentrics in comedy. He never changed winter theatres, and did not, indeed, play anywhere in London but Covent Garden, aside from a few scattered benefits at the Haymarket and a single performance at Drury Lane. He could usually depend, as a favorite of two generations, on drawing good benefit houses. His salary rose but slowly. Arthur Murphy gave it as £1 per diem as of 14 September 1767. Other surviving manuscript pay sheets show him paid in 1778–79 for 178 days at £1 6s. 8d. for a total of £237 6s. 8d. for the season. In 1782–83 he was paid for 192 nights at £1 6s. 8d. or £256. His attendance at the theatre was constant, except during the end of the 1767–68 season and the beginning of the next. On 20 April his part of Tullus Aufidius in *Coriolanus* had to be supplied by Younger, and he was out of action because of some ailment for the rest of the season. He was in frail health during the 1768–69 season also, appearing in only 20 scattered performances.

Among Clarke's characters, added carefully year by year, were the following: Elder Wou'dbe in *The Twin Rivals*, Bellamy in *The Suspicious Husband*, Frederick in *The Miser*, Jasper in *Miss in Her Teens*, the Duke in *Venice Preserv'd*, Narbal in *Mariamne*, Cosroe in *The Prophetess*, Cunningham in *The Amorous Widow*, Freeman in *A Bold Stroke for a Wife*, Henry VIII in *Anna Bullen*, Caesar in *Julius Caesar*, Hotspur in *1 Henry IV*, Polydore in *The Orphan*, Osmond in *Tancred and Sigismunda*, Paulet in *Cleone*, Constable of France in *Henry V*, Cloten in *Cymbeline*, Charles in *The Busy Body*, Debonair in *The Lady's*

Harvard Theatre Collection

MATTHEW CLARKE, as Antonio
artist unknown

Choice, Elder Brother in *Comus*, Springlove in *The Jovial Crew*, Lovewel in *The Spirit of Contradiction*, Hubert in *The Royal Merchant*, Le Noble in *The Country House*, Bassanio in *The Merchant of Venice*, King Philip in *King John*, Cassander in *The Rival Queens*, Bertran in *The Spanish Fryar*, Macduff in *Macbeth*, the King in *The Mourning Bride*, Scandal in *Love for Love*, Richmond in *King Henry III*, Gloster in *Jane Shore*, Roderigo in *The Pilgrim*, Sullen in *The Stratagem*, Clytus in *The Rival Queens*, Offa in *The Royal Convert*, Elder Worthy in *Love's Last Shift*, Young Knowel in *Every Man in His Humour*, Colonel Standard in *The Constant Couple*, Blunt in *No One's Enemy But His Own*, Hussar in *Perseus and Andromeda*, Farewell in *Sir*

Courtly Nice, the Bastard (Edmund) in the Tate alteration called *King Lear and His Three Daughters*, Dolabella in *All for Love*, Manly in *The Provok'd Husband*, Medley in *The Man of Mode*, Marcian in *Theodorus*, Morton in *The Albion Queens*, Sir William Honeywood in *The Good-Natur'd Man*, Archbishop of York in *2 Henry IV*, the Duke in *The Double Falsehood*, Smith in *The Rehearsal*, Antonio it *The Merchant of Venice*, Bellarius in *Cymbeline*, Thorowgood in *George Barnwell*, Earl Belmont in *The Sister*, Older Belfield in *The Brothers*, Sciolto in *The Fair Penitent*, Pembroke in *The Earl of Warwick*, both Claudius and the Ghost in *Hamlet*, Ventidius in *All for Love*, Guardian in *The Guardian*, Mathusius in *Timanthes*, Angelo in *Measure for Measure*, Clytus in *The Rival Queens*, Kent in *King Lear*, Strickland in *The Suspicious Husband*, Dionysius in *The Grecian Daughter*, Stockwell in *The West Indian*, Astyages in *Cyrus*, Lafeu in *All's Well that Ends Well*, Sealand in *The Conscious Lovers*, the Abbot in *King Henry*, and Brumpton in *The Funeral*.

In addition to his long London service, after 1758 Clarke acted regularly at Jacob's Wells Theatre in Bristol in the summers. In 1764 he was named, along with William Powell, John Arthur, and John Palmer (all celebrated London actors) to manage the projected new theatre to be erected by 1766 between King Street and Baldwin Street in Bristol. Their lease was drawn up for fourteen years, but at the end of the first season all but Arthur declined to accept it. Clarke nevertheless played second leads at Bristol in every season following until 1780. He re-entered the management at Bristol, along with Dodd, after the death of Powell in 1769.

The *Theatrical Biography* reported in 1772 that the Bristol managers "having always two benefits in the season, and Mr Clark being universally liked by that sober, industrious people, they have always turned out as very considerable appendages to his emoluments in town." As a Bristol critic described him, Clarke was "the chief favourite at our old Theatre. He was very respectable both in appearance and performance, seldom out of his latitude; and if he never mounted to a great height, he never sunk below a proper level." This might do for an assessment of Clarke's career overall. As the chronologically arranged list of characters given above shows, Clarke was far less restricted to given "lines" of characters than most actors of his period, and, although he showed ability in mature and old men (along with youthful fops and beaus) during his early years on the stage, it was not until his final five seasons that he nearly abandoned more youthful parts for ones of eld, like Corvino in *The Fox*, the Old Shepherd in *The Winter's Tale*, and old Capulet in *Romeo and Juliet*.

Clarke was an inoffensive man, but in his earlier years seems to have given an impression of having a disposition somewhat sour. The anonymous author of *The Rosciad of C——v——nt G——rd——n* (1762) saw him thus:

NEXT sullen C——KE advanced, with
    pensive air,
Cloudy his brow, and overhung with
    care.
Spight of himself, in ev'ry varied scene,
He mixes with his part his native
    spleen . . .
But, when he shines OSMOND, in whose
    breast
Are all the passions of his own ex-
    press'd,
So strong his feelings, and so just each
    pause,
That ev'n envy can't deny applause:
Then for the ruffian, I dare bet a shilling,
M——CKL——N himself ne'er look'd a
    thorougher villain;
Altho' my friend, once stript him of his
    part,
'S a very honest fellow at his heart.

In 1766 Hugh Kelly in *Thespis* praised his manly voice and form but found him usually too rough and unmusical, capable of few strokes of tenderness, and advised him to eschew the flimsier comical characters in favor of the graver business of the stage— the judge, the cautious parent, the sage, and so on. Other writers agreed. A critic in the *Macaroni and Savoir Vivre Magazine* (1773) praised him "Where he is confined to his own natural walk," characters like Sciolto, Abudah, and Kent. William Hawkins in *Miscellanies in Prose and Verse* (1775) echoed the judgment: in his "rough, honest parts of tragedy. . . . There is a manliness in his person, with a sound and just tone of voice which renders him in this walk second to none on either of the stages."

There were, of course, dissenters. The *Rational Rosciad* (1767) summed him up in a quatrain:

> *With a strong voice, and a good person graced,*
> *But destitute of feeling and of taste,*
> *Clarke, to no greater characters pretends,*
> *Than trusty valets, or advising friends.*

Francis Gentleman in *The Theatres* (1772) dismissed him as "tolerable third rate Clark" who did a good job in "the medium style."

In his final season Clarke played only from 22 September to 21 October 1785. His last appearance was as the King in *1 Henry IV*. He fell ill shortly thereafter and took to his bed in his house at No 15, Great Russell Street, Covent Garden. The Covent Garden playbill for 6 May 1786, his benefit night, read sadly:

> Mr Clarke begs leave to inform his Friends, [of] his violent Indisposition, and Incapacity to perform for his Benefit. . . . Mr Clarke hopes his present severe Indisposition, which had prevented his playing for several Months past, will be considered by his Friends as a sufficient Apology for his not performing at his Benefit, and solicits their Patronage this Evening.

Clarke died the same night. He was buried on 10 or 12 May in the churchyard of St George, Hanover Square.

In 1772 the *Theatrical Biography*, a publication not always known for its strict accuracy, had reported that

> Previous to his going on the stage, Mr Clark married the daughter of a general officer, a Lady possessed of many useful and ornamental virtues; by her he has had six or seven children, all of whom he has educated with a tenderness and attention that deserve to be mentioned with a particular compliment when it is considered he is a player.

This good lady was never on the stage. She survived her husband less than five months, dying on 24 September 1786.

Portraits and prints of Matthew Clarke include:

1. As Antonio in a large painting by Zoffany, with Charles and Maria Macklin, Michael Dyer, and Robert Bensley, in the trial scene of *The Merchant of Venice*. The painting, now in the Tate Gallery, is reproduced in this dictionary with Charles Macklin's biography.

2. As Antonio, by an anonymous engraver, published by Smith and Sayer, 1769.

3. As Henry VIII, by an anonymous engraver, published by J. Wenman, 1778.

4. As Henry VIII, engraved by C. Grignion, after J. Roberts, for *Bell's British Theatre*, 1776.

5. As Lord Brumpton, with John Quick as Sable, in *The Funeral*, engraved by W. Walker, after R. Dighton, for the *New English Theatre*, 1777.

6. As Othman, with Savigny as Selim, in *Barbarossa*, by an anonymous engraver.

7. As Procles in *Eurydice*, engraved by Pollard, after J. Roberts, for *Bell's British Theatre*, 1777.

8. As L. Virginius, by an anonymous engraver, published by Harrison, 1781.

Clarke, Nathaniel *1699–1783, actor, dancer.*

Nathaniel Clarke was first named in playbills on 29 January 1728 at Lincoln's Inn Fields when he played Filch in the first performance of *The Beggar's Opera* — a role for which he was remembered many years later. He may have made stage appearances before this, his thirtieth year, but he is not to be identified as the Clarke who was a harlequin at Drury Lane from 1726 to 1728, for then two Clarkes acted simultaneously. Nathaniel Clarke went on to play Sancho in *The Successful Strangers* on 25 June 1728 and Maiden in *Tunbridge Walks* on 2 July. He then appeared on 9 August at the Haymarket Theatre as the Colonel in *The Spanish Fryar* and on 24 August as Captain Slicer in *Bateman* at the Hall-Miller booth at Bartholomew Fair.

In 1728–29 Clarke was again at Lincoln's Inn Fields, but he was infrequently mentioned in the bills. He played Slender in *The Merry Wives of Windsor* on 28 December and Roger in *Flora* on 7 May 1729; billed as "Young Filch" he danced on 9 May; and with two others he shared a benefit on 12 May which brought in £196 19s. 6d. In August he again appeared at Bartholomew Fair, this time as a Sailor in *Maudlin* at the Hall-Oates booth. His 1729–30 season was similar: he added a Prisoner in *A Woman's Revenge* and a Brideman in *The Wedding* to his repertory, but apparently nothing more. In 1730–31 at Lincoln's Inn Fields his only new part was Lycophron in *Periander*, but he acted Archer in *The Stratagem* at York Buildings on 20 August 1731, playing opposite his wife's Mrs Sullen. The performance was for the benefit of Mr and Mrs Clarke and its playbill contained the first indication that Nathaniel was married. His wife was presumably the Mrs Clarke who sang and acted from 1727 to 1747. Clarke finished the summer of 1731 at Southwark Fair playing Tipple in *The Banished General* and Perriwinkle in *A Bold Stroke for a Wife*.

The pattern of Clarke's activity during the rest of the 1730s was much the same. He performed at Lincoln's Inn Fields and then Covent Garden during the winters and, through 1736, played in late summers at Bartholomew Fair. His repertory expanded slowly. By 1740 it included such roles as Brush in *Love and a Bottle*, Harlequin in *The Farrier Nicked*, Supple in *The Double Gallant*, Osric in *Hamlet*, Daniel in *Oroonoko*, Robert Faulconbridge in *King John*, the title role in *The School Boy*, the Shoemaker in *The Relapse*, Cogdie in *The Gamester*, Tom in *The Constant Couple*, Gloucester in *Henry V*, Donalbain in *Macbeth*, and Pistol in *The Merry Wives of Windsor*.

Clarke stayed with Rich at Covent Garden in 1740–41 and 1741–42, adding a few new parts: Galloon in *The Gamester*, Barnaby in *The Old Bachelor*, Prince John in *1 Henry IV*, Blunt in *Richard III*, and others. But on 6 May 1742 he shared a benefit with three other actors and concluded his association with the company. The *Memoirs of Charles Macklin* contain an anecdote about Clarke:

His chief employment, after the run of the Beggar's Opera, was as an under Harlequin to Rich, whom he much resembled in size and figure, and which gave rise to the following whimsical accident. One of the Actors having had some words with Clarke, during the representation of a Pantomime, waited till he should find an opportunity of shewing his resentment. Unluckily, Rich being in the way of this angry person, as he came off the stage, he, thinking it was Clarke, struck him such a blow on the breast, as for a time deprived him of the power of breathing. The man instantly made every apology for his mistake. "But pray, Muster," says Rich, "what provocation could Clarke possibly give you to strike so hard?"

Davies in his *Dramatic Miscellanies* noted that Clarke sometimes substituted for Rich "in such situations of the pantomimes as were least interesting" — which arrangement explains why Clarke received few billings for such work. Of Clarke's salary under Rich we know only that in 1735–36 he was allowed 172 days at 3*s*. 4*d*. daily and no benefit.

Perhaps after leaving Covent Garden, Clarke toured the provinces. There was a Mr Clark at Norwich in 1742–43, but the evidence is too thin to make a positive identification. On 8 September 1743 at Southwark Fair a Mr Clark played Gudgeon in *The Blind Beggar of Bethnal Green*; on 10 May 1744 at the Haymarket Theatre a Clark acted Hellebore in *The Mock Doctor*; and on 7 September 1750 at Southwark Fair a Mr Clark acted Elen in *Jeptha's Rash Vow*.

At some point Nathaniel Clarke retired to Hammersmith where he "lived at ease, and often treated his visitors with good ale, and much theatrical anecdote," related Tom Davies, who was one of his frequent visitors. Clarke was never a major figure, though in "under parts of Tragedy and Comedy" he was a useful performer, and his "meagre countenance" and "shambling gait" made him a perfect Filch, according to the Macklin *Memoirs*. Nathaniel Clarke (erroneously called Edward in some sources) died on 12 August 1783 at the age of 84.

Clarke, Mrs ₁Nathaniel?₁ ₁*fl.* 1727–1747₁, *actress, singer.*

A Mrs Clarke, who very likely was the wife of the actor Nathaniel Clarke, made her first appearance on any stage on 17 October 1727 playing Lady Wealthy in *The Gamester* at Lincoln's Inn Fields. In the months following she appeared as Jenny Diver in *The Beggar's Opera* and the Judge's Lady in *Love and a Bottle*. At her shared benefit with two others on 23 May 1728 she may have acted in *The Jew of Venice*, but no role was listed for her. The receipts came to £151 7*s*. The 1728 edition of the opera *Penelope* assigned Mrs Clarke the title role, but the work, performed on 8 May 1728 at the Haymarket Theatre, was advertised with no cast listed.

On 2 January 1729 Mrs Clarke played Abigail in *The Lottery* at the Haymarket; on 25 February she was the first Countrywoman in *The Humours of Harlequin*; and on 29 May she acted Strummer in *The Beggar's Wedding*. Yet the Haymarket bill for 26 July 1729 listed a Mrs Clarke as playing the title role in *Flora*, with Ray acting Hob, "being the first Time of their appearing on this Stage." That reference may have been to some other Mrs Clark. On 25 August 1729 at Bartholomew Fair a Mrs Clark played an unnamed role in *The Beggar's Wedding* at Reynolds's booth, and a Mrs Clarke acted Friendly in *Flora* at Bullock's booth. Though two different performers are implied, it is noteworthy that the Reynolds bill stated carefully that *The Beggar's Wedding* would be played until 8:00 P.M. *Flora* was scheduled as an afterpiece, and so it probably would have started after that hour. One actress could have played in both performances.

On 12 November 1729 *Love and Revenge* was presented at the Haymarket, and the 1729 edition of the work lists Mrs Clarke as Charlot. Most of her performing in late 1729, however, was seen at Goodman's Fields. There she acted Mrs Foresight in *Love for Love*, Widow Lackit in *Oroonoko*, Araminta in *The Old Bachelor*, Lady Wealthy in *The Gamester*, Honoria in *Love Makes a Man*, and Lady Darling in *The Constant Couple*. She was active at the Haymarket in early 1730, and in August and September she played at both Bartholomew and Southwark fairs, taking the roles of a Forester and a Woman Peasant in *Harlequin's Contrivance*, first under Reynolds and then under Pinkethman.

Mrs Clarke made a few appearances at the Haymarket in 1730–31, playing Lady Kingcall in *The Author's Farce*, Gipsey in *The Stratagem*, Good Scratch in *The Welch Opera* and other roles. On 20 August 1731 at York Buildings she played Mrs Sullen in

The Stratagem and Phillida in *Damon and Phillida* for her shared benefit with Mr Clarke—presumably her husband and probably the dancer Nathaniel Clark.

During the 1731–32 season Mrs Clarke was in the company at Drury Lane, but no roles are known for her and she seems not to have stayed the full season. On 8 March 1732 she was at the Haymarket again, playing Jenny in *Tunbridge Walks*, and by the end of the month she had also acted Lady Beauslire in *The Wanton Jesuit* and Sarah in *A Bold Stroke for a Wife*. At Bartholomew Fair on 23 August 1732 she played Anna Bullen in *Henry VIII*, and after a year of silence she turned up at the Fair again on 23 August 1733 to act Flora in *Jane Shore*.

Mrs Clarke was associated with Theophilus Cibber and his Drury Lane malcontents at the Haymarket in the fall of 1733 and played Isabinda in *The Busy Body*, a Shepherdess in *An Impromptu Revel Masque* (also called *The Festival*), and Venus in *Chrononhotonthologos*. On 24 August 1734 she was Eboli in *Don Carlos* at the Fielding-Oates booth at Bartholomew Fair while her husband (if we have identified him correctly) acted at a different booth. At Tottenham Court on 28 May 1735 Mrs Clarke played Abigail in *The Drummer*; during 1736–37 she was listed on the Covent Garden roster but was not named in any bills; on 29 December 1746, after a long period of silence, she played the title role in *Anna Bullen* at a "concert" at the James Street Theatre; on 24 March 1747 she popped up at the Haymarket again as Alicia in *Jane Shore*; and on 24 September 1747 at Southwark Fair she made her last known appearance playing the title role in *Jane Shore*.

Clarke, Richard [*fl. 1730–1760?*], *violinist.*

Richard Clarke was a member of the string section of the Drury Lane Theatre's band toward the middle of the eighteenth century. He is said by Grove's *Dictionary*, to have succeeded Richard Jones as "leader" (i.e., first-chair violinist) of the band at some unspecified time.

Clarke, Robert *1777–1853, dancer.*

The R. Clarke who danced and swelled stage crowds a few times at Covent Garden during the season of 1798–99 has been identified in a clipping affixed to a manuscript in the Harvard Theatre Collection as the Robert Clark who died on 18 March 1853, aged 76. His wife Anne had died at Brompton Crescent on 20 February 1853, whereupon reportedly her husband, until then "in excellent health [and] full of spirits," declined and expired.

Clarkson, Mr [*fl. 1723–1728*], *pit office keeper.*

Mr Clarkson may have been working at Lincoln's Inn Fields for some time prior to the first appearance of his name on the bills, on 3 June 1723. He then shared with three others a benefit that brought in £111 19s. On 22 May 1724 he shared £141 13s. 6d. with two others, and on 10 May 1725 he split £177 6d. with Harrison, one of the pit office keepers.

The Lincoln's Inn Fields accounts for 1724–28 make it clear that Clarkson was a house servant, probably a pit office keeper who occasionally served as a boxkeeper when the boxes and pit were laid together. The accounts show payments to him for "incidents" almost every week in the 1724–25 season, and occasionally thereafter, of amounts ranging from 5s. 3d. to £8 10s. Clarkson also handled the issuing of free tickets for the managers and actors. He was last mentioned in the accounts on 9 March 1728 when he replaced the boxkeeper Redfern for a month. Clarkson, along with Wilmer and Verhuyck, appears to have been one of the supervisors who occasionally substituted for other servants when they were absent.

Clarkson, Mr [*fl. 1750–1765*], *actor.*

A Mr Clarkson acted Horatio in a single performance of *The Wife's Relief* at the Haymarket on 26 July 1750, given by a company which included Lewis Hallam. Probably this Clarkson was the one who, with other London actors, sailed to Virginia with Hallam on the *Charming Sally* in 1752. Despite T. Allston Brown's claim that Clarkson had made his first appearance on any stage at Goodman's Fields, the above noted performance at the Haymarket is the only recorded instance in the extant bills of a Clarkson acting in London prior to the departure of the Hallam company.

Clarkson made his debut on the American stage as Antonio in *The Merchant of Venice* at Williamsburg on 5 September 1752, in the first performance given by the company. He made his first appearance in New York on 17 September 1753 at the Nassau Street Theatre, as Myrtle in *The Conscious Lovers*. At the New Theatre in Water Street, Philadelphia, between 15 April and 24 June 1754, Clarkson played Altamont in *The Fair Penitent*, Flash in *Miss in Her Teens*, Sir Thomas Testy in *Flora*, and Omar in *Tamerlane*. According to Seilhamer, his other roles in the repertory of the Hallam company included Gifford in *The Albion Queens*, Gibbet in *The Beaux' Stratagem*, Abel Day in *The Committee*, Clincher, Junior, in *The Constant Couple*, Phoenix in *The Distrest Mother*, Butler in *The Drummer*, Dawson in *The Gamester*, Edmund in *King Lear*, Foresight in *Love for Love*, Richmond in *Richard III*, Friar Laurence in *Romeo and Juliet*, Jack Meggot in *The Suspicious Husband*, Young Woudbe in *The Twin Rivals*, Old Gerald in *The Anatomist*, Corydon in *Damon and Phillida*, Aesop in *Lethe*, Uncle Michan in *The Stage Coach*, the bailiff in *Tom Thumb*, and Goodwill in *The Virgin Unmask'd*. After the company's performances at Charleston in January 1765, the actors departed for Jamaica and, with the exception of the Hallams, never were seen again

on the American stage. Clarkson's name does not appear in any extant notices of performances in the West Indies, where presumably he died or from whence he at some time returned to England.

Clarkson's wife, of whom there is no record on the London stage, was also on the *Charming Sally* and acted minor roles for the company in America until 1754.

Clarkson, Mr [*fl. 1778*], *booth proprietor.*

A Mr Clarkson was the proprietor of a booth at Bartholomew Fair in 1778.

Clarridge. *See* CLARIDGE.

Clary, Mr [*fl. 1791–1795*], *costume designer.*

Newspaper advertisements credit a Mr Clary with designing the dresses—"in character"—at Astley's Amphitheatre for *The King and The Cobbler* on 6 May 1791 and *Harlequin Invincible* on 22 August 1795.

Clary, Mme [*fl. 1757–1758*], *dancer.*

Madame Clary danced in a ballet, *Le Carneval de Venice*, at the Haymarket on 26 December 1757 and 6 January 1758.

"Clatterbane" [*fl. 1774*], *musician.*

A person by the pseudonym of "Clatterbane" performed on the saltbox in a *Comic Ode*, written by Bonnell Thornton, at the Haymarket on 15 March 1774, in a program which also featured such performers as "Dingdong" and "Bladderbridge."

"Claudio." *See* ROGIER, CLAUDIO.

Clavigney. *See* CHAVIGNY.

Clawood, Robert [*fl. 1765*], *musician.*

Robert Clawood, described as a musician living in Blackfriars, became a freeman and was admitted to livery in the Worshipful Company of Musicians on 12 September 1765.

Claxton, Mr [*fl. 1703–1707*], *dancer.*
On 3 February 1703 at Drury Lane Mr Claxton performed an Irish dance, and on the twelfth he danced *The Whip of Dunbyn* with his pupil, the "Devonshire Girl" (Mrs Mosse). The pair appeared again at the Dorset Garden Theatre in April, and on 18 June, back at Drury Lane, Claxton danced *The Highland* and *The Whip of Dunbyn* with his son. Claxton and the Devonshire Girl appeared again at Drury Lane on occasion in the 1703–4 and 1704–5 seasons, and Claxton was billed once more at the theatre on 21 January 1706. The last notice of him was for 19 November 1707 at York Buildings when he danced and his son composed music for a concert.

Claxton, Mr [*fl. 1703–1707*], *dancer, composer. See* **CLAXTON, MR** [*fl. 1703–1707*], *dancer.*

Clay, Joseph [*fl. 1709–1710*], *musician.*
In late January 1710 Joseph Clay and other "Musitians living in the Parish of St. James'" were complained against for having played music for money during the previous year without authorization. Clay and the others were ordered to appear before the Court of Burgesses of Westminster to answer the charges, but no record has survived of the results of the case.

Clay, Samuel [*fl. 1784?–1794*], *singer? instrumentalist? music copyist.*
Samuel Clay was listed in 1794 in Doane's *Musical Directory* as a "tenor" and music copyist, living at No 26, Great St Andrew's Street, Seven Dials, and a participant in the performances commemorating Handel which were given at Westminster Abbey in 1784 and several later years.

Clay, William [*fl. 1784–1794*], *singer.*

William Clay was listed in 1794 by Doane's *Musical Directory* as a bass singer, from Greenwich, a member of the Handelian Society, and a participant in "the grand performances at Westminster Abbey." He is probably the same Mr Clay listed by Burney as a bass in his account of the Handel Memorial Concerts at Westminster Abbey and the Pantheon in May and June 1784.

Claysack, S. [*fl. 1794*], *musician.*
Two conflicting entries in the Drury Lane accounts at the Folger Shakespeare Library dated 14 June 1794 concern a musician named either S. Claysack or Clayshort. One entry puts Claysack down for 6*s*. daily as an added musician, while the other puts Clayshort down for 5*s*. daily.

Clayshort. *See* **CLAYSACK.**

Clayton, Master [*fl. 1763*], *dancer.*
Master Clayton and Miss Street, both apprentices to Gerhardi, performed a provincial dance at the Haymarket Theatre on 5 August 1763. "Clayton" may have been a misprint for "Clinton."

Clayton, John [*fl. 1762–1778*], *scene painter.*
It is likely that the Mr Clayton who was paid £2 on 30 May 1768 for painting scenery at Covent Garden was John Clayton, who exhibited a number of still lifes and landscapes in watercolors, crayons, and oils at the Society of Artists of Great Britain and at the Free Society of Artists at various times between 1762 and 1778. He was living at Mr Vincent's in the Little Piazza, Covent Garden, in the 1760s, and by 1778 he had moved to Mr Alleyn's in Great Compton Street, Soho.

Clayton, Thomas *1673–1725?, composer, impresario, violinist?*
Thomas Clayton, son of William and Elizabeth, was baptized at St Paul, Covent

Garden, on 28 October 1673. His father was a violinist in the King's Musick and, in later years, a sharer in the United Company at Drury Lane. On 16 July 1689 young Thomas, then nearing 16, was given a position in the King's Musick without fee and served thus until 8 July 1693, when he replaced the deceased John Goodwin. Since Goodwin, like Thomas's father, was a violinist, it is probable that Thomas was also. The younger Clayton seems never to have distinguished himself in any way in the royal musical establishment, for the references to him in the Lord Chamberlain's accounts have only to do with his annual livery payments of £16 2s. 6d. and his yearly salary of £40. He served at court until 1702.

The elder Clayton died in 1697, leaving the bulk of his estate to his son and widow. Thomas, by the terms of the will, was to receive William Clayton's house in Little Bridges Street (Vinegar Yard), half the plate, all the musical instruments, and four ground rent shares in Drury Lane, and upon his mother's death or remarriage he was to have her house in Arlington Street. The will was proved only by Mrs Clayton, Thomas apparently renouncing, but after she died in August 1700 Thomas proved the will again on 14 November and came into his full inheritance.

In 1702 Thomas went off to Italy, presumably to study music, and when he returned in 1704 he chose to pursue a career as an opera composer and musical impresario rather than return to the security of performing at court. The *Diverting Post* of 28 October 1704 announced that Clayton was preparing an opera for the Queen's Theatre in the Haymarket which Sir John Vanbrugh was then building. The musician and his associates in this venture, Nicola Haym and Charles Dieupart, changed their minds, and *Arsinoe* was presented at Drury Lane on 16 January 1705. Clayton wrote 23 of the 27 songs in the opera, which was "after the Italian manner" but in an

English translation by Motteux. An anonymous critic scornfully commented that "there is nothing in it but a few sketches of antiquated Italian airs, so mangled and sophisticated, that instead of Arsinoe, it ought to be called the Hospital of the old Decrepid Italian Opera." None of the songs have been traced to Italian originals, however, and Clayton has been exonerated from the charge of plagiarism if not of having composed third-rate music. Burney called *Arsinoe* mean in melody and incorrect in counterpoint, yet the work was popular, and it received 36 performances in two years.

Clayton next turned his attention to *Rosamond*, which was first performed at Drury Lane on 4 March 1707 but failed. The anonymous critic was ready with another blast at the composer: he felt the new work had "mounted the stage on purpose to frighten all England with its abominable musick." Clayton did not give up his efforts after this, but he wisely shifted locale. It is said he went to Dublin for a period; he seems not to have been noticed in London documents again until 27 April 1710. On that date he advertised for his benefit a *Pastoral Masque* at York Buildings to be performed on 3 May. Steele in the *Tatler* gave him a puff on 1 May and asked him, in return, please to have the instrumentalists tune up before the audience arrived. Clayton not only agreed but promised to "order the *heels of the performers to be muffled in cotton*, that the artists, in so polite an age as ours, may not intermix with their harmony, a custom, which so nearly resembles the stamping-dances of the West Indians or Hottentots."

Steele's interest in Clayton's efforts were renewed in 1711 when Clayton, Haym, and Dieupart, with Steele's assistance, produced a series of concerts in Clayton's house in York Buildings featuring recitals of English poems with musical backgrounds. On 24 May 1711 Harrison's *The Passion of Sappho* and John Hughes's revision of Dryden's *Alexander's Feast* were presented with settings by Clayton, and on the following 16 July Prior's *If Wine and Musick Have the Power* was offered. The problem with these presentations appears to have been Clayton's mediocre talents as a composer. Hughes was especially critical of the musician's settings and wrote to Steele in April 1711:

That which seems to me to strike most, are the Prelude Bases, some of which are very well fancy'd; but I am afraid they are in themselves too long, especially when repeated; for Prelude Bases are only to begin the subject of the Air, & do not shew any Composition (which consists in the union of parts) so that if they are not artfully worked afterwards with the Voice part, they are no proof of Skill, but only of Invention.

The Symphonies in many places seem to me perplex'd, and not made to pursue any Subject or Point.

The last Air of Sappho begins too cheerfully for the sense of the Words. As well as I can guess, without seeing the score, it is in D sharp, from which it varies (in another movement of Time) into B flat 3d, & so ends, without returning to the same Key either flatt or sharp. This being one continued Air (though in two Movements of Time) let it be asked of some Master Whether it is allowable (I am sure, 'tis not usual) to begin an Air in one Key sharp, and end it in a different key flatt? For though y° passage is natural, the Closing so is, I believe, always disallowed.

The Overture of Alexander ought to be great & noble; instead of which, I find only a hurry of the Instruments, not proper (in my poor Opinion) & without any Design, or Fugue, & I'm afraid, perplex'd & irregular in the Composition . . .

—and so on. Hughes picked Clayton's work to shreds, yet Addison and Steele, anxious to encourage the use of English words with English music, gave Clayton and his cohorts another puff in the 26 December 1711 issue of the *Spectator*.

Concerts of poems and music were presented on 24 and 29 May, 16 July, and 14 December 1711 and on 18 January 1712. Clayton and his partners also offered subscription concerts on 26 December 1711, 18 January and 15 February 1712, and subsequent dates, but in time their efforts faded and Steele took over the rooms in York Buildings for his own "Censorium." Clayton's setting for *Alexander's Feast*, his *Ode design'd for the Prince's Birth-Day*, and an *Ode on the King* were presented at Hickford's Music Room on 13 December 1716. The last mention of Clayton in the musical life of London was on 15 November 1718 when a concert was presented at Lincoln's Inn Fields Theatre as an after-entertainment to *Cymbeline*. The music was that which Clayton had written for *Sappho*.

Perhaps the musician was the Thomas Clayton who was buried at St Paul, Covent Garden, on 23 September 1725, though some sources say that he died about 1730.

Clayton, William   *c. 1636–1697, instrumentalist, singer.*

His marriage license offers evidence that William Clayton was born about 1636. He was appointed to the King's Musick as a violinist (with a second position among the wind instruments) sometime before 24 January 1661, when he was listed with others to receive a New Year's gift. On 12 April he was granted a special livery allowance for playing at the coronation of Charles II. He was one of the small group of musicians chosen on numerous occasions to accompany the King on journeys out of London, typical examples being a trip to Portsmouth in April 1663 and visits to Windsor and Turnbridge in the summer of 1663.

By the end of 1664 Clayton was earning £66 2s. 6d. annually plus a livery allowance and was a member of the elite group of 12 violins within the regular band. For 1668 a warrant in the Lord Chamberlain's accounts shows his salary to have been £45

10*s*. 10*d*., which amount must have been his pay for only one of the two positions he occupied, for the higher figure listed in 1664 was mentioned again on 9 January 1669.

A curious warrant dated 21 July 1669 admitted William Clayton as a musician in ordinary without fee—to have a salary at the next vacancy in the King's private music—and on the following 3 September Clayton was appointed to replace the deceased Edward Coleman for "voice and lute" at £40 yearly. Though this reference might have implied the existence of a second and younger William Clayton, it was probably an administrative method of providing the musician with his arrears in salary, for Charles II was frequently behind in his payments to court entertainers.

During the rest of the reign of Charles II, Clayton was regularly in attendance on the King on journeys to Dover, Windsor, Hampton Court, and Newmarket. He also was given, on 10 July 1673, an additional post left vacant by the death of Thomas Mell. On 15 February 1675 he played in the court masque *Calisto* as one of the regular band of 24 violins, and ten years later he and other court musicians played at a ball held in the court theatre. At the accession of James II, Clayton was reappointed a member of the private music and finally received some of his arrears in salary stretching back to as early as 1670 (on 21 September 1686 he was ordered to receive £145 2*s*. 6*d*.) As sometimes in the previous reign, William Clayton was sent on trips outside London to entertain the court of James II. For such extra duties over the years he always received an extra fee, sometimes as much as 8*s*. daily. Clayton was reappointed under William III at £30 annually plus livery (some others of his positions he seems to have lost over the years). He saw his son Thomas join the King's Musick in February 1682.

William Clayton is known to have been engaged in public theatres and to have had interesting ties with the King's Company and its players. On 3 August 1663, not long after he had become firmly established in the King's Musick at court, Clayton married Elizabeth Wintershall. He described himself as a bachelor about 27 years old from the parish of St Clement Danes; she was a spinster of about 18 from St Paul, Covent Garden, and the daughter of the King's Company actor William Wintershall. Perhaps because of this alliance Clayton was chosen on 20 December 1664 as one of the court musicians to attend Thomas Killigrew, the King's Company manager, at the Bridges Street Theatre whenever the players should need him. How frequently he played in the theatre's music room is not known.

William Wintershall made Clayton his heir and executor, by which means Clayton came into possession of four of the 36 shares in the United Company by June 1683. Thus, willy-nilly, he was involved in occasional litigation involving the players, as when Charles Killigrew's mismanagement of the acting company and theatrical property led to a court case in 1683. Again on 14 January 1696 Clayton was in court, petitioning against the actor Edward Kynaston for £100 due him as Wintershall's executor, according to articles of agreement drawn up in May 1676; Kynaston was named as one of the trio of players who managed the King's troupe for a short time in 1676 when the agreement was made.

By the beginning of 1697 William Clayton was ill. On 28 January John Shore was appointed to replace Clayton in the King's Musick. Clayton must have died that day or shortly before, for he was buried on 30 January 1697 at St Paul, Covent Garden, described as from the parish of St Martin-in-the-Fields.

He was the William Clayton who had made his will on 11 May 1696, one of the witnesses being an Andrew Card—probably the theatre concessionnaire of that name. The will was proved by Clayton's widow,

Elizabeth, on 11 February 1697. To Elizabeth Clayton he left his house in Arlington Street as long as she remained unmarried; upon her death or remarriage the property was to go to William's son Thomas. Mrs Clayton was also to receive all the household items in Clayton's houses in London and Windsor and half of all his plate; the remainder of the plate was to go to Thomas Clayton. To his daughter Margaret the musician left £500, to be given her at her marriage or when she reached 21, until which time she was to receive £20 maintenance. To his son Thomas he left all his musical instruments and books, his house "in little Bridges Street alias Vinegar Yard wherein I now dwell" (which was very close to the Drury Lane playhouse), and all his rental shares and interest in the theatre. To his sons-in-law Charles Longland and Thomas Brayne and their wives and to his daughter Margaret, Clayton left £5 each for mourning rings. Elizabeth Clayton and her son Thomas were to divide the rest of the estate and serve as executors of the will.

Clayton's will and information in the St Paul, Covent Garden, parish registers make possible a partial reconstruction of his family. William and Elizabeth Clayton had the following children:

Elizabeth, baptized 7 February 1669, buried 13 March 1677

Thomas, baptized 28 July 1672, buried 5 August 1672

Thomas, baptized 28 October 1673, (buried 23 September 1725?)

Charles, buried 2 May 1677

William, buried 23 July 1679

William, buried 7 December 1679

Margaret, baptized 18 November 1681

John, buried 24 January 1682

Wintershall, buried 19 July 1683

Milicent, baptized 18 April 1686 (died in infancy)

Milicent, baptized 3 February 1688

First names are not known for the Clayton girls who married Charles Longland

and Thomas Brayne. William Clayton's widow, Elizabeth, was buried on 24 August 1700. When Thomas Clayton proved his father's will a second time on 14 November 1700 some of William's livery allowances from years before were still unpaid.

Clear, Richard ₁fl. 1659–1662₁, carver.

Richard Clear, a carver, worked on the Lord Mayor's shows in October 1659 and October 1660, contributed his talents to the coronation entertainment for Charles II in 1661, and was carver for *Aqua Triumphalis* on 23 August 1662.

Cleater. *See also* CLEETER.

Cleater, Mrs ₁fl. 1745–1765₁, dresser.

On 19 November 1745, Covent Garden paid Mrs Cleater, a dresser for Mrs Cibber, 7s. 6d. for five days. A Mrs Cleeter, apparently the same person, was being paid 1s. 6d. per day (9s. per week) as a women's dresser at Drury Lane in 1764–65.

Cleavely, Price ₁fl. 1732₁, singer.

Price Cleavely (or Clevly), possibly a Gentleman of the Chapel Royal, sang Habdonah in a private performance of Handel's oratorio *Esther* at the Crown and Anchor Tavern on 23 February 1732.

Cleaver, William. *See* CLAREMONT, WILLIAM.

Cleer. *See* CLEAR.

Cleeter. *See also* CLEATER.

Cleeter, Mr ₁fl. 1708₁, bill carrier.

Among Vice Chamberlain Coke's papers at Harvard is a salary list for the Queen's Theatre in the Haymarket dated 8 March 1708; Mr Cleeter is noted as one of four bill carriers, all of whom were paid 4s. daily.

Clegg, John *1714–1750?, violinist.*

John Clegg was born in Dublin in 1714, a son of the well-known Irish violinist and teacher, William Clegg. He studied violin with his father and with William Viver, master of the band at Dublin Castle.

There was a performance on 24 May 1723 at the Haymarket Theatre, "by Particular desire of several ladies of quality, for the benefit of John Clegg, a youth of nine years of age, lately arrived from Ireland." Clegg must have dropped out of all but private playing for almost a year, for it was not until the benefit performance for the singer Mrs Barbier at Lincoln's Inn Fields Theatre on 13 April 1724 that he was again seen in the bills. He played "Two Concertos" and again was said to be "nine years old." Van der Straeten says that he was "A pupil of Dubourg, afterwards of Bononcini," and if that is true, the tutelage may have occurred during the idle year.

For 8 May 1724 was announced a performance at the Haymarket for the benefit of "J. Clegg (from Ireland), a Youth of Ten Years of Age, who play'd at Mrs Barbier's Benefit." There were to be "Several choice Concertos by the Youth, never perform'd in Publick; particularly a Concert[o] of Vivaldi's called *La Temista di Mare*, the song by Mr Kitch, the Violin by the Youth . . . a solo of Sig Germeniani's [*sic*] by the Youth."

If the assertion of J. S. Sainsbury, in the *Dictionary of Musicians* (1824) is true, that "He travelled with Lord Ferrers to Italy, and much improved his taste during his stay in that country," it is probable that he went on this tour at some time during the 11 years before his next recorded London appearance in solo concert. This was on 17 April 1735, at Hickford's Great Room, Dean Street, Soho, when he played "Two new solos on Violin . . . the music composed by Geminiani." On 11 February 1736 he was "First Violin" in a concert for the violoncellist Caporale's benefit at the Swan Tavern, Swan Alley, Cornhill, and on 8 March following he had his own benefit at Lincoln's Inn Fields at which Caporale reciprocated, and Arrigoni the lutenist also played. The admission was 5*s*. On 8 March 1737 Clegg was again on a program at the Swan with Caporale. There is not another record of his concert performance until 3 February 1741 when he was one of an instrumental quartet with Caporale, Weideman, and Miller at the Haymarket for a charity benefit.

There is hardly any doubt that, in view of his great celebrity for tone and technical brilliance, Clegg was heard in many more public performances than surviving announcements show. He is said to have been a favorite of Handel's and to have been chosen by him to succeed Castrucci as leader of the band at the Opera. He must also have been concerned in the oratorios. He was one of the original subscribers to the Royal Society of Musicians of Great Britain, according to the Declaration of Trust dated 28 August 1739.

Clegg's career was cut short by madness. On 21 January 1744 he was confined in Bedlam Hospital where, said Burney, "it was long a fashionable, though inhuman amusement, to visit him there . . . in hopes of being entertained by his fiddle or his folly." He was discharged as cured on 20 July but readmitted on 15 December 1744. He was allowed to leave again on 13 October 1746. He died about 1750.

Clegg had two sisters who were singers in Dublin in the 1740s. One of them may have been the Mrs Davis who sang in London at various periods from 1726 to 1745.

Clegg, William *[fl. 1784?–1794], singer, actor?*

William Clegg, a tenor singer, resided at No 1, Poppin's Court, Fleet Street, in 1794. He was, according to Doane's *Musical Directory* of that year, a veteran of at least some of the performances commemorating Handel in Westminster Abbey (held al-

ternately there and at the Pantheon in May
and June 1784, and revived in 1785, 1786,
1787, and 1791), and a member of the
"Choral Fund." *The Thespian Mirror . . .
of the Theatres Royal, Manchester, Liverpool and Chester* (1793) cites a Mr Clegg,
possibly the same performer, who had recently performed Douglas in Home's tragedy at one of these provincial places, and
had been imperfect in the part.

> *Some traits indicated discernment and
>   sense,*
> *While others conspired to give judgment
>   offence*
>
> . . . .
>
> *His vocal endowments without cultivation,*
> *Must fail in the tribute of rich admiration.*

Cleland, Miss, stage name of Miss Buttery *b. 1762, actress.*

The actress Miss Cleland, according to
the untrustworthy *Authentic Memoirs of
the Green Room* (1804), was born of "respectable" parents at Boston, Lincolnshire,
in 1762. Her father, "a builder of much
credit" named Buttery died when she was
still a child. Her mother was the mistress
of an inn at Boston in the 1770s. At the
age of 17, Miss Buttery went down to
London to become apprentice to a milliner,
but after two years her childhood interest in
the stage led her to take lessons in acting
from Charles Macklin. Eventually put off
by his "harsh manners," she left Macklin to
take up an engagement, "at liberal terms"
arranged by a friend, with the Edinburgh
theatre in 1780–81. Acting there under her
assumed stage name of Miss Cleland, she
was favorably received in her first appearance, as Cordelia. Her benefit at Edinburgh,
patronized by the Duchess of Gordon, was
brilliantly attended.

In the following season Miss Cleland
was engaged at Covent Garden where she
made her first appearance, billed as a
"Young Lady," as Maria in *George Barn-*

well on 26 December 1781. Still unnamed in the bills, she next acted Lavinia in
The Fair Penitent on 1 January 1782.
These were her only two billed appearances
that season, a season for which she was
paid £20 on 3 April 1782, a sum large
enough to suggest that she probably acted
some supernumerary roles as well. In
1782–83 she returned to Covent Garden
to perform on a regular basis at £2 per
week. On 27 September 1782, the bills
now carrying her name, Miss Cleland
again played Lavinia. She then acted Florimel in *The Positive Man* on 16 October,
Sukey Tawdry in *The Beggar's Opera* on
22 October, Elmira in *The Sultan* on 20
December, Anne Bullen in *Henry VIII* on
30 December, Hero in *Much Ado About
Nothing* on 19 February, and Serina in *The
Orphan* on 31 March 1783.

At the end of her second year at Covent
Garden, Harris the manager recommended
her to the Bath theatre "for the sake of
practice." There she remained for some
years, and also played at Bristol from 1784
to 1790. In 1791 she joined Wilkinson's
company at York for two seasons, but "this
manager being fond of new faces, she was
under the necessity of leaving him," and
engaged at Birmingham. In the fall of 1792
she acted at Chester, then went to Manchester for a season, and during the rest of
the last decade of the century worked her
way through the circuit managed by
Hughes at Weymouth, Exeter, and Plymouth. In 1793 the author of *The Thespian
Mirror . . . of the Theatres Royal, Manchester, Liverpool and Chester* advised her:

> *As you hope to escape Melpomene's rage
> In parts of much consequence never engage*
>
> . . . .
>
> *Then suffer the feelings of tender compassion,*
> *To curb the excesses of tragical passion.*

Miss Cleland returned to London in
1803 to join Colman's new company at the

Haymarket, making her debut as Mrs Chloe Wiggins in *Mrs Wiggins* on 3 June 1803. She took on the title of Mrs, instead of Miss, as she did not conceive the latter "suitable to her years," and continued to act supporting roles, such as Mrs Balance in *Guilty, or Not Guilty* and Lady Dunder in *Ways and Means*, during summers at the Haymarket through 1810.

Clement, Franz *1780–1842, violinist, composer, conductor.*

Franz Clement, the Austrian violinist, was born on 17 November 1780, the son of a butler and musician in the house of Count von Harsch. He was tutored in the violin from the age of four by his father and from the age of seven by Kurzweil, concert-master of Prince Grassalkowitsch. At the age of nine, in March 1789, Clement played with great success at the Imperial Opera House in Vienna and was then taken by his father on a concert tour of Germany, Holland, and England. Notices in the *Allegemeine Musik Zeitung* of Franz's rendition of a concerto by Rode extolled his "extraordinary technique, elegance of style and purity of intonation," but stated that he yet lacked certain qualities of tone and deep emotion.

On 2 June 1790, young Clement played a concerto with G. A. P. Bridgetower, another prodigy of similar age, at a concert in London sponsored by the Prince of Wales, and both became pupils of Giornovichi during their stay in that city. Clement played at Bristol in January 1791 and on 11 March of the same year he made his first appearance at Drury Lane, offering a concerto in an oratorio concert of Handelian music. He gave similar performances on 23 and 30 March, 8, 13, and 15 April, and then at the King's Theatre on 19 May 1791. For his own benefit on 10 June 1791, he played at Ranelagh Gardens in a concert organized by Haydn, and on 24 June he played for the benefit of the Chevalier D'Eon at the same place. He also played at other concerts conducted by Haydn and Salomon, and at a concert at Oxford given on the occasion of the conferral of the degree of Doctor of Music on Haydn, in July 1791.

When he returned to Vienna soon after, Franz became solo violinist at the Court Theatre, and assistant to the *kapellmeister*, Süssmayer, and in 1802, at the age of 12, he was appointed conductor to the new Theatre am der Wien, a position he held until 1811, when he left Vienna to tour Russia with a Polish nobleman. At Riga, Clement was arrested as a spy, brought to Petersburg, and, although found innocent, was deported. Apparently in severe financial straits, he worked his way back to Vienna by giving concerts in small Hungarian and Bohemian towns. Finding his posts at Vienna occupied, Clement was obliged to take a position as violinist in the orchestra at Baden. But soon, in 1813, he became *konzertmeister* to the national theatre at Prague, under its new conductor C. M. von Weber. After a tour in Germany in 1817, Clement was recalled as conductor to the Theatre am der Wien in 1818, where he remained until 1821, at which time he became manager and conductor of Madame Angelica Catalani's concert tours. After 1829 he lived at Vienna, in distressed circumstances brought on by his bad management and irregular habits, until his death there on 3 November 1842.

Clement was, by all accounts, both a brilliant violinist and a gifted musician, for whom Beethoven wrote his violin Concerto in D, which was first played in public by Clement at Vienna on 23 December 1806. At this same concert, according to the program, Clement also played some variations with the violin held upside down. The musician had an extraordinary memory, and it was reported by the tenor Roeckel that one time at the palace of Prince Lichnowsky, when Beethoven was persuaded by his friends to contract the three acts of *Fidelio* to two, Clement played the whole score on the violin from memory, including the solo passages of the other instruments. Spohr related that after hearing *The Creation* only a few times, Clement made a complete pianoforte arrangement, with the help only of the word book. When it was shown to Haydn, the composer at first believed his score had been stolen or secretly copied, so perfect was it, and then finding the arrangement so satisfactory, Haydn adopted it for publication. According to Spohr, Clement also played from memory several long pieces from the oratorio *The Last Judgment* after hearing two rehearsals and a performance. Such virtuosity, however, sometimes tempted him to low tricks of musicianship to impress his audiences, according to the *Wiener Musik Zeitung* (1820).

Clement composed a number of concertinos, concertos, airs, and studies for the violin and some for the pianoforte. It is reported that he also wrote an opera and music for a melodrama, the scores and titles of which have gone into oblivion.

Clement, John ₁*fl. 1660–1688?*₁, *singer, theorbo player.*

John Clement was admitted to the private music of Charles II on 9 November 1660 replacing William Lawes, who had died during the Interregnum. His duties were singing and playing the theorbo, for which he was to receive annual livery payments of £16 2s. 6d. plus a yearly salary of £40 to commence from the Feast of St John the Baptist, 1660. As happened to many court musicians, Clement was seldom paid on schedule, and the story of his life is a series of warrants in the Lord Chamberlain's accounts, detailing his arrears and debts.

In 1666, for instance, he was waiting for his livery payment for 1663, and in 1667 he still had not received his fees for 1664, 1665, and 1666. In October 1671 he borrowed from his colleague Humphrey Madge and petitioned to have his back pay for 1669, 1670, and 1671 paid to Madge in

return for an unspecified loan. On 15 August 1673 Clement was to be paid £80 12s. 6d. for liveries still owing from 1664 to 1667 and for 1671, but he never received it, for on 25 February 1686 Clement still had arrears due him from 1662, 1664, 1665–67, and 1678–84. Under the circumstances, it is a wonder he survived, and perhaps he did not. James II made an effort to pay his brother's debts, and on 21 September 1686 Clement was to be given £179 11s. in back pay. But a 23 March 1688 warrant noted that Clement had been one of Charles II's musicians and had received livery "unto St. Andrew, 1684" – evidence that after that date he had retired, or perhaps had died.

Clemente. *See* CLEMENTINE.

Clementi, Signor ₁*fl. 1739*₁, *singer.*

A manuscript notation in the Burney papers at the British Museum for 1739 reads "Nov 23 Sigʳ. Clementi arrived here from Italy & is engaged to sing at the Little Thea. in the Haymarket." No other notice of this Signor Clementi is known to us.

Clementi, Muzio *1752–1832, organist, harpsichordist, pianist, composer, conductor.*

Muzio Clementi was born at Rome on 21 January 1752 (not on 23 January as indicated by Grove). His father was a silver craftsman whose principal trade was providing embossed vases and figures for Roman Catholic worship. Anxious to encourage the obvious musical precocity which his son exhibited, the elder Clementi provided Muzio with a series of excellent teachers. The first master was Buroni, a family relation and choirmaster of one of the churches in Rome, who later became a principal composer at St Peter's. In 1759, at the age of seven, Clementi was instructed in thorough bass by the organist Cordicelli. By the age of nine, Clementi had

Harvard Theatre Collection

MUZIO CLEMENTI

engraving by Scriven, after Lonsdale

passed his examination for admission as an organist. The examination, it is reported, consisted "in giving a figured bass from the works of Corelli, and making the scholar execute an accompaniment, after which he is obliged to transpose the same into various keys." He studied counterpoint with Carpani, "the deepest contrapuntist of his day," and voice with Santarelli, "the last great master of the true vocal school."

At the age of 12, in 1764, Clementi's oratorio, *Il martirio de' gloriosi Santi Girolamo e Celso*, was performed in Rome. Within the next few years he composed several contrapuntal works, including a mass for four voices which was publicly performed to great acclaim. When Carpani, who was unaware that Clementi was writing the Mass, heard it sung he is said to have remonstrated, "Why did not you tell me you were about to write a mass? This is very well, to be sure; but if you had con-

sulted me, it might have been much better." Under Carpani he wrote fugues and canons, and the master was reported to have said in later years that had Clementi remained his student a year longer he probably would have passed the examination in counterpoint.

Clementi's fortunes, however, were to take him from Italy. By the age of 14, he had also developed an extraordinary proficiency on the harpsichord. In 1766 Clementi's father was persuaded to allow the prodigy to go to England for further education under the patronage of an English gentleman, Peter Beckford, M. P., a nephew of Alderman Beckford. Clementi was taken to the Beckford seat in Dorsetshire (Grove states Wiltshire) where he learned English and studied assiduously the works of Corelli, Scarlatti, Handel, and Paradies. In 1773 he came to London to enjoy immediate success in his engagement in the orchestra of the King's Theatre. From 1777 to 1780 he was the conductor of the Opera. His Op. 2, introduced to the public in 1773, has been described by Edward Dannreuther in *Grove's Dictionary* as "the basis on which the whole fabric of modern sonatas for the piano-forte has been erected." Johann Christian Bach praised it highly, but would not attempt its performance, although he was a celebrated player on the instrument. When Schroetter was asked upon his arrival in London if he could play the works of Clementi, he replied "they could only be performed by the author himself, or the devil!"

In 1780 Clementi embarked on a professional tour of the Continent, beginning with concerts in Paris. The books of the firm of Broadwood & Son indicate that in 1781 they "Shipped a harpsichord and a piano-forte for Mr. Clementi to Paris." In that city he enjoyed enormous success, and received "the most unqualified applause" of the French Queen. While at Paris he composed his Op. 5 and Op. 6, and published a new edition of his Op. 1, with an additional fugue. In 1781, passing through Strasbourg and Munich, where he was received with honors both by the Prince of Deux Ponts (later King of Bavaria) and the Elector, he traveled to Vienna. There he became acquainted with the celebrated musicians of this musical capital, including Haydn and Mozart. Emperor Joseph II invited him to the palace late in 1781 where before the emperor and the Grand Duke Paul of Russia and others, Clementi engaged "in a sort of musical combat" with Mozart, at the harpsichord, a joust which is described in *Grove's Dictionary*:

Clementi, after a short prelude, played his Sonata in B♭ (Op. 47 No. 2)—the opening of the first movement of which was long afterwards made use of by Mozart in the subject of the 'Zauberflöte' overture—and followed it up with a toccata in which great stress is laid upon the rapid execution of diatonic thirds and other double notes for the right hand, esteemed very difficult at the time. Mozart then began to prelude and played some variations; then both alternately read at sight some manuscript sonatas of Paisiello's, Mozart playing the allegros and Clementi the andantes and rondos; and finally they were asked by the emperor to take a theme from Paisiello's sonatas and accompany one another in their improvisations upon it on two pianofortes. The victory, it appears, was left undecided.

At the time Clementi was 29 years of age and Mozart 25. Writing of Clementi in a letter in the following year, Mozart criticized him as "a mere mechanician, strong in runs of thirds, but without a pennyworth of feeling or taste." Clementi, however, was more charitable and admiring of Mozart's touch "and exquisite taste," and influenced by the encounter with the Austrian genius turned from a less mechanical approach to cultivation of "a more brilliant execution." One of Clementi's later pupils, L. Berger, explained that his master "subsequently achieved a more melodic and noble style of performance after listening attentively to famous singers," and that Clementi turned his attention to perfecting the "mechanism of English pianos, the construction of which formerly stood in the way of a cantabile and legato style of playing."

Clementi returned in 1782 to London, where, except for a concert tour to Paris in 1785, he remained, establishing himself solidly in many branches of his profession: conductor, teacher, performer, composer, music seller, and instrument manufacturer. At the King's Theatre on 4 March 1784 he played a sonata on the harpsichord between the first and second act of *Demofoonte*, and at the same theatre on 11 June 1789 he, John Baptiste Cramer (one of the most brilliant of his numerous pupils), and James Cervetto performed a trio for pianoforte, violin, and violoncello. Reporting the event, which was for Mme Storace's benefit, the *Morning Post* praised Clementi's "prodigious execution on the pianoforte." Between 19 February and 26 March 1790, Clementi played in the orchestra for the oratorios at Covent Garden Theatre. Also in March of 1790 he participated in concerts organized by Johann Peter Salomon at the Hanover Square Rooms. In the early 1780s Clementi resided in Titchfield Street. By 1794 he was living in Upper Marylebone Street.

Between 1791 and 1795 Clementi was an official composer to the Professional Concerts and became an acquaintance of Haydn during the latter's two visits to London. Their names appeared on the same program for 24 February 1792 when an overture by Clementi was followed by a new symphony by Haydn. Both composers exhibited an energy and impetuosity in their works, devoted to the pursuit of a single musical theme, which anticipated Beethoven. Clementi's esteem for the German composer was manifested in his gift to Haydn of a coconut-shell goblet, richly adorned with silver. It was Clementi who brought out the score for piano and voices

MUZIO CLEMENTI
by T. Hardy

for *The Creation* immediately after its performance on 27 April 1800. Among others of Haydn's works published by Clementi were the eighth of the London symphonies, and piano sonatas and quartets, some of which he obtained English rights for by an exchange agreement with Pleyel, who was publishing Haydn's music in Paris.

In August of 1802 Clementi took one of his most talented pupils, John Field the pianist, on a continental tour which began in Paris. At the age of 11, Field had become apprenticed to Clementi for a fee of 100 guineas in 1793, and in addition to being a pupil he had also worked as a salesman-demonstrator in Clementi's shop, displaying the firm's pianos. Field, about whom Clementi was supposed to have remarked that "such was the quickness of conception, retentiveness of memory, and

facility of execution, which this highly gifted boy possessed, that he seldom had occasion to make the same remark to him a second time," delighted Paris audiences by his playing of the great fugues of Sebastian Bach "with such precision and inimitable taste, as to call forth . . . the most enthusiastic applause." They then traveled to Vienna, where they experienced equally enthusiastic receptions. Presumably it had been Clementi's intention to leave young Field at Vienna under the instruction of Albrechstberger, but when the time came for Clementi to continue on his tour, he was persuaded by the tearful Field to take him along to St Petersburg, where they arrived in December 1802. In this city, Clementi himself played "with the greatest distinction," and he established a showroom for the sale of his pianos, using young Field again as a demonstrator. It was reported that Clementi's parsimonious nature kept his pupil short of food and without an overcoat for the Russian winter, despite the large profits Field's playing brought him. In his earlier diary Spohr had described Clementi as "a man in his best years, of an extremely lively disposition, and very engaging manners," but after he visited him and his pupil in St Petersburg Spohr presented Clementi in an unflattering manner in his *Autobiography*:

In the evening I sometimes accompanied him after dinner to his large pianoforte warehouse, where Field was often obliged to play for hours, to display the instruments to the best advantage to the purchasers. . . . I have still in recollection the figure of the pale, overgrown youth, whom I have never seen since. When Field, who had outgrown his clothes, placed himself at the piano, stretched out his arms over the keyboard, so that his sleeves shrunk up nearly to his elbows, his whole figure appeared awkward and stiff in the highest degree; but as soon as his touching instrumentation began, everything else was forgotten, and one became all ear. Unhappily, I could not express my emotion and thankfulness to the young man otherwise than by a silent pressure of the hand, for he spoke no other language, but his mother tongue.

Even at that time, many anecdotes of the remarkable avarice of the rich Clementi were related, which had greatly increased in latter years when I again met him in London. It was generally reported that Field was kept on very short allowance by his master, and was obliged to pay for the good fortune of having his instruction with many privations. I myself experienced a little sample of Clementi's true Italian parsimony, for one day I found teacher and pupil with turned up sleeves, engaged at the washtub, and Clementi advised me to do the same, as washing in St. Petersburg was not only very expensive, but the linen suffered greatly from the method used in washing it.

When he left Russia in 1803, Clementi also left Field behind, and his former student became a most esteemed pianist and teacher in St Petersburg where he remained for many years. With a new pupil, the young musician Zeuner (who was to become perhaps "the most exact fugue player in existence," according to Sainsbury), now in his entourage, Clementi then went to Berlin for several months and on to Dresden, where Zeuner remained to make his reputation. But Clementi picked up yet another pupil, the young Klengel, with whom he returned to Vienna for some months, then toured Switzerland, and afterward returned to Berlin.

In Germany, Clementi acquired Ludwig Berger and Meyerbeer as students and also made the acquaintance of Beethoven. In Berlin on 15 September 1804 he married the daughter of J. G. G. Lehmann, cantor of St Nicholas Church in that city. After a journey with him to Italy, she died in childbirth at Berlin in August 1805. Clementi then took up his continental travels again, revisiting Russia and Austria. He lived for brief periods in Milan, and also was called to Rome by the death of his brother.

After eight years of grand touring which he filled with a substantial amount of teaching, performing, and composing, Clementi returned to England in the summer of 1810. He was married again, by a license from the Faculty Office, St Pancras, on 3 July 1811, to Emma Gisborne, spinster, of St Giles in the Fields, whom Sainsbury characterized as an "amiable and accomplished" woman.

Except for journeys again to the Continent in 1820 and 1821 (he spent an entire winter at Leipzig), Clementi lived out the remainder of his life in England, passing his latter years at Lincroft House near Lichfield, Staffordshire, and then at Elm Lodge in Evesham, Worcestershire. A public dinner in his honor in London on 17 December 1827 demonstrated the high respect and affection of his many pupils and admirers. The records do not establish that Clementi was a member of the Royal Society of Musicians, but on 1 May 1796 he was voted thanks by the Society for collecting some money due it. He died at Evesham on 10 March 1832, at the age of 80, and was buried (with a public funeral from No 26, Newman St, Oxford St) in the South Cloister of Westminster Abbey.

For many years Clementi had been a principal party in a series of business enterprises. In his earlier years he had held an interest in the establishment of Longman & Broderip, "manufacturers of musical instruments and music-sellers to their Majesties." He suffered heavy losses by the bankruptcy of that firm in 1798, but soon joined in a new partnership with John Longman at No 26, Cheapside. After Longman left him in 1801 to set up at No 131, Cheapside, Clementi formed a new firm at No 26, Cheapside, with Banger, F. A. Hyde, F. W. Collard and D. Davis, with premises also at No 195, Tottenham Court Road from about 1806. In March 1807 damage to their property in the amount of £40,000 was caused by fire.

The firm was originally established as

Clementi, Banger, Hyde, Collard & Davis. As the several partners withdrew or died the name changed: in 1810 Hyde's name disappeared, in 1819 Banger's; in 1822 the name was Clementi, Collard & Collard, and after Clementi's withdrawal in 1830 it continued to publish music at the two addresses until 1834 under the name of Collard & Collard. During most of his connection with the business, however, the firm was known commonly as Clementi & Co., and the account books of the theatres show frequent payments to the "Messrs Clementi" for music paper. The business served as a ticket agency for the Royal Circus Theatre during the first decade of the nineteenth century, and it enjoyed a great trade in pianofortes and violins.

According to Grove, Clementi was married three times and fathered children in his old age, but we find record of only two wives. Perhaps he had been married prior to his wedding to Fraulein Lehmann in 1804, but Sainsbury records her as his first wife. Emma Gisborne, whom he married in 1811, was presumably the Emma referred to by Clementi as his wife when he made his will on 2 January 1832. By his commercial talents he left Emma a substantial legacy including his house at Evesham, "all other houses he may be possessed of," his carriages, utensils, watches, and specifically his books, which were enumerated in a list dated 21 May 1827. She was also to receive £500 upon his death and another £500 within six months. He bequeathed £400 to be divided equally among the children of his late brother Gaetano Clementi and of his sister Regina Clementi Malton. Other bequests included mourning rings to William Frederick Collard and William Horsley (of the Kensington Gravel Pits). All his books other than those reserved for his wife he left to the Rev John Smith of St John's College, Cambridge; Frederick Fielding of Newman St, Marylebone; Thomas Hall of Walsall, Staffordshire; a Mr Currier; and John Theobald of Kentish

Town, in trust, with specific instructions for distributing the library among his children. The residue of his estate, including mortgages he held and £800 of 3½% bank annuities and unspecified amounts of East India stock, he left to his wife, in trust for his children, whom he did not name. Clementi was evidently too feeble to sign his name to the will, but managed to make his mark. On 2 April 1832, several weeks after his death, his former partners F. W. Collard and W. F. Collard appeared to swear familiarity with his hand writing as it appeared on the list of books Clementi had made for his wife. The will was proved at London on 24 April 1832. The only child of Clementi known to us by name was Charles Clementi, who wrote to Sainsbury from No 26, Cheapside, on 20 January 1824 that his father would attain the age of 72 "to-morrow." Charles also provided Sainsbury with a list of 52 musical compositions by his father.

As composer of at least 100 sonatas, 64 of which are for the pianoforte, Clementi, says Dannreuther in *Grove's Dictionary*, "left a deep and indelible mark upon everything that pertains to the pianoforte." His *Introduction to Practical Harmony*, originally titled *Clementi's Selection of Practical Harmony, for the Organ or Pianoforte*, written evidently during his eight-year visit to the Continent, was an important work in its day. His series of 100 studies, *Gradus ad Parnassum* (1817) remains, according to Dannreuther a work "upon which to this day the art of solid pianoforte playing rests." Between 1786 and 1832 Clementi also composed about 20 symphonies, 12 of which were performed in London between 1815 and 1825. For many years, the scores could not be found and were presumed irrevocably lost. In 1934, however, Alfredo Casella identified four symphonies by Clementi in the Library of Congress. The manuscripts had come to that library through Dr Carl Engel, who after 1917 had purchased them in a collection from the estate

of Dr William H. Cummings. The latter, in
turn, had obtained the manuscripts from the
Rev P. Clementi Smith, grandson of the
composer, who had found them in the
cellar of his house. Many of Clementi's
manuscripts, including symphonies and a
sketch for the oratorio "Daniel," however,
had been thoughtlessly burnt by a maid.
The surviving symphonies, none complete
but reconstructed by Casella, include one
in C major, in D major, a "Great National"
symphony (1824?), and a last symphony
in D major. These compositions are characterized by Alfredo Casella in *Grove's Dictionary* as follows:

The style of the re-edited symphonies is
that of a musician whose life spans the period
from the death of J. S. Bach to the ripe romantic era. The spirit is essentially classical,
the outcome of disciplined studies and an ex-
ceptional command of polyphonic technique
and of form. Clementi obviously attempts to
revive in his symphonies the classical heritage
and to combine it with 19th-century restless-
ness. It thus happens that, side by side with
pages of a Haydnesque quality, one finds
others which suggest Beethoven and even
hint prophetically at Verdi and Brahms.

Lists of Clementi's compositions are found
in Grove and in the British Museum
Catalogue of Printed Music. The list of
compositions published by Sainsbury in his
Dictionary of Music (1827) was provided
to that editor in 1824 by the composer's
son, Charles Clementi, and that manuscript
list is in the Glasgow University Library.

Portraits of Muzio Clementi include:

1. Engraving by T. Hardy, published by
Bland, 1794.

2. Anonymous engraving, printed by
W. Richardson, 1803.

3. Engraving by F. W. Bollinger, after
Albert, published at Berlin, 1804.

4. Engraving by H. Cook, after J. Lonsdale, published as a plate to Jerdan's *National Portrait Gallery,* 1833. Lonsdale's
portrait was also engraved by E. Scriven.

5. Engraving by Hillemacher, published
1870.

6. An engraving by S. Rosciani, dedicated "A sua Eccellenze Sig. Contessa
Amalio Gallo nato Gubiani."

7. Clementi was included in a large
group portrait of musicians by Luigi Scotti
and engraved by Bettelini, about 1805.

8. J. F. Bolt engraving after V. Kin-
ninger.

9. Engraving by A. Lemoine.

10. Engraving by T. Mollo.

11. Engraving by A. Schall.

Clementina. *See also* **CREMONINI,
CLEMENTINA.**

Clementina, Sobieska *[fl. 1772],
equestrienne.*

A Miss Sobieska Clementina was advertised in the press as doing trick riding in
performances at Hughes's Riding School,
Blackfriars Bridge, in June 1772.

Clementine, Signor *[fl. 1699], singer.*

The *Post Boy* of 13–15 April 1699 reported that

the Masters of the Theatre Royal have engag'd
Signior Clementine, the famous Eunuch, Servant to the Elector of Bavaria, to Sing on their
publick Stage, for the short time of his stay
in England. There is very great Expectation
from his Performance as being a Person of
that extraordinary Desert in Singing, that his
yearly Salary on that Account is 500 *l.* a Year.

When *Feign'd Friendship* was performed at
the rival Lincoln's Inn Fields Theatre soon
afterward, the epilogue chided the audience:

*Of late your Stomachs are so squeamish
    grown,
You are not pleas'd with Dainties of our
    own,
And 'tis meer folly to think to win ye
Without Balon [the dancer] or Seignior
    Clementine.*

And *A Comparison Between the Two Stages* in 1702 still remembered the singer: Ramble says, "But above all commend me to *Signior Clemente*—he got more by being an *Eunuch* than if he had the best Back in Christendom; the Ladies paid more for his *Caponship* than they wou'd ha' done for his virility."

Clench. *See* CLINCH.

Clendening, Clendiling, or **Clendillon.** *See* CLENDINING.

Clendining, Miss [*fl.* 1798], *actress.*
Miss Clendining, the daughter of the singer and actress Mrs Clendining and William Clendining of Dublin, made her first and apparently only appearance on the London stage on 24 May 1798 as Little Bob in *The Poor Sailor,* for her mother's benefit at Covent Garden.

Clendining, Mrs William, Elizabeth, née Arnold *1768–1799, actress, singer.*
Elizabeth Clendining was born in 1768 at Stourhead, Wiltshire, the daughter of a Mr Arnold whose family had had roots in the area for over a century. Her father had been educated in the choir at Salisbury, and at an early age had received an offer of the Duke of York's patronage to study in Italy, which, however, he did not accept. About 1770, Arnold sang with great success in Linley's concerts at Bath where he earned from Tenducci, according to *The Secret History of the Green Room* (1795), the eulogium of being "the best English singer and master he had ever heard." After filling a lucrative position in the choir at Wells, Arnold took an appointment at the Dublin Cathedral, "which he did not enjoy entirely," for he died after two years there, at the age of 29.

After the death of her father, Miss Arnold was allowed by her mother to sing in 1785 at the Dublin Rotunda which was under the particular patronage of the Duchess of Rutland. There Miss Arnold received a good salary and a benefit. Before the Rotunda season expired, Miss Arnold married William Clendining, a surgeon, who owned "handsome landed property" in County Longford. Although the proprietors of the Rotunda concerts offered her advantageous terms for the next season, her new husband's pride would not allow her to reengage, and Mrs Clendining withdrew from professional singing for six years. Clendining, however, because of "professional inattention" and "indiscriminate hospitality," fell into debtor's prison at Dublin, so to protect him and her "young family" from poverty Mrs Clendining resumed her profession. In mid-December 1791 she left Ireland, "with a few guineas in her pocket," for London. There she was taken in and provided for by the singer Mrs Billington, whom she had met on a summer tour in Dublin. Unsuccessful in obtaining engagements at Covent Garden or Vauxhall, and Dr Linley, to whom she applied, having "no leisure for instruction," upon the suggestion of Mrs Billington she went to Bath in February 1792 and was introduced by the flutist Ashe to Rauzzini who "immediately took her under his tuition." Mrs Clendining made her first appearance at Bath in a benefit concert for Ashe, and her ballad of "Auld Robin Gray" brought extravagant plaudits. Immediately she was engaged by the Catch Club for the remainder of the season, during which she also continued under the tutelage of Rauzzini.

At the music festival in Bath Abbey, she rendered Handel's "He was despised," written for countertenor, "with such tone, expression, and steadiness," according to *The Secret History of the Green Room,* "as to excite the wonder and approbation, not only of the amateurs but of the professional judges." Consequently, on the recommendation of a Mr Sarjant, she was invited by Lewis of Covent Garden to come up to London. At season's end, in order to make it possible for her to go to London, a committee of Bath gentlemen got up a benefit for her in the town hall, which was allowed free of expense by the mayor. She realized so much money from the occasion that she was able to effect the release of her husband, who joined her in London several months later.

In June 1792 Mrs Clendining arrived at London to meet Harris, the manager of Covent Garden, whose terms she did not immediately accept, reportedly because of her own dubiety over her ability to perform stage roles. She eventually articled for three years and made her first appearance at Covent Garden on 3 November 1792 as Clara in *Hartford Bridge*, being encored in her first song. The *Thespian Magazine* found her to possess a pretty figure and to sing "with great taste," while the daily press—which sometimes called her Mrs Clendillon—pronounced that she had "musical talents of the very first rank" with an uncommon "sweetness of voice," but no claims to beauty. Mrs Clendining enjoyed considerable success for the rest of the season, playing Clara a total of 36 times. On 22 December 1792 she also played the role of Clara in *The Duenna*, and on 9 January 1793 Lorenza in *The Castle of Andalusia*. She made her first attempt at Rosetta in *Love in a Village* on 25 January, and when Madam Mara became indisposed, she substituted for her on 13 March in a concert of sacred music, singing Handel's "He was despised." Her other roles that season included a vocal part in *The Relief of Williamstadt* on 23 March, when she sang Dr Arne's "Gentle Soldier, oft you've told me," Rosamund in *The Armourer* on 4 April, Rosolea in *Money at a Pinch* on 25 April, Mary in *Sprigs of Laurel* on 11 May, and Lucy in *Love and War* on 15 May. For her benefit on 16 May 1793 (at which she took receipts of £273 17s. less about £105 house charges) and when tickets could be had of her at No 19, Martlett Court, Bow Street, she played Yarico in *Inkle and Yarico*, with extra songs.

Her husband, William Clendining, who had become a navy surgeon and was serving on the frigate *Inconstant*, died at Portsmouth on 27 April 1793, but from the bills it would seem that Mrs Clendining did not interrupt the momentum of her first season at Covent Garden for any special mourning.

In 1793–94 she was at Covent Garden again, at a salary of £4 per week. She played the Claras of *Hartford Bridge* and *The Duenna*, and Mary in *Sprigs of Laurel*, and added to her repertory Adelais in *The Midnight Wanderers*, Celia in *Fontainebleau*, Matilda in *The Ward of the Castle*, a Bacchant in *Comus*, Julia in *The Travellers in Switzerland*, and vocal parts in *A Comedy of Errors* and in the funeral processions in *Romeo and Juliet* and *Hamlet*. At her benefit on 3 June 1794 she played Sophia in *The Road to Ruin*, taking £301 10s. (less about £105 house charges). The bill announced that tickets were available from her at No 5, Bow Street, although Doane's *Musical Directory* in that year gave her old address, No 19, Martlett Court. On that night her sister, Miss Arnold, played the title role in *Rosina* on the same stage, but with little success. In the summer of 1796 her sister also acted with her at Birmingham.

Mrs Clendining continued at Covent Garden for four more seasons. In 1794–95 her salary was £5 per week; it was raised to £6 in 1795–96. Shortly after she performed Yarico on 30 December 1794, she had a severe fall, on New Year's Day, which dislocated her shoulder and collar bone, and according to the *Morning Herald*, 5 January 1795, she was "dangerously ill." By 6 April 1795, however, she had recovered sufficiently to play a villager in *Windsor Castle* and Cupid in a *Grand Masque* devised by Noverre in honor of the wedding of the Prince of Wales to Princess Caroline of Brunswick. She played Huncamunca in *Tom Thumb* on 6 and 21 May, a villager in *The Battle of Hexham* on 14 May, Yarico on 16 May, and the Page (with a song) in

The Follies of a Day for her benefit on 6 May 1795. Her net benefit receipts were about £100 and she was now living at No 13, King Street, Covent Garden. In this year, in *Candid and Impartial Strictures on the Performers Belonging to . . . Covent Garden,* F. G. Waldron called her "A sweet singer with a tolerable person, and pleasing countenance. The least we say of her acting the better." She was praised by the *Monthly Mirror* of January 1796 for her performance as Lothaire in *The Days of Yore* by Cumberland: "the pretty ariette of Clendining will most probably live longer than the play." That season she also played an Arabian Girl in *Harlequin Treasurer,* Mrs Casey in *Fontainebleau,* Jesse in *The Lad of the Hills,* Victoria in *The Castle of Andalusia,* and the title role in *Artaxerxes;* for her benefit on 18 May 1796 she performed Yarico, with the added songs of "Mad Bess" and "Where is that tow'ring spirit fled," accompanied on the harp by Weippert. She was still living at No 13, King Street, and her net receipts were about £133. In the summer of 1797 she acted at the Crow Street Theatre, Dublin. Back in London in 1796–97 she took only about £52 for her benefit on 24 May, when she sang Rosetta in *Love in a Village* for the first time. In her last season she played Philippo in *The Castle of Andalusia,* for the first time, on 29 September 1797. At her benefit (and last London performance) on 24 May 1798, she played Eliza in *The Poor Sailor.* On this night her daughter made her first appearance on any stage in the role of Little Bob. Mrs Clendining's net receipts were again low, only about £25. She was then living at No 22, Southampton Street.

According to the *Authentic Memoirs of the Green Room* (1799), Mrs Clendining was discharged from Covent Garden at the end of 1797–98. She went to act at Edinburgh, but was so frequently ill the audiences there saw little of her. She died at that city on 16 July 1799, at the age of 31.

Songs published as sung by her included

Reeve's *Hey down!* from *Merry Sherwood* (1795), *The Minstrel's Song* from *The Days of Yore* (1796), Reeve's *Come buy my Earthern Ware* from *Harlequin's Return* (1798), and Reeve's *Victorious La Pucelle* from *Joan of Arc* (1798).

Clendon, Eliza. *See* **Baker, Mrs David Lionel Erskine.**

Cler. *See* **L'Cler.**

Clerici, Roberto   [*fl.* 1711–1748], *scene painter.*

Roberto Clerici was probably the son of designer Giovanni Leonardo Clerici (fl. c. 1691–1708). He was a student of Ferdinando Bibiena at Parma. In 1711 he went to Vienna as a scene painter and perhaps from there came to England. He was in London by 1716, and on 15 May the King's Theatre in the Haymarket advertised that the opera *Pirro e Demetrio* had a scene "in Perfection of a Royal Palace, which exceeds any thing that has been seen in England, containing about One Thousand Yards of Painting by Sig Roberto Clerici." At the King's on 21 March 1719 a concert was presented "in a Magnificent Triumphant Scene, exceeding 30 Foot in Length any Scene ever seen before." This, too, was Clerici's work. He became the designer and machinist—or "engineer"—for the Royal Academy of Music when it was established in 1719, and for this society he provided scenery for *Numitore* at the King's on 2 April 1720. He is said to have worked in Portugal in 1735, at the Comédie Française in 1740, and to have returned to Parma by 1748.

Clericus, Josephus. *See* **Clark, Joseph.**

Clerk. *See also* **Clark** and **Clarke.**

Clerk, Mr   [*fl.* 1784], *singer.*

The Rev Mr Clerk was one of the countertenors who participated in the Handel

Memorial Concerts at Westminster Abbey and the Pantheon on 26, 27, 29 May and 3, 5 June 1784.

Clerke, William *d. 1663, musician.*

All that is known of William Clerke is contained in his will, written on 4 March 1662 and proved by his wife Jane on 3 August 1663. He described himself as a "Cittizen and Musitian of London" and left his sister Mary Fossan 20*s.*; Richard Clerke, William Clerke, Katherine Vincent, Ann Aystne, and Jane Turner 12*d.* each and the rest of his estate to his wife.

Clermont. *See* CLAREMONT.

Cleve. *See* DE CLEVE.

Cleveland, Mr *[fl. 1728], dancer.*

A Mr Cleveland, otherwise unknown, danced at the Haymarket Theatre on 15 October 1728.

Cleveland, Thomas *[fl. 1792–1799], actor.*

Thomas Cleveland first appeared under that name in a London playbill when he played Sir Walter Blunt in *1 Henry IV* at the Haymarket on 6 August 1792, a role he repeated on 10 August, and probably on 12 August. He also played Smith in *The Rehearsal* on 9 August. It seems, however, that Cleveland had played at London earlier under the curious name of "Uncle." A person billed as "A Young Gentleman" made his announced first appearance at the Haymarket on 16 April 1792 as Catesby in *Richard III* and on 4 July 1792 acted Charles Euston in *I'll Tell You What* (repeated 14 July). The "Young Gentleman" is identified as a Mr Uncle in a manuscript list (now in the Harvard Theatre Collection) of new performers at the Haymarket for the 1792 summer season. The *European Magazine*, however, identified the person who acted Charles Euston as Cleveland, and stated that he had already performed Doug-

las at Bath. He was described by the *European Magazine* as short, with a strong clear voice—"His action was too redundant but he sustained his character with feeling and obtained applause."

The above-noted performances proved to be the only ones Cleveland ever gave at London. He acted juvenile roles at Bristol in 1792–93, including Trip in *The School for Scandal* on 31 December 1792. In May 1793, it was announced that Cleveland had been engaged by "a respectable company in America." According to T. Allston Brown, it was not until 13 February 1796 that Cleveland and his wife made their debuts—mistakenly stated as "their first appearance on any stage"—at the John Street Theatre in New York as Zaphna and Palmira in *Mahomet.* The Clevelands, however, had acted earlier at Philadelphia, he making his first appearance there as a bandit in *The Castle of Andalusia* and as Granger in *Who's the Dupe?* on 17 February 1794. On 19 February he played Belford in *Isabella* and on 21 February Neville in *The Dramatist.* He remained at Philadelphia through 18 July 1794, and returned there in 1795.

From 2 November 1795 to 20 January 1796, the Clevelands acted with Hodgkinson's company at the Federal Street Theatre, Boston. Clapp described Cleveland as "a good actor" who had "a peculiar knack for making apologies" for cast or play changes, and getting applause for them. Cleveland also played at Hartford in the summer of 1795. During the 1796 season at the John Street Theatre, New York, Cleveland acted some 23 roles, mostly in comedies and farces but several in serious plays, among them being Lord Minikin in *Bon Ton*, Pallet in *Better Late than Never*, Souffrance in *My Grandmother*, Orlando in *As You Like It*, Clodio in *Love Makes a Man*, Don Carlos in *A Bold Stroke for a Husband*, Harry Thunder in *Wild Oats*, Catesby in *Jane Shore*, a Senator in *The Independence of America*, Sifredi in *Tancred and Sigismunda,* the King in *Hamlet,* Claudio in *Much Ado About Nothing,* and Charles Ratcliffe in *The Jew.*

After another summer engagement at Hartford in 1796, Cleveland played the 1796–97 season at Boston, acting Bulcazin in *The Mountaineers,* Sneer in *The Critic,* Glenalvon in *Douglas,* the Prince of Wales in *Henry the Fourth,* Callooney in *The Irishman in London,* Manly in *The Provok'd Husband,* Richmond in *Richard III,* Joseph Surface in *The School for Scandal,* Henry in *Slaves in Algiers,* Pierre in *Venice Preserv'd,* Sir Brilliant in *The Way to Keep Him,* Rakeland in *The Wedding Day,* and the title role in *Percy.* He was at Hartford again in August and September 1797, and then in the fall went to make his first appearance at Charleston, where he is known to have acted Richard III on 6 December 1797, and Young Rapid in *A Cure for the Heart-Ache* on 30 December and 1 January. In the latter role, the press praised him for "the alacrity with which he executed the eccentric and highly diverting but very difficult character." Cleveland was still at Charleston in the winter season of 1799, when he acted Greville in *Secrets Worth Knowing* on 25 January, and an American officer in *Charleston's Celebration* on 5 February. He took his benefit in *The Monk* on 8 April 1799. After that date, Cleveland and his wife, who was also with him at Charleston but seems never to have acted on the London stage, disappeared from theatrical records.

Clevly. *See* CLEAVELY.

Clifford, Mr [*fl.* 1781–1794?], *actor.*

A Mr Clifford acted the role of Brandon in *Richard III* at the Crown Inn, Islington, on 30 March 1781. The bill did not specify him as one of the "Performers from the the Theatre Royal, London," as it did many others in the cast. At the Crown Inn on 9 April 1781 Clifford played the title role George Barnwell, Leander in *The Mock Doctor,* and the Clown in *Linco's Travels.* On the same program, Mrs Clifford, presumably his wife, who had previously appeared at the Haymarket as Clarinda in *The Humours of Oxford* on 15 March 1779, acted the Dumb Lady in *The Mock Doctor.*

The London Stage has identified this Mr Clifford as the Henry Clifford, who, after being prompter at Norwich for 37 years, died on 8 June 1837. But the identification cannot be correct, for the Norwich Henry Clifford, by the testimony of the *Gentleman's Magazine* for August 1837, was 68 at the time of his death, and would have been only 12 years of age in 1781.

Possibly the Clifford who acted at the Crown Inn was the same Mr Clifford—announced as from the Bath Theatre—who made his debut in Charleston, South Carolina, on 22 January 1794, playing Valentine in *The Farmer* and speaking an occasional address. At Charleston in May of the year a Mr Clifford announced his intention to open a school for fencing. On 18 June he sang a comic duet with Mrs Chambers, and for his benefit on 27 June he sang the duet "Time has not thinned my flowing hair" with a Mr McGrath. A notice in the *Columbia Centinal,* a Boston newspaper, on 1 October 1794 reported that Mr Clifford, of the "Company of Comedians in Charleston," had recently died in Charleston. The obituary is curious, since a Mr Clifford made his debut at Boston on 29 December 1794—three months later—as Valentine in *The Farmer,* the same role in which the Mr Clifford of Charleston had made his first appearance there. According to Seilhamer, Clifford demonstrated "execution superior to any yet heard on the Boston boards." Either two Mr Cliffords were acting in eastern America at this time, or the Mr Clifford of *The Farmer* survived his death notice.

On 12 August 1800, the Bristol press announced the marriage of Mrs Clifford, "widow of the late Mr Clifford, of our theatre, and daughter of Mr Robins, the drawing master," to George Sims, son of Sims of Lilliput Alley, Bath. This Mrs Clifford now began to act under her new married name. As Mrs Sims she played at Bath and Bristol from 1805 through 1809. She may well have been the Miss Robins who many years before, on 1 December 1774, had made her debut at Drury Lane Theatre, at the age of 17.

Clifford, Mr ₍fl. 1792–1793₎, *singer.*
A Mr Clifford sang at Vauxhall Gardens in 1792 and 1793.

Clifford, Mr ₍fl. 1796₎, *actor.*
On 22 February 1796, a Mr Clifford played Gonzalez in *The Mourning Bride* and Colonel Tivy in *Bon Ton* at the Haymarket Theatre.

Clifford, Mr ₍fl. 1799₎, *manager.*
A manuscript list of the rules of the Richmond Theatre, Surrey, signed by James Winston, and dated 23 February 1799 (now in the Richmond Library), declared under rule 22 that Messrs Neville, Noble, and Clifford were to be acting managers that season. (Perhaps he was the Henry Clifford who later served as prompter at Norwich for 37 years until his death on 8 June 1837.) In 1799, the year in which Mr Clifford was an acting manager at Richmond, a Mrs Clifford was acting in that company.

Clifford, Mrs, née Robins, later Mrs George Sims ₍fl. 1779–1809?₎, *actress. See* **CLIFFORD, MR** ₍fl. 1781–1794?₎.

Clifford, Mrs ₍fl. 1799₎, *actress. See* **CLIFFORD, MR** ₍fl. 1799₎.

Clinch, Mr *c. 1664–1734, imitator.*
Born about 1664, "Clinch of Barnet," as he was usually billed, became known in London at the end of the seventeenth century. On 12 September 1699 Tom Brown

wrote to George Moult about the flood of novelties at the fairs and theatres. Among these, he said, was "the famous Mr Clinch of Barnet, with his kit and organ . . ." who had apparently already appeared at Drury Lane or Dorset Garden offering his imitations. He was popular enough that references to him in prologues began appearing as early as 1700, a typical one being that for *The Ambitious Step-Mother* which said that if audiences were less jaded in their tastes the actors would not need to import French dancers, and

Clinch and his Organ-Pipe, his Dogs and
    Bear,
To native Barnet might again repair.

On 22 August 1702 Clinch advertised his offerings at Drury Lane: he would imitate an organ with three voices, the "double Curtell," the flute, bells, huntsmen, and hounds—and the entertainment would include vaulting on a horse. On 18 June 1703 he gave a similar group of imitations, "All which he performs with his Mouth on the open Stage, being what no Man besides himself could ever yet attain to." When he returned on 5 June 1704 he had added a quaint new imitation of "an old Woman of Fourscore Years of Age nursing her Grand-Child."

As time went on and his novelty diminished Clinch played wherever he could gather a crowd: in Bartholomew Lane behind the New Exchange (1712), at the Cross Keys in St John Street (1730), and at the Lord Cobham's Head in Coldbath Field (1731). Oddly, he did almost nothing to expand his repertory over the years except to add an imitation of a harp.

Clinch was probably in his element at provincial fairs, and the fullest description of his abilities comes from a perfectly dreadful poem by John Davies written in 1721 as a class exercise at Cambridge. In 1724, *Bury-Fair*, as Davies called it, was actually published and a whole section, complete

with footnotes (here placed in the margin),
dealt with Clinch. Davies was unhappy
about one of the exhibits, but

*Picqu'd at the Loss—yet pleas'd, I onward
bend,
When thus accosted by a tatter'd Friend:
Walk in and see, Sir,—here with various
Sounds,
Or Flute, or Bagpipe, Quack,
or Cry of Hounds,**   * Clinch
                                     o'*Barnett*
*Drunkard, Old-Woman—or some twenty
more.
No time, Sir, lost—begin in half an Hour.
Fam'd CLINCH o'*Barnett *all the World
well knows.
With what inimitable *Art *he shows—
Elegant Sir, conduct me—
When soon the *Artist **   * He imitates
                                     a Quack-
                                     Doctor
Quack,
       with dex-
       t'rous Skill,
Expounds the Use and Virtue of each Pill;
From Head to Foot, he'll firmly set you
right,
Or failing that, why—*you're a Loser by't.
*From this he chang'd—and sent diverting
Noise,
As if from toothless **   * Old-woman
Gums, a jarring Voice;
Now Gammar, vers'd in Genealogy,
And tedious Forms of far-fetch'd Pedigree,
Mumps out with tatling Tale the Wonders
seen
In good Queen BESSE's Days, and Golden
Reign;
With * complicated Yelps,*   * He imitates
                                 the Cry of
                               Hounds
*and Medley Strains,
We hear full scented Cries
       upon the Plains,
The distant Sounds distinctly we can trace,
And *Springer's *Treble, note, from *Jowler's
Base.
An * Instrument he Took,*   * He imitates
                                 the Flute
                                 with his
                                 Voice

*he play'd, he sung,
Our Ears attentive, on
the Numbers hung,
And justly preferr'd the *Mimick-Tongue.
*So *STRADA'S *Artist with un-
erring Note **   * See, Strada's
                                   Prolusions.
*And equal Emulation long had try'd
Till *Philomela *burst her warbling Throat,
Inferior still, till, as He *play'd,* She *dy'd.
Variety of Matter gave Content,
I thought my *Splendid Shilling *hap'ly spent.*

Ten years after the poem was published,
shortly before 24 December 1734, according to the London *Daily Post,* Clinch of
Barnet died.

Clinch, Herbert [*fl. 1697*], *musician.*

On 4 January 1697 Herbert Clinch was
appointed a musician without fee in the
King's Musick. Since the Lord Chamberlain's accounts did not mention him again,
he doubtless never achieved full status and
he may have left the court.

Clinch, Lawrence *d. 1812, actor.*

Lawrence Clinch, a native of Dublin,
made his earliest appearances on the stage
in Ireland, playing at the Crow Street Theatre, Dublin, in 1768 and at Cork in the
summers of 1769 and 1770. He was a
member of the company at Norwich in
1771–72, and on 17 January 1772 the proprietors of that theatre offered to renew his
contract for a period of up to three years
at his usual salary of £1 11*s.* 6*d.* per week,
but Clinch apparently declined. According
to the headnote for the season of 1771–72
in *The London Stage* he was an actor at the
Haymarket in that year, but we do not find
his name in the bills. His first recorded appearance at London was on 16 October
1772, at Drury Lane, when, announced as
"A Young Gentleman," he played the title
role in *Alexander the Great, or The Rival
Queens.* On that night the prompter Hopkins wrote in his "Diary" that "Mr Clinch
made his first appearance in the part of

Alexander tolerable figure & Voice a Little too much upon the Brogue, he is wild & Aukward—but was receiv'd with Applause." Clinch repeated the role on 19 and 26 October and 3 December. His name is found in the bills for no other role that season until he played Albert in *Alonzo* on 27 February (and nine other times through 22 March). He received a number of payments from the treasury in the interim—£5 5s. by order on 17 October, £20 by order on 28 October, amounts of £5 5s. on account on 31 October, 21 November, 26 December, and 16 January, and £1 "short advance" on 29 November—lending credence to the statement by the *Thespian Dictionary* (1805) that "Garrick, repenting the engagement, offered him some money

to be off, which the other declined; and consequently, the manager gave him characters which were disagreeable." On 27 January, he had been paid £12 14s. in full of his salary "to 23rd Instant." (He was on the salary list at £2 10s. per week.) Indeed, the only other role he seems to have acted in his first year at Drury Lane was Oswald in *King Arthur* on 28 April 1773.

Despite this inauspicious debut season, and after playing leading roles at Bristol in the summer of 1773, Clinch was nevertheless re-engaged by Garrick for 1773–74. Although payments continued to him, again he was used but slightly; his name appeared in the bills only for King Edward in *The Earl of Warwick* on 26 March and 23 April 1774, on which latter date he had a benefit night which brought him a profit of £55 10s. 6d. He was paid, however, £12 10s. on 13 November 1773 for 30 nights, though he was not on the salary list, and again £2 1s. 8d. on 27 May 1774 for five days due him from the beginning of the season. Probably he served the repertory in a number of unbilled roles.

Clinch played at Cork and Limerick in the summer of 1774, and then joined Covent Garden, where he made his first appearance on 4 October 1774 as Alexander. Apparently the management there thought more highly of his abilities. He acted in *The Rehearsal* on 11 October, Pharamond in *Philaster* on 20 October, Richmond in *Richard III* on 23 October, and Dionysius in *The Grecian Daughter* on 31 October. In a review of new performers at Covent Garden, the *Westminster Magazine* (October 1774) wrote of his performance of Alexander:

Critical justice must own, that Mr. *Clinch* has acquired a rust; but at the same time it must also be allowed that his *present* exceeds his former performance of the Macedonian hero, altho' he did not exhibit that perfection we wish him to attain. It is true, he gave his passion utterance more naturally than before; but he was extremely deficient in the tender

Harvard Theatre Collection

LAWRENCE CLINCH, as Alexander, with MRS MELMOTH

engraving by Walker, after Dodd

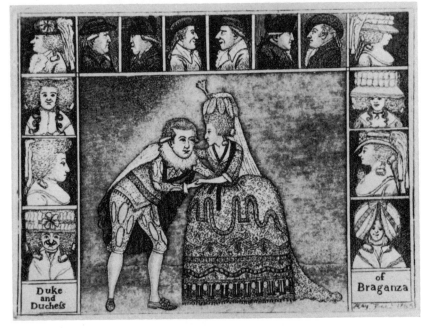

LAWRENCE CLINCH, with MARY ANN YATES, as the Duke and Duchess of Braganza

artist unknown

scenes. His voice has a very unmusical tone in it, which we cannot but think may be in a great measure got the better of, with care and attention. He has since performed *Richmond* in *Richard III* and *Pharamond* in *Philaster*, with applause. He caught Barry's manner, but he is far behind him in his persuasive and eloquent delivery.

William Hawkins in *Miscellanies in Prose and Verse* (1775) was not as enthusiastic, reporting that "he clinches so vociferously [as Alexander], that if he is not less violent, he will inevitably tear himself, and his parts to rags." He advised Clinch "not to be so lavish with his superfluous fire and action." On 7 January, Clinch played Pylades in *The Distrest Mother*. When Sheridan's *The Rivals* was given its first performance on 17 January 1775, Clinch was not found in the original cast, but by the play's third performance on 28 January, he had replaced Lee in the revised role of Sir Lucius O'Trigger, and his performance contributed greatly to the subsequent success of the play, which Sheridan had worked over considerably since the first night. So grateful (it was said) was Sheridan to Clinch for having saved *The Rivals* from ruin that he wrote the afterpiece *St Patrick's Day* for the actor, who played Lieutenant O'Connor in its first performance on 2 May 1775.

In the following season at Covent Garden, Clinch again performed Sheridan's two Irishmen, and acted Charles in *The Jealous Wife*, Bedamar in *Venice Preserv'd*, Axalla in *Tamerlane*, Portius in *Cato*, Salisbury in *King John*, and his other roles of Pylades, Alexander, Richmond, and Dionysius. From 3 July to 16 September

1776 he acted at Liverpool for £2 per week, and was at Cork again from 25 September to 14 October.

In a poem entitled *Drama,* Downman wrote in 1775 that

> *Nature has dealt to Clinch with lib'ral*
>   *hand,*
> *Talents, which cultur'd, might applause*
>   *command;*
> *But vain the grant, and slow must rise*
>   *his fame,*
> *Unless the manager will fan the flame.*

The Covent Garden managers did not "fan the flame," but indeed, for reasons unknown, failed to reengage Clinch for 1776–77. He returned to play successfully at Crow Street for several years. In the summer of 1777 he was at Liverpool again, but at a reduced salary of £1 per week. His marriage about 1780 to a lady of independent wealth allowed him to perform when, where, and on what terms he preferred, according to the *Thespian Dictionary.* He was, however, not again engaged at London, except for a single performance of Young Pedant in *The Temple Bar* in a specially licensed performance at the Haymarket on 21 September 1782.

Clinch acted summers at Cork in 1783, 1784, 1786, 1787, and 1788, at Limerick in 1783 and 1788, and at Waterford in 1786. He was also at Edinburgh in 1784–85 and 1785–86. After a quarrel with Daly, the manager of Crow Street, where he also had played regularly during the 1780s, Clinch became the manager of Sir Vere Hunt's theatrical enterprises at Limerick and Waterford in 1790–91, at a salary of £3 13s. 6d. per week.

Clinch died at Dublin in 1812. His wife had died in that city, at their residence on Grafton Street, in November 1789.

A crude anonymous engraving of Clinch and Mrs Yates as the Duke and Duchess of Braganza, presumably at Dublin, was published in May 1785. The print is made

curious by the borders which contain four full-face and ten profile portraits of men and women, apparently other characters in the play. Clinch is also shown as Alexander with Mrs Melmoth as Roxana in *The Rival Queens* in an engraving by W. Walker, after D. Dodd, published for the *New English Theatre,* 1776.

Clinford, Mr (*fl.* 1792), *actor.*

A small company of irregulars, a mixture of novices and experienced hands, rented the Haymarket Theatre on 15 October 1792 and for the benefit of one of their number, Mr Sims, presented *The Country Girl* and *Who's the Dupe?* In the afterpiece a Mr Clinford played Granger. Whether he was an amateur out for a lark or a youngster from the provinces hoping to attract managerial attention is not known. He did not appear again in London in the eighteenth century, unless he was the Mr Clifford who was active in London in the 1790s.

Clingo, Mr (*fl.* 1759–1763), *pit doorkeeper.*

Mr Clingo was a pit doorkeeper at Covent Garden from about 1759–60 through 1762–63. On 19 May 1760, 15 May 1761, and 26 May 1763, he shared benefit tickets with other house servants. In 1760–61 he was paid 10s. per week.

Clinton, Master (*fl.* 1763–1765), *dancer.*

Master Clinton made his first noticed appearance on the London stage on 11 August 1763 at the Haymarket in a *Provincial Dance* with the young Miss Street. Both were scholars of the ballet master Gerhardi. On 15 August, again with Miss Street, who was to be his dancing partner throughout his brief career, Master Clinton performed a new comic dance. Both pieces were repeated throughout the summer until 7 September.

He was engaged at Drury Lane for

1763–64, making his first appearance, again with Miss Street, in a *Provenzale* on 14 October, at which time the prompter Hopkins noted in his "Diary" that they were "greatly applauded." This number was repeated numerous times during the season, in which Master Clinton also performed a dance of *Venetian Gardeners* (10 November), a *Fairy Dance* (23 November), *The Shepherdesses, or, La Faux a Veugle* (13 January), *The Hunters* (24 February), and *The Gipsies* (23 May). He returned to the Haymarket for the summer of 1764 to appear regularly in such pieces as *The Carpenter and the Fruit Dealer* and *The Dutchman and the Provincials*. Master Clinton seems not to have been re-engaged at Drury Lane for the next winter season. In the summer of 1765 he was, however, again at the Haymarket, adding to his repertory *The Carpenter*, *Le Chausseur*, and *Le Berge* (all three on 8 July), and a new hornpipe on 7 August. His last known performance was in the hornpipe on 13 September 1765.

Clitherow, Benjamin *fl. c. 1740–1774*, *pyrotechnist.*

The pyrotechnist Benjamin Clitherow was "associated" with displays of fireworks at Cuper's Gardens in the 1740s; intermittently between 1750 and 1755 he was the "engineer" of the fireworks at that pleasure resort and was also engaged at Marylebone Gardens. On 19 September 1754, at Hill's theatrical booth on the Bowling Green, Southwark, Clitherow exhibited "*Italian Fireworks,*" by "permission of his Majesty's Officer of Ordnance," at which time he advertised himself as "the real Engineer to Cuper's and Marylebone Gardens." On 23 June 1755 he prepared fireworks to accompany a concert at Cuper's which commemorated the accession of George II. Later that summer he was obliged to apologize in the newspapers for the failure on 2 August 1755 of an elaborate naval battle in the gardens "owing to

part of the machinery for moving the shipping being clogg'd by some unaccountable accident" and the powder in the ships "having unfortunately got a little damp." It appears that this was the last summer for fireworks at Cuper's.

In the summer of 1762 Clitherow advertised a display of fireworks at Jamaica House, Rotherhithe. He worked at Ranelagh in 1766 and 1771 and probably in other years. In the late summer of 1769, he supervised the preparations of the fireworks for the ill-fated Shakespeare Jubilee at Stratford, dampened by constant heavy rains which caused the pyrotechnics to fizzle. In 1772, 1773, and 1774 he shared the exhibitions of fireworks at Marylebone Gardens with such notable pyrotechnists as Caillot, Clanfield, and Torré.

During most of his long career, Clitherow lived with his family at the King's Arms, No 10, Rose and Crown Court in Moorfields, where he also maintained a shop for the making and selling of his explosive wares. In the Harvard Theatre Collection is a large broadside sheet (undated, but printed sometime after the accession of George III in 1763) in which the fireworker, billing himself as "Clitherow, Sen. The Britannic Artist," advertised an extensive range of fireworks, "Sold by none else in England." These included "Vertical Wheels," "Globe Wheels illuminated," "Brilliant Fountains," "Gold Flower Pots to fire in Rooms," "Pyramids of Fire Pumps," and "The Metamorphose Wheel, or Wheel of Folly," which the maker offered to ship to any part of Britain. On the bill he claimed to be the "Real Engineer to Ranelagh and Mary-Le-Bone Gardens," who had exhibited fireworks before the King and the Royal Family at Kew and Gunnersbury, and at Ranelagh "for the Entertainment of his Danish Majesty." The advertisement also carried a print illustrating the various types of firework mechanisms, with explanations.

How long Clitherow remained active as

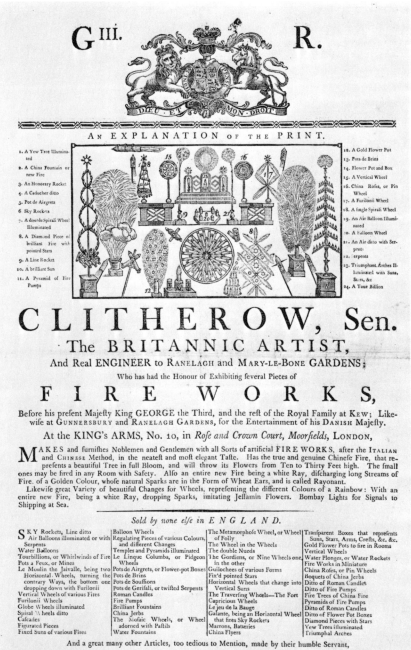

1. A Yew Tree Illuminated
2. A China Fountain or new Fire
3. An Honorary Rocket
4. A Caducher ditto
5. Pot de Airgreta
6. Sky Rockets
7. A double Spirali Wheel Illuminated
8. A Diamond Piece of brilliant Fire with pointed Stars
9. A Line Rocket
10. A brilliant Sun
11. A Pyramid of Fire Pumps

12. A Gold Flower Pot
13. Pots de Brins
14. Flower Pot and Box
15. A Vertical Wheel
16. China Rofes, or Pin Wheel
17. A Furilonii Wheel
18. A fingle Spirali Wheel
19. An Air Balloon Illuminated
20. A Balloon Wheel
21. An Air ditto with Serpents
22. Serpents
23. Triumphant Arches Illuminated with Suns, Stars, &c
24. A Tour Billion

CLITHEROW, Sen.
The BRITANNIC ARTIST,
And Real ENGINEER to RANELAGH and MARY-LE-BONE GARDENS;
Who has had the Honour of Exhibiting feveral Pieces of

FIRE WORKS,

Before his prefent Majefty King GEORGE the Third, and the reft of the Royal Family at KEW; Like-wife at GUNNERSBURY and RANELAGH GARDENS, for the Entertainment of his DANISH Majefty.

At the KING's ARMS, No. 10, in *Rofe and Crown Court, Moorfields,* LONDON,

MAKES and furnifhes Noblemen and Gentlemen with all Sorts of artificial FIRE WORKS, after the ITALIAN and CHINESE Method, in the neateft and moft elegant Tafte. Has the true and genuine Chinefe Fire, that reprefents a beautiful Tree in full Bloom, and will throw its Flowers from Ten to Thirty Feet high. The fmall ones may be fired in any Room with Safety. Alfo an entire new Fire being a white Ray, difcharging long Streams of Fire of a Golden Colour, whofe natural Sparks are in the Form of Wheat Ears, and is called Rayonant.
Likewife great Variety of beautiful Changes for Wheels, reprefenting the different Colours of a Rainbow: With an entire new Fire, being a white Ray, dropping Sparks, imitating Jeffamin Flowers. Bombay Lights for Signals to Shipping at Sea.

Sold by none elfe in ENGLAND.

SKY Rockets, Line ditto
Air Balloons illuminated or with Serpents
Water Balloons
Tourbillions, or Whirlwinds of Fire
Pots a Feux, or Mines
Le Moulin the Jaivalle, being two Horizontal Wheels, turning the contrary Ways, the bottom one dropping down with Furilonii
Vertical Wheels of various Fires
Furilonii Wheels
Globe Wheels illuminated
Spiral Wheels ditto
Cafcades
Figurated Pieces
Fixed Suns of various Fires

Balloon Wheels
Regulating Pieces of various Colours, and different Changes
Temples and Pyramids illuminated
Le Linque Columba, or Pidgeon Wheels
Pots de Airgrets, or Flower-pot Boxes
Pots de Brins
Pots de Souffions
Pots de Gerifali, or twifted Serpents
Roman Candles
Fire Pumps
Brilliant Fountains
China Jerbs
The Mofaic Wheels, or Wheel adorned with Paftils
Water Fountains

The Metamorphofe Wheel, or Wheel of Folly
The Wheel in the Wheels
The double Nueds
The Gordiens, or Nine Wheels one, in the other
Guilochees of various Forms
Fix'd pointed Stars
Horizontal Wheels that change into Vertical Suns
The Traverfing Wheels—The Fort
Capricious Wheels
Le jeu de la Bauge
Galante, being an Horizontal Wheel that fires Sky Rockets
Marrons, Batteries
China Flyers

Tranfparent Boxes that reprefents Suns, Stars, Arms, Crefts, &c. &c.
Gold Flower Pots to fire in Rooms
Vertical Wheels
Water Plonges, or Water Rockets
Fire Works in Miniature
China Rofes, or Pin Wheels
Boquets of China Jerbs
Ditto of Roman Candles
Ditto of Fire Pumps
Fire Trees of China Fire
Pyramids of Fire Pumps
Ditto of Flower Pot Boxes
Diamond Pieces with Stars
Yew Trees illuminated
Triumphal Arches

And a great many other Articles, too tedious to Mention, made by their humble Servant,

BENJAMIN CLITHEROW, Sen.

⁎ To prevent Miftakes, Orders directed as above will be carefully and expeditioufly fent to any Part of GREAT BRITAIN, &c.——Reafonable Allowance to Shopkeepers to fell again; and all Goods to be paid for on Delivery.

Harvard Theatre Collection

Advertisement by BENJAMIN CLITHEROW

The Dreadful FIRE, in Rose & Crown Court, Long Alley
MOORFIELDS.

1

Good people hear the sad relation,
Of the Moorfields late Conflagration,
Which was at One in the morning done,
The Second of November, Ninety One.

CHORUS

Let all in future, with care remember,
Fire Works for the fifth of November.

2

The Widow Clitherow by name,
Made Fire Works and sold the same:
The Fifth of November drawing nigh,
She had made up a great quantity.

3

None knows how this mischance befell,
They're all blown up who best could tell,
But some Gunpowder fire took,
The House blew up all Moorfields shook.

Publish'd Nov.r 5.th 1791, by C. Sheppard, N.o 19, Lambert Hill, Doctors Commons, London.

4

Two adjoining houses the shock did raze,
Two houses opposite set on blaze,
Folks all got up being fill'd with wonder,
Some cried an Earthquake, some said Thunder.

5

Mrs Clitherow, and her three Children small,
With Seven more poor souls were blown up all,
Their limbs were scatter'd in the Air,
And after found some here some there.

6

Young Mr Clitherow being not at home,
By that means scaped the dreadful doom,
But when he knew their wretched state,
He almost wish'd he'd shar'd their fate.

7

A Woman slept in the garret there,
Was thro' the roof blown in the air,
Yet fell unhurt in the court yard,
By God Almighty's Mercy spared.

THE WIDOW CLITHEROW and family, killed in an explosion
artist unknown

a fireworker after 1774 is not known, and his billing of himself on his advertisement as "Clitherow, Sen" suggests that at some time a son was also engaged in the business. The elder Clitherow was dead, however, before 1791, for on 2 November of that year his wife, "The Widow Clitherow by Name," died in an explosion while making fireworks for sale in preparation for Guy Fawkes Day. Her house in Moorfields blew up along with two adjoining houses in Rose and Crown Court, and two other houses were set afire. The accident also killed three of Mrs Clitherow's "small" children and seven other persons. "Young Mr Clitherow," presumably an elder child, was spared by not being at home at the time. A print showing the explosion, and Mrs Clitherow flying through the air, was published on 5 November 1791 by C. Sheppard of No 19, Lambert Hill, Doctors' Common, accompanied by seven stanzas of verse describing the tragedy.

Clive, Mrs George, Catherine, née Raftor *1711–1785, actress, singer.*

Catherine Raftor Clive, known universally as Kitty, was the most vivacious comedienne and the best female comic singer on the London stage in the middle of the eighteenth century. She was also one of England's most amusing and most celebrated personages.

According to the only plausible account we have of her parentage and early life, that of W. R. Chetwood in his *General History of the Stage*, Kitty was the daughter of William Raftor, a lawyer of Kilkenny, Ireland, and heir to a considerable estate which was forfeited because of his adherence to the cause of James II at the battle of the Boyne. Raftor followed James to the Continent "and, by his Merit, obtained a Captain's Commission in the Service of Lewis the Fourteenth; but, gaining a Pardon . . . he came to England, where he married Mrs. Daniel, daughter of an eminent Citizen on Fishstreethill with whom he

Harvard Theatre Collection

CATHERINE CLIVE
engraving by A. Van Haecken, after J. Van Haecken

had a handsome Fortune: By her he had a numerous Issue." The names of all these children except Catherine and her younger brother James are unknown. William Raftor was still alive in 1734.

Kitty was born in 1711, on 15 November, she told Jane Pope in a letter of 1782. Her spelling, barbarous even for a century which had little interest in exact orthography, is usually adduced as proof of neglect of her early education. But, her spelling and odd syntax aside, her letters and memoranda show wide knowledge and alert good sense. She wrote a few farces, sang in French and Italian, and mingled on terms of equality with people of the highest cultivation. It is probable that the degree of her educational deprivation has been exaggerated.

Kitty told Chetwood that when she was about 12 years old she and Jane Johnson (later the first wife of Theophilus Cibber) "used to tag after the celebrated Mr Wilks (her own words) whenever they saw him in the streets." Charles Lee Lewes, who was not born until a decade after Kitty's debut, confidently recounted in 1805 a story he had heard many years before which purported to relate how she got on the stage. The account is minutely circumstantial:

Mrs. CLIVE was originally servant to Miss Eleanor Knowles, afterwards Mrs. Young, mother to the present Sir George Young, and Mr. Thomas Young, who, in 1774, came out at Covent-garden Theatre in Macheath, which he performed nine nights with much celebrity. When Mrs. Clive lived with Miss Knowles, who then lodged at Mrs. Snell's, a fan-painter in Church-row, Houndsditch, Mr. Watson, many years box-keeper at Drury-lane and Richmond, kept the Bell Tavern, directly opposite to Mrs. Snell's. At this house was held the Beef-steak Club, instituted by Mr. Beard, Mr. Dunstall, Mr. Woodward, Stoppalaer, Bencraft, Giffard, &c. &c. Kitty Rafter, being one day washing the steps of the door, and singing, the windows of the club-room being open, they were instantly crowded by the company, who were all enchanted with her natural grace and simplicity. This circumstance alone led her to the stage, under the auspices of Mr. Beard and Mr. Dunstall.

That indefatigable collector of theatrical anecdote James Winston, writing at the turn of the century, introduced another element to the complexity by claiming that John Beard had taken her to his friend the song writer Henry Carey, who was really responsible for bringing her to Drury Lane when she was 17.

Chetwood's recollection in 1749 was over half a century nearer in time and perhaps factually closer also, inasmuch as he was in 1728 prompter at Drury Lane Theatre:

Miss Raftor had a facetious Turn of Humour and infinite Spirits, with a Voice and Manner in singing Songs of Pleasantry peculiar to herself. Those talents Mr. Theo Cibber and I (we all at that time living together in one House) thought a sufficient Passport to the Theatre. We recommended her to the Laureate [Colley Cibber] whose infallible Judgment soon found out her Excellencies; and the Moment he heard her sing, put her down in the List of Performers at twenty Shillings per Week.

However it was that she came to the attention of managers and public, Chetwood seems perfectly correct in claiming that "never did any person of her age fly to perfection with such rapidity." He says that she was first given the trifling part of Ismenes, the page to Robert Wilks's Ziphares in *Mithridates, King of Pontus*, in April 1728. It was reported that she pleased the town with an entr'acte song especially written by Sir Car Scroop. The story is probably true, though the surviving playbill of 13 April, the first and last time the tragedy was offered that season, does not name Kitty. But when the 1728–29 season began, she was put into rehearsal for larger parts and at once began to take her destined place as the chief comedy favorite of the Drury Lane audiences for the next four decades.

In that first full season, Kitty was cast first as Bianca in *Othello* on 12 October but quickly moved into singing parts and sprightly secondary comedy roles. She learned Minerva in *Perseus and Andromeda*, Dorinda in the Dryden-Davenant-Shadwell alteration of *The Tempest*, Honoria in *Love Makes a Man*, Rosella in *The Village Opera*, Valeria in *The Rover*, Flora in *The Lover's Opera*, Bonvira in *The History of Bonduca*, the title role in *Phebe*, Arethusa in *The Contrivances*, and Maria in *Whig and Tory*. By 10 April the bills were also able to advertise that she was singing "her usual song."

There had been a near riot of "the Hydra-Headed Multitude" when on 7 January 1729 Colley Cibber brought out his *Love in a Riddle*. But, says Chetwood, when Miss Raftor came on in the part of Phillida, the monstrous Roar subsided. A Person in the Stage-Box, next to my Post [as Prompter] called out to his Companion in the following elegant Style—'Zounds! *Tom!* take Care! or this charming little Devil will save all.'

Her presence did not, in fact, keep the play alive and Cibber withdrew it after the second night, but evidently Kitty had made a personal success for she was at once painted by Schalken and engraved by Faber in the part, and her roles increased in number and importance.

As in the previous season she opened in 1729–30 with Bianca (a role she was to have until Mrs Butler annexed it in 1732–33). She added the part of Night in *The Scene of Apollo and Daphne* in the new afterpiece *The Comical Distresses of Pierot* (from which may have come the song

Harvard Theatre Collection

CATHERINE CLIVE, as Phillida
engraving by Faber, after Schalken

See! the radiant Queen of Night, published that year "as sung by" Miss Raftor) and was the original Kitty in *The Humours of Oxford* and the original Isabella in *The Stage Coach Opera*. She played Rosella in *The Chambermaid* and Dulceda in *Bayes's Opera*. She took over Mrs Booth's part of Serena in *The Orphan* in April. Several of these roles were in afterpieces, and many obliged her at some point to sing, but despite her vocal abilities she kept clear of harlequinades this season, except for singing in the title part of *The Fairy Queen: or, Harlequin Turned Enchanter* for Surel's benefit on 15 May. (Evidently she was never a good dancer; as late as 6 February 1733 her "minuet" was derided by *The Auditor*.)

Kitty performed less frequently than in her first year, principally because of the popularity of tragedy during the 1729–30 season. For by then the managers had discovered that she was no tragedienne, though she herself had not. There were also longish runs of plays she was not cast in, like Benjamin Martyn's *Timoleon*, utilizing Mrs Porter, and James Thomson's *Sophonisba*, mainly devised as a vehicle for Mrs Oldfield. Kitty at 18 was not yet in competition with these grandes dames, either in comedy or in tragedy, but rather with the feebler Mrs Shireburn, and with Mrs Horton, who had years of effective playing ahead still but who was at 30 waning as an ingenue.

In 1730–31 Kitty Raftor added to her repertoire Procris in *Cephalus and Procris*, Amphitrite in the Dryden-Davenant-Shadwell alteration of *The Tempest*, Phillida in *Damon and Phillida*, Jenny in *The Amours of Billingsgate*, Rachel in *The Jovial Crew*, Farcia in *Bayes's Opera*, and Kitty in *The What D'Ye Call It*. During the season she was the first representative of Nanny in *The Highland Fair*, "A new Scots Opera" by Joseph Mitchell, and, for the benefit of the author Thomas Cooke, Urania in his new play *The Triumphs of Love and*

Honour. But her own triumph of the season was her memorable performance as Nell in a revival of Charles Coffey's ballad opera called *The Devil to Pay*, which threw the critics into raptures and, if Thomas Whincop is to be believed, caused her trifling salary to double. A favorite character with both Kitty and her audiences for the rest of her career, it gave scope for her two principal enchantments, her voice and her wry comic ability.

Kitty's steady conquest of her audience continued in 1731–32 as she added to her already lengthy string of roles: Mrs Littlewit in the revival of *Bartholomew Fair*, Jenny in *The Provok'd Husband*, Miss Sprightly in *The Tragedy of Tragedies*, Busy in *The Man of Mode*, and Margery in *The Country Wedding*. She was the original Flametta in the new and popular "Farcical Ballad Opera of one Act" *The Devil of a Duke*; she played Martin's Wife in the first performances of the anonymous *Comical Revenge*. She was given loud acclaim as she showed for the first time, at 21, that she was qualified to step to the head of the line of interpreters of Polly in *The Beggar's Opera*, singing the role 11 times before the season's close. Most importantly of all perhaps, she attracted the interest and friendship of Henry Fielding. He wrote for her Isabel in *The Old Debauchees* and Kissinda in *The Covent Garden Tragedy*, and she played them both on their joint opening night, 1 June 1732. She was also Fielding's first Chloe in *The Lottery*. Oftener and oftener her clear soprano was heard singing entr'acte and other specialty songs, such as Purcell's "Rosy Bowers" and Carey's "Oh! jealousy thou raging Pain." Audiences and critics agreed that, as Thomas Cooke said in *The Comedian, or Philosophic Enquirer*, "Miss Raftor is without a Superior, if we except the foremost voices in the Italian Operas." Again and again her droll manner was exploited in comic prologues and epilogues.

Kitty Raftor's unbroken sequence of suc-cesses continued in 1732–33 as she repeated favorite parts and added: Silvia in *The Old Bachelor*, Leonora in *Sir Courtly Nice*, Cydaria in *The Indian Emperour*, Thalia in *The Judgment of Paris*, Edging in *The Careless Husband*, Deborah in *Deborah; or, A Wife for You All*, Belinda in *The Man of Mode*, Mrs Fanciful in *The Imaginary Cuckolds*, Prue in *Love for Love*, and Aranthes in *Theodosia*. During the season she was the original Cicely in the anonymous afterpiece *Wat Tyler*, the first Jenny in Charles Coffey's farce *The Boarding School*, the original Thirsis in Theophilus Cibber's *Damon and Daphne*, the original Phillis in the new ballad opera by Edward Phillips called *The Livery Rake*, and the Venus of a new masque, *Cupid and Hymen*, with music by Seedo. Henry Fielding provided another of her permanently popular characters in Lappet in his new comedy *The Miser*.

The maturing Kitty was by far the most talented and most popular among the actresses who remained in the "loyal" company at Drury Lane with John Highmore when in the fall of 1733 the disgruntled Theophilus Cibber led his seceders away to the Haymarket. She remained the first actress in the company when Highmore sold the patent to Charles Fleetwood early in 1734. But about that time squibs and jokes concerning her abrasive tongue and difficult, forthright temperament began to find their way into the public prints and coffee houses. In the ephemeral penny-catching commentary on the secession of 1733 called *The Theatric Squabble; or, The Patentees*, one side of her growing reputation was reflected but exaggerated:

> *Then R——ft——r, follow'd by the*
> *Wise and Bold,*
> *A pleasing Actress, but a Green-Room*
> *Scold;*
> *Puff'd with Success, she triumphs over*
> *all,*
> *Snarls in the Scene-Room, Curses in the*
> *Hall:*

She'as Learning, Judgment, Wit, and
    Manners too:
Ay and good Sense,—if what she say's be
    true.
Her Virtue too, the purest of the Age,
She'll scarcely be a Whore—upon the
    Stage:
Yet she that rails 'gainst vicious Talk so
    strong,
Makes no Objection to a Bawdy Song

Though the author of this doggerel was reasonably accurate about Kitty's irascibility, he was far off target with his innuendo on her morals. She was already famous for her militant chastity, and she disappointed predatory beaus and managers for the rest of her life. Kitty determined instead upon marriage, and she married outside the profession. Her voice, vigor, and virginity had already caught the ear and heart of George Clive, a nonpracticing barrister, whose more eminent father, also George, was shortly (in 1735) to be appointed Cursitor Baron of the Exchequer. (Young George's second cousin was the famous Robert, Lord Clive "of India".) George and Kitty were married, apparently at some date between the change of her name in the bills from "Miss Raftor" on 1 October 1733 to "Mrs Clive" on 5 October, (though this may only reflect a lag in the printer's understanding, inasmuch as 1 October was the first night of the new season).

It is difficult to imagine what the attraction could have been between the oddly assorted pair. But love was already fading fast by early 1734, when Henry Fielding wrote in the preface to his farce *The Intriguing Chambermaid* an encomium on her filial piety and her chastity:

Great favourite as you are with your audience, you would be much more so were they acquainted with your private character; could they see you laying out great part of the profits which arise from entertaining them so well, in the support of an aged father; did they see you, who can charm them on the stage with personating the foolish and vicious characters of your sex, acting in real life the part of the best wife, the best daughter, the best sister, and the best friend.

George Clive and his wife parted company in 1735 or earlier and lived separately thereafter but were never divorced. Seemingly a cultivated but weak man, he became the companion of the wealthy and aged Mr Ince (reputedly the original of the Templar in the *Spectator*) and faded into provincial obscurity. Kitty had many attractive male friends—indeed, she seems to have got on better with men than with most of her own sex—but no real scandal ever attached to her name. Nor did she hold a grudge against Clive. Thirty-five years after the separation she replied to some news of her husband sent by the gossipy Garrick: "You are very much mistaken if you imagine that I shall be sorry to hear Mr Clive is well; I thank God I have no malice or hatred to anybody: besides it is so long ago since I thought he used me ill, that I quite forgot it. I am very glad he is well and happy."

The brief marital interlude had no effect one way or the other on Kitty's career. She continued at Drury Lane with growing power and popularity until her retirement on 24 April 1769, except for her two years at Covent Garden (1743–44 and 1744–45) and a Dublin summer excursion of 1741. (Her first appearance in Ireland was at the Aungier Street Theatre on 20 June 1741.) She also charitably played several benefit performances at Lincoln's Inn Fields, Goodman's Fields, and Southwark over the years.

Kitty continued to add characters and admirers—and with them jealous enemies—as she added years and experience. Like all actors in repertory companies, as time went on her yearly number of new roles diminished as she acquired her basic repertoire of favorite characters in older plays. Still, thanks first to the talented exertions of Henry Fielding, then of James Miller, and then of others who discovered that upon her sturdy talents they could successfully erect comic structures even out of flimsy materials, she did go on annexing parts until the very end of her career.

In 1733–34 Kitty added Estifania in *Rule a Wife and Have a Wife*, Diana in *Harlequin Doctor Faustus*, Elvira in the *Spanish Fryar*, Kitty in *The Harlot's Progress*, Dollalolla in *The Opera of Operas*, Miranda in *The Busy Body*, Mercury in *Timon in Love* by John Kelly (its first performance), the Chambermaid in *The Intriguing Chambermaid* by Fielding (first), Columbine in *Cupid and Psyche*, anonymous (first), and Flippanta in *The Confederacy*.

In 1734–35 she added: Primrose in *The Mother-in-Law*, Phillis in *The Conscious Lovers*, Lucy in *An Old Man Taught Wisdom* by Fielding (first), Mrs Pinchwife in *The Country Wife*, Margaret in *A Cure for a Scold* by James Worsdale (first), Lady Wou'dbe in *Volpone*, Nell in *The Merry Cobler* (a sequel by Coffey to *The Devil to Pay*, which allowed her further scope for her favorite characterization), Maria in *The Man of Taste* by James Miller (first), Cherry in *The Stratagem*, and Hoyden in *The Relapse*.

In 1735–36 Kitty presented Doll Common in *The Alchemist*, Lady Froth in *The Double Dealer*, Lady Sadlife in *The Double Gallant*, Aurelia in *The Twin Rivals*, Clymene in *The Fall of Phaeton* ("A New Dramatic Masque . . . Invented by Mr Pritchard Musick composed by Mr Arne"), and Biddy in *The Tender Husband*.

For the benefit of the town, though she did not intend it, Mrs Clive this season furnished the most spectacular of her professional contentions, that with Mrs Theophilus Cibber. The genesis of the quarrel may have lain as much in her childhood friendship with the beautiful and pitiable Miss Johnson, who had married the disreputable Theophilus Cibber and died young, as with any natural rivalry with his

second wife, Susanna Maria Arne Cibber. But the rivalry would have been sufficient; for Mrs Cibber (and Theophilus) seem to have convinced the shifty Fleetwood that the lovely voice and figure of Mrs Cibber were more meet for Polly in *The Beggar's Opera* than were the attributes of Mrs Clive and that Kitty could be satisfied with the excellent—but nonetheless secondary—part of Lucy. It was hardly so. Kitty defended her right to the part of Polly with savagery and found just so many more champions in the press and among people of influence in the theatre than her rival did that she retained the role. For three months the journals were in a hubbub—*Fog's*, the *Grub-Street Journal*, the *Daily Journal*—and Henry Giffard at Goodman's Fields Theatre made hay by producing *The Beggar's Pantomime; or Contending Columbines*, which was not only played but hawked about the town. In the third edition, an eminent comedian at the rival house, Henry Woodward, furnished (for the tune of the ballad *Chevy Chase*) a long mock-heroic rhyme on the affair. Some of it is irresistible:

> *Cibber, the Syren of the Stage,*
> *A Vow to Heav'n did make,*
> *Full Twenty Nights in Polly's Part,*
> *She'd make the Play-house shake.*
>
> *When as these Tidings came to Clive,*
> *Fierce Amazonian Dame;*
> *Who is it thus, in Rage she cries,*
> *Dares rob me of my Claim.*
>
> *I, who have charm'd the Pit so low,*
> *And eke the Gallery High,*
> *Shall I be rival'd thus? Ye Gods!*
> *O rather let me die.*
>
> *With that she to the Green-Room flew,*
> *Where Cibber meek she found;*
> *And sure if Friends had not been by,*
> *She had fell'd her to the Ground.*
>
> *O had these Rival Nymphs engag'd,*
> *How scratch'd had been each Face;*
> *What Slaughter there had been to see*
> *Of Silks, and eke Bone-lace.*

and much more, with the pantomime itself a pitched battle between Madam Squall and Madam Squeak.

Kitty joined the fray with her usual verve. In a lengthy letter to the *London Daily Post and General Advertiser* of 19 November 1736, she replied to an ill-tempered allegation in a letter of 4 November in the *Daily Gazeteer* (which she intimates came directly from Mrs Cibber's faction at the theatre) that *The Beggar's Opera* has been "suppress'd" at Drury Lane "*from an obstinate refusal in me to act the Part of Lucy in that play.*"

I can only say in Answer that by my Articles *it is not in my Power* to refuse That or any other Part; but that I have shewn an Unwillingness to surrender my own Part of Polly and to act the inferior Part of Lucy, I confess is true. But then I must declare this Unwillingness did not proceed from my Jealousy of Mrs Cibber, or from any Intent of mine to obstruct the Progress of her Merit: No; the true and only Reason is this: Not only the Part of Polly, but likewise other Parts (as could be made to appear) have been demanded of me for Mrs Cibber, which made me conclude (and, I think with Reason) that there was a Design form'd against me, to deprive me by degrees of every Part in which I had the Happiness to appear with any Reputation; and at length, by this Method, to make me so little useful to the Stage, as not to deserve the Sallary I now have, which is much inferior to that of several other Performers.

She added, most interestingly, "a receiv'd Maxim in the Theatre, *That no Actor or Actress shall be depriv'd of a Part in which they have been well receiv'd, until they are render'd incapable of performing it either by Age or Sickness.*" Management vacillated for three months, then gave Polly back to Kitty.

Kitty's vocal contributions increased in number during 1735–36. She was particularly praised when on 22 April she joined "Philippo Palma, lately arrived from Italy," and Isabella and Esther Young in *A Grand*

Epithalamium for Thomas Augustine Arne's benefit. He was the brother of Mrs Cibber, and the benefit may have been intended as a peace offering.

In 1736–37 Kitty played for the first time: Isabella in *The Squire of Alsatia*; Arabella in *The Wife's Relief*; Aurelia in *The Twin Rivals*; singing with Stoppelaer as the "Ghosts of Darius and Statira" in *The Rival Queens*; the Wanton Wife in the anonymous farce *The Amorous Widow* (first), Liberia in *The Universal Passion*, an adaptation by James Miller of *Much Ado About Nothing* (first); and Lady Fanciful in *The Provok'd Wife*.

In 1737–38 she added Narcissa in *Love's Last Shift*, Laetitia in *The Old Bachelor*, and Doris in *Aesop*. She was by 26 January 1738 famous enough to play herself ("Miss Kitty," opposite "Cibber a Comedian– Cibber") in James Miller's afterpiece *The Coffee House* (first), was Violetta in Miller's *Art and Nature* (first), played Miss Kitty (again, more or less *in propria persona*) in *Sir Cockle at Court* by Robert Dodsley. She and the golden tenor John Beard teamed, singing in concert, for the benefit of Master Ferg on 3 March.

In 1738–39 Kitty essayed for the first time Viletta in *She Wou'd and She Wou'd Not*, Hillaria in *Tunbridge Walks*, Ann Lovely in *A Bold Stroke for a Wife*, Chloe (Lady Lace) in *The Lottery*, Loveit in *The Man of Mode*, Miss Notable in *The Lady's Last Stake*, Olivia in *The Plain Dealer*, and Phoebe in *The Beggar's Wedding*.

In 1739–40 she was the Daughter in *An Hospital for Fools* by James Miller (first) and Kitty, alias Donna Americana, in *Britons Strike Home; or, The Sailors' Rehearsal* by Edward Phillips (first). She played Millamant in *The Way of the World* for her benefit.

In 1740–41 she added Manto ("with the Hymn to Apollo") in the revival of *Oedipus, King of Thebes*, Emilia ("with two new songs") in the revival after 20 years of *A Fond Husband*, Caelia in the revival of *As You Like It* ("Not acted these Forty years"—but it had been acted, adapted, as *Love in the Forest* in 1723), Lady Townly in *The Provok'd Husband*, the title part in *Rosamond*, and Bessy in *The Blind Beggar of Bethnal Green* by Robert Dodsley (first). She also tried Portia in *The Merchant of Venice* for the first time on 14 February 1741, on the same night that Charles Macklin revived Shakespeare's original for the first time in the century, and offered his fierce new Shylock. Kitty's interpretation of Portia, which involved a take-off of the mannerisms of Justice Mansfield, earned her more hostile criticism than anything she ever did. Characteristically, she ignored the strictures. During the summer of 1741 she acted in Dublin at the Aungier Street Theatre, making her first appearance in that kingdom as Lappet, on 20 June.

In the winter season of 1741–42 Kitty added Lady Lurewell in *The Constant Couple* and Pallas in *The Judgment of Paris*, and was the original Lucy in *Miss Lucy in Town* (a sequel to *The Virgin Unmask'd*) by Henry Fielding, London's only new play that season. But Kitty was out of the bills for several periods during the fall of 1741, and on 16 December the *Daily Advertiser* reported: "We hear that Mrs Clive, who has been so dangerously ill that her life has been despaired of, is now judged to be in a fair way of recovery." She was acting once more by 21 December but was ill again for several days in January 1742. The Countess of Hertford wrote to her son Lord Beauchamp censuring Mrs Phillips, Kitty's replacement in the part of Nell, on 17 January. In another letter of 23 January the Countess alluded to the illness again, preserving for us by the way one of the most effective bits of repartee from a century which cherished such exchanges in proportion to their acerbity:

About ten days ago Mrs Woffington and Mrs Clive met in the Green room. Mrs Woffington came up to Mrs Clive and told her she had long looked for the favour of a visit from her and begged she would let her know when she designed her that pleasure, for she was often engag'd in an afternoon. Mrs Clive paused a little and then answered, Madam, I have a reputation to lose. Madam, said Mrs Woffington, so should I have too if I had your face.

Her benefit for the 1742–43 season was again patronized by the Prince and Princess of Wales and was said to be very profitable, notwithstanding the attempt at fraud of one Mrs Catherine Penny, who went to Bridewell for selling counterfeit tickets to this popular annual event. Kitty was in the spring of 1743 chosen by Handel himself to sing the part of Dalila in his oratorio *Samson*, and she also sang parts in the *Messiah* and *L'Allegro*. Horace Walpole, not yet her close friend, derided Handel for hiring "all the goddesses from farces." But Kitty added only two new dramatic roles, still another "Kitty" in *The Lying Valet* and (in one of those stubbornly tasteless acts which she, despite all advice, was occasionally prone to) for the benefit of her brother James Raftor, she essayed the male role of Bayes in *The Rehearsal*. As James Winston long afterward explained it, she was "instigated to it by Cibber [as an] act of envy to Garrick, but he missed his aim, for she did it most wretchedly. It was believed she would not have gone through the part. A Great House. If she had succeeded she meant to repeat it for her own Benefit." The *Daily Advertiser* at the time believed that the attempt was "in imitation of the late celebrated Mrs Verbruggen." But whatever impelled Kitty to do it, the idea was clearly disastrous, and her detractors did not very quickly let her forget it.

At the beginning of the season of 1743–44 Kitty and a number of the more prominent Drury Lane players, led by Macklin and Garrick, incensed at Fleetwood's stinginess, duplicity, and neglect of business, determined to secede and act as a new company at the Haymarket. The project failed, and an extensive paper war ensued in which Kitty Clive took an enthusiastic part. She was personally attacked by the authors of *Theatrical Correspondence in Death An Epistle from Mrs Oldfield in the Shades to Mrs Br——ce——dle* (1743), in which several of the spirits satirized Kitty as "the Sing-Song Girl." Old Joe Miller's ghost claimed that

that plaguy part NELL has actually overset the Girl—She is *metamorphosed* indeed with a Witness, and fancies herself the real Lady Loverule off the Stage, she represents on—add to this the little Gipsy's natural Temper is inclinable to be Shrewish—the Servants, her high Salary enabled her to keep, if unembodied and with us, would justifie my assertion.

By that time Kitty had accepted an offer by John Rich at Covent Garden for the 1743–44 season, where she was not much better pleased than she had been under Fleetwood, though she continued with Rich during the following season. In the middle of her tenure with him she burst out bitterly in a lengthy diatribe, *The Case of Mrs Clive Submitted to the Publick* (published on 12 October 1744), in which she called down a plague on both patent houses and explained acidly her belief that Fleetwood and Rich had formed a "cartel" to drive down actors' salaries. Before the dispute and secession she had (she said) signed with Fleetwood for £300 "and at the expiration of my Agreements the Manager offered me an additional Salary to continue at that Theatre." But when want had forced the other victims back to Drury Lane and had exiled Charles Macklin, she had been offered a small salary, not at all in proportion to her worth relative to other players and much smaller than her former articles had provided for. She had refused to sign and had gone at Rich's urging over to Covent Garden where, once she had

slammed the door on Drury Lane, Rich had offered her exactly the same terms as those she had just refused. He had added as well the indignity of demanding that she pay house charges for her benefit, destroying "an Advantage the first Performers had been thought to merit for near Thirty Years, and [which] had grown into a Custom." As for Fleetwood, he at the time she wrote still owed her "a Hundred and Sixty Pounds, twelve Shillings, which he [had] acknowledged to be justly due, and [had] promised Payment of it by last Christmas."

Kitty claimed that her "Labour and Application have been greater than any other Performers on the Stage." She declared:

I have not only acted in almost all the Plays, but in Farces and Musical Entertainments; and very frequently two Parts in a Night, events to the Prejudice of my Health. I have been at a very great Expence in Masters for Singing; for which article alone, the Managers now give five and six Pounds a Week.

She had spent, she added, upwards of £100 a year for clothes and other necessaries.

This effusion had no effect on the hardened heart of management, but it did not get her permanently fired, either. Both Fleetwood and Rich were by then well acquainted with the rough side of Kitty Clive's tongue, and she was far too valuable a commodity for a manager to lose. Rich did discipline her a bit by refusing to engage her for the next season until November of 1744, but her staunch friends the Prince and Princess of Wales leapt into the breach, lending their "Command" to a benefit concert of vocal and instrumental music at the Haymarket on 2 November.

At Covent Garden in 1743–44 Kitty had gone to the head of the bill and had continued to add roles to her repertoire: the Shade of Hero in *The Necromancer*, Rhodope in *Orpheus and Eurydice*, and Morayma in *Don Sebastian, King of Portugal*. On 21 March 1744, also, Kitty, John

Beard, Miss Edwards, and Savage sang in *Love and Friendship*, "A New English Pastoral Serenata. Set to Musick by William de Fesch," at the Crown and Anchor Tavern. Kitty resolutely played Portia for her benefit on 13 March 1744, again by command of the Prince and Princess of Wales. Her interpretation was again roundly abused in the press.

In 1744–45, after an illness which kept her off the boards for a week or so even after she had signed that tardy agreement with Rich, Kitty began to act late in November, playing her favorite role of Lappet. Though she played often during the season she added only two new characters to her list, Lucy in *The Beggar's Opera* (she voluntarily relinquished Polly to her protégée Mrs Vincent) and Melissa in Shadwell's alteration of *Timon of Athens*.

For the season of 1745–46 Kitty went back to Drury Lane, late in November and very reluctantly, Lacy having succeeded Fleetwood as manager of that house. She unwisely chose her low-comedy Portia for her reappearance there, the bill erroneously stating this to be the first time of her playing at that theatre in three years. Again, the more sensitive critics complained of her aberration, but she quickly appeased them by displaying five of her most brilliant comedy characters in quick succession: Nell on 25 November, and then her droll Lady Fanciful in *The Provok'd Wife*, her bouncing Hoyden in *The Relapse*, Lettice in the favorite afterpiece *The Intriguing Chambermaid*, and her newly developed Lucy in *The Beggar's Opera*. An indication that she was finally done with Polly was the announcement that Miss Edwards (afterwards Mrs Mozeen) that night was assuming the part "first time at this theatre." Tom Davies wrote that she generously gave up Polly to Miss Edwards on her own initiative and had instructed and encouraged the girl.

But Kitty was not at all finished with the part of Portia, and she stubbornly retained her "interpretation" despite a renewed critical barrage. During the remainder of the season she added to her repertoire the following: Ariel "(with proper songs)" in *The Tempest;* the original Columbine in a new pantomime with music by Dr Arne called *Harlequin Incendiary* (with scenes in Scotland and allusions to the recent suppression of the Jacobite rebellion); Melantha in *The Comical Lovers;* Lucinda in *The She Gallant;* Leonora in *Sir Courtly Nice;* and Clarinda in the revival of *The Sea Voyage; or, The Commonwealth of Women.*

To open the Drury Lane season of 1746–47 Kitty again came before her public as Portia. Her new characters were Sophronia in the revival, after 25 years, of Cibber's comedy *The Refusal*, Betty in *Marry or Do Worse*, and Phaedra in *Amphitryon.*

Kitty Clive entered a new phase of her career and her life when David Garrick came to the management of Drury Lane in the 1747–48 season. They were to clash often and bitterly, but gradually an understanding of their mutual professional need and respect and even a reluctant affection developed. Their first two or three seasons together seem to have been a quiescent time, with a cautious testing of strength by both parties. Once again, in 1747–48, Kitty opened as Portia. She added two new characters: Margery in *The Dragon of Wantly*, Olivia in *Twelfth Night.*

In 1748–49 she was Lady Wronghead in *The Provok'd Husband*, Tag in *Miss in Her Teens*, Mrs Riot in the revival of *Lethe*, a Shepherdess in Dodsley's masque *The Triumph of Peace*, and Clarinda in *The Suspicious Husband.* On 16 May 1749, the next-to-last night of the season, she reassumed Polly (both Miss Edwards and Mrs Cibber being by then departed from the theatre). She suffered illness again from before 30 March until she played again on 10 April, but she cannot have been very well during late April and May, for other actresses took some of her habitual roles.

In 1749–50 she presented Lady Harriet

in *The Funeral; or, Grief à la Mode,* Pastora in *The Chaplet,* and Lady Squeamish in the revival after 30 years of *Friendship in Fashion.* She also commenced author, playing Bayes in her own farce *Bayes in Petticoats.* She encountered a certain amount of ribbing for this breeches part, her figure being by now somewhat awkward for display. Typical criticism was "Harry Rambler's" in *Bays in Council* (Dublin, 1751), which purports to report a meeting of principal actors at Drury Lane planning strategy against John Rich's Covent Garden competition in which Mrs Clive was made to suggest vaingloriously that *she* alone could prevail. Bottom-like, she would play all the parts, from "Jemmy Brute" to Bajazet.

In 1750–51 Kitty was again publicized, though this time kindly, in a picture. The *General Advertiser* of 18 September 1750 ran a notice:

This day at Noon will be publish'd and sold by the proprietor and print shops, two portraits of those celebrated Comedians, Mr Woodward and Mrs Clive, in the characters of the Fine Gentleman and Lady in *Lethe* (as they are to perform them tonight, at Drury Lane) curiously engraved (in Miniature) from Original drawings of the same size. By J. Brooks, Engraver of Silver and Copper plate. (N. B. the above prints may be had together or separate).

She also shone as Diana in the revival of Dryden's *Secular Masque,* Bisarre in *The Inconstant,* Leonora in *Sir Courtly Nice,* Girtred in *Eastward Hoe; or, Ye Prentices,* and Daphne in *The Shepherd's Lottery,* "a new Musical Masque" by Moses Mendez, set by Dr William Boyce.

Audiences in 1752–53 saw Kitty for the first time as Mrs Marwood in *The Way of the World* and Lady Haughty in *Epicoene.* She suffered another *lapsus* in insisting upon appearing as Zara in *The Mourning Bride,* a lugubrious high-tragedy part utterly unfitted to her figure, style, or personality. It was cruelly jeered in the press, although it did not faze her devoted public. In this season, in addition, she appeared *in propria persona* in Henry Woodward's farce *A Lick at the Town,* in which actors revolt amusingly against their roles.

In 1753–54 Kitty added Mrs Frail in *Love for Love* and Princess Theoraz in *The London 'Prentice,* "A new Operetta" with music by De Fesch, for her benefit. ("Farce dull & hiss'd at ye End," wrote Cross, the Drury Lane prompter, in his diary.) The season was enlivened by a famous altercation in the Green Room between Kitty and Peg Woffington, swelling to fisticuffs between their respective champions, Kitty's brother James Raftor and Owen Swiny, and inspiring a facetious print called "The Green Room Scuffle."

In 1754–55 she was for the first time Abigail in the revival (after 10 years) of

Harvard Theatre Collection

CATHERINE CLIVE, as the Fine Lady engraving by Mosley after Van Vleeck

The Drummer. She played Jacintha in the revival (after 30 years) of *The Mistake*, and also offered the Mother in *The Chances* and Mrs Kitely in *Every Man in His Humour*.

In the season of 1755–56 Kitty added to her repertoire Catherine in Garrick's alteration called *Catherine and Petruchio*. Cross noted in his diary concerning the first performance that "Mrs Clive fell down in yᵉ Farce, and accused Woodward wᵗʰ doing it on purpose." Davies says that on another occasion while this farce was playing Woodward, accidentally or not, stuck a fork in her finger. Kitty was also that season Lady Wronglove in *The Lady's Last Stake*.

In 1756–57 Kitty tried for the first time Flora in *The Wonder*, revived after 14 years, and was the first Mrs Cadwallader in Samuel Foote's new farce *The Author*. She also carried on her feud with Woodward. Cross the prompter noted on 1 November 1756:

This Night when Busk (Mr Woodward) was reading the Verses with Lady Froth (Mrs Clive) instead of observing, with the Author, that her Ladyship's coachman, John, had a red Face, said *because yr. Ladyship has a red face*, & as Mrs Clive is of that Complexion the Audience burst into a loud roar, to her no small Mortification; but she behav'd well & took no Notice of it.

Kitty played only one new character in 1757–58, but one so important and so exactly in her vein that the managers seem culpable not to have tried her in it before: Lady Wishfort in *The Way of the World*. As it happened, she herself chose it, for her benefit on 16 March 1758. Cross's laconic pronouncement was, surprisingly enough, "bad." But Kitty refined the part in after years and finally made it one of her most notable. In 1758–59 she again acquired only one new part, Patch in *The Busy Body*, and again it was destined to become one of her most appreciated efforts.

Kitty was, according to Cross, "taken ill" on 2 October, 1759, and the Mistresses Abington, Young, Cibber, and Pritchard filled in for her until she returned in Lady Wishfort on the sixteenth. In October also she several times played Kitty in the new farce *High Life Below Stairs* by James Townley. Cross says that it was "hiss'd," despite the efforts of a fine cast which included Mrs Abington, Tom King, and Yates. But parts of it were commended by Goldsmith in *The Bee*, though he thought it on "too narrow a plan," and the author must have taken the hint, for after revision it entered the repertory and was much employed as a claptrap by Mrs Clive and the others in the following seasons. Kitty was once again "indisposed" on 23 November 1759, but she played Lucy in *The Guardian* for the first time on 30 November and later in the season added Termagant in *The Upholsterer*.

In April 1761 she was involved in a furious paper war with Ned Shuter, the leading comedian of Covent Garden Theatre. He and his partisans had attempted to stir up anti-Gallic feeling over the use by Mrs Clive of a translation from the French called *The Island of Slaves* as the farce on her benefit night, 26 March 1761. Their motive, she charged, had been to anger her audience and send it over to Shuter's own benefit the same night. After a pyrotechnic exchange of discourtesies the feud sputtered out. The season was in other ways a disappointment: there was the loss of 19 days to mourn the death of George II, and Kitty suffered some more illness. But she added two new parts which were useful to her, Muslin in *The Way to Keep Him* by her friend Arthur Murphy (first), and Lady Freelove in *The Jealous Wife* by her friend George Colman (first). She also succeeded splendidly with her singing. The announcement that Mrs Clive would give her "Mimic comic opera song" was enough to send even opera lovers scurrying to the theatre. Tate Wilkinson reported her opinion of the foreign singers—"a set of Italian squalling devils who come over to England to get our bread from us, and I say curse them all for a parcel of Italian bitches." Sylas Neville confided to his *Diary* in 1767 that she "took off the ridiculous sing-song at yᵉ Opera House charmingly." (But Kitty had been perfecting this satire for years. As early as 26 May 1742 Horace Walpole wrote to Horace Mann "There is a little simple farce at Drury Lane, called *Miss Lucy in Town,* in which Miss Clive mimics the Muscovita [Signora Panichi] admirably".) A reviewer writing in *The Old Maid* for 8 May 1756 had seen a performance of *Lethe* at which he was particularly diverted

with Mrs Clive's Italian Song, in which this truly humourous Actress parodys the Air of the Opera, and takes off the action, of the present favorite female at the Haymarket [probably Signora Giulia Frasi], with such exquisite ridicule, that the most zealous partisans of both, I think, must have applauded the comic genius of Mrs Clive, however they might be displeased with the application of it.

In the season 1761–62 William White-head wrote for Kitty *The School for Lovers,* in which she played Lady Beverly. In 1762–63 she brought out her own odd afterpiece *Sketch of a Fine Lady's Return from a Rout* for her benefit on 21 March 1763. The *Theatrical Review* roundly condemned the piece, remarking (among other pleasantries) that the Irish comedian John Moody's role was so badly written that, to save his credit with the audience, he "commenced Hibernian in his dialogue." During the season Kitty added to her repertoire the title character in *The Old Maid.*

In 1763–64 Mrs Frances Sheridan kindly created the character of Mrs Friendly in *The Dupe* for Kitty. In 1764–65 a new farce of Kitty's authorship, *The Faithful Irishwoman,* was given on her benefit night, 18 March 1765; alas for her literary ambition, it was never played again. Kitty was

learning that, for all her sensitivity in interpreting other people's humor, and for all her own possession of much impromptu wit, she could not write farces. This season she was the first Lady Fanshaw in *The Platonick Wife,* a comedy by Mrs Elizabeth Griffith, and the first Lisetta "(with a *mock Italian Song*)" in *The Capricious Lovers,* a comedy by Robert Lloyd.

In the new season 1765–66 she added two new characters of the utmost importance: Widow Blackacre, the litigious eccentric in *The Plain Dealer,* and old Mrs Heidelberg in *The Clandestine Marriage.* The latter play had to be deferred because, according to the prompter's notes, Kitty was "taken extremely ill" on 15 February 1766; but she bounced back with 12 successive nights playing Mrs Heidelberg, from 20 February through 13 March. Sylas Neville mentioned in his *Diary* that she did the part "inimitably," and she chose it for her benefit night on 23 March 1767 and did it again for her friend Vernon's benefit on 7 April.

Kitty added no new parts in 1766–67. A manuscript pay list transcribed by James Winston gives her salary that year as £10 10s. per week. Perhaps feeling her age, she subscribed £2 2s. to the new Drury Lane retirement fund. In 1767–68 she introduced her next-to-last new character to the stage, Lady Fuz in Garrick's burlesque *A Peep Behind the Curtain.* She was still playing Phyllis in *The Conscious Lovers* well after her fifty-fifth birthday.

Kitty learned her last new character in 1768–69 when she played Mrs Winifred in Elizabeth Griffith's new comedy *The School for Rakes* on 4 February 1769 and spoke a sprightly epilogue furnished her by Garrick. Her retirement was forecast to the public by the announcement on 17 April that her appearance as Lady Fuz would be the last in that role. The bill for her benefit on 24 April 1769 announced that her performance that night would be "the last time of her appearing on the

Stage." Garrick generously insisted on playing his engaging Don Felix as she acted Flora in *The Wonder*. In the same bill, supported by Tom King's marvelous Lord Chalkestone and Dodd's hilarious Fine Gentleman, she delighted her audience with the broad satire of her Fine Lady in *Lethe*. But for over a year she had planned to withdraw. Horace Walpole had written to George Montagu on 15 April 1768 that "I have quitted the stage and Clive is preparing to leave it."

Kitty had been attracted to Horace Walpole and he to her perhaps as early as 1738. Certainly by 1741 her virago courage had been the object of his amused admiration. He wrote to Lord Lincoln in his fastidious way that he had been to the theatre and had despised its noise and confusion. Mrs Clive had desired "leave to harangue the pit . . . 'Hear her! Hear her!'—'Gentlemen, they have flung an halfpenny at me; it might have cut out my eye, and I can't stand to bear that.'"

The odd and (so far as any reliable evidence shows) entirely sexless relationship lasted until Kitty died. We cannot be certain of the point at which the strange friendship between the cultivated master of Strawberry Hill and the outspoken comedienne became sufficiently strong to make her think of establishing her domicile near him. On 20 March 1738 she had been living at her house in Cecil Street, off the Strand, and she was still there in 1740. Her benefit bill for March 1741 gave her address to those seeking tickets as "at Mr Dandridge's in Great Queen Street." In 1743 she acquired a house at No 59, Great Queen Street, which she occupied through 2 March 1750. But on 6 March she was lodging at Mrs Burlacy's, milliner, in Tavistock Street, Covent Garden, near the theatre. On 15 March following, the date of her benefit, her supporters were asked to apply for tickets at the box office. In 1751 she was to be found at an inn conveniently near her work, the Naked Boy in Henrietta

Street, and she remained there through March 1753. From March 1754 to March 1756 she lodged at another inn, the Wheatsheaf in Henrietta Street. The next address that we have, and the one to which buyers of her benefit tickets were sent after 18 March 1765, was the sign of the Two Red Lamps, also in Great Queen Street. It is very likely therefore, as P. J. Crean and others have argued, that Kitty had given up her *permanent* residence in town and was already at Twickenham, but not at Little Strawberry Hill, by December 1749. That may have been the date on which she wrote her letter from Great Queen Street to Walpole in the country in which she said: "Tho' I am now representing women of qualitty and coblers wives etc. etc. to crowded houeses; the charecture I am most desierous to act well is; a good sort of countrey gentlewoman at twickenham."

R. S. Cobbett, quondam a curate of St Mary's, Twickenham, testified in his *Memorial of Twickenham* (1872) that "Near Marble Hill, very sweetly situated, is a beautiful villa originally called Spencer Grove. . . . This villa stands upon the site of a cottage once occupied by Mrs Clive, who removed from this place to Little Strawberry Hill."

It would appear, then, that Kitty had established a residence near Marble Hill perhaps five years before accepting Walpole's offer of a rent-free tenure of the cottage which became known as Little Strawberry Hill or (in Horatio's whimsy) "Clive-den." The cottage was, in the Reverend William Cole's words, "a little box, contiguous to Mr Walpole's garden, and close almost to the Chapel. Here she lives retired, and her brother, Mr Raftor, with her." That she had removed from Marble Hill to Little Strawberry Hill by at latest the fall of 1754 seems certain, since Walpole wrote to Richard Bentley on 3 November that his "chief employ" was "planting at Mrs Clive's, whither I remove all my superabundances. I have lately planted the green lane, that leads from her garden to the common: 'Well,' said she, 'when it is done, what shall we call it?'—'Why,' said I, 'what would you call it but Drury Lane.' "

Walpole had already interested himself intensely in her affairs. On 4 August 1755 he had "just come from supping at Mrs Clive's" when he reported to Bentley "I have contracted a sort of intimacy with Garrick, who is my neighbour" and had offered him a Latin motto for his Temple to Shakespeare, then being constructed. "The truth is, I make the most of this acquaintance to protect my poor neighbor at *Cliveden*."

Steadily the two households merged almost into one ménage, with free exchange of servants, amenities, and acquaintances. Walpole began lacing his vast correspondence with references to anecdotes of "Lady Cliveden," or "Dame Clive," and her wit and cherished crotchets were reported as well to blind Madame Duffand in France as to Mary Berry in Italy. Yet Walpole the protector never became the lover, despite some published insinuations at which Horace secretly laughed in his journal. (In December 1769 two medallion portraits, engraved on one plate, of "Mrs Heidelberg" and "Baron Otranto" illustrated a "history" in the *Town and Country Magazine* which alleged the former to be the latter's mistress and that "it is generally reported some beautiful pledges of their loves are now visible at Mulberry-hill, which naturalists account for upon the principles laid down in a well-known book, under the title *Lucina sine concubitu*." The canard has been laid to the resentful Thomas Chatterton.)

Kitty and Horace were fond of playing at loo, gossiping, and regaling at occasional feasts either at her little house or his steadily evolving "Gothick" castle. On 13 January 1760 Horace dined delightedly at Little Strawberry Hill with Cecilia West, daughter of the seventh Baron (afterwards first Earl) Delawarr, "my niece Chomley"

(really the wife of Walpole's nephew Robert Cholmondeley, née Woffington, ex-actress and Peg Woffington's sister), and Arthur Murphy, "the writing actor." On 5 July 1761 Walpole scolded George Montagu for cancelling a proposed visit and used Kitty as lure: "she had proposed to play at quadrille with you from dinner to supper, and to sing old Purcell to you from supper to breakfast next morning." It was only persiflage; their hours were exceedingly decorous, like their assemblies. On 16 December 1766 Walpole thanked Montagu on Kitty's behalf for a haunch of venison to make "a figure at her Christmas gambols!" and "Catherine, I do not doubt, is up to the elbow in currant jelly and gratitude." "All the morning," Walpole testified to a friend, "I play with my workmen or animals, go regularly every evening to the meadows with Mrs Clive, or sit with my Lady Suffolk." On 25 September 1761 he wrote that "I carried Lady Townsend, Lady Hertford, Lady Anne Connelly, my Lady Hervey, and Mrs Clive to my deputy's house at the gate of Westminster Hall" to see the coronation of George III.

Kitty was never abashed by the fantastic congeries of titled folk and divines, painters and members of parliament, nabobs and diplomats who came to look at the curios and partake of the hospitality at Strawberry Hill. She was first accepted by them for Walpole's sake and then enjoyed for her radiant personality and impudent sallies. It was not long before her magnetism rivaled Walpole's in attracting people to Strawberry Hill in summers, at Christmas, and in Passion Week—seasons when a remission of her professional duties released her from London. By the time she retired she had become a figure as well-known in the fashionable countryside near Twickenham as David Garrick was. She displayed a rather childish pride in the legacy of £50 left her by John Robardes, Earl of Radnor, but she was really no snob, and she remained loyal to her friends of the theatre.

Fortunately, Walpole seemed amused by theatrical people, though he had deplored his nephew's marriage with Miss Woffington. In a rhymed invitation sent to Lady Cecilia Johnson he boasted that "Our abdicated Monarch Lear [Garrick] / And bonny Dame Cadwallader [Kitty] / With a whole theatre in one from France [Le Texier]" would dine with him "next Saturn's day."

Though Little Strawberry Hill was a grateful retreat from stage business and green-room tensions, the life was not invariably comfortable. Kitty wrote to Jane Pope on 3 November 1770:

retirement—no such thing I promise you, I have ten times more business now than I had when I playd the Fool as you do, I have engagements every day of my life. Routs either at home or abroad every night all the nonsense of having my hair not done time enough for my parties as I used to do for my parts with the difference that I am losing money instead of getting some but I dont mind that for I am in such good health, and such fine spirits that it is impossible for any one to be happyer than the triumvirate as you call us, as to my Raftor I sometimes think he is going mad his joy is so great at his new kind of life; all my neighbours like him mightily, he goes every where with me.

More seriously, there were actual attacks against her domestic peace. Walpole wrote to Viscount Nuneham on 6 December 1773:

Except being extremely ill, Mrs Clive is extremely well, but the tax-gatherer is gone off [absconded with his collection] and she must pay her window-lights [window tax] over again; and the road before her door is very bad, and the parish won't mend it, and there is some suspicion that Garrick is at the bottom of it.

Kitty sustained three frightening experiences with footpads. Walpole wrote their mutual friend the Countess of Ailesbury on 25 June 1778, "Poor Mrs Clive has been robbed again in her own lane, as she was last year and has got the jaundice, she thinks, with fright." And on 14 August 1784 he wrote to Henry Conway that "Mrs Clive has been broken open," adding mischievously "and Mr Raftor miscarried and died of the fright."

Kitty's health, indeed, had never been as robust as her spirit, and attacks of what her doctor diagnosed as jaundice increased in frequency as the years mounted. She was in much physical distress in the spring and summer of 1782, and Walpole asked the Reverend William Mason to "tell Lord Harcourt that poor Clive is better, yet her fits of the jaundice return so often that I much doubt her recovery. Indeed the apothecary fears her liver is affected—she is shrunk to an astonishing degree." But by September she was out "cruising on all the neighbours," and by October "she even [partook] of the diversion of the carnival."

Kitty had earned financially what the century called "a competence," and socially she had found her perfect milieu. Walpole sent her from Paris "a cup and saucer with roses on a blue ground"; he thinned out his goldfish ("which breed with me excessively, and are grown the size of small perch") and took three fat ones "for a present to Madam Clive." She, a respectfully religious woman, entertained the minor clergy and listened appreciatively to the preaching of the Reverend Mr Ashton. ("She says she is always vastly good for two or three days after his sermons, but by the time Thursday comes, all their effect is worn out.") She sang to "The Cherokee majesty" when the chiefs dined with her at Lord Macclesfield's (though Walpole disdained that "mob—don't imagine I was there"). Her close friend Jane Pope came for protracted visits. According to Letitia Hawkins, Kitty "worked for the Holbein Chamber, at Strawberry Hill, the carpet with blue tulips, and yellow foliage." She gardened, she gossiped, she cooked, she sewed. From every aspect Kitty's life in the small villa in the well-manicured countryside not too far away from what Johnson called "the high-tide of human existence" seems to have been the judicious blend of urban sophistication and rural delight that the century's philosophers sought, a *summum bonum* found in a *via media*.

Kitty died on 6 December 1785 at 75 full years and was buried in Twickenham Churchyard on the midnight of 14 December. Walpole wrote to Lady Browne:

My poor old friend is a great loss; but it did not much surprise me, and the manner comforts me. I had played cards with her at Mrs Gostling's [Whitton Place, Twickenham] three nights before I came to town, and found her extremely confused, and not knowing what she did: indeed, I perceived something of the sort before, and had found her much broken this autumn. It seems the day after I saw her, she went to General Lister's burial and got cold, and had been ill for two or three days. On the Wednesday morning she rose to have her bed made; and while sitting on the bed, with her maid by her, sunk down at once, and died without a pang or a groan. Poor Mr Raftor is struck to the greatest degree, and for some days would not see anybody.

The Reverend Mr Cole had obtained, on a visit to Strawberry Hill many years earlier

Harvard Theatre Collection

MRS CLIVE's residence at Twickenham by Storer

(October 1774), a copy of a verse "lately composed" by Walpole and "meant as a sportive and innocent amusement . . . written by way of epitaph, and on a supposition that Mrs Clive was dead." Walpole had preserved the verses too, and now he caused them to be engraved on a memorial urn set up in the shrubbery beside her cottage:

> *Ye smiles and jests still hover round!*
> *This is mirth's consecrated ground.*
> *Here lived the laughter-loving dame,*
> *A matchless actress, Clive by name;*
> *The comic muse with her retired,*
> *And shed a tear when she expired.*

Kitty's old friend Jane Pope was not to be denied her own marmoreal sentiment, and she erected a stone on which Kitty's excellences were extolled at somewhat greater length, if with less finesse:

> *Clive's blameless life this tablet shall pro-*
> *claim,*
> *Her moral virtues and her well earn'd*
> *fame.*
> *In comic scenes the stage she early trod,*
> *"Nor sought the critic's praise nor fear'd*
> *his rod."*
> *In real life was equal praise her due,*
> *Open to pity and to friendship too;*
> *In wit still pleasing, as in converse free*
> *From all that could afflict humanity:*
> *Her gen'rous heart to all her friends was*
> *known*
> *And ev'n the stranger's sorrows were*
> *her own.*
> *Content with fame, ev'n affluence she*
> *wav'd,*
> *To share with others what by toil she*
> *sav'd;*
> *And, nobly bounteous, from her slender*
> *store,*
> *She bade two dear relations not be poor!*
> *Such deeds on life's short scenes true*
> *glory shed,*
> *And heav'nly plaudits hail the virtuous*
> *dead.*

Kitty Clive's career was more than an illustration of the beneficent effects of combining alert intelligence and resolute industry. She was by all accounts a comic genius. Endowed with a voice of operatic quality, a marvelously malleable face, and an infallible sense of timing, she had instinctively also a sensitive rapport with audiences which was almost unmatched in her century. Her prodigious talents underwent a slow and careful maturation, usually under sympathetic management, and she remained on the stage long enough—over 40 years—to perfect every technique of comedy then known. Against some very tough competition she fought for and won permanent rights—particularly in farce—to some of the most popular and therefore most valuable roles in the repertory. But what Kitty's roles did for her were as nothing compared to what she did for her roles. Some of the most trifling catchpenny potboilers of petty poetasters, or the occasional inconsiderable *jeu d'esprit* of some gentleman amateur, absolutely vapid when read, were brought to sparking life by her vibrant *vis comica* and approved by audiences and critics alike. She came to grief only on those rare occasions when she deserted her natural vein and tried roles which were thwart to her psychology.

Kitty was fortunate in having David Garrick as her manager during the last two decades of her long career. Often he was to her an intolerable annoyance, as she to him. His small affectations disturbed her sometimes as much as his talent stirred her rivalry and envy. But, as she once said through clenched teeth as she watched him from the wings, "He could act a gridiron!" and she grew to feel respect for him and a kind of grudging affection. Walpole was perhaps correct in his partisan remark that "Clive is at least as perfect [as Garrick] in low comedy," but he surely was incorrect as well as callous in assuring the Countess of Upper Ossory on 1 February 1779, the day of Garrick's funeral, that the great actor-manager "hated Mrs Clive, till she quitted the stage, and then cried her up to

the skies, to depress Mrs Abington." Garrick often had trouble controlling a stage which had contained at one time Mrs Woffington, Mrs Cibber, Jane Pope, Mrs Pritchard, Mrs Abington, and Kitty Clive, not to speak of various divas and dancers, but he was no hater. He and Kitty learned from each other and honed their talents on each other's performances, and the frequent clashes between them were the effects only of high professionalism and opposition temperaments.

When she heard of Garrick's intention to leave the stage, settle down in his villa at Twickenham and take over the duties of a local squire as churchwarden, justice of the peace, and so on, she wrote him, on 31 January 1773:

I schream'd at your parish business. I think I see you in your churchwardenship, quareling for not making their brown loaves big enough; but for God's sake never think of being a justice of the peace, for the people will quarel on purpose to be brought before you to hear you talk, so that you may have as much business upon the lawn as you had upon the boards. If I should live to be thaw'd, I will come to town on purpose to kiss you; and in the summer, as you say, I hope we shall see each other ten times as often, when we will talk and dance and sing, and send our hearers laughing to their beds.

A transcript by the early nineteenth-century Drury Lane stage manager James Winston of Kitty's letter of 2 October 1775 to some unknown gentlewoman in Dublin ("your ladyship") asking social sponsorship there for her protégée Jane Pope sarcastically touches on the old charge that Garrick was stingy: "she comes to Dublin by my advice Mr Garrick & she having had a dispute, about sallary She wanted to be a little *Richer*, and he being *Poor* could not afford to let her." And in a later letter to Jane, Kitty speaks of "Mr Garrick's avarice." In still another, David's vanity and susceptibility to flattery are alluded to:

Mr Garrick told me he was much pleased with you we talked an hour about you—always take care to keep him your friend it will always be in his power to do you a great deal of good—or Mischief—give him now and then a *spoonful. We all* love it.

The last sentence shows a humorous and indulgent turn toward generality which seems characteristic and somehow central to her tough, candid, and philosophical personality—unsparing of others, yet after all conceding her own kinship with the rest of weak, crass, vulgar, vainglorious, and sentimental humanity.

Mrs Clive was one of the four or five master mimes of the age, of whose powers critics, both friend and foe, were unstinting in admiration. Churchill in his rough *Rosciad* swept off his hat:

> Original in spirit and in ease,
> She pleas'd by hiding all attempts to
>   please.
> No comic actress ever yet could raise
> On Humor's base, more merit or more
>   praise.

Francis Gentleman in *The Dramatic Censor* (1770) believed Mrs Heidelberg in *The Clandestine Marriage* to have been "lost to the public when Mrs Clive retired; the ignorant affectation, volubility of expression, and happy disposition of external appearance, she was so remarkable for, will render it difficult to find an equivalent." She was "luxuriantly droll."

The discerning eye of Henry Fielding had picked her out thirty years before in the *Apology for the Life of T:.... C.....*: "as she has a prodigious Fund of natural Spirit and Humour off the Stage, she makes the most of the Poet's on it. Nothing, though ever so barren, even though it exceeds the Limits of Nature, can be flat in her Hands."

Chetwood, who spanned two ages, testified:

I believe that of all Actresses who have appeared in the comic vein, Mrs. Clive's superior talents have always been pre-eminent. Notwithstanding the lavish encomiums which have been bestowed on the late Mrs. Bicknell and Mrs. Mountfort; yet those who recollect them, and have compared the merits of each with those of Mrs. Clive, are unanimously agreed in giving her the preference.

Examples of laudation could be multiplied endlessly. Yet Kitty, like most performers, occasionally exposed her Achilles heel of vanity and, as with many other comedians, this was an aspiration toward tragic parts. Year after year she insisted on opening her season with Ophelia, though no female less Ophelia-like ever lived. Her "comic" Portia was stubbornly retained, one suspects almost *because* it was so often attacked. Samuel Foote early cautioned her in *The Roman and English Comedy Considered* (1747): she is "the best Actress in her Walk, that I, or perhaps any Man living, has seen" but she has "been a little unhappy in her Choice of some Parts." He advised her never to attempt characters "which require a Delicacy of Figure, and an Elegance of Behaviour; . . . as both Nature and Habit have denied Mrs. Clive the Possession of these Requisites." He delicately added a little *coda* on behavior:

This Lady has now and then perhaps (owing to an Earnestness for the Success of the Business) expressed herself behind the Scenes in too loud and forcible a manner.

This Circumstance has (I am afraid) given some part of the Audience not a very favourable Opinion of her Temper. But when the Public are assured, that this Vehemence is assumed in order to procure a more decent Entertainment for themselves, I doubt not but they will convert their Resentment to Approbation.

Burney thought that "her singing, which was intolerable when she meant it to be fine, in ballad farces and songs of humour was, like her comic acting, everything it should be." Not the least valuable of the vendable talents which she brought to the total bill of the play were her ingratiating ability to prop up a staggering comedy by speaking prologues and epilogues which put audiences in properly indulgent moods, and the lovely singing voice with which she enthralled her hearers in "specialty" songs. Sometimes the two excellences were combined, as in the "Occasional Ballad by way of Epilogue [to *The Drummer*] in the character of Abigail." The "Celebrated Irish Ballad Elin a Room [Aileen aroon] sung by Mrs Clive, in Irish," was often demanded and was published in two editions. She sang "The Charms of Polly Willis" to great applause and was encored in many other songs which were then profitably published: "The Life of a beau" and "The card invites," from *Lethe*, "Preach not me your musty rules" and "The wanton god who pierces hearts," from *Comus*, Arne's setting of "Blow, blow thou winter wind" and his "O peace," from *Alfred*. Her "While gentle Parthenissa walks," also set by Arne, helped make the revival of Steele's *Tender Husband* successful, and her "Life of a belle" performed the same service for *The Confederacy*.

Her good friend Samuel Johnson is reported by Boswell as having said: "Mrs Clive in the sprightliness of humor, I have never seen equalled . . . she was a better romp than any I ever saw in nature." Johnson, said Boswell,

had a very high opinion of Mrs Clive's comic powers, and conversed more with her than any of the actresses. He said, 'Clive, sir, is a good thing to sit by; she always understands what you say.' And she said of him, 'I love to sit by Dr. Johnson; He always entertains me.'

There is in the Folger Library a collection of letters from Kitty to her protégée Jane Pope, but in the hand of James Winston, endorsed "NB All these letters were copied from the Originals in Mrs Thomas

possession lent by her to me She was the neice of Miss Pope JW." None have been published and all bear the distinctive imprint of the Clivean personality. A few excerpts from these private reflections on people and events, written after her retirement, from 1769 to 1794, may serve to add useful coloring to our brief sketch of the vivid Kitty.

6 November 1769:

How you will smile when I tell you I have so much business I have not a moment to spare and (thank god my business is pleasure) people calling in a morning who have nothing to do but to lounge about and then my engagements in the evening wherewith shuffling and cutting till we are tired to death but that will soon be over. I begin now to shed my neighbours, as my trees do their leaves my dear Garden is now as naked as a Grecian Venus, but like that is still beautifull tho I think they both look best with their cloaths on—.

31 December 1772:

I dine out allmost every day this week so that we are apeing the old English hospitality as well as we can, but we want a great many plumb puddings, with the Boars Head with an Orange in its Mouth to make it the Old Town our great fear is getting cold coming home and getting robbed for the thieves swarm like May flies but we go notwithstanding. . . . Nothing surprising that the Yates do, except lowering their pride in going a stroling; as to there having so much money it is a monstrous lie, there is not so much in Scotland; I am not at all lowered at O'Brians Mortification how should he write plays he is a puppy; and I hear *a poor one*; He had much better have kept to his high life *below stairs*; his going *up* has not succeeded.

24 March 1774:

I have had my long walk ["Drury Lane"] measured because I may know what I do it

want three quarters of a yard of half a mile
. . . I set out after Breakfast and walk five
miles up and down till I am tired—I call it
going to Rehearsal.

23 November 1773:

My pen Trembles in my hand when I think
what a situation that poor mad Ideot Macklin
has brought him self into from his infernal
vanity. Not that I think he was half so mad as
the Managers who let him play [Macbeth]. I
knew from the first moment I saw it advertised, that there would be great confusion
but I only supposed they would laugh him to
scorn I think they have carried it much too
far for tho I believe very few people love
Macklin I think in this affair he has been very
cruelly treated for a man is not to be starved
because he cannot act Macbeth, tho he certainly ought to be hiss'd for attempting it . . .
I cannot help being sorry for him that he
should be so bold, when he is so old and I
hear so poor.

15 December 1774:

I am sorry to hear you have an indifferent
part [Lucy?] in the new Comedy [*The
Choleric Man?*], but I don't at all wonder
when you tell me the author [Richard Cumberland?] he is a *wretch* of *wretches*, however
I charge you to make a good part of it let it
be never so bad. I have often done so myself
therefore I know *it is to be done* turn it &
wind it & play it in a different manner to his
intention and an hundred to one but you
succeed.

3 January 1775:

How dreadful was the end of poor Mossop
and how very sorry I am that I cannot pity
him but I really will not put on what I cannot feel he was a poor proud conceited man
without any humanity or feeling for any body
perhaps it may be a lesson to some of our
great Tragedians that are left. . . . I have
had so much vexation for these last months
(of different kinds) that it has been more

than my spirits coud bare and has thrown me
into the jaundice, I am as yellow as a guinea
& at present I believe no one would give one
for me.

10 January 1778:

What shall we say for the dear Garrick
whose soul is never at rest, who has the
sweetest place in the World and is hardly
ever there who instead of admiring the beauties of the Country from his Temple of
Shakespeare is freting to see how the last
Scene goes off in a new pantomime or trudg-
ing in a Morning with a Tragedy Packet under his arm to Rehearse his new play, to
teach the Actress, and order the scenes and
dresses then come home tired to death and
swears he will never undertake such a thing
again poor Man he does not know why, but
he certainly is not happy and indeed I believe few people are who have every thing to
make them so a very pretty philosophical ob-
servation—pray Mrs Clive are you happy for
you have every thing to make you so that a
reasonable woman can desire—I answer—
Yes—No—just as it hapens far be it from me
to be unlike the rest of the World.

25 December 1780:

[Mr Clive] has left his fortune which I believe
was considerable to his Landlady where he
. . . lodged at Bath poor man his heart was
too hard to feel any compunction for the in-
juries he has occasioned me I shall send you
. . . his will . . . he has not left me even the
shilling he has cut me off with
'And as for and concerning my Wife
Catherine Clive whom it is well known has
been separated from me for many years I give
her no part of what I die Leased or possessed
of but I give or rather confirm to her everything she shall be posses'd of at my death it
being my will and intention that she should
have nothing to do with my executors &
representatives nor they with her—' this last
clause I am obliged to him for it must put it
out of the Power of his Exers to molest or
trouble me and has given me a right to leave
a pair of Gloves to those I love.

Original portraits of Kitty Clive are not so numerous as might be expected, considering her popularity over so many years. A census of them and their derivative engravings follows:

1. Oil by Richard Cosway. In the Countess Tolstoy Collection.

2. Oil by Jeremiah Davison. Once at Strawberry Hill; now at Longleat.

3. Oil, painter unknown. Described by the catalogue of the Augustin Daly sale in 1912: Kitty is "seen seated wearing a low cut white dress with a blue scarf falling from her left shoulder. . . . Height 48 inches; width, 36 inches." Present whereabouts not known.

4. Oil by Willem Verelst. At the Garrick Club.

5. Oil, painter unknown; sometimes attributed to Hogarth. Kitty as Mrs Riot, the "Fine Lady" in Garrick's *Lethe*. At the Garrick Club.

6. A phosphatic porcelain figure of her as the "Fine Lady," made at Bow c. 1750–55. Evidently inspired by an engraving about 1750 by Charles Mosley, after Van Bleeck. A companion figure of Henry Woodward as the "Fine Gentleman" was fired at the same time.

7. Wash drawing. Kitty attired half in men's, half in women's, clothes. Described by W. J. Lawrence in "The First English Stage Costume Design," *The Printseller* (July, 1903), as a costume worn in a new prelude to Fielding's *Tom Thumb*, 1733. Now at the British Museum.

8. Engraved portrait by A. Van Haecken after J. Van Haecken, and printed for Bowles and Carver. The same picture was engraved by Davison and published by Bentley in line and stipple in 1840 and issued again in 1857.

9. Engraving in miniature as the Fine Lady by J. Brooks, after an anonymous artist, 1750.

10. As Mrs Heidelberg in Garrick and Colman's *The Clandestine Marriage*. "From an original in the possession of the Duchess of Northumberland," by an anonymous engraver. Published by R. Sayer and J. Smith, 1769.

11. As Mrs Heidelberg with Baron Otranto (Horace Walpole) by an anonymous engraver as a plate to *Town and Country Magazine*, December, 1767.

12. As Isabella in Fielding's *Debauchees*, when Miss Raftor. Published by Harrison and Company, 1780.

13. As Phillida in Cibber's *Damon and Phillida*. Drawn and engraved by P. Van Bleeck, Jr.

14. The above picture was engraved, reversed, by J. Faber, Jr.

15. The same was engraved, without the figure of Damon, by W. J. Alais.

16. As Phillida, with Damon, engraved by J. Faber, Jr after G. Schalken.

17. As Mrs Riot, the "Fine Lady" in *Lethe*. Engraved by Charles Mosley in 1750, after Van Bleeck.

18. By W. Greatbach after J. Davison.

19. By I. Tinney after L. Ellys.

20. An anonymous satirical engraving, "The Green Room Scuffle," 1754.

Storer drew and engraved a picture of her Little Strawberry Hill residence which was reproduced in *Histrionic Topography*, London, 1818. Also in that volume is a representation of the urn on which were engraved Walpole's lines and which was placed "in a shrubbery, attached to the former residence of Mrs Clive."

Cloathier. *See* CLOTHIER.

"Clodio." *See* ROGIER, CLAUDIO.

Cloesong. *See* CLOSSON.

Clogget. *See* CLAGGET.

Closson, Mr [*fl. 1738–1755*], *actor, dancer, animal imitator.*

A Mr Closson had a benefit at the New Wells in 1738 in which he sang, danced, and imitated "An Aviary of Birds"—"Mr

Closson will likewise sing the songs of the Lark, Chafinch, Canary Bird, and many other birds; and is allow'd to be happy therein, as to excel most, if not all the birds he attempts to imitate." As late as 1755, a Mr Cloesong, no doubt the same person, entertained with bird and animal imitations on 5 September at the Great Tiled Booth, George Inn Yard, West Smithfield, at the time of Bartholomew Fair.

A person by the name of Closson was with the Lee-Phillips company in the summer of 1740, when he appeared in the dancing roles of Pierrot in *Harlequin Happy* at Tottenham Court Fair on 4 August, Noodle in *Harlequin Restored* at Bartholomew Fair on 23 August, and a servant and a "fury" in *Harlequin Doctor Faustus* at Southwark Fair on 9 September.

Closson, Mlle (fl. 1740), dancer.

A Mlle Closson played a milkmaid in the performance of *Harlequin Restored* on 23 August 1740 at Bartholomew Fair.

Clothier, Devereux (fl. 1662–1699), drummer.

Devereux (or Deverick) Clothier was appointed to the King's Musick as a drummer on 7 April 1662, replacing Edward Ottley. Oddly, his appointment was twice reaffirmed in later years, once on 13 April 1665, when it was noted that he was to receive the usual £16 2s. 6d. annual livery plus wages of 1s. daily, and again on 26 March 1670, when his daily wage was listed as 12s. Both later warrants specify that Clothier's appointment was to commence on 25 December 1664, because the drummer had for a month or so been placed in the service of Prince Rupert, had deserted, had been arrested, and had to be reappointed. Clothier was one of four drummers specially decked out with scarves of crimson taffeta with fringes of gold at the coronation of James II. He was reappointed under William III and was still serving as late as 1699 for £24 per year. Devereux

Clothier was presumably the father of John, whose career began as Devereux's ended.

Clothier, John d. 1753, drummer.

John Clothier, probably the son of the drummer Devereux Clothier, was appointed to the King's Musick as a drummer on 29 April 1699 at a yearly salary of £24. He rose to Drum-Major General on 8 September 1719 and served as the head court drummer until his death on 30 September 1753.

Clough, Mrs (fl. 1670–1673), actress.

Mrs Clough played small roles and breeches parts for the Duke's Company in the 1670s, though only a few of her roles are known. She acted Isilia in *The Forc'd Marriage* on 20 September 1670 and the second Lady in *Six Days' Adventure* on 6 March 1671 at Lincoln's Inn Fields. At the new Dorset Garden Theatre she was Hillaria in *The Careless Lovers* on 12 March 1673 and probably Mariana in *The Reformation* in May 1673. On the last date cited the actress listed was "Mrs Caff," and it is probable that this was an error for "Clough." She may have continued acting, but the only other reference to her is a scurrilous poem in a manuscript collection of lampoons at Harvard:

Clough and Jackson yee Whores debaucht by fine Cloaths
Have a care of returning to pack thred in Shoes
Silly Jackson is poor and has gott a Clapp
Bloody Clough makes Farse ware a Cardinalls Capp.

Clough, Miss (fl. 1748), actress.

On 3 September 1748 Horace Walpole wrote of seeing a new actress, Miss Clough, at Richmond: "an extreme fine tall figure and very handsome; she spoke very justly and with spirit. Garrick is to produce her next winter." Garrick, indeed, was in the audience that night at Richmond, but since Miss Clough's name appeared in no Drury Lane bills, evidently she was not hired.

Clough, Thomas *d. 1770, actor.*

The actor Thomas Clough began his theatrical career as a performer in the fair booths of London. He made his first appearances as Flout in *The Devil of a Duke* and an attendant in *The Matrimonial Squabble* on 22 August 1741, in Hippisley and Chapman's booth at George Inn Yard, West Smithfield, at the time of Bartholomew Fair. In the following season he was a member of the company at Goodman's Fields Theatre, where one of his fellow actors was the young David Garrick. There Clough played Dicky in *The Constant Couple* on 14 September 1741, Trapland in *Love for Love* on 16 September, Bagshot in *The Stratagem* on 30 September, a role in *Trick for Trick* on 2 October, the Turnkey in *The Imprisonment, Release, Stratagem, and Marriage of Harlequin* on 9 October, Stratocles in *Tamerlane* on 4 November, and Benjamin in *Pamela* (in which Garrick played Jack Smatter) on 9 November. On 23 December he acted Blunt in *Richard III*, the production in which Garrick as Richard was creating a sensation that season at the little "outlaw" theatre. Clough's other roles included Barnaby in *The Old Bachelor* on 5 January 1742, Daniel in *Oroonoko* (with Garrick as Aboan) on 23 January, and the King of Brentford in *The Rehearsal* on 3 February.

With Goodman's Fields closed in 1742–43 by the pressure of the patent house managers, the enterprising Henry Giffard moved his company to the old Lincoln's Inn Fields house (but without Garrick, who went to Drury Lane), where they managed to survive until the middle of April. At Lincoln's Inn Fields, Clough continued mostly in his line of low comedy and pantomime roles, playing again the King in *The Rehearsal* and Appletree in *The Recruiting Officer*, Blunder in *The Honest Yorkshire Man*, Blunt in *Richard III*, Gibbet in *The Stratagem*, the Cook in *The Devil to Pay*, a Citizen in *Bickerstaff's Unburied Dead*, Filch in *The Beggar's Opera*, and Ben in *Love for Love*. He also acted Frederick in *The Miser* at the Haymarket on 14 April 1743. That summer he returned to the booths to play a part in *The Cruel Uncle* at Tottenham Court Fair on 23 August and Gamester in *The Blind Beggar of Bethnal Green* at Southwark Fair on 8 September 1743.

Unable to secure an engagement at one of the Theatres Royal, Clough did not perform at London for another six years, during which time he probably worked in the provinces. His name did not reappear in the bills until he played Solomon Overzeal in *Modern Madness* in Cross and Bridge's booth at Bartholomew Fair on 22 August 1749 and again on 26 and 28 August. Cross, who was also prompter of Drury Lane, perhaps was responsible for securing for Clough his first engagement at a patent house, for in 1752–53 Clough was a member of Garrick's company, making his first appearance as Jeremy in *The Double Disappointment* on 11 October 1752. That season he also acted Sexton in *Much Ado About Nothing*, Sancho in *Love Makes a Man*, Formal in *Every Man in his Humour*, parts in *The Rehearsal* and *Harlequin Enchanted*, and Bardolph in *The Merry Wives of Windsor*. On 16 May 1753 he shared benefit tickets with several other minor actors.

In the following season he added to his repertory James in *The Miser*, Shift in *Scapin*, Tom Errand in *The Constant Couple*, Supple in *The Double Gallant*, Hotman in *Oroonoko*, Robin in *The Knights*, the Duke in *Venice Preserv'd* a drunken man in *Lethe*, and parts in *Harlequin Ranger, An Englishman in Paris*, and *Fortunatus*. On 2 July 1754, also at Drury Lane, he acted Bardolph in *The Humourists*, at a benefit given for old Colley Cibber. On the twenty-fourth of the same month, Clough acted in a barn at Eltham for his own benefit, moving Arthur Murphy to the comments in the *Gray's Inn Journal* (27 July 1754) about the several parts Clough performed in an unidentified play—obviously *Romeo and Juliet*—comments which also provide some indication of his physical appearance: "he was a little too fat for the Apothecary, but in the Part of the Fryar he looked exactly like our Curate, rosy and Jolly, only his Dress was a little outlandish; and when he took off his Wig, before the Audience, his Head was shaved in a new Manner." Clough was next to appear at Eltham in the character of Sir Charles Easy in *The Careless Husband*, according to Murphy's report, "and there will be a Cricket Match for twenty Pounds before the Play begins; after the Play, Mr. *Clough* is to repeat for the second time his *Epilogue* to the Cricketters, and it is thought the Barn will be very full."

Clough returned to Drury Lane for 1754–55 and remained there in a similar line of roles for another 15 years. By 1764–65 he was being paid 5s. per day, £1 10s. per week, and he received the same in 1766–67. In addition to the repertory of roles cited above, an incomplete list of his parts includes: Pedro in *Catherine and Petruchio*, Rigdum Funnidos in *Chrononhotonthologos*, Jasper in *The Mock Doctor*, Saygrace in *The Double Dealer*, Alguzile in *The Wonder*, Bernardine in *Measure for Measure*, Harry in *The Modern Fine Gentleman*, Block in *The Reprisal*, an Old Man in *The Toy Shop*, Sandys in *Henry VIII*, Tom in *The Jealous Wife*, a Servant in *The Witches*, Bardolph in *1 Henry IV*, a Committee Man in *The Committee*, the Welchman in *Harlequin's Invasion*, the Boatswain in *The Tempest*, Old Gerald in *The Anatomist*, the Surgeon in *The Chances*, a Citizen in *Coriolanus*, Sir Hugh Evans in *The Merry Wives of Windsor*, Sampson in *Romeo and Juliet*, Follower in *The Tragedy of Tragedies*, and unspecified roles in *The Fair Quaker of Deal, The Chinese Festival, The Genii, Harlequin Mountebank, Mercury Harlequin, The Hobby Horse,* and *The Jubilee.*

In the summer of 1759, Clough acted at Plymouth in John Arthur's new theatre and in the summer of 1769 at Richmond, when on 1 July—according to a surviving bill—he played in *Comus* and *The Recruiting Officer.* He also played once at Covent Garden, on 27 May 1757, as Filch in *The Beggar's Opera* for the benefit of Morgan, who was then said to be the oldest living actor in England.

Clough's last performance was on 5 June 1770 in *The Jubilee* at Drury Lane. His name was somehow included in the bill for *The Jubilee*, 3 October 1770, but he had already died during the summer, on 2 July 1770. His name was removed from the bill for *The Jubilee* on 4 October. Clough had subscribed £1 1s. to the Drury Lane fund book in 1766 but had died before the fund was established. In his will dated 3 June 1770, he described himself as a "Gentleman" of the Parish of St Paul, Covent Garden. Among his bequests were £5 for a mourning ring to his sister Elizabeth Dutton and £5 and all his linen and apparel ("Save and Except my last New Suit of Clothes," in which he was undoubtedly buried) to his brother John Clough. (A John Clough, who acted at Charleston in the first decade of the nineteenth century, died on Sullivan's Island, South Carolina, in May 1810.) The balance of his unspecified estate he left to his "good friend" and executrix, Mrs Sarah Sawyer, spinster, of the parish of St James, Westminster, to whom administration was granted on 3 July 1770.

The *Theatrical Examiner* in 1757 described Clough as a performer, who "tho' little used in other matters, is yet extremely well and of service in the pantomimes." He was said to be a very close friend of Ned Shuter, the comic actor. Charles Dibdin remembered Clough as an habitué of all sorts of brutal amusements such as cockfights, bull-baitings, and especially hangings. He had, apparently, made a full study of the lack of concern with which the hardened criminal approached the gallows and he was full of anecdotes about such popular spectacles.

Clough was depicted as a watchman in a famous painting by Zoffany of the drunken scene in *The Provok'd Wife*, with Garrick as Brute, and Watkins, Henry Vaughan, William Parsons, and Thomas Phillips as other watchmen.

Clun, Walter *d. 1664, actor.*

Walter Clun was trained for women's roles at the Blackfriars Theatre, one of his parts probably being Arethusa in *Philaster* about 1638–42. A manuscript cast discovered at the Folger Library by David George has "Wat" down for that part and Charles (Hart?) for Euphrasia. The use of first names or nicknames for boy actors seems appropriate. Aubrey noted that Ben Jonson "had one eie lowre than t'other, and bigger, like Clun, the player; perhaps he begott Clun"—but, except for the helpful physical description, that remark should probably be taken lightly.

Of Clun's Commonwealth years nothing is known, but he retained his interest in theatre and joined the troupe at the Red Bull as early as 1659, just before the two official Restoration companies were organized. He was one of the signers of an agreement with Sir Henry Herbert on 14 August 1660 to pay the Master of the Revels for plays acted at the Red Bull, which fact suggests he was one of the more important members of the group. In October he played with a combined company at the Cockpit in Drury Lane, and in November he became a member of the King's Company under Thomas Killigrew. During this poorly documented period Clun is known to have acted Prig in *The Beggar's Bush* and, as early as 11 October 1660, also at the Cockpit, Iago in *Othello*.

Once Killigrew's troupe began acting at their converted tennis court in Vere Street,

Clun played Falstaff in *1 Henry IV*, Subtle in *The Alchemist*, possibly Clinias in *Erminia*, and Smug in *The Merry Devil of Edmonton*—all during the 1660–61 season. Almost as soon as they settled in Vere Street, the King's Company laid plans for a new theatre in Bridges Street, and on 20 December 1661 Clun was one of the actors who signed the indenture for the property. On 28 January 1662 he was sold two shares in the building, presumably at £66 13s. 4d. each, which interest ranked him equally with all the other actor-sharers except Edward Kynaston, who held four shares. The main holders were Sir Robert Howard and Thomas Killigrew, with nine shares each. Also, on 10 January 1662, Clun had bought one share in the acting company (as opposed to the theatre building), the annual income from which may have turned out to be about £280.

During this time he was busy acting, though only a few of his roles were recorded: the Clown in *The Royal King*, D'Auolos in *Love's Sacrifice*, Cacafogo in *Rule a Wife and Have a Wife*, and Titere Tu in *The Cheats*. On 7 May 1663, when *The Humorous Lieutenant* opened the new Bridges Street playhouse, Clun, for that performance only, played the title role. His other probable parts before his untimely death were Traxalla in *The Indian Queen* and a Plebeian in *Julius Caesar*, though it is clear from the importance of some of his roles that he must have played many other parts of significance.

On 10 June 1663 Clun and five other actors leased one of three houses which they had recently built in the parish of St Martin-in-the-Fields to a widow, Margaret Nephway, for £24 yearly. About this time Clun also sold his two building shares to Thomas Johnson, a barber-surgeon, for a handsome £430. Pepys observed how rich and proud the actors had grown, and Clun may have been in his mind. But the diarist liked Clun's acting, and years later, on 6 February 1669, when he saw Mohun act

Iago, he felt Clun had been better; and when he saw Wintershall play Subtle on 17 April 1669, he lamented: ". . . I do miss Clun, for the Doctor."

From Pepys, too, we learn of Clun's death. On 4 August 1664 he wrote: "Clun, one of their best actors, was, the last night [2 August], going out of towne (after he had acted the Alchymist, wherein was one of his best parts that he acts) to his country-house, set upon and murdered; one of the rogues taken, an Irish fellow. It seems most cruelly butchered and bound. The house will have a great miss of him." The next day Pepys wrote of being with his cousin and passing the place where the actor had been killed; it was apparently his cousin who told Pepys that Clun "was not killed by any wounds, having only one in his arm, but blead to death through his struggling." Soon after the event was written "An Elegy upon the most excrable murder of Mr Clun, one of the comedians of the Theatre Royal, who was robbed and most inhumanly killed on Tuesday night, being the 2nd of August 1664, near Tatnam Court, as he was riding to his country house at Kentish Town."

Clynch. *See* CLINCH.

Coaff. *See* CORFE.

Coakayne. *See* COKAYNE.

Coan, John *1728–1764, dwarf.*
John Coan, "the Norfolk Dwarf," was born at Twisthall in Norfolk in 1728 according to the *Newcastle General Magazine* (September 1751). When he was a year old, Coan seemed to be developing a normal physique, but by the age of 16 he had grown only to a height of 36 inches and weighed only twenty-seven and a half pounds. At the time he was exhibited in Norwich in April or May 1750, he was described as weighing 34 pounds fully clothed and as being 38 inches high, including shoes, wig, and hat, "with limbs no bigger than a child of three or four." He wrote and read English well, had a sprightly temper, and discoursed "readily and pertinently," though his speech was "a little hollow." At Norwich he was reported to have sung "tolerably" and to have amused the company that came to see him "with mimicking a Cock's crowing, which he imitates very exactly."

At London in January 1751, Coan was brought for an introduction to the Prince of Wales and other members of the Royal Family at Leicester House, where (according to clippings at the Huntington Library) "he stay'd upwards of two Hours; and by the Pertinency of his Answers, Actions, and Behaviour, their Royal Highnesses were most agreeably entertained the whole time, and made him a very handsome Present." An undated clipping of about the same time announced that "Mr John Coan, the famous Norfolk Dwarf, or perfect Man in Miniature" would be exhibited to the curious at the watchmaker's facing the Cannon Tavern, Charing Cross, for an admission charge of 2s. 6d., and claimed that Coan had recently had the honor of being seen by his Majesty at his Royal Palace at St. James's and by the members of the Royal Society, "who allow him to be the greatest Perfection of the Dwarf Kind that ever Nature produced . . . quite reverse to those shocking Spectacles that, under the Name of Dwarfs, appear distorted, and unfit for publick View, especially the Fair Sex."

On 3 February 1758, Coan could be seen for sixpence, from nine in the morning until nine at night, at the Ship, Anchor, and Windmill, outside of Temple Bar, near Butcher's Row, when he promised to deliver "an Oration in Praise of the Glorious King of Prussia," a performance he apparently gave "to most of the nobility and gentry in London, at different times." About 1762, Coan, "the jovial Pigmy," served as majordomo to the Dwarf's Tavern, in Chelsea Fields, on a spot called Spring Gardens (not to be confused with Spring Gardens, Knightsbridge) between Ebury Street and Belgrave Terrace. The proprietor also kept the neighboring Star and Garter Tavern. Visitors were invited to adjourn to the tavern after fireworks set by Carlo Genovini, "there to sup on a most excellent ham, some collared eels, potted beef, etc., with plenty of sound old bright wine and punch like nectar." *Owens' Weekly Chronicle or Universal Museum,* for 5–12 June 1762, printed a prologue reported to have been spoken by Mr Gibson to a performance of *The Orphan* at the Haymarket on Monday, 31 May 1762 (this performance is not listed in *The London Stage*), in which an allusion was made to Coan:

Blest Conduit House! what raptures does it yield:
And hail, thou wonder of a Chelsea field!
Yet Zucker still surpasses
Your Conduit-house, your pigmy, and your asses.

Coan died on 24 March 1764, according to a clipping in the Huntington Library (but on 28 March, according to the *London Magazine,* 1764). An effigy of him was then exhibited at Rackstraw's Museum of Anatomy and Curiosities in Chancery Lane. He was pictured with the giant Edward Bamfield in an engraving by J. Roberts, which is reproduced in Volume I (p. 244) of this dictionary.

Coary. *See* COREY *and* CORY.

Coates, Mr [*fl.* 1793–1803], doorkeeper.

A Mr Coates was a doorkeeper at Covent Garden from at least 1793–94 through 1802–3, at a constant salary of 15s. per week.

Coates, Mr [*fl.* 1799], proprietor.

A Mr Coates held a one-eighth interest (five shares) in Sadler's Wells in 1799.

The other co-proprietors were Thomas Arnold, Richard Hughes, William Siddons, and Richard Wroughton. Coates was reported by Charles Dibdin the younger to have been originally a tanner of Bermondsey. An Elizabeth Joanna Coates, "from Bermondsey" and perhaps his wife, was buried in the vault under the chancel at St Paul, Covent Garden, on 23 April 1803, at the age of 34.

Coates, Mrs [*fl.* 1797–1822?], singer, actress.

A Mrs Coates (not to be confused with Mrs Elizabeth Coates) was a minor actress and chorus singer at Drury Lane from 1797–98 through 1805–6 at least, at a regular salary of £1 per week. Although not specified in the bill, she is noted in a manuscript index of the Drury Lane season (in the Harvard Theatre Collection) as making her first appearance on 12 October 1797 as an old lady in *Rule a Wife and Have a Wife.* On 8 November 1797 she was one of the chorus of peasants in *Richard Coeur de Lion,* and on 14 November 1799 she was billed as a peasant in *The Captive of Spilburg.* Mrs Coates played Bianca in *Catherine and Petruchio* on 3 May 1799. Her name was regularly in the Drury Lane pay lists through 1805–6, and she may have been the Mrs Coates whose name reappeared on the pay list in 1821–22 at £1 16s. per week. She served in a similar minor capacity at the Haymarket in summers from 1799 through at least 1802.

Coates, Elizabeth [*fl.* 1788?–1830], actress.

Elizabeth Coates is said to have made her professional debut at the Crow Street Theatre, Dublin, on 19 November 1789. She may, however, have been the Mrs Coates who had acted at Edinburgh and York in 1788–89. Under the management of Michael Atkins, she played at Belfast in the season of 1790–91, acting Ophelia on 8

November and Jane Shore on 10 November; according to the local press, in the former she "acquitted herself with singular propriety" and in the latter she was "remarkable for chastity and correctness." On 12 November she played Lord Rutland in *The Earl of Essex* and then went to act at Crow Street for a month, after which engagement she returned to Belfast to play Laetitia Hardy in *The Belle's Stratagem* on 13 December. On 26 January 1791 she took her benefit at Belfast in the role of Lady Teazle in *The School for Scandal*.

She was at Derry in the spring of 1791; in the summer she returned to Belfast where she had a benefit on 10 August. Mrs Coates also was at Belfast in the winter of 1792 when on 15 February she acted Lady Amaranth in *Wild Oats* with great success. Billed as from Dublin, Mrs Coates engaged at the Orchard Street Theatre, Bath, in 1793–94. In 1794–95 she was again at Belfast, where she acted Lady Macbeth, Juliet, and Estifania in *Rule a Wife and Have a Wife*. The reviewer in the *Belfast News Letter* found "her manner and her voice are as happily suited to comedy as they are totally unfit for tragedy," but the critic of the *Northern Star* praised her performance of Juliet as a "finished piece." From 5 January to 11 January 1796 she had a special engagement at Manchester, taking her benefit on the latter date, when *The Provok'd Husband* and *High Life Below Stairs* were performed.

On 22 September 1797 Mrs Coates made her first appearance in London at Covent Garden Theatre in the role of Clarinda in *The Suspicious Husband*. Her debut was favored by the critics who found her a handsome woman, "passed the bloom of youth," with a good figure, attractive personality, and a definite brogue in her voice. The *Monthly Mirror* was reminded of the manner of Elizabeth Farren but thought her voice was "thin and reedy" for a London theatre; if she were "to impart a little more *spirit* to her dialogue, that deficiency

would be less obvious to the audience." Mrs Coates next played Miranda in *The Busy Body* on 4 October 1797, Mrs Fainall in *The Way of the World* on 28 October, and Mrs Lovemore in *The Way to Keep Him* on 8 December. In the next season, 1798–99, she was re-engaged at Covent Garden at £3 10s. per week, an increase over the £2 per week she had earned in her initial season.

Elizabeth Coates continued as a member of the Covent Garden company during the first decade of the nineteenth century. In 1809 she signed her full name to a pay receipt. She should not be confused with another Mrs Coates who was a singer at Drury Lane during the same period.

It is possible that our subject was the Elizabeth Coates of the parish of St Paul, Covent Garden, who married James Ricketts, of the precinct of the Savoy, on 29 February 1784. The marriage was registered at St Paul, Covent Garden, and was witnessed by Francis and Susanna Collis and Mary Ann Yeates, theatrical people. If the marriage was that of the actress Elizabeth Coates, it occurred some five years before we can establish the beginning of her provincial career, and it suggests she was not Irish in origin but was from the theatrical district of London, perhaps the daughter of a theatrical couple. In any event, Elizabeth Coates always was billed as "Mrs Coates." It should also be noted that a Mr Coates was a doorkeeper at Covent Garden from 1793–94 through 1802–3. A notation in a manuscript at the British Museum informs us that Mrs Coates was still alive in 1830.

Coats, Miss [*fl.* 1779–1780], *singer.*
A Miss Coats sang in the chorus at Drury Lane in 1779–80, appearing as one of the spirits in *The Tempest* on 3 November (and four other times) and in the funeral procession of *Romeo and Juliet* on 27 December. In the following season she again sang in *The Tempest*, on 23 Septem-

ber 1780, but her name was omitted the next time the piece was given on 12 December. A Miss "Coates" played at Kilkenny in December 1790 and at Newry in August 1792, according to Clark, but that person perhaps was Mrs Elizabeth Coates, the Dublin actress.

Cobb, James   d. 1697, singer, composer.

James Cobb, a tenor singer, served as a Gentleman of the Chapel Royal under Charles II, James II, and William III. He seems to have been appointed at the Restoration. He enjoyed exemptions from subsidies levied by Parliament in 1661, was in attendance on Charles II when the King visited Windsor in the summers of 1671, 1674, 1675, and 1678, marched in the coronations of James and William, composed some songs and catches that were published by Playford in 1679, and died on 20 July (or August, according to Grove) 1697. He was probably related to John Cobb, the organist and composer who was active before the Restoration.

Cobham, Mr   [fl. 1769], performer?

A Mr Cobham was a minor member of the Sadler's Wells company in the winter season of 1769.

Cobham, Charles   1774–1819, violinist, violist.

The violinist Charles Cobham was born at London on 9 March 1774, the son of James and Jane Sarah Cobham, and was baptized on 20 April 1774 at St James, Clerkenwell. By 1794 he was listed by Doane's *Musical Directory* as a member of the Academy of Ancient Music and a performer at Ranelagh Gardens then living at No 9, Poole's Buildings, Mount Pleasant, Gray's Inn Lane. When recommended by John Ashley for membership in the Royal Society of Musicians on 5 April 1795, Cobham was given the usual testament of having practiced music for a livelihood "for

upwards of seven years" and was described as a performer on the violin and tenor, engaged at Drury Lane Theatre, at Ranelagh, and at other concerts. At this time he was a single man. He was unanimously elected to the Society on 5 July 1795, and on 2 August 1795 attended the meeting of the Governors to sign the book of members. Cobham's name appeared on the Society's list for playing at the annual concerts at St Paul's for benefit of the clergy from 1796 to 1800, 1802–4, and 1806. In 1802 he also served as a Governor of the Society.

Cobham played regularly in the band at Covent Garden for the spring oratorios from 1794–1801, at £2 5s. per week. No doubt he continued in that capacity well into the nineteenth century. On 16 September 1807 his name was on the Covent Garden list as a regular band member at the same salary, and in 1817 he was a violinist in the orchestra at the King's Theatre.

The Minute Books of the Royal Society of Musicians record the sad story of Cobham's last year of life. On 7 February 1819, Cobham was granted 25 guineas for medical relief in consequence of a recent "paralytic affliction"—a stroke—which grant he acknowledged in a gracious note on 7 March, saying he hoped soon to be well enough to acknowledge in person. But he shortly suffered a second attack, which deprived him of the entire use of his left side and placed him "in eminent Danger of his Life" and therefore rendered him unable to provide for his large family. On 6 June 1819 the society granted another 10 guineas in relief which was this time acknowledged in a long letter by his wife, Amelia Cobham, born Stedman, originally of the parish of St James, Clerkenwell, whom he had married on 6 November 1806 at St Clement Danes.

Gentlemen, I had the honour of addressing you last month soliciting your assistance for my afflicted husband and unprotected family, when you kindly presented him with ten guineas for which I beg to offer our grateful acknowledgment. I was in great hopes I should not have had the painful necessity of again troubling you but the protracted illness of Mr. Cobham obliges me to request the favour of your taking him under your care until it shall please the Almighty in his mercy to restore him the power of providing for his helpless children. The paper Mr. Simcock will present you I hope you will find correct as likewise the certificate of our marriage and I trust I need only represent our destitute situation to induce you to render us every assistance the laws of your Society can or may allow, out of the money I received I have paid six guineas to physicians besides a nurse for the last month, having been rendered incapable of attending Mr. Cobham alone, from the constant fatigue I have undergone Day and Night for the last five weeks, had it not been for the trifle I have received for the concert that takes place tomorrow evening, we must have wanted the common necessaries of life. I have now £11.16. to pay for medicines besides rent and taxes. I have enclosed the bill for your perusal that you may see my statement is correct, the letter I received from Dr. Maston on my application to him will I am convinced exculpate me from the idea of having incurred unnecessary expense. Dr. Pemberton was out of town; I had therefore no other resource for I could not see my husband perish for want of medical advice under these afflicting circumstances. I commit Mr. Cobham, myself and unprotected Children to your attention, trusting you will afford us every assistance in your power. I have the honour to remain, Gentlemen,

Your obedient and humble servant,
Amelia Cobham.
Church Street, Chelsea.

The Society granted another £8 on 3 July 1819, and on 1 August 1819 also granted £8 10s. 8d. per month, exclusive of money for tuition, for the support of five of Cobham's children who were under the age of 14. In a statement sworn by Mrs Cobham on 30 July 1819, the four boys and a daughter were named and their birthdates were given: Charlotte, 18 January 1806;

George, 6 September 1808; Maurice, 26 November 1809; Frederic, 1 May 1812; and Francis, 29 September 1814.

On 5 September 1819, Cobham himself wrote a long letter from No 5, Church Lane, Chelsea, to the Society expressing his wish to move his family out of expensive London:

Gentlemen and Friends,
You are no strangers to the very melancholy situation in which it hath pleased the Almighty to place me. I certainly have to thank God for the allowance I receive from the Society, I consider it a great Blessing as I am now totally incapable of earning one Farthing towards the support of my numerous young family, but really with every economy it is insufficient to provide even an existance for so many in such a dear place like this. I therefore find it absolutely necessary to remove to some part of the country such as Wales where House Rent and provisions are cheap. Mrs. C will then keep a school to help to support me and my Children, and that with the income you Gentlemen allow me from the Society may afford me some little comforts above the common necessaries of life for at present I am sorry to say I have no means of procuring sufficient nourishment and strengthening things necessary for one in my situation. Rest assured Gentlemen the moment Mrs. Cobham can do it she will endeavour to get me off being a Burthen to the Society, which she hopes to do in a short time if she can establish a school in the country. I am sure those Gentlemen who have families must know it is impossible to keep a family on sixpence a day each in London, which is the amount I have to keep my family with when divided among so many. It is far from my wish to impose on so good a Society or to wish them to go beyond the bounds of those Laws so admirably made for the Benefit of us all, but under these distressing circumstances I hope the Gentlemen of the Society will be kind enough either to subscribe a trifle each or vote me something to remove my family with. I feel assured Gentlemen you will not think this an unreasonable request but am convinced the

goodness of your Hearts will direct you to do what you possibly can, therefore [I rest] entirely on your Mercy.

With compassion, the Society formed a committee to provide Cobham with the funds, not to exceed £30, to defray the costs of moving to the country. But poor Cobham never got out of London, for on 3 October 1819 his wife wrote to the Society that he had died, after 17 weeks of great illness, and would be buried on the following day. Advising also that her landlord would, within several days, be putting her family out of their lodgings at No 5, Church Street, Chelsea, for nonpayment of rent, and that she would also lose her "trifling articles of furniture which would be increasing my dreadful misfortune," she implored for further assistance. The Society granted £12 for the funeral and a full widow's allowance. Mrs Cobham also asked the governors "to put me in a way of placing" for son William, a sixth child, older than fourteen, as an apprentice. In subsequent correspondence a seventh child, Charles, also older, was mentioned.

Mrs Cobham received a benefit concert at the Argyle Rooms in 1820 which brought her £45. The Minute Books of the Royal Society continue to reveal her various transactions, mainly concerning the care and apprenticing of her children, until her death in January 1824, when the responsibility for caring for two of her children, still underage, passed on to Charles Cobham, the eldest son.

Cobonell. *See* **CABANEL.**

"Cocchetta." *See* **GABRIELLI, CATERINA.**

Cocchi, Gioacchino *1715–1804, composer, musical director, conductor.*
Although born at Padua in 1715, Gioacchino Cocchi was described as "Napoletano" on the title pages of his numerous published works. He was at Naples in 1735, and his first opera *Adelaide* was produced at Rome in 1743. Over the following 15 years he wrote some 35 operas which were performed in the principal cities of Italy. In 1750 he took up the post of *maestro di cappella* at the Ospedale degli Incurabili at Venice. For the Ospedale he wrote several oratorios and while there he collaborated occasionally with Goldoni.

In 1757 Cocchi was engaged by Signora Mattei as resident composer for the King's Theatre at London. His first work there was *Demetrio, re di Siria,* a *pasticcio* which opened on 8 November 1757 and enjoyed numerous performances during that season. He composed music for *Zenobia* on 10 January 1758 and for *Issipile* on 14 March 1758, and provided a song "Mia vita mio bene," sung by Potenza in a concert which benefited the Musicians' Fund on 6 April 1758. For the King's Theatre he composed and conducted about a dozen operas until 1761–62, when J. C. Bach became his successor. These works included *Il Ciro reconosciuto* on 16 January 1759, *La clemenza di Tito* on 15 January 1760, *Tito Manlio* on 7 February 1761, and *La famiglia in scompiglio* on 3 April 1762. He also conducted some of Galuppi's operas including *Attalo* on 11 November 1758, *Il mondo nella luna* on 22 November 1760, and *Il filosofo di campagna* on 6 January 1761.

Cocchi returned to direct music at the King's Theatre in 1765–66, when he produced *Eumene* and *La clemenza di Tito.* He was again at the King's in 1770–71 and his *Semiramide riconosciuta* was performed on 9 February 1771, announced as a new serious opera "with music entirely new." The work had been given at Venice in 1757, however.

As a composer Cocchi enjoyed little success in London, although upon his arrival there he did please with several of the works which had been in favor in Rome and Naples. But his creativity diminished quickly, and the public, according to Dr Burney, soon tired of the frequent repetition of stale works. Burney's assessment of Cocchi was most unflattering:

Cocchi was quite exhausted long before his comic operas were produced. His invention did not flow in torrents, it was but a rill at its greatest swell; and now, with hardly a single smile upon any one of the airs, his heavy and thread-bare passages were doubly wearisome. Indeed, his resources in the serious style were so few, that he hardly produced a new passage after the first year of his arrival in England; but in attempting to clothe comic ideas in melody, or to paint ridiculous situations by the effects of an orchestra, he was quite contemptible. Without humour, gaiety, or creative powers of any kind, his comic opera was the most melancholy performance I ever heard in an Italian theatre.

While in London, Cocchi taught singing, by which he gained "a considerable sum of money," and served for some time as musical director of Mrs Cornelys's subscription concerts at Carlisle House. He also published at London collections of music which included duos for cellos and other instrumental works. He wrote music

Civiche Raccolte d'Arte ed Incisione, Milan

GIOACCHINO COCCHI, with J. A. Hasse and Saratelli

detail from a large group, engraving by Scotti

for the "grand musical entertainment" called *Il tempio della gloria* which was given at the King's Theatre on 31 January 1759 in celebration of the alliance of George II with Frederick the Great, and a double cantata *Le speranza della terra* for the birthday of George II, and *Le promese del cielo* for the wedding of that monarch to Queen Charlotte, the latter two pieces being produced on 3 June and 19 September 1761. He also composed a double cantata, *La vera lode* and *Il marito coronato*, for the installation of John Fane, seventh Earl of Westmorland, as Chancellor of Oxford University on 2 July 1759.

Cocchi was back at Venice in 1773, at which time apparently he retired. He died in Venice in 1804. Details of Cocchi's continental career may be found in the *Enciclopedia dello spettacolo*. A list of his printed compositions is in the British Museum *Catalogue of Printed Music*. His wife, a Venetian, who was a *buffa* singer on the Italian stage, had accompanied him during his stay in England, but had never performed publicly in London.

Cocchi appears in a group of composers engraved by Luigi Scotti between 1801 and 1807.

"**Cochetta.**" *See* GABRIELLI, CATERINA.

"**Cochinino, Signor**" [fl. 1754], musician.

On 13 September 1754 at the Haymarket Theatre *Mrs Midnight's New Carnival Concert* was presented with "Signor Cochinino" (one of the "best Italian masters") playing, as close as one can estimate, two wooden spoons. The playful entertainment was a concoction of the zany poet-producer Christopher Smart, and who Cochinino really was is not known.

Cochois, Francis H. [fl. 1734–1735], dancer, actor.

Master Francis H. Cochois, son of Michel Cochois and his wife, came to London with his parents and their other child (or possibly children) in 1734 to play at the Haymarket Theatre as part of Francisque Moylin's French company. The group performed from 26 October 1734 through 4 June 1735. Francis was both a dancer and an actor. On 7 November 1734, his first London notice, he offered a *Wooden Shoe Dance*; on 9 December he played Lord Houssay in *Le Français à Londres*; on 27 December he danced a Harlequin Man in a new chaconne; on 6 February 1735 he shared a benefit with the rest of his family and was probably a part of Cochois's Lilliputian group that danced *La Polissone*; on 16 April he played Joas in *Athalie*; and on 9 May he acted Colin in *Georges Dandin*.

Cochois, Michel, ₁*fl. 1719–1735₁, actor.

Michel Cochois (or Cochoy) married the sister of the famous Francisque Moylin and performed with Moylin's troupe at the "Theatre Royal in Paris." The company came to England for a series of performances at Lincoln's Inn Fields in 1718–19 at John Rich's request. One of Cochois's roles was mentioned in the bills: on 13 January 1719 he played the small part of Loyal in *Tartuffe*, and his wife acted Dorine. The troupe performed in London with some success but with the usual criticism from the chauvinists, from 7 November 1718 to 19 March 1719, their last month being at the King's Theatre in the Haymarket after their contract with Rich ran out. A total of 40 performances was given.

In 1734–35 the company returned, and in addition to Mons and Mme Cochois, Master Francis H. Cochois and at least one other Cochois youngster were in the troupe. Cochois on this trip commanded a group of Lilliputians, who may simply have been the Cochois children. During their stay at the Haymarket Theatre, Cochois appeared again as Loyal in *Tartuffe* and also played Cogdie in *Le Joueur* (13 December 1734),

Scaramouch—his specialty—in *Arlequin balourd* (27 December), the Grand Prevost in *Le Festin de Pierre* (8 January 1735), Scaramouch in *La Fille captain et Arlequin son sergeant* (30 December), Scaramouch in *La Fausse coquette* (19 March), and, at Goodman's Fields, the Taylor in *L'Embarras de richesses*. The troupe gave about 116 performances between 26 October 1734 and 4 June 1735. Cochois and his family took their benefit at the Haymarket on 6 February 1735, at which Cochois's Lilliputians danced *La Polissone*.

There were two female dancers named Cochois in Berlin in the early 1740s who were doubtless related to Michel: Babet Cochois, who joined Jean Baptiste Boyer's troupe at the court of Frederick the Great in 1740, is said to have been Marie Sallé's second cousin. Marianne Cochois came into the same troupe in 1742 and in 1749 married Boyer (the Marquis d'Argenson).

Cochois, Mme Michel, née Moylin ₁*fl. 1719–1735₁, actress.

Sister of the famous harlequin Francisque Moylin, Madame Cochois was married to the scaramouch of Moylin's troupe, Michel Cochois (or Cochoy). The company acted in Paris at the "Theatre Royal" before coming to London at John Rich's request to play a season at Lincoln's Inn Fields. During their stay, from 7 November 1718 to 19 March 1719, Mme Cochois is known to have acted Dorine in *Tartuffe*, but most of the other casts were not publicized.

When the troupe returned in 1734 to play at the Haymarket Theatre, at least two Cochois children were in the company, Francis H. and another. Mme Cochois's parts were more frequently listed in the bills during this second engagement: the Woman Captain in *La Fille captain et Arlequin son sergeant* (30 December 1734), Amarille in *Le Festin de Pierre* (8 January 1735), Angelique in *La Fausse coquette* (19 March), Zacharias in *Athalie*

(16 April), Claudine in *Georges Dandin* (9 May), and, at Goodman's Fields, Floris in *L'Embarras de richesses* (23 May). With her husband and children, Mme Cochois shared a benefit at the Haymarket on 6 February 1735.

Cockayne. *See* COKAYNE.

Cockburn, Mr [*fl.* 1784–1785], *actor.*

Mr Cockburn acted the role of Roger in *The Gentle Shepherd* out of season at the Haymarket on 9 February 1784 and 24 January 1785. Performances of *The Gentle Shepherd* were usually given annually at the "request of several of the Scotch Nobility" by a mixture of professional and amateur actors.

Cockey. *See* COCKYE.

Cocklin, Mr [*fl.* 1764–1765], *violinist.*

Rendle's *Old Southwark and Its People* cites a Mr Cocklin (or Cocklyn) as leader of the band at Finch's Grotto Gardens in 1764. Cocklin was also in the bills of the Gardens during the summer of 1765, listed in accompaniment to singers.

Cockye, Miss [*fl.* 1685–1691], *actress.*

Miss Cockye, "the Little Girl," played Pipeau in *The Bloody Brother* at either Drury Lane or Dorset Garden on 20 January 1685. She also acted Arbella in *Madam Fickle* at Drury Lane about 1690–91.

Coco, Antony [*fl.* 1796], *acrobat?* *See* COCO, CONCETTO.

Coco, Concetto [*fl.* 1796–1797], *posture maker.*

Signor Concetto Coco was one of a troupe of Sicilian posture makers, headed by Signor Saccardi, which performed at Sadler's Wells in the summer of 1796.

According to a press bill dated 24 May 1796, Signor Coco balanced "upon his feet and hands (for the first time) a moving cross Platform, with from 12 to 16 people upon it at different elevations." Probably he accompanied the troupe which Saccardi brought to entertain at the Cambridge Fair in 1797. Also listed in the Sicilian company was Antony Coco, perhaps Concetto Coco's son.

"Codgerino, Signor" [*fl.* 1752], *dancer.*

Signor and Signora "Codgerino," certainly pseudonyms, performed a new comic dance at Bence's Booth on the Bowling Green, Southwork, on 22 September 1752, at the time of the Southwark Fair.

"Codgerino, Signora" [*fl.* 1752], *dancer. See* "CODGERINO, SIGNOR."

Codi. *See* LODI.

Coe, Mr [*fl.* 1719–1723], *pit office keeper.*

At Lincoln's Inn Fields the pit office keeper, Mr Coe, received annual benefits from 11 May 1719 through 28 May 1723, all of them solo except the last, which he shared with Brook. Once, on 17 May 1721, he excused himself to his friends for not waiting on them personally, for he had been "very ill." His receipts on that date came to £83 12s., the highest recorded for him over the years. Coe was active one year at Southwark, for on 18 February 1723 he was granted a benefit at the Great Booth in Bird-Cage-Alley when *Oroonoko* was performed—possibly by a group from Lincoln's Inn Fields where the play had been done two days before.

Cogan, John *d. c. 1673, actor.*

A minor actor in the Duke's Company, John Cogan is recorded for only two roles: the Duke of Exeter in Boyle's *Henry V* on 13 August 1664 at Lincoln's Inn Fields and Roderigo in *The Duchess of Malfi* on 31 January 1672 at Dorset Garden. He probably served in the troupe between these dates playing roles too small to gain mention in cast lists. The prompter Downes said that Cogan died about 1673–74, and Clark's edition of Boyle's works states that he lost his life in the King's service.

"**Coghetta, La.**" *See* GABRIELLI, CATERINA.

Cogun. *See* COGAN.

Cohen, Mr [*fl.* 1770], *musician.*
The "celebrated" Mr Cohen played a concert on the French horn at Marylebone Gardens on 10 September 1770, announced as "musician to the Stadtholder, being the first time of his performing since his arriving in England." There appears to be no further record of London performances by him.

Coindé, Mr [*fl.* 1788–1789], *ballet master.*
Mr Coindé was assistant ballet master under Noverre at the King's Theatre in 1788–89 at a salary of £165 for the season and with the privilege of a free benefit. On 1 July 1789, the *World* announced a program of dancing by performers from the King's Theatre to take place at Covent Garden on the following night, for the benefit of Mr Coindé, tickets to be had of him at No 37, Silver Street, Golden Square. No newspaper of 2 July seems to have carried the bill, so perhaps the performance did not occur.

Cointe. *See* LE COINTE.

Cointrie. *See* DE LA COINTRIE.

Coish. *See* COYSH.

Cokayne, Mary [*fl.* 1753–1775], *actress.*

Announced as "A Young Gentlewoman" making her first appearance on any stage, Miss Mary Cokayne acted the role of Peggy in *The King and the Miller of Mansfield* at Covent Garden on 5 October 1753. Again billed as a young gentlewoman she played the role for the second time on 8 October but was named in the bills for the third performance on 20 October. In that season she also acted Phoebe in *As You Like It* on 22 October and Jenny in *Love for Love* on 13 May. On 4 May 1754 she shared a benefit with Crudge and Miss Young.

Miss Cokayne (occasionally "Cockayne" in the bills, the way she spelled it when signing her full name on a letter to George Colman, along with other actors, in November 1768) remained at Covent Garden for 18 years, during which time she never ascended above the roles of tertiary young women and was often employed for the parts of maids and as a supernumerary. Occasionally, even late in her career, she acted the roles of young boys, such as Lord William in *The Countess of Salisbury* on 26 October 1768, the Page in *The Orphan* on 20 October 1769, Prince John in *1 Henry IV* on 29 December 1769, a Child in *Isabella* on 5 May 1769, and the Duke of York in *Richard III* on 26 September 1770. Peggy in *The Miller of Mansfield*, Phoebe in *As You Like It*, Jenny in *The Knights*, Betty Doxy in *The Beggar's Opera* (first played on 13 April 1757), and the maid in *The Upholsterer* (first on 26 October 1763), were usually hers.

Her other roles (with date of first performance) included Doll Trull in *The Beggar's Opera* (30 November 1754), Phoebe in *The Humorous Lieutenant* (10 December 1756), Ann Page in *The Merry Wives of Windsor* (23 September 1761), Terminta in *The Wife's Relief* (31 October 1762), Phlorimel in *The Frenchify'd Lady* (27 March 1762), a part in *The Merry Counterfeit* (29 March 1762), the maids in *The Inconstant* and *The Citizen*

(25 October 1763), Rose in *The Recruiting Officer* (5 May 1764), Arabella's maid in *The Fair Quaker of Deal* (15 April 1766), Julia in *All in the Right* (26 April 1766), Trifle in *The Old Maid* (27 February 1768), Gratilla in *Edgar and Emmaline* (22 March 1770), and Cupid in *Harlequin Outwitted* (31 March 1770). Usually sharing benefit tickets with other minor performers, she took a profit of £2 6s. on April 1760, £5 on 27 May 1768, and £5 4s. 6d. on 18 May 1767. Her salary was 3s. 6d. per day in 1760–61, 3s. 4d. per day in 1767–68, and £1 per week in 1771–72.

In the summer of 1761 Miss Cokayne acted at Drury Lane. She played a small role in *All in the Wrong* on 15 June (and five other times) and Corinna in *The Citizen* on 2 July (and six other times), her only appearances at that theatre. The latter role, which she then acted at Covent Garden on 10 October 1764, also became one of her regulars. She also made two appearances at the Haymarket. The first was as Dorinda in *The Beaux' Stratagem*, the best role of her career, on 27 September 1771. The second, some four years after her retirement from Covent Garden in 1771–72, was on 2 February 1775 when she acted Debora in *Love in a Village* at a special benefit performance for Mrs Woodman, the widow of the Covent Garden actor. The performance seems to have been Miss Cokayne's last.

Coke, Mr ₁fl. 1784₁, *singer.*

Mr Coke was listed by Burney as one of the bass voices in the Handel Memorial Concerts at Westminster Abbey and the Pantheon in May and June, 1784.

Coker, Mr ₁fl. 1715–1721₁, *actor.*

Of Mr Coker very little is known beyond a series of small roles he played at Lincoln's Inn Fields over a period of six years. His first recorded part was a Companion in the first performance of *The Slip* on 3 February

1715, and his second was a Servant in *The Doating Lovers* when it opened on 23 June. He played the full 1715–16 season, taking such roles as a Captain in *The False Count*, Jeremy in *The Fond Husband*, Starveling and Gamut in *Pyramus and Thisbe*, Tinsel in *The Northern Heiress*, and Wildman in *The Woman Captain*.

All that is known of Coker's 1716–17 season is that he received a shared benefit with two others on 16 May 1717. On 10 December 1719 he probably played Lord Willoughby in *Richard II*, for he was so listed in the 1720 edition, and during the rest of the 1719–20 season he is known to have acted Saywell in *Hob's Wedding*. He played Polixenes in *Love's Triumph* at Bartholomew Fair on 23 August 1720, his only known appearance outside Lincoln's Inn Fields. His last notice was on 19 May 1721 when he shared a benefit with four others and played the Mad Welshman in *The Pilgrim*.

Coker, Mr ₁fl. 1733₁, *dancer.*

A Mr Coker danced the "Irish Trot" at the Haymarket Theatre on 19 March 1733.

Coker, Mrs ₁fl. 1731–1739₁, *actress.*

The Mrs Coker who acted at the fairs in the 1730s may have been related to the actor of that name who played at Lincoln's Inn Fields some years earlier. She is known to have appeared as Lettice in *The Devil to Pay* and the Bawd in *Whittington* on 8 September 1731 at the Lee-Harper booth at Southwark Fair, the Aunt in *The Innocent Wife* at the Old Playhouse at the bottom of Mermaid Court at Southwark Fair on 7 September 1736, and the Wapping Landlady in *The Sailor's Wedding* at Hallam's Bartholomew Fair booth on 23 August 1739.

Colborne, John ₁fl. 1775–1784₁, *boxkeeper.*

John Colborne was a boxkeeper at Covent Garden at least from 1780–81 through 1783–84, at a salary of 12s. per week. He shared benefits each season with other house servants. On 2 July 1775 he signed his full name as witness to the will of Alexander Johnston, and on 28 July 1780 to that of Francis Heath. Both Johnston and Heath were employees of the theatre.

Coldell. *See* CONDELL.

Cole, Mr *d. 1730, harpsichordist.*
On 12 March 1720 Mr Cole played "A Lesson on the Harpsichord" at Lincoln's Inn Fields, and he repeated this a year later on 18 March 1721. He was organist of St Martin-in-the-Fields and died a lunatic on 20 April 1730 at the Hospital of St Mary of Bethlehem in Lambeth.

Cole, Mr *[fl. 1749], house servant?*
The Covent Garden account books cite a Mr Cole on 29 September 1749 to be paid 11s. for two days. His function is not known, though he may have been a house servant.

Cole, Mr *[fl. 1760–1761], billsticker.*
On 22 September 1760 the Covent Garden constant charges included a daily salary for Mr Cole the billsticker of 1s. 6d. On 15 May 1761 either he or the men's dresser of the same name shared a benefit with several others and had to settle for a half-value sum of £9 4s. 6d. The Mr Cole who was one of the men's dressers earned a daily salary of 1s. The two men were probably related.

Cole, Mr *[fl. 1761], dresser. See* COLE, MR *[fl. 1760–1761], billsticker.*

Cole, Mr *[fl. 1784], violinist.*
Mr Cole was a first violinist who played at the Handel Memorial Concerts at Westminster Abbey and the Pantheon on 26, 27, 29 May and 3, 5 June 1784.

Cole, Mr *[fl. 1785?–1794], violist.*
A Mr Cole of Oundall, Northamptonshire, is listed in Doane's *Musical Directory* for 1794 as a performer on the viola who had assisted at the "grand performances" in Westminster Abbey, commemorating Handel (probably the 1785, 1786, 1791 celebrations, inasmuch as he was not listed by Charles Burney as playing in 1784). He may have been the violinist of the previous entry.

Cole, Mr *[fl. 1795–1799], box-keeper.*
A Mr Cole served as one of 21 box-keepers for Drury Lane Theatre in 1795–96, 1796–97, and 1797–98. He was perhaps the Cole who was in a manuscript pay list of the theatre at Richmond, Surrey, dated 1799, and whose function there was "gallery money-taker."

Cole, Mrs *[fl. 1696], actress.*
A Mrs Cole acted Isabella in *The Lost Lover* in March 1696 and Mirva in *Ibrahim* in late May at Drury Lane.

Cole, Miss *b. 1729, actress, dancer, singer.*
Born in 1729, Miss Cole was probably the daughter of the actor and prompter E. D. Cole. She made her first stage appearance at the age of four playing the young Princess Elizabeth in *Virtue Betray'd* at Goodman's Fields on 8 January 1733. The rest of the season found her speaking a number of epilogues, but she also acted the Duke of York in *Richard III* on 11 April and Joyce in *The What D'Ye Call It* on 24 April. At her shared benefit with Evans on 11 May she delivered an epilogue in boy's clothes. Her popularity was such that she was asked to present epilogues at the Haymarket Theatre on 28 May (still billed as aged four years) and at the Cibber-Griffin-Bullock-Hallam booth at Bartholomew Fair on 23 August. Back at Goodman's Fields in 1733–34

she added to her parts Cordelio in *The Orphan* and Cupid in *Britannia*. On 8 May 1734 at her shared benefit, again with Evans, she acted the Boy in *The Contrivances,* spoke the epilogue, and sang ("Her first attempt of that kind"). By 24 September 1734 she had passed her fifth birthday.

Drury Lane snatched her away from Goodman's Fields in 1734–35 and cast her for her first appearance there as Agnes in *The Mother-in-Law* on 19 October 1734. She remained at Drury Lane through the 1749–50 season, making occasional appearances elsewhere, but after a promising start her career withered gradually as she grew older, only to blossom again during her last season. From 1734–35 to 1738–39 she did fairly well, playing many parts suited to a little girl: Falstaff's Boy in *2 Henry IV*, Robin in *The Merry Wives of Windsor*, Harlequin's Good Genius in *The Fall of Phaeton*, Cupid in *Poor Pierrot Married*, Pistolet in *Harlequin Restored*, and Mab in *Robin Goodfellow*. She was often chosen as an epilogue speaker, sometimes joining with Master Green, and she showed enough promise at dancing to offer a *minuet* with Master Weeks at her shared benefit on 20 May 1736. Her most important assignment was Ariel in *The Tempest*, which she first played on 10 February 1737. (On 12 August 1735 at the Haymarket Theatre—if the bill was not in error—she had attempted Polly in *The Beggar's Opera*.)

By 1738–39 the number of new roles assigned her at Drury Lane dropped noticeably, and in that season she received no benefit. She was cast as Tom Thumb in *The Tragedy of Tragedies* on 17 April 1740; yet that spring she was again refused a benefit. In 1740–41 Miss Cole was infrequently noticed in the bills, though she shared a benefit with three others at the end of the season. She acted Tom Thumb in *Tom Thumb the Great* on 21 April 1741 at Goodman's Fields at E. D. Cole's benefit, he having turned to prompting there after a rather undistinguished performing career at Drury Lane and elsewhere. In 1741–42 Miss Cole acted a few small roles at Drury Lane, including Fleance in *Macbeth*, but her benefit in the spring had to be shared with some six or seven others. By this time she was 13 and no longer a novelty. The little boy and girl roles were perhaps no longer suitable, yet older parts were still beyond her reach. In 1742–43 she was not with the Drury Lane company. A benefit was held for her when *George Barnwell* was played at the Haymarket on 23 March 1743. She offered an epilogue, billed as "Miss Cole who lately belong'd to the Theatre Royal in Drury Lane," but the bill gave no indication that she was to act in the play.

She was back at Drury Lane in 1743–44, and for the following several seasons she seems to have played whatever she could get, hoping to establish a suitable line. She was a Waiting Woman in *The Anatomist*, Lettice in *The Devil to Pay*, Mincing in *The Way of the World*, Betty in *Flora*, Prince John in *1 Henry IV*, Jack in *The Committee*, Edward V in *Richard III*, Cleora in *The Tragedy of Tragedies*, Mrs Vixen in *The Beggar's Opera*, Charlotte in *The Mock Doctor*, Mrs Ann in *Love's Last Shift*, Jenny in *The Provok'd Husband*, a Nun in *Measure for Measure*, Donalbain in *Macbeth*, Iras in *All for Love*, Prince Henry in *King John*, and (at the James Street playhouse on 29 December 1747) Elizabeth in *Anna Bullen*.

In 1747–48 she began dancing more, perhaps hoping to find her specialty there. She appeared in large group entr'acte offerings such as a *Polish Dance* or *The Gardener's Dance*, and she was in time cast in minor pantomime roles such as a Shepherdess and a Spaniard in *The Triumph of Peace*. At the same time she continued being seen in plays: Serena in *The Orphan*, a Lady in *Jane Shore*, Myrtilla in *The Provok'd Husband*, Milliner in *The Suspicious Husband* (the *Mrs* Cole listing for this role in 1748–49 is surely an error for *Miss Cole*), Lucinda in *The Conscious Lovers*, Ursula in *Much Ado About Nothing*, and Jessica in *The Merchant of Venice*.

Finally, in 1749–50, when Miss Cole would have been reaching her majority, her years of dogged utility work paid dividends. She danced, sang, played several of her earlier roles, and added to her repertory such parts as Abigail in *The Relapse*, Maria in *The London Merchant*, Angelica in *The Constant Couple*, Flametta in *A Duke and No Duke*, Miranda and Dorinda in *The Tempest*, Cephisa in *The Distrest Mother*, Julietta in *Don Saverio*, Lucilla in *The Fair Penitent*, Miss Biddy in *Miss in Her Teens*, Mrs Tattoo in *Lethe*, Ismene in *Merope*, and Lettice in *The School Boy*.

But then she left Drury Lane. With Thomas King she went to Dublin, and in 1750–51 at Smock Alley she is known to have acted Isabinda in *The Busy Body* on 19 September 1750 and Clarinda in *The Double Gallant* on 8 October. Miss Cole remained with the Smock Alley troupe for the 1751–52 season, but she seems not to have pursued her career beyond that.

Cole, Miss [*fl. 1774*]. *See* **ROBINS, MISS.**

Cole, E. D. [*fl. 1707–1741*], *actor, dancer, prompter.*

It is likely that the E. D. Cole who was active in the 1730s was the Mr Cole who played small parts in the early years of the eighteenth century. The first reference to Mr Cole seems to have been on 25 October 1707 when he acted Sancho in *Love Makes a Man*, at Drury Lane. He appeared at that playhouse again on 27 March 1710 as a servant in *Bickerstaff's Burial*, and on 21 April he shared a benefit with Giles. Cole spent the summer of 1710 at Pinkethman's theatre in Greenwich, playing Appletree in *The Recruiting Officer* for his first role on 27 July and the Prince of Tanais in *Tamerlane* for his last on 30 September. In be-

tween he essayed a Plebeian in *Oedipus*, the Dutch Boor in *The Royal Merchant*, the Starved Apothecary in *Caius Marius*, and Clip in *The Confederacy*.

Perhaps after this, Cole toured, for his name came up in London records only three times in the following 22 years. A Mr Cole was in the Mob in *The Contrivances* at Drury Lane on 9 August 1715; about June 1716, according to a British Museum manuscript, a Cole played Decius in *Ignoramus* somewhere in London; and on 17 December 1720 at Drury Lane a Mr Cole acted Wart in *2 Henry IV*. After these sporadic appearances, he (if these Coles were E. D. Cole) did not appear in London again until 1732, whereupon he settled down for almost ten years of fairly steady activity.

On 16 February 1732 Cole played Sly in *The Cheats of Scapin* at the Haymarket Theatre. He stayed at that house through May, acting Nimposto in *The Blazing Comet*, Mons Chaudon in *The Wanton Jesuit*, Freeman in *A Bold Stroke for a Wife*, Plume in *The Recruiting Officer*, Chamont in *The Orphan*, Lorenzo in *The Spanish Fryar*, and a role in *The Coquet's Surrender*. He finished his summer acting in *The Envious Statesman* on 22 August 1732 at the Fielding-Hippisley booth at Bartholomew Fair.

In the early months of 1733 Cole acted at the Goodman's Fields playhouse, playing Aegon in *Damon and Phillida*, Oxford in *Richard III*, and Westmoreland in *1 Henry IV*. His benefit tickets were accepted on 3 May, after which he moved to Covent Garden for July and August to appear as Varro in *Sophonisba*, Crambo in *The Stage Mutineers*, Blandford in *Oroonoko*, Harry in *The Fancyed Queen*, and Palmenio in *The Tuscan Treaty*. During the 1732–33 season while Cole was working at Goodman's Fields, a Miss Cole who was probably his daughter made her debut at the age of four.

Cole was not mentioned in the bills during the regular 1733–34 season, but he turned up at the Haymarket in the summer of 1734 to act the Justice in *The Humours of Sir John Falstaff*, Sullen in *The Stratagem*, and Clerimont in *The Miser*. He also made an appearance at York Buildings, playing Haly in *Tamerlane* on 8 August 1734. It seems clear that only when he acted with pick-up companies did he play roles of much significance, for at Drury Lane in 1734–35 he was Lepidus in *Julius Caesar* (on 8 November 1734, his first appearance there), Dr Proby in the pantomime *The Plot*, the Messenger in *Trick for Trick*, and Blunt in *The London Merchant*. He interrupted his engagement at Drury Lane to appear as Sancho in *Love Makes a Man* at York Buildings on 21 March 1735, and he was back at the Haymarket the following summer to play Subtleman in *The Twin Rivals*, the Doctor in *The Anatomist*, the Beggar in *The Beggar's Opera*, and Sir Charles in *The Stratagem*. Offstage, on 10 May 1735 in the Drury Lane scene room, Cole happened to be on hand when Macklin killed Thomas Hallam; it was into Cole's arms that the dying Hallam fell.

Cole's career during the rest of the 1730s followed a similar pattern. He acted most of the time at Drury Lane in plays and pantomimes, seldom in large roles; once he played at Lincoln's Inn Fields, as Corydon in *Damon and Phillida* on 14 April 1736. At Drury Lane during these years he was seen as a Justice in *The Harlot's Progress*, a Captain in *The Twin Rivals*, Hellebore in *The Mock Doctor*, the Surgeon in *Poor Pierrot Married*, Scrapeall in *The Squire of Alsatia*, Jemmy in *The Beggar's Opera*, the Friar in *Measure for Measure*, the Lawyer in *Love's Last Shift*, Buckram in *Love for Love*, and the second Murderer in *Macbeth*.

Cole's most noteworthy achievement was getting into a paper battle with Henry Giffard of Lincoln's Inn Fields in December 1736. Giffard was accused in the *Daily Journal* of 25 December of having created a disturbance at a Drury Lane performance

of *Harlequin Restored* in which, coincidentally, Miss Cole appeared. Giffard published a rejoinder, backed up with affidavits, accusing Cole of having hired persons at 2*s.* each to attend Lincoln's Inn Fields and hiss "the entertainment of The Contending Columbines" (*The Beggar's Pantomime*). The Drury Lane player, signing himself E. D. Cole, then published a denial of the charge, and the paper war ended. After this incident Cole was not given a new role at Drury Lane for almost five months, and it is likely that this was punishment for his having been the guilty claque-master.

After this rather undistinguished career as an actor and dancer, Cole took up prompting at Goodman's Fields in 1740–41. On 21 April 1741 *Tom Thumb the Great* was presented for his solo benefit, and Miss Cole was allowed to come over from Drury Lane to play the leading role. After that season, Cole's name disappeared from the London bills.

Cole, Mr J. [*fl.* 1785?–1794], *singer.*
Mr J. Cole, an "alto" (i.e., countertenor) who lived at No 12, Hoxton Market, Hoxton, in 1794 was concerned in the Cecilian Society's concerts and the oratorios at Drury Lane, according to Doane's *Musical Directory* (1794). He had sung in at least some of the grand commemorations of Handel at Westminster Abbey (probably the 1785, 1786, or 1791 celebrations, inasmuch as he is not listed by Charles Burney as singing in 1784).

Coleman. *See also* COLMAN.

Coleman, Mr [*fl.* 1670s?], *impresario.*
In 1682 Coleman's Music House with its large and well-planted gardens was offered for sale. It was situated near Lamb's Conduit and was demolished when Ormond Street was built. Presumably a Mr Coleman operated the establishment, probably in the 1670s.

Coleman, Mr *(fl. 1749–1750),* *actor.*

Mr Coleman is known to have made two appearances at Southwark Fair: on 2 January 1749 he played Filch in *The Beggar's Opera* and on 7 September 1750 he acted Toby in *Jeptha's Rash Vow.* In both instances he played at the Great Tiled Booth in Bowling Green operated by the Yeates family.

Coleman, Charles *d. 1664, instrumentalist, singer, composer.*

Charles Coleman the elder may have started his performing career on 4 May 1617 acting Hymen in a masque at the Ladies' Hall, Deptford. By 1625 he was a member of the King's Musick under James I, and on 15 July 1628 he was listed as one of the musicians for lutes and voices. On 17 April 1641 Coleman was described also as one of the "Musicians for the Waytes" and exempt from paying subsidies. During the Commonwealth he made a livelihood teaching the viol at Richmond, and since he had Puritan friends, when a committee was sent to Cambridge to reform the University, one of their recommendations was a degree for Coleman. Instrumental in this may have been one of Coleman's students, Colonel Hutchinson, one of the signers of the death warrant of Charles I. On 26 June 1651 Coleman was recommended for a Mus. D. degree at Cambridge even though he had not stood for an A.B., and on 2 July the doctorate was conferred.

By 1651 Dr Coleman had already distinguished himself sufficiently as a composer of secular music to have some of his pieces included in *The Musicall Banquett.* The next year John Playford published some Coleman works in *Select Musical Ayres and Dialogues,* and in 1653 Playford's next collection included more. *Court Ayres* and *Musicks Recreation on the Lyra Violl* in 1656 gave further evidence of his talent.

Coleman collaborated in 1656 with Sir William Davenant on the historic *First Day's Entertainment at Rutland House,* sharing with Henry Lawes the responsibility for the music. This was soon followed by the still more important *The Siege of Rhodes,* for which Coleman and George Hudson wrote the instrumental music. In both productions, Dr Coleman's brother(?) Edward and his wife also participated as singers. The Restoration was in the offing, and, along with many others, Coleman changed his affections: in 1660 he wrote *An Ode Upon the Happy Return of King Charles II. to his Languishing Nations,* with words by James Shirley.

As early as 16 June 1660 the King returned the favor by appointing Dr Coleman to Thomas Ford's place as a viol player in his private music. Coleman was to receive an annual livery allowance of £16 2s. 6d., though Charles II was notorious for not paying such bills on time. By 20 April 1661 Coleman's son Charles joined him in the King's Musick, both sharing the same position and probably splitting the £40 annual salary and £20 allowance for instrument strings. A curious warrant dated 4 July 1661 indicates that Dr Coleman and some of the other court musicians had their own private practice room which they rented and for which the crown reimbursed them; the warrant ordered a payment of £50 to Coleman and four others for the rent of two rooms used for practice and instrument storage from 24 June 1660 to 24 June 1661. Similar warrants paid them for 1661–62 and 1662–63.

Because he was a distinguished member of the King's Musick, Dr Coleman's works continued to appear in print. John Playford had put out another collection in 1659 which included some of his pieces, and Playford's *Courtly Masquing Ayres* in 1662 contained still more. It was not a surprise, then, when Coleman was appointed on 9 November 1662 to the composer's position at court left vacant by the death of Henry Lawes, at a salary of £40 yearly. This was, apparently, in addition to his position as one of the lutes and voices.

On 28 October 1662 Dr Coleman became a member of the revived Corporation of Music, but he was by this time getting on in years, and his professional activity waned. On 2 July 1664, "an Antient man" and "weake in body," Coleman made his will, describing himself proudly as a "Doctor of Musick" from the parish of St Andrew, Holborn. He left his estate to his wife Grace with the provision that she in turn should provide for Coleman's three younger children, Charles, Reginah, and Grace. Very soon after this Dr Charles Coleman died at his home in Churchyard Alley, Fetter Lane. He was buried at St Andrew's on 8 July 1664, and on 16 July his widow proved his will.

As was usual then, though it may seem unduly hasty now, Coleman's various positions were granted to others immediately after his death. On the day of his burial Henry Cooke was appointed to Coleman's post as composer for voices in the King's private music; on 19 July Thomas Purcell took Coleman's place in the Corporation of Music; and Coleman's son Charles took over his father's regular position in the King's Musick at the same livery fee. Typically, too, as late as 1667, fees due to Dr Coleman from as early as 1663 were still to be paid to his widow.

In addition to the numerous collections of music which contained his compositions printed during his lifetime, Dr Coleman also contributed, in 1658, articles on musical words for Edward Phillips's *New World of Words*. After his death his music continued popular and appeared in *Musick's Delight on the Cithern* (1666) and *Musick's Recreation on the Viol, Lyra-way* (1669). Many musical manuscripts, almost certainly attributable to Coleman the elder, are in the collections at the British Museum, Oxford, and Cambridge. He was, as Wood said, "an approver of the viol lyra way and an improver of it by his excellent inventions."

Coleman, Charles *d. 1694, musician.*

The son of the more famous Dr Charles Coleman by his wife Grace, Charles the younger was appointed on 20 April 1661 to a position in the King's Musick shared with his father, a rather unusual arrangement which suggests that Charles was still fairly young. Presumably what the father and son shared were the £16 2s. 6d. annual livery (when it was paid, which was seldom), the £40 annual salary, and the £20 allowance for strings for their instruments. Like his father, Charles was one of the musicians for lutes and voices, though his special instrument was the viol. After the death of Dr Coleman in 1664, the younger Charles was given his father's livery (on 4 May 1665, retroactive to 29 September 1664); one assumes that the shared position now became fully his.

The Lord Chamberlain's accounts make frequent mention of Coleman, but most of the references have to do with livery payments. A few, however, hint at his activities through the years. On 25 March 1667, for example, Coleman turned over his livery payment to John Lilly "for attending in his place," which suggests that Coleman may have been ill or traveling for a year. On 15 February 1675 we know he played in the court masque *Calisto* on the viol or the viola da gamba, or perhaps both. In the summer of 1675 Coleman attended the King at Windsor. He was reappointed to the King's Musick under James II on 31 August 1685 as a bass viol player in the private music, and King James was able to pay off his brother Charles's debts and order £129 in back fees paid to Coleman on 21 September 1686. Coleman continued in the court musical establishment under William III at £30 annually, the salary he had received under James.

Shortly before 22 June 1694 Charles Coleman died, for on that date his position at court was given to Robert Lewis. Of Coleman's personal life nothing is known unless the following references are to him: A Charles Coleman of New Inn, styled a gentleman, bachelor, and aged about 25, married Mrs Elizabeth Gritton of St Clement Danes, a widow of about 24, on 27 July 1672. If this was the musician, he would have been about 14 when he joined the King's Musick; this would help explain the shared position he was granted with his father. A couple identified as Charles and Elizabeth Coleman of St Margaret, Westminister, baptized a son Charles on 16 April 1673 and a son Benjamin on 18 September 1674. They may have been the musician and his wife, now moved to a parish closer to his work. Edward Coleman the singer was certainly related to Charles; they were probably uncle and nephew, though some sources suggest that they were brothers.

Coleman, Edward *d. 1669, singer, composer.*

Though *The Dictionary of National Biography* identifies the singer Edward Coleman as the son of Dr Charles Coleman, much evidence points to their being brothers. They seem to have been about the same generation, involved in many similar musical activities at about the same time, and they died within five years of one another. Dr Charles Coleman's son Charles, on the other hand, seems clearly to have belonged to a younger generation and to have died 25 years after Edward. Dr Coleman's will in 1664, incidentally, speaks of his son Charles in terms which suggest a very young man and which make no mention of Edward.

Edward Coleman was already a teacher of voice and viol by 1651. Ten years later the "rarely accomplished Virgin" Susannah Perwich, one of Coleman's pupils, testified to her master's talent in *The Virgin's Pattern.* Coleman was described as having "rare abilities in *singing* and as deserving "no *less* thanks and commendations for the *care* and *delight* he took in perfecting her in this *Art*, than any of her other masters." Coleman was also a composer, and some of his pieces were included in John Playford's *Select Musicall Ayres and Dialogues* in

1653. In this year, too, his music for Shirley's *The Contention of Ajax and Ulysses* came out.

On or about 23 May 1656 "Ned" Coleman sang in Davenant's *The First Day's Entertainment at Rutland House*, the first step in Davenant's efforts to bring "opera" to the English public stage. In September the more important *The Siege of Rhodes* was presented, with Coleman singing Alphonso and his wife Catherine, who had also participated in the May venture, singing Ianthe.

On 30 November 1660 Edward Coleman was granted the usual £16 2s. 6d. annual livery as a singing member of the King's Musick, replacing John Lanier, a position Coleman held until his death. His salary was probably £40 yearly throughout his tenure. He seems not to have attracted much attention at court, and the Lord Chamberlain's accounts mention little more than his livery payments, which were often in arrears. He was, as we learn from Pepys, something of a man of the town, and perhaps he did not take his court work very seriously.

Indeed, what little more we know about Edward Coleman comes from Samuel Pepys, who ached to move in Coleman's circle. Coleman and his wife were at Pepys's house on 31 October 1665, and Catherine sang "very finely, though her voice is decayed as to strength but mighty sweet though soft . . ." She sang some excerpts from "the Opera"—presumably *The Siege of Rhodes*—"though she won't owne that ever she did get any of it without book in order to the stage; but, above all, her counterfeiting of Captain [Henry] Cooke's part, in his reproaching his man with cowardice . . . she did it most excellently." Except for her appearances at Rutland House before the Restoration, Mrs Coleman made no known public appearances as a singer, and, indeed, Pepys seemed to suggest that she (and presumably her husband Edward) were now no longer young. Curiously, Pepys made no mention of Edward's doing any private singing.

Pepys delighted in the musical society in which the Colemans shone—"the best company for musique I ever was in, in my life," he wrote on 6 December 1665, "and I wish I could live and die in it . . ." On 2 August 1667 Pepys worried himself sick that Coleman and Pepys's father might have caught a glimpse of Samuel carrying on with a woman at Brampton—and perhaps they did, for afterwards Mrs Pepys was more than usually testy with her husband. Mrs Pepys, in fact, turned the tables and developed quite a liking for Coleman. On 23 December 1667 Pepys was with his friend Creed at the Exchange and saw Coleman, "of whom my wife hath so good an opinion, and [Creed] says that he is a very rogue for women as any in the world; which did disquiet me, like a fool, and run in my mind a great while." Later, on 12 January 1668, Pepys's father and Mrs Pepys were much at odds because Coleman had spent some time with her.

Edward Coleman died at Greenwich, apparently quite poor, on 29 August 1669. His place in the King's Musick was filled on 3 September by William Clayton. Administration of Coleman's estate was granted to his creditor Thomas Loup on 16 September, Catherine Coleman renouncing.

An entry in the parish registers of St Andrew, Holborn (Dr Charles Coleman's parish) may refer to Edward: an Edward Coleman, gentleman, of Hatton Garden, buried a son Edward on 9 December 1664. This indicates, however, burial of a young boy, and not knowing Edward's and Catherine's ages in 1664, one can scarcely decide whether or not this might have been their son.

Coleman, John [fl. 1668], musician.

John Coleman, apparently not related to the more famous musical family of Colemans earlier in the 1660s, was a member of the King's private music for lutes, voices, theorbos, and virginals, but just what his specialty was is not clear. Warrants in the Lord Chamberlain's accounts mention him rarely, and the only one clearly dated does no more than signify Coleman's membership in the private music in 1668. He may have been the John Coleman whose wife died about 1665; administration of her estate was granted to her husband on 7 November 1665. Her maiden name had been Frances Adams, and she and her husband were of the parish of St Leonard, Shoreditch.

Coleman, William [fl. 1794], violinist.

According to Doane's *Musical Directory* of 1794, William Coleman was a violinist living at No 4, King's Court. He performed for the New Musical Fund and played in the Handel Memorial Concerts at Westminster Abbey.

Coles, Charles [fl. 1760–1770], house servant?

An employee named Coles, who worked in some capacity at Covent Garden Theatre, was on the list there in May 1760 when he shared in a benefit. He testified during the litigation between the contending managers of the theatre (Harris and Rutherford versus Colman and Powell) in July 1770, concerning events in 1767 and 1768. At this time he was identified as Charles Coles.

Coles, John d. 1800, violinist.

John Coles played in the band at Drury Lane during the 1778–79 season and until sometime in 1793. He was numbered by Burney among the second violins in the large band which played in the Handel Memorial Concerts alternating at Westminster Abbey and the Pantheon on 26, 27, 29 May and 3, 5 June 1784.

When he was proposed by John Parke for membership in the Royal Society of Musicians on 4 January 1778, he was said to have "practised music seven years for a livelihood" (a usual formula) and to have been a single man. On 2 January and 6 March 1785 the Minute Books listed him as a Governor of the Society. On 1 November 1795 his name was withdrawn from the rolls of the Society at his own request. He lived at Carlton House in 1794, according to Doane's *Musical Directory*.

Coles died by his own hand on 20 October 1800. The *Gentleman's Magazine* obituary section for that date gives a circumstantially convincing account of his life and death:

This morning Mr. John Coles, formerly one of the band at Drury-Lane theatre, destroyed himself, at his apartments in Newman-street, by firing one pistol through his right side, and another through his head which blew out his brains. He was originally a pupil of the famous violin player, Pinto, and was patronized by Garrick. About 20 years ago he married a sister of Sir Thomas Apreece, who brought him a handsome fortune; but, being much attached to the situation he held, he continued in the theatre 13 years, and quitted the orchestra and the profession together, about 1793. By his wife he had two children, a son and a daughter; the son who is bred up to the church, is now at the university; he will in a short time be possessed of 400 £. a year. About two years ago Mr. C's wife died, since which he has been observed to be much dejected; and, on the night of the last performance of "The Beggar's Opera" at Drury Lane, he told Mr. Shaw that he was very unhappy; he said that, his wife being dead, his son at college, and his daughter at a boarding-school, he was lost for want of society; but, if he could be re-engaged at the theatre, he should recover his wonted spirits. Mr. Shaw promised him the first vacancy. His despondency increased hourly; he appeared much disordered during the whole of last week, frequently walking about his room for hours together. Independent of his own private property, he was allowed 50 £. a year by Sir Thomas Apreece, which was paid quarterly. The fortune of his wife was settled on herself and children. He was free from

any pecuniary embarrassments. In his apartments were found 40 £. in cash, and many valuable articles. The jury brought in a verdict of lunacy.

Coles, William   [*fl.* 1784–1794], oboist.

William Coles was listed by Burney as a "2nd hautbois" among the instrumentalists assisting at the concerts commemorating Handel given alternately at Westminster Abbey and the Pantheon on 26, 27, 29 May and 3, 5 June 1784. Doane's *Musical Directory* gave his address in 1794 as No 2, New Court, Bow Lane, Cheapside, and affirmed that he belonged to the New Musical Fund.

Colinette, Rose. *See* DIDELOT, CHARLES-LOUIS.

Colla, Mrs Giuseppe. *See* AGUIARI, LUCREZIA.

Collard, Mr   [*fl.* 1736], dancer.

A Mr Collard danced a hornpipe on 19 January 1736 at the Haymarket, under the management of Henry Fielding, and also appeared as one of the watchmen in Fielding's *Tumble Down Dick* on 29 April 1736.

Collard, Archangello Corelli   *b.* 1772, violinist, violoncellist.

Archangello Corelli Collard, the son of Philip and Mary Collard, was baptized at Wiveliscombe on 2 July 1772. When he was recommended by F. Chabran for admission to the Royal Society of Musicians on 6 July 1806, it was attested that Collard, violinist and violoncellist, was then a single man of 34 years of age, who had practiced music for upwards of seven years and at the time was engaged at the Opera and was a teacher of music. Collard was unanimously elected to the Society on 5 October 1806, and on 7 June 1807 was ordered to appear at the annual general meeting to explain why he had not attended the rehearsal for the annual concert at St Paul's. His name was on the lists for the St Paul's concerts in 1811, 1812, and 1813. In 1817 and 1818, Collard was a violinist at the King's Theatre together with Cobham and Condell. By 1829, Collard had apparently retired from professional life, and on 4 January of that year he withdrew his name from membership in the Royal Society of Musicians because he was going to reside in the country.

Collard was a member of an important eighteenth-century musical family, best known as musical publishers and makers of musical instruments, located at No 26, Cheapside, as early as 1767. He was related to William Frederick Collard and Frederick William Collard, both of whom were associated with Muzio Clementi in the making of high quality pianofortes. F. W. Collard, who became a freeman of the Worshipfull Company of Musicians on 22 January 1799, took patents as early as 1811 for improvements in these instruments, which carried, successively, the names of Clementi, of Collard & Collard, and of Longman & Broderip. A John Collard, violinist, of Barnstable, Devonshire, and a member of the New Musical Fund in 1794, was no doubt also related. A John Collard, of No 1, Exeter Street, was buried at St Paul, Covent Garden, on 4 May 1841, at age 34.

Collens. *See* COLLINS, CLEMENTINA.

Colles, Mrs Joseph, Hesther, née Boyde [fl. 1776–1780], *actress, singer.*

Hesther Boyde was first noticed in a Drury Lane bill for 10 December 1776, as singing in the funeral procession in *Romeo and Juliet*. That season, in which she was paid £1 5s. per week, she sang three more times in the same piece, at least 28 times in *Harlequin's Invasion*, and 18 times as one of the chorus of spirits in *The Tempest*. Billed as "A Young Gentlewoman," she made her first appearance at the Haymarket

on 19 June 1777 when she acted and sang the title role in the premiere of Colman's *Polly*, and the next day the *Morning Post* identified her as the "Miss Boyde, who filled a very inferior cast of parts last season at Drury Lane." The *Morning Chronicle* of 21 June 1777 confirmed that identification, said that she was from Bath, and added that she was now Mrs Colles, "lately married." For the seventh performance of *Polly* on 9 July 1777, she was called Mrs Colles in the bills.

Also during that summer, under Colman's management at the Haymarket, Mrs Colles played Lady Percy in *1 Henry IV* (24 July and six other times, a production in which Henderson acted Falstaff for the first time in London); Mrs Epigram in *The Advertisement* (9 August); Lucia in *Cato* (14 August); a part in *The Rehearsal* (25 August); Anne Bullen in *Henry VIII* (29 August); Ann Page in *The Merry Wives of Windsor* (3 September); and Lady Grace in *The Provok'd Husband* (19 September).

Returning to Drury Lane in 1777–78, Mrs Colles continued in a similar line of minor and supporting roles for three seasons. In 1777–78 she appeared (with dates of first performance) as: Gymp in *Bon Ton* (31 October); a country girl in *The Elopement* (10 November); Juliet in *Measure for Measure* (13 November); Lady Blanch in *King John* (29 November); Cloris in *The Rehearsal* (13 December); a bacchant in *Cymon* (15 December); Sabina in *The Battle of Hastings* (a new play by Cumberland, 24 January 1778); Ursula in *Much Ado About Nothing* (10 February); Iras in *All for Love* (23 April); Miss Godfrey in *The Lyar* (5 May); and Harriet in *The Jealous Wife*. The last-named was her best (and only featured) role, and was used for her benefit on 16 May 1778, at which she shared a profit of £136 18s. with Chambers and Fawcett.

Continuing with many of the listed roles in 1778–79, she also acted Regan when

HESTHER COLLES, as Polly

by J. Roberts

Henderson first played King Lear in London on 22 March 1779. At her benefit on 19 May 1779 she shared a profit of £120 15s. with the Widow Legg and Miss Kirby. In 1779–80 she acted the Player Queen in *Hamlet* (18 September), Mrs Williams in *The Times* (a new play by Elizabeth Griffith, 2 December), Lady Charlotte in *High Life Below Stairs* (8 December), and Lamorce in *The Inconstant* (3 April). For her benefit on 6 May 1780, when she played Arabella in *The Committee* for the first time, she shared profits of £113 4s. 6d. with Abrams and Miss Kirby. At the time she lived at Smith's, No 10, Bow Street, the corner of Martlet Court, Covent Garden.

No doubt she was the Hesther Colles, wife of Joseph Colles, whose son Thomas was christened at St Paul, Covent Garden, on 16 August 1779.

A colored drawing by J. Roberts (1778)

of Mrs Colles as Polly is in the British Museum.

Collet, Mr [*fl.* 1729–1734], *actor.*

A Mr Collet was a member of the company at Goodman's Fields Theatre from 1729–30 through 1733–34, playing a wide variety of roles but specializing in low comedy. He made his first recorded appearance on 31 October 1729 as Brazen in *The Recruiting Officer.* In that season he also acted Scrub in *The Stratagem*, Polydore in *The Orphan*, Jeremy in *Love for Love*, Squib in *Tunbridge Walks,* Bellmore in *Jane Shore*, Sir Francis in *The Busy Body*, Gomez in *The Spanish Fryar*, Daniel in *Oroonoko*, Obadiah in *A Bold Stroke for a Wife*, Setter in *The Old Bachelor*, Hector in *The Gamester*, Antonio in *Venice Preserv'd*, Charino in *Love Makes a Man*, Teague in *The Committee*, Old Mirabel in *The Inconstant*, Pearmain in *The Recruiting Officer*, Smugler in *The Constant Couple*, and Shallow in *The Merry Wives of Windsor.*

Collet continued in many of the above roles for the time of his tenure at Goodman's Fields, and in the next four years he also added Moody in *The Provok'd Wife*, Vulture in *Woman's a Riddle*, Perriwinkle in *A Bold Stroke for a Wife*, Bardolph in *1 Henry IV*, Coxen in *The Fair Quaker*, Foresight in *Love for Love*, an Old Woman in *Rule a Wife and Have a Wife*, Sir Jealous in *The Busy Body*, Polonius in *Hamlet*, Butler in *The Devil of a Wife*, Boor in the *Royal Merchant*, Sir Thomas in *Flora*, Tipkin in *The Tender Husband*, Indent in *The Fair Quaker*, Trifle in *The Fashionable Lady*, Lucius in *Cato*, Burgundy in *King Lear*, Porter in *The Pilgrim*, Sir William in *Love's Last Shift*, Testimony in *Sir Courtly Nice*, Granieus in *The Cynick*, Butler in *The Drummer*, Sancho in *The Rover*, Sir Avarice in *The Temple Beau*, Mustacha in *Tom Thumb*, Solomon in *The Double Gallant*, Clinch in *The Man's Bewitch'd*, a Witch in *Macbeth*, Menander in *Sopho-*

nisha, Ventoso in *The Tempest*, Father in *Father Girard*, Diego in *She Wou'd and She Wou'd Not*, Micher in *The Stage Coach Opera*, the Lieutenant in *Richard III*, a Citizen in *Julius Caesar*, Sealand in *The Conscious Lovers*, Jemmy in *The Beggar's Opera*, Corydon in *Damon and Phillida*, Justice Bridleman in *The Decoy*, Harry in *The Mock Doctor*, and Sly in *Love's Last Shift*.

In the summer of 1730, Collet performed Justice Gripeall in *Mad Tom of Bedlam* at Tottenham Court Fair and Jack Straw in *Wat Tyler and Jack Straw* at Bartholomew Fair. At the Tottenham Court Fair in August 1731, he acted Wantbrains in *Amurath* and Scrip in *Phebe*.

A Mrs Collet was a member of a company which played *The Beggar's Opera* at the Theatre in St Augustine's Back in Bristol about 1729.

Collet, Mr [fl. 1770–1771], *actor*.

A Mr Collet acted an officer in a performance of *Douglas* at the Haymarket on 21 November 1770. He and Mrs Collet joined Foote's summer company in 1771 at the Haymarket, where Collet acted the minor characters of Cobb in *Every Man in His Humour* (17 May), one of the mob in *The Mayor of Garratt* (20 May), Obadiah in *A Bold Stroke for a Wife* (27 May), the Constable in *The Provok'd Wife* (5 June), Jonathan in *The Brothers* (10 June), and a Watchman in *The Upholsterer* (28 August). On 16 September 1771 he shared benefit tickets with Fearon, Mrs Granger, Dancer, and Mrs Didier.

Possibly this Mr Collet was the father of Miss Catherine Collet, who was a child performer at Drury Lane as early as 1767.

Collet, Mr [fl. 1785–1822?], *dancer, singer, equestrian, machinist?*

A Master Collet, who may have been the younger brother of the dancer and actress Catherine Collet, was dancing and singing at Astley's Amphitheatre as early as 1785.

He was on the company list for 1788, and on 6 May 1791, he offered, with others, exhibitions of tumbling and also performed in a new musical piece, *The Irish Fair*. At Astley's in 1793 he appeared in the pantomime *Foret Noire, or, the Natural Son* on 31 January and performed feats of horsemanship on 21 August. Still billed as Master Collet, he performed one of the haymakers in *Harlequin Invincible* on 22 August 1795.

A Mr Collet, presumably the grown-up Master Collet, performed at the Royal Circus in May 1800 and August 1801. On 8 October 1804 he danced his "Military Hornpipe"—for that night only—his first appearance of the season. Probably he was the same Collet who devised machinery at the Royal Circus in 1803, with Honour, Male, and Rust. As machinist, he was also on the bills of *The Rival Statues, or Harlequin Humourist* (April) and *Louisa of Lombardy* (May). A Mr Collet was on the Drury Lane pay list in 1821–22 at £1 10s. per week.

Collet, Mrs [Ann?] [fl. 1765–1771], *actress, singer*.

A Mrs Collet sang under the auspices of Thomas Lowe at Marylebone Gardens in the summer of 1765. She may have been the same Mrs Collet who, with her husband, was a member of Foote's summer company at the Haymarket in 1771. That Mrs Collet made her first appearance as Harriet in *The Upholsterer* on 22 May. Her other roles that summer included a part in *The Lame Lovers*, Arabella in *The Author*, Mrs Prim in *A Bold Stroke for a Wife*, Mrs Subtle in *The Englishman in Paris*, Dolly in *The Commissary*, Bianca in *Catherine and Petruchio*, Lucy in *The Brothers*, Miss Godfrey in *The Lyar*, Miss Linnet in *The Maid of Bath* (a new play by Foote, on 26 June 1771), Lady Loverule in *The Devil to Pay*, Melissa in *The Lying Valet*, an unspecified part in *Dido*, Madge in *Love in a Village*, Lady Grace in *The*

Provok'd Wife, Tag in *Miss in her Teens,* and Nerissa in *The Merchant of Venice.*

A Mrs Collet was listed in the Drury Lane account books for 1774–75 as a dancer, but that entry was probably intended to refer to Miss Catherine Collet; it is possible, however, that Mrs Collet was Catherine's mother and that her Christian name was Ann. On 27 May 1767, the treasury of Drury Lane paid an Ann Collet £10 10*s.* for a gold brocaded silk.

Collet, Catherine, later Mrs Tetherington *[fl. 1767–1800], dancer, actress.*

The theatrical career of Miss Catherine Collet (or Collett), which spanned at least 34 years, began when she appeared as a child dancer in the ensemble of the initial performance of *Cymon* on 2 January 1767. Garrick's enormously successful spectacular enjoyed numerous performances for the rest of the season. She also filled the roles of the young Duke of York in *Richard III* on 11 April 1767 and Grotilla in *Edgar and Emmaline* on 29 April; and she danced a minuet with Miss Giorgi on 8, 16, and 26 May, at which times the bills stated she was a scholar of Signor Giorgi, the dancing master. Miss Collet filled a repertory of young people's roles for most of her career, graduating eventually to those minor supporting parts of youngish women in the comic afterpieces. In 1767–68 she again performed the Duke of York and her dancing role in *Cymon.* She played the title role in *Queen Mab* and Robin in *The Merry Wives of Windsor,* as well as dancing parts in *Harlequin's Invasion* and *Daphne and Amintor,* the latter piece being performed before the King of Denmark in a special program on 18 August 1768.

Her other roles, typical of her line, through 1782–83 included little Lord William in *The Countess of Salisbury,* Pages in *1 Henry IV* and *The Orphan,* parts in *The Rehearsal, The Register Office,* and *Pigmy Revels,* and chorus roles in *The Christmas*

Tale, the procession in *Romeo and Juliet, St Helena, The Tempest, Macbeth,* and *The Camp.* She also played Billy Violet in Dr Arne's *The Rose,* Fleance in *Macbeth,* a country girl in *The Elopement,* Fatima in the first performance of the new musical piece, *Selima and Azor* (on 18 October 1776), Louisa in *The Deserter,* a Nymph in *Comus,* a principal character in the original performance of *The Wonders of Derbyshire* (30 September 1779), Clara in *Rule a Wife,* Gillian in *The Quaker,* Lucinda in *Love in a Village,* a niece in the first performance of Sheridan's *The Critic* (30 October 1779), Diana in *A School for Fathers,* Theodosia in *The Maid of the Mill,* Spitfire in *The Times,* a new mainpiece by Elizabeth Griffith (3 December 1779), and Columbine in both *Fortunatus* and *The Genii.* She sang in the gala *Fête Champêtre* which was performed in *The Maid of the Oaks* (28 February 1780). Miss Collet also danced at Sadler's Wells in 1773, 1775, and 1779, and at Bristol in 1771.

On 10 July 1772, the Drury Lane treasury paid out £2 8*s.* 10*d.* for "Miss Collet's schooling," probably for coaching she received in dancing or singing. Her name was put in the Drury Lane fund book for subscriptions of 10*s.* 6*d.* in 1775 and 1779, and on 20 March 1775, the theatre gave her, "per order," a gratuity of £5 5*s.* Her salary in 1776–77 was £1 5*s.* per week.

By 1780–81 she had grown out of adolescence into young womanhood. On 24 January 1781 she sang the title role in Arne's *Artaxerxes* for the first time; by 1782–83 she was found in such roles as the flirtatious chambermaid in *The Clandestine Marriage,* Myrtilla in *The Provok'd Husband,* Melissa in *The Lying Valet,* Lucinda (with a song) in *The Englishman in Paris,* Bridget in *Too Civil by Half* and *Every Man in His Humour,* Jenny Diver in *The Beggar's Opera,* and Nerissa in *The Merchant of Venice.* On 6 December 1782, Miss Collet danced a minuet with Williamson.

After 1782–83, Miss Collet's name disappeared from the London theatre bills for four years, during which time she may have toured the provinces. On 22 February 1787, however, she returned to Drury Lane to sing Lucy in *The Beggar's Opera*, and two days later her name was added to the pay list for 13*s.* 4*d.* per day. During the balance of the season, she performed Diana in *A School for Fathers*, Alice in *The Strangers at Home*, Margery in *Love in a Village*, and Jenny in *The Deserter*. She continued in a similar line at the same salary the next season and in the summer of 1788 was engaged at the Haymarket, where she made her first appearance on 11 June as Lucy in *The Beggar's Opera*.

Her other roles that summer were Patty in *Inkle and Yarico*, Mary in *The Prisoner at Large*, Araminta in *The Young Spectator*, Emma in *Peeping Tom*, Gillian in *The Quaker*, Miss Plumb in *Gretna Green*, Inis in *A Key to the Lock*, Comfit in *The Dead Alive*, and Tatlanthe in *Chrononhotonthologos*. She was back at Drury Lane in 1788–89, but by then her usefulness to the theatre seems to have greatly diminished, for she appeared only a few times: as Lesbia in *Selina and Azor* (14 October 1788) and singing in choruses to *Macbeth* (16 October) and to *Romeo and Juliet* (17 November). But when *Romeo and Juliet* was repeated on 11 May 1789, Miss Hagley was singing in her place, and on 18 May Miss Collet's name was taken off the pay list.

What happened to Miss Collet for some 10 years after she left Drury Lane is not known, but perhaps she performed at Sadler's Wells during this period for which very few bills of that theatre have survived. Some time after her departure from Drury Lane in 1789, she married a Mr Tetherington, apparently not a performer. According to the Dublin *Public Register* he had died in Fleet Prison a few days before 26 November 1796. In 1800, as Mrs Tetherington, she was a member of the company at Sadler's Wells and was noted in the *Memoirs* of the young Charles Dibdin as "formerly Miss Collet, a celebrated Columbine of the Theatres Royal."

Catherine Collet may have been the daughter of the Mr Collet (fl. 1770–1771) and Mrs Collet (fl. 1765–1771) who performed at London in 1770–71. Indeed, many of the roles which Mrs Collet acted in Foote's company at the Haymarket in the summer of 1771 later were found in the young Miss Collet's repertory at Drury Lane. She may also have been related to the Mr Collet (fl. 1785–1804), who danced at Sadler's Wells as Master Collet in 1785.

Collet, John   [fl. 1754?–1770], violinist.

Although he probably made earlier appearances, John Collet was first noticed as a violinst in a performance of the *Messiah* at the Chapel of the Foundling Hospital in May 1754, for which he was paid 15 shillings. He played in a similar concert there, at the same salary, on 27 April 1758. In 1763, John Collet was listed by *Mortimer's London Directory* as living in Queen Street, Golden Square. At London in 1770 he published six solos for the violin, with a thorough bass for harp.

The violinist may have been either the John Collet who, according to the *Whitehall Evening Post* for 9 July 1771, had died "lately" in Good Street or the John Collet whose will was proved at London on 29 January 1771, by oath of his son, John Collet.

Collet, Richard   [fl. 1737–1767], violinist.

Richard Collet made his first noticed appearance playing the violin at Hickford's Room on 24 March 1737, for his own benefit, but very likely he had been active in London concert circles before that date. On the same program were Vincent, the harpsichordist, and Valentine Snow, the trumpeter. Bills and notices of subsequent concerts did not always provide a first name, and in some instances the Collet listed may not have been Richard but either John or Thomas, also violinists and certainly related to Richard. Probably Richard was the Collet who played the violin at Castle Tavern on 2 May 1737 for the benefit of the singer William Savage. A Collet played at Hickford's Room on 5 February 1741 for the benefit of John Lyne, at the Haymarket on 26 February 1741 for the benefit of Snow, and at Drury Lane on 16 April 1741.

When the Royal Society of Musicians was instituted by a "Declaration of Trust" on 28 August 1739, Richard Collet was listed among the charter members. By 1745 he was considered one of the principal English performers on the violin. "His tone was full, clear, and smooth, and his hand strong," in the words of Dr Burney, but "having neither taste nor knowledge of Music he always remained an inelegant player."

In 1745 he was leader of the band at Vauxhall Gardens, a position he held at least until 1748 and probably beyond. On 29 February 1748, a Mr Collet played first violin for a concert at the Haymarket. By 1753 Richard Collet was in the band at Drury Lane; *Midwife, or Old Woman's Magazine* (1751–53) told of Collet, like Orpheus, tweedling Harlequin into existence by his playing—"his Skill has the desired Effect, and Harlequin comes to Life gradually to a very pretty tune, and in exceeding good Time." In 1763, he was listed as "Richard Collet Senior" (suggesting a younger Richard Collet) and as the first violinist at Drury Lane Theatre by *Mortimer's London Directory*. He was still working there on 28 February 1767, when the theatre paid him and Johnston a total of £41 4s. 6d. for their "Music Bill." A Collet had a benefit with Legg and Miss Davis at Marylebone Gardens on 6 August 1765.

On 4 December 1785, a Miss Isabel Collet (perhaps Richard Collet's granddaughter?) was bound by the Royal Society of Musicians to an unspecified person, and the Society voted to pay for her room, board, washing and other necessities. On 4 December 1791, the Society was informed by her mistress that Isabel had served her apprenticeship with "industry and fidelity."

Collet, Thomas [*fl.* 1739–1743], *musician.*

Thomas Collet was one of the charter members of the Royal Society of Musicians when it was established in a "Declaration of Trust" on 28 August 1739. On 15 March 1743 he shared a benefit with Bosch, Carter, and Gair at Lincoln's Inn Fields Theatre. Several of the notices mentioned in the entry of Richard Collet may refer to Thomas.

Colley, Mr [*fl.* 1774–1784], *house servant.*

A Mr Colley was a minor house servant at Covent Garden from as early as 1774–75 and through 1783–84, sharing benefit tickets in each season with other minor personnel.

Collier, Mr [*fl.* 1725?–1731], *actor, dancer.*

A Mr Collier is recorded in a single performance in the London area, that of 8 September 1731 at the Great Theatrical Booth in Half-Moon Inn Yard, during the time of Southwark Fair. He played and danced the harlequin part of Merlin in the pantomime *The British Enchanters*. He may have been the Collier who played at Norwich off and on from 1725 through 1728.

Collier, J. [*fl.* 1702], *orator.*

At Stationers' Hall on 7 May 1702 was presented a concert for the benefit of "Poor Decay'd Gentlemen, and Maintenance of a School for the Education of Youth" in which one of the features was an oration by one J. Collier, M.A.

Collier, William [fl. 1709–1714], proprietor.

William Collier was a barrister, a Member of Parliament for Truro from 1713 to 1715, a shareholder in the Drury Lane Theatre, an "Inspector of the Playhouses," and a Gentleman of the Privy Chamber to Queen Anne. He had considerable influence at court, a casual mercenary interest in theatre, and was, according to Colley Cibber, "a lawyer of an enterprising head and jovial heart."

When Christopher Rich was forced to close the doors of Drury Lane because of his oppressive management in 1709, Collier offered the investors £4 instead of £3 rent per day and was given a license to reopen the playhouse. On 19 November 1709 Sir James Stanley wrote Collier that Queen Anne had approved of Collier's producing plays beginning 23 November and that Collier was "not to suffer Mr. Rich or any other person" to be in any way concerned with the management. Armed with this authority, Collier gathered the players on 22 November for a celebration around a bonfire in front of the theatre. The players entered the playhouse, apparently forcibly, and found that the wily Rich had run off with the costumes. At the reopening of the theatre the next day, *Aureng-Zebe* was played with the actors wearing their own clothes.

Having no managerial experience, Collier turned over the operation of Drury Lane to Aaron Hill and a committee of seven actors. The 1709–10 season was not a prosperous one. The company was torn by fights between Hill and the actors, and in mid-season the public's attention was drawn to the trial of Dr Sacheverel. So Collier decided to make a trade with Owen Swiney at the Queen's Theatre in the Haymarket; Swiney signed a new agreement with Wilks, Cibber, and Doggett at Drury Lane on 6 November 1710, and Collier took over the control of the Queen's Theatre and its opera company. Collier arranged to have himself paid £200 annually by the Drury Lane management, since it was understood that opera would not make as much money as plays. He also persuaded the Drury Lane managers not to perform on Wednesdays in competition with opera performances. Having arranged all this, Collier then farmed out the management of the Queen's Theatre to Aaron Hill for an estimated £600 per year.

But Collier was no happier at the Queen's than he had been at Drury Lane. With the aid of Sir John Vanbrugh he arranged on 17 April 1712 for a new license, putting Swiney again in charge of the opera house, with Collier again acting as proprietor of Drury Lane. The new bargain he drove with Cibber, Wilks, and Doggett, who ran the company for him, brought him £600 yearly "neat Money," plus £100 of the £200 annually which he had previously received as the opera proprietor. The actors offered him an equal share in the company, but Collier rather stupidly turned that down in favor of the assured £700. Cibber noted that Collier might have earned £1000 as a sharer.

The trio of actors chafed under the new arrangement, and when Barton Booth, using *his* considerable court connections, forced his way into the Drury Lane management, the players stopped paying Collier his annual fee. Before Collier had a chance to go to litigation, fate took matters in hand. With the death of Queen Anne in 1714, a new patent had to be drawn up. The actors reasoned that if they had to put up with a costly inactive partner, they would prefer anyone to Collier. They approached Sir Richard Steele, knowing that all they needed was to have Collier's name quietly replaced by Steele's on the new license. Steele applied to the Duke of Marlborough, the Duke procured a new license on 18 October 1714, and William Collier, fleeced again, disappeared from the theatrical world.

Collin. *See* COLLINS.

Collings, Mr ₁*fl. 1792–1804*₁, *actor, scene painter.*

A Mr Collings played the second officer in a production of *Othello* in a specially licensed performance at the Haymarket on 6 February 1792. He perhaps was the Mr Collings who was paid £8 15*s*. by Drury Lane on 3 May 1794 for "Painting the Flies"—i.e., the backdrops. The name appeared again on the Drury Lane pay list in 1803–4.

Collingwood, S. ₁*fl. 1794*₁, *singer.*

Mr S. Collingwood was listed in 1794 by Doane's *Musical Directory* as a bass, living at Woolwich, Kent, a member of the Handelian Society, and a singer in the Handelian performances at Westminster Abbey.

Collingwood, William ₁*fl. 1793–1794*₁, *singer.*

William Collingwood was listed in 1794 by Doane's *Musical Directory* as a tenor, living in Church Street, Greenwich, a member of the Choral Fund and the Handelian Society, a singer at the Oxford Meeting in 1793, and a participant in the Handelian performances at Westminster Abbey.

Collins, Mr ₁*fl. 1771*₁, *actor.*

A Mr Collins acted three times in specially licensed performances at the Haymarket in the spring of 1771: Belcour in *The West Indian* on 15 April, the title role in *Athelwold* on 24 April, and Lopez in the afterpiece of *The Wrangling Lovers* on 17 May. The Mrs Collins who acted Miss Rusport in the same performance of *The West Indian* presumably was his wife. This Mrs Collins also played ingenue roles in Foote's company at the Haymarket that summer, including Tag in *Miss in her Teens* on 26 June 1771, Bell in *The Deuce is in Him* on 8 July, Iris in *Dido* on 24 July, Mrs Fulmer in *The West Indian* on 26 July, Araminta in *The Old Batchelor* on 2 September, and a part in a new mock tragedy, *Madrigal and Truletta,* on 18 September.

Collins, Mrs ₁*fl. 1771*₁, *actress. See* COLLINS, MR ₁*fl. 1771*₁.

Collins, Mr ₁*fl. 1774–1781*₁, *doorkeeper, supernumerary.*

The name of a Mr Collins was put on the Drury Lane list for 1774–75 as a supernumerary, with no salary given. Probably he was the same Collins who was a stage doorkeeper there from at least 1775–76 through 1780–81. He probably died soon after the latter season, for on 26 May 1783, the "Widow Collins" shared in benefit tickets with Drury Lane house servants.

Collins, Charles ₁*fl. 1667–1670*₁, *scenekeeper.*

Charles Collins was listed on a Lord Chamberlain's warrant dated 29 May 1668 as a scenekeeper in the King's Company at the Bridges Street Theatre. He was with the company for the 1667–68 through the 1669–70 seasons and probably earlier and later as well.

Collins, Clementina, ₁née Hayward?₁, later **Mrs Thomas Woodfall** ₁*fl. 1776–1837*₁, *actress.*

According to a brief memoir in the 1790 edition of *The Secret History of the Green Room,* Clementina Collins's birthplace was at Perth, she being the only actress then "in London who was born North of the Tweed." The 1804 edition of *Authentic Memoirs of the Green Room* gave her birthplace as Edinburgh. Miss Collins was reportedly the daughter of a linen draper who turned actor; he played in Scotland in

William Fisher's company, which he served also as a carpenter. He was probably the J. Collins who performed at Scarborough and Margate and who was at the Haymarket in 1782.

Clementina's mother was also an actress in Scotland. Presumably she was the Mrs Collins who acted at Covent Garden on 16 July 1790. Some confusion, however, is created by several notices which occurred at the time Clementina married Thomas Woodfall in 1796. The *Oracle* of 16 March 1796 announced the marriage of Miss Collins to Thomas Woodfall on 12 March 1796 at St Andrew, Holborn. The marriage register of St Andrew's for this date, however, identified her as Clementina Hayward, spinster, of York. That Clementina was Miss Collins's first name is established by a notation in the Winston copy of the Drury Lane fundbook, when she subscribed 10s. 6d. in 1791. The real family name perhaps was Hayward, with the name "Collins" being adopted by her parents for professional reasons.

Miss Collins, at any event, acted as a child at York in 1776. Her mother was a member of the same company. Probably the young girl acted wherever her itinerant parents took her—Liverpool in 1776, York again in 1776, 1777, and 1778, Bristol in 1778, Edinburgh in 1783 and 1784, and Ludlow also in 1784. On 26 April 1785, Miss Collins made her first appearance at Drury Lane in the girlish role of Maria in *The Citizen*. It was her only appearance of the season. She played Cordelia at Richmond on 26 September 1785, for the benefit of Waldron, and then took up an engagement at Drury Lane which was to last for ten years, during which period she played a variety of supporting roles in tragedy, farce, and pantomime but specialized in young secondary or tertiary women in the comic afterpieces.

Her roles in her two earliest full seasons were typical: Clarissa in *All in the Wrong* (26 October 1785), Inis in *The Wonder* (31 October 1785), (walking as) Cordelia in *The Jubilee* procession (18 November 1785), Arethusa in *Philaster* (1 December 1785), Nanette in *Hurly-Burly* (19 January 1786), Cleone in *The Distrest Mother* (4 March 1786, with Mrs Siddons as Hermione), Maria in *Twelfth Night* (9 May 1786), Diana in *The Humourist* (19 September 1786), Rosara in *She Wou'd and She Wou'd Not* (10 October 1786), Harriet in *The Miser* (30 October 1786), Lucilla in *The Fair Penitent* (18 November 1786), Sukey Chitterlin in *Harlequin's Invasion* (26 December 1786), Charlotte in *The First Floor* (13 January 1787), Serina in *The Orphan* (7 February 1787), Charlotte in *Who's the Dupe?* (17 April 1787), and Ninny in *The Distrest Baronet* (3 May 1787). On 22 May 1787, she also played at Covent Garden as Serina in *The Orphan*. In the summer of 1786 she acted at Liverpool, taking £10 10s. in her benefit there.

In 1789–90, Miss Collins's salary at Drury Lane was £3 per week, the figure at which it stood during the rest of her stay there. *The Secret History of the Green Room* (1795) described her:

tall, of a fair complexion, and very handsome; nor have we yet heard that she has been contaminated by the morals of the Green-Room, which may be principally attributed to her mother's precaution, under whose care she lives. . . . Her voice is very well calculated for a Theatre; but there is a continual grin on her countenance both in Comedy and Tragedy, which, however she may imagine it sets off her charms, greatly lessens her merit as an Actress; but . . . she is very young . . .

Of her performance as Princess Catherine in *Henry V* on 1 October 1789, one critic wrote that, despite the role having been shortened to about a dozen lines, it "was nevertheless, by Miss Collins, kept forward in the drama, and preserved an air of consequence." It was generally agreed that, in the short parts she sustained, "her exertions have been approved."

In 1789–90, Miss Collins added to her repertoire: Mincing in *The Way of the World*, Kitty Sprightly in *All the World's a Stage*, Matilda in *Arthur and Emmaline*, Lucy Weldon in *Oroonoko*, Peggy in *The Miller of Mansfield*, Emily in *Cross Purposes*, Charlotte in *The Apprentice*, Sophia in *The Deaf Lover*, Florival in *The Deuce is in Him*, and Harriet Bramble in *The Adventurers*. On 16 June 1790 she again appeared at Covent Garden when she acted Alithea in *The Country Girl* for the benefit of the Widow Fearon.

A notice in *The World* of 27 October 1788 indicated that on 25 October Miss Collins had married a Mr W. Spencer at Lee, in Kent. Confirmation of this marriage is lacking; no record can be found in the register of the Lee Church. During the summer of 1792 the actress performed at Richmond, where she lived, it was said, with the actor Matthew Williames (d. 1801), leading *The Secret History of the Green Room* (1792) to believe "that matrimony it is supposed will result." The supposition proved false.

In the summer of 1794 she played at Bristol and Bath and then returned for her last season at Drury Lane, making her final appearance at that theatre as the First Constantia in *The Chances* on 6 June 1795. A selected list of her other roles at Drury Lane follows: the Niece in *The Critic*, Miss Godfrey in *The Haunted Tower*, both Aurora and Marcella in *The Pannel*, Donna Anna in *Don Juan*, Charlotte's Maid in *High Life Below Stairs*, Jenny in *The Provok'd Husband*, Lady Anne in *Richard III*, Blanch in *King John*, Agatha in *Henry VIII*, Venus in *Neptune's Prophecy*, Miss Tintem in *The Dupes of Fancy*, Lurewell in *The Constant Couple*, Cherry in *The Beaux' Stratagem*, Mrs Blandish in *The Heiress*, the Widow Brady in *The Irish Widow* (when Mrs Goodall was ill on 3 November 1792, and according to the *Thespian Maga-*

zine, December 1792: "the Farce should have been changed, for Poor Miss Collins was a lamentable Mrs Brady; before the second act was half over, the greater part of the audience quitted the theatre"), Dorinda and Miranda in *The Tempest*, Clara in *Cheats of Scapin*, Phoebe and Celia in *As You Like It*, Young Lady Lambert in *The Hypocrite*, Miss Godfrey in *The Lyar*, Lady Lydia Graveairs in *Anna*, Nerissa in *The Merchant of Venice*, Harriet in *False Colours*, Susan in *The Mariners*, Aurelia in *The Female Duellist*, Lady Grace in *The Provok'd Husband*, Anna in *Douglas* (on 4 October 1795, with Mrs Siddons as Matilda), Fatima in *The Siege of Belgrade*, a character in *Nobody*, Lucy in *The Devil to Pay*, Mrs Foresight in *Love for Love*, Corinna in *The Confederacy*, Diana in *The Triumph of Hymen*, Flora in *She Wou'd and She Wou'd Not*, Angelica in *The Constant Couple*, and the Duchess in *The Deserter*. On 20 May 1795, preceding the mainpiece of *The Country Girl* (in which she acted Alithea), Miss Collins danced with the D'Egvilles.

Miss Collins returned to Richmond in the summer of 1795 and in the winter joined the company at York, where on 31 December 1795 (as "Miss Collins of Drury Lane") she acted Lady Townly in *The Provok'd Husband*. At that time the *Monthly Mirror* (December 1795) reported that although "struggling even with her own resolution" to cross the Atlantic, she still preferred "Old England" to the distant though hospitable shores of America. This notice tempts one to suppose some connection with the Mr and Mrs Collins who made their first appearance on the American stage at Boston in September 1794, but no evidence suggests these Collinses as Clementina's parents. Indeed, the reason given by the *Monthly Mirror* for Miss Collins's reluctance to leave England ("Friends—kindred—country—all at once to quit")—would suggest that her parents were still in "Old England" and not in New

England. She, however, did not go to America, for, as noted above, on 12 March 1796 she married Thomas Woodfall, the publisher and the printer of bills for the theatres. He was the son of William Woodfall (1746–1803), proprietor of the *Public Advertiser*, publisher of the letters of "Junius," and also founder of the *Morning Chronicle*. Using the name of Adams, William Woodfall had acted in Scotland as a member of Fisher's company at the time Miss Collins's parents were also there.

Upon her marriage Clementina Woodfall retired from the stage for six years. In the summer of 1803 she returned to act under the name of Woodfall as a member of Colman's company at the Haymarket, playing Lady Percy in *1 Henry IV*, Zorayda in *The Mountaineers*, Isabel in *The Voice of Nature*, Melissa in *The Lying Valet*, and a role in *The Maid of Bristol*. Her extended illness in the summer of 1804 prevented her acting for Colman's company in that season, but Mrs Woodfall continued to act in the Haymarket summer company, on occasion, through 1810. Her sister-in-law, Sophia Woodfall, later Mrs John McGibbon, who acted at Edinburgh and Nottingham, also was at the Haymarket from 1804 to 1810. Mrs Woodfall was known still to be alive in 1837.

Collins, J. ₁*fl. 1763–1792*₁, *actor, carpenter.*

Mr J. Collins spent almost all of his professional life as an actor in the provinces, performing in Edinburgh, it seems, by 1763 and remaining there in William Fisher's company at least through 1771. He was probably the Collins who, according to various green-room memoirs, had first been a linen draper and then served Fisher's company as a carpenter as well as an actor. His wife also acted with him in Scotland and her name was found in the bills at the various provincial places where Collins performed. They were the parents of the London actress, Clementina Collins (fl. 1776–1837), and their real name may have been Hayward.

Collins seems to have specialized in playing old men. His only roles known at Edinburgh, however, were Ramilie in *The Miser* on 30 June 1764 and Sir Jealous Traffick in *The Busy Body* on 19 November 1770. He acted at Birmingham in the summer of 1776, and from 12 October through 20 December of that year he was performing at Liverpool for a salary of £1 7s. per week. Probably he was the "Collin" who performed clown roles at Bristol in 1778–79.

The only known performances by J. Collins at London were in the summer of 1782, when he acted a masquerade character of "Reviving Death" in *Harlequin Teague* on 17 August and 22 subsequent times. Collins was back at Edinburgh, acting in Jackson's company, between 1782 and 1784. He was at Norwich from 1785 to 1787 and at Plymouth in 1789. On 10 July 1792, when the new Theatre Royal at Margate opened under the direction of Wilmot Wells, Collins was a member of the company. According to the *Thespian Dictionary* (1805), for many years Collins acted low comedy roles at Exeter and Scarborough and "latterly at Margate, where he died and was interred." Collins resembled the actor William Parsons in feature and figure, "of which he was not a little vain; but here the resemblance ends." He showed merit in several parts, and was, it was said, an honest man. There is no evident connection between J. Collins and the two performers named Collins who acted in America, one making his debut in Boston in 1794 and the other at New York in 1797.

Collins, Mrs J. ₁*fl. 1770–1796*₁, *actress.*

Mrs J. Collins, wife of the actor J. Collins (fl. 1763–1792) and mother of the London actress Clementina Collins (fl. 1776–1837), was acting at Edinburgh by

1770–71. She was performing at York from 1773 to 1777 and was at Birmingham in 1775 and at Liverpool in the winter of 1776, where she was paid 18*s.* per week. She was at Edinburgh again in 1781 and perhaps was the Mrs Collins who acted at Belfast in 1787, at Kilkenny, Waterford, and Wexford in 1792, at Wexford again in 1793, and at Galway in 1795.

Mrs Collins made at least one appearance in London, as Flora in *She Wou'd and She Wou'd Not*, at a benefit given for Lee Lewes at Covent Garden on 16 July 1790. Evidently she lived in London for some time between 1789 and 1796, caring for her young daughter, Clementina, an attractive actress at Drury Lane.

Collins, John *c. 1725–c. 1757, scene painter, landscape painter.*

John Collins was born about 1725. In his earlier career he enjoyed the patronage of the Duke of Ancaster, the Marquis of Exeter, and others, who sent him to travel and study in Italy. Upon his return, according to the *Gentleman's Magazine*, he painted scenery for one of the principal London theatres, probably Covent Garden, in the 1750s. When the new theatre at Norwich opened on 31 January 1758, it was announced by the Norwich *Gazette* (28 January 1758) that the scenes, "so highly finish'd and executed," had been painted by "the late ingenious Mr. Collins" and were "accounted far superior to any of the kind."

In addition to his theatrical scenes, Collins painted Roman landscapes in a romantic style. The most notable were in a set of views from Tasso's *Gerusalemme liberata*. Engravings of these were done by Sandby, E. Rooker, and P. C. Canot.

Collins died at a silversmith's house in Henrietta Street, Covent Garden, in late 1757 or in January 1758. "His death was occasioned by some neglect after taking Dr James's powders," stated the *Gentleman's Magazine*, "in an infectious fever caught by a visit to a comedian, one of his intimate acquaintance." Collins left a wife and two children.

Collins, John *1742–1808, monologuist, actor, singer, poet, publisher.*

John Collins, known in his time as "Brush" Collins because of his evening's entertainment of song and monologue called *The Evening Brush*, was born at Bath in 1742, the son of a tailor. After an apprenticeship to a staymaker, Collins turned to the stage, making his first appearance in his native city, where he developed an extensive repertoire of roles "extending to tragedy, genteel comedy, low comedy, and old men and country boys in farces and opera." He may have been the Collins who acted at Birmingham in July 1762. Several years later, announced as from Edinburgh, he acted Mirabel in *The Inconstant* at Smock Alley, Dublin, in October 1764, and in a variety of parts he soon proved "a very respectable acquisition to the Irish stage." Probably he was the Collins who was with Roger Kemble's touring company at Coventry in August 1766 and at Bath from 18 September 1767. A manuscript notebook record of Kemble's company, in the Harvard Theatre Collection, reveals Collins's unpredictability at the time; Kemble noted that, on 30 April 1768, Collins suddenly left the company— "being his second disappearance in that Character in Bath."

Presumably it was John Collins whom the Duchess of Portland had sent round to see Garrick for an audition and interview in October 1767. Garrick wrote to her on the twenty-ninth of that month that he had assured a Mr Collins that at the end of the season he would examine his qualifications. "I think he has the most unpromising Aspect for an Actor I ever saw—a small pair of unmeaning Eyes stuck in a round unthinking face are not the most desirable requisites for a Hero, or a fine Gentleman," wrote Garrick. Despite the influence of the

JOHN COLLINS
frontispiece to his *Scripscrapologia* (1804)

artist unknown

Duchess, Collins was not engaged. In his *Memoirs*, Charles Lee Lewes stated that Collins had played Captain Plume in *The Recruiting Officer* at Covent Garden "many years ago" but had suffered a severe cold which had marred success and sent him back to the provinces. No record, however, of such an appearance is found by us in the bills, and Lewes perhaps was confusing him with William Collins, who was at Covent Garden from 1747 to 1762, or another Collins who was at the Haymarket in 1771.

Collins soon evolved a particular type of theatrical entertainment of pleasant stories and songs, similar to acts found in cabarets today. He refined the monologuist's art first made popular by G. A. Stevens's *Lecture Upon Heads* into a most engaging program of music and poetry, with most of the lyrics written by himself and punctuated with imitations of the most famous stage personalities of the time. Endowed with different names at different periods, the program remained essentially the same in format. In 1775 it was called his "Lecture Upon Oratory," which he gave at the Devil Tavern, London. Dr Thomas Campbell of Clogher, a visitor to London at the time, went to the performance and noted in his *Diary* that "the fellow displayed good enunciation and good sense" and that his ridiculing of the Scots, Irish, and Welsh went "passing well." At Belfast in January 1776 Collins called it "The Element of Modern Oratory," which he delivered in a "Humorous, Satirical, Critical, and Mimical Exhibitions" for several nights at McKane's Assembly Rooms, in the course of which offerings he afforded illustrations of the use and abuse of speech in the characters of a schoolmaster, a schoolboy, a public reader, a pedant, a Scotch orator, a Welsh orator, and others.

In his advertisement Collins avowed that the "Exhibition" had been repeated 42 successive nights in London and "also several times with equal success at the Universities of Oxford and Cambridge." He, therefore, declined "the fulsome (tho' too common) Practice of Self Encomium; choosing much rather to submit the Decision of its Merits to the well known Candour and Judgment of an Irish audience."

He also acted Major O'Flaherty in *The West Indian* at the Mill Gate Theatre in Belfast on 2 February 1776, giving his lecture after the play. Collins returned to Belfast for one night on 30 May 1781. In the fall of 1784, he was at Norwich, where he was seen on Saturday evening 6 November by Sylas Neville who told his *Diary*:

His imitations differ from Cary's in this that he gives specimens of bad as well as of good acting &c no imitation of actresses—Cary the best mimic of the two. The audience was numerous &c genteel. Imitations in which he succeeded best—Garrick in Hamlet, Barry in Alexander, Maclin in Shylock, Powel in Hamlet.

After enjoying great success at Bath in 1788 with his one-man program, now called *The Evening Brush*, Collins returned to London to perform at the Free Mason's Tavern, Great Queen Street, beginning on 8 March 1788. By 26 March he had moved to the Great Exhibition Room in Panton Street, Haymarket, and by 16 July to the Royalty Theatre in Wellclose Square, where he continued every evening during the summer season. At this time was published his song *The Golden Days of Good Queen Bess*, in nine stanzas. He distributed this song gratis at his benefit on 28 July 1788, at which he performed the *Annals of the Green-Room*, a review for which he wrote the words and music. His address at this time was No 7, Shorter Street, Wellclose Square. The newspapers lauded his performances in the highest terms, a notice (perhaps a puff) on 24 June being typical:

Of all the entertainments which this town can boast, 'The Evening Brush of Collins,' deserves, perhaps, the preference. There is such a fund of miscellaneous wit, humour, and character, in the whole exhibition, that the warmest eulogium in the power of language to bestow, would not exceed the deserts of the author.

One song in the entertainment, "Date Obolum Belisario," it was concluded, "never was, nor possibly, never will be, equalled." Displaying a complete mastery of the various dialects of the English, the Welsh, the Scotch, and the Irish "that ever appeared before an audience," Collins presented the characters of a Yorkshire "senator" making an important motion for mending a window pane, a Somerset collier describing a country christening, a Highlander declaiming on elocution, a Welsh exciseman reading Cato, and an Irish pastor exhorting his flock. In an advertisement on

6 June 1788, Collins announced his intention to publish the entertainment, with all the songs and others not yet in print, claiming he already had nearly 3000 subscribers and warning his patrons against "any spurious catch-pennies which may possibly anticipate the said publication." But no such publication seems to have been immediately forthcoming. *The Brush* was published at Newcastle about 1800, and *The Theatrical Banquet or the Actor's Budget. Together with Collins' "Evening Brush"* was published by William Oxberry in 1809.

After the summer at the Royalty, Collins gave other performances around the town, such as the one called *Petty Curry*, in the Concert Room of the Red Lion Tavern, for his own benefit on 25 November 1788.

When the bookseller Paterson gave up

By permission of the Trustees of the British Museum

JOHN COLLINS, as Belisario
initialed J. C. B.

his shop and auction room at No 38, King Street, Covent Garden, in 1790, it was taken over by King, Chapman, and Collins, who continued to sell books during the day, but in the evening Collins again offered his mélange of story, song, and sentiment. In February 1790, the *Biographical and Imperial Magazine* declared that the claim of these performances in King Street "to the union, so seldom met with, of classical wit with eccentric humour, is not to be disputed. The song on the destruction of Troy is excellent, as indeed are most of the songs; and that of *Date obulum Bellisario* can never be too often repeated."

During the winter of 1791–92, Collins took over the Lyceum Theatre for 52 nights with *The Evening Brush*. He was at Cork in the summer of 1790, and in Dublin probably in 1791. According to a manuscript notation at the Folger Library, Collins went to America in 1791 with Mrs Sage, the first female aerial traveler. This report, however, seems confused, as the Collins known to have performed in America in the 1790s could hardly have been John. In January 1793, he played at Birmingham and occupied a house in Great Brook Street, Ashted. For a while, according to a James Winston manuscript at the Folger Library, he kept an inn at Plymouth. Not succeeding in this venture, he went in 1795 to take up auctioneering at Bath, where he knocked down "the lots of folly and dissipation as adroitly with his hammer, as he formerly did with his tongue." By 1799 he was an honorary professional member of the Bath Harmonic Society.

Collins seems to have made his final appearances at York in 1795. On 18 May of that year Collins's *Evening Brush* was announced there with alterations and additions; and it was again announced for 20 May, as "the last but two of the author's appearances in public." Sometime after, endowed with a "well-earned competency" obtained by his many performances, Collins

became partners with a Mr Swinney in the *Birmingham Chronicle*. The many poems and essays which he published in that newspaper, mostly about local events, were offered with the by-line of "Brush" and were often, as he complained, reproduced by others without acknowledgment. His wife, a Miss Shellard, to whom he was married at Walcot Church, Bath, on 24 January 1768, was reputed to have been a beautiful woman, who painted likenesses in profile at a half-guinea each, "frame and glass included." She died at an unknown date as the result of an operation for breast cancer. They had no children, but a Miss Brent, a niece, lived with Collins at Birmingham.

John Collins died at Birmingham on 2 May 1808, in his sixty-sixth year. He had brought the art of monologue to a high point during his forty-odd years of professional activity, and the *Brush*, of course, spawned many bad imitations. Perhaps the best appreciation of his achievement is that given in an undated newspaper clipping:

Collins's *Brush*, like Stevens's *Heads*, seems to have set all Menander's sons a madding! Stevens, by his success, stirred up Head-Lecture in every part of the kingdom, but, alas, all heads but his own were unfurnished with brains! Collins, as a fellow of oddity and whim, has from the good fortune which followed his Farrago, raised Whims and Oddities in the heads of others, which have not been quite so successful as his own. . . . And this is Collins's peculiar boast. From the beginning to the end of his Brush, nothing lags nor drags; happy in his subjects, quick in his transitions, and versatile in his powers, his spectators never yawn, his auditors never doze, his *Animal Magnetism*, singular in its quality, makes with the loadstone for laughter, and what few Philosophers can do, he electrifies us without a shock.

An original manuscript of "The Brush," according to *The Dictionary of National Biography*, was the property of Samuel Trimmins, of Birmingham, at the beginning of the twentieth century. As noted above, it was printed about 1800 and in 1809. Among the many songs which were written and sung by Collins and published at London are *Date Oblatum Belisario* (1790), *The Despairing Negro*, with music by Reeves, as sung at the Lyceum (1792), *The Bucket of Water*, music by Jonas Blewitt, as sung at the Lyceum (1792), *The Joys of the Bottle*, music by Blewitt, as sung at the Lyceum (1792), *The Romans in England they once did sway* (1795?), and *In the Fields, when to Phoebe, one sweet Summer's Day* (1797?). At Birmingham in 1804 was published *Scripscrapologia, or Collins's Doggerel Dish of All Sorts*, a volume of his collected poems, with an apostrophe to Mr Meyler, bookseller and printer in the Grove, Bath, and with a portrait of Collins by an anonymous engraver. A colored drawing, initialed J. C. B., of him as Belisario in *The Evening Brush* is at the British Museum.

Collins, William   *d. 1763, actor, dancer.*

During his 21 years on the London stage, William Collins played mainly utility and supporting roles in comedy and received little critical notice. His first recorded appearance was as the father to Columbine in the pantomime *Harlequin Sorcerer* at Lee and Woodward's booth "near the Turnpike," on 4 August 1741, at the time of the Tottenham Court Fair. His second notice was at the Yates, Warner, Rosomon booth at Bartholomew Fair on 23 August 1743 when he performed an unspecified role in *The Cruel Uncle*.

In the following season, 1743–44, Collins joined the Drury Lane company where he remained for four years, making his first appearance there on 27 October 1743 as Gomez in *The Spanish Fryar*. His roles which followed that season were typical of the lot he would have for the rest of his life: Clearaccount in *The Twin Rivals*, Dorant in *The Gamester*, Rugby in *The Merry Wives of Windsor*, Don Lopez in *The Wonder*, Harlico and a dancing servant in *The Amorous Goddess*, Filch in *The Beggar's Opera*, Old Gerald in *The Anatomist*, Harry in *The Mock Doctor*, a beggar in *The Jovial Crew*, Jaqueline in *The Fatal Marriage*, Sir Harry in *The Double Gallant*, Tom Errand in *The Constant Couple*, Sir Thomas in *Flora*, Peto in *1 Henry IV*, and his best part, the title role in *The Miser*, which he played on 8 May 1743, when he shared a benefit with Auretti, Gray, Miss Bradshaw, and the two Misses Scott.

In 1744–45, Collins added to his list of parts dancing-clown roles in *The Fortune Tellers*, *Robin Goodfellow*, and *Harlequin Shipwreck'd*, the Taylor in *The Provok'd Wife*, Poundage in *The Provok'd Husband*, and Foresight in *Love for Love*. His shared benefit was announced for 8 May 1745, but it was advertised for the next night that tickets "deliver'd out by Collins that could not get in last night will be taken."

Collins opened the season 1745–46 as Abel Drugger in *The Alchemist* on 28 September, a performance which Foote in his *Roman and English Comedy Considered* (1747) compared favorably with that of Garrick: Garrick "persuades you that he is the real Man," Collins, less realistic, "gives you to understand, that he is but personating the Tobacco-Boy: But then to atone for the Loss of the Deception, you are ready to split with Laughter, at the ridiculous Variations of his Muscles." His features, reported Foote, were formed with "peculiar Pleasantry."

Other new roles in 1745–46 included Daniel in *The Conscious Lovers*, Coupler in *The Relapse*, Uncle in *The Stage Coach*, Cymon in *Damon and Phillida*, Argus in *The Contrivances*, the Miser in *Harlequin Incendiary*, the Poet in *The Scornful Lady*, Gripe in *The Double Disappointment*, Simon in *The Lying Lover*, Smock in *The Vintner Trick'd*, Abhorson in *Measure for Measure*, and Pilfer in *The Humours of the Army*. In 1747–48, his last season at Drury

Lane, Collins added the Surgeon in *The Lady's Last Stake*, a Citizen in *Julius Caesar*, Mercury in *Amphitryon*, and Razor in *The Provok'd Wife*.

Not re-engaged when Garrick took up the patent at Drury Lane in 1747–48, Collins went over to Covent Garden, making his first appearance as Filch in *The Beggar's Opera* on 31 October 1747, and playing 26 other roles in the repertory that season. He was kept similarly busy at Covent Garden for another 14 years. In 1749–50 his salary was 6s. 8d. per day, and by 1761–62, his last season, it was still only about 8s. 6d. per day.

Collins's last performances were as Sir William Meadows in *Love in a Village*, the very successful pastiche by Bickerstaffe which opened on 8 December 1761. He played in 22 performances through 15 January 1762, but for the next performance on 18 January, evidently very ill, he was replaced by Bennet. He died on 30 March 1763. On 14 May 1763, his widow was given a share of the benefit night with Lewis, Redman, and Gardner.

An incomplete list of the roles played by William Collins totals 85 in number, and, in addition to those mentioned above, includes: Scrub in *The Stratagem*, Francis in *1 Henry IV*, Wiseacre in *The London Cuckolds*, Squire Richard in *The Provok'd Husband*, Sancho in *The Rover*, Daniel in *Oroonoko*, Corbaccio in *Volpone*, Dicky and Young Clincher in *The Constant Couple*, the Shoemaker in *The Man of Mode*, Sham in *The Gentleman Gardener*, Sir Paul Pliant in *The Double Dealer*, Sir Solomon in *The Double Gallant*, Lord Sands in *Henry VIII*, James in *The Miser*, Tom in *The Funeral*, Timothy in *The What D'Ye Call It*, Trapland in *Love for Love*, Day in *The Committee*, Sampson in *Romeo and Juliet*, Fretful in *The Lover His Own Rival*, Shallow and Sir Hugh Evans in *The Merry Wives of Windsor*, Lucianus in *Hamlet*, the Welch Collier in *The Recruiting Officer*, a Witch in *Macbeth*,

Soto in *She Wou'd If She Cou'd*, Timothy in *The County Lasses*, Lord Dryse in *Taste*, Muckworm in *The Honest Yorkshireman*, Tester in *The Suspicious Husband*, Puritan in *A Duke and No Duke*, William and Touchstone in *As You Like It*, Lewis in *Love Makes a Man*, Fondlewife in *The Old Bachelor*, Polonius in *Hamlet*, Peachum in *The Beggar's Opera*, Oldcastle in *The Intriguing Chambermaid*, and an Old Woman in *Rule a Wife and Have a Wife*.

Collis, ₁**Francis?**₁ ₁*fl. 1777–1784?*₁, *house servant? supernumerary?*

Although his name was not on the regular pay list, a Mr Collis was paid £2 14s. 2d. for 14 days at Drury Lane on 18 October 1777, perhaps as a supernumerary or house servant. A Mrs Collis, presumably his wife, was paid the same amount for 13 days on 14 October 1777, and on 19 May 1779, she shared gross benefit receipts of £120 14s. 6d. with Mrs Legge and Miss Kirby. Francis Collis and Susanna Richardson Collis, along with Mary Ann Yeates, witnessed the marriage of Elizabeth Coates to James Ricketts at St Paul, Covent Garden, on 29 February 1784.

Collis, Mrs ₁**Francis, Susanna, née Richardson?**₁ ₁*fl. 1777–1784*₁, *house servant? See* **COLLIS, FRANCIS.**

Collis, John ₁*fl. 1672*₁, *musician.*

On 2 October 1672 John Collis and a number of other musicians were ordered apprehended for performing without licenses.

Colmack, John ₁*fl. 1699*₁, *musician.*

John Colmack was one of seven musicians of Princess Ann of Denmark who received a share in £22 1s. 6d. paid them on 23 October 1699 for playing at two balls and a play.

Colman. *See also* **COLEMAN.**

Colman, Mr *[fl. 1749], actor, singer.*

One Colman, probably a very young man, played the part of Filch in *The Beggar's Opera* at the Great Tiled Booth on the Bowling Green in Southwark "For one night only. Benefit Mrs Yeates," on 2 January 1749. Except for this one instance, he appears on no surviving bills.

Colman, George *1732–1794, manager, playwright.*

George Colman was the son of Francis Colman, aristocratic diplomat and amateur of the arts, and his wife Mary Gumley, daughter of a wealthy manufacturer and sister of the Countess of Bath. George was born about 15 April 1732 at Florence, where his father was British ambassador to the Court of the Grand Duke of Tuscany, and was baptized in the Church of San Giovanni on 18 April. He was given the Christian name George because his baptismal sponsor was George I, as was Queen Caroline for his sister Caroline.

Francis Colman, who seems to have been responsible for bringing Senesino and Carestini to England, was a passionate devotee of opera. He wrote the libretto for Handel's *Ariadne in Crete* (1734) but never heard it sung, for he died at Pisa on 20 April 1733. Mrs Colman returned to London to live in St James's Park in a house furnished by the government, and she continued in residence there until she died, in May 1767. But Mrs Colman's brother-in-law, William Pulteney, Earl of Bath, reputedly England's wealthiest man, assumed George's guardianship and in 1741 sent him to join his own son William at Westminster School.

George Colman was an excellent student and after four years at Westminster he successfully undertook the examination which made him a King's Scholar. He also formed many friendships valuable to him in later life, with William Cowper, Charles Churchill, Edward Gibbon, William Cumberland, William Henry Cavendish-Bentinck, later Duke of Portland, Hamilton Boyle, later Earl of Cork, and Robert Lloyd. At Westminster, George wrote his first hesitant poetry, dedicated to his cousin William, "Verses to the Right Honorable Lord Viscount Pulteney." He also took part in the traditional Latin plays which had been offered by students at Westminster for 400 years or more. But he failed to gain first place among the King's Scholars at his first attempt in 1750, a victory desired by his patron, an Oxonian, as entitling him to go to Oxford. The Earl suggested that he should remain at Westminster an additional year. George did so, and with that advantage he gained his first and was "elected" to Christ Church, Oxford, in the spring of 1751.

George seems to have heeded the admonitions of the Earl, delivered in frequent correspondence, that he avoid the fleshpots of London. But he itched to write, and while he was still an undergraduate a stream of miscellaneous productions, which was not stemmed until the end of his life, began to issue from his pen. His first printed work was an essay of criticism called "A Vision," sent anonymously to Hawkesworth's *Adventurer* and published 15 September 1753. From 1754 to 1756 he collaborated with Bonnell Thornton (and occasional "guest" writers like "Orator" Henley and William Cowper) in the 140 weekly numbers of *The Connoisseur* by "Mr Town." It was one of the best of the essay periodicals of mid-century. Colman and Thornton also collaborated in a perfunctory collection of verse by 17 female poets (with attached "lives" filched from Ballard's *Memoirs of Learned Ladies* and Theophilus Cibber's *Lives of the Poets*) called *Poems by Eminent Ladies*.

Colman left Oxford in May 1755 for Lincoln's Inn, to combine the study of the law with the enjoyment of London. He helped Thornton and others form a seven-member Thursday night society, the Nonsense Club, devoted to hoaxes and practical

National Portrait Gallery
GEORGE COLMAN, the Elder
by Gainsborough

jokes. He was called to the bar on 24 January 1757 and spent several months trying cases on the Oxford judicial circuit between 1758 and 1761. In 1757 he had written the largely autobiographical sketch *The Law Student* (published in altered form in 1762) in which he confessed himself already "Deep in the drama, shallow in the Law."

The years 1760 and 1761 were busy ones. He and Robert Lloyd collaborated on two odes, "To Obscurity" and "To Ob-livion," burlesquing Gray and Mason, respectively. He began his long and fruitful friendship with Garrick, ingratiating himself with the great actor-manager by publishing the pamphlet *A Letter of Abuse to D—— G——k, Esq.*, actually an encomium on the actor, followed by flattering remarks in his *Critical Reflections on the Old English Dramatists* (1761). He also, apparently, this year took into "keeping" Sarah Ford, sometimes described as an actress, though she does not appear to have

Harvard Theatre Collection

GEORGE COLMAN, the Elder

engraving by Smith ?, after Thurston's copy
of a portrait by Zoffany

performed in London. Miss Ford had met
Colman in 1760, very soon after she was
deserted by the Irish actor Henry Mossop,
for whom she had borne a daughter, Harriet. For some years Garrick thought ill of
Colman's choice. Writing to his brother
George Garrick from Munich on 23 August
1764 Garrick mentioned Sarah with disapproval. He did not "like y[e] wench, &
never thought of her & yet I would not
offend Colman, who I fear will be much
harassed with her—an Idiot—" Yet in time
—and especially after Colman married her,
Garrick came to accept Sarah, and even
paid her much compliment, for his friend's
sake.

Colman's first stage offering was an excellent short afterpiece, *Polly Honeycombe,
a Dramatick Novel in One Act*, which
amiably satirized the vogue for novel-read-
ing. It came out anonymously at Drury
Lane on 5 December 1760, and was

thought to be Garrick's until he disavowed
it. Certainly Colman had Garrick's assistance on it, as a letter of May or June 1760
from Garrick, praising the characters but
calling the plot "very deficient," shows.
Two months later, on 12 February 1761,
Garrick guided Colman's first full-length
comedy to the boards. *The Jealous Wife*,
based in part on hints from *Tom Jones*,
was brought on with Garrick himself and
Kitty Clive in the leading roles. But before
long Garrick was writing to Colman ex-
cusing himself from playing the part of
Oakly because of the necessity of learning
other strenuous roles to which he had committed himself. The work entered the standard repertory, where it remained for many
years. It was published with an effusive
dedication to the Earl of Bath.

But Colman's satisfaction was marred by
a quarrel with and temporary estrangement
from Arthur Murphy, very likely caused by
Murphy's jealousy over the success of *The
Jealous Wife*. Colman turned for awhile
away from the theatre, and, with Bonnell
Thornton and Garrick as partners, launched
the *Saint James's Chronicle* on 18 April
1761. He traveled for the last time that
spring on the Oxford judicial circuit. In
June he began contributing to the *Chronicle* his series of very popular "Genius"
papers, some of them under the signature
"Rhapsodista." In the second of these
papers he proffered a "Portrait of the Author, and Description of his Person": "In
a word, it is my irreparable misfortune to
be, without my *shoes*, a little more than
five feet in height." Certainly he was very
short. If the description was accurate he
was one of the few prominent men of the
theatre whom Garrick could literally look
down on.

On 6 March 1762 Garrick brought out
Colman's mildly successful afterpiece *The
Musical Lady*, which ran for another 10
nights. On 15 September 1763 Garrick
left for his continental tour and gave over
the care of Drury Lane to Lacy his co-

manager, but gave the principal direction of plays to George Colman, with whom David maintained a brisk and cordial correspondence. On 8 October Colman took advantage of his new influence by staging his alteration of *Philaster*, with the remarkable young actor William Powell, as Philaster, making his first appearance. On 21 October Sarah Ford gave birth to Colman's son, George. On 4 November Colman's short comedy *The Deuce is in Him*, borrowed from a tale of Marmontel, caused the prompter William Hopkins to note in his diary: "The Novelty of the Subject, together with its being extremely well perform'd; gave the Audience such entire Satisfaction that I never heard Such Bursts of Applause; crying out Bravo! Bravo! &c.&c."

Colman fell ill from fatigue in the spring of 1764, necessitating a recuperative trip to Paris in May, and it was not a good year in other respects. His close friends and literary allies Robert Lloyd and Charles Churchill died late in the year.

On 25 April 1765, George Colman demonstrated the depth and tenacity of his love for the classics by producing an edition of the plays of Terence, translated into blank verse, with an excellent scholarly introduction. Each of the six plays bore a dedication to one or several friends, including Garrick. Before Garrick's departure for the Continent (where he had remained a full year longer than he had intended) he and Colman had roughed out nearly three acts of their modified sentimental comedy *The Clandestine Marriage*, which Garrick puckishly called "our bastard." On Garrick's return they finished it. But now a contention arose between the authors, first because of Garrick's refusal to play the comic part of Lord Ogleby, and then over which one of the authors was responsible for the conception of Ogleby, then broadening into what threatened to be a full-blown quarrel over their respective shares of credit in the writing as a whole. But

their friends intervened, Colman became resigned to accepting Tom King as Ogleby (as it turned out, a most fortunate insistence on Garrick's part), and the play blossomed on 20 February 1766 to great critical and popular acclaim, running for 19 performances during the spring. The authors were reconciled and resumed something like the old friendship.

Colman again visited Paris in 1766, taking along Sarah Ford and her daughter by Mossop, while young George, then three, was left at Richmond where the theatrical carpenter Saunders was building a fine new villa for Colman, Northumberland House, in Petersham Road. George and Sarah did not remain long at Paris, Sarah being dissatisfied and anxious to return soon after their arrival. While they were away Garrick assiduously visited and amused young George and worried sincerely over Colman's health, which had momentarily worsened at Paris, due, thought David, to "Nothing but ye Change of air, & the Seine-Water."

In 1766 Colman finished a translation of Plautus's *The Merchant* for an edition supervised by Bonnell Thornton which appeared in March 1767. He also wrote two prologues, one for *The Clandestine Marriage* and one for Dr Thomas Francklin's new tragedy *The Earl of Warwick*. The latter was severely chastized, along with Garrick's epilogue and the play itself, by the author of *A Letter from the Rope Dancing Monkey in the Haymarket to the acting Monkey of Drury Lane . . .* (1767).

On 21 February 1767 Colman adapted Voltaire's *L'Ecossaise* as *The English Merchant*. Highly sentimental and moral—and much complimented for these qualities—it was not as successful as *The Clandestine Marriage*. It was full of chauvinism and fustian, and Sylas Neville in his diary thought it would "take, tho it had nothing to support it but the character of Freeport," the merchant. On his author's third night

Colman cleared £97 8s. 6d., and on his ninth, £151 14s.

Another brief coolness arose between the friends when Garrick discovered, before Colman was quite ready to tell him, that Colman was preparing to close a deal which would make him a partner in the rival patent theatre, Covent Garden. John Beard sold the patent and property on 1 July 1767 to Thomas Harris, a soap manufacturer, John Rutherford, a wine merchant, Colman, and young William Powell, Garrick's best actor, for £60,000. No one but Colman had the slightest experience with theatrical management. He assumed from this obvious fact that he would be given a free hand regarding choice of plays and the hiring and assignment of actors. He added to £9,000 of his own money a borrowed £1,000 and mortgaged his share for £5,000. Trustfully, and perhaps naively, he signed a vague and ambiguous agreement with his partners which in the event left him exposed to years of ignorant interference and insolent demands from Harris and Rutherford, who, it was soon revealed, had joined the enterprise principally to enlarge their scope for gallantry and to make money without assuming any burdensome responsibility.

Colman at once went diligently to work trying to bolster the acting company, a thing he found at first difficult to do, for Beard had let drama deteriorate while musical spectacle flourished and Garrick had acquired much of the dramatic talent. Still, with a nucleus which included the excellent Powell, William "Gentleman" Smith, George Ann Bellamy, Harry Woodward, Ned Shuter, Lee Lewes, Mr and Mrs Yates, John Quick, Mrs Bulkley, Dubellamy, Mrs and Miss Ward, the singers headed by Mattocks, and the dancers including Larivier, Aldridge, and the Fishars, Colman was far from crippled. He quickly won the loyalty and cooperation of most of his troupe and of the house servants. He opened on an optimistic note on 14 Sep-

tember 1767 with a special prologue written by the satirist Paul Whitehead and spoken by Powell.

Trouble with his partners quickly arose and Colman was harried during the entire 1767–68 season by the arrogance and folly of Rutherford and Harris. Fortunately he had an answering stubbornness, stiffened by Garrick's advice to resist. Before the season was a month old he was confronted with demands for private dressing rooms and favored consideration for roles from Jane Lessingham, Harris's new inamorata, and also from Rutherford's expensive favorite, George Ann Bellamy. A dispute over the hiring of the Yateses and one over the inventory of properties kept in Powell's house adjoining the theatre ballooned into threats of legal action, then open warfare in newspapers and pamphlets, then attempts by Rutherford and Harris to commandeer the properties, followed by Colman's padlocking the theatre door at season's end. On 17 July Harris brought a band of hired bullyboys and forcibly entered the theatre early in the morning. Colman was denied entrance to the house for three weeks.

Almost miraculously, however, considering his distractions, the exertions of Colman had given the undeserving Covent Garden patentees a season highly successful both from the artistic and the financial points of view. The theatre had given 79 different plays and afterpieces in 192 performances. Five new productions had been brought forth, including Goldsmith's first play, *The Good-Natur'd Man*, on 29 January 1768, and Colman's own farce *The Oxonian in Town*. That had had a run of 22 performances—but only after the pacification of the London Irish, who threatened to foment a riot because the villains in the play were Irishmen. Bills emphatically denying anti-Hibernianism were distributed at the theatre on the third night and Colman published compliments to the Irish, extracted from the piece, in the *Public*

Advertiser on 12 November. The play was also attacked in a pamphlet as having an immoral tendency, being filled (it was charged) with pickpockets and whores. But total receipts on the author's night were a satisfactory £230 6s. 6d. The season's gross receipts were £31,105. William Powell, whom Garrick was now missing sorely at Drury Lane, drew large houses, starring especially in Shakespearean characters: King John, Richard III, Othello, Romeo, Macbeth, and Lear. For the performance of *King Lear*, Colman rewrote the Tate version, excising the absurd sentimental love story of Edgar and Cordelia and restoring many of Shakespeare's lines, but retaining the happy ending and failing to return the Fool to the play.

The season's successes and the season's contentions would perhaps have balanced except for two deaths that spring and summer. The first, on 9 May 1768, was of Colman's old school-fellow and collaborator Bonnel Thornton, who left "Twenty Pounds to be laid out in Remembrance of me To George Colman Esquire." The more shocking death of young William Powell on 3 July 1768, at Bristol, from pneumonia, taken after overheating in a game of cricket, was a terrible blow to Covent Garden Theatre. The most important event of 1768 from Colman's point of view was his regularization of the four-year association with Sarah Ford. They were married by the Reverend Mr Richard Penneck on 12 July at St John's, Southwark. She was to die suddenly on 29 March 1771, when their son George was eight years old.

Colman continued resolutely and adroitly to prosecute the management in 1768–69. He produced 75 plays and afterpieces, including four new ones, and ended with a profit of £6,724, despite practically continuous harassment from Harris, now joined by the Messrs Dagge and Leake, who had purchased Rutherford's share for £18,500 on 8 September 1768. He sustained in 1768, in such "satires" as *The Managers*

Managed, some attacks by poetaster partisans of the Harris group. That year in *The True State of the Differences Subsisting Between the Proprietors of Covent Garden Theatre* he scolded the playwright William Kenrick for intruding into the theatrical dispute because, as Colman supposed, Kenrick wished to oust him from Covent Garden and take his place. Kenrick replied with vigor in *An Epistle to G. Colman . . . ,* in which he blasted Colman's management, writing, and direction of the acting. He attributed Colman's early success to the tutelage of Thornton and Lloyd, charged that it was "notorious" that *The Jealous Wife* had been a success only because Garrick had rewritten it, and said that Colman and Powell had made a "seraglio" of the green room. In February 1769 Colman's estranged partners filed suit in Chancery, naming as codefendant Powell's widow Elizabeth, charging among other allegations that all but Colman had been frozen out of their managerial rights and that Colman had been wildly extravagant in hiring actors and laying out money for properties.

Undaunted, Colman pressed on, continuing to make money for the ungrateful combine. For instance, he immediately exploited the publicity generated by Garrick's strange and abortive Stratford Shakespeare Jubilee of 6 through 9 September 1769. The alert Colman swiftly wrote his own *Man and Wife; or, the Shakespeare Jubilee,* introducing a colorful procession of Shakespeare characters, each introduced by music appropriate, and Covent Garden produced the entertainment on 7 October. It brought the theatre a total of £2,872 in 11 nights and had played six times before Garrick brought out his more elaborate production *The Jubilee* on 14 October. Certainly Garrick was able to recoup the considerable sums he had lost in the September fiasco in rainy Stratford, but equally certainly Colman had skimmed some of the cream off the theatrical profits of Jubilee processions. It did not improve relations between Garrick and the young manager whom he still regarded as his protégé. The 1769–70 season saw 89 plays and afterpieces in production at Covent Garden over 192 nights. Six productions were new.

On 16 July 1770 began the delayed suit in Chancery between Colman and the Harris faction. It terminated on 20 July after voluminous testimony, with the Commissioners not only finding in Colman's favor but roundly scolding the plaintiffs for coming "with a very ill grace" and "playing with a Court of Equity." Colman's attorney John Dunning experienced little difficulty with the defense. The only testimony really hostile to Colman came from Henry Woodward, Isaac Bickerstaffe, and Charles Macklin, and in each of these depositions it was apparent that some selfish personal consideration and not the health of Covent Garden Theatre was the motivation. The great Harlequin Harry Woodward, "Lun, Jr," still remembered the glorious days of pantomime under his mentor and patron "Lun," the manager John Rich, and he blamed Colman for diminishing the importance of harlequinade in the total scheme of Covent Garden. His testimony was both passionate and eloquent. Colman, he said, had inherited pantomime appurtenances worth at least £10,000. But he had

so injudiciously used those pantomines as to have all or the greatest part of them in use in the same season & by frequent Repetition has made them lose all their former power of attraction besides which the s⁴. Geo. Colman hath employed a capital & famous set of scenes designed at a vast expense by the Sieur Servandoni as to make them also lose the Lucrative Effect they most probably would have had.

Colman made a great mistake

in tacking them to an Old Entertainment. . . . The Rape of Proserpine [which] sunk with the scenes because many Popular Effects were curtailed to make way for them all. [he,

Woodward] can the better depose to the purpose & Effect afores⁴. because he knows that by a contrary & opposite conduct & use of the same Pantomines the sd. Mr Rich preserved the part of the Stock of Representations & made them a constant round of Novelty . . .

and this had made Rich succeed even in a time when all the best actors were at the other theatre.

Charles Macklin chose another point of attack, and his testimony gives us valuable information about contractual practices. He was scandalized over Colman's departure from accepted conventions in the matter of players' articles:

. . . it hath been usual for the space of 35 years last past or thereabouts for Managers of Theatres to contract & Enter into written Arcles for Terms of Years at Salaries with Captl or Established performers & with pformers of distinguished & rising Parts & Merits. But Dept sayth that in all his knowledge of the business of sd Theatre for 40 years & upwards Dept never knew or was Informed that it was usual or Customary to enter into such Engagemtˢ for years with Inferior players as Deft Colman hath done and Dept saith that it is hurtful in his Opinion & belief to the Managers of the s⁴ Theatre to Contract in manner af⁸ᵈ with under Actors & performers for any certain Term or Number of yʳˢ because that by tying such kinds of actors or Performers to a Theatre by Articles is loading it with such an Expence as never can produce any special Profit to a theatre & will disable the proprietors thereof from getting rid of such Expence at pleasure when necessary and to pay for Merit when it might be had. . . . Saith when under or inferior Actors Officers Door Keepers Carpenters & Scene Drawers are tied by articles to a Threatre [*sic*] they will be and do grow negligent & Careless & perhaps Impudent Encouraged thereto by this Reflection that they may be forfeited but cannot be discharged.

Macklin certainly had a prudential point, but Colman had perhaps demonstrated a better one: that keeping a dependable group of secondary performers loyally together was as important as enforcing "discipline" by the dubious threat of annual discharge. As for Bickerstaffe, his complaint was concerned solely with his spleenful dissatisfaction with the manner in which Colman had staged Bickerstaffe's own musical pieces "merely when he had not any thing Else to perform . . ."

Freed now from some of the petty bickering and constant tension, Colman had entered more fully into the enjoyments of the intellectual society of London to which his birth, education, and literary attainments entitled him. On 17 October 1767 he had been inducted into the Sublime Society of Beefsteaks. He was soon admitted to the "Club" of the Johnsonian circle, joining Burke, Goldsmith, Reynolds and other notables, and he frequented other gatherings at Tom's Coffee House with Johnson, Foote, Murphy, Reynolds and Steevens.

In the 1770–71 season Covent Garden theatre lost the estimable but difficult Harry Woodward, whose parts were taken by Lee Lewes. Ross came down from Dublin, and Thomas Death came in from Norwich, and the excellent John Palmer, the scandalous but competent Miss Catley, Savigny, and others joined the company, now grown to 89 actors, five dancers, six singers, and four instrumental musicians. Colman turned now to writing burlettas, coming out first with *The Portrait*, with music by Dr Samuel Arnold, on 22 November 1770. A great success of 22 performances persuaded Colman and Arnold to try another burletta immediately. *Mother Shipton* had an even greater success—57 performances during the season, and Colman began himself to be called "Mother Shipton" about the town. "Nicholas Nipclose, Bart." (the actor-critic Francis Gentleman) in his *The Theatres: A Poetical Dissection* after condemning *Mother Shipton*, scourged Colman on several other of his sore spots:

COVENT—alas!—for many years had been
Of pantomime and frippery the scene;
Like the piazza females, trick'd with show,
Most meanly high, most eminently low;
Gods, devils, ostriches, and such a train,
As ne'er were jumbled into human brain
'Till RICH existed, have usurp'd this spot,
Of childish insipidity the lot;
RICH mark'd a path, and BEARD pursu'd his plan,
Now tiny GEORGE, that mere poetic span,
In nought but human Fantoccini dealing,
Wages fell far 'gainst genius, sense, and feeling;
Bold in patch'd coat and pageantry alliance,
Taste and his colleagues sets at bold defiance;
Fenc'd with a shield of subtle legal cunning,
Kindly produc'd by shrewd, sarcastic DUNNING,
Throws down goose quills, takes up the wooden sword,
A Mede or Persian law his ev'ry word;
Works wonders with the thunder of his tongue,
And, miller like, converts the old to young
Makes Harass'd VINCENT, verg'd on sixty-three,
Smirk, cant, and trip thro' girls in tragedy;
Makes SAVIGNY—but Soft—let him appear
In proper season, and his destin'd sphere—
Field officer—oh scandal of the age!—
Amidst our wretched train bands of the stage.

In September 1771 Colman and Harris were reconciled at a dinner party and thereafter observed a mutual civil forbearance, if not friendship. On 12 November Colman brought out his *Fairy Prince*, a three-act piece borrowed from Ben Jonson's *Masque of Oberon*, with songs added from Dryden,

Gilbert West, and Dr Thomas Augustine Arne. It included ceremonies at Windsor relative to the installation of Knights of the Garter. Profits to Colman on his author's first night were £125 15s. But Colman's health was not good, and on 30 November, while at the theatre, he was "seized with a fit," either a mild stroke or an attack of epilepsy, and had to suspend activity for several weeks. However, he recovered to direct the company during the rest of a successful season which gave 82 different mainpieces and afterpieces to the public and nearly £4,000 to the theatre.

At the beginning of the next season on 21 September 1772, Jane Barsanti, one of the most enchanting singing actresses of the century, and the pupil and protégée of Dr Burney, was introduced to the public anonymously as "A Young Lady." Colman had written a dramatic "Occasional Prelude" contrived so as to display her ability as a mimic of leading Italian and English singers. Her success that night and in 11 repetitions earned her her first big role, Estifania in *Rule a Wife and Have a Wife*, under her own name, and she went on to become one of Colman's most dependable actresses during the short remainder of his tenure at Covent Garden. In 1771–72 also Colman pleased the public but angered William Mason by producing that poet's closet drama *Elfrida* without his knowledge. Colman himself reduced the length of John Dalton's 1738 stage version of Milton's *Comus* and turned it from a masque into something like a musical comedy. The account-book entry for 11 January 1773 showed for "Mr Colman's Night" receipts of £254 15s. 6d., all of which Colman received "for the Alterations of *Elfrida* & *Comus* & for the *New Occasional Prologue*."

It was with great reluctance that Colman was persuaded by his fellow Club member Oliver Goldsmith to accept a piece, for production in the 1772–73 season, which Goldsmith called *The Mistakes of a Night,*

or She Stoops to Conquer, by which its author hoped to stem or deflect the tide of sentiment and tears which had engulfed British comedy for more than fifty years. It was of course immediately and greatly successful, though its appearance on 15 March 1773 put it too late in the season for it to build up full momentum.

But though that year the managers had sponsored four new mainpieces of worth—including Goldsmith's immortal one—things were not entirely satisfactory at Covent Garden. The first number of the *Westminster Magazine* immediately revealed its Garrickian bias and condemned Colman's version of *Comus*, "picked down like a skeleton," his production of *Henry VIII*, and his new farce *Cross Purposes*, and charged him with wholesale plagiarism—a charge ridiculous in a milieu in which unceremonious borrowing was epidemic. There were more serious rumblings in Covent Garden Theatre itself. Maria Macklin wrote her father Charles on 3 February 1773 that the atmosphere was disturbed, that Colman kept aloof from his company, that Savigny had gout, and that Younger (the prompter) was arrogantly usurping all the business of the theatre. She declared that the house was never filled. On 13 March she reported the terrible ruction of 6 March, begun by a faction incensed at Colman's having refused to let Mrs Yates play for the benefit of the popular William "Gentleman" Smith. The house was in imminent danger of demolition until an announcement was made of the satisfactory resolution of the matter.

Even rougher water was ahead. After repeated application by the aged Charles Macklin, Colman had rehired him on the same terms which the actor had enjoyed in the seasons 1767–68 through 1770–71, notwithstanding the fact that Macklin during the interim had been a vocal and venomous partisan of the Harris faction. Macklin now proposed, for the new season 1773–74, an elaborate schedule of capital

Shakespearean roles. He got only so far as Macbeth on 23 October 1773 before he managed, typically, to involve himself in a broil. Macklin had acted the title part and had dressed his actors, for the first time in London, in reasonable replicas of the tartan. It was in that respect at least an historic production. But it was hissed, and even at age 73 the irascible Macklin was not complacent about that. The irate Irishman addressed the audience on 30 October, accusing the comedians Isaac Sparks and Samuel Reddish of instigating the hissing. The matter swiftly ballooned and involved Garrick and others. Factions formed, and on 13 November a serious riot prevented Macklin from acting, the house being threatened with destruction unless he should be discharged on the spot. Colman was forced to acquiesce and to bar Macklin thenceforth from his stage. Macklin began an action against Colman for 1,000 guineas which dragged on for ten years until Lord Chief Justice Mansfield finally persuaded a compromise, and Colman paid Macklin £500.

Colman was involved in other disputes in 1773 – in one with the blackguardly William Kenrick over the failure of his *The Duellist*, in another with Henry Fielding's brother, the blind chief magistrate Sir John Fielding, who sought to keep a production of *The Beggar's Opera* off the Covent Garden stage because he felt it would be a stimulant to criminal activity, and in a third involving a physical attack on him by the frantic Reverend Mr Penneck, B. D., F. R. S., Keeper of the Reading Room at the British Museum (the same clergyman who had married Colman and Sarah Ford), who mistakenly suspected Colman of rivaling him in the affections of Miss Miller, an actress. Colman seemed innocently unable to escape contention that year. One July evening in 1773 when he was sitting inoffensively at Vauxhall with the beautiful actress Mrs Hartley and her husband and another violent clerical type,

the Reverend Henry Bate (later Sir Henry Bate Dudley), boxer, duellist, and journalist, Mrs Hartley was insulted by ruffians. They were immediately braved by Bate and a brawl began. Evidently Colman avoided physical involvement in the affair, but he figured nonetheless prominently in the backwash of newspaper squibs and doggerel which followed.

Colman's health was poor and he had lost for the moment a good deal of his managerial zest and most of his creative sparkle. He seems also to have become unusually sensitive. Evidently his feelings were ruffled over having been excluded from membership on the board of trustees of the players' annuity of Covent Garden. A mollifying assurance was sent from the trustees – Smith, Mattocks, Reinhold, Hull, Bensley, Clarke, Younger, Rotton, (Wroughton), and Dunstall – explaining the constitutional grounds of his exclusion and deploring "the most distant supposition of our having been wanting in respect or attention to Mr Colman." His last adaptation as Covent Garden manager appeared on 16 December 1773 when he presented *Achilles in Petticoats*, altered from John Gay, with Thomas Augustine Arne's new music. On 31 January he produced the first full-length comedy of his own after he assumed the managership, *The Man of Business*, a weakly sentimental thing, which ran for 13 nights but only because of Colman's determination to see it do so. It was badly reviewed and poorly attended. John Hampden in his *Journal* called it "a very confused miscellany of several plays and tales." Colman made only £37 12s. on it.

On 26 May 1774 Colman's perplexed, but on the whole successful, seven-year reign at Covent Garden ended with an epilogue of his authorship, spoken by the dependable Jane Barsanti:

Of mortal men how equal is the date!
Kings and Mock Kings submit alike
to Fate.

*Abroad, in state, one mighty monarch
    lies;
While here, his Mejesty of Brentford
    dies.
Hung be the Stage with black! and
    Juliet's Bell,
Midst flashing Resin, toll our monarch's
    knell!
While we with tragick plumes and
    mournful verse,
In slow procession all attend his hearse.*

. . . .

*Six Beggar's-Opera Ladies tend the bier,
Parted, like Hector's wife, 'twixt Smile
    and Tear;
Elfrida's Virgins too proceed before us,
A   Modern-Antient,   English-Grecian,
    Chorus.
Scene-shifters, Candle-snuffers, and Stage-
    keepers,
Bill-stickers, Pickpockets, and Chimney-
    sweepers,
The Mob without doors, and the Mob
    within,
Close the Procession, and complete the
    din.
Thus having buried him let's waive Dis-
    section!
'Tis now too late to give his faults cor-
    rection.
Peace—if peace may be—to his shade!
    He died
Felo de se, poor soul! a Suicide:
Yet he confess'd with his departing
    breath,
And in the very article of death,
Oft did your favour cherish his pretences,
Which now defrays his Funeral Ex-
    pences.*

Colman had, in this final season, with 99
performers in his acting company, performed 185 nights and gleaned the respectable profit of £4,500 for putting on 89
pieces, four of them new. He sold his share
of the patent and properties to the actor
Thomas Hull for £20,000, which sum, considering inflation of money and property
values since the time of purchase, did not
represent much profit to him.

Colman, with a perfectly obvious sense

of relief, repaired to "the Bath" for six
months, remaining into Christmas week
1774. His social calendar became crowded
through the winter at the residence in Great
Queen Street and through the summer at
his villa at Richmond. His guest lists in this
period contained the names of London's
foremost intellectual makers and shakers:
Johnson, Reynolds, Garrick, Foote, Wilkes,
Lord Mansfield, Lord Kellie, the publishers Woodfall, Becket and Baldwin, Gibbon, the Burkes, Topham Beauclerk, the
Wartons.

In the summer of 1775 Colman made a
tour of the western and northern provinces
of England, spending several days at Oxford to familiarize his son George with the
colleges (he was enrolled at Christ
Church). Father and son extended their
progress through Woodstock, Stratford,
Birmingham, Liverpool, York—where, at
the races, in the party of Captain Phipps,
they met the Otaheitan Omai, a "noble
savage" who had been brought to England
in 1774 by Captain Furneaux. Also in the
party was Mr (later Sir) Joseph Banks.
The Colmans travelled on with the party
to Scarborough and then to Mulgrave, the
seat of Captain Phipps's father Lord Mulgrave, thence to "Crazy Castle," Cocken
Hall, Durham, the residence of Sterne's eccentric friend Hall-Stevenson.

From January 1770 Colman had been
interested as a proprietor in the *London
Packet*, along with Captain Edward
Thompson, Richard and Henry Baldwin,
Lockyer Davis, Thomas Lowndes, Thomas
Davies, Woodfall, Christopher Henderson,
Garrick and others. From July to December
1775 he contributed a series of six long
essays under the general title "The Gentleman" and several biographical sketches of
his literary friends, including Bishop Hurd
and Samuel Johnson, signing these "Chiaro
Oscuro." He had continued also to write re-
views for both the *Public Advertiser* and
the *London Chronicle*. In April 1775 he
had re-established contact with the stage,

furnishing a prologue for Garrick's farce *Bon Ton* for which Garrick wrote profuse thanks, and allowing his version of *Comus* to be put on at Drury Lane. On 13 January 1776 at Drury Lane Garrick produced Colman's short adaptation of Ben Jonson's *Epicoene,* but this was not very successful, even though Mrs Siddons played the title role. The *Westminster Magazine* for January said:

Upon the whole we cannot esteem this a striking comedy, even with the assistance it has now received, – the fine manner in which it is got up, and the great expence which the managers have been at in habiting the whole *dramatis personae* in splendid and characteristic Old English dresses. All the actors except Mr. King and Mr. Parsons performed but indifferently. Bensley is the worst Old Man we ever saw. He presents the countenance of a sickly old woman; and the uniform goggle of his eye, by which he means to express infirmity and distress is the look of a man in anguish from the colic. Mr. Palmer, Mr. Brereton, and Mr. Davis have a bloated vulgarity about them, which should ever deter the manager from assigning them the parts of cavaliers or men of fashion. Baddeley, as usual, overdid his part, and Mr. Yates, as usual, was not very perfect in his.

This estimate was confirmed by the prompter in his diary: "Characters New Dressed in the Habits of the Times. This play is alter'd by Mr Colman and receiv'd with Some Applause, but it don't seem to hit the present Taste a few hisses at the End."

On 7 March 1776 Colman's two-act farce *The Spleen, or Islington Spa,* taken partly from Molière's *Malade imaginaire,* came on at Drury Lane, earning Colman £169 17s. His old adversary Kenrick, who affected to believe that the central character Jack Rubrick was a caricature of him, retorted with a vicious satire *The Spleen; or, the Offspring of Folly,* signed "Rubrick," and embellished with a vicious frontispiece

caricature, in which the mildest thing said about Colman was a restatement of the old canard that he was the Earl of Bath's bastard.

Garrick retired from the Drury Lane management at the end of the 1775–76 season. There are many indications that Garrick had hoped to see Drury Lane Theatre, physical property and patent, come under the financial and artistic direction of his friend George Colman. Extant letters show that Garrick annoyed and frustrated R. B. Sheridan and Thomas Linley the elder in the winter of 1775–76. They felt that he was obstructing their desire to buy Drury Lane by his insistence on offering Colman the first refusal. On 29 December 1775 Garrick wrote Colman, asking £35,-000 for his share. Colman replied that he would be interested only in acquiring the controlling interest. This exchange seems to have been a charade. Garrick had little real expectation that Colman would buy his share. Colman knew that he had no chance to buy a controlling interest. (Long after Garrick's death in 1779 gossip in the *Morning Herald* in 1782 reported Colman and a Captain Thompson as then in treaty for the purchase of Drury Lane. The rumor seems to have been without foundation.)

For the opening of the season of 1776–77 Richard Brinsley Sheridan asked Colman to write a prologue introducing his own management at Drury Lane. *New Brooms! An Occasional Prelude* on 21 September 1776 referred in complimentary terms to both Garrick and Sheridan and derided the popularity of the opera at the King's Theatre. (An entry for 7 October 1777 in a manuscript Drury Lane account sheet in the British Museum shows "Mr Colman [paid] for New Broom from Debt Fund 84.18.6.") Sheridan then commissioned him to write the epilogue for the introduction of *The School for Scandal;* it was spoken when that coruscating comedy took the boards at Drury Lane on 8 May 1777. Also in 1777 Colman got out his

Dramatick Works (up to that point) in four volumes, a total of some 17 productions. The publisher, Colman's friend Thomas Becket, was in financial straits and wished the author to lend him £200, partly to satisfy £60 outstanding on a debt to Jonathan Garton, to whom Colman had previously assigned Becket's note to Colman for £300 in payment for the volumes. Through a lamentable misunderstanding on Colman's part and cruel severity from Garton, poor Becket, who had once loaned Colman £1000, went to debtor's prison for a time. Colman suffered much criticism over the affair and his friendship with Becket ended.

The "English Aristophanes," the great mimic and author of farces Samuel Foote, wearied with management, retired at the end of the summer season of 1776 and sold his theatre in the Haymarket to Colman for a guaranteed annuity of £1,600, to be paid in semiannual instalments. Sadly, as it turned out, Colman got a bargain, for Foote had received but one payment of £800 when, on 23 October 1777, he died.

Colman continued to manage the Haymarket under an annual license. The *Gazetteer* of 19 September 1777 published a puff for the new enterprise which sounds suspiciously like Colman's work:

At the close of the last theatrical winter campaign, there was great lamentation, weeping and mourning among the lovers of the drama, on account of a deserted stage. Barry, Woodward, Shuter, Weston, and other theatrical genii, all swept away by unrelenting death . . . Garrick, the great luminary of the stage, to complete the total darkness, had withdrawn his radiant being. . . . All was given up for lost, all was cloudy, gloomy, and downright desperate! When Colman rose with summer splendour . . . not as an *actor*, but something more, an *actor-maker!* that is, a manager, who by intuition, if not by sympathy or instinct, can see and bring forth into open blaze of day the latent seeds of brilliant genius. . . . This summer manager

has, under all the disadvantages of heat and faintness, an empty town and dejected few inhabitants, made full houses well entertained and insatiable after more . . .

and so forth in that vein.

The Haymarket enjoyed its most distinguished era under George Colman the elder. He set about at once acquiring new scenery, a finer wardrobe, and more players to supplement those who habitually came over from the winter patent theatres for a summer of work. As early as March 1777 he had provided for his coming first season by the acquisition of the fine comedian John Edwin and of the excellent Shakespearean John Henderson from Bath. He also signed to his roster the charming Miss Farren, then only about 18 years old. Colman's expedients to attract summer audiences were various and imaginative. He introduced daily performances for the first time; he brought Gay's *Polly* onto the stage for the first time since its creation (and banning) in 1729; his own pared-down version of *The Winter's Tale* which he called *The Sheep-Shearing* was only mildly successful, but another adaptation, that from *Le Barbier de Seville* of Beaumarchais, which Colman called *The Spanish Barber*, had a good run. In addition to innovation, Colman offered a solid season of 81 nights of plays in the summer of 1777.

After Foote's death in October 1777 his unpublished plays began to appear in pirated editions. Colman had bought all rights to them from Foote for £500. On 4 February 1778 the Court of Chancery granted injunction against the piratical practices, and Colman collected, edited, and published *English Plays by Samuel Foote*. In 1778 also emerged the important edition in 10 volumes of *The Dramatick Works of Beaumont and Fletcher* which he edited and for which he wrote a preface. He employed an incident from *The Coxcomb*, by that famous partnership, in his new satirical comedy *The Suicide* when it took the Haymarket boards on 11 July 1778. That summer season he staged 89 nights of plays, including on 18 May his farce *The Female Chevalier*, taken from Taverner's old comedy *The Artful Husband*, but satirizing the antics of the transvestite diplomat and swordsman the Chevalier D'Eon.

In the winter of 1778–79 Colman employed his unique social and theatrical position as volunteer director of the mixture of genteel amateurs and professionals in the famous private Christmas theatricals of Sir Watkyn Williams-Wynn at Wynnstay, Denbighshire, Wales. Evidently he acted a little also. There is an anecdote in the *Monthly Mirror* of September 1796 which has him admitting to having performed Richard III "execrably." (Both the elder and the younger Colman came back to Wynnstay during the Christmas seasons of 1779–80 and 1780–81.) On 1 February 1779 Colman sadly shared a coach with Sheridan, Banks, Chamier, and Gibbon in the funeral cortege of David Garrick. In the summer of 1779 he directed another successful season of 87 nights and produced his own new comedy of four acts, the satire of the *haut monde* he called *The Separate Maintenance*.

Colman made the mistake on 1 March 1780 of renting the Haymarket Theatre to Charles Dibdin for the puppet show *Pasquin's Budget*. The audience, attending under the impression that live actors were performing, rioted when the curtain went up on the puppets and demolished the interior of the theatre. Only when Colman rushed onstage to disclaim any personal responsibility was the burning of the house averted.

On 5 May 1780 the *Morning Chronicle* reported:

A formidable combination seems to be forming against Mr. Colman's campaign this summer. That useful veteran, Parsons of Drury-Lane, for reasons unknown, has withdrawn himself from the Haymarket Corps;

and the Hussar, Lee-Lewes, is to revive the Lecture upon Heads at Covent Garden. . . . In the meanwhile, the Little Summer General is, we hear, preparing to take the field with more than usual spirit, having . . . enlisted under his banner, that Camilla of the Theatre, Mrs. Crawford.

Colman opened the season on 30 May 1780 with his *The Manager in Distress*, satirizing debating societies, particularly the Belle Assemblée, which met at Mrs Theresa Cornelys's rooms in Carlisle House, Soho. He ended the season with his excellent satirical farce *The Genius of Nonsense*, which poked fun at the quack Doctor Graham and his "Temple of Health." By summer's end he had staged 91 nights of plays and afterpieces, including five new ones. After the theatre closed Colman went to Ireland, on the invitation of the brother-in-law of Lord Fitzgibbon, Lord Chancellor of Ireland, to investigate the possibility of building or buying a Dublin playhouse in conjunction with the Irish actor Tottenham Heaphy. He decided against the project.

In the summer of 1781, with the usual mixture of comedy and tragedy and farce, Colman's small company of experienced actors put on a total of 93 nights, including two new mainpieces and eight new afterpieces and the atrocious but evidently profitable travesty *The Beggar's Opera Reversed*, which featured John Edwin as Lucy, Mrs Cargill as Macheath, and the like.

In 1782 Colman collaborated with O'Keeffe on a pantomime called *Harlequin Teague*, altered *Volpone* and Lillo's tragedy *Fatal Curiosity*, and, signing himself "Signor Novestris," composed a "Ballet Tragicomique" to some music by Gluck. Probably also in 1782, as Howard P. Vincent has conjectured, Mrs Sophia Croker, the estranged wife of an army officer, supplanted the last of a series of mistresses, among them Mrs Theodosia Mills and a Mrs Sulston, in the affections and the household of George Colman.

The years passed. Colman's winters were spent in literary pursuits and in the intricate social-professional minuet which the proprietor of a summer theatre had perpetually to dance with the chief actors and proprietors of the patent houses in order to insure a constant summer company. His theatre steadily improved but his health gradually worsened. His own production for the stage declined, and one is perhaps not too imaginative to suppose that he felt a twinge of regret that he had not spent more time cultivating his marked scholarly and editorial abilities. In 1783 he brought out 91 nights of plays, among which were six new pieces. He also published his long-preparing translation of Horace's *Epistola ad Pisones, de arte poetica* in rather fine decasyllabic couplets. His elegant friend Horace Walpole made graceful allusion to that work when he wrote on 19 September 1785 to explain his own gift, sent by that same post, a translation into French of Walpole's *Essay on Modern Gardening*, fresh from his own little press at Strawberry Hill:

I beg your acceptance of a little work just printed here; and I offer it as a token of my gratitude, not as pretending to pay you for your last present. A translation, however excellent, from a very inferior Horace, would be a most inadequate return. . . . I flatter myself you will excuse my troubling you with an old performance of my own, when newly-dressed by a master-hand. As, too, there are not a great many copies printed, and those only for presents, I have particular pleasure in making you one of the earliest compliments.

In the summer of 1784 he put on 50 plays, among them nine new pieces, and in December he went to Bath to "take the waters" for his gout, which had that fall grown more troublesome. After a few weeks he felt sufficiently recovered to return to London and make preparation for his new season, the summer of 1785, in which he again offered 95 nights, but only six new pieces. At the close of the summer's theatrical activity he went to Margate for sea bathing for several weeks and afterwards seemed to be in fairly good health. But in October, preparing to accompany Dr Samuel Arnold to Canterbury, he had a stroke which left one side of his body paralyzed. Newspaper exaggerations of his illness irked him; still he realized that his activity had to be strictly limited. Young George, now rising 25, was assuming more and more responsibility, and with his assistance Colman, still nominally in charge, put on 53 plays and afterpieces, with four new pieces, in the summer of 1786.

That year Colman had the satisfaction of renewing acquaintance with the gentle poet William Cowper, his old school fellow, from whom, over the years, he had drifted away. That year he altered Joseph Atkinson's comedy, which had failed at Dublin, into *Tit for Tat* and prepared a three-volume collection of his nondramatic works which was published in 1787, *Prose on Several Occasions, Accompanied with Some Pieces in Verse.* The collection was dedicated to his old and close friend Sir Joseph Banks, at that time president of the Royal Society. In addition to his "Genius" essays, his first *Adventurer* essay, the *Terrae-Filius* series, newspaper contributions, his *Critical Reflections*, and many prologues and epilogues, the volumes contain one or two new pieces of interest, especially the essay "Orthopaedia, or Thoughts on Public Education." The precarious state of his health also impelled him to write a pamphlet, which was not, however, published until after his death, *Some Particulars of the Life of George Colman*, evidently principally designed to refute the still rankling charge that he was the natural son of the Earl of Bath.

The attempts of one of Colman's favorite actors, John Palmer, to establish a theatre in Wellclose Square in 1787 vexed him greatly and he probably authored the warnings to Palmer which appeared in the *Morning Chronicle* of June 1787, signed "Dick Whittington." He certainly wrote the stern pamphlet *A Very Plain State of the Case, or the Royalty Theatre versus the Theatres Royal*, which appeared on 9 July.

George Colman's last piece for the theatre was the burletta *Ut Pictura Poesis!; or, The Enraged Musician*, suggested by Hogarth's print, which enjoyed 15 performances from 18 May 1789. By this date the direction of all the Haymarket's affairs had devolved upon the younger George Colman. His father had suffered another paralytic stroke and was declining into the state in which he languished pitifully until his death, with his mind, as the younger George wrote in his *Random Records*, sometimes "filled like a cabalistic book, with delusions, and crowded with the wildest flights of morbid fancy," and sometimes "comparatively lucid." He was placed in an asylum in Paddington and remained there until his death on 14 August 1794. On 24 August he was buried in St Mary Abbots Church, Kensington.

Colman had signed a will on 30 April 1789 appointing his friends "Sir Joseph Banks of Soho Square, Baronet and Richard Jackson of Gray's Inn, Gentleman" executors of his estate. His son George was to receive his "Theatre and Leasehold premises in the Hay Market . . . with the Appurtenances and my Wardrobe Scenes Machinery and other things therein and thereunto belonging" *if* "a Grant patent or License shall be obtained . . . for the like times or term as I have heretofore enjoyed a License . . . to carry on or perform plays . . ." If it should happen that no patent or license could be obtained, then the physical theatre should be sold and the money derived from the sale should go to his son's benefit. But whichever course of action should be taken, from either the theatre's profits or its sale, "Sophia Croker, wife of Richard Croker late a Captain in the fifth Regiment of ffoot," should benefit by £250

a year in the first case or to the extent of £1,000 invested for her benefit in the second. Sophia was also to have £1000 from his personal estate invested for her benefit, she to draw interest on the amount during life.

Out of the theatrical profits (if any) the following persons were to receive benefits: "To Lady Wittenrouge widow of the late Sir John Wittenrouge Baronet and to Elizabeth Wittenrouge of the Parish of Saint Mary Le Bone . . . Spinster two distant but distrest Relations a clear annuity or yearly sum of Ten pounds ten Shillings each. . . . To Theodosia Mills late of Bristol but now of Tavistock Street Covent Garden . . . Spinster" £20 per year. "To Mary Hawlyn of Shire lane," an annuity of £4 4s., and "To Ann Barker Daughter of the Reverend Mr Barker deceased," £100 per year.

In addition, Colman added, "I give and bequeath to Henry Dally my man servant ffifty pounds and all Wearing Apparel (my Linen . . . excepted) and unto Sarah Hobbs my Maid Servant ffifty pounds and all my Shirts Stocks Thread Stockings Night Caps and pocket Handkerchiefs . . ." Finally, Banks was to receive £300 in cash and Jackson £200.

Colman's assets, in addition to theatrical real estate and properties, lay in his life insurance policies with the Equitable Insurance Office "in Serjeants Inn, Fleet Street," and "certain hereditaments and premises assigned to me by one John Browne by Indenture dated the twenty-eighth Day of July one thousand seven hundred and eighty four," but the proceeds from the policies were to go "in payment on as far as the same will extend with the Sum of Six hundred pounds due from me to the representative of William Scott late of the parish of St George Hanover Square Brickmaker deceased . . ."

But at the onset of George Colman's lunacy the estate had been encumbered by debts so large that for years considerable financial adroitness was required of George Colman the younger in managing the income from the theatre and other property so as to pay off the creditors. One of the more galling expenses had been the payment on the £600 mortgage of the elder Colman's Gower Street house, which he had given to Sophia Croker on 15 March 1788. After his father's death, young George sued to recover the house from Sophia, whom he stigmatized in his complaint as a "kept Mistress or Common Prostitute." His suit failed, however, as Howard P. Vincent has shown.

There is a generally trustworthy full-length modern study by E. R. Page, *George Colman the Elder*, 1935, which has been employed in this entry, heavily supplemented by contemporary sources and the data of *The London Stage*.

Portraits of George Colman the elder are numerous:

1. An oil by Thomas Gainsborough. In the National Portrait Gallery. This is probably the painting engraved by J. Hall and published by T. Cadell, 1787; by A. Smith, undated; and by an anonymous engraver as a plate to the *European Magazine*, 1785.

2. Oil by Sir Joshua Reynolds. Painted for Lord Mulgrave in 1767 and exhibited at the Royal Academy in 1770. This portrait has disappeared. It may be the picture which was engraved by G. Marchi and published in 1773; by N. Schiavonetti, published by John Sharp, 1807; by E. Scriven as a plate to *Contemporary Portraits*, 1813; as a plate to *Modern Standard Drama*, by J. Halpin; and by S. Fisher as the frontispiece to R. B. Peake's *Memoirs of the Colman Family*, 1841.

3. Oil, copy of the above. In the possession of Lord Faringdon.

4. Oil, copy of No 2, above. In the L. Gow sale, Christie's, 1937. Bought by Vicars.

5. Oil, copy of No 2 above. In the National Portrait Gallery.

6. Oil painting after Johann Zoffany. In

the Garrick Club. "Similar to a portrait in the possession of Lord O'Hagan, reproduced in Williamson's *Zoffany*." Engraved by E. Smith in 1822.

7. Engraving by Ridley, from "an original painting in the possession of Mr Jewell [treasurer of the Haymarket]." Published as a plate to the *Monthly Mirror*, 1797.

8. By an anonymous engraver, an oval frame supported by the comic and tragic muses, undated.

9. By an anonymous engraver, with title "The Manager in Distress," on plate with another of "The Adorable Alicia" (Jane Lessingham), for the *Town and Country Magazine*, 1780.

10. By an anonymous engraver. On plate with another engraving, of David Garrick. Undated. Plate to the *Lady's Magazine*.

11. "View Colman in the Lap of Mother Shipton / A Better Subject Satire Never Whipt On." Engraved by M. D[arly]. From the first page of the second part of *The Theatres*, 1772.

12. By an anonymous engraver. Frontispiece to *The Spleen or the Offspring of Folly*, 1776.

Colman, George *1762–1836, manager, dramatist, critic.*

George Colman the younger was born in London on 21 October 1762 to Sarah Ford, sometimes described as an actress (though no records now extant confirm the description) and George Colman the elder, playwright and theatrical patentee. Miss Ford had met the elder Colman in 1760, soon after her desertion by the Irish actor Henry Mossop, for whom she had borne a daughter Harriet. She and Colman began living together about 1761 but did not marry until 12 July 1768.

Young George began life in a household through which surged crowds of the literary, theatrical, and social *luminati* of the later eighteenth century, for his father was not only well born and the protégé of his kinsman the Earl of Bath, but was also gifted and charming and, successively, the master of two of the most active London theatrical enterprises, Covent Garden and the Haymarket. Young George remembered being dandled on Oliver Goldsmith's knee at five years of age, being greeted with Samuel Foote's "usual salutation of 'Blow your nose, child!'" and having David Garrick entertain him by making grotesque faces. When he was in his fourth year his father and mother went on a summer excursion to Paris and left him at the Colmans' Richmond estate. Garrick visited him regularly and wrote to his father that "We have work'd very hard in the Garden togeather, & have play'd at Ninepins till I was oblig'd to declare off — He is well taken care of indeed . . . & be assur'd that you may set y^r tender hearts at rest about him. . . . We are to have a day at Hampton, & he is to make love to my niece Kitty, & a plumb-pudding . . ." Samuel Johnson frightened the child, but Gibbon condescended to chat with him, and R. B. Sheridan was a frequent and fascinating visitor. Among others who appeared at Richmond and at the winter residence in Great Queen Street were Sir Joshua Reynolds, Lord Mansfield, Arthur Murphy, John Wilkes, Bonnell Thornton, Edmund Burke, and Topham Beauclerk. The brilliant Drury Lane actor William Powell, just before his death in 1769, gave the seven-year-old George a pony — which tossed him hard enough to make him give up riding for over a year. These and other recollected incidents of his earliest youth yield a picture of a bright boy, inquisitive, happy, and indulged by his elders.

At eight years of age George was placed in a fashionable school in Marylebone. He recalled in his *Random Records* (1830) that "The head-master . . . old Doctor Fountain ('Principium et Fons') was a worthy good-natured *Domine*, in a bushwig." Fountain began the inculcation of the classics. But after a few months George left

Harvard Theatre Collection

GEORGE COLMAN, the Younger
engraving by Greatbach, after De Wilde

the school, on the day of his mother's death, Good Friday, 29 March 1771: "My mother had died that morning; she had been for a short time ill, but not dangerously so, till on the preceding night; she had . . . swallow'd, by mistake a wrong medicine." Her death left a deep impression on the boy, as well as on his father, who never married again.

When he was ten George was enrolled at Westminster School, where the "plaguily severe" undermaster Vincent was a hard flogger in the tradition of Dr Busby. The Westminster of the time offered one of the finest classical curricula in England, and George seems to have thrived on the regimen. He boarded at a house kept successively by a Mr Jones and a Mrs Clapham in Great Dean's Yard, where among his fellows were Vernon, later Archbishop of York, "Bob Hobart, the late Earl of

Buckinghamshire (whose *fag* I was in particular), and Cocks, the present Earl of Somerset." There were also Frederick Reynolds, later the dramatist, "Germaine, now [1830] Duke of Dorset; and Paget, now the Marquis of Anglesea." Colman was almost drowned bathing in the Thames, but was saved by yet another noble schoolfellow, "a younger brother of the then Lord Cranstoun."

In the summer of his thirteenth year, 1775, young George and his father went on a tour through the North of England, visiting Oxford en route to show the lad the site of his future studies. In the course of the journey, which led from Oxford to Woodstock, through Warwickshire, Staffordshire, Derbyshire, Lancashire, and Yorkshire, father and son encountered Captain Phipps (later Lord Mulgrave) and a party which included the eccentric botanist Joseph (later Sir Joseph) Banks, and that celebrated "noble savage," the tattooed Omai of Otaheite, who at Scarborough took young George graciously on his brown shoulders and swam with him some distance to sea and back.

On one of several visits to Bath, in 1776, young George's father borrowed from Palmer the proprietor of the Bath Theatre a costume for Prince Arthur and attired his son in it to show him off at the "select mummery" of the Bath cotillion.

George had since early childhood viewed the stage from his father's private box. But in 1777, when the elder Colman acquired the Haymarket from Foote and the son was 15, he began to frequent the green room and consort with the company. In the Christmas vacation of 1778–79 he accompanied his father to Wynnstay, the estate of Sir Watkin Williams Wynn in Denbighshire, Wales, to act among the genteel amateurs in Sir Watkin's celebrated private theatricals. The Colmans returned for the next three Christmases.

In January 1779 George matriculated at Christ Church College. Oxford proved

Harvard Theatre Collection

GEORGE COLMAN, the Younger

artist unknown

scholastically unrewarding for the student and financially painful for his father. George remained at Christ Church during term time, diverted by games and supper parties and squandering considerable cash (on one occasion he generously cosigned bad notes to the amount of £1000 for one of his friends who was in the hands of money lenders). But he rushed at once to the Haymarket green room and its seductions during the long vacation. On 13 September 1781 the *Morning Chronicle* reported that "Mrs Cargill [the actress] and her husband took it into their heads to set off suddenly for Bath last week; the consequence was the audience were on Tuesday evening [7 September] disappointed of their Macheath" in *The Beggar's Opera*, which she was supposed to have played. J[ames] W[inston], however, in a manuscript note on the Haymarket bill of 8 September, remarked, "Mrs Cargill run away this day with Colman Jun." But whether or not the lad succumbed to this particularly notorious temptation, Mrs Cargill was only one of many such lures.

So in the fall of 1781 George's indignant parent packed him off to King's College, Aberdeen University, under the escort of William Jewell, the Haymarket treasurer, "to be turned over to the *surveillance* of Professor Roderick Macleod," a move which, it was hoped, would remove him "from scenes of idleness and dissipation."

Aberdeen served no better than Oxford the causes either of economy, education, or discipline. Professor Macleod failed in his surveillance, and Colman found the studies meager and the opportunities for roistering extensive. As he admits, he quickly earned the "appellation of the 'Muckle De'il'" among the Aberdeenites, though his sins appear from this distance to have been venial. In a wild January horseback excursion with two English fellow exiles, he stayed the night at an inn at Laurence-Kirk, and there wrote his first verse, a ballad, in the "album" kept to memorialize guests. Astonished and charmed to find that he "could tag rhymes," on his return to school George wrote his first long poem, called *The Man of the People*, a satire on the Whig statesman Charles James Fox, who had so termed himself. Colman knew "little more of Politicks, and the Man of the People, than the Man in the Moon!" but, vain of his work, he had the verses published at his own expense, anonymously. They were, he says, "downright school-boy trash."

His next effort, and his first for the stage, was a musical farce, *The Female Dramatist*, which an indulgent father thrust on at the Haymarket on the benefit night of the hapless William Jewell, his long-suffering treasurer, on 16 August 1782. "It was uncommonly hiss'd," Colman remembered. Fortunately for him the authorship was not known at the time, and Sarah Gardner was later rumored to have written it. It was never printed.

Still nominally in residence at the University of Aberdeen, Colman next produced a three-act comedy, *Two to One*, for which Dr Samuel Arnold wrote the music. It was delayed in production, however, until 19 June 1784, by which time George had been released from his Scottish bondage and was at the Haymarket to witness his triumph. The piece played 18 times that summer season and was in the repertory for several years. Reviewers were exceedingly kind, partly out of regard for his father.

The elder George Colman, probably disturbed by the younger's growing interest in a young actress of the Haymarket company named Catherine Morris, sent him on a tour of the Continent in August 1784, with an older friend as companion. Young George returned, however, in late September, and took advantage of his father's absence from town "on a party of pleasure" to fly to Gretna Green with Miss Morris, marrying her there on 3 October. The marriage was kept secret until 10 November 1788, when at Mrs Colman's insistence they were married again, by the Rev Erasmus Middleton at St Luke's, Chelsea, with David Morris her brother and Edward Pritchard as witnesses.

George had been entered at Lincoln's Inn to study law on 9 August, and for some years he lived in chambers in the Temple, but his mind, as well as his heart, was now irretrievably dedicated to the theatre. His third play, *Turk and No Turk*, was brought on at the Haymarket on 9 July 1785, with an epilogue by his friend Edward Topham. It played 10 times that season. On 4 August 1787 the Haymarket company performed Colman's sentimental comic opera *Inkle and Yarico*, based on the slight sketch in the *Spectator*. Dr Arnold furnished some bright airs, a few of them adapted from Paisiello, and Rooker painted exotic scenes. This romantic fancy was wildly popular, playing 20 times at the Haymarket during the season and remaining in that theatre's (and Covent Garden's) repertory far into the next century. It was the most admired comic opera of its era.

With his next *oeuvre* Colman had trouble from the beginning. He wrote it first in four acts as *More Ways than Means*, then reduced it to three acts and produced it on 10 July 1788 as *Ways and Means*. Colman's epilogue, spoken by Palmer in the character of Johnny Grub, a scandal-mongering newspaper editor, gave serious offense to the London journals, and Colman suffered their enmity for months.

Young George Colman, like his father, made some perfunctory gestures toward training for the law. He was a few terms at Lincoln's Inn and continued to occupy his chambers in King's Bench Walk. But this interest, never very strong, gradually faded as he was drawn more and more into theatrical activity. The health of the elder Colman began to fail after 1785 and by 1789 he was so enfeebled in body and mind that the duties of managing the Haymarket fell entirely on his son.

In his first summer season of management, 18 May through 15 September 1789, Colman, just 27 years old, presented 89 nights of 50 plays with his company of 57 actors and actresses, six dancers, and nine singers. He had the assistance of the faithful William Jewell, who presided over the cash box, and of the veteran prompter James Wrighten. James Aickin, the younger Bannister, Mr and Mrs Stephen Kemble, the two John Edwins, and Robert Palmer led the superior company. Nine of the plays produced were new, but Colman found time away from executive duties to contribute only two of his own, the mainpiece *The Battle of Hexham*, which was a success, playing 20 times after its introduction on 11 August, and the afterpiece *The Family Party*, which received a wan reception, playing only six times during the season. Though it was published on 19 July, it was never revived. Music for both productions was by Samuel Arnold.

After the lapse of a year, in which he was hard beset by financial and organizational worries and distress over the accelerated deterioration of his father's health, Colman wrote, for production on 30 July 1791, *The Surrender of Calais*, a lavish melodrama of Edward III's age, employing the entire company, and with romantic scenery by Rooker. The costume designer Whitfield promised "The Characters will be dressed in the Habits of the Times." "The new Musick (with a Martial Overture) by Dr Arnold," was particularly commended, and helped the piece to 28 performances that season. On 15 June 1792 came Colman's "prelude" *Poor Old Haymarket*, which played eight nights. On 3 August 1793 opened the melodrama *The Mountaineers*, which was repeated for 26 nights. On 9 June 1795, to open the new season, *New Hay at the Old Market* was produced. Another "prelude," it was, however, employed as an afterpiece an astonishing 32 times during that summer and (as *Sylvester Daggerwood*) was in demand for many years.

On 14 September 1793 Colman had closed his regular season at the Haymarket. Five days later he had reopened it with the bulk of the Drury Lane company, who were then without a stage because of the demolition and rebuilding of their theatrical home. Colman presided over this talented group—with the Drury Lane management happily acquiescing in the scheme—until 21 April 1794. On that date the first dramatic performance was presented in the enormous new Drury Lane Theatre. Colman turned the Drury Lane company back to its regular management and supplied a long epilogue for Miss Farren to speak on the occasion.

George had remained his father's responsible agent at the Haymarket until the elder Colman's death on 14 August 1794. By the terms of his father's will he received the "Theatre and Leasehold premises . . . with the Appurtenances and . . . Wardrobe Scenes Machinery and other things therein and thereunto belonging" *if* "a

Grant patent or License shall be obtained . . . for the like time or term as I have heretofore enjoyed a License." That formulation of his father's had implied both a fear and a hope. The Haymarket had never had a patent, and its license was fragile, needing annual resuscitation, depending always on the Lord Chamberlain's good whim. But the Lord Chamberlain's accounts at the Public Record Office show licenses being granted to the Haymarket proprietor with regularity for each summer through 1814, usually 15 May through 15 September, though in 1811 and 1812 to 15 October, and in 1813 and 1814 all the way to 15 November. It was a valuable concession, and relations with successive Lords Chamberlain were maintained with some care by both Colmans.

On 3 March 1796 George Colman's gothic melodrama *The Iron Chest*, derived from Godwin's novel *Caleb Williams*, was presented, with music by Stephen Storace, at Drury Lane. It was a dismal failure, playing only four nights, although John Philip Kemble himself had assumed the leading role of Sir Edward Mortimer. In a witty and bitter preface to the published play Colman laid the blame for the disaster on Kemble for bringing the work to production insufficiently rehearsed and while Kemble, the composer Storace, and Colman himself were ill. The charge caused a breach between Colman and Kemble which lasted for some years.

For his friend Palmer's benefit at Drury Lane on 28 April 1797 Colman furnished a hastily written afterpiece called *My Nightgown and Slippers*. It was a trivial and rather scurrilous monologue; the *Monthly Mirror* reported that "this *slipshod* amusement was absolutely *hooted from the stage*." But the comedy *The Heir at Law*, staged on 15 July 1797 at the Haymarket, was given 28 showings that season, and has been one of the most durable of all of Colman's works, being revived occasionally still.

On 16 January 1798 the Drury Lane management expended £2,000 (according to the *London Chronicle*) on the costumes and scenery for Colman's melodrama *Blue-Beard; or, Female Curiosity*. The scenemen blundered and delays in the performance kept the audience up until past midnight. Critics smote the piece brutally. But it was a roaring success with box, pit, and gallery, was exploited 64 nights that season, and rolled triumphantly on into the nineteenth century. It was the first of Colman's pieces for which Michael Kelly "selected" the music. Less admired by audiences was *Blue Devils*, a rather transparent theft from Joseph Patrat's *L'Anglais; ou, Le Fou Raisonnable*, staged once at Covent Garden, on 24 April 1798 for Fawcett's benefit. It was revived in later years, however.

Feudal Times; or, The Banquet Gallery, another of Colman's florid "historical" melodramas, was sold to Drury Lane for production on 19 January 1799 and dazzled patrons 39 times that season "with new Musick, Scenery, Machinery, Dresses and Decorations." Kelly composed incidental music and Jan Ladislav Dussek contributed the overture. The *Morning Chronicle* described it as "an exhibition of music and dialogue, pantomime and dancing, painting and machinery, antique dresses and armour, thunder and lightning, fire and water, illumination, processions, banquets, battles, sieges, explosions, and everything that can surprize, enchant or terrify the spectators."

On 29 September 1800 the Haymarket staged Colman's hastily written "operatic farce" *The Review; or, The Ways of Windsor*. His sensibility-ridden "comedy," *The Poor Gentleman* was brought out at Covent Garden on 11 February 1801. But on 5 March 1803, his immortal *John Bull; or, The Englishman's Fireside* appeared at Covent Garden introducing the excellent Irish character Dennis Brulgruddery and the honest yeoman Job Thornberry, marking the apogee of their respective types.

John Bull had a run of 47 nights. Also in 1803, on 25 July at the Haymarket, Colman launched his farce *Love Laughs at Locksmiths* (an adaptation of Bouilly's *Une folie*) under his new *nom de plume* "Arthur Griffinhoofe."

His slight operatic farce *The Gay Deceivers* (purloined from Hell's *Les Événements imprévus*) was produced at the Haymarket on 22 August 1804, his comedy *Who Wants a Guinea?* at Covent Garden on 15 April 1805, and his operatic farce *We Fly By Night; or, Long Stories* at Covent Garden on 28 January 1806. Michael Kelly had seen the latter in Paris as *Le Conteur, ou Les Deux Postes* and had pilfered it for Colman. The "book" of an "operatic romance" entitled *The Forty Thieves*, produced at Drury Lane with music by Kelly on 8 April 1806, has also been ascribed to Colman, but now appears to have been only partly his.

Kelly furnished the music also for Colman's melodrama *The Africans; or, War, Love, and Duty* at the Haymarket on 23 July 1808. Critical disapproval caused revisions, after which the piece succeeded. Colman's next attempt, the farce *X. Y. Z.*, was a casualty of the furious dispute between him and his brother-in-law Morris who obtained an injunction in Chancery to keep the work off the boards after it had been performed once at Covent Garden, on 11 December 1810. It was a very small loss to the dramatic repertory, however. The farce *The Quadrupeds of Quedlingburgh; or, The Rovers of Weimar*, based on Canning and Frere's burlesque of German sentimental tragedy, *The Rovers* (1798) drew large audiences to the Haymarket following its introduction on 18 July 1811. *Doctor Hocus Pocus; or, Harlequin Washed White* was a routine pantomime at that house on 2 August 1814.

Colman wrote no more until the mildly successful farce *The Actor of All Work; or, First and Second Floor* was prepared for the Haymarket on 7 August 1817, and he

was again silent until, on 22 April 1822, Covent Garden staged his three-act melodrama *The Law of Java*. A year later, on 27 September 1823, at Drury Lane, *Stella and Leatherlungs; or, A Star and a Stroller* rather sadly terminated his career of 41 years as a writer for the London theatres. R. B. Peake called it "a hasty production . . . written at the earnest desire of Elliston, to exhibit the extraordinary precocious powers of Clara Fisher." It failed utterly.

Colman's managerial enterprise had at first prospered, due in large part to the general success of his musical pieces and farces. But he was a high liver and improvident to a degree. He was also quarrelsome and litigious. An interesting example of his several actions-at-law was one he pressed against George Wathen, manager of the theatre at Richmond, Surrey, in May 1793 for performing John O'Keeffe's *The Agreeable Surprise*, with songs by Samuel Arnold. The farce had indeed been purchased 12 years before by the elder Colman, but it had been seen dozens of times, and Wathen was not really harming anyone's interests. The jury found for the plaintiff but Mr Justice Buller sensibly set that verdict aside.

Colman often voiced the more reasonable complaint that the winter patent theatres sometimes made difficulties about the actors they employed in common with the summer Haymarket. Once or twice they deliberately encroached on Colman's season, making it impossible for him to employ certain stars. The summer of 1802 was particularly unsuccessful, from this and several other points of view, and Colman began to canvass the provinces for fresh faces. He heard of Charles Mathews's successes at York and engaged him in September 1802 for the summer of 1803. In March Colman and his son George, a captain in the army, arrived in York to inspect their purchase, and an immediate and lasting friendship sprang up. Mathews was the most talented and financially the most profitable of the several discoveries Colman made and was the Haymarket's principal draw for years.

But such lucky acquisitions were not frequent enough. In 1805 Colman was forced, largely by his own extravagance, to part with a number of shares in his theatre to his brother-in-law Morris, James Winston (James Bowes) later stage manager at Drury Lane, and an attorney named Tahourdin, who afterwards sold his shares to Morris. The company continued excellent.

In 1807 Colman's finances received an unexpected boost from the generosity of Jack Bannister, from whom Colman had borrowed £700. Colman had later taken a collection of loose comic materials for a dialogue which Bannister had brought him, had put them in order and had fleshed them out, thus providing the comedian with the famous "Bannister's Budget," which he had taken on a highly profitable tour. On his return Bannister gallantly tore up Colman's bond.

In 1808 Colman engaged in a paper war with Mrs Elizabeth Inchbald over her denigratory remarks about his *Heir at Law* and some of his father's productions in her collection of plays called *The British Theatre*. In 1810 a long-simmering factional feud within the Haymarket burst into litigation between Colman and Morris, now the treasurer. A motion brought forward in the High Court of Chancery on 20 July 1811 caused the Lord Chancellor to order Morris to pay the salaries of the players, which he had refused to do. Morris demurred and sought to bring the question to a Court of Equity. By 25 July Morris had relented sufficiently for the season to proceed. But the feud broke out afresh in May 1812, with Morris placing public notices to the effect that he would endorse neither theatrical engagements nor repairs agreed to by the other partners. Again, peace was made. But the quarrel continued to smoulder through 1814. In that season disaster

took another form when Mathews and Terry were thrown from a gig and injured. Mathews dislocated his hip and was lamed for many months, delaying his all-important contributions to the theatre's health.

Furthermore, not all of Colman's creditors were as generous as Bannister. During some three years, with only brief and infrequent respites, he was forced into residence in the liberties of the King's Bench debtor's prison at the suit of his erstwhile friend and collaborator Samuel Arnold. He was occasionally allowed to sally forth to transact business, however. On one occasion the Duke of York obtained permission for him to come to Carlton House to dine with the Prince Regent. (R. B. Peake has an account of some roughly jovial impertinences which Colman offered to the heir to the throne on that occasion, exactly calculated to please such a man. When he was crowned as George IV he continued his friendship to Colman, appointing him to the honorary post of Lieutenant of Yeomen of the Guard on 13 May 1820. Colman in 1830 dedicated his *Random Records* to the monarch.) In 1819 Colman gave up the fight and disposed of his share of the Haymarket to the tenacious Morris.

On 19 January 1824, John Larpent, the previous functionary, having died, the Lord Chamberlain appointed George Colman "Examiner of all Plays, Tragedies, Comedies, Operas, Farces, or any other entertainment of the stage, of what denomination soever." Curiously, although Colman was never scrupulous to exclude profanity, impious expressions, or licentious situations from his own works, when he assumed the censorship he became rigorously and even ludicrously puritanical. To his new-found abhorrence of "improper" and "impious" expressions he added a detestation of anything which could conceivably be interpreted as denying any sort of authority. "Hell" or even "Heavens!", "damn" (or even "demme"), invocations to the "God of Truth," a young man's addressing his mistress as "angel"—all were mercilessly excised, along with all political commentary or allusions of the most distant sort to rebellion or revolution, and such inflammatory words as "thighs." Yet once the manuscript left his hands for the theatre Colman was indifferent to its representation and he was ready to wink at evasion, as his letter of 27 April 1829 to Frederic Yeates the manager demonstrates:

My Dear Yates [*sic*],

I hear that Beazley complains I have reduced all his full-grown angels into cherubims, *id est,* cut them in half and left them neither heaven or cloud to rest upon; that his comedy will be d——d by the public, owing to the removal of some devilish good jokes by the Examiner, and further, that the Licenser's Deputy has taken most unlicensed liberties with the dramatist.

Cannot you, my dear Fred, instruct him better? The play, you know, must be printed in strict accordance with my obliterations; but if the parts be previously given out, it will be difficult to induce the actors to preach from my text.

A vein of cupidity also surfaced in Colman's character and he attempted to impose a separate license on the new songs or musical interpolations to old plays at a fee of two guineas each, and asserted a claim to license oratorios—a claim which was fortunately not upheld, in view of his abhorrence of biblical allusions.

Like his father, Colman suffered from gout. The complaint grew worse in February 1830, and so did an infection of his bladder and liver. In November of that year he had a disabling attack followed by a severe illness of some three months. Removing to the residence of Henry Harris at Greenford on orders of his physician, Dr H. S. Chinnock, he improved somewhat. He remained at Greenford until August 1836 when he came back to his house at No 22, Brompton Square, where he died on 17 October 1836. His funeral was private.

He was buried beside his father in the vault of Kensington Church.

Colman and his first wife had discovered —and apparently very early—that their marriage was a mistake. (Evidently Colman's elder son George was the offspring of this union, though his birthdate is not known.) By 1795 Colman's interest in Mrs Maria Gibbs, a pretty and talented comedienne who had come to the Haymarket company in 1793, had ripened into an affair well known to London and alluded to satirically in the *Monthly Mirror*, by "Peter Pindar" in *The Cap*, and elsewhere. They lived together openly for many years and were said to have been married in 1809. There are, however, no known records to substantiate the union, neither notices of license and marriage nor of the events which would have made the marriage possible—the deaths of Catherine Morris Colman and Mr Gibbs, or of the requisite divorces. There seems no doubt, however, that Colman's only other known child, Edmund Craven Colman, born in 1802, later a captain in the army like his half-brother George, was Mrs Gibbs's son. In a letter of 22 September 1796 to Henry Woodfall, who contemplated his biography, Colman wrote candidly on the "grating subject" of his marriage to Catherine Morris: "Mrs. C—— and I have long been mutual plagues. A year ago we determined to separate: the proposal came first from her, and I accepted it instantly. She wished afterward to retract, but I would not." He had provided her, he said, with £800 per year.

The younger George Colman was, like his father, a small, smart-looking man, neat in his dress and precise in his gestures. In his later years he inclined to corpulency.

Portraits of the younger George Colman include the following:

1. Engraving by W. Ridley. Plate to the *Monthly Mirror*, 1797.

2. Same picture, engraved by Freeman, 1806.

3. By Cheesman after De Wilde, with

title "Proprietor of the Haymarket Theatre." 1807.

4. By Ridley and Blood after S. Drummond. Plate to the *European Magazine*,
1808.

5. By W. T. Fry after F. C. Turner,
1820.

6. Same as No 5, by an anonymous engraver, undated.

7. In dress of a Lieutenant of the Yeomen of the Guard. By T. Lupton after
J. Jackson.

8. By T. Lupton after J. Jackson. Published by Jackson, Colnaghi & Co., 1832.

9. By W. Greatbach. Frontispiece to
Bentley's *Miscellany*, 1837. Reprinted
1838 and 1841.

10. Same as No 8, vignetted. Printed by
C. Hullmandel. Published by Henry Colburn and Richard Bentley. Anonymous and
undated.

11. By R. Cooper. Published by Richardson, undated.

12. *The Genius of the Times*. Caricature
engraving by Williams, published 1812 for
proprietors of *Town Talk*.

13. *Hocus Pocus; or, Conjurors Raising
the Wind*. Caricature engraving by Williams. Published 1814 by W. N. Jones.

*George Colman the Younger 1762–
1836* by Jeremy Bagster-Collins (1946) is
the standard book-length biography.

Colman, Mrs George the first, Catherine. *See* MORRIS, CATHERINE.

Colman, Mrs George the second, Maria. *See* GIBBS, MARIA.

Cologne. *See* COULON.

Colomba, Giovanni Battista Innocenzo *1717–1793, scene painter, machinist, costume designer.*

The Swiss painter and decorator Giovanni Battista Innocenzo Colomba was
born at Lugano in 1717 and was schooled
in painting by his uncle, Luca Antonio

Columba. For some time Giovanni was a
decorator and scene painter at the courts
of Württemberg, Hanover, and Frankfurt,
and he painted the ceilings in the Ludwigs-
burg Opera House. Colomba was a painter
and costume designer for about five years
for the pantomime manager Niccolini,
traveling to Mainz, Hamburg, Mannheim,
Vienna, Prague, and elsewhere. In 1764 he
painted the new theatre at Como and also
worked at Turin for the King of Sardinia.

Coming from Milan, in 1773–74 Colomba joined the King's Theatre in London
as scene painter and machinist, a post he
held through 1779–80. His name was
specified in the bills for scenes and machines for *Armida* on 8 November 1774,
Montezuma on 7 February 1775, and
Didone on 7 November 1775, but no doubt
he provided similar services for most of
the productions at the King's Theatre
during this period. Rosenfeld and Croft-
Murray credit him also with: (1773–74)
Perseo, Antigono, Nitteti; (1774–75)
*Alessandro nell'Indie, Piramo e Tisbe, La
difesa d'amore, La donna di spirito*;
(1775–76) *La vestale, Le ali d'amore, Cajo
Mario*; (1776–77) *Germondo, Telemaco*;
(1777–78) *L'amore soldato*; (1778–79)
*L'avaro deluso, Demofoonte, Enea e La-
vinia, La Governante or The Duenna*, a
masquerade ball; (1779–80) *Quinto
Fabio, Rinaldo*, and *Il duca d'Atene*. In
1775 he equipped a theatre for Sir Henry
Bridgeman at Weston Hall and also
painted the scenery.

Colomba died at Lugano in 1793. Details of his continental career are in the
Enciclopedia dello spettacolo.

Colombani. *See* COLOMBATI.

Colombati, Elisabetta *[fl. 1791–1811], singer.*

Before coming to England in 1794,
Signora Elisabetta Colombati sang in Italy.
Her full name is found on the libretto of
Li due castellani which was published at

Pisa in 1791. She made her first English appearance at the King's Theatre, London, as Merlina in *Il capriccio drammatico* on 1 March 1794, when she also sang a role in *Don Giovanni*. On 18 March she sang Vespina in *La bella pescatrice* and on 28 April Azema in *Semiramide*.

Signora Colombati continued as the second woman in serious opera at the King's Theatre for another two seasons in which she sang Donna Eugenia in *L'amor contrastato*, a role in *Zenobia in Palmira*, a role in *I zingari in fiera*, Isabella in *La scola de maritati*, Dorinda in *Aci e Galatea*, Zelma in *L'isola del piacere*, a role in *Le nozze di Dorina*, Alena in *La bella Arsene*, and Zulima in *Piramo e Tisbe*.

Absent for a season, Colombati returned to the King's Theatre in 1797–98 to sing Elisa in *Nina*, Lisotta in *La Cifra*, Ernesto in *La sposa in equivoco*, Costanza in *Il consiglio imprudente*, Fidalma in *Il matrimonio segreto*, and her roles in *Semiramide*, *La scola de maritati*, and *Il capriccio drammatico*. Her name is not found in the Opera bills again until the season of 1801. She then continued at the King's Theatre until 1811. The operas in which she sang between 1801 and 1811, in addition to some of those already cited, included *Le gelosie villane* (20 January 1801), *La pastorella nobile* (17 January 1801), *I viaggiatori felice* (1 March 1803), *Fernando nel Messico* (31 March 1803), *Calipso* (31 May 1803), *Le astuzie femminili* (21 February 1804), *Il trionfo dell'amor fraterno* (22 March 1804), *Argenide e Serse* (4 March 1806), *Il principe di Teranto* (23 December 1806), *Il ritorno di Serse* (24 February 1807), and *La morte di Mitridate* (16 April 1807). Signora Colombati's last known performance at the King's Theatre was in *Il fanatico per la musica* on 19 February 1811.

Colombe, Émilie [fl. 1788–1789], dancer.

Mademoiselle Émilie Colombe was en-gaged at the King's Theatre in 1788–89 at a salary of £300, plus a benefit free of charges and the payment of the expenses of her journey. Brought from Paris with several other principal dancers in an attempt by Gallini, manager of the Opera, to stem the rising tide of public dissatisfaction with his dance troupe, Mademoiselle Colombe made her first appearance on 10 January 1789 in a *New Divertissement* and a new ballet *L'Embarquement pour Cythère*.

That season she also danced in new ballets *La Nymphe et le chasseur*, *La Jalousies du sérail*, *Admète*, *Annette et Lubin*, and *Les Caprices de Galatée*. For her benefit on 19 March, tickets could be had at her address, No 37, Silver Street, Golden Square. When the King's Theatre was burned down by an arsonist on 17 June, Gallini's company moved to Covent Garden for three weeks, where Mademoiselle Colombe first danced on 27 June. She made her last recorded appearance in London at Covent Garden on 11 July 1789, in *Les Fêtes provençales*.

Mlle Colombe may have been related to the singer and dancer of the same name (1751–1830) who performed at the Comédie-Italienne at Paris in the 1760s. According to the *Enciclopedia dello spettacolo*, that Mlle Colombe was more noted for scandal and extravagance than for artistic merit and in 1784 was obliged to give up the theatre.

"Colossus" [fl. 1745], giant.

The *Daily Advertiser* of 23 February 1745 reported that there was

a young Colossus to be seen at the Sign of the French Horn and Mansion House, opposite the Mansion House, being a boy fifteen Years of Age, Seven Feet high, and every way proportioned; born at Hurtfield, in Sussex, and allowed by several Judges to be a greater curiosity then the famous Sweede [Daniel Cajanus] that was shewn at the above Place some time ago. He is to bee seen any time, from Ten in the Morning till Nine at Night;

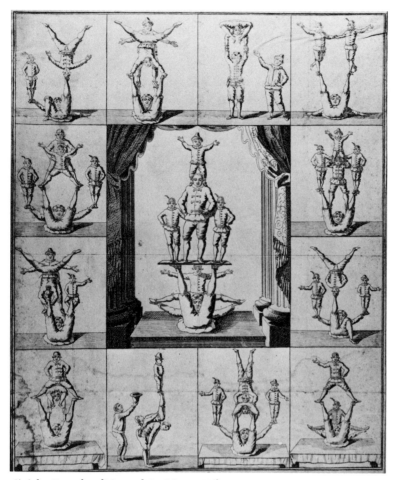

Civiche Raccolte d'Arte ed Incisione, Milan
SIGNOR COLPI, in a variety of postures
artist unknown

and never was exhibited to public view before.

On the following 3 August the same paper announced that "The Wonderful Young Giant will perform on the Rope this present Saturday, at the New Wells near the London Spaw, Clerkenwell."

"Colossus of Equestrians." *See* DUCROW, ANDREW.

Colpi, Signor ₁*fl. 1764–1789₁, posture maker, ropedancer.

On 28 December 1764 "the celebrated Signor Colpi" performed on the slack rope at the Crow Street Theatre, Dublin, announced as the person "who exhibited all last season in London with universal Applause," probably at Sadler's Wells. The Crow Street advertisement promised

Particularly he will hang by his toe on the rope in full swing:/He will also per-

form a continual somerset/With the quickness equal to the Flier of a Jack/he will hang by his teeth/he will lie across the rope on his back/he will turn himself into all the forms of a monkey/and the rope all the while in full swing./He will do such things as are incredible.

The incredible Colpi was back at London in 1765, "turning a fast Catherine Wheel on the slack-wire with fireworks at his feet" on the stage of Sadler's Wells. Sylas Neville saw Colpi, billed as the Venetian, perform with his children at Sadler's Wells on 13 June 1767 and described the event in his *Diary*:

Postures in which the Venetian and his children (a boy and a girl particularly) excel greatly. One stands on his hands, turns his feet backwards to his haunches, and walks in this position or forms an arch with his breast, while the other stands on his head upon it, the father carries one on his hand around his body, one stands on his head on his father's hand. These I mention as a specimen of many more, equally curious, tho' seeing these postures is disagreeable to a humane mind. The father balances too the slack rope. . . .

The Colpis were at Sadler's Wells again in 1769, and on 13 September 1770 arrived at Glasgow where they took the theatre to present their exhibitions. No doubt they gave similar performances throughout the three kingdoms over the years. By 1777 they were back at London, and Colpi displayed "Surprising Attitudes" at Astley's equestrian amphitheatre, on 7 May. On 23 September of that year Colpi and his children took a benefit at Astley's. He performed tricks on the slack wire, and with his children he raised six persons from the ground and balanced them all at one time. Signora Colpi also performed "Several Equilibres on the Slack Wire."

By 1789 Colpi was in Montego Bay, Jamaica, where on 11 July it was announced that Mr Bernard and the Venetian would give various performances on the tight and slack ropes, and would offer exhibitions of tumbling, balancing, and magic. These exhibitions were repeated on 2 and 4 September and 27 October 1789, and Colpi was not heard from again. A print was published c. 1825, depicting Colpi in a variety of postures.

Colpi, Signora [*fl.* 1777], *ropedancer. See* **COLPI, SIGNOR.**

Colpi, Signorino [*fl.* 1767–1777], *ropedancer. See* **COLPI, SIGNOR.**

Colpi, Signorina [*fl.* 1767–1777], *ropedancer? See* **COLPI, SIGNOR.**

Colter, Mrs. *See* **WHEELER, ELIZA.**

Coltman, Mr [*fl.* 1794], *organist.*
Mr Coltman was listed in 1794 by Doane's *Musical Directory* as organist at the Temple of Flora.

Columba. *See* **COLOMBA.**

Columbine, Mrs Peter. *See* **BRUNTON, ELIZABETH.**

Colvill, Mr [*fl.* 1779], *singer.*
At the end of the mainpiece in a specially licensed performance at the Haymarket Theatre on 27 December 1779 a Mr Colvill sang "Blow High, Blow Low." The company was an impromptu collection of professionals brought together to introduce to the stage "A Gentleman [unidentified, but not Colvill] well known in the literary world, who has been prevailed on by his Friends to make his first attempt on the stage."

Comanni, Mr [*fl.* 1734], *dancer.*
A Mr Comanni played the dancing role of Euryale in *Perseus and Andromeda* at Covent Garden on 25 January 1734.

Comano. *See* COMMANO.

Combes. *See* COOMBES.

Comelati, Mr [*fl.* *1735–1741*], *singer?*

A Comelati was on the Covent Garden pay list at the end of the season of 1735–36 at the rate of 1*s.* 6*d.* per night. His function was unstated. From 26 September 1740 through 14 March 1741 he received 14 payments of various sizes, all of them specifically paying him for his work in the opera *Orpheus and Eurydice* at the rate of 5*s.* per performance and most of them mentioning other performances "besides." He was evidently hired by the performance and was not in the regular company.

Comer, Henry [*fl.* *1660–1676*], *violinist.*

Henry Comer was appointed to the King's private music as violinist on 16 June 1660, replacing Richard Comer—possibly his father. A warrant dated 9 November specified his annual salary as £46 12*s.* 8*d.*, in addition to which he presumably received the usual livery payment each year. On 6 March 1662 he was paid £10 for a treble violin, which he had purchased for the King's service, and a month later he journeyed to Portsmouth with his Majesty to meet the Queen. It was doubtless Comer to whom Evelyn talked on 21 December 1662, though the diarist called him "Cromer . . . a greate Musitian."

Henry Comer was chosen to be a member of the elite group of 12 violins within the regular band of 24 on 14 March 1667, but on 25 March he was granted leave to travel for some years. This permission appears to have been renewed a year later when William Aleworth was given Comer's place and £23 of his salary for the period 25 March 1668 to 27 March 1669. By 16 May 1670 Comer seems to have returned to Court, for he was to attend the King at Dover from that date until 4 June. By 5

December he was absent again, Richard Browne serving in his place, and on 21 February 1672 a warrant was issued to stop Comer's salary and pay it to Browne. Though the violinist's absence from court was referred to as temporary, on 8 May 1676 it became permanent: James Banister was appointed to Henry Comer's place "with all rights and profitts." What Comer was doing during his frequent absences is not known. Once, apparently in error, the Lord Chamberlain's accounts cited Comer as John.

Comer, John. *See* COMER, HENRY.

Comerford, Mr [*fl.* *1789–1794*], *prompter's assistant, actor.*

A young man named Comerford—probably the son of the actor Henry Comerford (d. 1778)—served as "prompter's boy" at Drury Lane in 1789–90, when he was paid 4*s.* 6*d.* per week, and in 1790–91. In the summer of 1793 he acted a minor unspecified role at the Haymarket in *The London Hermit* (on 6 July and nine other times) and Perequillo in *The Mountaineers* (on 3 August and 25 other times). He was also a member of Colman's acting company at the Haymarket in 1793–94, when he performed the role of a Turnkey in *Royal Clemency* on 10, 11, and 12 October and an unspecified role in *The Box-Lobby Challenge* on 22 February and 11 other times, concluding on 27 March 1794. Perhaps he was the Comerford who acted at Birmingham in 1802 and at Manchester in 1813.

Comerford, Henry *d. 1778, actor.*

Henry Comerford's first noticed appearance on the London stage was as Connolly in *The School for Wives* and Sileno in *Midas* on 23 September 1776 at the China Hall Theatre, Rotherhithe. At China Hall in that autumn he also acted the Duke of Norfolk in *Henry VIII*, Othman in *Barbarossa*, Colonel Feignwell in *A Bold Stroke for a Wife*, the title role in *Oro-*

onoko, King Henry in *Richard III*, Cassander in *Alexander the Great*, Loader in *The Minor*, King Arthur in *Tom Thumb the Great*, the Uncle in *The London Merchant*, the King in *The Mourning Bride*, the title role in *Cato*, Lord Duke in *High Life Below Stairs*, and, in his last appearance on 18 October 1776, Captain Plume in *The Recruiting Officer*. When the actors from China Hall took the Haymarket for occasional performances during the winter, Comerford acted Worcester in *Henry IV* and Prattle in *The Deuce is in Him* on 11 February 1777 (at the desire of the Noble Order of Bucks), with benefit tickets delivered out by Comerford to be taken in. On 1 May 1777 at the Haymarket he played Sir John Dormer in *A Word to the Wise*. He may also have been the Comerford who acted at Chester in Joseph Austin's company during the summer of 1776.

On 24 July 1778 the *Morning Chronicle* announced that Henry Comerford had died "lately" at Bristol. A Comerford, very likely his son, was a prompter's assistant at Drury Lane, 1789–91, and acted at the Haymarket in 1793–94. Drury Lane Theatre loaned "Mrs Cummerford" £1 1s. on 3 July 1792, another 10s. on 3 August 1793, when it was noted she was "in great distress," and another 10s. 6d. on 23 September 1793.

A James Camerford, "Comedian," was a subscriber to Bell's edition of Shakespeare's plays in 1773, but unless the name was a variant for Henry Comerford, there is no record of this person's acting in London.

Comins, Mr ₍fl. 1784₎, *singer*.

A Mr Comins of Penzance was listed by Burney as one of the tenor singers in the Handel Memorial Concerts at Westminster Abbey and the Pantheon in May and June 1784. Also listed separately as a countertenor was the Rev Mr Comins of Exeter. They may have been related to the Thomas Comins who was left a bequest in the will of his uncle, the musician Thomas Billington, in 1828.

Commano, Giovanni Giuseppe ₍fl. 1730–1732₎, *singer*.

On 3 November 1730 at the King's Theatre in the Haymarket, Giovanni Giuseppe Commano, a *basso*, sang Ernando in *Scipione*. He followed this with Timagene in *Poro* on 2 February 1731 and Mago in *Rinaldo* on 6 April. It is probable that he also sang Boschi's old role of Garibaldo in *Rodelinda* on 4 May. He returned to Italy after this, but (unless a different singer was involved) went again to England and sang Discord in *Britannia* at the Haymarket Theatre on 16 November 1732.

Commerford. *See* COMERFORD.

Como, Antonio ₍fl. 1770–1776₎, *dancer, ballet master*.

On 10 January 1770 Lord Pembroke wrote from Milan to David Garrick to recommend that the manager engage a dancer and ballet master named Antonio Como, who was a "goodish performer, & a very civil, easy kind of man." Although Como preferred a contract for two or three years, he was prepared to accept any reasonable offer. In another letter from Pembroke, 10 March 1770—which indicated Garrick had replied—Pembroke regretted having heard that it was already too late to take on Como but said that he would tell the dancer that Garrick had promised to send a contract for two years, to begin after the engagement of the incumbent Drury Lane ballet master concluded. Pembroke further noted that Count Firmian, whom Garrick had met, was a great and warm protector of Como.

It seems, however, that Como may not have waited for Garrick's contract to arrive before leaving for London, for on 19 May of the same year, a Mr Como danced in a single performance of the opera *Il disertore* at the King's Theatre. But there was, indeed, no other notice of him at London until he made his first appearance at Drury Lane on 30 September 1773 in a new comic dance called *The Mountaineers*, with Signora Crespi. William Hopkins, the prompter, noted in his "Diary" that they were "very Indiff[erent]." The facetious Drury Lane actor Thomas Weston, according to a newspaper clipping, had exclaimed extempore upon seeing the two new dancers at practice before their debut:

> *Signior Como*
> *Is not the Homo.*
> *Signiora Crispi*
> *She will hiss'd be.*

Como made his second appearance in *The Mountaineers* on 2 October. On 9 October he danced in the masque of *Alfred* and on 25 November in a *Bacchanalian Jubilee* with Signora Crespi, Giorgi, and Atkins. His other performances that season included dancing in *A Christmas Tale*, *Florizel and Perdita*, and *Amphitryon*. For his benefit on 22 April 1774, when he performed in a *New Grand Spanish Dance* and a *Grand New Serious Dance*, he shared a profit of £26 12s. with Signora Crespi.

Como remained at Drury Lane for another two seasons. In 1774–75, when his salary was £3 13s. per week, he appeared in a new *Dance of Foresters* in *As You Like It* on 1 October, in a *Dance of Slaves* on 27 October, in the dances to *The Tempest* on 26 December, and in a new dance, *The Pirates*, on 22 April. On the occasion of Monsieur La Rivier's dancing debut at Drury Lane on 3 April 1775, Como performed in a new ballet, *The Force of Love*, with Signora Como and "Two Children." Signora Como had previously danced at Drury Lane on 16 March 1775. On 8 May Como again danced with his wife in a *Grand New Spanish Dance* and *The School Master*.

In 1775–76, his last season at Drury Lane and evidently in London, Como performed in *The Hunting of the Savages*, *The Genii*, *The Sultan*, a *Grand Provencalle* ("with Allemande"), and a *Grand Dance* of *Fantastic Spirits*. On 2 March 1776 he danced a *Grand Garland* with Slingsby and on 3 May a *Grand Chaconne* with Signora Crespi. On 3 June 1776 the treasurer paid Como and Crespi £3 8s. 3d. each, "in full."

Como, Signora Antonio ₁*fl. 1775*₁, *dancer.*

On 16 March 1775, Signora Como, the wife of the ballet master Antonio Como, replaced Signora Crespi in the *Fête* in *The Maid of the Oaks* at Drury Lane. She danced with her husband and two others in a new ballet, *The Force of Love*, on 3 April 1775, and again with him in a *Grand New Spanish Dance* and *The School Master* on 8 May 1775.

Compton, Rouse ₁*fl. 1784–1794*₁, *violinist.*

Mr Compton was one of the second violinists who played at the Handel Memorial Concerts at Westminster Abbey and the Pantheon on 26, 27, 29 May and 3, 5 June 1784. By 1794 he was in the King's Band at Buckingham House.

Concy. *See* CORCY.

Condell, Charlotte *d. 1759, actress.*

Miss Charlotte Condell, the daughter of the Covent Garden boxkeeper John Condell the elder (d. 1779) by his first wife Jane, born Wilcox, shared in benefit tickets at Covent Garden on 30 April 1755 and 19 May 1756, but for what reason is uncertain. *The London Stage* suggests she may have been the "Young Gentlewoman who never appeared on any Stage" who acted Semanthe in *Ulysses* on 23 March 1756. In her second appearance "on any stage" she played Ismene in *Phaedra and Hippolitus* on 1 November 1756.

That season she also acted Dorinda in *The Stratagem* on 15 December, Lucilla in *The Fair Penitent* on 21 February, and Serina in *The Orphan* on 25 April, and shared a benefit with the prompter Carmichael, Holtom, and Miss Helm on 30 April 1757. The *Theatrical Examiner* (1757) regretted that Miss Condell was "hourly ruining herself" by attention to John Rich's instructions and by copying Mrs Woffington's manner of speaking: "the little part of Lucilla in [*The Fair Penitent*] shews it. . . . She has other means in her power."

In 1757–58 she acted Rutland when David Ross (1728–1790) made his first appearance at London in the title role of *The Earl of Essex* on 7 October. She also played Dorinda and Serina again and Angelica in *Love Makes a Man* on 7 November, Drusilla in *The Prophetess* on 1 February, Philadelphia in *The Amorous Widow* on 11 March, Volumnia in *Coriolanus* on 14 March, Clariana in *The Country House* on 3 April, and Lady Diana Talbot in *Anna Bullen* on 10 April. The treasurer paid out £4 4s. on 11 February 1758 for a pair of earrings for her, and on 8 April she took £9 1s. 6d. as her share of benefit tickets. Her last performance at Covent Garden was as Philadelphia on 28 April 1758. Evidently too ill to play in 1758–59, Miss Condell died on 23 May 1759 and was buried at St Margaret's, Westminster, on 28 May 1759.

Charlotte was the sister of John Condell (fl. 1779–1784) the younger, also a box-keeper at Covent Garden, and the half-sister of the musician Henry Condell (1757–1824).

Condell, Henry *c. 1757–1824, harpsichordist, violinist, composer.*

Henry Condell was born at London about 1757, the son of Covent Garden box-keeper John Condell (d. 1779) by Ann Wilson, his common-law wife from about 1752. For information on Henry Condell's parentage and family see the entry of John Condell.

How Henry Condell became educated in music is not known. No doubt he benefited from the associations and friendships which

his father must have enjoyed among the personnel of Covent Garden Theatre and by living with his family for some years, at least between 1773 and about 1790, at Cross Court, Bow Street, in the heart of Covent Garden. He gave his first performance in public, billed as Master Condell, on 23 May 1771, playing a concerto on the harpsichord at Covent Garden Theatre. Two years later, on 25 May 1773 at the same place, he performed another concerto on the harpsichord, this one of his own composing, for his father's benefit.

By the time Condell was recommended by the musician John Parke, on 4 January 1778, as a proper person to be admitted to the Royal Society of Musicians, he had practiced music for a livelihood for at least seven years and was still a single man. He was elected on 1 March 1778. During his mature years Condell served the Society regularly as a member of the Court of Assistants, between 1793 and 1818. In 1815 he was a member of the committee for the annual concert at St Paul's and of the house committee.

By 1783, Condell was engaged as a member of the band for the operas at the King's Theatre. In May and June 1784, he was a first violinist in the Handel Memorial Concerts given at Westminster Abbey and the Pantheon; he was in the band as first violinist when the King's Theatre company played at the Pantheon in 1790–91. By 1794, according to Doane's *Musical Directory*, he was living at St Alban's Street and, in addition to the appointments already mentioned, was also a participant in the Concerts of Ancient Music and the Professional Concerts.

Between 1800 and 1818 Condell continued as a musician at the King's Theatre, at a salary of £2 5s. per week in 1801 and £3 per week by 1807–8. According to *The Dictionary of National Biography*, he also played during this period at Drury Lane and Covent Garden. About 1785 six of his songs were published, including a setting of

Edward Jerningham's poem "Matilda," but most of his composing took place after the turn of the century. In 1802–3 he provided overtures for Michael Kelly's new operas, *A House to be Sold*, *The Hero of the North*, and *Love Laughs at Locksmiths*, and music for Fawcett's ballet *The Enchanted Island* at the Haymarket on 20 June 1804.

Condell set music for Allingham's musical farce *Who Wins, or, the Widow's Choice*, at Covent Garden, 25 February 1808. In 1810 he wrote music for Reynolds's *The Bridal Ring* at Covent Garden on 16 October and for *Transformation*, attributed to Allingham, produced by the Drury Lane company at the Lyceum on 30 November. With other composers he furnished tunes for T. J. Dibdin's *Up to Town*, at Covent Garden on 6 November 1811. He contributed incidental music for *Aladdin, or The Wonderful Lamp*, 19 April 1813, and for the younger Charles Dibdin's *The Farmer's Wife*, 1 February 1814, both at Covent Garden. In 1811, Condell had won a prize at the Catch Club for his glee "Loud blowe the wyndes." A number of his songs as well as several harpsichord duets were published after 1810.

On 7 December 1823, it was reported to the Royal Society of Musicians that Condell was suffering an illness which prevented him from attending the meetings. He lingered six months, until his death at Cave House, Battersea, on 24 June 1824. In his will, dated 5 April 1821, Condell described himself as of Frith Street, Soho, but late of St Alban's Street, Pall Mall. Evidently his wife and his daughter Jane (mentioned in the will of her grandfather John Condell) had died before him, as neither they nor any other issue were mentioned in his will.

To his executors and nephews, Edward Long of Limehouse and William Long of the Bank of England, sons of his sister Ann Long and the musician John Long, he left all his funded properties in trust to carry out his several bequests: an annuity of £30 and his diamond ring to his "best of friends," Sophia Varle (?), of Frith Street, the sum of 19 guineas to Caroline Sherwood, who lived with the aforesaid Sophia (Sophia Varle may have been the Mrs Varley who was a dresser at the King's Theatre in 1783), and 19 guineas each to the executors Edward and William Long and to his niece Elizabeth Long. To the latter he also gave his silver watch, the ground rent for his property in New James Street, Oxford Road, amounting to £29 per year, the lease of his house at Battersea, with the furnishings, pictures, wardrobe, musical instruments, and manuscripts of his own composing. Condell also mentioned another nephew, the late John Long, and his widow Elizabeth and their children, of Beaufort Row, Chelsea.

A portrait of Henry Condell by John Opie, in the possession of H. F. Long early in the nineteenth century, was twice sold by Puttick and Simpson, the dealers: on 4 March 1864 and on 15 November 1866. Its present location is unknown.

Condell, John   *d. 1779, boxkeeper, concessionaire.*

John Condell (sometimes Cundell) was a boxkeeper at Covent Garden Theatre for at least 33 years from 1746 to 1779. His name was in the pay list at 2*s.* per day, or 12*s.* per week, in 1746–47 and remained at that level throughout his career. Despite this low salary, other emoluments made him quite well off financially (and suggest incidentally, the advantage to which boxkeepers could put their conspicuous positions to curry favor with the public). His annual benefit, usually taken with several other house servants, brought him handsome amounts if the figure of £238 9*s.*, which he shared with Green and Vaughan on 16 May 1760, is typical. In May of 1758 and 1759, he was given payments of 10*s.* 6*d.* as salary for serving as a house servant for the performances of the *Messiah* at the Foundling Hospital.

Moreover, Condell had fruit concessions

at Covent Garden from 1760–61 and at Drury Lane from at least 1771–72 to the end of his life, paying each theatre £60 per year in rent for the sales space. He also sold "books" of the oratorios at Covent Garden from his address in Cross Court, Bow Street. In his later years he seems also to have established himself in the jewelry trade.

Condell may have come into a substantial annuity through a bequest in the will of his friend John Hardham, who was for many years an undertreasurer at Drury Lane and a well-known snuff merchant. By his will, dated 6 February 1772 and proved in October of that year, Hardham left the dividends and interest of £15,500 in three-percent bank annuities to his housekeeper Mary Binmore and after her death to John Condell "for and during the term of his natural life," after which the principal was to go to the town of Chichester "to ease the inhabitants" in their poor rate. The bequest became available to Chichester in 1786, suggesting that Mary Binmore had outlived Condell. For John Condell died at Battersea on 11 December 1779.

By his first wife, born Jane Wilcox, who died about 1752, he had a son, John Condell, who also was a boxkeeper at Covent Garden in the 1770s and 1780s, and a daughter, Charlotte Condell, who acted at Covent Garden in the 1750s and died in 1759. His common-law wife Ann Wilson (niece of Richard Chadd, a jeweler in New Bond Street), was described by Condell in his will dated 3 November 1779 as the woman "who has lived and cohabited with me as my Wife from about the year one thousand seven hundred and fifty two or thereabouts and is now called Ann Condell." By Ann he had a son, the musician Henry Condell (1757?–1824) and a daughter Ann, who became the wife of the Covent Garden musician John Long.

John Condell's will was proved on 24 December 1779 at which time administration was granted to Henry Condell and Ann Wilson, otherwise Condell, "spinster."

In the will, the younger John Condell was to receive £300 – "to be paid to him within two years after my decease" – provided he did not "molest" Ann Condell, the executrix, in the performance of her duty. Henry Condell received £300, upon trust, to buy securities in his name, the interest of which was to be paid to Henry's daughter Jane. John Condell's brother, James Condell of Leith, received 10 guineas, his sister Jane Marshall 10 guineas, and his servant Martha Brandon 80 guineas. The rest of his estate, including his leasehold at Battersea, was bequeathed to the said Ann Wilson Condell. After her death half of the estate was to pass to his son Henry Condell and the other half was to be placed out at interest for his daughter Ann Long and then to her children.

Condell, John [fl. 1779–1784], boxkeeper.

John Condell, the younger, was the son of the Covent Garden boxkeeper John Condell, by his first wife Jane Wilcox Condell, who died before 1752. The younger Condell also became a Covent Garden boxkeeper by 1779–80, perhaps earlier, at a fixed salary of 12s. per week at least through 1783–84. On 20 May 1780 and 24 May 1782, he shared benefits with several other boxkeepers.

In his father's will, dated 3 November 1779 and proved on 24 December 1779, John was left £300, to be paid him within two years after his father's death, provided he did not interfere in the duties as executrix of the father's second wife, Ann Condell. Details of his other relatives are found in the entries of John Condell (d. 1779) and Henry Condell (1757–1824).

Conegliano, Emanuele. See **Da Ponte, Lorenzo.**

Coningham, Mr [fl. 1768–1772], equestrian.

About 1768, a Mr Coningham performed original feats of horsemanship at the Mulberry Gardens, Burr Street, near Tower Hill. Later, having bought the horses of the equestrian Sampson, in 1771 and 1772 he exhibited in the evenings in a field adjoining the Three Hats public house, in the High Street, Islington. One of his handbills describes his remarkable antics:

First—He rides on gallop, standing upright, on a single horse, three times round the room without holding. Second—He rides a single horse on full speed, dismounts, fires a pistol, and performs that boasted feat of Hughes', leaping over him backwards and forwards for forty times without ceasing. Also flies over three horses on full speed, leaps over one and two horses on full speed as they leap the bar, plays a march on the flute, without holding, upon two horses, standing upright. The public are desired to take notice, that I do not throw myself over the horses with my feet touching the horses' hind legs, but my feet over the saddles, and will perform every other feat that is performed by any horseman. . . . Mr Coningham will engage to fly through a hogshead of fire upon two horses' backs, without touching them, and, for a single person, will perform activity with any man in the world.

Coningsby, Gilbert [fl. 1674–1682], singer.

On 7 November 1674 Gilbert Coningsby was paid 3s. daily as one of the Chapel boys under John Blow for attending Charles II at Windsor from 18 May to 3 September 1674. He sang in the court masque *Calisto* on 15 February 1675 and was in attendance at Windsor again from 14 August to 26 September 1678. By 24 December 1679 his voice had broken, for on that date he was granted a black felt hat and a black castor (beaver) hat as a former Chapel boy. Subsequent warrants provided him with Spanish cloth, shoes, hose, and another castor, the last item granted him on 16 August 1682. Coningsby's name is found in the Lord Chamberlain's accounts variously spelled: Coninsby,

Conisby, Cunisbo, and Cunisbey, but Coningsby seems to be the most common form.

"Conjurer, Bottle." *See* NICHOLLS, WILLIAM.

Connard, Miss [fl. 1794], actress, singer.

A Miss Connard performed the role of the maid in a production of *The School for Scandal* given at the Windsor Castle Inn, King Street, Hammersmith, on 24 March 1794, for the benefit of Mr Kent and his family. Tickets could be had in Union Court from Miss Connard, who also rendered a song. Several other productions were offered by the same company during the remainder of that month, including *The Road to Ruin* and *The Poor Soldier*, for which no casts are known.

Connel, Henry [fl. 1668–1669], barber.

A warrant dated 4 December 1668 in the Lord Chamberlain's accounts identifies Henry Connel as the Duke's Company barber in 1668–69, and one may suppose that he served both before and after that season.

Connell, Master. *See* CORNEL, MASTER.

Connell, E. d. 1801, singer, actor.

Mr E. Connell was a singer and actor in the minor theatres of London from about 1774 until his death in 1801. About 1774 he played Bundle in a performance of *The Waterman; or, the First of August* by Mrs Baker's Sadler's Wells company at the Greyhound Yard Theatre. By the summer of 1780, Connell was a performer in the burlettas at Astley's Amphitheatre, Westminster Bridge, a situation he seems to have held regularly for many years.

Connell's name appears in the bills at Astley's over a period of some 20 years, for such roles as principal parts in *The Lilliputian World* (7 July 1780), *The Air Balloon; or, All the World in The Clouds* (7 April 1785, when tickets could be had of him at No 4, Surrey side of Westminster Bridge), the Knave Diamond in *The Marriage of the Knave of Hearts* (24 July 1786), Trout, the fisherman, in *Love from the Heart* (4 September 1786), Henry the Eighth in *The King and the Cobbler* (6 May 1791), the Lord of the Manor in *The Tythe Sheep* (July 1791), Philemon in *The Good and Bad* (11 June 1792), Farmer Sledges in *Bagshot* (August 1792), Ward in the musical farce *The Miser* (31 January 1793), the Father in *La Forêt noire* (31 January 1793), roles in *Maternal Affection* (8 April 1793) and *The Generous Turk* (April 1793), and the Lord of the Manor in *The Reasonable Wife* (22 August 1795). He also played in burlettas at the Royal Circus in 1785.

He was no doubt the same Mr Connell who acted several roles at the Haymarket in the winter of 1784–85, including Lockit in *The Beggar's Opera*, Sir Patrick O'Neale in *The Irish Widow*, the title role in *King Charles I*, a character, with a new Irish song, in *The Fair Refugee*, and Sir Gilbert Pumpkin in *All the World's a Stage*. In the next season he appeared once at the Haymarket when he played Sir Jacob Jollup in *The Mayor of Garratt* on 6 March 1786. A Mr Connell acted at Fishamble Street, Dublin, in 1795 and at Cork in March 1800. *The Pad*, a song which he sang at the Royal Saloon in an entertainment called *The Disembarkation of the Light Horse from on Board the British Transports at Ostend*, was published in 1798.

Connell's wife, Maria, was a ticket seller and boxkeeper at Astley's during the 1790s, and she appeared once at the Haymarket, as Diana Trapes in *The Beggar's Opera*, on 15 March 1785. Her first name was provided by De Castro in his *Memoirs*. In July 1801, the *Monthly Mirror* an-

nounced the death of "Mr E. Connel, of Mr. Astley's Theatre."

Connell, Mrs E., Maria [*fl. 1785–1793?*], *ticket seller, boxkeeper, actress.*
See CONNELL, E.

Connelle. See CONNELLY.

Connelly, Mr [*fl. 1793–1795*], *doorkeeper.*
A Mr Connelly was a doorkeeper at Covent Garden Theatre, with a salary of 12s. per week, from 1793–94 through 1794–95, or longer.

Connelly, [Miss?] [*fl. 1724*], *house servant?*
A Miss or Mrs Connelly shared a benefit with two others at Lincoln's Inn Fields on 29 May 1724, the total receipts being £127 7s. 6d. The account books give her salary as 3s. 4d. daily on 25 September 1724. She may have been one of the house servants, but her function was not specified.

Connelly, [Miss] [*fl. 1799*], *dancer.*
A Miss Connelly performed in the chorus of peasants in the dance of *Moggy and Jemmy* at Drury Lane on 5 February 1799.

Connolly. See CONNELLY.

Connor, Mr [*fl. 1741?–1750*], *house servant?*
A Mr Connor shared benefit tickets at Covent Garden with house servants in 1742–43, 1743–44, and 1744–45. In 1746–47 and 1749–50 his salary was about 6s. 8d. per week. He may have been that Mr Connor who received a benefit at Drury Lane on 24 March 1741, and who was described in the bills as the person who kept the Key and Garter Tavern in Pall Mall.

Connor, Mr [*fl. 1788*], *actor.*
A Mr Connor acted Russet in *The Jealous Wife* at the Haymarket in two specially

licensed performances on 9 and 29 April 1788. (Possibly he was the Mr Connor who acted at Manchester in the 1780s and 1790s and who died in that city on 6 July 1808.)

Constable, Mr *(fl. 1749–1803),* *house servant.*

A person, or persons, by the name of Constable served as a minor house functionary at Covent Garden Theatre for at least 54 years between 1749 and 1803. In 1749–50 a Mr Constable was on the pay list as doorkeeper of that theatre for 2 shillings per day. In 1767–68 and 1775–76, a Mr Constable shared benefit tickets with other house servants. As late as 1802–3, a Mr Constable was receiving two shillings per day as a house servant.

Constance, Mlle *(fl. 1784–1787),* *dancer.*

Announced as "from the King's Theatre in Paris," Mlle Constance made her first, and evidently her only, appearance at Covent Garden, when she danced with Le Boeuf on 17 April 1784. In an *Entertainment of Music and Dancing,* given at the Haymarket a month later on 10 May, she performed a new *Pastoral pas de deux* with Duquesney. Although she may have remained in London as an obscure chorus dancer, her name did not appear again in the known bills until 31 October 1787, when she danced in the entertainment of *Don Juan, or, the Libertine Destroyed* at the Royalty Theatre, after which all record of her activity is lost.

Constantini. *See also* COSTANTINI.

Constantini, Signor *(fl. 1741–1742),* *dancer.*

Signor Constantini was first mentioned in the bills on 21 October 1741, when he danced in *Le Genereux corsaire* at Drury Lane. On the following 11 November he was Cupid in *A Voyage to the Island of Cytherea,* and during the rest of the season

he appeared in such dances as *Le Jardiniers Suédois, Les Masons & les sabotiers, Les Satires puny, The Peasants,* and a "new grand ballet."

Constantini, Signora *(fl. 1726–1727),* *dancer.*

A member of the *Commedia dell'arte* troupe which visited England in 1726–27, Signora Constantini was billed as dancing in December and April and sharing a benefit with the harlequin of the company on 16 March 1727. Her only named part was Corisea in a dance on 25 April. The troupe played throughout at the King's Theatre in the Haymarket.

Constanza. *See* COSTANZA.

Contair. *See* DE LA COINTRIE.

Conti. *See also* DE LA COINTRIE.

Conti, Anna *(fl. 1754–1755), dancer.*
On 3 September 1754 the *Daily Advertiser* announced that a dancer named Ninna Conti would be at the Opera that winter. The only person by this surname found this season in the bills, however, is Anna Conti, who danced at the King's Theatre on 9 November 1754 and probably a number of times thereafter.

Conti, Giacchino. *See* GIZZIELLO.

Conti, Ninna. *See* CONTI, ANNA.

Conti, Vincenzo *(fl. 1766–1796),* *scene painter.*

Born at Bologna, and the student of Antonio Bonetti, Vincenzo Conti (sometimes called Longino) became a scenographer in the post-Bibiena manner. He came to London in 1766 to work with his fellow Bolognese, Francesco Bigari, at the King's Theatre, where he painted scenes in 1766–67 for *Gli stravaganti, La buona figliuola,* and *Carattaco.* In 1767–68 he painted scenery for *Il signor dottore, Sifare, Ifigenia in Aulide, Sesostri,* and *Il ratto della sposa.* Thereafter, Conti returned to Italy to work on operas at Venice, 1776–77, at Modena, during the long period 1776–1796, and at Bologna. Information on his Italian career can be found in the *Enciclopedia dello spettacolo.*

Contini, Giovanna (*fl. 1742–1743*), singer.

During her single season in the opera at the King's Theatre, Signora Giovanna Contini sang Zama in *Gianguir* on 2 November 1742, Floridan in *Mandane* on 4 December, a role in *Enrico* on 1 January, Aspasia in *Temistocle* on 22 February, and Lesbano in *Sirbace* on 5 April 1743.

Contri. *See* DE LA COINTRIE.

Convers. *See* CONYERS.

Conwy, Mr (*fl. 1797*), actor.

A Mr Conwy acted the role of Brownlow in a specially licensed performance of *The Romance of an Hour* at the Haymarket on 10 May 1797.

Conyers, Mr (*fl. 1744–1752*), singer, actor.

The first notice of Mr Conyers in the London bills was for the occasion on which he sang with Miss Clarke in Daniel and Smith's booth at May Fair on 1 May 1744. He appeared as Tribulation in *The Alchemist* at Drury Lane on 11 August 1746, and in that summer he was also a member of the company at Twickenham and Richmond. Thereafter Conyers seems not to have played again at London. He acted at Norwich in 1747 and at Edinburgh in 1749 and 1750, making his first appearance in the latter city as Sir Harry in *The Constant Couple* on 17 November 1749. During this season at Edinburgh, he played Harlequin for some 40 nights, sang, and acted Richard III.

On 13 April 1752 Conyers made his first appearance at Smock Alley, Dublin, as Jack Maggot in *The Suspicious Husband.* He then played Macheath on 25 April, Valentine ("with the proper Songs") in *The Mock Lawyer* on 27 April, and the Miller in *Harlequin Ranger* on 15 May. In the following season at Smock Alley he acted Damon in *Damon and Phillida* on 17 October 1752, after which we lose track of him.

Cook. *See also* COOKE.

Cook, Mr (*fl. 1694–1718*), singer, violinist?

Mr Cook's earliest appearance as a singer may have been late in 1694 in *Macbeth* at Drury Lane or Dorset Garden, for a British Museum manuscript of the music used in that production has his name substituted, on various songs, for Wiltshire, Hodgson, Sherburn, or Spalding. He sang in *Pausanius* in April 1696 at Drury Lane, and the British Museum *Catalogue of Printed Music* lists an Eccles song published about 1700 and sung by Cook at the Lincoln's Inn Fields Theatre in a performance of *The Mad Lover*—a work not otherwise known to have been given at this time.

In the opening years of the eighteenth century Cook appeared frequently at Lincoln's Inn Fields; on 21 August 1703 he sang at a concert in Hampstead; on 11 December 1703 he played the violin at a York Buildings concert (unless this billing was for a second Mr Cook); he sang "Cloe blush't and frown'd and swore" in *The Biter* at Lincoln's Inn Fields on 4 December 1704; and on 16 January 1705 he sang Delbo in *Arsinoe* at Drury Lane. In 1706 he was at the Queen's Theatre in the Haymarket singing as a Satyr in *The Temple of Love* on 7 March and doing a comic dialogue with Doggett on 20 April.

By 1704 Cook was probably earning £20 annually, a salary comparable to most of the ordinary theatre songsters but only half what the popular Richard Leveridge could command. Cook continued appearing at concerts and occasionally sang at the Queen's Theatre, one of his engagements there being on 14 December 1708, when he was Brennus in *Piro e Demetrio*. Between 1710 and 1712 he was not mentioned in the bills, but on 24 November 1712 he sang at a concert for his benefit at the Barbers and Surgeons' Hall. Then he was not mentioned until 25 January 1715, when he sang in *The Island Princess* at the new theatre in Lincoln's Inn Fields. He stayed there for the rest of the season, singing in *The Beau Demolished* on 9 February and sharing a benefit with Rawlins on 3 June. He sang regularly at the same house through 29 October 1716, though only two roles were named for him in the bills: Jupiter in *The Presumptuous Lover* and the Lion in *Pyramus and Thisbe*. On 19 July 1718 William Pinkethman opened his theatre in Greenwich, listing among the company personnel for the summer "the Cookes"—possibly the singer and his wife, though there is insufficient evidence to prove the identification.

Cook, Mr ₁*fl.* 1716–1732₁, dancer.
In 1716–17, Mr Cook danced various specialties, sang a dialogue with a young "Gentlewoman" making her first appearance on 18 December, and danced in *Woman's a Riddle*, for his benefit on 28 May 1717, which he shared with Eaton. In 1718–19, some distinction was made in the bills between two Cooks. The elder performer danced in *Macbeth*, *Platonick Love*, *Julius Caesar*, and *The Emperor of the Moon*, while the younger one was specified for the Englishman in *Amadis* (in which the other Cook danced as a Scaramouch) and for dancing in *The Busy Body*, *Woman's a Riddle*, *The Gamester*, *The Committee*, and *The Old Bachelor*. One of them also danced that season in *The Devil of a Wife*, *The Rival Queens*, *Love for Love*, and *Love Makes a Man*.

In 1720–21 one of them—perhaps each at different times—danced in *The Fair Quaker of Deal*, *The Amorous Widow*, *Coriolanus*, *Macbeth*, *The Beggar's Bush*, *The Emperor of the Moon*, *Oroonoko*, and a number of other pieces. On 1 May 1721, Mr Cook shared gross benefit ticket receipts of £126 14s. with Sandham's son. The last appearance recorded for a dancing Cook during this period was on 7 June 1721, in *Woman's a Riddle*, but the bills for this early part of the century are incomplete, and these dancers may have continued for some years unnoticed. On 25 February 1732, a Mr Cook shared a benefit at Lincoln's Inn Fields with Angel. Either Cook senior or junior may have been the Mr Philip Cooke, the dancing master who worked at Covent Garden from 1738–39 until the early 1750s. Cook senior may have been the husband of the actress Mrs Mary Cooke, who was at Lincoln's Inn Fields during the same period.

Cook, Mr ₁*fl.* 1718–1750?₁, dancer. *See* **COOK, MR** ₁*fl.* 1716–1732₁.

Cook, Mr *d.* 1731, boxkeeper.
A Mr Cook was a boxkeeper at Drury Lane from at least 1716–17 until his death in January 1731. Each season he shared benefits regularly with either Williams or Wilkins, also boxkeepers. Soon after his death, his wife took on his job at Drury Lane until at least through 1736–37.

Cook, Mrs ₁*fl.* 1726–1737₁, boxkeeper.
A Mrs Cook assumed the position of boxkeeper at Drury Lane made vacant by the death of her husband in January 1731. On 17 February 1731 advertisements stated that "places may be taken at the Widow Cook's, Boxkeeper, in the Playhouse Passage." She shared a benefit that season on 13 May 1731. The last notice of the Widow Cook was on 30 May 1737, when she shared benefit tickets with Erwin and

Allen, other house servants. Her name, as the boxkeeper's wife, was on the theatre free list in 1726–27 and 1728–29.

Cook, Mr (fl. 1735), *musician.*

On 21 February 1735 at Hickford's Room, a Mr Cook, probably a musician at the Opera, played on the French horn.

Cook, Mr (fl. 1765), *singer.*

A Mr Cook sang at Sadler's Wells in the fall of 1765, according to the *Jester's Magazine*, October 1765. One of the songs he offered, *My Dog and My Mistress are both of a Kind*, was published about this time.

Cook, Mr (fl. 1785), *tumbler.*

A Mr Cook was in the bill for tumbling at Astley's Amphitheatre, Westminster Bridge, on 7 April 1785.

Cook, Mr (fl. 1793–1800), *singer.*

A Mr Cook, not to be confused with James Cooke (1791–1825), was a chorus singer at Drury Lane from at least 1793–94 through 1799–1800. The name Cook or Cooke was entered many times in the Drury Lane pay books during the first 20 years of the nineteenth century for persons who were either minor house servants or chorus singers.

Cook, Mr (fl. 1794), *singer.*

A Mr Cook was listed by Doane's *Musical Directory* in 1794 as an alto (counter-tenor), a member of the Titchfield Chapel Society, and then living on Green Dragon Wharf.

Cook, Mr (fl. 1795), *costumer.*

According to advertisements on 22 August 1795, a Mr Cook, with Gotleb and Clary, designed the costumes for a production of *Harlequin Invincible* at Astley's Amphitheatre, Westminster Bridge.

Cook, Mr [S.?] (fl. 1797–1819), *doorkeeper?*

A Mr Cook was a house servant at Drury Lane as early as 1797–98. In 1799–1800 his salary was £1 per week. A Cook was paid nine shillings per week as a door-keeper from 1801–4. An S. Cooke, perhaps the same person, was paid 18 shillings per week as a doorkeeper at Drury Lane between 1812–13 and 1818–19.

Cook, Mrs (fl. 1718), *performer. See* **Cook, Mr** (fl. 1694–1718).

Cook, Mrs (fl. 1730), *actress.*

A Mrs Cook played the part of Teresa in *The Comical History of Don Quixote*, part two, at the Lincoln's Inn Fields Theatre on 23 May 1730.

Cook, Mrs (fl. 1740–1741), *dancer.*

A Mrs Cook is listed by *The London Stage* as a dancer at Covent Garden in 1740–41, but her name is not found in the bills. Probably she was the Mrs Cook whose name was in the pay list that season for 3s. 4d. per day.

Cook, Mrs (fl. 1748), *actress.*

A Mrs Cook acted the role of Mrs Sullen in *The Stratagem* at the Haymarket, usually dark at that season, on 30 March 1748, for the benefit of Mrs Rawlinson.

Cook, Mrs (fl. 1763), *dancer.*

A Mrs Cook danced as a follower of Ceres and the element of Air in the pantomime *The Rape of Proserpine* at Covent Garden some dozen times between 26 January and 25 April 1763.

Cook, Master (fl. 1737), *singer, harpsichordist.*

A boy of ten, called "Young Cook," and a scholar of Waltz, sang with his teacher at a concert given at Hickford's Room in James Street on 7 April 1737. He also accompanied Waltz in "several new Duettos" on the harpsichord.

Cook, Arthur [fl. 1794], *violinist.*

Arthur Cook, a violinist, was listed by Doane's *Musical Directory* in 1794 as a member of the New Musical Fund. He was then living at Bath.

Cook, John [fl. 1767–1801], *puppeteer, exhibitor.*

John Cook was active in London and the provinces as a puppet showman from at least 1767 to 1801. He is known to have performed with his puppets at the Stourbridge Fair, near Cambridge, in the years 1767, 1768, 1773, 1777, and 1778, at London in 1773, and at Bartholomew Fair in 1801. His show also included waxworks and a menagerie.

Cook, Joseph [fl. 1702], *performer.*

Along with several other strollers, Joseph Cook was cited in the *Post Man* of 8 September 1702 as being required to pay 2s. daily to town constables when he performed. Since he was named in a London paper, presumably he had been performing in the city, but what his specialty was is not certain. The order applied to "Stage-players; Mountebanks, Rope-dancers, Prize-players, Poppi[t]-showers, and such as make the shew of motions and strange sights . . ."

Cook, Layton [fl. 1794], *singer.*

Layton Cook was listed by Doane's *Musical Directory* in 1794 as a singer living at No 24, James Street, Westminster, a member of the Chapel Royal Choir and of the Academy of Ancient Music, who sang in the Concerts of Ancient Music.

Cook, Thomas [fl. 1766–1768], *house servant.*

A Thomas Cook was a house servant, perhaps an assistant office keeper, at Covent Garden from at least 1766 through 1768. He was sleeping in the theatre when Harris, the deposed manager, seized the building from Colman in the early hours of 17 June 1768. In a deposition Cook stated that Harris's mob had "beat him most unmercifully" and that he was covered with blood from a severe cut on his head before the sheriff arrived.

Cooke. *See also* **COOK.**

Cooke, Mr [fl. 1719], *musician.*

A Mr Cooke performed a composition of his own on the harpsichord in a concert given at Hickford's Room in James Street, Haymarket, on 18 February 1719.

Cooke, Mr [fl. 1751–1770], *equilibrist.*

A Mr Cooke performed equilibres on a small wire at the Great Tiled Booth on the Bowling Green on 7 September 1751, at the time of the Southwark Fair. He was advertised as an Englishman, a citizen of London, "who, with the utmost elegancy performs all the Ballances, in full swing, the Turk [Caratta] ever did." Perhaps he was the same Mr Cooke who, with two children tied to his feet, walked a wire at the Haymarket on 10 December 1770, a performance for his own benefit.

Cooke, Mr [fl. 1758], *harpsichordist.*

A Mr Cooke played the harpsichord in a presentation of *Acis and Galatea* at the Great Room in Dean Street, Soho, on 1 April 1758. He may have been the young Benjamin Cooke, later Doctor of Music.

Cooke, Mr [fl. 1761–1762], *actor.*

A Mr Cooke, identified by Reed in his manuscript "Notitia Dramatica" as "Son to the City Marshall," appeared for the first time on any stage as Lord Chalkstone in *Lethe* at Covent Garden Theatre on 13 April 1761. He made his second appearance there on 23 June 1761, when he acted Cassio in *Othello*, for his own benefit, and his third as Marplot in *Marplot in London* on 29 April 1762. Probably he was the same Cooke who acted the Professor in *The*

Orators at the Haymarket Theatre on 25 October 1762.

Cooke, Mr [*fl.* 1782–1784], *actor.*

A Mr Cooke played Dr Calomel in the interlude *Dr Last's Examination Before the College of Physicians* at the Haymarket Theatre on 30 December 1782. Probably he was the same person who played an unspecified part in a performance of *The Reprisal* there on 23 February 1784.

Cooke, Mr [*fl.* 1796–1797], *singer.*

A Mr Cooke was a member of the chorus at Covent Garden Theatre in 1796–97. His name appeared on the bills for a musical character in *The Mountaineers* on 6 October and for an Irish peasant in *Bantry Bay* on 18 February and 10 other times.

Cooke, Mrs [*fl.* 1735–1736], *dresser.*

A Mrs Cooke was a dresser at Covent Garden Theatre in 1735–36, receiving a salary of £12 18s. for 172 days.

Cooke, Mrs [*fl.* 1756–1757], *actress?*

A Mrs Cooke shared a benefit at Drury Lane Theatre with Scrase, Ackman, and Sturt on 9 May 1757. Her name appeared in no bills or accounts that season; she may have been an obscure supernumerary or servant.

Cooke, Arthur [*fl.* 1669], *musician.*

Arthur Cooke and four others were ordered apprehended on 17 December 1669 for performing music in London without a license.

Cooke, Benjamin *d. c. 1743, musician, music seller, publisher.*

Benjamin Cooke, the father of the more celebrated musician, his namesake Dr Benjamin Cooke (1734–1793), was a music seller and publisher with premises at the Golden Harp, in New Street, Covent Garden, between 1726 and 1743. The elder Cooke was listed as one of the original subscribers—"being musicians"—on the "Declaration of Trust" which established the Royal Society of Musicians on 28 August 1739. Cooke published a large number of vocal and instrumental works, some under official license and others evidently unofficial pirated editions, including the music of Thomas Roseingrave, Arcangelo Corelli, Charles Avison, G. F. Handel, and William De Fesch. A list of his publications is found in *Grove's Dictionary*.

Cooke was married to Eliza Wayet, of a Nottinghamshire family. Their known issue included the aforementioned second Benjamin Cooke and a daughter, Philippa Cooke, who was living as a spinster in Hampton Court at the time her brother made his will in 1792. Benjamin Cooke died about 1743, when his son was nine years of age.

Cooke, Benjamin *1734–1793, organist, composer, choirmaster, conductor.*

Benjamin Cooke was born in 1734 at the Golden Harp, the shop and dwelling house in New Street, Covent Garden, where his father Benjamin carried on a music selling and music publishing business between 1726 and 1743. His mother's maiden name was Eliza Wayet. She was of a Nottinghamshire family. At the age of nine, soon after the death of his father, young Benjamin was placed under the instruction of Dr John Pepusch (who left him a piece of gold worth five guineas in his will dated 9 July 1752). So precocious was the lad that by 1746, at the age of 12, he was appointed deputy to John Robinson, organist of Westminster Abbey. In 1749, Cooke succeeded Howard as Librarian of the Academy of Ancient Music, and three years later in 1752 he succeeded Pepusch as conductor of that organization, a position he held until 1789, when changes in the constitution of the Academy made it necessary to relinquish it to Dr Arnold. So disturbed was Cooke by this necessity that he refused for some time to join a little musical club

BENJAMIN COOKE
engraving by Skelton

called "the Graduates Meeting" because Arnold was a member.

Other appointments came to Cooke in quick succession. In September 1757, upon the resignation of Bernard Gates, he was made master of the choristers of Westminster Abbey and on 27 January 1758 he was appointed a lay vicar. He succeeded Robinson as the Abbey's organist on 1 July 1762. Several years before, on 2 November 1760, Cooke had been elected a member of the Royal Society of Musicians. He joined the Catch Club on 6 April 1767 and subsequently was awarded prizes there for his compositions (five glees, a canon, and a catch). During his lifetime Cooke published a collection of glees, at the composing of which he was most skillfully adept, and after his death a second collec-

tion was put out in 1795 by his son Robert. In Warren's collections are to be found 29 glees and 11 rounds, with catches and canons, by Cooke. On 9 August 1769, Cooke became a member of the Madrigal Society. Some of his madrigals were published between 1791 and 1793 in a collection called *Amusement for the Ladies*.

In 1775 Cooke earned the degree of Doctor of Music at Cambridge University, presenting for the occasion an anthem "Behold how good and joyful," which he had originally composed in 1772 for the installation of the Duke of York as a Knight of Bath. In 1782 he received the honorary doctorate from Oxford, and in that same year he obtained, over Dr Burney, the election as organist of St Martin-in-the-Fields. Cooke served as an assistant director to Burney for the great Handelian concerts held at Westminster Abbey and the Pantheon in May and June of 1784, and he received one of the commemorative medals which George III commanded to be struck for the occasion. In 1787–88, about a year before he was obliged to resign as conductor of the Academy of Ancient Music, he was paid a total of £52 10*s*. for his services to that organization as well as for the use of his choir boys. Indeed, throughout his career, Cooke earned a handsome extra income by the employment of his choir boys, especially at Drury Lane. The accounts of that theatre show regular payments to Dr Cooke for the children's singing in such pieces as *A Christmas Tale* between 1771 and 1793. In 1777–78, for example, he received a total of about £19, in 1778–79 about £35 14*s*., in 1786–87 about £75, and in 1792–93 (the season before he died) about £77 14*s*., with the final payment of £12 12*s*. being made to him on 4 March 1793.

In 1790, 1791, 1792, and 1793, Dr Cooke passed his summers, successively, at Ramsgate, Brighton, Oxford, and Windsor. While at the latter place in the summer of 1793, he suffered a severe attack of gout, a malady which had plagued him for many years, and he was obliged to return to his house in Dorset Court, Westminster, where he died on 14 September 1793. He was buried in the West Cloister of the Abbey on 21 September, near his wife Mary Cooke, who had died on 19 March 1784 at the age of 52. A mural tablet, bearing a canon of his composition and an inscription written by T. J. Mathias, marks Dr Cooke's grave.

Benjamin Cooke had married Mary Jackson on 22 May 1758. She was the daughter of Mrs Mary Shelvocke (d. 1761) by her first marriage, to a Mr Jackson. Mrs Shelvocke's second husband, whom she married at Greenwich on 26 May 1758, was George Shelvocke (d. 1760), a Secretary to the General Post Office. By Mary his wife, who was "a most amiable and affectionate woman, and possessed good property," Dr Cooke had ten children, five of whom died in infancy and were also buried in the West Cloister: George Cooke, born 28 May 1759 and died 16 June at the age of 3 weeks; Mary Elizabeth Cooke, died 7 October 1760 at the age of 16 days; Dorothy Cooke, died 13 April 1764 at the age of 8 months; Margaret Cooke, died 9 March 1765 at the age of 7 months; and William Cooke, buried on 27 February 1766 at the age of six months and three weeks. A sixth child, Benjamin Cooke, born 13 August 1761, died at the age of ten years and six months on 25 January 1772.

Four children survived to adulthood. Mary Cooke was born on 28 July 1762 and baptized at St Margaret, Westminster, on 14 September 1762. She died a spinster, while living in Palace Yard, Westminster, on 28 February 1819 and was buried in the West Cloister on 6 March 1819. Her brother Henry administered her estate on 27 May 1819, when her net worth was sworn to as under £3000. Henry Cooke, born in 1766, was for many years connected with the General Post Office. He edited some of his father's music and pub-

lished a short biography of him and "Some Remarks on the Greek Theory of Tuning Instruments." Henry died, unmarried, at the age of 74 on 30 September 1840 at his house, No 2, Little Smith Street, Westminster, and was buried in the North Cloister on 6 October 1840. His sister Amelia administered his estate on 19 November 1840 when his worth was sworn to amount to less than £6000. Amelia Cooke, born 7 October 1768 and baptized at St Margaret, Westminster, on 1 December 1768, died a spinster at No 2, Little Smith Street, on 16 May 1845 and was buried in the West Cloister on 22 May 1845. Robert Cooke, born in 1768, was a composer and organist, who succeeded upon his father's death in 1793 to the post of organist of St Martin-in-the-Fields. In 1802 he became organist and master of the choristers of the Abbey. Robert Cooke died unmarried on 23 August 1814; according to the Abbey Funeral Book, he drowned in the Thames, evidently a suicide. He was buried in the West Cloister on 30 August 1814. His brother Henry administered his estate on 7 September 1814.

By his will, dated 22 June 1792 and proved on 17 October 1793, Dr Benjamin Cooke left £100 to his sister Philippa Cooke, spinster, of Hampton Court, and five guineas to his "kinswoman" Hannah Cooke, of Newton, near Bath. He then divided his remaining property equally among his four surviving children. To his son Henry he gave his organ with the condition that his son Robert have the option to purchase it for ten guineas within 12 months after Dr Cooke's death. He also gave Henry one of his bass viols, his gold watch, and one of his Catch Club medals. To Robert he left his other instruments, a gold medal from the Academy of Ancient Music, and his commemorative medal from the great Handel festival in 1784. He gave his daughter Mary his double harpsichord, a picture of his wife, an oil picture of himself, and a diamond ring. To his daughter

Amelia he left a yellow diamond ring and her mother's single harpsichord.

According to Letitia-Matilda Hawkins, Benjamin Cooke was a most affectionate parent and "one of the worthiest and best-tempered men that ever existed." His door was always open to his large circle of acquaintances, and in the streets "he was perpetually stopt." He was an average-sized person, "latterly rather corpulent, though when young extremely thin," with a "fine face" and "a soft concealed eye." He was reported to have kept a diary, but it has not been found. Among Cooke's many pupils were James Bartleman, T. L. Bellamy, John Crosdill, Charles Evans, Thomas Greatorex (who in his will asked to be buried as close to Cooke as possible), Charles Hague, Knyvett, Sir William Parsons, Rock, and Spofforth.

For the theatre, Cooke wrote music for Delap's tragedy, *The Captives*, which was produced at Drury Lane on 9 March 1786. His setting of the song "Hark! the Lark at Heaven's Gate sings" was used regularly in performances of *Cymbeline* in the 1780s and 1790s. A critical appreciation of some of Cooke's nontheatrical music may be found in *Grove's Dictionary* as well as an account of his voluminous compositions for church, special occasions, and choruses. Some of his works are listed in the British Museum's *Catalogue of Printed Music*. The library of the Royal College of Music holds a large collection of his manuscript music. An engraved portrait of Dr Cooke was done by W. Skelton. The painter and the present whereabouts of the oil painting which Cooke bequeathed to his daughter Mary are both unknown.

Cooke, George Frederick 1756–1812, actor.

George Frederick Cooke, whose reputation for appearances before audiences in a drunken stupor has often overshadowed the fact that he was one of the very great actors of the English stage, was born, according

Pennsylvania Academy of the Fine Arts, Philadelphia

GEORGE FREDERICK COOKE, as Richard the Third

by Sully

to his own account given to his biographer William Dunlap, in Westminster on 17 April 1756. It is likely, however, that he was three years older. (Other accounts suggest that he was born in Berwick or in a Dublin barracks.) His father, whom Cooke described as "a dashing officer," died when George was a young child, presumably leaving his widow in financial straits. If it was true, as Cooke claimed, that his mother was the daughter of the Laird of Renton, near

Lamberton, then John Renton and Lady Susanna Montgomerie Renton (d. 1754), daughter of Alexander, ninth Earl of Eglinton, were George's grandparents. Soon after her husband's death, Mrs Cooke took George to live at Berwick-upon-Tweed, where he was educated. When his mother died, he was cared for by her two sisters who bound him apprentice to John Taylor, a printer at Berwick.

Stimulated as a youth by the visits of touring actors, Cooke organized his friends into an amateur theatrical group. He claimed to have played Lucia in *Cato* in such a company on 5 November 1770, at the age of 14. In June 1771, having obtained a release from indentures to Taylor, at the age of 15 he set off for London, where he frequented the theatres. Cooke wrote that in November 1771 he was in Holland, but he did not elaborate; perhaps it was during this period that he served as a midshipman or cabin boy aboard a British naval vessel. (He also claimed to have been an ensign during the American Revolution, and during his engagement in America in 1811 was inclined to point out to his companions the places he had visited earlier.) Curiously enough, though he made no mention of it in his journal, Cooke may have acted professionally prior to his first going to London, and some five years earlier than commonly assumed. A playbill (now at Hall's Croft) for a performance of *Hamlet* "at the New Theatre at the Unicorn in Stratford" on 2 March 1771 lists the actor of Horatio as a Mr Cooke. Of all the other performers of this name known to us, in respect to dates and other data, none seems to have been a better candidate for this attribution as Horatio than George Frederick himself, though he was young for the part. Moreover, an actor named Cooke was a leading man with a provincial troupe at King's Lynn from mid-February through 15 May 1774, and again George Frederick seems the likely person.

According to Dunlap, early in 1772

Cooke had returned from Holland to Berwick. Now 18, he went again to London in 1774 to visit the theatres, and as he wrote "I began to see acting." How he occupied himself at Berwick for two years before this excursion to London is not known. Dunlap suggests the time was spent in reading plays "with his usual assiduity," but the bills for Stratford and King's Lynn suggest the possibility that he had already begun his career. In his journal, however, Cooke placed his first appearance as a professional actor at Brentford in the spring of 1776 when he played Dumont in *Jane Shore*. On the following evening he acted Ensign Dudley in *The West Indian*. The progress of his budding career over the next 15 months or so remains a secret, but in the summer of 1777 he joined Standen's company which played at Hastings and Rye in Sussex. Taken with "a fever and ague" in Rye, Cooke returned to London by the first of November.

Cooke's first appearance on the London stage occurred at the Haymarket Theatre on 9 April 1778 when he acted Castalio in *The Orphan*. At the same theatre on 29 April he acted Modely in *The Country Lasses* and on 30 April Lovewell in *The Clandestine Marriage*. In the following month he joined a company which played at China Hall, Rotherhithe, from 25 May until their theatre burned down on 26 July, and afterward held forth in a temporary booth. His roles at China Hall included Gayless in *The Lying Valet* (25 May 1778), Frederick in *The Wonder* (25 May), Glenalvon in *Douglas* (27 May), Hortensio in *Catherine and Petruchio* (29 May), Young Marlow in *She Stoops to Conquer* (29 May), Young Wilding in *The Citizen* (1 June), Lord Hastings in *Jane Shore* (1 June), the Conjurer in *The Devil to Pay* (3 June), Charles in *The Busy Body* (3 June), Harry in *The Mock Doctor* (8 June), Harlow in *The Old Maid* (9 June), Trueman in *The London Merchant* (9 June), Tibalt in *Romeo and Juliet*

GEORGE FREDERICK COOKE, as King Lear

engraving by Edwin, after Leslie

(10 June), Bedamar in *Venice Preserv'd* (15 June), a character in *The Comical Courtship* (15 June), Freeman in *A Bold Stroke for a Wife* (18 June), Sir Harry's Servant in *High Life Below Stairs* (18 June), Captain Constant in *The Ghost* (19 June), Southampton in *The Earl of Essex* (19 June), Lord Aberville in *The Fashionable Lover* (22 June), George Bevil in *Cross Purposes* (22 June), Frederick in *The Miser* (24 June), and Tressel in *Richard III* (26 June)—a number and variety of roles which suggest considerable previous experience in the provinces. In August he acted Edgar in *Lear* three times in the temporary booth set up by the China Hall company.

In the following spring he acted several more times at the Haymarket: Young Belmont in *The Foundling* and Medium in *The Prejudice of Fashion* on 22 February 1779 and Glenalvon in *Douglas* on 10 May, but evidently he attracted little attention from the patent house managers. In September 1779 he joined Fisher's company at Sudbury where he remained until February 1780. He then moved as a strolling player from company to company and from town to town, including Loughborough, Nottingham, Derby, and Stamford, until he came, in Cooke's words, "to a more important era in my theatrical career," namely an engagement at Manchester where he made his first appearance on 2 January 1784 as Philotas in *The Grecian Daughter*.

Leaving Manchester in June of 1784, Cooke joined the circuit troupe under the management of Joseph Austin and Charles Edward Whitlock at Lancaster, for a salary of two guineas a week, reported to be the highest in the company. He toured with them to Preston and to Liverpool, appearing in the latter city for the first time in September 1784 as Frankly in *The Suspicious Husband*. After returning with the company to Manchester in December, Cooke left them in February 1785 for three months because of a dispute over the role of Sir Peter Teazle in *The School For Scandal*. The part had been his at Manchester in the previous season, but at Liverpool it was given to Moses ("a doubtful actor"); when the latter left the company abruptly, Cooke refused to take the role back and he, too, in a fit of self-righteousness, resigned.

By now Cooke had built a good reputation on the northern circuit as a "correct actor," but already he was drinking heavily —"he would sometimes abstain from excess for three months, and behave with great propriety," wrote Dunlap, "but when he broke from this restraint, he was not to be heard of for several days." He rejoined Austin and Whitlock at Lancaster in June

1785. In the fall they played at Chester, where on 14 September he acted Adam in *As You Like It*. In the role of Celia ("with the Cuckow Song") was a "Mrs Cooke," who had played with him at Liverpool. For a benefit he shared with her at Chester on 26 October 1785 Cooke acted Hamlet and recited Garrick's *Ode on Shakespeare*. (Cooke's promptbook copy for this Chester performance now belongs to the Newcastle-upon-Tyne Literary and Philosophical Society.) While at Chester the Cookes lived at Mr Tilston's in Foregate Street. Supposedly Cooke's first legal wife was the actress Alicia Daniels, whom he did not marry until 1796, and no mention of an earlier wife was made in his journal. It is possible that in this instance Cooke had formed an alliance in everything but the form, but the woman, whoever she was, remains unknown. During this stay at Chester, which lasted until 7 November 1784 (when he was advertised for Hamlet again), Cooke also played Bertoldo in *The Maid of Honour*, and no doubt other roles in pieces for which the bills and advertisements are not extant.

On 29 July 1786 Cooke made his first appearance with Tate Wilkinson's company at York as Count Baldwin in *Isabella*, with Sarah Siddons, fresh from her great successes in London, in the title role. On 15 October 1787 he played Macbeth at Chester. By January 1788 he was acting in the new Theatre Royal, Newcastle, where his Othello, he claimed, "met with most flattering applause." Wilkinson reported that he excited a real frenzy at Newcastle. For his own benefit there he played Richard III. In this manner, he continued in the Midlands throughout the rest of the century. In 1789 he acted again at Newcastle, with Mrs Siddons, and for his benefit on 23 March he played Cato. At Chester again in 1789 at his benefit, he recited Collins's *Ode on the Passions* to music by James Saunderson. At Sheffield his roles included Shylock, Hamlet, Iachimo, Petruchio, Oakly in *The*

Jealous Wife, Loveless in *Reparation*, Sir John in *Word to the Wise*. In 1790 he made the circuit again in the Austin-Whitlock company. At Buxton in August of 1791 Cooke acted Tancred in *Tancred and Sigismunda*, O'Flaherty in *The West Indian*, Joseph Surface in *The School for Scandal*, Moody in *The Country Girl*, and Rover in *Wild Oats*. After an engagement in Manchester he went again to Liverpool for the summer where on 8 June 1792 he acted Sciolto in *The Fair Penitent*. Cooke recorded in his journal that he also had played King Lear for his benefit during this time at Liverpool.

In the 1794 season at Manchester, a place which was very much his home base, Cooke seems to have reached his maturity as an actor. He was now being called "the Manchester Roscius." No finer piece of acting than his Shylock on 2 April 1794 had been witnessed by the critic of the *Monthly Mirror* "for a long time," and it was a performance not "to be equalled by any other actor in this kingdom." For his benefit on 7 April he acted Don Juan in *Braganza* and Colonel Talbot in *He Would Be a Soldier*. The *Monthly Mirror* found him "sadly too old for Barnwell" on 9 April; his Lord Davenant in *The Mysterious Husband* on 21 April was "very respectable," and his Edward in *The Irishman in London* on the same date was "very pleasing," but "very wicked." On 23 April he played Octavian in *The Mountaineers* ("Cooke, in the distracted Lover, almost out-does himself") and at the end of the first act gave Collins's *Ode on the Passions* in a very masterly manner, and "drew forth a just applause."

He returned to Buxton in July 1794 where he acted for the summer and occupied himself with considerable reading (according to Dunlap) and much drinking. The author of *The Thespian Mirror . . . of the Theatres Royal, Manchester, Liverpool, and Chester* (1793) had already publicly taken him to task for being too partial to "the cheering juice of the Lesbian wine." In the journal he kept while he was at Buxton Cooke described, on 13 August 1794, a clergyman who had been reduced by drink to a pitiful object—"Drunkenness is the next leveller to death" he wrote, and he thought and hoped he would "never forget him." If, indeed, Cooke continued to be haunted by the image of what might become his own end, he seems nevertheless, to have been incapable of turning from drink. He was now 38 years old and had been an actor for at least 18 years (possibly 23). Only about five months of that time had been spent on the London stage and none yet at a winter patent house. One must wonder why this theatrical hero of the North remained away from London for

so long a period while numerous less worthy talents came in a constant parade. Perhaps there is truth in Dunlap's assertion that actually Cooke had want "of proper ambition," owing to "his attachment to what he called conviviality." It is also possible that his reputation for "conviviality" had outstripped his reputation as an actor and no London manager would have him, although Cooke claimed to have turned down an offer from Covent Garden in 1793.

During the summer of 1794 Cooke had negotiated an engagement for the ensuing season at the Crow Street Theatre in Dublin. He made his debut there in the role of Othello on 19 November 1794—and, Dunlap wrote, "He took possession of the Dub-

Newcastle Literary and Philosophical Society

GEORGE FREDERICK COOKE's promptbook for Hamlet

lin stage without a struggle: there was no competitor; the throne was his own." During the season there he acted numerous capital roles including Macbeth, Richard III, and Shylock. He left Crow Street at the beginning of March 1795, claiming in his journal to have become "heartily sick" of the undisciplined and mediocre company under Richard Daly's parsimonious management, but the real reason was his debilitating drunkenness which on one night, it was reported, led to his destroying the windows and furniture in his lodgings. Mad with drink, he had then ventured out into the night—"and was brought home the next day beaten and deformed with bruises." This binge extended into a stupor which kept him off the stage for a year. "In a fit of drunkenness and despair," he enlisted in a regiment bound for the West Indies but his sickness at Portsmouth prevented his embarkation. At Portsmouth he appealed to Maxwell, the manager of the theatre there, to help him obtain his discharge. Maxwell wrote to Ward and Banks, the managers at Manchester, for their assistance in the matter. Dunlap related the outcome:

Maxwell heard no more of it for some weeks, when a boy came to him at his theatre in Portsmouth, and accosted him with "a poor sick man, Sir, who has been a soldier, is now at my mother's, and begs to see you before he dies." He went to a miserable public house, and there found George Frederick Cooke in a state of the most abject misery. . . . Banks and Ward had procured his discharge, and sent him money to pay his way to them at Manchester, but the money was spent or thrown away, sickness ensued, he was ashamed to apply to them again, he had crawled from Southampton to Portsmouth to see Maxwell, and had sunk exhausted on his arrival at this public house.

Maxwell got him clothes and a physician and eventually sent him off to Manchester with just enough money for expenses, but

Cooke stopped on the road between London and Manchester "for another taste of his beloved madness, while the managers had to disappoint a great concourse of people who crowded the theatre to witness his return." He managed finally to proceed, and on 17 March 1796 made his reappearance at Manchester as Octavian in *The Mountaineers*. Soon he was on the circuit again.

At Chester on 20 December 1796 he married Alicia Daniels at St Peter's Church. They were both engaged for Ireland in 1797–98. On 20 November 1797 he again acted Othello at Dublin, this time at Fishamble Street while the company awaited the opening of its new Theatre Royal in Crow Street. He played Shylock at Cork on 17 September 1798 and Delaval in *He's Much to Blame* on 26 September, and then set off for Limerick, where he made his debut as Shylock on 1 October. From a mail coach inn at Clonwell Cooke wrote to Frederick Edward Jones, the Irish manager, on 19 November 1798 (letter now in the Harvard Theatre Collection), to explain his delay in getting back to Dublin. He had, he said, experienced an accident at Limerick which had prevented his departure until 12 November, but on that date had been stricken after supper at the inn in Clonwell; he was much recovered but unable to travel: "Since I left Dublin I have had one Physician, two Surgeons & two Apothecaries. . . . The excursion has been a miserable one." But at Dublin he again fell into debt and drink, and his wife left him. (Several years later on 4 July 1801 at London she had her marriage to Cooke declared null and void before Sir William Scott in Doctors' Commons. Later she acted at Bath and the Haymarket as Miss Daniels and at Bath again after 1804 as Mrs Windsor. She died at Bath in 1826.)

In February of 1800 Cooke received a letter from Covent Garden advising him of an opening for the next season. By June 1800 the negotiations with the manager

Thomas Harris, through his agent Lewis, were concluded. Cooke later told Dunlap he had accepted the same offer which he had rejected seven years before. The Covent Garden account books for 1800–1 show him to have been engaged at £1 per day or £6 per week. Cooke's departure from Ireland was conducted in his usual fashion. He finished appearances at Cork in September and became dead drunk soon after the drop of the final curtain. When he was found in "the Bulk," a cobler's tenement near the playhouse, he had no money, so his friends collected funds which they gave to the packet master who took Cooke—"as happy as a Lord"—across to Bristol on 13 October.

He arrived at London on Sunday 26 October, attended rehearsal on Wednesday the 29th and on Friday 31 October 1800 in the character of Richard III he returned to the London stage after 21 years. He was now 44 years old. The management took extraordinary care to assure that his debut would be a special event. New scenes and costumes were created, additional supernumeraries were employed for the soldiery and were given better rehearsal training, and new music for the marches was composed by Attwood. Cooke's success was brilliant and immediate. He wrote in his journal: "never was a reception more flattering; nor ever did I receive more encouraging, indulgent, and warm approbation than on that night, both through the play and at the conclusion. Mr Kemble did me the honour of making one of the audience." The reviewer in the *Monthly Mirror* (November 1800) offered an unusually detailed analysis of Cooke's Richard, a performance which excited more public attention than any actor had had for many years. After general observations on the arduous challenge which the character presents to any actor—"the performer who undertakes the task must bring to it a mature judgment and extensive powers;—the most skilful discrimination, an exhaustless spirit, and a voice that will sustain itself through a rapid series of the most difficult transitions"— the critic reported at length:

Such a man is COOKE—who seems to possess an active and capacious intellect, with a profound knowledge of the *science* of ACTING. He has read and thought for himself. He appears to have borrowed neither from contemporary nor deceased excellence. He sometimes passes over what have been usually conceived to be *great points* in the character; and he exalts other passages into importance which former *Richards* have not thought significant enough for particular notice. His

Harvard Theatre Collection

GEORGE FREDERICK COOKE, as Sir Archy Macsarcasm

engraving by Woodman, after De Wilde

object seems to have been to form a grand, characteristic, and consistent *whole*—and that whole is the result of deep thinking, and well-directed study, judiciously adapted to his individual powers of action;—for Mr. Cooke not only *thinks* originally, but he looks, speaks, and walks unlike any other man we ever saw. *"He is himself alone:"*—he is, therefore, in some degree, a *mannerist*; but his *settled habits* are not injurious to the characters he has hitherto played, or is likely to play, in Covent-Garden; and his talents are so uncommonly brilliant, that though we cannot be altogether blind to his defects, they are forgotten almost as soon as noticed. Admiration supersedes objection; and such are the insinuating effects of his acting, that the peculiarities, which rather offend at first, grow more pleasing by degrees, and, before the close of his performance, have lost nearly all their weight in the scale of criticism.

Mr. Cooke has introduced three lines from the *Third Part of King Henry VI.* which are very suitable to his manner of playing the part.

> *"Why I can smile, and murder while I*
> *smile,*
> *"And cry content to that which grieves*
> *my heart;*
> *"And wet my cheeks with artificial tears,*
> *"And frame my face to all occasions."*

In all the subtle, ludicrous, sarcastic turns of the character, he conveyed the poet's intention with uncommon force—this, indeed, seems to be the governing excellence of his performance. We have seen *Richard* rendered more awful and terrific, but never more thoroughly detestable; and this is the proper feeling that he should excite during nearly the whole of the first four acts. In the last he becomes an object of deeper interest—as his fate approaches, commiseration of his sufferings, and admiration of his valour, are blended with our disgust at his crimes. Perhaps Mr. Cooke is somewhat deficient in the *kingly* and heroic part of the character; and his expression of terror, after the dream, is not so vivid and impressive as it should be; but there must always be imperfection somewhere, and Mr. Cooke's merits can afford to suffer some abatement.

Especially interesting was the fact that Cooke not only made Richard revel in his deformity and his satisfaction at doing evil, but his performance revealed a constant design—"the grand object he had in his eye"—which attested to the great "preparatory feature" of his acting:

The soliloquies were all finely given; not addressed, as too commonly is the case, to the audience, like a chorus to explain the play; but they actually appeared to be the secret deliberations of the soul, forming themselves into words as they arose in the mind. Nothing was ever more natural than his management of the short soliloquy in which he meditates upon the place where the young king is to hold his court. *"The Tower—ay, the tower"*—there was no side glance at the pit; no grin of malignant delight at the arrangement he had planned. He seemed to settle the point as a man of *Richard's* policy, studious of his own immediate interest, *would* settle it, and who was satisfied that he had settled it rightly.

Richard had a common habit of gnawing his lip when he was offended. *"The king is angry; see, he gnaws his lip"*—and this peculiarity Mr. Cooke exhibited with great effect in several parts of the play: indeed, his perturbation, under all circumstances, is extremely natural, and forcibly expressed.

During the *murder of the princes*, where Richard reflects, for the first time, upon the enormity of his conduct, and its probable consequences, Mr. Cooke was highly interesting; and his hesitation and *walking to and fro*, just before the *tent scene*, with some admirable *bye-play*, which to be properly estimated must be seen, finely denoted the misgivings of his mind as to the event of the approaching battle, and suitably prepared the audience for the awful visitation that was at hand, when the ghosts of those he had murdered were to sit heavy on his soul,

> "And weigh him down to ruin,
> shame, and death."

It will be impossible, in an article like this, to notice all the particulars in which Mr. Cooke varies from, or improves on, the manner of other representatives of *Richard*; but it would be unpardonable to forget the mingled irony and displeasure in his reply to

Stanley, father-in-law to Richmond, and, of course, an object of mistrust to his enemy. "Well—as you *guess*." It is easy to discover new points, but the skill consists in making them, as is done here conformable to season, place, and character.

Cooke achieved another triumph with Shylock, the second character he introduced to London, on 10 November 1800. Again the reviewer of the *Monthly Mirror* captured the quality of the performance which was compared in greatness to Macklin's in the previous century:

In voice, feature, and external appearance altogether, he was perfectly the Jew of Shakespere. His general cast of expression conveyed that deep, heart-rooted, diabolical malignity which the poet intended. His caution, cunning, servility and moroseness were strictly in character, and in the great scene of the third act, he was hailed with shouts of applause: —the break was exquisite—*"Let him look to his bond."* The gloomy satisfaction that seemed to accompany the recollection of the deed by which he had Antonio "on the hip," and the savage exultation of his *laugh*, when the full amount of his enemy's losses is stated, were frightfully impressive. The transitions were made in a masterly manner, and the speech in which Shylock urges his own wrongs, and vindicates his tribe, formed a climax of as well-wrought passion as can be conceived. The amateur will not soon forget his stifled emotion at the word *'Passions'*— and other fortunate discriminations, which gave value and originality to this part of his performance of Shylock.

In the *Trial Scene*, the 'lodg'd hate' of the impenetrable Israelite was observable throughout. And here, likewise, there were some striking novelties which surprised and delighted us: for instance, the abrupt reply to Portia's request that he would let her *tear the bond*—"When it is *paid* according to the tenour;" indicating a degree of apprehension lest she *should* tear it, and, at the same time, a malignant recognition of the penalty due: — the earnestness of his enquiry "Is it so nominated in the bond?" and his triumphant *chuckle*, when he returned it to Portia, "I cannot find it—'tis not in the bond:"—the division in this passage "I take this offer then; pay the bond—thrice:"—and the eagerness with which he adds the last word, lest he should be excluded the benefit of the offer that had been made him—in fact, the whole of this scene was inimitable, and his last look and groan, on retiring from the court, expressed despair, hate, and disappointed malice.

On 13 November 1800 Cooke displayed his virtuosity at comedy by assuming Sir Archy Macsarcasm in *Love a la Mode*, another role in which he was measured against Macklin. In the words of Dr John W. Francis, who saw Cooke play Sir Archy later in New York (and was a physician at his deathbed), "no actor in any one part within the compass of the entire drama ever excelled therein to an equal degree as did Mr Cooke in the Scotch character." In his first season at Covent Garden Cooke acted 62 times, 44 as Richard, and also played Iago, Macbeth, Sir Giles, and Kitely. For his benefit on 27 January 1801, when he acted *The Stranger*, vast numbers had to be turned away. Harris gave him the benefit free of the normal £160 house charges; according to Cooke's journal he took in £560 (the accounts books indicate the total receipts were £530).

It was inevitable that Cooke would be measured against John Philip Kemble, at that time regarded as the greatest actor in London, and about whom Cooke had felt contentious since the earlier days when they had acted together at Dublin. The German writer Goede compared their persons and styles (as related by Dunlap):

Of the two, Kemble's countenance is the most notable and refined, but the muscles are not so flexible and subject to command as Cooke's. Cooke is a great comedian as well as tragedian, but Kemble has no favor with the comic muse. . . .

Cooke does not possess the elegant figure

Harvard Theatre Collection

GEORGE FREDERICK COOKE

engraving by Cooper, after Dunlap

of Kemble; but his countenance beams with great expression. The most prominent features . . . are a long and somewhat hooked nose, of uncommon breadth between the eyes, which are fiery, dark, and at times terribly expressive, with prominent lids and flexible brows; a lofty and broad forehead, and the muscles around the mouth pointedly marked. His countenance is certainly not so dignified as Kemble's, but its expression of passion, particularly the worst passions of our nature, is stronger. His voice, though sharp, is powerful, and of great compass, a pre-eminence which he possesses by nature over Kemble, and of which he skilfully avails himself. His attitudes are far less picturesque than those of Kemble, but they are just, appropriate, and natural.

In *The Old Play-goer*, William Robson, a champion of Kemble, allowed that Cooke's energy and genius placed him at least equal with Kemble as Shylock, Richard, Sir Giles, Kitely, Glenalvon, and King John, but "in the noble walk, where pity was to be stirred, deep grief was to soften, elegance to

charm, or lofty bearing to impose," then Kemble was very far superior. Cooke, however, had "a sort of humour" in his acting, which Henry Crabb Robinson, in his *Reminiscences*, did not find in Kemble.

During his auspicious first season at Covent Garden Cooke evidently managed to control his drinking. In early summer of 1801 he played at Edinburgh and Glasgow to large and appreciative audiences. Later at Liverpool the house on the opening night of his Richard amounted to £240, and he took £112 at his benefit. In commenting on his performance of Richard at Edinburgh the *Monthly Mirror* found Cooke's voice to be very extensive and sonorous but "being deficient in harmony and softness, is incapable of many of the necessary intonations." He represented the designing villain admirably, but did not exhibit "the mingled power of light and shade" necessary to the character:

His beauties in the part were almost always blended with faults. The former chiefly prevailed in his soliloquies. Those in the first act, and when planning the destruction of his nephews, were truly excellent. That upon securing the crown had the greatest merit. His transient gleams of remorse, before the interview with Tyrrel, were excellently pourtrayed. His tent scene, though a powerful piece of acting, is not so impressive as it should be. Upon the whole, his Richard, though a forcible, was not a fine representation. It resembled the image of Nebuchadnezzar, described by the prophet Daniel, much iron, much brass, much clay, some silver, and a little gold.

Upon his entrance as Richard in Manchester on 24 August 1801 he was greeted as a returning hero. At Manchester he offered a selection of the roles which had won him acclaim in London, and then went on to Newcastle. A return to his old habits at this time evidently caused him to miss the opening night at Covent Garden on 14 September 1801 for which he was advertised to play Richard. He did not show up in London until a month later (Cooke claimed he never received notice of the opening from the manager, a really silly statement, since he knew he was engaged for the season). When he offered Richard on 19 October 1801 he delivered a public apology. During the season of 1801–2 (now being paid £7 per week) he introduced his portrayals of Stukely in *The Gamester* (27 November), Jaques in *As You Like It* (2 January), Zanga in *The Revenge* (4 January), Lear (8 January), Orsino in *Alfonso* (15 January), and Sir Pertinax in *The Man of the World* (10 April 1802). Of his performance as Sir Pertinax, Hunt wrote that "You may see all the beauties and all the faults of Cooke in this single character. . . . The Scotch dialect, which he so inimitably assumes, is in vain undervalued by those who persuade themselves that he was born in Scotland. . . . The sarcasm of Cooke is at all times most bitter," continued Hunt

but in this character its acerbity is tempered with no respect either for its object or for himself. His tone is outrageously smooth and deep; and when it finds its softest level, its under monotony is so full of what is called hugging one's self, and is accompanied with such a dragged smile and viciousness of leer, that he seems as if he had lost his voice through the mere enjoyment of malice.

It is thus that in characters of the most apparent labour, as well as in a total neglect of study, this excellent actor surpasses all his contemporaries.

During this season Cooke also acted several times at Bath and Bristol and took "a flying excursion" to play Richard at Portsmouth. At Covent Garden on 28 April 1802 he acted Falstaff in *The Merry Wives of Windsor* and on 7 May Sir Edward Mortimer in *The Iron Chest*. On 11 May he was too drunk to finish the performance of Orsino in *Alfonso*. He created a masterpiece of villainy in the role of Pierre in *Venice Preserv'd* on 29 May 1802, thereby

establishing a new tradition for the character. Earlier Pierres were bluff, honest, and plain-spoken, but not hypocritical. The interpretation was a turn away from the republican sentiments fostered by the Revolution, but probably more realistically caught the post-revolutionary political mood. If Cooke had been in the French theatre during the Revolution, posited Hunt, "When actors became legislators, he might have become the most finished statesman of his day. He can be either a gloomy hypocrite, like Cromwell, or a gay one, such as Chesterfield would have made his son." It was indeed this great versatility at displaying fierceness and hypocrisy which caused Hunt to dismiss Cooke as a tragic actor, for even his Richard was too "occupied by the display of a confident dissimulation, which is something very different from the dignity of tragedy."

Cooke's salary for 1802–3 at Covent Garden was substantially raised, to £14 14*s.* per week. In October 1802 he was living at No 4, Boulton Street, Piccadilly, according to a manuscript in the Harvard Theatre Collection; on 5 February 1803, in his journal, Cooke gave his address as No 9, Piccadilly West. His first London attempt at Hamlet on 27 September 1802 was a failure. Hunt characterized the performance as one painful to recall, for Cooke had made Hamlet "an unpolished, obstinate, sarcastic madman." When George III heard that Cooke was to act the Dane he was reported to exclaim, "Won't do, won't do. Lord Thurlow might as well play Hamlet." On 23 December 1802 he essayed Cato for the first time in London, and played the part exquisitely, thereby redeeming himself. In the spring of that season he was hooted off the stage for being drunk in the middle of his performance of Sir Archy Macsarcasm. Again he apologized to the audience but such aberrations became common during the remainder of his career at Covent Garden, which extended through 1809–10. In the fall of 1803, for example, he destroyed the most exciting week of acting to be seen in London for years. On 3 October, Cooke, playing Richmond and Kemble, playing Richard, appeared together for the first time at Covent Garden amidst great excitement. Three nights later *Douglas* was produced "as it has never been seen before or since," with Cooke as Glenalvon, Kemble as Old Norval, and Mrs Siddons as Lady Randolph. For the following night, 7 October, the bills announced Cooke in the title role of *Pizarro*, with Kemble as Rolla and Mrs Siddons as Elvira, but Cooke was so drunk he could hardly walk. He staggered forward to confess to the audience, "Ladies and Gentlemen—the old complaint—the old complaint!" and the curtain came down to muffle the hoots of derision.

The pay ledgers of Covent Garden show his salary to have been £347 14s. for the season of 1805–6. The theatre burned down on 20 September 1808, and Cooke acted at the King's Theatre with the Covent Garden company in 1808–9 and until the new theatre was opened on 18 September 1809. During the summers he continued his provincial excursions, which are detailed by Dunlap. His performance of Richard III at Manchester in 1803 was reported by *The Townsman* (28 December 1803) as "one of the finest pieces of acting the British stage can boast." The press continued to report his recklessness and improvidence; typical were the lengthy verses which appeared in *The Thespian Review . . . of the Performers on the Manchester Stage* (1806):

> COOKE, who can act—strange skill!—
> and reach the goal,
> When liquid robbers have his reason
> stole:
> COOKE never elegant—almost sans
> grace,
> Trusting to genius to display his face!
> Who, in despite of figure and of voice,
> For Roscius' chair, would still be Shake-
> speare's choice.
> Great as he is, his faults are clear as day,

> And he that mimics, must those faults
> display;
> Faults which our reason ne'er can over-
> look;
> Yet we must bear them—they are part of
> COOKE.
> His strong sarcastic grin—sardonic
> smiles!
> His bolt-like eyes, when, threat'ning, he
> reviles!
> His sneer!—his "Guess"—applause will
> always tax—
> And ev'ry actor bows to Pertinax.
>
> . . . . .
>
> Revere his talents, actors! but reject
> His orgies, vile! if ever you expect
> To reap or honour, or the golden need,
> For breathing sweetly on the Thespian
> reed.

In the fall of 1808 Cooke married a Miss Lamb, of Newark, a woman he had frequently seen in Edinburgh. Although Dunlap asserted that "the marriage was agreeable to all parties concerned," the new Mrs Cooke had disappeared from his life by the time he left for America two years later.

Cooke's last season at Covent Garden was a pitiful exhibition. On 26 December 1809 he was incapable of speaking when he came on as Horatius in *The Roman Father*, and two days later he failed to arrive at the theatre for his announced performance of Shylock, so Charles Kemble substituted at the last moment. On 5 May 1810 Cooke drew public abuse when he acted Henry VIII for the first time with little success. He was announced to perform Falstaff in *1 Henry IV* on 5 June 1810 but, characteristically, he did not show up for the performance. His last London appearance was at Covent Garden on 22 June 1810, when he played Shylock for Mrs Clarke's benefit. While playing for the summer at Liverpool, he was persuaded by Thomas A. Cooper to engage in America at a salary of 25 guineas per week for a ten-month season, plus benefits, transatlantic passage, and an allowance of 25¢ per mile for traveling around to New

York, Boston, Philadelphia, and Baltimore. Cooke, already suffering symptoms of delirium tremens, broke his articles with Covent Garden and sailed on the *Columbia* bound for New York on 4 October 1810. He was, despite his indulgences, the first truly major British actor to engage in the former colonies. Wags commented that visiting America would be punishment enough for his desertion of the English theatre; even when he was announced to be in New York, unbelieving Englishmen in that city claimed he must be an imposter— "Cooke come to America! Pooh!"

After a voyage of 43 days during which he was forced to abstinence after the alcoholic stock on board was exhausted, Cooke landed in New York on 16 November 1810 in the best health he had known in years. He made his debut as Richard III on 21 November 1810, an event described by Dunlap, who was in the audience, as one of tremendous confusion and excitement. More than 2200 people paid in excess of $1820 to the box office. In his journal Cooke wrote that "it was said to be the greatest house ever known in America." Despite a violent snowstorm the receipts were $1420 for his performance of Sir Pertinax on 23 November. For his third appearance on 24 November, again as Richard, he was drunk and could barely speak above a whisper, but the audience generally assumed he was hoarse from the effects of a bad cold. On 28 November he acted Shylock. Meanwhile, Stephen Price the manager took Cooke into his home in an attempt to control him.

Cooke made his debut in Boston as Richard on 3 January 1811. His misadventures during the month he acted there as well as those at Philadelphia, Baltimore, and Providence, are given at length by Dunlap and by Bernard in his *Retrospections of America*. (Don B. Wilmeth's article, "Cooke Among the Yankee Doodles," *Theatre Survey*, November 1973, digests and corrects Dunlap and Bernard

and adds much new matter, providing an excellent account of Cooke's triumphant and tragic final days and his death.) From Boston on 14 January 1811 Cooke wrote to Incledon in England:

Dear Sir.—This is the first letter I have written to Europe, from which my departure was only the result of a few hours' deliberation. On the 4th of October last I sailed from Liverpool, and arrived at New York on the 16th of November. The latter part of the voyage was very tempestuous, and many vessels were lost. I was received by Mr. Price, one of the managers, in a very friendly and hospitable manner, and at whose house I remained while I continued in that city. On Wednesday, the 21st of November, I made my first appearance before an American audience, and was received by a splendid and crowded assemblage in a most flattering manner. I acted seventeen nights to some of the greatest houses ever known in the New World. My own night exceeded four hundred guineas.

On the 29th of December, in company with Mr. Price, I set out in one of the best passage-boats I ever saw, for Newport, Rhode Island, which we reached after a most pleasant trip, in 22 hours, and after a short stay left it in a commodious carriage for this town. We slept on Sunday at Taunton, and arrived here on Monday. My first appearance on Thursday following in the *new* play of *Richard*, which was repeated the next night. This was also my first play in New-York, where they had it three times, and so will the good people here. The house filled as at New-York, and my reception equally flattering. New-York is the handsomest and largest house. We return to the city on Saturday the 29th, and about the 10th of March journey on to Philadelphia, from thence to Baltimore, where my engagement ends; but I shall return to New-York to embark for Liverpool. My time was passed in the last mentioned city in a most agreeable manner, as almost every day, not of business, we had parties at Mr. Price's, or at the houses of some of the principal inhabitants. We are going on the same way here, with this exception, we are lodged at the Exchange Coffee-House, one of the largest and most extraordinary buildings I ever saw, and of consequence, I miss and regret the kind, polite attention of Mrs. P. at whose house I imagined myself in my own, and feel highly gratified at the near prospect of returning to it. Mr. Bernard is one of the managers here, but I believe retires from it at the conclusion of the season. Theatricals are conducted at both Theatres in a very respectable manner, and the companies superior to what I expected to meet. I may add, much so.

I am going to trouble you, my Dear Sir, with a small business, which I request you will be so friendly as to settle for me. If I mistake not the time for paying the Fund, by absentee, is by the 1st of June, if you would take that trouble upon yourself, you would highly oblige me, & I should gratefully acknowledge it on my return.

To Mrs. Incledon, whom I sincerely hope is well, pray present my best regards. I send my warm remembrance to all the family. Mary and my young godson I suppose I shall find grown out of knowledge.

For his debut at Providence on 13 July 1812 he acted Shylock and then played Richard III, Sir Pertinax, Macbeth, Penruddock in *The Wheel of Fortune*, Zanga, Sir Archy Macsarcasm, Lear, Falstaff, and for his final performance on 31 July Sir Giles Overreach. The nine nights brought him $574. One of the richest citizens of Providence, Thomas Lloyd Halsey, sitting in his box watching Cooke play Sir Giles, at the climax "became so excited that he involuntarily rose from his seat, and ejaculated in the presence of a crowded audience, 'Throttle the damned infamous villain!' to the amazement and horror of the whole assembly." Cooke was reported to have attended regularly to his professional responsibilities at Providence; he walked the distance of three-quarters of a mile from his lodgings to the theatre and back every day and never missed a rehearsal. Nevertheless there were occasions during his stay when he was so drunk he fell in the street and had to be assisted home. The Providence engagement took place only several months before he died, so a characterization of him

in that city at the time is of special interest.

Mr. Cooke was about five feet ten inches in height, and scrupulously neat in his dress. His manners were dignified, self-possessed, and courteous. . . . He wore when in Providence, a blue coat with gold buttons, breeches, and top boots, his hair being powdered and worn in a queue. No one would suppose from his appearance that he had any proclivity for indulgence in intoxicating liquors; but would set him down as a precise, well-bred 'gentleman of the old school.' In society he was affable, and his conversation gave evidence of excellent judgment, and a well-stored mind. At those intervals when he gave way to his only vice he never lost his precise air, though he became overbearing in his assumption of superiority, and occasionally fierce in his vituperations. At such times, in the very tempest and whirlwind of his passion, he never evinced any malignity, but, on the contrary, by some chance expression, gave indisputable evidence of a noble nature.

Cooke returned to New York in early September to his lodgings at Mechanics' Hall at the corner of Broadway and Park Place (then Robinson Street). There he died on 26 September 1812, at the age of 56, attended to the end by his new wife, the former Mrs V. M. Behn. (She was the widow of a German merchant in New York. Her father, James Bryden, kept the Tontine Coffee House, which Cooke had frequented. They had been married in New York on 20 June 1811, according to the New York *Commercial Advertiser* of 24 June 1811.) The cause of Cooke's death was reported as dropsy but from the long account provided to Dunlap by Dr David Hosack (1769–1861), who performed the autopsy, it seems obvious that Cooke died from cirrhosis of the liver. On 27 September 1812, he was buried in the Strangers' Vault of St Paul's Church in New York City, with an impressive funeral cortège headed by a carriage containing Governor Tompkins of New York, Mayor DeWitt Clinton, and Elisha Jenkins, Secretary of State. Also in attendance were representatives from the arts, sciences, and clergy.

Stores were closed and flags were flown at half mast. When Edmund Kean, the next great English actor and addict of the bottle, visited New York in 1820–21 he persuaded the church authorities to allow Cooke's remains to be moved to another location in the center of St Paul's Churchyard. Over the new grave Kean had a monument placed with the inscription "Erected to the Memory of George Frederick Cooke by Edmund Kean of the Theatre Royal, Drury Lane, 1821." Below was the couplet by Fitz-Green Halleck:

Three Kingdoms claim his birth
Both hemispheres pronounce his worth.

John Reubens Smith's engraving of the monument, with figures of Kean and Dr Francis standing next to it, was published in New York in 1821; a slightly altered copy was published in London in 1822. In his *History of the American Theatre* (1832) Dunlap wrote somewhat cryptically: "it may hereafter be found that his surgeon possesses his scull, and his successor, Kean, the bones of the finger of his right-hand,—that dictatorial finger,—still the monument covers the *remains* of George Frederick Cooke." That statement along with other legends about his burial spawned numerous spurious stories including one that Edwin Booth used to carry Cooke's skull onstage in performances of *Hamlet*. In a fascinating article, "The Posthumous Career of George Frederick Cooke," in *Theatre Notebook* (Winter 1969–70), Don B. Wilmeth has provided an account of the monument and its subsequent history (it became a shrine for such pilgrim actors as Macready, Charles and Fanny Kemble, Rachel, and Forrest) and has also cleared away many legends about Cooke's skull and forefinger. The skull had indeed been taken by Dr Francis, one of the attending physicians, and was in later years passed along to his son Dr V. Mott Francis who gave it to Dr George McClellan, Dean of the Jefferson Medical College in Philadelphia. It now rests in a display case in

the library of that institution. Indeed, Dr John Francis acknowledged that on one occasion when the skull was still in his possession he actually did provide it in an emergency to an unnamed actor for use in a New York production of *Hamlet*. A tooth from the skull was sent by one of Dr McClellan's friends to Edwin Booth, who sent it to the Player's Club. It is now in the City Museum of New York. The legend that Kean had taken Cooke's forefinger back to England as a sacred relic only to have his disgusted wife throw it away cannot be verified. A death mask of Cooke is in the Harvard Theatre Collection.

Cooke had at least three wives, possibly four, if the woman who acted as Mrs Cooke at Chester in 1785 was married to him. Alicia Daniels Cooke, who had their marriage annulled in 1801, died as Mrs Windsor at Bath in 1826. What happened to Miss Lamb of Newark or the former Mrs Behn who was with him when he died is not known to us. No children of Cooke by any of these women are known. In his history of the American stage T. Allston Brown claimed that the George Cook who made his first appearance on the American Stage at Philadelphia on 11 March 1830 in *Richard III* was a "Nephew of George Frederick Cook."

The judgment of a critic cited by Genest that "Cooke did not play many parts well, but that he played those which he did play well better than anybody else" seems appropriate. He was the first of the great romantic actors who sacrificed grace and dignity for energy and passion and who possessed an extraordinary ability, in the words of Dunlap, "of seizing the perfect image of the person he would represent, and identifying it with his own feelings, so as to express every emotion designed by the author, as if that emotion were his own." But all was not really by intuition. He carefully worked out his transitions and his gestures, punctuated with a number of tricks calculated to catch applause. Dunlap described a copy of the part of Sir Archy

which Cooke had carefully marked for in-
flection and volume. He wrote out his roles
as if in prose in order to avoid a sing-song
delivery, a defect which marred J. P. Kemble's acting. Cooke "spoke with two voices,"
reported Boaden, one "harsh and acrimoni-
ous," another "mild and caressing," and he
often employed both in the same sentence
or speech.

Just as he spoke "with two voices" so he
lived with two psyches, which contested
for one human being with intense and opposite commitments—Cooke sober and
Cooke drunk. For some periods he was a
dedicated artist and a scholarly affable gentleman, at other times he was "a maniac
and a sot." He was, of course, his own worst
enemy, "always debasing himself below the
level of the men he despised." But at his
best he was truly a great actor, indeed, for
many persons of discrimination and taste,
the greatest actor they had ever seen. "He
always presented himself to me in the light
of a discoverer," said the distinguished
American actor John Howard Payne, "one
with whom it seemed that every action and
every look emanated entirely from himself;
one who appeared never to have had a
model; and who depended entirely upon
himself for everything he did in the character he represented." Edmund Kean pro-
claimed that Cooke had never been
equalled as an actor. On the other hand,
Leigh Hunt, who acknowledged that Cooke
"was intelligent and peremptory, and a hard
hitter" who seized attention, regretted that
"he was never pleasant" on stage. He was
too harsh in his "smiling malignity" for
Hunt, who also accused him of reducing
Shakespeare's poetry to "indignant prose."
In 1807 Hunt wrote in *Critical Essays* that

Mr. Cooke is the Machiavel of the modern
stage. . . . He can render all his passions
subservient to one passion, and one purpose,
and can—
Smile, and smile, and be a villain.
Like most statesmen, however, he can do

nothing without artifice. His looks and his
tones invariably turn him from the very appearance of virtue. If he wishes to be seriously
sentimental, he devolves into irony; if he endeavors to appear candid, his manner is so
strange and inconsistent, that you are merely
inclined to guard against him the more. It is
for these reasons that his gentlemen in sentimental comedy become so awkward and in-
efficient, that his *Jacques* in 'As You Like It,'
instead of being a moralizing enthusiast, is
merely a grave scoffer, and that his *Macbeth*,
who ought to be at least a majestic villain,
exhibits nothing but a desperate craftiness.

In his ten years at Covent Garden Cooke
"created" comparatively few original char-
acters, all rather slight: Orsino in *Alfonso*
(15 January 1802), an unnamed char-
acter in *Word of Honour* (26 May 1802),
Peregrine in *John Bull* (5 March 1803),
Sandy MacTab in *Three per Cents* (12
November 1803), Lt Seymour in *Love
Gives the Alarm* (23 February 1804),
Lord Avondale in *School of Reform* (15
February 1805), Lavensforth in *To Marry
or Not to Marry* (16 February 1805),
Prince Altenberg in *Adrian and Orrila* (15
November 1806), and Colonel Vortex in
Match-making (24 May 1808). Engravings
of him in his major roles were profusely
made and circulated and he sat for his
portrait for many artists.

The Garrick Club holds 11 original
paintings or drawings of Cooke:

1. A portrait by Gilbert Stuart. Painted
for the manager Stephen Price and finished
on 6 January 1811.

2. A small panel, head and shoulders.
Artist unknown.

3. A set of nine silhouettes on paper.
Artist unknown.

4. A pencil drawing on paper, head and
shoulders. Artist unknown.

5. A painting by Thomas Sully. Bequeathed by J. W. Wallack. Dunlap mentioned three portraits of Cooke done by
Sully in 1811: one for Wood, the manager
at Philadelphia; one for Mr Wilcocks; and

one as Richard III. The painting in the Garrick Club is one of the first two or a replica. See No 40 for the original by Sully of Cooke as Richard III.

6. As Iago. An oil by James Green, which was exhibited at the Royal Academy in 1801. An engraving by J. Ward was published in 1801, and another engraving by an anonymous artist appeared at about the same time.

7. As Kitely in *Every Man in his Humour*. An oil by Henry Singleton.

8. As Richard III. A watercolor on paper by De Wilde. A portrait of Cooke in this part by De Wilde was exhibited at the Royal Academy in 1809. The Garrick Club version was engraved by Cheesman for the *Theatrical Inquisitor* in 1813 and for *Le Beau Monde*. An engraving by Anderson also appeared.

9. As Richard III. An oil by C. R. Leslie in 1813. Engraved by Thomson for Oxberry's *New English Drama* in 1818.

10. As Shylock. An oil by Thomas Phillips, painted about 1803.

11. As Sir Archy Macsarcasm. A painting by De Wilde, signed by the artist on 16 May 1806. In his journal for that day Cooke recorded sitting at De Wilde's for this painting. The picture was variously engraved by R. Woodman and published by John Cawthorn in 1808, by A. Cardon and published in Cawthorn's *Minor English Theatre* in 1806, and by Kennerley and published in Oxberry's *Dramatic Biography* in 1826. Some of the Woodman issues are incorrectly titled "Mr Cooke as Sir Pertinax Macsycophant."

Other original paintings and drawings and numerous engravings of Cooke include the following: (Unless otherwise noted, copies of the engravings are in the Harvard Theatre Collection.)

12. A watercolor on ivory. Artist unknown. In the Shakespeare Memorial Theatre Gallery at Stratford-upon-Avon.

13. A bust silhouette engraving by "J. B."

14. A bust portrait by J. Corbett, engraving by J. Whessell. Published by T. Simpson and Thompson in 1801, and reissued by Thompson in 1804. The same picture (reversed), by an anonymous engraver, was published in the *Thespian Dictionary*.

15. A caricature entitled "Cook the Actor; the Dirty Beau and Big Ben." Drawn and engraved by G. Cruikshank.

16. Portrait by Drummond. Engraved by J. Rogers for Oxberry's *Dramatic Biography* in 1827.

17. A miniature, by William Dunlap. Engravings by H. R. Cook and published by J. Miller in 1813; by Leney; and by Cooper for Dunlap's *Life* which was published by H. Colburn in 1813.

18. Engraving by Ridley & Co. Published in the *European Magazine* in 1807.

19. Portrait by Slater. Engraving by Towes.

20. Portrait by S. J. Stump. Engravings by J. Hopwood and published by Mathews & Leigh in 1807; by P. Maguire and published in the *Cyclopaedian Magazine*; by an anonymous engraver and published in the *Cabinet*, 1811.

21. Bust portrait by Sully. Engraving by D. Edwin for the *Mirror of Taste and Dramatic Censor* in 1811.

22. As Falstaff in *1 Henry IV*. Engraving by J. Alais. Published by J. Roach in 1802.

23. As Falstaff in *1 Henry IV*. Engraving by F. Lambert, after "A. B.", from an original in the Dick Collection.

24. As Falstaff in *1 Henry IV*. Engraving by Wedgwood, after Singleton. Published by Longman & Co.

25. As Falstaff in *The Merry Wives of Windsor*. Engraving by Rhodes, after Thurston. Shown with characters of Mistress Ford and Mistress Page.

26. As Iago. Engraving in stipple by W. Ridley, after J. Corbett. Published in the *Monthly Mirror* in 1800. The picture was engraved by P. Maguire, also.

27. As Iago. Engraving by Chesham, after Cruikshank. Published by Macpherson in 1802.

28. As King John, in tent with Prince Arthur. Engraving by J. K. Shirwin.

29. As King Lear. Engraving by D. Edwin, after C. R. Leslie. Published in the *Mirror of Taste*, 1811.

30. As Macbeth. Engraving by Parker, after De Loutherbourg. Published by Kearsley, 1803.

31. As Richard III. Oil painting by an unknown artist. In the Folger Shakespeare Library.

32. As Richard III. Miniature by J. T. Barber Beaumont. In the possession of Robert Eddison, London. Shown in an exhibition of paintings, drawings, and stage designs ("Shakespeare and the Theatre") arranged by the Guildhall Art Gallery in collaboration with the Society for Theatre Research in 1964. A version was engraved by A. Cardon and published by J. P. Thompson in 1805.

33. As Richard III. Vignette engraving by Benwell.

34. As Richard III. Engraving by Brook.

35. As Richard III. By R. Dighton. Engraved and published by the artist, 1800.

36. As Richard III. Engraving by D. Edwin, after C. R. Leslie. Published in the *Mirror of Taste*, 1811.

37. As Richard III. Oil painting by J. R. Lambden, copied after Thomas Sully. This painting was in the Augustin Daly Collection which was sold at the Anderson Galleries in 1912. In 1962 it was sold by the Folger Shakespeare Library to the American Shakespeare Festival Theatre, Stratford, Connecticut, where it now hangs.

38. As Richard III (at Cork, September 1800). Watercolor, "Taken from Life by W. Loftis." In the Folger Shakespeare Library.

39. As Richard III. Engraving by E. Scriven, after G. Bullock, from a model in rice paste. Published by V. Zanetti, 1812.

40. As Richard III. Oil painting by Thomas Sully, 1811. Sold by the artist for $300 to the Pennsylvania Academy of Fine Arts, Philadelphia, where it still hangs. An engraving was published by Gebbie & Co in 1888.

41. As Richard III. Engraving by an unknown engraver. Published by N. Jones, 1802.

42. As Shylock. Engraving by J. Alais. Published by J. Roach, 1804.

43. As Shylock. Engraving by J. Archer. Published by Oliver & Boyd, Edinburgh, and D. Arnott, London.

44. As Shylock. Engraving by Skelton, after De Loutherbourg. Published by Kearsley, 1803.

45. As Sir Archy Macsarcasm. Engraving by an unknown engraver. Published by Oliver & Boyd, Edinburgh, 1811.

46. As Sir Giles Overreach in *A New Way to Pay Old Debts*. Engraving by Stalker, after Singleton. Published by Longman & Co.

47. As Sir Pertinax Macsycophant in *The Man of the World*. Engraving by D. Edwin, after C. R. Leslie. Published in the *Mirror of Taste*, 1811.

48. As Sir Pertinax. Engraving by J. E. Walker, after Singleton. Published by Longman & Co, 1806.

49. As Sir Pertinax. Engraving by an unknown engraver. Published by Oliver & Boyd, Edinburgh.

50. As Strictland in *The Suspicious Husband*. Engraving by J. Archer. Published by Oliver & Boyd, Edinburgh.

51. As Stukeley in *The Gamester*. Engraving by Rogers. Published in Oxberry's *New English Drama*, 1823.

52. As Timon in *Timon of Athens*. Engraving by Warren, after De Wilde. Published by Kearsley, 1805.

Cooke, Mrs George Frederick the second. *See* DANIELS, ALICIA.

Cooke, Henry *c. 1616–1672, singer, composer, teacher.*

Henry Cooke was probably the son of John Cooke, a Gentleman of the Chapel Royal under James I, and it is likely that he was born at Lichfield about 1616. Young Henry was a boy chorister in the Chapel before the civil wars, but by 1640 he was a lieutenant in the regiment of foot commanded by Colonel George Goring after the retreat from Newcastle into Yorkshire. Two years later he had gained the rank of captain, and even after the wars he so styled himself.

Cooke may have married in the early 1640s, and it is probable that he was the Henry Cooke of St Thomas, Southwark, who married Marie Reyner of St Mary Woolnoth on 1 January 1643. By 1651 Cooke was earning a living teaching music, and at some time he may have visited Italy to study voice. On 28 October 1654 he played the theorbo and sang at John Evelyn's house, and the diarist called Cooke the "best singer after the Italian manner of any in England."

On 23 May 1656, or perhaps a day or two before, Henry Cooke participated in Davenant's production called *The First Day's Entertainment at Rutland House.* He, Edward Coleman and his wife, and what a government spy called "other inconsiderable voyces" were the singers. Cooke also contributed to the writing of the music. The following September he sang Solyman and composed the second and third entries for Davenant's next Rutland House production, *The Siege of Rhodes.*

Captain Cooke was appointed on 29 June 1660 to replace Thomas Day as "master of the boyes in the private musick" at court, an office of great importance in which he acquitted himself well for the rest of his life. He also replaced Nicholas Duvall in the lutes, voices, theorboes, and virginals at court on 9 November 1660. In recompense he received the livery payments of £16 2s. 6d., which had previously been paid to Day and Duvall, plus a yearly stipend of £60, plus £20 for instrument strings, plus £24 for teaching the Chapel children, plus £10 each for two boys under his particular care. In addition, at the death of Dr Charles Coleman in 1664, Cooke became composer for voices in the King's private music and had £40 annually added to his income. These sums, plus extra fees which he was paid from time to time for special services, made Captain Cooke one of the highest paid musicians in the King's service. But, as will be seen, he was seldom paid on schedule.

Cooke was a basso and attracted the attention of the music-loving Samuel Pepys, who frequently mentioned him in his diary. On 12 August 1660, for instance, Pepys heard Cooke sing a "brave anthem" of his own composing at the Whitehall chapel that "well pleased" King Charles, and on 27 July 1661 at a tavern Cooke sang a song that made Pepys feel that "without doubt he hath the best manner of singing in the world."

The following 14 September Pepys heard some more of "Captain Cooke's new musique. This the first day of having vialls and other instruments to play a symphony between each verse of the anthem; but the musique more full than it was the last Sunday, and very fine it is. But yet I could discern Captain Cooke do overdo his part at singing, which I never did before." Pepys was to have other misgivings about Cooke as he grew to know him better, but his admiration at this early point was great.

What little we know of Cooke's wife also comes from Pepys. On 22 November 1661 the diarist wrote of a dinner at the Dolphin where were

. . . Captain Cook and his lady, a German lady, but a very great beauty . . . and there we had the best musique and very good songs, and were very merry, and danced, but I was most of all taken with Madam Cook and her little boy. . . . But after all our mirth comes a reckoning of 4*l.*, besides 4*s.* of the musicians, which did trouble me, but it must be paid, and so I took leave.

At Lord Sandwich's on 21 December 1663 Pepys found "Captain Cooke and his boys, Dr Childe, Mr Madge, and Mallard, playing and singing over my Lord's anthem which he hath made to sing in the King's Chapell . . . And after that was done Captain Cooke and his two boys did sing some Italian songs, which I must in a word say I think was fully the best musique that I ever yet heard in all my life, and it was to me a very great pleasure to hear them." But as time went on, Pepys developed mixed feelings about Cooke. He stated them most fully on 13 February 1667:

[A]mong other vanities, Captain Cooke had the arrogance to say that he was fain to direct Sir W. Davenant in the breaking of his verses into such and such lengths, according as would be fit for musick, and how he used to swear at Davenant, and command him that way, when W. Davenant would be angry, and find fault with this or that note—but a vain coxcomb I perceive he is, though he sings and composes so well. . . . After dinner Captain Cooke and two of his boys to sing, but it was indeed both in performance and composition most plainly below what I heard last night [Draghi and Mrs Knepp singing], which I could not have believed. Besides overlooking the words which he sung, I find them not at all humoured as they ought to be, and as I believed he had done all he had sett. Though he himself do indeed sing in a manner as to voice and manner the best I ever heard yet, and a strange mastery he hath in making of extraordinary surprising closes, that are mighty pretty, but his bragging that he do understand tones and sounds as well as any man in the world, and better than Sir W. Davenant or any body else, I do not like by no means, but was sick of it and of him for it.

Disenchanted, Pepys subsequently had little to say about Cooke.

The Lord Chamberlain's accounts for the 1660s are filled with references to Cooke and his work as master of the children of the Chapel Royal. He was, apparently, a fine teacher, strict in his discipline and demanding of his students, and under him such boys as Michael Wise, Pelham Humphrey, John Blow, and Henry Purcell learned their Latin, writing, musical composition, virginal, organ, lute, and violin. The accounts show frequent payments to him over the years for clothes for the boys, transportation to Windsor when he and his students were needed there for services, strings for instruments and fire for the music room where they practiced, books and paper, fees for nurses and doctors—the everyday expenses of training young boys for musical careers and giving them their primary education. His group apparently numbered about 12, two of whom at any given point were under his special care and had to be looked after when their voices broke and they left the Chapel Royal. Sometimes Cooke received reimbursement for his expenses on time, but, judging by his will, King Charles frequently forced Captain Cooke to take care of the boys out of his own pocket and hope for recompense later.

In addition, Cooke had his duties as a regular Gentleman of the Chapel Royal: writing music, attending the King when he visited outside London, looking after the organ loft at the Chapel, and performing at services. By 9 April 1669 he was living "at the further end of the Old Bowling Alley at Hampton Court," for on that date an order was issued for repairs to his lodgings. And as of 21 January 1670 Cooke added to his own duties by serving as a marshal in the Corporation of Music. His life was clearly busy and full of expense, but, despite arrears in payment, lucrative and satisfying. Though no great musician himself, except perhaps as a singer, he contributed importantly to the musical life of the Restoration.

On 24 June 1672 Captain Cooke asked the Corporation of Music to find a replacement for him as marshal, for sickness had prevented him from attending to business. Less than a month later, on 13 July, he died. He had made a will on 6 July 1672 which asked that he be buried near his daughter Mary in the Cloisters of Westminster Abbey, with a space left between for his wife. He left land in Pluckly, Kent, to his widow (Christian name not given), after whose death the property was to be divided between his surviving daughters. To his daughter Katherine Cooke he left £300 of £500 due him from the Exchequer, plus 120 broad pieces of gold, and to his daughter Amy he left £200 from the same source. Mourning rings worth 10s. each he bequeathed to those Gentlemen of the Chapel Royal who attended his burial.

Much of Cooke's will concerned itself with the money owed Cooke and debts he owed others and is indicative of the sorry state of Charles II's finances. In addition to the £500 the King owed him, Cooke had yet to receive from the Crown £180 in salary, £112 for traveling expenses when he went to Windsor in 1671, the remainder of a £50 bill at Windsor, an unspecified sum for teaching the boys in the Chapel, £5 for the boys' lute strings, £20 allowance for fire in the music room, £96 15s. for six liveries (presumably for the boys), at least £200 "without they have set their hand to the book for me" (whatever that may imply), and £215 due Cooke at Michaelmas 1672. Cooke was also owed £230 for having been the executor of Mr Thorne's will, £5 from Dr Cunstable of Deptford, and 20s. from Mr (Alphonso?) Marsh. His debts were small by comparison: he owed Mr Boughy £200, for which Boughy held a mortgage on Cooke's house at Longditch, and he was in debt to John Harding for £10 and to Edward Hooten for £4. If Cooke looked after his duties in the Chapel as closely as he looked after his own finances, he must have been well worth what the King was supposed to pay him.

On 15 July 1672, two days after Cooke's death, William Turner was appointed to his position of lute and voice in the King's Musick, and Cooke's ex-pupil Pelham Humphrey replaced him as composer for voices and master of the children. Cooke was buried at Westminster Abbey on 17 July 1672, in the East Cloister. Wood claimed that he had died of grief because Pelham Humphrey excelled him on the lute, but that sounds rather fanciful, however vain Cooke may have been. As of 4 December 1676 Captain Cooke's widow was still alive and some of the debts owed him had apparently been paid.

Though Cooke wrote much music, little of it was memorable. Manuscripts of some of his works have been preserved at the British Museum and at Oxford, and some of his short pieces were published in *Court Ayres* (1655).

Cooke, James   [*fl.* 1791–1825], *singer, actor.*

Prior to his engagement at Drury Lane Theatre in the season of 1790–91, James Cooke had been employed by the musical instrument makers and song publishers Longman and Broderip as a singer to introduce their songs into choral societies. He made his first appearance at Drury Lane on 1 January 1791 as Anselm in the premier performance of *The Siege of Belgrade*, a music drama by Cobb and Storace. The piece was performed with Cooke another nine times through 15 January, but on 18 January he was replaced by Sedgwick. On the pay list for £1 10s. per week, he probably continued in the chorus for the rest of the season.

In 1791–92 when the Drury Lane company played at the King's Theatre, he was again engaged at £1 10s. per week and acted and sang a variety of minor roles including Perez in *Don Juan*, Gadshill in *1 Henry IV*, the Boatswain (with song) in *Don Juan*, Scroop in *Henry V*, Dorilus in *Cymon*, a character in *Huniades*, Thomas in

The Virgin Unmask'd, Durande in *Venice Preserv'd*, a Herald in *King Lear*, Leonardo in *The Merchant of Venice*, and choral parts in *The American Heroine*, *The Surrender of Calais*, and *Dido, Queen of Carthage*. On 13 June 1792, Cooke shared benefit tickets with 15 other people.

Cooke continued in a similar capacity at Drury Lane through the rest of the eighteenth century. In 1796–97, his salary was £2 per week. Perhaps he was the Cooke who received £1 5s. per week in the chorus regularly from about 1800–1801 through at least 1816–17.

No doubt he was the J. Cooke, bass singer, listed in Doane's *Musical Directory* in 1794 as a member of Drury Lane Theatre and singer in oratorios, a performer at the Handel commemorations in Westminster Abbey, and then living at No 2, Upper John Street, Golden Square. He had a good bass voice, according to the *Authentic Memoirs of the Green Room* (1799), and was "very useful in his line; but as a colonel or a gentleman" he was "ridiculous." The author of *Candid and Impartial Strictures on the Performers* (1795) called him "a wretched singer, and a worse actor." Among his other parts at Drury Lane in the 1790s were one of the horde in *Lodoiska*, an Officer in *The Cherokee* and *Isabella*, Robin of Bagshot in *The Beggar's Opera*, a Gentleman in *A Bold Stroke for a Wife*, Francisco in *Hamlet*, a Sailor in *Harlequin Captive*, and a Huntsman in *The Honey Moon*.

Our subject was probably the James Cooke mentioned by Wewitzer in his *Dramatic Biography* as a provincial actor in 1825 and the uncle of Mrs William West, of Bath, who was a London actress in the 1820s. Reputedly the theatrical Cookes of Bath were related to George Frederick Cooke. The composer J. Cooke wrote the songs *My Thyrsis was the Gentlest Youth*, sung by Mr Dignum, and *The Turn of her Eye*, both published about 1795.

Cooke, Mary *1666?–1745, actress, singer.*

The Mrs Mary Cooke (sometimes Cook) who performed at Lincoln's Inn Fields Theatre during the first half of the eighteenth century was possibly the wife of the dancer Mr Cooke who was at the same theatre between 1715 and 1721. Her Christian name is found in a manuscript dated 1722, now in the British Museum. But as the addition "Mrs" was also a common style for single women on the stage at this time, it is possible that the performer Mary Cooke was not a married woman and may have been the Mary, daughter of John and Alice Cooke, who was baptized at St Margaret, Westminster, on 25 February 1665/66, or Mary, the daughter of Peter and Rebeka Cooke, who with her twin brother Thomas was baptized at the same place on 4 October 1666. These birth dates are consistent with the report that Mrs Cooke was 80 years of age at her death in 1745.

Mrs Cooke's first recorded appearance was at Lincoln's Inn Fields on 17 January 1715 when she sang a duet, "Since times are so bad," with Richard Leveridge. A week later, on 25 January, she sang in *The Island Princess*. Her name was in the bills for Lady Swish in the first performance of *The Northern Heiress* on 27 April 1716. Perhaps she was the Mrs Cook who performed in Pinkethman's company at Richmond in the summer of 1718. She shared a benefit, certainly, with Mrs Hodgson at Lincoln's Inn Fields on 18 May 1719.

Playing primarily in the line of mature women in comedy, Mary Cooke remained active at that theatre for another 14 years. Her roles (with dates of first known performances) included: Hostess in *1 Henry IV* (2 October 1719), Charlotta in *Oroonoko* (13 February 1720), Johayma in *Don Sebastian* (26 April 1720), a role in *The Old Bachelor* (17 May 1725), Mrs Goodfellow in *Tunbridge Walks* (5 July 1726), Mrs Snore in *The Wits* (19 August 1726), a role in *The Country Wife* (17 May 1727), Lady Plyant in *The Double Dealer* (19 April 1727), Mrs Mopus in *The Cheats* (11 December 1727), Mrs Prim in *A Bold Stroke for a Wife* (23 April 1728), Teresia in *Don Quixote* (24 April 1728), Bulfinch in *Love and a Bottle* (22 May 1728), a role in *The Fortune Hunters*, and the Governess in *The Fond Husband* (14 February 1732).

Mary Cooke's salary in 1724–25 was 10 shillings per day, and by 1726–27 it had been raised to 15 shillings. On 17 May 1727 she shared benefit receipts of £197 6s. with Gwinn, Mrs Atkins, and Mrs Warren. Mrs Cooke's known performances at the various fairs were: Hob's Wife in *Love's Triumph* at Southwark Fair on 23 August 1720, a role in the droll *King Saul* at Southwark on 2 September 1721, and Madam Doodle in *Semiramis* at Bartholomew Fair on 23 August 1725. No doubt she made many other similar appearances.

When the Lincoln's Inn Fields company transferred to Rich's new Covent Garden Theater in 1732, Mrs Cooke was with them. She acted Bulfinch in *Love and a Bottle* on 30 March 1733. Thereafter she appeared only occasionally in the small roles of old women. In 1733–34 she played Mrs Cloggit in *The Confederacy*, Ruth in *The Squire of Alsatia*, the Aunt in *The London Cuckold*, and Lady Pride in *The Amorous Widow*. From 1734–35 through 1739–40 she gave only several performances each year of the latter two roles. Her last performance on record was as Lady Pride on 7 May 1740. According to Isaac Reed's manuscript "Notitia Dramatica" at the British Museum, Mrs Cooke died on 18 March 1745, at the age of 80.

Cooke, Matthew (fl. 1780–1800?), *instrumentalist, singer, composer.*

Matthew Cooke was one of the vocal performers in the Handel Memorial Concerts at Westminster Abbey and the Pantheon in May and June 1784. In 1794 he was listed in Doane's *Musical Directory* as a player on the tenor violin, the pianoforte, and the organ, a member of the New Musical Fund. He was then living in Charles Street, Berkeley Square. For some time he was organist of St George, Bloomsbury. His pupils included his nephew, Nathaniel Cooke (1773–1827), an organist and composer living at Brighton, and Joseph Binns Hart (1794–1844), composer, who became chorus master and pianist at the English Opera at the Lyceum in 1818.

Compositions by Matthew Cooke are listed in the *Catalogue of Printed Music at the British Museum*. The earliest, "A Set of Country Dances as performed at the Grove, the Seat of the Earl of Clarendon," dates from about 1780. His song *Our Bottle and Friend* was published about 1785 and another, *The Wooden Walls of Old England*, about 1790. Collections of settings of Psalms were printed in 1790 and 1795. Instrumental music which he published included *Six Lessons for the Harpsichord or Piano Forte* (1780?), *The Celebrated Dutch Minuet, and a Favorite New Waltz . . . adapted for the Piano Forte* (1800?), and an arrangement of Mozart's overture and march from *Die Zauberflöte*, for two performers on one pianoforte (1800?).

Cooke, Philip (fl. 1739–1755), *dancing master.*

The dancing master Philip Cooke was no doubt a member of the Covent Garden Theatre's company when he received a benefit there on 16 January 1739, the night when his son, Master Philip Cooke, made his first appearance on the stage. The elder Cooke did dance at Drury Lane Theatre in 1739–40, appearing in *Comus* on 28 November, as a Haymaker in *Harlequin Shipwrecked* (in which his son played a Sea God) on 5 January, as a Pilgrim in the entertainment *A Voyage to the Land of Cytherea* on 15 January, in a *Shepherd and Shepherdess Dance* on 13 February, as a pilgrim in *The Fortune Tellers* on 29 April, and dancing with Mrs Walter in a dance called *Maggot* on 7 May 1740.

Although Cooke had fallen into bankruptcy as a dancing master in 1739 (according to a notice in the *Daily Advertiser* of 22 May 1739, which also provided his full name), he apparently retired from stage dancing at the end of 1739–40 to try again as a private teacher. By 1744 he was living in Great Ormond Street, near Queen Square. He was still alive in September 1755, and was, according to the death notice for his son in the *Daily Advertiser* on the twelfth of that month, still functioning as a dancing master at an address in Chancery Lane. He may have been related to the Cookes who danced at Lincoln's Inn Fields in the 1720s.

Cooke, Philip *d. 1755, dancer.*

Philip, son of the dancing master Philip Cooke (fl. 1739–1755), made his first appearance on any stage, billed as Master Cooke, at Covent Garden Theatre on 16 January 1739, when he danced for his father's benefit. He danced again on 7 April 1739, with Miss Scot. When his father went over to Drury Lane in the following season, Master Cooke joined him, playing a Sea God in *Harlequin Shipwrecked* on 10 December 1739, dancing in a ballet of *Shepherds and Shepherdesses* on 11 April 1740, and performing a minuet with Mrs Walter on 15 May 1740. The latter performance was for his own benefit, for which tickets could be had at his father's lodgings at the Blue Flower Pot, in Devonshire Street, near Red Lion Square.

At the end of 1739–40, the elder Cook seems to have retired from stage dancing to devote full time to his dancing school. Master Philip Cooke, by now approaching manhood, went to Paris, where he obtained a position with the Opéra. He returned to England in the fall of 1742 and (now billed as Mr Cooke and as making his first appearance since his arrival from the Paris Opéra) danced at Covent Garden on 23 October 1742 with the two Auretti sisters, also from Paris and making their English debuts. Two nights later Cooke danced a *Grand Ballet* with them, and alone, a *Dutch Skipper* and a *Tambourine*; the last piece proved very popular and was repeated regularly throughout the season. For his benefit on 24 March 1743, Cooke danced a piece called *Les Matelots*, a French *Peasant Dance*, and a minuet. His residence in this year and in the following was at his father's house in Great Ormond Street, near Queen Square.

Cooke continued as a very busy specialty dancer at Covent Garden through 1745–46, appearing in such pieces as the masque in *Comus*, dancing as a Rural Swain in *Orpheus and Eurydice*, and performing a variety of unnamed entertainments. On 22 October 1746 he was paid £10 10*s*. on account by the Covent Garden treasury, but he seems not to have performed there that season. Instead, he took an engagement at Drury Lane, making his first appearance there since 1740 on 21 January 1747. A writer to the editor of the *General Advertiser* on the next morning praised the dancing of Cooke, Signor Saloman, and Mlle Violette as being excellent in every way, and without offence to decency. Cooke remained at Drury Lane for three seasons, living during this period at the house of Mr Clarke, an upholsterer, in James Street, Covent Garden.

In 1749–50 Cooke returned to Covent Garden, where he remained for the rest of his career, continuing to lodge at Mr Clarke's in James Street. In the summer of 1751 he played at Richmond and Twickenham and in September 1751 at Southwark Fair. Soon afterward he was rumored to be dead, but on 19 November 1751 the *General Advertiser* assured its readers that "The Death of Mr Cooke mentioned in the papers is a mistake, he being in a fair way of recovery."

During his last season at Covent Garden, he regularly performed a *Dutch Dance* and minuet with Miss Hilliard. For his benefit on 4 April 1754 he danced a louvre and a minuet with her. On 26 January 1754 the *Gray's Inn Journal* printed two pages of satiric comment about pantomimes at both theatres, where it was alleged that Cooke's use of a hare and gun in his pantomime role (probably in *Harlequin Skeleton*) was an encouragement to poaching. Cooke's last performance was in a *Peasant Dance* with Miss Hilliard on 6 May 1754. He must have been too ill to perform in 1754–55. On 12 September 1755 the *Daily Advertiser* announced that he had died on 9 September and identified him as the son of Mr Cook, the dancing master of Chancery Lane. On 11 October 1755 administration of his will was granted to Angelina Cooke, his widow, of the parish of St Marylebone.

Cooke, Robert *1768–1814, organist, composer, singer.*

Robert Cooke was born at Westminster in 1768, the son of Dr Benjamin Cooke by his wife Mary, born Jackson. Educated in music by his father, he was among the tenor vocalists in the Handel Memorial Concerts at Westminster Abbey and the Pantheon in May and June 1784, for which his father was the assistant director. Robert Cooke succeeded, upon Dr Cooke's death in 1793, to the position of organist at St Martin-in-the-Fields. In 1794 Doane's *Musical Directory* listed him also as a teacher of music then living in Dorset Court, Westminster. When Dr Arnold died in 1802, Cooke was appointed organist of Westminster Abbey, and in 1806 he became master of the Abbey choristers. These posts he held for the rest of his life.

At the age of 46, on 23 August 1814 Robert Cooke, suffering from madness, committed suicide by throwing himself into the Thames. (This death date, taken from the Abbey burial register, differs from that of 13 August 1814, given by Grove.) He was buried in the West Cloister on 30 August. Cooke died unmarried. Administration of his estate was granted to his brother Henry on 7 September 1814.

His compositions included an "Evening Service in C, Major," an "Ode to Friendship," which was sung on the first night of the British Concerts, a canzonet for two voices with an accompaniment for the pianoforte, which was entitled "The Tear that Breaks for Others' Woe" and was set from Erasmus Darwin's poem *The Botanic Garden*, plus a number of glees and catches. Three of the glees won medals at the Catch Club. A collection of nine glees was published in 1795 and another collection of eight in 1805. His other works are listed in the *Catalogue of Printed Music in the British Museum*.

For bequests received by Robert Cooke from his father and for information on his brothers and sisters, see the entry for Benjamin Cooke (1734–1793).

Cooke, Sarah *d. 1688, actress.*

According to the *Satyr on the Players* (c. 1684), Sarah Cooke's mother was a vendor of herbs. Her aunt held a loftier station, being the governess of the maids of honor to the Duchess of York, and probably through her influence Sarah (sometimes called Susan) became one of the maids. *The Memoirs of Count Grammont*, though fictionalized, may truly report Sarah's service in 1665 or 1666. Sarah's aunt, it seems, became concerned that Miss Hobart, one of the maids of honor with lesbian tendencies, was paying undue attention to her niece, so she spoke to Lord Rochester of this. He recommended that Sarah be "removed from Miss Hobart's clutches; and performed his office so well that she immediately fell into his own." The Duchess of York thereupon appointed Sarah to serve about her person and, since the young girl was blessed with a good memory, used her as a source of information and gossip. In time both Sarah and her aunt were dismissed by the Duchess for spreading rumors about Miss Hobart, upon which Rochester is said to have whisked them both to his country house, where he discovered Sarah's dramatic talent and encouraged her to pursue a stage career.

The *Memoirs* state that Rochester placed Sarah in the King's Company at the Bridges Street Theatre the next winter and that "the public was obliged to him for the prettiest, but also the worst actress in the realm." Some or all of this tale may be true, and the dates, at least, fit with what little we know about Sarah Cooke's stage career. She was named as Luciana in *The Comedy of Errors* in a copy of the play at the University of Edinburgh containing manuscript prompt notes, and the other performers noted were, most of them, associated with the King's Company; the prompt notes seem to date about 1667–73 and may be either for a touring company headed by John Coysh or for the young players who performed at the Nursery operated jointly by the King's and Duke's companies about 1671–72. A related promptbook for *The Wise Woman of Hogsdon*, which shows Sarah playing the second Luce, also dates about 1671–72 and pertains to Coysh's touring company. Sarah Cooke was cited as a member of the cast of *Sir Salomon* about 1674–75, also on tour. Rochester, then, may very well have introduced Sarah to the King's players about 1667, whereupon she may have been placed by Thomas Killigrew in Coysh's strolling group to gain experience. And she may have ended up at the Nursery with other young players in the early 1670s.

Her first recorded role with the King's Company proper was Gillian in *The Country Innocence* at Drury Lane in March 1677. The following September Charles Killigrew tried to form a separate company made up of many of the newer members of the King's players, including Sarah, but the end result was simply a reconstituted King's Company. In late February 1678 Sarah played Flora in *The Rambling Justice* and spoke the prologue, after which she may have gone touring again, possibly to Edinburgh in 1679, for her name did not appear again in London casts until 8 December 1680, when she delivered the epilogue to *The Sicilian Usurper*. At Drury Lane in 1681 she is known to have played the Countess of Rutland in *The Unhappy Favourite*, and the following season she acted Livia in *Sir Barnaby Whigg* and Semanthe in *The Loyal Brothers* (and also spoke the epilogue).

Sarah Cooke joined the United Company when it formed in 1682 and was chosen for Spaconia in *A King and No King*, Estifania in *Rule a Wife and Have a Wife*, the epilogue to *The Duke of Guise*, Portia in *Julius Caesar*, Serena (and the epilogue) in *Constantine*, Oldrent's Cook in *The Jovial Crew*, the prologue to *Valentinian*, Erminia in *The Disappointment*, Edith in *The Bloody Brother*, Aminta in *The Commonwealth of Women*, Dona Elvira in *The Banditti*, Lady Lovemore in *The Devil of a Wife*, Leticia in *The Lucky Chance*, Elaria in *The Emperor of the Moon*, and Quisara in *The Island Princess* (her last new role, performed at court by the United Company on 25 April 1687). During this period Sarah was also considered for Octavia in *All for Love* (about September 1684), but Mrs Butler took the role.

Along with other players, Sarah Cooke was ridiculed in the *Satyr on the Players* about 1684, one of the cleaner versions of which runs:

> *Impudent Sarah thinks she's praised by*
> *   all,*
> *Mistaken Drab, back to thy Mother's*
> *   stall,*
> *And let true Savin whom thou hast*
> *   proved so well;*
> *'Tis a rare thing that belly will not swell,*
> *Though swived and swived and as de-*
> *   bauched as hell.*

(The third line in another version is clearer about her background: "And sell there Savin [herbs], which thou'st prov'd so well.")

Etherege, writing from Ratisbon at the beginning of 1688, commented that "Sarah Cooke was always fitter for a player than for a Mrs., and it is properer her lungs should be wasted on the stage than that she should die of a disease too gallant for her." She was, apparently, sick at this time and her life despaired of. She was reported dead by 5 May 1688. Most evidence seems to suggest that she died in March and of a venereal disease.

Cooke, Susan. *See* **COOKE, SARAH.**

Cooke, Mrs Thomas Simpson the first. *See* **HOWELLS, FANNY.**

Cooke, William   [*fl.* 1763–1800], *deputy treasurer.*

William Cooke was a deputy treasurer at Covent Garden Theatre for 22 years between 1763 and 1785. In a deposition given in legal proceedings between the managers Colman and Harris in 1768, Cooke testified that he had begun his appointment in 1763. In a letter dated 17 February 1800, sent from his house in Charlotte Street, Bloomsbury, to Samuel James Arnold, Cooke stated that he had left the theatre in 1785. Possibly he was the William Cooke who witnessed the wills of the actor James Bencraft on December 1764 and the prompter James Wrighten on 28 March 1793.

Coombes, Mr   [*fl.* 1789–1805], *property man, actor, singer.*

Before settling in London (by 1789), Mr Coombs kept a public house at Portsmouth, opposite a theatre built in 1787. It was from the front of Coombes's establishment, according to Gilliland, that the inebriated actors Brereton, Williams, and Staunton pelted the carriage of the magis-

trate Sir John Carr and consequently were required to make a public apology. By 29 May 1790, when he shared tickets with other house servants, Coombes was employed at Covent Garden as a property man, a situation he continued in until at least 1805. He was being paid £1 per week in 1793–94 and £1 10s. per week by 1800–1801.

Coombes frequently appeared on stage in supernumerary roles, some of which required at least basic skills in dancing and singing. On 31 March 1792 he was a singing character in the burletta portion of *A Peep Behind the Curtain,* and on 10 May 1792 he filled a vocal part in *Just in Time.* In 1792–93 he was a Creolian insurgent in *The Governor* and a bather in *The Invasion.* He acted six times as the porter in *The Bank Note* between 1 May and 5 June 1795. Similar turns in minor parts included several as a traveler in *1 Henry IV* and the Town Clerk in *The Way to Get Married,* both in 1795–96; 25 performances as a Danish chief in *The Round Tower,* 1797–98; and regular performances as a tradesman in *The Road to Ruin.* In the summer of 1797, a Mr "Coombs" acted at Richmond, Surrey.

On 31 July 1798, the *Morning Post* announced the death, on 20 July, of Mrs Ann Coombes, wife of Coombes of Covent Garden. According to Gilliland, Coombes was still a property man in 1805.

Coombes, Miss   [*fl.* 1795–1802], *dancer.*

Miss Coombes, who was probably the daughter of Coombes the property man, first danced at Covent Garden as an English Amazon in the spectacular production of *Lord Mayor's Day* on 16 November 1795. This was repeated a week later on 23 November. The next notice for a Miss Coombes did not occur until 29 January 1799, when she appeared in the chorus of *The Magic Oak,* a very successful piece which was offered 32 times that season through 27 May. In 1799–1800 she filled an unspecified role in 29 performances of the pantomime *The Volcano* between 23 December and 22 January. Miss Coombes was at Covent Garden again in 1800–1801, and she performed at the Royal Circus in September 1802.

Cooper, Mr [fl. 1695–1701], *singer.*

The "Mr Coper" who sang in *The She-Gallants* at Lincoln's Inn Fields in late December 1695 was probably the Mr Cooper who sang Daniel Purcell's "Corinna with a Gracefull Air" in *The Reform'd Wife* at Drury Lane in March 1700. The Purcell song was published in 1700 with Cooper cited as the singer. Another song, which Cooper sang with Mrs Haynes, was "The loud, the loud alarums," published in the March–April 1701 *Mercurius Musicus*. The playbills of the period make no mention of Cooper.

Cooper, Mr [fl. 1729–1746], *boxkeeper.*

Mr Cooper served as a boxkeeper at Drury Lane from 1729–30 through 1740–41, after which he worked at Covent Garden until 6 May 1746, the last mention of him in the bills. Throughout the years he was mentioned for shared benefits, or his benefit tickets were cited as acceptable at the theatre.

Cooper, Mr [fl. 1749], *actor.*

A Mr Cooper, who cannot be certainly identified with any other Coopers of the time, was paid 13s. 4d. for appearing on 11 and 18 November 1749 at Covent Garden. The bill on 11 November was *Cato* and *Merlin* and on 18 November *Volpone* and *Phebe*. Cooper was probably a supernumerary in the afterpieces.

Cooper, Mr [fl. 1767], *performer.*

The Treasurer's Book of Drury Lane Theatre bears the entry for 10 February 1767, "Paid Mr Cooper for 21 nights in *Cymon* £11 6d." The new dramatic romance, by David Garrick, with music by Michael Arne, had been brought out on 2 January and had proved very popular. It required "New Scenes, Dresses, Machinery and other Decorations" and probably extra musicians and dancers. Judging from the mode and amount of payment, we assume Mr Cooper was neither a regular in the company nor a performer of very great consequence.

Cooper, Mr [fl. 1787], *dancer.*

A Mr Cooper was listed among the 20 "Principal Dancers" for the summer season at Hughes's Royal Circus, St George's Fields, in 1787.

Cooper, Mr [fl. 1795], *scene painter, machinist.*

The playbill of the Royal Circus, St. George's Fields, for 17 April 1795 clumsily states "The Scenery Machinery, and Decorations, [are] painted by Mr Cooper." The work referred to was for a new pantomime called *The Prophecy; or, Mountain in Labour.* How long Mr Cooper himself labored to bring forth the frequent spectacles at the Circus we do not know, as the remaining bills are incomplete and fragmentary and often do not bother to name all personnel concerned in the productions.

Cooper, Mr [fl. 1798], *actor.*

According to the *Authentic Memoirs of the Green Room* (1799), a Mr Cooper and Elizabeth Mansel, from Liverpool, were given an opportunity to perform at Covent Garden in 1798. There seem to be no records of Cooper's having appeared, though he may well have worked at Covent Garden briefly without being cited in the bills.

Cooper, Mr d. 1809, *actor.*

A Mr Cooper (if he is always the same Cooper) tried off and on for fifteen years to attract the favorable notice of the managers of the London patent houses, but with no success. Very likely, between forays into the minor stages of the metropolis, he acted in the country. Evidently the country is where he ended.

Cooper was in at least five specially licensed winter performances at the Haymarket Theatre, normally a summer playhouse: as a Servant in *King Charles I* on 31 January 1785, as Varland in *The West Indian* for Griffith's benefit on 12 March 1787, as Charles in *The Jealous Wife* and Nephero in *The Irish Widow* on 9 April 1788, as Lord Trinket in *The Jealous Wife* and Fribble in *Miss in Her Teens* on 29 April 1788, and both as Fribble and as Lovemore in *Barnaby Brittle* on 30 September 1788.

He was probably the same Cooper who played Rowley in *The School for Scandal* at the Windsor Inn, King Street, Hammersmith, on 24 March 1794 for the benefit of Mr Kent "By Desire of Her Serene Highness the Margravine of Anspach." Kent was evidently the manager of this small company of adventurers which had, it seems, played there before, inasmuch as the advertisement asserted that patronage would contribute to "Kent's extricating himself from a Situation obvious to all acquainted with the Expence he has been at, and the ill Success he has met with." The next night the company offered *The Road to Ruin* and *The Poor Soldier*, but no casts were published. No other bills for this troupe survive.

On 15 May 1799 at the Old Crown Inn, Highgate, a Mr Cooper played a Messenger in *Douglas* and Bagatelle in *The Poor Soldier* among a company of unknowns, apparently for the benefit of one Frimbley.

It may be that the Cooper we have been following was the subject of the obituary in the *Gentleman's Magazine* for June 1809.

[Died 16 May 1809] At Peterborough Mr Cooper, comedian. He had just recovered from a long illness, and walked to the bridge to congratulate his friends (belonging to Mr Robertson's company) on their arrival from Wisbech, when he fell down; and expired immediately.

Cooper, Mrs *[fl. 1722–1734]*, actress.

The Mrs Cooper who played Aurelia in *The Wife's Relief* at the Haymarket Theatre on 17 December 1722 may have been the Mrs Cooper who was at Drury Lane on 3 January 1734 to play Julia in *The Cornish Squire* and on 4 February to be Juno in *Cupid and Psyche*. Presumably the same Mrs Cooper "attempted" Lady Easy in *The Careless Husband* at Lincoln's Inn Fields for her own benefit on 26 April 1734.

Cooper, Mrs *[fl. 1775–1777?]*, wardrobe assistant?

A Mrs Cooper was paid £1 per week at Drury Lane Theatre through at least the seasons 1775–76 and 1776–77. She was apparently an assistant to Mr and Mrs Frank Heath, who were for many years master and mistress of the wardrobe at the theatre, for she was usually listed with them in the treasurer's book.

Cooper, Master *[fl. 1795]*, actor.

A Cooper, probably a juvenile, played a fairy in *Chevy Chase; or, Douglas and Percy* at Sadler's Wells on 4 August 1795.

Cooper, Miss *[fl. 1785–1787?]*, dancer.

A Miss Cooper was in the pantomime *Don Juan* in a specially licensed performance at the Haymarket, under the ballet master Delpini's direction, on 15 and 18 April 1785. She may have been the Miss Cooper who was added to the Drury Lane list at 10*d.* per diem, according to the notation of 6 October 1787 in the manuscript account books.

Cooper, Miss *[fl. 1793]*, singer, actress.

"A Young Lady," who was said to be making her first appearance on any stage,

played the title role in the farce *Polly Honeycombe* at the Haymarket Theatre on 26
August 1793. She is identified in a manuscript list in the Haymarket playbills at the
Harvard Theatre Collection, and so by *The
London Stage*, as a Miss Villers. But the
European Magazine in August 1793 remarked: "A young Lady, whose name is
said to be COOPER, made an unsuccessful
attempt at the Haymarket, in the character
of Polly Honeycomb," adding, frustratingly
enough, "More than this is unnecessary to
record." Neither this Miss Cooper nor any
Miss Villers appeared again.

Cooper, Francis *[fl. 1671]*, *musician.*
Francis Cooper and several other musicians were cited on 4 August 1671 for
teaching or performing music "in companys
or otherwise" or "at publique meetings
without the approbation or lycence of the
Marshall and Corporation of musick."

Cooper, George *[fl. 1794]*, *musician.*
Doane's *Musical Directory* of 1794 listed
George Cooper of No 39, Gloucester Place,
Islington, as a music seller, organist, and
bass (player, presumably, though he may
have been a singer). He participated in the
oratorios at Drury Lane and the Handelian
commemorative concerts at Westminster
Abbey.

Cooper, Henry *[fl. 1790?–1819?]*,
violinist, violist.
Henry Cooper, violinist, and "Tenor"-
player (violist), of Castle Street, Holborn,
was said by Doane's *Musical Directory*
(1794) to have belonged to the New Musical Fund and the band of the Drury Lane
Theatre and to have played in "Oratorios"
(at Covent Garden under the Ashleys).
He may have been the Cooper who occurs
in a British Museum manuscript list of
Drury Lane personnel under date of 5 November 1790: "adv[ance]d on acc[ount]
of sal[ar]y [£]2. 2[d.]," raised 4s. 2d. per
week on 11 December.

Henry was doubtless the Cooper who on
14 June 1794 was added to the music list
at Drury Lane and raised to 10s. from a
base not stated. On 1 August 1799
"Cooper, band, arrears 1/15/0" was entered. The British Museum list and the
Folger manuscript account book disagree
as to the amount of his benefit share on 9
June 1803: £198 15s. versus £211 15s.
The account books entered a Cooper in the
company in 1802–3 and gave him £1. 5s.
per week in 1815–16 and 1816–17, and
this may have been our musician. A
Cooper, violinist, was in the band of the
opera at the King's Theatre in 1818, and
a Garrick Club manuscript also listed a
Cooper at Drury Lane in 1818–19, but
with no indication that he was a musician.

Cooper, Joseph *[fl. 1794]*, *singer?*
Joseph Cooper was listed in Doane's
Musical Directory of 1794 as an alto—a
countertenor, presumably, though he may
have been a horn player—living at the Red
Cross, Borough, Southwark. He performed
with the Longacre Society and the Handelian Society and participated in the Westminster Abbey Handelian concerts.

Cooper, Maria. *See* HUNTER, MARIA.

Cooper, Ralph *[fl. 1763]*, *singer.*
Mortimer's London Directory of 1763
listed Ralph Cooper of Surrey Street as one
of the Gentlemen of the Chapel Royal.

Cooper, Richard *[fl. 1794]*, *singer?*
Richard Cooper was listed in Doane's
Musical Directory of 1794 as an alto
(singer probably, or possibly a horn
player) living at No 1, Bear Lane, Southwark. He participated in performances offered by the Handelian Society.

Cooper, Rose Mary. *See* KATER,
MRS.

Cooper, Thomas Abthorpe *1775–
1849, actor, manager.*

Thomas Cooper (he added the middle name "Abthorpe" after his arrival in America) was born on 16 December 1775 at Harrow-on-the-Hill, the son of Thomas Cooper, a prominent physician of Irish descent, and his wife Mary Grace Cooper. Mrs Cooper was the first cousin of the mother of the philosopher William Godwin (1756–1836). When Dr Cooper died destitute in India in 1787, Godwin placed Thomas under his personal instruction in the classics and later assisted him in what W. B. Wood said was "an excellent English education at a principal seminary."

Thomas was certainly also exposed to the liberal intellectual circle which surrounded the Godwins. One of their acquaintances, Thomas Holcroft, the actor-dramatist and revolutionary, was sympathetic to the boy's desire at 16 to become an actor and introduced him to Stephen Kemble, then managing at Edinburgh. At 17 Cooper played a few minor parts in the Scottish capital and then was given Malcolm in *Macbeth*. He forgot the last lines in the play, was summarily sacked by Kemble, and left Edinburgh to play for a few months with the manager Collins at Portsmouth, Southampton, Chichester, Winchester, and Newport. By October 1794 he had quit Collins and had joined a group of strollers in Stockport, Cheshire, a group which he described as "a wretched set of mummers."

Cooper's London debut, made possible through Holcroft's intercession, and after his intensive tutelage in acting, was at Covent Garden on 1 October 1795. He came forward as Hamlet, under the protective anonymity often employed by hesitant young adventurers, billed only as "A Young Gentleman.'" But the disguise was instantly penetrated, and some of the critics who knew him for the friend of Holcroft and Godwin praised or condemned him more on the grounds of his supposed political opinions than for his qualities as a performer. The *Monthly Mirror* of December 1795 took note of this fact, after

Harvard Theatre Collection

THOMAS ABTHORPE COOPER

engraving, after Jarvis

Cooper had played Macbeth and Horatio in *The Fair Penitent* and after elaborate protestation of its own strict impartiality, and decided:

Mr Cooper is, in person, of the middle size, his features are not strongly impressive of any particular character; there is more softness and playfulness, than spirit or energy about them; yet, with artful management, they may suit either tragedy or comedy: — naturally inclinable perhaps to the latter.

His voice is, in tone, pleasing; capable of more modulation than he seems to know how to give it; firm and extensive in the upper division; in the lower, musical and articulate.

In general his performance of Hamlet was thought too tame in spots, too passionate in others, but never that picture of grief which Shakespeare intended to draw. This reviewer continued to toy with *Hamlet* and

Cooper's interpretation of Hamlet from issue to issue through May 1797, summing Cooper up at year's end: "he possesses understanding and powers, but in his utterance he is disgustingly broad and provincial, in his action embarrassed, and, in the general disposition of his person, inattentive to all the rules of grace and proportion."

But in truth, and politics aside, Cooper, though strikingly handsome and a willing student, was as yet far too immature for the prominent parts he was thrust into. So in December there were newspaper rumors that he had been engaged at Norwich by Brunton; in February 1796 he had joined the company at the Orchard Street Theatre in Bath; and by April he was playing young heroes at Bristol. He had, according to Joseph Ireland's *Memoir*, proudly refused the secondary parts which Harris had offered him at Covent Garden and had gone to the provinces to learn.

Early in 1797 in *A Pin Basket to the Children of Thespis* the cruel John Williams asked (and answered):

Where, where is young COOPER, that Tyro so vain,
Who Hamlet re-kills, who's so often been slain?
But my memory urges, he'll vex us no more,
As he's sought with a troop the transatlantic shore. . . .
Ev'ry man is a tyrant, or greater or lesser,
From Phalaris down to the cook at his dresser;
And when no other object approaches his reach,
He will torture the parts and the idiom of speech:
Hence COOPERS arise to transform what was right,
And decline and express their verbs wrongly in spite.
As idiots, from singular motives, will goad
Their steeds to offend all who journey the road —

Though the dolt knows his fault, yet his hope's to amaze,
And be noted for error, despairing of praise!

By this time, as Williams surmises, Cooper was out of the reach of British critics, both hostile and friendly. Thomas Wignell, the co-manager with Reinagle at Philadelphia's Chestnut Street Theatre, had in the fall of 1796 made his second foray into England after recruits to the American stage. He had brought back Cooper, Anne Brunton Merry, and several others who had shone but dimly in the London firmament but were to be stars of the first magnitude in America.

Cooper made his American debut at the Chestnut Street Theatre as Penruddock in *The Wheel of Fortune* on 11 November 1796, announced impressively as "from Covent Garden." He made a modest success of Macbeth on 9 December and did well in other tragic roles (on one occasion playing Richard II before President Washington) but his career was shadowed by the popularity of the theatre's leading tragedian Fennell. However, when Wignell took over the Greenwich Street Theatre in New York in the summer of 1797, Wood says, "Cooper, by his performance of Hamlet, Iago, Lothario, Chamont, [and] Sir E. Mortimer . . . established a reputation on which his future fame and fortunes were built."

In January 1798 he performed for Hodgkinson at the John Street Theatre and was sued for £500 by his managers Wignell and Reinagle, who alleged breach of articles. An attempt was made to buy his contract and retain him at John Street, but the Philadelphia company refused to sell. In the summer of 1798 Cooper accompanied Hodgkinson and the American Company to Boston, first appearing there at the Haymarket on 27 July. In February of 1800 the lawsuit by the Philadelphia managers was settled amicably and Cooper re-

Harvard Theatre Collection

THOMAS ABTHORPE COOPER

photograph

turned to Chestnut Street. He was with the Philadelphia company at the newly opened Washington Theatre in the summer of 1800. About this time, apparently, he married Joanna Upton, née Johnson, the widow of a Captain Upton.

In the 1801–2 and 1802–3 seasons Cooper signed on with Dunlap at the Park Street in New York. In January 1803 he returned to England where on 7 March 1803 he was favorably criticized as Hamlet. He was received in the British provinces as "The American Roscius" and acted at Manchester off and on from mid-December 1803 through late February 1804. The good and bad points of his Hamlet and Richard III were minutely canvassed by the critic of the *Townsman*.

Somewhat distorted news of what American theatre-goers resented as unfair

treatment of Cooper by the English had reached New York, and on his return to the Park Street Theatre on 19 November 1804, he was greeted with a cordial uproar. Boston audiences were also enthusiastic in 1805, and in January 1806 he applied to the trustees of the Federal Street Theatre for a three-year lease of the house. He was refused because the management had already been committed to Snelling Powell. At the Providence, Rhode Island, Theatre in 1805 he played Othello in Moorish Costume and was violently assailed by the critics for the innovation.

Cooper first appeared in Charleston on 14 April 1806 and during that summer at Richmond and Petersburg. In the fall of 1806 he obtained the lease of the Park Street Theatre, where he remained in active management until 1815, when he turned the direction of all performance affairs over to Stephen Price, whom he had brought into partnership in 1808. But he continued to act both at New York and elsewhere, and he acted most profitably. For instance, a tabulation of receipts of nine nights during which he played at Boston in January and February of 1807, show total receipts of $6945, a huge sum. Of this amount, after house expenses, sharing with the management, and a clear benefit, he received a net profit of $2530.

In 1810 Cooper was again performing. From before 1813 he made annual visits to Boston; in 1822 he played for the first time at New Orleans and in 1827 at Mobile. In the fall of 1827 he traveled once more to England to play under the management of Stephen Price, who had leased Drury Lane.

Cooper's first wife had died in 1808, and on 13 June 1812 he married Mary, the eldest daughter of the socially prominent Major James Fairlie and Maria Yates Fairlie. The second Mrs Cooper was a brilliant and gracious hostess and strikingly beautiful, and the Coopers moved in the best society of the Eastern seaboard.

Cooper made a small fortune through his acting and his interests in management. But the handsome Thomas was fond of wine and dancing, of cards and fast horses and field sports; and by 1830, much of his fortune gone and the conditions of American management radically altering, Cooper found also that his popularity with the public was waning. He had, moreover, nine children by his second wife to support. In 1833 the first of a series of compassionate benefits was arranged for him by his friends. In 1834 he brought his daughter Priscilla to the stage, but whatever hopes he had of a theatrical career for her were cut short by her marriage to Robert Tyler, son of the future President of the United States. She later, for some time before President Tyler's second marriage, acted as his hostess at the White House.

Cooper's last appearance on the New York stage was at Hamblin's benefit on 24 November 1835, though he evidently acted in the American hinterland until 1840. His last recorded appearance was as Damon in *Damon and Pythias* for his own benefit, which yielded him $37. He is said to have appeared by the end of his career in at least 165 plays and to have acted in every state in the Union.

T. Allston Brown in the *History of the American Stage* says that in 1841 he was appointed Military Storekeeper to the Arsenal at Frankfort, Pennsylvania, and "was afterwards Surveyor of the Ports of Philadelphia and New York." In 1843, according to Ireland, he was appointed Superintendent of the United States Mint at Dahlonga, Georgia, and held the position for six years; and during President Polk's administration he was made inspector in the New York Custom's House. He died at the home of his daughter Mrs Tyler in Bristol, Pennsylvania, on 21 April 1849 and was buried there. He was survived by six daughters and a son.

John Bernard the actor has left a number of anecdotes in his *Retrospections* illustrative of Cooper's charm and his personal courage. On one occasion Cooper extracted an apology from a member of Congress named Dawson (who had hissed his performance at Georgetown) by threatening to "horsewhip him before the senate-house." Bernard summed him up:

Harvard Theatre Collection

THOMAS ABTHORPE COOPER, as Leon engraving by Edwin, after Leslie

It would be hard to say whether he were the greatest favorite in public or private, with the men or the women. With the one he would ride, drive, shoot, or bet. For the other he had the eye of Caliph Vathek—'instant annihilation.' Such an emptying of Cupid's quiver as on the nights of his performance I suppose had never previously been known in the Union. . . . Endowed with great genius, and the highest qualifications in face, voice, and person, he had little or no art, which he never strove to acquire, being content to cover its want by his impulse and freshness. Thus, as he grew older, he failed to improve, while his luxurious habits abated his force, and left but gleams of the fire which, at first, was continuous. . . . Still, with all his defects, I look back to his youth as displaying a power which I can only rank second to the greatest I have seen. I still think his Macbeth was only inferior to Garrick's, and his Hamlet to Kemble's; while his Othello, I think, was equal to Barry's itself.

Thomas Abthorpe Cooper was the subject of several portraits, including the following:

1. A photographic portrait of him as an elderly man. Photographer anonymous.

2. Oil portrait by Rembrandt Peale. Now owned by the New York Historical Society.

3. Oil portrait by Gilbert Stuart. Now in the Players' Club, New York.

4. Oil portrait by John Wesley Jarvis. Now in the Cleveland Museum of Art.

5. Engraved portrait by C. H. Meyer after J. Wood.

6. Engraved portrait by S. Harris. Plate to *The Polyanthus*, 1806.

7. Anonymous woodcut, undated; bust, full face, oval decorated with laurel spray. Same picture, vignette, woodcut.

8. As Hamlet. Engraved by Edwin.

9. As Leon in *Rule a Wife and Have a Wife*. Engraved by Edwin after C. R. Leslie, as plate to the *Mirror of Taste*.

10. As Pericles. Engraved by W. Skelton after Graham. Plate to Bell's *British Theatre*, 1796.

11. As Pierre in *Venice Preserv'd*. Engraved by J. O. Lewis after C. R. Leslie.

This entry is indebted in several of its details to "A Biography of the Actor Thomas Abthrope Cooper (1775–1849)," a University of Minnesota doctoral dissertation, 1971, by Fairlie Arant, a de-

scendant of Thomas Cooper. Miss Arant made extensive use of manuscript records of her family.

Cope. *See also* **CAPE.**

Cope, Mrs ₁*fl. 1770–1771₁, *dancer.*
A Mrs Cope danced a hornpipe at the Haymarket Theatre on 5 October 1771. She was probably the same Mrs Cope who was a dancer at the Norwich theatre in 1770–71.

Copeland, Mrs ₁*fl. 1729₁, *dancer.*
A Mrs Copeland replaced Mrs Cantrell as a country lass in the dancing chorus of *The Rape of Proserpine* at Lincoln's Inn Fields Theatre on 16 and 19 December 1729.

Copell. *See* **GOPELL.**

Copen. *See* **COPIN.**

Coper. *See* **COOPER.**

Copin, Mrs Roger, Elizabeth ₁*fl. 1733–1773₁, *actress, singer.*
Mrs Elizabeth Copin (sometimes Copen) acted at York about 1736. She was married to Roger Copin, a provincial player. Their daughter (who survived only a week or so) was baptized at Holy Trinity Christ Church at York on 15 February 1733 (and buried on 17 February 1733). Billed as "Miss" Copin, Elizabeth made her first appearance in London at Drury Lane as Melinda in *The Recruiting Officer* on 26 September 1745. On 1 October 1745 she acted Desdemona. She repeated Melinda on 7 November, 9 December, and 1 February, and on 27 December acted Mrs Coaxer in *The Beggar's Opera*. In her first London season she had little success. Mrs Cibber wrote Garrick on 26 February 1746 that Mrs Copin had "met with disgrace the first night of her appearance" and had now been dismissed from the house. The bill

of *The Beggar's Opera* on 3 February 1746 listed Mrs Horsington as her replacement in the role of Mrs Coaxer, and Mrs Copin's name appeared in no other bills that season.

Despite her dismissal in the previous season, Mrs Copin was again at Drury Lane in 1746–47. She was employed but sparingly, however. She was Molly Brazen in *The Beggar's Opera* on 30 September and again was Melinda in *The Recruiting Officer* on 21 November. On 19 March 1747 she shared in benefit tickets.

In the following season she was engaged at Covent Garden, where she was given slightly more to do. After making her first appearance at that theatre on 13 November 1747 as Melinda, she played Ruth in *The Committee* on 17 December, Miranda in *The Busy Body* on 23 December, Angelina in *Love Makes a Man* on 7 January, Lady Wronghead in *The Provok'd Husband* on 15 January, Lucy Weldon in *Oroonoko* on 16 January, Clarinda in *Woman's a Riddle* on 19 January, Clara in *Rule a Wife and Have a Wife* on 10 February, and Jiltup in *The Fair Quaker* on 13 April 1748. On 28 March 1748 she filled the role of Mrs Novel in an "Operatic Puppet Show, call'd the Pleasures of the Town," which was introduced into a performance of *The Author's Farce*. In her next season at Covent Garden she played Dolly Trull in *The Beggar's Opera*, Teresa in *The Spanish Fryar*, Araminta in *The Old Bachelor*, Florinda in *The Rover*, Lucy in *Oroonoko*, Francisca in *Measure for Measure*, Mincing in *The Way of the World*, Trusty in *The Provok'd Husband*, and Aemilia in *The Man of Mode*.

Mrs Copin then went to play for two seasons under Thomas Sheridan's management at Smock Alley, Dublin, making her first appearance there on 4 October 1749 as Lady Fanciful in *The Provok'd Wife*. At Dublin she also played Clarissa in *The City Wives Confederacy* on 11 October, Dorinda in *The Beaux' Stratagem* on 18

October, Melinda in *The Recruiting Officer* on 1 November, Jacintha in *The Suspicious Husband* on 15 November, Sophronia in *The Refusal* on 17 November, Camilla in *The Mistake* on 20 December, Arabella in *The Committee* on 28 December; and in the following season Mrs Stocks in *The Lottery* on 5 October 1750, Lady Bountiful in *The Beaux' Stratagem* on 18 October, the Landlady in *The Suspicious Husband* on 14 January 1751, Lady Pride in *The Amorous Widow* on 18 January, Lady Lovewell in *The Provok'd Wife* on 18 March, and Mrs Midnight in *The Twin Rivals* on 24 April 1751.

Upon her return to Covent Garden in 1754–55, Mrs Copin settled into the line of older matrons, which she had developed at Dublin (and no doubt in the provinces for two years after Dublin) and which she acted thereafter for 18 consecutive seasons. Her salary was fixed at 3s. 4d. per day, at least between 1760–61 and 1767–68.

In addition to those mentioned above, her other roles included (with date of first performance): Mrs Motherly in *The Provok'd Husband* (13 January 1754), Lady Darling in *The Constant Couple* (22 January 1755), Mrs Chat in *The Committee* (6 February 1755), Dora in *Appius* (6 March 1755), the Nurse in *Romeo and Juliet* (3 April 1755), Mrs Wisely in *The Miser* (16 April 1755), the Governess in *The Humourous Lieutenant* (10 December 1756), Moretta in *The Rover* (19 February 1757), Fardingale in *The Funeral* (20 October 1758), Anne in *The London Cuckolds* (9 November 1758), Mrs Quickly in *The Merry Wives of Windsor* (26 September 1759), Diana Trapes in *The Beggar's Opera* (10 October 1759), Lady Manlove in *The School Boy* (22 October 1759), Hob's mother in *The Country Wake* (18 March 1760), the Mother in *Flora* (9 April 1760), a Lady in *Rule a Wife and Have a Wife* (25 March 1761), Mrs Peachum in *The Beg-*

gar's Opera (27 April 1762), Mrs Clogitt in *The City Wives Confederacy* (13 May 1762), Mrs Hackum in *The Squire of Alsatia* (18 November 1763), Penelope in *The Knights* (5 January 1764), the Aunt in *The What D'Ye Call It* (27 March 1764), the Nurse in *Polly Honeycombe* (19 October 1765), a role in *Harlequin Doctor Faustus* (2 December 1766), Mrs Motherly in *Orpheus and Eurydice* (6 January 1768), Margery in *The Miller of Mansfield* (25 February 1768), a Passenger in *Man and Wife, or, the Shakespeare Jubilee* (7 October 1769), and a character in *Mother Shipton* (26 December 1771).

During her last several seasons she appeared only occasionally. In 1772–73 she acted just once, as the nurse in *Polly Honeycombe* on 20 May 1773, her last performance on the record.

Copland, Mr ₍fl. 1756₎, *boxkeeper.*
A Mr Copland was a boxkeeper at Sadler's Wells in 1756.

Copland, Mr ₍fl. 1789–1791₎, *house servant.*
A Mr Copland shared benefit tickets as a house servant at Covent Garden on 8 June 1790 and 9 June 1791.

"Copper Captain." *See* BROWN, HENRY.

Coppinger, Matthew *d. 1695, actor.*
Matthew Coppinger was a performer of drolls at the fairs in the late seventeenth century. On 9 September 1689 he was ordered arrested for performing without a license. He was also a poet, and a volume of his verse was published in 1682. His chief interest, however, was robbery, counterfeit coinage, and clipping coins. He impudently impersonated an officer pretending to search for clippers and in that manner "robbed many houses."

The authorities finally caught up with Coppinger and hanged him at Tyburn in 1695. He had become so notorious that a short biography with a long title was written about him in the same year: *An Account of the Life, Conversation, Birth, Education, Pranks, Projects, Exploits, and Merry Conceits of the Famously Notorious Mat. Coppinger, once a Player in Bartholomew Fair, and since turned bully of the town; who, receiving sentence of death at the Old Bailey on the 23rd of February, was executed at Tyburn on the 27th, 1695.*

Coppola, Giuseppe ₍fl. 1777–1779₎, *singer.*
Giuseppe Coppola was a principal singer at the operas in the King's Theatre in 1777–78 and 1778–79. He made his first appearance singing Lucindo in *Le due contesse* on 4 November 1777. His other roles (with dates of first performances) included Ciro in *Creso* on 8 November 1777, Il Conte di Rapalta in *Vittorina* on 16 December 1777, Marchese Ernesto in *La vera costanza* on 20 January 1778, Cresfonte in *Erifile* on 7 February 1778, Titta in *L'amore artigiano* on 3 March 1778, a role in *La buona figliuola* on 2 April 1778, Marzio in *La clemenza di Scipione* on 4 April 1778, a role in *L'amore soldato* on 5 May 1778, Agenore in *Il re pastore* on 30 May 1778, Cherinto in *Demofoonte* on 28 November 1778, a role in *La Frascatana* on 22 December 1778, Turno in *Enea e Lavinia* on 25 March 1779, Ferdinando in *La governante* on 15 May 1779, and a role in *L'Olimpiade* on 29 May 1779. Burney thought that Coppola was "a languid and uninteresting soprano."

Coradini, Signora ₍fl. 1767–1768?₎, *dancer.*
On 9 September 1767, the *Public Advertiser* announced that Signora Coradini, a new dancer, was among those people engaged for the opera during that coming

season. Perhaps she did dance at the King's Theatre, but her name does not appear in any extant bills.

Coraill. *See* CERAIL.

"Corallina." *See* COSTANTINI, DOMENICA.

Corar. *See* CURRER.

Corbally, Miss [*fl. 1732*], *actress.*
Miss Corbally, otherwise unknown, played Lucy in *The Beggar's Opera* at the Haymarket Theatre on 4 September 1732.

Corbet, [Neeves? *d. 1761?*], *singer.*
A Mr Corbet sang at the playhouse in James Street on 30 May 1748. Perhaps he was the musician Neeves Corbett of St Olave, Silver Street, who died in early 1761.

Corbet, Symon *b. 1675?, singer.*
Symon Corbet was a boy singer in the Chapel Royal at the coronation of James II on 23 April 1685, but by 5 July 1689 his voice had broken and he was to be paid £20 for a year and given clothing as a former Chapel boy. In view of this, perhaps he was the Simond Corbett, son of Simond and Elizabeth, who was christened at St Margaret, Westminster, on 26 September 1675.

On 11 December 1691 the former Chapel boy, his voice matured, was sworn a Gentleman of the Chapel Royal extraordinary—without salary until a place was vacated. After this, however, the Lord Chamberlain's accounts make no mention of Corbet, and presumably he grew tired of waiting for a permanent position and left the court. Perhaps the following parish register entries concern the singer: Simon, son of Simon and Jane Corbet, was born on 19 December 1696 and he was baptized the same day at St Martin-in-the-Fields;

Simon, son of Simon Corbet from St James, Westminster, was buried at St Paul, Covent Garden, on 19 March 1697; Anne, daughter of Simon and Jane Corbet of St James, Westminster, was born on 28 April 1698 and baptized the same day at St James. A possibly related Simon Corbet had a considerable family in the 1660s and 1670s and christened most of his children at St Martin-in-the-Fields but buried them at St Paul, Covent Garden.

Corbett, Mr [*fl. 1780*], *actor.*
A new prologue was spoken by a Mr Corbett, in the character of one of the City Associators, at a performance of *The City Association* at the Haymarket on 13 November 1780.

Corbett, Mary [*fl. 1670?–1682?*], *actress.*
Mary Corbett may have acted Portia in *Julius Caesar* at the Bridges Street Theatre as early as 1670, for a manuscript cast in the British Museum which dates about this time mentions her; but the first certain role we have for her is Dainty Fidget in *The Country Wife* at Drury Lane on 12 January 1675. She may have played Portia at some later date. Mrs Corbett also acted King Andrew in *Psyche Debauch'd* on 27 August 1675, Melesinda in *Aureng-Zebe* on 17 November, Narcissa in *Gloriana* on 29 January 1676, Monimia in *Mithridates* in February 1678, Clevly in *The Man of Newmarket* and Sabina in *Trick for Trick* in March 1678, the Countess of Nottingham in *The Unhappy Favourite* in May 1681, Gratiana in *Sir Barnaby Whigg* in the summer of that year, and possibly a role in *Like Father, Like Son* in March 1682 (the Epilogue refers to a "Mistriss Corall," but this may have been a reference to Mrs Corey or Mrs Currer).

In *All the King's Ladies*, J. H. Wilson suggests that the actress may have been the Mrs Corbett, cousin of Mrs James

Pierce, who met Pepys on 9 November 1666. There is also a chance that Mary Corbett was the wife of William Corbett the instrument maker of St Martin-in-the-Fields. He made his will on 18 October 1674, and it was proved by his widow Mary on 11 December. He left his wife all his household stuffs and made bequests to a daughter Elizabeth Corbett, his father and mother John and Ann Corbett, his sister Hannah Corbett, and his brother (in-law?) Harward Darke and his wife Elizabeth. At the time the will was drawn, Mary Corbett was pregnant.

Corbett, William *1680–1748, violinist, composer.*

Nothing is known of William Corbett's birth, though probably he was the William Corbett, son of Henry and Sarah, who was baptized at St Margaret, Westminster, on 18 July 1680. The birth year would fit with later facts, and the musician's will cites St Margaret's as his family's parish.

On 17 March 1699 William Corbett, already an established composer, was given a benefit concert at York Buildings. He then became associated with Thomas Betterton's company at Lincoln's Inn Fields, for which he composed music for *Henry IV*, performed at the playhouse on 9 January 1700 and, according to the separately printed music, played "all the time of the Publick Act in Oxford" at some time after this. He also wrote music for *Love Betray'd*, presented in February 1703, and *As You Find It*, performed on 28 April of the same year. On 29 March 1704 he held a benefit concert at York Buildings; on 18 May some of his music was played there; and on 8 June at Lincoln's Inn Fields "A new Set of Airs for the Trumpet, Hautboys and Violins," by Corbett, was performed. In 1705 he published *A New Set of Tunes Compos'd . . . for the Theatre*.

When the Queen's Theatre in the Haymarket opened on 9 April 1705, William Corbett was leader of the band, a position

WILLIAM CORBETT

engraving by Simon, after Austen

he retained for the following six years. For the new playhouse he wrote music for *The British Enchanters*, which was given there on 21 February 1706. For his work at the Queen's, Corbett was paid £40 annually, the highest salary paid to any of the musicians and matched only by his fellow violinist John Banister. On 19 March 1707 at York Buildings, Corbett made his first public concert appearance as a soloist, and from this time forward he augmented his salary by playing frequently at York Buildings, once (in August 1707) at Nottingham during the races, at the Duchess of Shrewsbury's at Kensington, at Home's Dancing School, and at Hickford's music room.

In 1711 when Handel's *Rinaldo* was produced at the Queen's Theatre, the entire band was replaced and Corbett's post as leader was lost to him. The violinist then went to Rome, where he probably made the acquaintance of Corelli, for that master's violin came into Corbett's possession about this time. By 25 March 1713 he was back in London, sharing a benefit with Signora Lodi at the first concert to be given in Hickford's New Room in James Street. He made other concert appearances there in 1714 and 1715 and in 1716 was appointed to the royal band of music, a position he held, despite absences from England, until 1747. He had continued his composing, having published, about 1713, six trio sonatas for two flutes or German flutes and a thorough bass and six trio sonatas for two violins and a thorough bass carried by spinet or harpsichord. In 1714 he published a Scotch song, *Mad Loons of Albany*, and in 1719 that song and "A Mock Address to the French King" were printed in *Wit and Mirth*.

Corbett returned to Italy, presumably at some point after 1716, and this time he stayed until 1724. He spent much of his time collecting valuable music books and instruments, and one story has it that he was able to support this costly activity by serving as a spy upon the Pretender. But the special annual stipend of £300 which it is said he received, apparently from the British government, may have been only to aid his collecting activities. He moved about a great deal during these years, visiting Venice, Milan, Florence, Cremona, Bologna, and Naples, but Rome was his base of operations. According to the historian of the violin, van der Straeten, Corbett came into possession of violins previously owned by Corelli, Cosimi, Torelli, and Gobby (probably C. A. Lunati).

On 18 March 1724, billed as "lately arriv'd from Italy, being the first Time of his Performance," Corbett played at the Haymarket Theatre "on the Viol de Venere, a particular New Instrument, never yet heard of in England, after the New Manner of Signiora Faustina," the famous singer. In May the *Session of Musicians* ridiculed Corbett's new fiddle; the

poem has all the prominent musicians of the day appear before Apollo to be judged:

> C——rb——t next him succeeded to the
>   Bar,
> And hop'd to fix his Fame by something
>   rare;
> Up to the God, with Confidence he made,
> And's Instrument De Venere display'd.
> How! cries the God (and frowning told
>   his Doom),
> Am I for such poor Trifles hither come?
> Pray tickle off your Venery at home,
> Or else to cleanly Edinburgh repair,
> And from ten Stories high breathe
>   Northern Air;
> With tuneful G[o]rd[o]n join, and thus
>   unite,
> Rough Italy with Scotland the polite.

Corbett may have become band leader at the Haymarket Theatre, as one report had it, but he was off to Italy again before long, where he published his *Le bizzarie universali* about 1728; and he was back in England in early 1728 with some new treats for British ears. On 20 March at Hickford's he offered his "New Bizzaria's; on all the New Gusto's of Italy, Pieces on the Viol d'Amore, and the two new Instruments call'd The Chamber-Horns, never heard in Publick." The bill lied a bit: the "Chamber-Horn" had been used at a concert at Hickford's five days before at Michael Festing's benefit. Still, Corbett was an attraction, and he advertised that his concert would be for his benefit and that he was "lately arriv'd from Italy, being the first and the last time of his Performing in Publick."

He soon returned to the Continent and was not heard in London again until 8 March 1734, when at York Buildings he offered "Several new concertos call'd *Bizzana Universall*, compos'd by Corbett in Travels . . . in Italy, he playing the first Violin." The following 5 April, billed as lately arrived from Italy, he presented for his benefit at York Buildings "An Essay of different Kinds of Harmony, intermix'd with some Pieces on the new Viol D'Venere of 22 Strings, and the Viol D'Amore." He seems to have stayed in England this time, serving in the court position that had been granted him years before. On 28 August 1739 he became one of the original members of the Royal Society of Musicians, and in 1742 he published his most ambitious collection, two books of *Concertos or Universal Bizzaries in Seven Parts for Four Violins a Tenor Violin and Violoncello with a Thorough Bass for a Harpsichord*. In 1742 he tried, apparently for the second time, to sell part of his collection of music and instruments, but with no success.

On 3 March 1748 William Corbett, of St James, Westminster, made his will. Four days later he died, and on 19 April the will was proved by Richard Dawson, Daniel Cogdell, and Bridget Bohannon, widow. Corbett requested burial in his family grave in the churchyard of St Margaret, Westminster, with his name and the time of his death inscribed on stone, along with the names of others of his family buried there. This request, which would have provided a great deal of helpful genealogical information, may have been carried out, but the tablet seems not to have survived. Corbett also asked for a private burial "at some short time" before midnight, with two coaches only in his cortege.

To his brother-in-law Isaac Watlington, late of St Leonard, Shoreditch, Corbett left a £60 bond; his executors Dawson and Cogdell were granted £10 for mourning rings; but his wife Ann was to receive 1*s*. only "if demanded." Corbett's largest and most interesting bequest concerned his collection of music, instruments, and other valuables. These he left to Gresham College "to be deposited and put in a Room belonging thereto," and he provided £10 annually during life for Bridget Bohannon, who was to be the curator of the collection.

The will provided an inventory, not everywhere decipherable, of Corbett's "Gallery of Cremonys and Stainer's Violins:"

Cremony's

Violin Andrea Amadi whole Back painted N°	1574
Ditto Andrea Amadi 2 pieces Back	1564
Antonino Hieronimus Amati whole Back	1621
Ditto ajoin'd Back	1592
Nicola Amati whole Back	1673
Ditto 5 holes and whole Back	1653
A whole Back of Hieronimus Amati	1710
[A pair?] with Nicola Amatis Name	1684

Stainer's

Rich Wood with 5 holes	1665
best Rosemary	1666
Bought of M^r ditto	1665
ditto 2 celones Lyon head	1668
10 holes ordinary 2 Celones	1666
A Brown of per	1660
Tenor Violin of Gramini Milan	1621
Violencello of Antonino Hieronimus Amati	1590
A double Bass of Caspar de Sallo	1540
A Lyon Head double Bass	
A violin brown coloured of Matias Albani which was Arch Angelo Corellis	1683
Another ditto which was Nico Colone's [Cosimi's?] both whole Backs same Year with ten Bows of the most emminent Masters	

The inventory also listed "One old Harpsichord made by Vite Cresentine of Viennia 1577" plus a number of pictures, candlesticks, Italian silks, and music books. Included in the music were three sets of concertos, seven books of operas, and 53 concertos "with the adjuncture, four setts of them are to be given every Year to strangers from Foreign Countreys if they are good performers"—but they were not to be sold on any account. Ironically, the authorities of Gresham College, having no place to house Corbett's splendid collection, turned down the bequest. In March 1751 the items were sold at auction.

Austen (or Austin) painted Corbett and displayed his coat of arms, which suggests for him a Shropshire ancestry. J. Simon made two mezzotints after the Austen painting.

Corbetta, Francesco *c. 1620–1681, guitar player.*

Born in Pavia about 1620, Francesco Corbetta became the most accomplished guitar player of his day and the favorite of courts all over Europe. In 1652 he was in Hanover; he traveled in Spain; he was attached to the court of the Duke of Mantua; and by 1656 he was in Paris as a participant in Lully's ballet *La Galanterie du temps.* Louis XIV patronized him, before the guitarist's wanderlust brought him to England. Charles II made Corbetta a Gentleman of the Queen's Chamber and apparently procured the musician a wife; the Duke of York hired him to teach his daughter Anne the guitar—at £100 a year; Pepys thought him an admirable musician; and the English court went mad for his guitar. A letter from Charles II at Whitehall to his sister in St Germain gives some indication of Corbetta's popularity:

Lords and ladies a like raved over his genius and tried to imitate his example. Hardly had he composed a sarabande than all the world played it. God knows the universal scraping that was heard wherever you went. . . . [Here are] some lessons for the guittar, which I hope will please you . . . and as Francesco makes any more that pleases me, I will send them to you . . .

This letter, dated 29 May 1665, is strikingly similar to passages in the *Memoirs of Count Grammont*: "This Francesco had composed a saraband, which either charmed or infatuated every person; for the whole guitarery at court were trying at it, and God knows what an universal strumming there was."

The guitarist visited France in 1669 or

Harvard Theatre Collection

FRANCESCO CORBETTA

engraving by Van den Berghe, after S. Harding

1670 (apparently he had also made a brief trip in 1664 but had been taken ill), but by 1674 he was back in London. He was one of four guitar players who participated in the court masque *Calisto* on 15 February 1675, and the following year he was appointed one of the Italian musicians of the King's bedchamber. Though he had become quite anglicized, even to the point of using "Corbett" instead of "Corbetta," he ultimately returned to France. He died in Paris in March 1681.

Corbetta published *Varii capricci per la ghittara spagnuola* at Milan in 1643, which collection contains a portrait of the musician. In 1671, during his stay in Paris, he published *La guitarre royalle*, dedicated to Charles II. Corbetta was painted by H. Gascar, who made an engraving of his own work; and S. Harding did a portrait which was engraved by van den Berghe.

Corbyn, Master [*fl.* *1785*], *dancer.*

In a performance specially licensed by the Lord Chamberlain, a group of unidentified players put on Aphra Behn's old extravaganza *The Amorous Prince* at the Haymarket Theatre on 26 December 1785, for the benefit of "a Performer, thirty years a Servant of the Publick at Covent-garden and Haymarket Theatres." At the end of the play there was a masquerade featuring a *Minuet de la Cour* by Master Corbyn and Miss Keen. Neither the one nor the other young dancer was ever in the bills at a public theatre again during the eighteenth century.

Corcy, Diancinto [*fl.* *1669–1671*], *scenekeeper.*

A scenekeeper in the King's Company at the Bridges Street Theatre in 1669–70 and perhaps earlier, Diancinto Corcy (or, on a warrant dated 30 July 1670, "Dracinto Concy") was sued on 9 September 1671 by "Baldasher Artima," his fellow scenekeeper, for debt.

Cordell, Thomas [*fl.* *1663–1670*], *scenekeeper.*

The London Stage lists Thomas Cordell as a scenekeeper in the King's Company at the Bridges Street Theatre in 1663–64, 1666–67, and 1669–70. He was cited in the Lord Chamberlain's accounts on 3 March 1665.

Cordoni, Signor [*fl.* *1760*], *violinist.*

Signor Cordoni [or Cardoni], a virtuoso on the violin, announced as "lately arrived from Italy, who never yet performed in public," directed the orchestra and performed a solo at a performance of *L'isola disabitata* at the Great Room in Dean Street, Soho, on 13 March 1760. He played the violin again at performances of the same piece at the Haymarket on 27 March 1760 for the benefit of Miss Provenzale and at Hickford's Room on 29 April 1760 for the benefit of Laura Rosa.

Core. *See* **COREY**.

Corer. *See* **CURRER**.

Corey. *See also* **CORY**.

Corey, John [*fl. c. 1699–1735*], *actor, playwright.*

John Corey (or Cory) was born in Barnstaple and was descended from an old Cornish family, according to *The Dictionary of National Biography*. That short account also states that he entered New Inn to study law before beginning a stage career and that he was the author of two plays, *A Cure for Jealousy*, performed at Lincoln's Inn Fields Theatre about December 1699 and printed in 1701, and *The Metamorphosis*, played at the same house in September 1704 and published that year. These facts would seem to preclude the possibility that he was the son of the Restoration actress Mrs John Corey (née Katherine Mitchell), since the actress seems to have been a Londoner throughout her career. But John could have been born in Barnstaple and christened in London; John and "Catherine Cory" christened a son John at St Clement Danes on 26 April 1668.

Young John Corey's first recorded stage appearance was about August 1701 at Lincoln's Inn Fields, when he acted Faithless in *The Gentleman Cully* by Charles Johnson. The author noted in his preface when the play was published that the piece "stole into the Theatre in the very Heat of last Summer (as if it would cunningly avoid the Critics, who instead of carping here were at Tunbridge, Bath, etc) was study'd in a Hurry, and play'd by what they call the Young Company." In the 1701–2 season Corey went on to play Seleuchus in *Antiochus the Great* in November 1701, Cratanor in *Altemira* and Mirvan in *Tamerlane* in December, and Colonel Manly in *The Beau's Duel* in June 1702—

or so the cast lists in the printed editions would imply. Before moving to the Queen's Theatre in the Haymarket in 1705, Corey went on to act such parts as Careless in *The Different Widows*, Cuproli in *Abra Mule*, Arbaces in *Zelmayne*, Dorante in *The Gamester*, and Don Pedro in *Careless of Love*. On 4 July 1704 he received a solo benefit at Lincoln's Inn Fields, his first on record. He had moved swiftly to a position of importance in the Betterton company.

At the Queen's Theatre from 23 November 1705 to 1 January 1708 Corey acted Lycinius in *The Faithful General*, Don Philip in *Adventures in Madrid*, Carlos in *The Fatal Marriage*, Lord Dartmouth in *Feign'd Innocence*, Seyton in *Macbeth*, Patrico in *The Jovial Crew*, and other roles. On 9 February 1708 he appeared for the first time at Drury Lane, playing Mustapha in *Irene*. There, for the rest of the decade, he acted such parts as Hotman in *Oroonoko*, Pedro in *The Rover*, Demetrius in *Timon of Athens*, Don John of Austria in *Don Carlos*, Alonzo in *The Tempest*, Juan de Castro in *Rule a Wife and Have a Wife*, Lodovico in *Othello*, Malcolm in *Macbeth*, Vasquez in *The Indian Emperor*, Dolabella in *All for Love*, Nestor in *Troilus and Cressida*, Arimant in *Aureng-Zebe*, Acasto in *The Orphan*, Tiresias in *Oedipus*, and Garcia in *The Mourning Bride*.

In the summer of 1710 he acted a busy season at Pinkethman's playhouse in Greenwich, playing Don Duart in *Love Makes a Man*, Renault in *Venice Preserv'd*, the Player King in *Hamlet*, Lenox in *Macbeth*, Charles in *The Busy Body*, and Frederick in *The Rover*. From the fall of 1710 to the spring of 1714 at Drury Lane, Corey's pace slackened considerably—or perhaps in addition to occasional acting he served the theatre in some other capacity. During those four seasons he was named in the bills only eight times, though he received benefits (shared with one other person). Maybe he longed to act more, for

he left Drury Lane to join John Rich's company after the 1713–14 season.

Corey stayed at Lincoln's Inn Fields from 1714–15 through 1718–19, playing such parts as Acasto in *The Orphan* (his first role at the new playhouse, on 3 January 1715), Cheatly in *The Squire of Alsatia*, Pontius in *Valentinian*, Courtley in *Love in a Sack*, Bertran in *The Spanish Fryar*, the Duke in *Don Quixote*, Laertes in *Hamlet*, Leontine in *Theodosius*, Alvarez in *Don Sebastian*, Worcester in *1 Henry IV*, Lucius in *Cato*, Touchwood in *The Double Dealer*, and Hemskirk in *The Royal Merchant*. He concluded his association with John Rich on 1 April 1719, sharing with three others a benefit, the total receipts for which came to £128 2s. During the summer of 1719 he acted Earl Douglas in *The Earl of Warwick* at Drury Lane, and in the fall he returned permanently to that theatre.

In the 1720s Corey added such new parts as Menenius in *The Invader of His Country*, Burleigh in *The Unhappy Favourite*, the Archbishop of Canterbury in *2 Henry IV*, Magas in *The Ambitious Step-Mother*, Lucius in *Theodosius*, the Duke of York in *Henry V*, Casca in *Julius Caesar*, King Edward in *Jane Shore*, Dervise in *Tamerlane*, and the Duke in *Othello*. His most popular old role during this decade was Lucius in *Cato*. In addition to acting at Drury Lane during the 1720s, Corey also appeared at the summer fairs, his first time being on 2 September 1721, when he acted Mountford in *The Injured General* at the Pinkethman-Miller-Norris booth at Southwark Fair. During this year another John Corey—the poet—died, and consequently several later sources record 1721 as the year of the actor's death. He was, however, far from the end of his lengthy career. On 2 September 1724 at Southwark Fair he played the Duke of Gloucester in *Merlin*, and on 21 August 1727 at Bartholomew Fair he repeated his role as King Edward in *Jane Shore*. After this, he appears to have given up summer acting.

In the 1730s Corey acted at Drury Lane such new parts as Sir William in *Patie and Peggy*, Ariston in *Eurydice*, and Prince Prettyman in *The Rehearsal*, but for the most part he continued in his earlier roles, infrequently expanding his repertoire. Briefly, in the winter of 1732–33, he appeared at Goodman's Fields, making his first appearance there on 18 November 1732 in one of his favorite parts, Acasto in *The Orphan*. There he also acted Sealand in *The Conscious Lovers* and Seyton in *Macbeth* before returning to Drury Lane in the fall. In 1733–34 he was one of the faithful who stayed at Drury Lane when Theophilus Cibber led a contingent to the Haymarket Theatre for a few months, but there is little indication that Corey gained new parts because of it. He played Stanley in *Richard III* and the Lord Chamberlain in *Henry VIII*, but his few other appearances during Cibber's absence were in old roles. His standing in the company had clearly slipped, and on 24 May 1735 he and four others had their benefit tickets accepted, a considerable falling off from the days of his solo or shared benefit nights.

His last season at Drury Lane was 1734–35, during which he played, in chronological order, Alphonso in *The Spanish Fryar*, the Lord Chamberlain in *Henry VIII*, Messala in *Julius Caesar*, Burleigh in *The Unhappy Favorite*, the Merchant in *Wit Without Money*, and, on 8 May 1735, at his last appearance, a repetition of his part in *Henry VIII*.

Corey, Mrs John, Katherine, née Mitchell *b. c. 1635, actress.*

Katherine Mitchell was one of the first actresses to appear on the English public stage, but we have only the sketchiest notion of what she played. We know only that she acted during the early years of the Restoration. She was born about 1635, and when *The Alchemist* was performed by the King's Company in December 1660, perhaps she played Dol Common, a role she was popular in later. In 1660–61 Flecknoe intended her for Alithea in *Erminia*, but there is no certainty that his preference was considered by the players. She may have appeared as Lady Mary Audley in *The Royall King* in 1661–62, but the source of this guess is a manuscript cast that lists "Widdow" for the role—and Katherine was a widow at this time.

Katherine Mitchell and John Cory (the playwright Corey?) were granted a marriage license on 17 October 1662. She described herself as a widow, aged about 27, of the parish of St Andrew, Holborn; John Cory, a bachelor aged about 25, was from the same parish. The license was alleged by William Cory of St Andrew's, probably John's father, but possibly his brother, and perhaps the William Corey who was a member of the Duke's Company at this time. When *The Cheats* was performed in mid-March 1663, Mrs "Covey" was cast as Mrs Whitebroth. Julia in *Love's Sacrifice* was played by Mrs "Coary" sometime between 1662 and 1664 at either the Vere Street or the Bridges Street playhouse. Other roles which Katherine Corey may have acted at this early period are Frances in *The Wild Gallant*, the Citizen's Wife in *The Knight of the Burning Pestle*, and Mrs Day in *The Committee*—but these are conjectures made by modern historians. She certainly played Dol Common in *The Alchemist* on 3 August 1664; Thomas Killigrew intended her for Anna in *Thomaso* about November; and she acted Lady Politick in *Volpone* on 14 January 1665.

Pepys found Mrs Corey to be a fine actress, dubbed her "Doll Common," and commented on 27 December 1666 that she did "Abigail most excellently" in *The Scornful Lady*. During this 1666–67 season she was also cast as Mrs Otter in *The Silent Woman*, Melissa in *Secret Love*, and the Duchess in *The Bloody Brother*. In 1667–68 she acted Cleorin in *The Black*

Prince, and in 1668–69 she played Quisana in *The Island Princess*, Sempronia in *Catiline*, and Arane in *A King and No King*. While acting in *Catiline*, Mrs Corey found herself in the midst of a court squabble. Pepys got the story from Sir W. Coventry, who told him of

my Lady Harvy's being offended at Doll Common's acting of Sempronia, to imitate her; for which she got my Lord Chamberlain, her kinsman, to imprison Doll: when my Lady Castlemayne made the King to release her, and to order her to act it again, worse than ever, the other day, where the King himself was: and since it was acted again, and my Lady Harvy provided people to hiss her and fling oranges at her: but it seems the heat is come to a great height, and real troubles at Court about it.

Mrs Corey was apparently in prison only a few hours, but one wonders if she might not have preferred to stay there than to continue playing under such circumstances.

During the mid-1660s John and Katherine Corey may have started a family. The St Paul, Covent Garden, registers record the baptism on 12 June 1665 of Frances, daughter of John and Katherin Corey; and the St Clement Danes registers show baptisms for Catherine Corye, daughter of John and Catherine, on 23 June 1666, and John Cory, son of John and Catherine, on 26 April 1668. An Edward Corey, son of John and Katherin, was baptized at St Paul, Covent Garden, on 14 May 1676. Though the theatrical records are incomplete for these years, Mrs Corey the actress is not known to have performed at any times which would have conflicted with the births of these children. John Corey, the eighteenth-century actor, may have been the John born in 1668, and, though he is supposed to have been born in Barnstaple, there is no reason he could not have been baptized in London.

During the 1670s with the King's Company, at the Bridges Street Theatre until it burned in 1672, then temporarily at Lincoln's Inn Fields, and from 1674 forward at the new Drury Lane, Mrs Corey played Sophonia in *The Roman Empress*, Mrs Joyner in *Love in a Wood*, Julia in (her husband's?) *Generous Enemies*, Teresa in *The Spanish Rogue*, the English Woman in *Amboyna*, Strega in *The Amorous Old Woman*, Agrippina in *Nero*, Lucy in *The Country Wife*, Cumana in *Sophonisba*, Ardelia in *Lucina's Rape*, Widow Blackacre in *The Plain Dealer*, Sysigambis in *The Rival Queens*, the School Mistress in *Scaramouch*, Octavia in *All for Love*, and Quickthrift in *The Man of Newmarket*. An amply-built woman, judging from descriptions of some of the characters she played, Mrs Corey seems to have been best at acting nurses, serving women, governesses, mothers, scolds, and bawds. Her flair was for comedy, though she made occasional appearances in tragedies.

Mrs Corey joined some of the dissatisfied actors from the King's Company who went to Edinburgh in 1679 and stayed for a year or so. Her name did not reappear in London casts until 4 February 1682, when she acted Begona in *The Loyal Brother*, just before the King's Company amalgamated with the Duke's. After the union she played such parts as the title role in *Dame Dobson*, Mrs Trainwell in *The Northern Lass*, Angelline's supposed mother in *The Disappointment*, Roselia in *The Commonwealth of Women*, Mopsophil in *The Emperor of the Moon*, Ruth in *The Squire of Alsatia*, Mrs Flirt in *The Widow Ranter*, Farmosa in *The Successful Strangers*, the Abbess in *The Merry Devil of Edmonton*, Bromia in *Amphitryon*, Crowstitch in *Love for Money*, Teresia in *Bussy D'Ambois*, the Aunt in *Greenwich Park*, Mrs Barebottle in *Cutter of Coleman Street*, Lady Fanciful in *Win Her and Take Her*, Mrs Teazall in *The Wives' Excuse*, Lady Bumfiddle in *The Marriage-Hater Match'd*, and Morossa in *The Traitor* (in March 1692, her last recorded role).

During the 1680s there were occasional other references to Mrs Corey. In 1683 she was named in the actor Charles Hart's will to receive a 20-shilling gold mourning ring; in the summer of 1686 she may have been one of the actresses who went off to Holywell (to pray, not to sin, said the prologue to *Titus Andronicus*); and in 1689 she ran into trouble with the Killigrews. On 11 March of that year she petitioned the Lord Chamberlain because she had been banished from the United Company. Henry Killigrew had tried to persuade Mrs Corey and some of the other players to bolt the company and join him in a new troupe. All were discharged, but all except Mrs Corey were readmitted, hence her plea to the Lord Chamberlain. She claimed that she had served Charles Killigrew and his family for 27 years and was "the first and . . . the last of all the Actresses that were constituted by King Charles the Second at His Restauration . . ." The Lord Chamberlain ordered on 11 March 1689 that she be readmitted, and within a few weeks she was acting again, as Lady Fantast in *Bury Fair*. Her salary about this time was 30s. weekly, nearly the highest in the company, for she was one of the most popular of Restoration actresses throughout her long career. Evidence presented in 1694, when Betterton pleaded for a separate company, spoke of Mrs Corey as though she were still alive, so it is probable that after the 1691–92 season, with over 30 years of acting behind her, Katherine Corey retired.

Corey, William *d. c. 1664?, actor.*

There is a possibility that William Corey, who was sworn a member of the Duke's Company on 24 September 1662, was the brother-in-law or father-in-law of the actress Katherine Mitchell Corey. Katherine married John Corey in October 1662, the license being alleged by William Cory of St Andrew, Holborn, who may have been John's father or, less likely, his brother. The William Corey in the Duke's

Company was probably an actor, though only one role can even be suggested for him: the "Will" who played Pecus in *Ignoramus* at Lincoln's Inn Fields on 1 November 1662 may have been either Corey or Will Peer.

Most of the references to Corey in the Lord Chamberlain's accounts have to do with litigation he was involved in, the first such occasion being on 6 June 1663 when he was sued by Richard Wrenford. On 4 February 1664 Richard Bayly sued him, and Bayly may have been the man of that name who was a Duke's Company sharer and became the company's counsel. Michael Arnold sued Corey on 23 March 1664, and on 25 June of the same year he was simultaneously sued by Mathew Cage and petitioned against by Colonel Careless, Edward Brook, William Dickerson, and Michaell Brighthouse. His name disappeared from the records after that date, and some historians have suggested that perhaps he had died. But he may simply have left town. The Mr Cory who acted with the King's Company in 1675 may have been William.

Corfe, Mr *b. 1718, singer.*

At the age of 12, the tenor Corfe (mistakenly listed as Corse by *The London Stage*) sang on 1 August 1730 in a booth operated at the Tottenham Court Fair by the comedians from Goodman's Fields Theatre. Billed as Master Corfe, he sang at Goodman's Fields on 6 November 1730 and again on 13 May 1731, in the latter instance rendering a Hayden cantata for the benefit of Prelleur and Giles. On 7 March 1733 he played a messenger and an angel in Thomas A. Arne's setting of *Rosamond* at Lincoln's Inn Fields. In the fall of 1733 Master Corfe was with Arne's group at the Haymarket, where he performed Glumdalca in *The Opera of Operas*, with music by Arne, and a shepherd in *An Impromptu Revel Masque*. With Henry Giffard's company at Lincoln's Inn Fields in 1736–37, now billed as *Mr* Corfe, he sang in the choruses of *King Arthur, Harlequin Shipwrecked, Britannia,* and *The Beggar's Pantomime.* From about 1735, Corfe also sang small parts in the oratorios, including *Saul, L'Allegro,* and *Acis and Galatea.* In the latter piece, there being no parts for tenors, Corfe sang soprano. On 3 November 1744 he sang the Chief Priest of Baal in *Deborah* at the King's Theatre. He may have been the "Mr Coaff" who sang at Bath in May 1745 in the oratorios *Alexander's Feast* and the *Messiah.*

Probably also he was related to the composer James Corfe (fl. 1735–1750) and the tenor Joseph Corfe (1740–1820).

Corfe, Arthur Thomas 1773–1863, *organist, harpsichordist, singer, composer.*

Arthur Thomas Corfe, the son of the tenor Joseph Corfe (1740–1820) and his wife Mary, was born at Salisbury on 9 April 1773. At the age of ten he was placed as a chorister under the instruction of Benjamin Cooke in Westminster Abbey, and he later studied the harpsichord under Clementi. *The London Stage* places Arthur as an instrumental performer in the oratorios at the King's Theatre in 1792, but we believe this person probably was his brother John Corfe (b. 1769). In 1804 Arthur succeeded his father as organist and choir master at Salisbury Cathedral. In August 1828, Corfe organized a successful music festival at Salisbury. In a letter dated 7 October 1823 he provided the biographical notices for his father and his brother which Sainsbury printed in his *Dictionary of Musicians.*

Compositions by Arthur Thomas Corfe included several anthems, one being "Lord thou art become gracious," for a countertenor; a *Te Deum, Jubilate, Sanctus,* and *Commandments* for a service; some pieces for piano; "The Principles of Harmony and Thorough Bass;" and an "Ordination Hymn."

He died at Salisbury on 28 January 1863

and was buried in the cloisters of the cathedral, where a memorial tablet was placed by his 13 children. In his will, proved on 28 February 1863, two of his sons were named as executors of his estate (which was valued at under £8000): John Davis Corfe, born at Salisbury in 1804 and organist at Bristol Cathedral from 1825 until his death there on 23 January 1876; and Charles William Corfe, born at Salisbury on 13 July 1814, organist at Christ Church, Oxford, from 1846 until his death there on 16 December 1883. For information about Arthur Thomas Corfe's legacies from his father's will and about his brothers and sisters, see the entry for Joseph Corfe.

Corfe, James [fl. 1735–1750], *musician, composer.*

James Corfe was named a charter member of the Royal Society of Musicians in the "Declaration of Trust" which established that organization on 28 August 1739. Between 1735 and 1750 a number of songs composed by him were published at London, including *The Mighty Bowl* (1735?), two editions of *Of all the Joys we are possest,* as sung at Goodman's Fields (1735?), *The Caution* (1740?), *Luckless Love* (1740?), and *The Lady of the May* (1750?). He may have been related to the tenor Corfe (b. 1718) and to Joseph Corfe (1740–1820) and his family of musicians at Salisbury.

Corfe, John b. 1769, *bass player, violoncellist.*

John Corfe, the son of the tenor Joseph Corfe (1740–1820) and his wife Mary, was born at Salisbury on 30 July 1769 and baptized at St Martin's Church there on 14 August 1769. Brought up as a chorister in the Chapel Royal, he was recommended by Sale for membership in the Royal Society of Musicians on 5 May 1793 (elected on 1 September 1793), at which time it was certified that he had been a professional musician for at least seven years, was a deputy at the Chapel Royal, played the violoncello and double bass, was single, and was engaged at the King's Theatre. Probably he was the Corfe who played at the oratorios there in the spring of 1792. In 1794 he was listed by Doane's *Musical Directory* as a singer in the oratorios, as a member of the Drury Lane band, as a player in the grand performances at Westminster Abbey, and as then living in Queen Street, Golden Square.

Corfe was named to play the double bass at the annual concerts given by the Royal Society of Musicians at St Paul's for benefit of the clergy in 1794 and 1795. On 1 April 1798 the Society gave him a vote of thanks for his services to it. John Corfe was not named in the will of his father, dated 22 February 1814, so presumably he was dead by that time. For information about his brothers and sisters, see the entry for Joseph Corfe.

Corfe, Joseph *1740–1820, singer, organist, composer.*

Joseph Corfe was born at Salisbury on 25 December 1740 and was instructed in music by Dr Stephens, an organist of that city. Corfe was a chorister of Salisbury Cathedral, and then, by the patronage of James Harris, grandfather to the Earl of Malmesbury, he came to the notice of Bishop Lowth, through whom he received an appointment as Gentleman of the Chapel Royal in 1783. On 2 March of the same year Thomas Barrow recommended Corfe for membership in the Royal Society of Musicians, certifying at the time that Corfe, aged 42, had practiced music upwards of seven years, was married, and was director of the concert at Salisbury and a vicar of the Cathedral. In a rare instance of such rejection, Corfe was not elected to membership.

In March 1775, Corfe sang in the oratorios presented by J. C. Bach and Abel. Between 1764 and 1768 he sang at the Three Choirs Festival, and in May and June 1784 he sang in the Handel Memorial Concerts at Westminster Abbey and the Pantheon. He succeeded Robert Parry in 1792 as organist and master of the choristers of Salisbury Cathedral, positions he held until he relinquished them to his son Arthur in 1804. At some time after his original refusal by the Royal Society of Musicians, he may have been reconsidered and elected, for in 1794 Doane's *Musical Directory* stated that he was a member. According to his son Arthur, who wrote his father's biography for Sainsbury's *Dictionary of Musicians*, "Few men stood higher, both in public and private estimation," than Joseph Corfe.

Corfe died at his house at New Sarum, Wiltshire, on 29 July 1820. His will, dated 22 February 1814, was proved on 7 October 1820 by his widow Mary Corfe, to whom he bequeathed all his furniture, library, plate, china, and dividends in stock, for her natural life. To his daughter and eldest child Mary Bernard Bolin (b. 1767) he left £100 which she was to receive after the death of her mother, "she having received less for her advancement in life than either of my other children." Also after the death of his wife, the residue of his estate was to be equally divided among three children: Mary, Arthur Thomas Corfe (1773–1863), and George Richard Corfe (b. 1778). Mary also received his pianoforte made by Broadwood. To George Richard Corfe he also gave his printed and manuscript music and £4700 in three-percent annuities as a marriage settlement, the annuities to be considered as part of the son's proportionate share of his estate. Three of Joseph Corfe's children, not named in his will, presumably died before him (their names are found in Thomas Barrow's original recommendation of Corfe to the Royal Society of Musicians): John Corfe (b. 1769), Joseph Corfe (b. 1772), and Louisa Corfe (b. 1775).

Compositions and publications by Joseph Corfe included three sets of glees, of

12 numbers each, from Scottish and other melodies; treatises on singing and thorough-bass; *The Beauties of Handel . . . arranged with separate Accompaniment for the Piano Forte* (1800); a collection in two volumes of *Sacred Music* (1800?), arranged by him; *Nine Vocal Trios arranged from the most Favourite Airs and Duetts of Purcell, Wise, Travers, Hayden & Harington* (1800?). He also edited and revised James Kent's *A Morning and Evening Service, a Sanctus, with eight Anthems* (1773–77?).

Corfe may have been related to the Mr Corfe (b. 1718) who sang at London between 1730 and 1747 and to the composer James Corfe (fl. 1735–1750), both entered separately. See also the entries for his sons Arthur and John.

Corie. *See* COREY *and* CORY.

Corifet. *See* DORIVAL À CORIFET, MARIE CATHERINE BRIDA.

Cornacchini, Emanuele   ₍fl. 1759–1760₎, *singer.*

Emanuele Cornacchini (sometimes Carnacchini, Cornacchiari, or Cornacini) replaced Rotenza as the first man in the opera at the King's Theatre in 1759–60. He made his first appearance in the title role of *Vologeso* on 13 November 1759. He sang Sesto in *La clemenza di Tito* on 15 January and again on 16 February after recovering from a cold. His other roles were Jupiter in *La Gran Brettagna emula della antico Roma* on 25 February, Curisteo in *Antigona*, and Ormonte in *Erginda regina di Livadia* on 31 May. Oliver Goldsmith in *The Bee* (1759) described him as:

a very indifferent actor, has a most unmeaning face, seems not to feel his part, is infected with a passion of showing his compass; but to recompense all these defects, his voice is melodious, he has vast compass and great volubility, his swell and shake are perfectly

fine, unless that he continues the latter too long. In short, whatever the defects of his action may be, they are amply recompensed by his excellency as a singer; nor can I avoid fancying that he might make a much greater figure in an oratorio than upon the stage.

The London Stage places Cornacchini in London again for a performance of *La clemenza di Tito* on 3 December 1765. It is very doubtful that he was at the King's Theatre that season, however, and although his name appears in the cast of the 1765 edition of the libretto, that list is simply a repetition of the cast found in the 1760 edition. Burney wrote that Cornacchini's "voice was not good, and his style of singing by no means grand or captivating."

Corne, Mr   ₍fl. 1782₎, *actor.*

A Mr Corne played Dr Camphire in a performance of *Dr Last's Examination Before the College of Physicians*, at the Haymarket, in a specially licensed performance on 30 December 1782.

Corneille. *See also* CORNWALL.

Corneille, ₍Mons?₎   ₍fl. 1675₎, *harpsichordist.*

One Corneille, presumably a Frenchman, played the "Harpsicall" in the court masque *Calisto* on 15 February 1675.

Corneille, Mons   ₍fl. 1735–1736₎, *acrobat.*

Monsieur Corneille was a tumbler in the French troupe which played at Lincoln's Inn Fields from 18 December 1735 to 28 February 1736, according to a British Museum manuscript. He was granted a benefit on 9 February 1736, on which date he had "a match in tumbling" with his compatriot de Broc (or du Brocq).

Cornel, Master   ₍fl. 1745–1747₎, *singer.*

A Master Cornel (sometimes Connell)

performed the role of the page in Thomas Arne's opera of *Rosamond* at Drury Lane on 31 January 1745 and 13 April 1747. On 3 April 1745 he had a principal musical role in *Alfred the Great*, and on 12 April 1746 he played the page in *The Orphan*. For the likelihood that Master Cornel was really Michael Arne (c. 1740–1786), see the latter's entry.

Corneli. *See* CORNELYS, TERESA.

Cornelius. *See also* CORNELYS, TERESA.

Cornelius, Mr [*fl.* 1675], *violinist.*
A Mr Cornelius played the "French violin" in the court masque *Calisto* on 15 February 1675. He was mentioned again on 27 May when he was to share in the £221 paid to 28 performers and their leader, Nicholas Staggins.

Cornelles. *See* CORNELYS, TERESA.

Cornellies. *See* CORNELYS, MRS JOHN.

Cornelys, Miss [*fl.* 1791–1801], *actress.*
The daughter of the well-known actors John and Margaret Cornelys made her professional debut at Crow Street Theatre, Dublin, on 7 March 1791 in a minor part not now known. She accompanied her parents to London when her father was invited by Colman to try out at the Haymarket Theatre, but she did not act in London during that summer of 1791 when John Cornelys was failing to win a contract. She did act once or twice at Brighton.

Miss Cornelys was probably with her mother and father acting at Chelmsford in September 1792. Mrs and Miss Cornelys (and perhaps John Cornelys) were together on the Liverpool circuit in 1793, and Miss Cornelys won some praise from the author of *The Thespian Mirror* . . .

of the Theatres Royal, Manchester, Liverpool, and Chester:

> *In characters wanting an arch comic spirit,*
> *Cornelys discovers the dawnings of merit,*
> *Pert, gay, and vivacious, brisk, nimble and airy*

This arbiter admitted

> *. . . What from her youth one would not expect,*
> *Her fancy is keen and her judgment correct*

But no doubt crushed the young creature with his decision that:

> *Her person so ill with her talents accords,*
> *No exquisite raptures her acting affords*

Her deficiencies notwithstanding, Miss Cornelys in the following year won a place on the Covent Garden roster. On 15 September 1794 she made her London debut as Jacintha, the ingenue in *The Suspicious Husband*. During the season following, she added Miss Neville in *She Stoops to Conquer*, Annette in *Robin Hood*, a Shepherdess in *Cymon*, Rosa in *Fontainebleau*, Miss Frolick in *The British Recruit*, Harriet in *The Jealous Wife*, Lucinda in *The Conscious Lovers*, the Duchess in *Barataria*, Nancy in *Three Weeks after Marriage*, another Nancy in the first performance of John Bernard's farce *The Poor Sailor* (29 May 1795), and Lucy in the first performance of the anonymous afterpiece *The Frolics of an Hour* (16 June).

Miss Cornelys was engaged at Richmond in the summer of 1795, was again at Dublin, with her mother, in 1795–96 ("in the line of Mrs Jordan"), and was at Hull in 1798, where the reviewer for the *Monthly Mirror* commended her acting in comedies as "sprightly, chaste, easy, and agreeable." She was at York, Hull, and Sheffield in

1799, and in 1801 at Liverpool, after which she can no longer be traced.

Cornelys, John *1735–1818, actor, singer.*

John Cornelys was very likely the Cornelys who was first seen at the Crow Street Theatre in Dublin on 28 October 1768. He was then 33 years old and had probably acted in the Irish provinces before his debut in the capital. His brief obituary in the *Gentleman's Magazine* of October 1818 says that he was native to Dublin and had once been apprenticed to a staymaker.

Cornelys joined Samuel Foote's company at the Haymarket in the summer of 1771, making himself useful in a variety of small and medium comic roles from 20 May onward: Roger in *The Mayor of Garratt*, Quildrive in *The Citizen*, Taylor in *The Provok'd Wife*, the Boy in *Taste*, Davy in *The Mock Doctor* (as "Carnelys"), a role in *Contrivances*, a servant in *The West Indian*, and Jaques in *Love Makes a Man*. He also sang, as Iarbas in Hooke's new comic opera *Dido*, on 24 July.

Cornelys surfaced next at the excellent little theatre in Norwich, where he appears to have been in financial straits by 13 August 1774, when the Committee Books of the theatre carried the recommendation: "That the Treasurer lend Mr Cornelys £30 or guineas on his Note on Condition that He article for two years." Evidently Cornelys refused the condition, for he departed the company.

Cornelys was married to his wife Margaret, a woman said to be twelve years his senior, by the January opening of the York season of 1775, and they were both acting in the company that season. The couple returned to Norwich (still with money troubles) late in 1775. The Committee Books note on 20 January 1776: "Ordered that the treasurer advance to Mr Cornelys twenty pounds on his note to be paid at £1 1*s*. p[er] week during the season, & the remainder to be discharged at his second

Harvard Theatre Collection

JOHN CORNELYS, as Lingo
artist unknown

yearly benefit." He was also advanced £20 in May 1778.

The Cornelyses remained at Norwich through 1780 and then went to Cork and on to Dublin. John made his Smock Alley debut on 1 November 1781. Margaret also secured an engagement. John O'Keeffe remarked in his *Memoirs*, "John Cornelius was a successful comedian . . . my original Lingo [in *The Agreeable Surprise*, 1781] in Dublin."

John evidently did not accompany his wife to Edinburgh in 1782–83, but the couple reunited in Dublin in 1783–84, and they acted also sometime that year at Newry and elsewhere in the North. On 27

September 1785 they were at Cork and by 30 January 1786 were again at Smock Alley, for on that date both John and Margaret signed a letter to the *Hibernian Journal*, along with other actors of that theatre. They were again at Cork in 1787 and at both Cork and the Crow Street Theatre, Dublin, in 1788 and 1789. In July of 1788 John played at Limerick. He and Margaret both went to Derry in May and June of 1790. On 7 March 1791 their daughter made her professional debut at the Crow Street Theatre, Dublin.

At the death on 31 October 1790 of the great comedian John Edwin, who had been for many years a fixture at Covent Garden in the winters and at the Haymarket in the summers, the Cornelyses made overtures to George Colman, who managed both theatres. They represented to him John Cornelys's eminent suitability to take over Edwin's roles. Colman gave him what the *Thespian Dictionary* called a "conditional" engagement. When the Haymarket opened on 13 June 1791, Cornelys played his notable Lingo in the afterpiece, announced as "from the Theatre Royal, Dublin." He was, alas, "a failure . . . which did not escape the notice of the audience," said the critic of the *European Magazine*. Much later the *Thespian Dictionary* analyzed the failure, doubtless correctly, as attributable to the audience's memory of Edwin in the character. Cornelys repeated the part for a few nights, and though he had somewhat better success with Mungo in *The Padlock*, his Haymarket engagement ended with the end of the season, and he was not hired for the winter company at Covent Garden. Cornelys, according to the *Thespian Dictionary*, "complained, that to the ill-nature of newspaper critics he was indebted for his dismission." Mrs Cornelys was not hired by any London theatre at this time. She may have been at Brighton that summer, for on 13 July 1791 their daughter made her English debut there, advertised as "from Dublin."

John Cornelys, and probably his wife and daughter, were acting at Chelmsford in September 1792. He may have remained to seek work in London while his wife and daughter were on the Liverpool circuit in 1793. His efforts to catch on with one of the London patent theatres in 1794–95 were futile, though his daughter was by that time articled to Covent Garden and his wife soon would be. He took himself off to Birmingham, where he acted through the summer of 1795.

Margaret Cornelys was playing at Covent Garden from January to June 1795 and at Dublin in 1795–96. The daughter was at Richmond in 1795, at Dublin in 1795–96, at Hull and elsewhere in the English provinces in 1798 and 1799, and at Liverpool in 1801.

John Cornelys went back to Dublin in 1795. He acted at Smock Alley in 1796–97 and then either went to the country or retired. He died in Dublin on 23 July 1818, aged 83. The *Gentleman's Magazine* for October of that year called him "the father of the Irish stage" and said that "Of late years Mr Cornelys had been precluded from an engagement in the Theatre. He was a man of intellect [and] unassuming manners, and was very generally respected."

An anonymously engraved plate for the *Hibernian Magazine* (1791?) depicts Cornelys as Lingo in *The Agreeable Surprise*.

Cornelys, Mrs John, Margaret *1723–1797, actress.*

Mrs John Cornelys, whose first name was Margaret, had perhaps acted elsewhere in the English provinces before her arrival in York, apparently a mature performer, in 1784. She was married to her actor-singer husband by the opening of the York season in January 1775 and acted there until the spring. She accompanied her husband to Norwich for the 1775–76 season and remained there with him through 1780. In February and March of 1777 she was in poor health, and her roles were taken by Mrs Hunter of the Haymarket.

In 1781 the Cornelyses went to Cork and Dublin. The *Thespian Dictionary* (1805) asserted that she had been engaged by Thomas Ryder at Crow Street Theatre, Dublin, and had played parts like Lady Teazle in *The School for Scandal*, "but from the then distracted situation of this theatre, she was soon glad to join the other company and perform as *second* to Mrs [Richard] Daly [the manager's wife at Smock Alley]. She produced a comedy for her benefit called 'The Deceptions,' which was acted but once."

Mrs Cornelys, apparently alone, crossed over to Jackson's Edinburgh company in 1782–83. She rejoined her husband at Dublin in 1783–84 and was also that year at Newry and other places in the North. In September 1785 they were at Cork and by 30 January 1786 were again at Smock Alley. They were again at Cork in 1787 and at both Cork and Crow Street, Dublin, in 1788 and 1789. In May and June of 1790 they were at Derry. On 7 March 1791 their daughter made her debut at Crow Street.

In the summer of 1791 Margaret Cornelys's husband John secured a summer job at the Haymarket Theatre in London. Margaret accompanied him but did not then act. She may have been in Brighton that summer, for on 13 July a *Miss* Cornelys, advertised as "from Dublin," acted there. *The Thespian Mirror . . . of the Theatres Royal Manchester, Liverpool, and Chester* (1793) gave qualified praise to both mother and daughter Cornelys. Mrs Cornelys may have remained on the Liverpool circuit for the next year or two.

Margaret Cornelys (sometimes "Cornellies" in the account books) was paid £2 per week at Covent Garden in the spring of 1795. She made her first appearance on that stage on 31 January 1795 as Clara in *Two Strings to Your Bow*. On 2 May she played Mrs Enfield in the first performances of Thomas Holcroft's *The Deserted Daugh-*

ter. She was last seen at Covent Garden (and in London) in that same piece on 15 June 1795. After brief appearances at Dublin in 1795–96, she disappeared from the record. She was, according to the estimate of George Parker in *A View of Society* (1781), "Equally fortunate both in her tragic and comic exertions . . . one of the best Breeches figures at present on the stage; not excepting even Mrs Inchbald."

Cornelys, Teresa, née Imer, *1723–1797, singer, entrepreneur.*

Teresa Imer was born in Venice in 1723, the younger daughter of the manager, actor, and librettist Giuseppe Imer, a friend of the eminent librettist and playwright Carlo Goldoni. Her older sister Marianna was an opera singer of some consequence.

By her eighteenth year Teresa was the mistress of the seventy-six-year-old Senator Malipiero. In his house she met, and was of course overcome by, Giacomo Casanova, by whom she had a daughter. At what point in her life she first went on the stage is not known, but in view of her theatrical parentage there is reason to think that it was quite early. Before she was 21 she had married the dancer Angelo Pompeati and was with him in Vienna in 1744–45. He later committed suicide by disemboweling himself.

According to Burney, Teresa appeared in London for the first time at the King's Theatre as Signora Pompeati, on 7 January 1746, in Gluck's new opera of *La caduta de' giganti*. Also in the cast was her sister Marianna. Burney thought that "though nominally the second woman [Teresa] had such a masculine and violent manner of singing that few female symptoms were perceptible." On 28 January she sang Eriphilis in *Il trionfo della continenza* and on 13 May Ismene in the *pasticcio Antigono*. These operas were repeated several times. Probably she was also in the performances of Gluck's *pasticcio Artamene* on and after 4 March and *Alessandro nell' Indie*, a *pas-*

ticcio by Lampagnani on and after 15 April, for which no casts were listed. Both Imer sisters had disappeared from London before the 1746–47 operatic season began, and by August 1746 Teresa was back in Vienna.

She sang at Hamburg in 1748 and at Copenhagen under Gimgotti's direction in 1749. Casanova saw her again in Venice in 1753. She then became the mistress of the Margrave Friedrich in Bayreuth.

At some time shortly after she lost the protection of the Margrave (which must have been about 1755), Teresa attracted the more honorable attention of Prince

TERESA CORNELYS
"Cupid Turn'd Auctioneer"

engraving by J. Taylor, after S. Wale

Charles of Lorraine who, according to Casanova, gave over to her the direction of all theatrical activity in the Austrian Netherlands. Frank Walker, writing in *Grove's Dictionary*, notes in confirmation of this seemingly incredible claim that a list of subscribers to Robert Daubat's *Cent contredanses* (1757) includes "Mlle Pompeati, directrice des spectacles en Flandre." Evidently it was at this time that she began to develop the appetite for management and direction which she later displayed in London. But the enterprise involved her in debts and Teresa went hastily (as "Madame Trenti") to Holland, where once again she met with Casanova, who acknowledged Sophie, one of her two children, as his daughter.

At Amsterdam she became wife or paramour to a wealthy burgher, Cornelis de Rigerbos. At any rate, when she came to England in 1759, she bore his name (which appeared in many forms in the playbills and newspapers: Cornelis, Cornelles, Cornelys, Corneli, and Cornelius).

In 1760 Mrs Cornelys bought a mansion on the east side of Soho Square which had been built for the Earl of Carlisle during the reign of James II. In November 1760 she began giving a series of subscription balls and *ridottos* in the house. The revels overflowed by way of a "Chinese Bridge" to a two-story "Chinese Pavilion" which she had erected in the Garden. This enterprise of the "Circe and Sultana of Soho" was immediately the rage of fashionable society and continued for many years to eclipse the private routs and balls of London's *ton*.

Mrs Cornelys showed from the first a complete mastery of the psychology of snobbery and public relations. She admitted none but certified aristocrats, and decorum was rigidly enforced in the luxuriously decorated assembly rooms. But in February 1763 she gave a ball "to the upper servants of persons of fashion, as a token of the sense she had of obligations to the nobility and gentry, for their generous subscriptions to her assembly." She had the support of the leaders of society and, being of German origin, even of the Court. Count Kilmansegge, for instance, on a visit to England, was given a ticket to her assembly by the Duke of Richmond. Her success was envied and was very soon imitated. On 16 December 1764 Horace Walpole wrote to George Montagu:

Mrs Cornelis, apprehending the future assembly at Almack's [Assembly Room], had enlarged her vast room, and hung it with blue satin, and another with yellow satin; but Almack's room, which is to be ninety feet long, proposes to swallow up both hers, as easily as Moses's rod gobbled down those of the magicians.

But Almack's did not at once swallow the Soho assemblies. Mrs Cornelys had shrewdly anticipated the competition and, on 24 February 1764, had added a more serious feature, "a grand concert of vocal and instrumental music," which was designed both to attract a more serious clientele and to expand to daytime hours the use of premises which were becoming frighteningly expensive. (She still had close connections with London's musical world, and, in fact, was listed in the 1764 edition of Dr Thomas Augustine Arne's oratorio *Judith* singing a principal part.) On 6 April 1764 the "Subscribers to the Society in Soho Square" were told that "the first meeting for the morning subscription music will be held this day." The subscription for gentlemen was five guineas, for ladies three guineas.

On 23 January 1765 Johann Christian Bach and Karl Friedrich Abel took over the joint conduct of the subscription concerts and ran them until about 1771. In April 1768 the Prince of Monaco was present at the assembly ball, escorted by members of the royal family of Great Britain; and in August that year the King of Denmark and his suite appeared at Carlisle House. In January 1769 more rooms were opened, along with "a new gallery for the dancing of cotillons and allemandes, and a suite of new rooms adjoining." On 6 June 1769 Gaetano Guadagni, the male soprano, supervised a festival and grand concert, with "illuminations," honoring the King's birthday. At a masked ball given by the Tuesday Night's Club on 27 February 1770, the wealthy Miss Monckton appeared wearing £30,000 worth of jewelry.

Testimonies about the atmosphere and clientele of the Soho Assemblies in their heyday are plentiful. The following are selected from two of the most ubiquitous chroniclers of the fashionable scene of the day. Both are from 1770, when the vogue for Mrs Cornelys's entertainments was at its height and not long before the utter debacle of the Carlisle House enterprise. Horace Walpole, writing to Horace Mann about a revel of 26 February 1770 which he attended, affects his usual amused indulgence:

Our civil war has been lulled asleep by a Subscription Masquerade, for which the House of Commons literally adjourned yesterday. Instead of Fairfaxes and Cromwells, we have had a crowd of Henry the Eighths, Wolseys, Vandykes, and Harlequins; and because Wilkes was not mask enough, we had a man dressed like him, with a visor in imitation of his squint, and a Cap of Liberty on a pole. In short, sixteen or eighteen young lords have given the town a masquerade; and politics, for the last fortnight, were forced to give way to habit-makers. The ball was last night at Soho; and, if possible, was more magnificent than the King of Denmark's. The Bishops opposed: he of London formally remonstrated with the King, who did not approve it, but could not help him. The consequence was that four divine vessels belonging to the holy fathers, alias their wives, were at this masquerade. A fair widow who once bore my whole name, and now bears half of it, was there, and with one of those whom the newspapers call *great personages*—he dressed like Edward IV.; she like Elizabeth Woodville, in grey and pearls, with a black veil. Methinks it was not very difficult to find out the meaning of those masks.

As one of my ancient passions formerly was masquerades, I had a large trunk of dresses by me. I dressed out a thousand young Conways and Cholmondeleys, and went with more pleasure to see them pleased than when I formerly delighted in that diversion myself. It has cost me a great headache, and I shall probably never go to another. A symptom appeared of the change that has happened in the people.

The mob was beyond all belief: they held flambeaux to the windows of every coach, and demanded to have the masks pulled off and put on at their pleasure, but with extreme good humour and civility. I was with my Lady Hertford and two of her daughters in her coach: the mob took me for Lord Hertford, and huzza'd and blessed me! One fellow cried out, "Are you for Wilkes?" Another said, "D——n you, you fool, what has Wilkes to do with a masquerade?"

In April of 1770 Fanny Burney accompanied her father Dr Burney and Nancy Pascall to the assembly but was not quite so amused as Walpole had been:

The magnificence of the rooms, splendour of the illuminations and embellishments, and the brilliant appearance of company exceeded any thing I ever before saw. The apartments were so crowded we had scarce room to move, which was quite disagreeable, nevertheless, the flight of apartments both upstairs and on the ground floor seemed endless. . . . The first person that we saw and knew was Lord Pigot [a Yorkshire baronet, who later died as Governor of Madras]. . . . The Rooms were so full and so hot that nobody attempted to dance. . . . I must own this evening's entertainment more disappointed my expectations than any I ever spent; for I had imagined it would have been the most charming in the world. . . .

In 1771 Mrs Cornelys, already in debt because of enormous expenditures on decorations and musicians and with her assemblies being gradually infiltrated by gamblers and prostitutes, made the tactical error which caused her downfall. She began a series of "Harmonic Meetings," involving vocal performances, with Guadagni again as organizer and chief singer, "as a sort of competition with the opera house," according to the *Monthly Mirror* of September 1797. For a time they were so successful as to inspire theatrical bills to carry occasional notices like that for Covent Garden on the night of 6 June: "Performance will be over time enough for those ladies and gentlemen who are engaged at Mrs Cornelys's." But the management of the King's Theatre procured a bill of indictment from the Grand Jury asserting, among charges more to the point of her usurpation oi the Opera's commercial rights, "that she does keep and maintain a common disorderly house, and does permit and suffer divers loose, idle, and disorderly persons, as well men as women, to be and remain during the whole night, rioting and otherwise misbehaving themselves." The magistrate Sir John Fielding took Guadagni into custody and Mrs Cornelys was obliged to desist from harmonic meetings. Teresa was, indeed, vulnerable, for while the indictment overstated the moral case, the assemblies at Carlisle House in 1771 were a far cry from the decorous gatherings of 1760. She was also unlucky in that the magnificent and well-conducted Pantheon opened at this time and began to draw away the best of her clientele. She was apparently defeated. The list of bankrupts in the *London Gazette* of November 1772 included "Teresa Cornelys, dealer," and in December the contents of Carlisle House were sold at public auction.

She still owned the house, and in 1773 she tried for a few nights to revivify her assemblies, but without success. She retired for awhile to Southampton where she was to be found in 1774 keeping a hotel. On 20 June 1775 she was paid 700 guineas to cater and manage a masked ball and supper at Ranelagh in conjunction with a grand regatta on the Thames. She tried several times more, with a masked ball at Carlisle House on 19 February 1776 and intermittently with *ridottos* and entertainments for a year thereafter, to attract the fashion of the town. Fewer and fewer patrons responded, however, and they were of lower and lower levels of respectability.

But Teresa Cornelys seems to have been nearly indomitable. In 1778, unable to attract her old custom in Westminster, she sold Carlisle House, retired to Knightsbridge Grove, and attempted to retrieve her fortunes with entertainments on the old plan, but scaled to the more modest requirements of the county gentry. She was able to keep afloat at Knightsbridge until about 1785, when she disappeared from public record. Her obituary in a *Monthly Mirror* of 1797 seems to be the *locus* from which several subsequent accounts of her latter years proceed:

She remained in obscurity for many years under the name of Mrs. Smith; but a year or two ago she came forward again—and here our readers will no doubt learn with surprise, not unmixed with risibility, the strange transition in her fate; for she who was once a *leader of fashion*, became literally the *attendant of asses*, for she kept a house at Knightsbridge, and was a vendor of *asses milk*. In this situation, however, she still retained a desire of resuming her former pursuits, and for this purpose ornamented a suite of rooms, in order to have occasionally a public *dejeuné* for people of fashion.

The manners of the times, however, were changed, and her taste had not adapted itself to the variations of fashion; and after much expence employed in gaudy and frivolous embellishments, she was obliged to abandon the scheme, and seek an asylum from her creditors.

Evidently the asylum she sought eluded her. Teresa Imer Cornelys died, after a long incarceration for debt, in the Fleet Prison on 19 August 1797. "Anthony Pasquin, Esq." (John Williams) wrote a 33-stanza

moral effusion for the October number of the *Monthly Mirror*—"An Elegy, Written in Soho Square, On seeing Mrs Cornelly's House in Ruins," which condemned her place of entertainment as a contaminator of innocence.

Mrs Cornelys had a son, "le petit Aranda" of Casanova's account, who, according to the *Monthly Mirror*, "was a tutor to the present Lord Pomfret. He was a very amiable man, and an excellent scholar. He allowed his mother an annuity till his death, which happened a few years ago." There was also the daughter Sophie, who had been educated at a Roman Catholic nunnery in Hammersmith, where Casanova said Teresa had a house. Sophie (who early took the name "Miss Williams") liked to pretend that, so far from being Casanova's daughter, she was of noble parentage. The *Town and Country Magazine* in 1775 stigmatized her and Lord Coventry in a pair of its "tête-a-tête" portraits," as "Peeping Tom of Coventry and Miss W——ms." She was given an allowance by Charles Butter and was kindly patronised by various others of her mother's former friends: Lady Spencer (who left her an annuity), the Duchess of Newcastle (with whom she lived for awhile), and the Princess Augusta.

Teresa Cornelys was the subject of an anonymous and undated vignette line engraving, depicting her wearing a bonnet, and of a contemporary caricature engraving, "Lady Fashion's Secretary's Office, a Peticoat [*sic*] recommendation the best," satirizing her supposed influence at court. Several satirical prints in the British Museum either present her as subject or allude to her assemblies or employ references to her establishment in some political allegory: No 4376, "Remarkable Characters at Mʳˢ· Cornellys Masquerade," engraved for the *Oxford Magazine*, 26 February 1770, is actually a political allegory aimed at the Earl of Bute's party; No 4928, titled the same, and published for the same magazine

"Remarkable Characters at M.rs Cornellys Masquerade"
artist unknown

on 1 March 1771, is different in content, representing some of the characters—Messrs Hooke, Hodges, and others—at the public masquerade of 6 February 1771; No 5066, "Cupid Turn'd Auctioneer, or, Cornelys' Sale at Carlisle House," a picture by S. Wale engraved by J. Taylor, was published 24 December 1772 as illustration to an article in the *Westminster Magazine* bearing that title. People, rather than objects, are being auctioned.

Cornet, Signor   [fl. 1726–1727], dancer.

One Cornet was a dancer in the Italian troupe which arrived in London in September 1726 and opened their season at the King's Theatre in the Haymarket on 28 September. He was named once in the bills, on 16 March 1727, when he danced a hornpipe.

Corney, Mr   [fl. 1661], singer.

The Westminster Abbey Precentor's book named a Mr Corney on 30 March 1661 as having been one of the Gentlemen of the Chapel Royal who participated in the funeral of Princess Mary, the King's eldest sister, for a special fee of 7s. 4d.

Cornish, James   d. 1804, oboist.

James Cornish was an oboist active in London between 1784 and 1804. He was no doubt the Mr Cornish listed by Burney as a "2nd hautbois" for the Handel Memorial Concerts at Westminster Abbey and the Pantheon in May and June 1784. Cornish was a member of the Royal Society of Musicians from at least 1789; in May of that year he played at the Society's annual concert for the benefit of the clergy at St Paul's. His name was also on the list for these concerts in 1790, each year from

1792 to 1797, and in 1799, 1800, 1802, and 1803. In 1794, Doane's *Musical Directory* listed him as a participant in the grand performances at Westminster Abbey, with engagements at Sadler's Wells Theatre, then living at Stangate Street, Lambeth. In that year, and between 1796–1800, he played in the band for the Covent Garden oratorios. Cornish's name, or that of one of his sons, also appeared regularly in the Drury Lane account books between 1794 and 1802 for playing the triangle and the tabor and pipe. Payments to him were irregular in amount and date, but he seems to have earned about £1 15*s.* per week, when employed.

On 1 January 1804, Cornish applied to the Royal Society of Musicians for relief and was granted four guineas a month until further notice. On 6 May of that year he reported that he was engaged at Sadler's Wells and relinqushed his claim, but on 2 September the allowance was renewed when Cornish's poor health prevented him from continuing at Sadler's Wells. Sometime between 19 November 1804, the date his will was made, and 6 January 1805, James Cornish died. In his will (proved 26 January 1805) he described himself as a musician of Mount Street, Lambeth, "weak in body," and he left all his household goods, stock in public funds, and other effects except his musical instruments and books, which he bequeathed to his son Thomas Cornish, to his second wife and executrix, Catherine Cornish. Another son, James John Cornish, also a musician, borne in 1767 by a previous wife named Mary, had died in 1803.

On 6 January 1805 the Royal Society of Musicians granted Catherine Cornish £8 for funeral costs and an allowance of £2 12*s.* 6*d.* per month. A month later she applied to the Society for medical assistance and was granted £4. On 3 March 1822 she received £6, being then above 70 years old. Catherine Cornish died on 15 March 1835, at the age of 85. Because she was possessed

with over £200 at the time, no money was granted by the Society for her burial, which took place at St Paul, Covent Garden, on 22 March 1835.

Cornish, James John 1767–1803, musician.

According to affidavits filed with the Royal Society of Musicians, James John Cornish was born on 26 February 1767 and baptized on 26 March 1767 at St Margaret, Westminster, the son of James Cornish, the oboist, by his first wife Mary. He was recommended for membership in the Royal Society of Musicians by J. Clarke on 5 May 1793, at which time he was described as having studied and practiced music seven years: "He performs on the Hautboy, Violin, and Clarinet, is engaged at the Theatre Royal in the Haymarket is 26 years of age a single man." He was elected to the Society on 5 August 1793. In 1794 he was listed in Doane's *Musical Directory*—as "Cornish Junr"—as an oboist, a performer in the oratorios and at the Apollo Gardens, and a participant in the grand performances at Westminster Abbey. At the time, he was living with his father in Stangate Street, Lambeth.

"Cornish Junior" is found on the list for the annual concert at St Paul's in 1798, given by the Royal Society of Musicians for benefit of the clergy. Cornish died in 1803, before 4 September, at which time his widow Jane was granted a funeral allowance of £8 and £2 12*s.* 6*d.* per month for living expenses. As an aged widow she received a donation of £1 from the Society on 1 January 1837 and a benefaction at Christmas 1837, for which she returned her gratitude on 4 February 1838.

Cornish, Thomas [*fl.* 1794–1818], oboist.

Thomas Cornish, an oboist active in London between 1794 and 1818, was a son of the musician James Cornish. In 1794 he was listed by Doane's *Musical Directory* as an oboist in the Second Regiment of Guards, and at the Royal Circus, living in Oxendon Street, an address separate from that of his father and his brother, James John, who then lived in Stangate Street, Lambeth. By his father's will, proved on 26 January 1805, Thomas inherited musical instruments and books. Little else is known of his career except that he was no doubt the Cornish, oboist, on the King's Theatre list in 1818, his father and brother having since died. A son was born to him in 1817, by his wife Mary, when they lived at No 28, Crown Street, in the parish of St Giles in the Fields. There is no record of his having been admitted to the Royal Society of Musicians.

Cornleys. *See* **CORNELYS.**

Cornwall. *See also* **CORNWELL.**

Cornwall, Mr *d. c. 1724, scene painter.*
An entry in the Lincoln's Inn Fields account books on 6 February 1724 cites a Mrs Cornwall, executrix of Mr Cornwall, "painter," who was paid £13 13s. "in full." The money was probably a settlement with Mrs Cornwall for her husband's unpaid wages at the theatre.

Cornwell, David ₁*fl. c. 1700–1713?*₁, *acrobat, conjurer, exhibitor.*
Morley's *Memoirs of Bartholomew Fair* cites David Cornwell as an exhibitor of about 1700 "who drew stumps for ten shillings and teeth for five, at the Ram's Head in Fenchurch Street . . ." Quoting an unidentified contemporary source, Morley offers a description of the "Bold Grimace Spaniard" whom Cornwell exhibited:

[He] liv'd 15 years among wild creatures in the Mountains, and is reasonably suppos'd to have been taken out of his cradle, an Infant, by some savage Beast, and wonderfully preserv'd, 'till some Comedians accidentally pass'd

through thos parts, and perceiving him to be of human Race, pursued him to his Cave, where they caught him in a Net. They found something wonderful in his Nature, and took him with 'em in their Travels through *Spain* and *Italy.* He performs the following surprising Grimaces, *viz.*: He lolls out his Tongue a foot long, turns his Eyes in and out at the same time; contracts his Face as small as an Apple; extends his Mouth six Inches, and turns it into the shape of a Bird's Beak, and his eyes like to an Owl's; turns his mouth into the Form of a Hat cock'd up three ways; and also frames it in the manner of a four-square Buckle; licks his Nose with his Tongue, like a Cow; rolls one Eyebrow two Inches up, the other two down; changes his face to such an astonishing Degree, as to appear like a Corpse long bury'd. Altho' bred wild so long, yet by travelling with the aforesaid Comedians 18 years, he can sing wonderfully fine, and accompanies his Voice with a thorow Base on the Lute. His former natural Estrangement from human Conversation oblig'd Mr *Cornwell* to bring a Jackanapes over with him for his Companion, in whom he takes great Delight and Satisfaction.

Though there is no proof, perhaps David Cornwell was the "Mr Cornwall' who augmented the puppeteer Powell's shows at Punch's Theatre in November 1713 by conjuring "(the egg bag)" and, apparently, tumbling.

Corny. *See* **COREY, CORNEY,** and **CORY.**

Corona, Teresa. *See* **COSTANTINI, SIGNORA GIOVANNI BATTISTA.**

Coror. *See* **CURRER.**

Corpora, Signor ₁*fl. 1722*₁, *violinist.*
"A Cantata, with Violins, by Seignior Corpora, lately brought by him out of Italy," was performed at the Haymarket Theatre on 26 January 1722.

Corporalli. *See* **CAPORALE.**

Correr. *See also* CURRER.

Correr, Signora Vittorio. *See* ANGE-
LELLI, AUGUSTA.

Corri, Angelo [fl. 1739], *manager?*
In 1739 Angelo Corri was granted a
license to produce operas at the theatre "in
St James's, Haymarket," or elsewhere in
the liberties of Westminster.

**Corri, Signora Domenico, née Bac-
chelli** [fl. 1771–1810], *singer.*
Before leaving her native Italy, the
singer Signorina Bacchelli married the composer Domenico Corri (1746–1825). By
1771 the Corris had settled at Edinburgh,
where she sang and he conducted concerts
of the Edinburgh Musical Society. In
1774–75 they were in London for the production of Corri's opera *Allessandro nell'
Indie* at the King's Theatre, 3 December
1774. During their stay Signora Corri sang
in the oratorios given by Bach and Abel in
March 1775 and performed a *duetto* with
Mrs Weichsel in the oratorio *Alexander's
Feast* at the King's Theatre on 24 March
1775. Both Corris also performed at various private concerts at London, including
several at Dr Burney's house. It is also probable that Mrs Corri was the person, called
Gori by *The London Stage*, who sang the
female role of Sandrina in *La Buona
figliuola* at the King's Theatre on 17 March
1774.
The Corris soon returned to Edinburgh,
where they remained for some 15 years.
About 1778, Domenico leased the Theatre
Royal, Edinburgh, but failed as a theatrical
manager. With his brother Natale Corri
(1765–1822) he set up a music publishing
business about 1779, but in 1790 he and
Signora Corri again moved to London,
where he composed several operas and entered into music publishing with his son-in-
law, J. L. Dussek, trading under the name
Corri, Dussek, & Co. for many years at

No 28, Haymarket, until they went bankrupt and Dussek ran off to the Continent.
While in London during this period,
Signora Corri seems not to have performed
in public, although she had been a regular
participant in the Edinburgh Musical Society concerts during the 1780s. She was
listed in 1794, however, by Doane's *Musical Directory* as a soprano, living with her
husband at No 67, Dean Street, Soho. In
the preface to Corri's *Singer's Preceptor*
in 1810, the public was informed that "Mrs
Corri also instructs in vocal and instrumental music."
The date of Signora Corri's death is not
known to us. Her husband, who seems
never to have performed on the London
stage, died at London on 22 May 1825, at
the age of 74. Their daughter Sophia Corri
(b. 1775), who sang and performed on the
harp in the 1790s, is entered in this work
as Mrs Jan Ladislav Dussek. Their sons
included John Corri, who operated his
father's business at Edinburgh; Montague
Corri (1784–1849), who was a music
publisher and a composer at the Haymarket in the nineteenth century; Philip
Antony Corri, a composer who promoted
the establishment of the Philharmonic Society and who died in America; and Haydn
Corri (1785–1860), a pianist and organist
who settled at Dublin. The family descending from Domenico and his brother Natale
was numerous in nineteenth-century musical circles in London and extends into the
twentieth century through Charles Corri
(1861–1941), a conductor for many years
at the Old Vic operas. For information on
Domenico and Natale Corri and other
members of the family during the nineteenth century, see Grove, *The Dictionary
of National Biography*, and the *Enciclopedia dello spettacolo*.

Corri, Sophia. *See* DUSSEK, MRS JAN
LADISLAV.

Corrie. *See* CORY.

Corse. *See* CORFE.

"Corsican Fairy, The." *See* TERESIA, MME.

Cortes, Mr [*fl.* 1790–1791], *rope-walker, dancer, tumbler.*

According to an advertisement in the *Kingston Daily Advertiser* of Jamaica, a Mr Cortes (sometimes Curtis) and his company performed feats of dancing, rope-walking, and tumbling at Dallas's Long Room in Church Street, Kingston, on 7 August 1790. About a year later, in May 1791, the company was at Montego Bay, where the *Cornwall Chronicle* announced that Cortes, from Rome, having "performed with great Applause, in London, Paris, Madrid, Lisbon, etc.," would walk the tight-rope and dance a hornpipe. He also danced "on a parcel of eggs, blindfolded, with sundry jumps and tumbles."

Cory. *See also* COREY.

Cory, Mr [*fl.* 1675], *actor.*

The Mr Cory who played Redstreak in *Psyche Debauch'd* at Drury Lane on 27 August 1675 may have been the William Corey who acted with the Duke's Company in the 1660s, but certain identification is impossible.

Cory, Thomas [*fl.* 1791–1808?], *actor.*

As a youth, Thomas Cory studied acting under Dr Barrow, who operated a training school at the Soho Theatre. According to a notation in a manuscript at the Folger Library, dated 22 January 1791, Cory was successful enough as a student to succeed Holman as the "Hero of the Soho Theatre" and had "lately" auditioned for Harris, manager of Covent Garden Theatre. Harris advised him to acquire provincial experience before attempting the London stage. After an apprenticeship to Mr White,

Solicitor of the Treasury, Cory took Harris's advice. He made his debut at the Crow Street Theatre, Dublin, billed as "A Gentleman," on 29 June 1796, and for his second appearance at Crow Street on 8 July his name was given as "Corrie." Later that summer and in the following summer he acted at Edinburgh. The *Authentic Memoirs of the Green Room* (1801) reported that he had also acted at Cheltenham, Manchester, and other theatres.

Cory's "growing reputation" in the provinces recommended him to Sheridan at Drury Lane, where he was engaged for 1798–99 at a salary of £5 per week. Billed as from the Manchester Theatre, Cory made his debut at Drury Lane on 17 November 1798 as Reginald in *The Castle Spectre*, a role he continued to play regularly during his London career. The *Monthly Mirror* (November 1798) found Cory to be a large man, with a voice "the most powerful we ever heard, or ever expected to hear, and not unsusceptible of pathos." He performed the role with judgment, but the critic reserved an opinion of Cory's promise until he played more roles. The author of the *Authentic Memoirs of the Green Room* (1799) was less cautious. He predicted that Cory, who appeared to be "between thirty and forty," would with practice become more graceful and that his talents would in time bring him status and favor in a London theatre. This critic confirmed that Cory's voice was deep, powerful, and melodious, with great compass, and that his tones were clear, distinct, and impressive.

After repeating the role of Reginald on 24 November, Cory performed Eustache de St Pierre in *The Surrender of Calais* on 4 December, a role which the critic of the *Monthly Mirror* (December 1798) judged he played "upon the whole, in a very creditable manner." The critic again called attention to the extraordinary strength and capacity of Cory's voice and passed along a rumor, which he called "a stupid report," that J. P. Kemble was jealous of Cory's talents and refused to act in any play with him. "If this be reported by Mr Cory's friends," wrote the reviewer, "his worst enemies could not have fabricated a story so superlatively ridiculous in itself, and so injurious to the interest of the young actor." There seemed at the time to be no substance to the rumor, for near the end of that season, on 24 May 1799, Cory played the role of the Old Blind Man in the first performance of Sheridan's *Pizarro*, a play in which Kemble as Rolla achieved enormous success, causing it to be performed a total of 31 times into the summer. Earlier, on 27 December 1798, Cory had made his first appearance as Glenalvon in *Douglas* and also played Abomelique in *Blue Beard*. In *The Dramatic Censor* (1800) Thomas Dutton came out as a firm advocate of Cory's Glenalvon, but reminded him that "to whom much is given, of the same will much, likewise, be required." Dutton, who praised Cory's powers of voice and range warned the actor about his "impetuosity" of delivery, by which he fatigued himself "with unnecessary exertion." On 19 January 1799, Cory acted Baron Fitzallen in *Feudal Times*, a new afterpiece by Colman. With Caulfield and Trueman, Cory shared £340 in net benefit receipts on 7 May 1799, when he again played Reginald. His address was given in the bills as No 19, Martlett Court, Bow Street.

Again engaged at £5 per week at Drury Lane in 1799–1800, Cory continued in the roles of Reginald and the Old Blind Man, and also acted a Dutchman in *The Embarkation*, an Egyptian in *The Egyptian Festival*, a role in *DeMontfort*, and Bulcazin Muley in *The Mountaineers*. On 18 June 1800, Aickin being ill, Cory played Iago for the first time and acquitted himself "satisfactorily," by the report of Dutton. Earlier that season, on 4 February, he had played Kemble's role of Rolla in *Pizarro*,

and, though he had betrayed nervousness at the comparison, he had done well.

Cory remained at Drury Lane for another season, at the end of which he was discharged by the management, an act which Cory claimed was illegal, because he had articles for two more years. Perhaps there had been some truth in the earlier rumor of Kemble's jealousy. Cory did not contest his dismissal, and "within an hour or two" he entered into articles for five years with Harris at Covent Garden. The appointment was not "at a rising salary," as reported, for the Covent Garden account books for 1801–2 show his pay to have been £4 per week, a reduction from the £5 he had been earning at the other house.

Cory made his first appearance at Covent Garden as Richmond to G. F. Cooke's Richard III on 14 September 1801. On 9 October he played a character in *Integrity*. On 21 October he acted Bassanio in *The Merchant of Venice*. He continued to serve as a useful actor at Covent Garden through at least 1804–5, playing such roles as Bulcazin Muley in *The Mountaineers*, Morrington in *Speed the Plough*, Claudius in *Hamlet*, and Solyman in *The Sultan*. In the summer of 1804 he acted at Richmond, Surrey, where for his benefit on 9 October tickets could be had of him at Mrs Emmett's in the Vineyard.

Presumably, Cory acted little after 1805. On 2 May 1808, from his address at No 125, Bond Street, he wrote to Brunton at Covent Garden Theatre seeking an engagement for his wife: Mrs Cory was "willing to engage to act the old women for the latter part of the season" if Brunton had already engaged someone for the earlier period. Perhaps his wife was the Mrs Cory who had acted at the opening of the New Theatre in Worthing in the summer of 1807. An actress who signed herself "Harriot Correy" was engaged at Drury Lane Theatre in 1812–13.

Illustrations

FRINGE THEATRICALS: PLEASURE GARDENS, CIRCUSES, FAIRS, MASQUERADES, AND MINOR THEATRES

515

Enthoven Collection, Theatre Museum

Bird's-eye view of Vauxhall Gardens in 1754 engraving by Carse after Wale

The Metropolitan Museum of Art, Elisha Whittelsey Fund, 1959
A concert at Vauxhall Gardens
etching by Rowlandson, 1785

Enthoven Collection, Theatre Museum
Interior of the music room at Vauxhall Gardens about 1765

View of Ranelagh Gardens in 1750

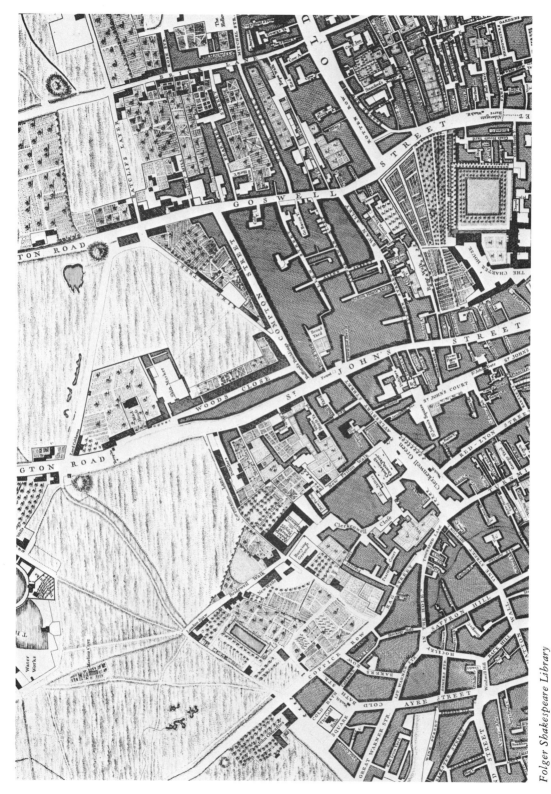

Folger Shakespeare Library

Clerkenwell and environs, site of the New Wells, Clerkenwell, and New Tunbridge Wells (Sadler's Wells)
from Roque's map of London, 1746

Folger Shakespeare Library
Clerkenwell and environs in 1794, showing the sites of Sadler's Wells and Bagnigge Well
from Horwood's map of London, 1794

Enthoven Collection, Theatre Museum
Exterior of Sadler's Wells
satirical print by Cruikshank, published in 1796

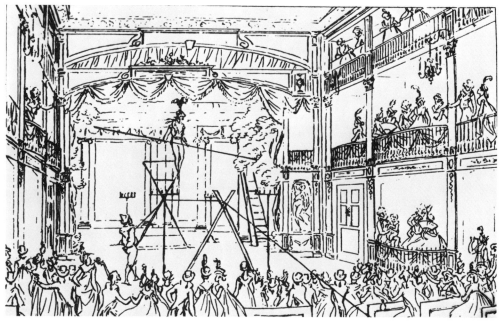

Islington Libraries
Rope dancing at Sadler's Wells in 1795

Stage of the Pantheon
engraving by Wise after G. Jones
from Wilkinson's *Londina Illustrata*, 1819–25

Henry E. Huntington Library
Ruins of the Pantheon in 1792
engraving by Wigstead, published by Rowlandson

Auditorium of the Royalty Theatre, Wellclose Square, 1785–1787
from Wilkinson's *Londina Illustrata,* 1819–25

Exterior and interior views of Astley's Riding School in 1770
from the collection of Edward A. Langhans

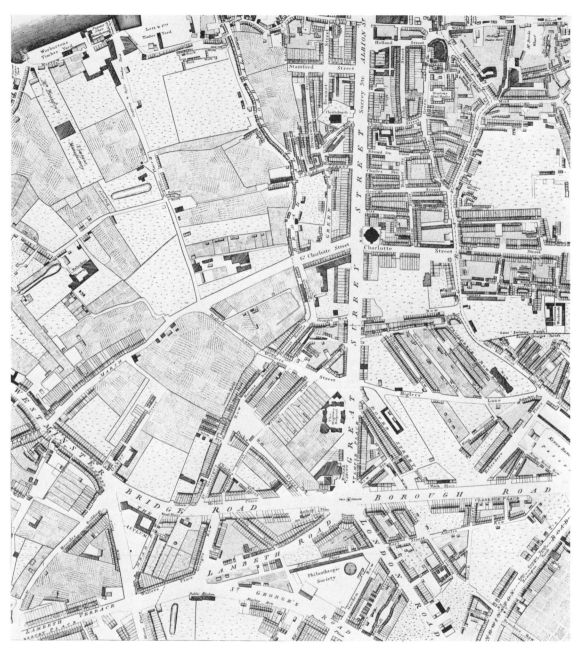

Folger Shakespeare Library
Site of the Royal Circus, near the Obelisk
from Horwood's map of London, 1794

Henry E. Huntington Library

Interior of Astley's Olympic Pavilion in 1807

Enthoven Collection, Theatre Museum

A masquerade at the King's Theatre in the Haymarket in 1735, during Heidegger's managership painting by Grisoni

Guildhall Library, City of London
Bartholomew Fair in 1721
engraving from a fan painting

BARTHOLOMEW FAIR. 1721. (Lee and Harper's Booth.)

Henry E. Huntington Library
Detail of Lee and Harper's booth at Bartholomew Fair in 1721

Hogarth's "Southwark Fair," 1733
engraving by Phillibron
from the collection of Edward A. Langhans

Folger Shakespeare Library
Greenwich and environs, site of William Pinkethman's playhouse and Greenwich Fair
from Roque's map of London, 1746

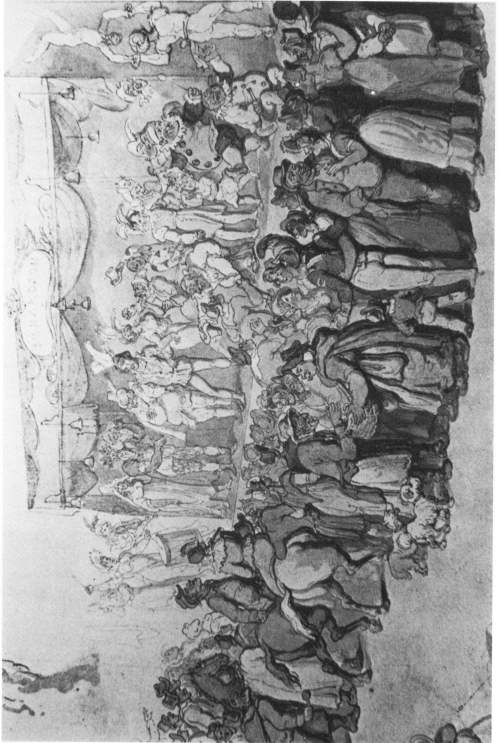

Trustees of the British Museum
Richardson's booth at Greenwich Fair
watercolor by Rowlandson

May Fair in 1716
from *London Society*, 1863

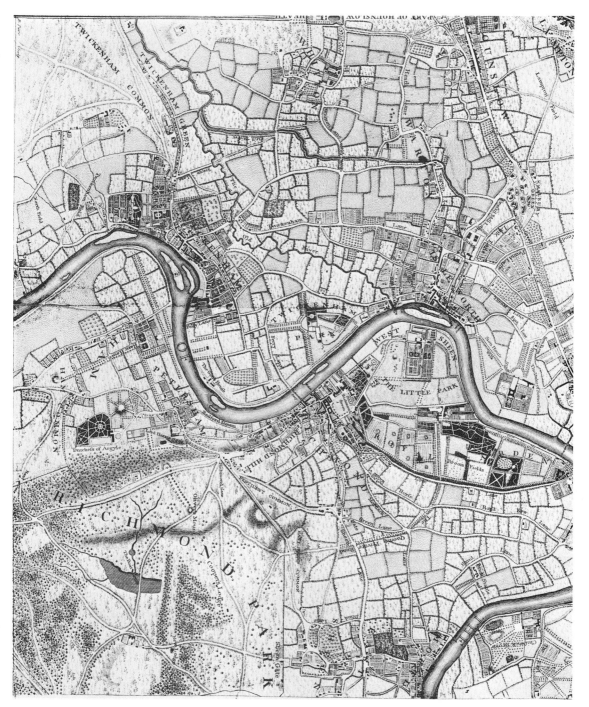

Folger Shakespeare Library

Richmond, Twickenham, and environs. Thomas Chapman managed a summer theatre troupe that played in these towns during the 1730s and 1740s
from Roque's map of London, 1746

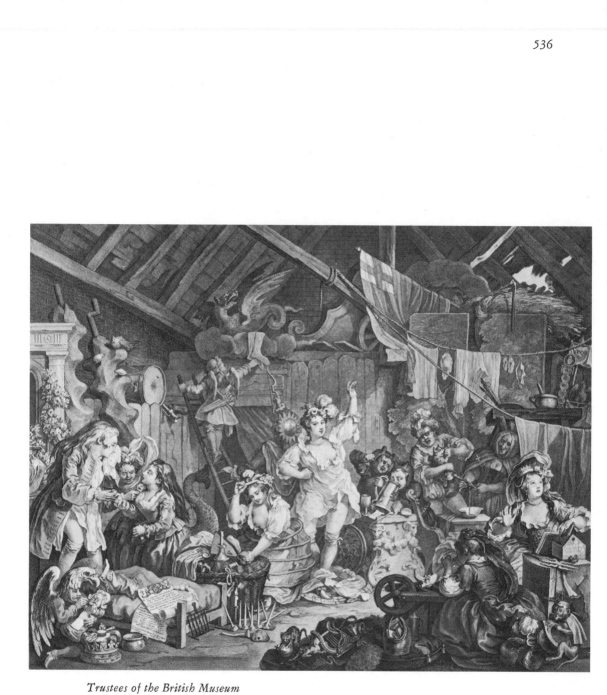

Actresses in a barn, by Hogarth, 1738